1923

PROGRESS

EVERY YEAR
AND EVEN
EVERY DAY
MUST SHOW
PROGRESS IN
THAT FINE ART
OF BUSINESS
MANAGEMENT

1922

VALUE

IT IS OUR
DETERMINATION
THAT SPLENDID
VALUE SHALL
ALWAYS
BE ASSOCIATED
WITH EVERY
ARTICLE SOLD

SHOPPING, SEDUCTION
& MR SELFRIDGE

By the same author
War Paint: Helena Rubinstein and Elizabeth Arden –
Their Lives, Their Times, Their Rivalry

SHOPPING, SEDUCTION & MR SELFRIDGE

LINDY WOODHEAD

P

PROFILE BOOKS

First published in Great Britain in 2007 by
Profile Books Ltd
3A Exmouth House
Pine Street
Exmouth Market
London EC1R 0JH
www.profilebooks.com

1 3 5 7 9 10 8 6 4 2

Typeset in Goudy Old Style by MacGuru Ltd
info@macguru.org.uk

Printed and bound in Great Britain by
Clays, Bungay, Suffolk

A CIP catalogue record for this book is available from the British Library.

ISBN 978 1 86197 888 2

The paper this book is printed on is certified by the © 1996 Forest Stewardship
Council A.C. (FSC). It is ancient-forest friendly. The printer holds FSC chain of
custody SGS-COC-2061

FSC
Mixed Sources
Product group from well-managed
forests and other controlled sources
Cert no. SGS-COC-2061
www.fsc.org
© 1996 Forest Stewardship Council

For Colin, Ollie and Max

Woman was what the shops were fighting over when they competed, it was woman whom they ensnared with the constant trap of their bargains, after stunning her with their displays. They had aroused new desires in her flesh, they were a huge temptation to which she must fatally succumb, first of all by giving in to the purchases of a good housewife, then seduced by vanity and finally consumed.

Emile Zola, *Au Bonheur des Dames* (1881)

When I die I want it said of me, 'He dignified and ennobled commerce.'

Harry Gordon Selfridge (1856–1947)

CONTENTS

ILLUSTRATIONS

Endpapers
To celebrate Selfridge's twentieth birthday in 1929, illuminated panels illustrating the year-by-year principles on which Harry Selfridge had built the firm's reputation blazed throughout the night across the entire façade of the store

The author and publishers wish to thank the following for permission to reproduce images: Plates 1, 3, 18, family archives of Simon Wheaton-Smith; 2, 4, 5, 6, 7, 8, 9, 10, 11, 12, 15, 19, 21, 22, 23, 24, *endpapers*, the Selfridges Archive, held at the History of Advertising Trust www.hatads.org.uk; 13, Otis Elevators; 14, *Chicago Daily News* Negatives Collection, Chicago History Museum; 16, private collection of James Gardiner; 17, private collection of Ian Stevenson; 20, Getty Images; 25, D.M. Booth, by kind permission of the Reverend Garry Taylor, St Mark's Church, Highcliffe; 26, Press Association.

INTRODUCTION

~

CONSUMING PASSIONS

The rise of the department store – or what in Paris were more gracefully called *les grands magasins* – in the second half of the nineteenth century was a phenomenon that encompassed fashion, advertising, entertainment, emergent new technology, architecture and, above all, seduction. These forces evolved to merge into businesses that Emile Zola astutely called 'the great cathedrals of shopping', and vast fortunes were made by the men who owned them as they tapped into the female passion for shopping. But arguably no one man grasped the concept of consumption as sensual entertainment better than the maverick American retailer, Harry Gordon Selfridge, who opened his eponymous store on London's Oxford Street in 1909.

In building the West End's first fully fledged department store, he quite literally changed everything about the way Londoners shopped. His visionary, larger-than-life Edwardian building perfectly reflected the character of its founder – the only modest thing about him being his height. It was Harry Gordon Selfridge who positioned the perfume and cosmetics department immediately inside the main entrance, a move that changed the layout – and turnover – of the sales floor for ever more. Selfridge created window-dressing as an art form, pioneered in-store promotions and fashion shows, and offered customer service and facilities previously unheard of in Britain. Above all, he gave his customers fun. At a time when there was no radio or television, when cinema was in its infancy, Selfridge's in Oxford Street offered customers entertainment as fascinating as that at a science museum, with as much glamour as on any music-hall stage. In giving his customers a unique 'day out', Harry Selfridge proudly boasted that after Westminster Abbey and the Tower of London, his store was 'the third biggest tourist attraction in town'. The public could buy much of what they needed at Selfridge's, and much that they never knew they wanted until they were seduced by the tantalizing displays.

Harry Selfridge perfected the art of publicity, spending more money on advertising than any retailer of his era. A consummate showman, he himself became a celebrity at a time when there were few identifiable, exciting personalities that the public could see at close quarters. When he arrived at work, there was invariably a cluster of customers waiting to meet and greet the 'famous Mr Selfridge'. His ritualistic 'morning tour' of the store, where his staff of thousands lined up anxiously by their counters in eager anticipation of a personal nod of approval from their boss, was the curtain-raiser to the daily show at Selfridge's – the only difference being that for his audience, entrance was free.

There was no shortage of shops or stores in London and many other wealthy provincial cities in Britain when – after twenty-five years working at the celebrated store Marshall Field & Co. in Chicago – Selfridge masterminded his grand plan to open in the imperial capital. The industrial transformation that had occurred in Britain had created a new spending population who were proud to show off their wealth by acquiring consumer goods, and retailers scrambled to cope with an almost insatiable demand. The new rich had large houses to equip, a prodigious number of children – not to mention an army of servants – to dress, and their own position in society to promote. Happily for retailers, conspicuous consumption, always so crucial in defining wealth and status, had found itself a much larger market.

That fashion became big business was because of big dresses. In the 1850s, when both the young Queen Victoria and the French style icon, the Empress Eugénie, both enthusiastically embraced the new caged crinoline, clothes billowed to unprecedented proportions. Women of substance were dressed from head to toe in as much as forty yards of fabric. As well as a muslin shift and fine-knitted cotton or silk underwear – not to mention the ubiquitous corset – the ensemble had hoops underneath, and at least three if not four petticoats, in layers varying from flannel through muslin to white, starched cotton. Add to this a lace fichu, bead-trimmed cape, fur or embroidered muff, hat, gloves, parasol, stockings, button boots and reticule – and consider that the entire paraphernalia was usually changed once a day and often again in the evening – and one can begin to comprehend the costs, not to mention profits, in supplying it all. As if this bonanza wasn't enough for retailers who stocked all of the above and ran vast workrooms making the finished gowns, there was the ritual of mourning the dead. This meant the whole thing all over again – but this time in black. Many a Victorian linen-draper's fortune was made merely by operating a successful 'mourning department', and one of the first diversifications into 'added-value customer services' was to offer funeral facilities – right down to supplying dyed black ostrich feathers for the horses that pulled the hearse.

As dress-reformers railed against 'the tyranny of women's fashion', the redoubtable feminist Elizabeth Cady Stanton used dress as a topic of debate: 'Men say we are frail. But I'd like to see a man who can bear what we do, laced up in steel-ribbed corsets, with hoops, heavy skirts, trains, panniers, chignons and dozens of hairpins sticking in our scalps – cooped up in the house year after year. How would men like that?'

The answer is that the men – or at least those who owned stores and factories – liked it very much. Fortunes were made in the textile trade – in cotton, wool, linen and silk, growing it, weaving it, dyeing it, and selling it. Associated businesses making all manner of goods from dye, needles and pins, ribbons and sewing thread to bleach and starch boomed. And as distribution systems improved, merchandise could be moved further and further from its point of production to its point of sale, meaning stores could offer a wider selection of goods than ever before.

The nineteenth-century passion for fashion wasn't the only factor in the rise of the great department stores. Just as the growth of credit had led to an explosion of shops in the seventeenth century, so the ability to buy in bulk – also on credit – benefited the new breed of retailers. The prosperous middle classes may have wanted quality, but above all, their Victorian ethics demanded value for money. Economies of buying in bulk enabled larger retailers to reduce their prices far below those of smaller, specialist shops. These independent shopkeepers – who had for decades catered to the upper echelons of society – were restricted by their credit systems. The richer the customer, the longer he or she took to pay. It wasn't unusual for accounts to be settled annually, and many speciality shops went bankrupt as a result. The emergent stores, however, were mainly cash businesses, with perhaps a monthly charge account offered to more select personal customers. Such stores developed awesome buying power – particularly as many of them operated a wholesale division servicing sales outposts in the Empire or throughout rural America – and they didn't hesitate to use it as a weapon against their suppliers, who were obliged not just to provide goods against a ninety-day payment policy, but often also to store merchandise for phased delivery.

The great stores acted as a catalyst for change in women's lives. For the first time women were able to 'cross the line', venturing out in public to buy goods for themselves, to experience shopping and be observed doing it without in any way jeopardizing their reputations. Not all stores were the size of cathedrals, but certainly fashionable women in London, Manchester and Newcastle, and further afield in Paris, New York, Philadelphia and Chicago, were spending a lot more time shopping than going to church. Small wonder when the stores were light, bright, warm and enticing. Neither did these stores cater exclusively for the carriage trade. The department store was the anchor in a rapidly expanding egalitarian, urban society, drawing its customer base from a mix of old and new money, and able to offer not just fixed prices but also sale bargains. For many people these stores were infinitely more glamorous and comfortable than their own homes. In 1880s Chicago, Harry Selfridge had pioneered the policy of browsing, making Marshall Field's an ideal location for those who were 'just looking', and opened a 'Bargain Basement' for those on a budget. He had also introduced a restaurant, a reading-room, a crèche and a ladies' rest-room complete with nurse, and so could justifiably claim to have helped emancipate women: 'I came along just at the time when women wanted to step out on their own. They came to the store and realized some of their dreams.'

He made his own dreams come true in turn-of-the-century London where, at the time he arrived, compared to the giant American department stores and *grands magasins* of Paris, many of London's 'stores' were just rather large shops. In the days before lifts and escalators, and in part due to onerous building restrictions, retail space was restricted to the ground, first and possibly second floors, with stock rooms below and workrooms above. Stores like Swan & Edgar, Dickens & Jones and Debenham & Freebody had in-house catering for their staff who ate breakfast, lunch and dinner on site. More often than not, staff lived in a store-tied hostel or in a grim and cold dormitory tucked away on the upper floor. Young people who had eschewed residential domestic service for jobs in retailing soon realized they had merely swapped the servants' hall for the staff canteen. Working hours were gruelling. When West End shopkeepers gave evidence before the Parliamentary Select Committee on Shop Hours in 1886, it transpired that average working hours were from 8.15 a.m. to 7.30 p.m. six days a week, with half an hour off for lunch and fifteen minutes for tea. If romance flourished on the shop floor, it was because workers had little time or opportunity to meet elsewhere.

Most leading drapery stores had, for the main part, evolved from a background in haberdashery, often expanding their floor space by buying sites to the left and right, knocking them through into a rabbit-warren of levels rather than rebuilding from scratch. From the main street entrance, customers entered a showroom space literally stuffed full with everything from garter elastic and dress pins to embroidery silks and bootlaces. The amount of time spent by a sales assistant in selling a shilling's worth of such goods – haberdashery being the training ground for all apprentices – was totally disproportionate to the return. The mindset of the day, however, was that ladies who bought their buttons would move further on in – or up to the first floor – to buy silks, satins, laces and lingerie.

Selfridge himself had already seen London's retailers and those of Manchester, Berlin, Vienna and Paris when he first toured Europe in 1888. Though admiring the William Morris fabrics in Liberty's and impressed by Whiteley's in Bayswater, in general he found the rest of the city's shops and stores disappointing. He particularly disliked floorwalkers. 'Is Sir intending to buy something?' asked one super-cilious man. 'No, I'm just looking,' replied Selfridge, at which the floorwalker dropped his pseudo-smart voice and snarled, 'Then 'op it mate!' Selfridge never forgot the incident and refused to hire 'walkers' when he opened in Oxford Street two decades later. Instead he employed knowledgeable, well-informed sales assistants who loved where they worked and who idolized their boss, whom they called 'the Chief'.

The time Selfridge spent time studying Au Bon Marché in Paris was crucial to his development as a retailing revolutionary. When he first saw the store in 1888, the final phase of rebuilding and expansion, orchestrated by the architect Louis-Charles Boileau and the brilliant engineer Gustave Eiffel, had been completed. What had started as a minor *magasin de nouveauté* opened by the Videau brothers on the fashionable rue de Bac in 1825, had grown to a massive enterprise under the direction of their ex-employee Aristide Boucicaut. Au Bon Marché was a masterpiece, and it set the standard for fine shopping throughout Europe. Monsieur Boucicaut was a great innovator, imposing fixed pricing, annual sales, an 'exchange' or 'money back' guarantee and *entre libre* (no obligation to buy) as well as running the first French retailing establishment to sell a huge variety of merchandise ranging from homewares, toys and perfume to sports equipment and children's clothes. Indeed, the bourgeois, taciturn Aristide Boucicaut, ably assisted by his thrifty wife Marguerite, took the Paris emporium to such majestic heights that it became the inspiration for Emile Zola's seminal novel *Au Bonheur des Dames*, a book so popular with business historians that it has tended to give the impression that innovation in retailing was the exclusive preserve of the French.

Across the Atlantic, however, another retailing pioneer was making his mark in establishing one of the world's first true department stores. In New York, an Irish immigrant called Alexander Turney Stewart established a sumptuous store so famous it had no name over the door but was simply known as 'The Marble Palace'. Among Stewart's many master-strokes in seducing shoppers was his decision to hire only the best-looking and most charming male sales assistants. He also introduced the first in-store fashion shows and live music, fitted the first plate-glass windows in America, and imported the country's first full-length mirrors, having spotted them first at Au Bon Marché. By the time the American Civil War ended in 1865, he had taken luxury shopping in New York to such heights that simply going to Stewart's was described by the press as 'being notoriously fatal to the female nerves'. *Harper's* considered this growing shopping mania 'a disease peculiar to women', even claiming it to be 'a species of insanity'. In the case of the assassinated President Lincoln's wife Mary, they were right. Poor Mary never got over the shock of her husband's death. Her already extravagant shopping habits became so bad that she ran up a bill of $48,000 (nearly a million dollars today) at Alexander Stewart's whereupon her family had her declared insane, insisting they weren't responsible for her debts.

Whatever the dangers of shopping, both Stewart and Boucicaut were men with an innate understanding of the powers of salesmanship, marketing, service and quality. It was their legacy, along with the enduring influence of Marshall Field, that inspired Harry Gordon Selfridge.

London's established retailers, although anxious to cultivate women customers, had some serious anomalies. Whiteley's was one of the rare retailers offering any sort of in-store catering, having opened a 'refreshment room' in 1872. However, when Mr Whiteley applied for a liquor licence – thinking that ladies who lunched might enjoy a glass of wine – Paddington's magistrates rejected his application in the 'interests of morality', saying that 'ladies, or females dressed to represent them, might make licensed premises a place of assignation'.

Even drinking tea or lemonade, however, necessitated a ladies' room, but there was no such provision for London's lady shoppers. Nor could respectable Victorian women be seen using one of the rare public conveniences. The only solution was to visit a hotel for afternoon tea.

Steeped in tradition, the city's retailers were alarmed by the idea of change. It was, however, long overdue. When Andrew Carnegie, the Scottish-American philanthropist millionaire, visited London in 1900 he was appalled. 'Just look at the jumble in the store windows – so much stuff you cannot take it in,' he said. 'When you go into a shop they treat you most indifferently. You are scowled at if you ask for goods out of the ordinary, and you are made to feel uncomfortable if you do not buy. These shop people drive away more customers than they attract. What London needs is a good shaking up.'

Nothing excited Harry Gordon Selfridge more than the idea of 'shaking up London', and the spirit of the age was on his side. The concept of selling to 'all classes of trade' was totally alien to existing British retailers. Stores were up-market or they were middle-market – and occasionally they catered to the better end of the lower market – but they never, ever did all three. Selfridge would change all that, just as he changed the traditional merchandise mix. When the trade press reported that he was going to sell everything from photographic equipment to glass and gloves, his drapery competitors derided such diversification, Marshall & Snelgrove stiffly announcing that 'We know what we are and mean to stick to it.'

Thanks to his commercial success, Selfridge enjoyed the lavish lifestyle of an impresario, having a penchant for large houses, fast women and regrettably slow horses. His greatest addiction other than work was gambling, which in one form or another dominated his life, from the risk he took in sinking all his money into a site arguably at 'the wrong end' of Oxford Street, to the hours he spent in casinos where he and one of his famous mistresses, the baccarat-addicted Jenny Dolly, won – and lost – hundreds of thousands of pounds. No one knows exactly how much Selfridge squandered over the three decades he lived in London, but it's reliably estimated at well over £3 million, or nearly £65 million today. The money vanished in a haze of extravagance, frittered away on jewels and furs for his mistresses, a fully crewed yacht that slept twenty, the maintenance of his three daughters' well-born but largely unemployed husbands and on his insatiable thirst for gambling.

None of these pastimes mattered when Selfridge and his store were making money. Indeed, his glamorous reputation added to the attraction of shopping there. Yet for a businessman involved in dealing with millions of pounds, Selfridge was curiously naïve, and his complex personal and social life and tumultuous business expansion ultimately brought about his downfall. In the late 1920s, advice from one of London's most flawed financiers trigged acquisitions of staggering proportions. Company revenues were drained and Selfridge was woefully unprepared when the Great Depression took hold. By the late 1930s, his personal lifestyle had left him deeply in debt to the store – and to the taxman.

In 1939, at the age of 83, thirty years after building Selfridge's, revolutionizing London's retailing and arguably creating what for years to come would be known as the greatest shopping street in the world, Harry Selfridge was ousted from what he had always thought of as 'his' store. The most celebrated retailer of his era, who had lived like a lord in Lansdowne House, was reduced to penury, dying in a small flat in Putney.

His legacy isn't just his gloriously iconic building in Oxford Street

– although the towering columns of Selfridges are an awesome monument for any man – it is that he modernized retailing, bringing to it his belief in 'the power of experience'. A man light years ahead of his time, a true accelerator of change, he deserves to be remembered as the man who put fun on to the shop floor and sex appeal into shopping.

1

~

THE FORTUNES OF WAR

'Fashion is the mirror of history. It reflects political,
social and economic changes, rather than mere whimsy.'
Louis XIV

In 1860, as America braced itself for civil war, businessmen began to stockpile goods. No one knew better than the store owners what would happen when fabric became scarce. It wasn't silks and satins that worried them, it was cotton – and they fretted more about the lack of it than the picking of it. In April 1861, when war was declared and President Lincoln issued his Proclamation of Blockade, speculation in cotton became rife, and panicking Northern mill owners were only too glad to forge associations with men who promised to continue the smooth flow of supplies from South to North.

When Union forces captured New Orleans in 1862, trade through the Mississippi Valley became particularly brisk. Cotton was also moved out via Memphis and Vicksburg, all of which kept the mills working – so much so that during the first two years of the war manufacturers still made a healthy profit. By 1863, however, supplies were dwindling and there was a shortage of men to run the machines. American spinning mills went on half-time production. As cotton goods became increasingly scarce, those who had filled a warehouse or two could name their price.

In New York, President Lincoln's friend Alexander Stewart, the acknowledged 'merchant prince' of the day, made enormous sums of money, having astutely cornered the market in domestic linen as well as cotton. Given that Mary Lincoln, a woman who clearly sought security through her possessions and for whom shopping was an addiction, spent thousands of dollars at Stewart's Marble Palace – on one memorable visit she ordered eighty-four pairs of coloured kid gloves – it is not surprising that Mr Stewart was also rewarded with lucrative contracts to supply clothing to the Union army. Indeed, the war seemed to have no effect on the shopping habits of New York's rich. The media criticized their 'hedonistic approach during the daily slaughter wrought by the war', but the pursuit of fashion carried on regardless.

Chicago too enjoyed a profitable war. The small town that had emerged out of the swampy Fort Dearborn just three decades earlier – and where some could still remember Chief Black Hawk and his warriors swooping in to attack – was now the hub of America's biggest railroad network and the collecting point for food to supply both the East and the army. Awash with opportunity and swimming in cash, sprawling, still muddy, 'rough and ready' Chicago became a boom town. As the farm boys joined the army, production of Cyrus McCormick's reaping machines increased – as did his fortune. He wasn't alone. Whether it was pork, which Philip Armour bought at $18 a barrel and sold for $40, or luxury Pullman Cars developed by the railwayman George Pullman, Chicago tycoons were making millions of dollars – and their wives were helping them spend it.

The destination of choice for Chicago's shoppers was Potter Palmer's store on Lake Street. Palmer, who went on to become a property developer of immense skill, had started his career in Chicago in 1839 as a small-time dry-goods retailer. There was nothing small about his ambitions, however, nor his ability to judge women's desire to shop. He sold goods at fixed and fair prices, let his ladies take clothes home to try on, and left copies of *Godey's Ladies Book* (the fashion magazine of the time) in the store for browsing. Better yet, he read it himself. His maxim was 'You've got to think big', and by the time war came, he had done so, stocking up on cotton goods, filling vast warehouses with everything from petticoats and pantalettes to sheets and tea towels, and advertising his stock with a 'money-back guarantee' – a revolutionary idea at the time.

Among the men who enlisted all over the North in 1861 was Robert Oliver Selfridge. At the age of 38 he left his home in Ripon, a hamlet in Wisconsin 170 miles north of Chicago, where he ran a general store, to go to war. Reputed to be a sober, hard-working man and described as 'a stalwart of local activity', he was also Master of the Ripon Freemasons' Lodge. Robert Selfridge and his wife Lois had three young sons – Charles Johnston, Robert Oliver Jr and Henry Gordon (known as Harry). Though there has always been uncertainty in the Selfridge family over precise dates of birth, it seems likely that Harry was born on 11 January 1856. He was just 5 when his father went to war – and never returned.

Not that Major Selfridge died in battle. He was honourably discharged in 1865, whereupon he simply vanished. No one ever knew why. Perhaps, having witnessed the carnage, he had a nervous breakdown. Perhaps he simply wanted to be free of responsibilities. Whatever the case, he left his wife to bring up her family on her own, on the meagre earnings of a teacher. Harry later described Lois as 'brave, upstanding and with indomitable courage'. She was indeed brave, and she needed to be. Not long after the war her eldest son Charles died, and then her middle son Robert. She was now left alone with young Harry.

Moving with her son to Jackson, Michigan, Lois found work as a primary school teacher, earning around $30 a month. Making ends meet was a constant struggle, so she supplemented her salary by painting Valentine and other novelty cards. Still with no word from her husband, she was left to assume that he was 'missing, presumed dead'. Only years later did she learn that he had been killed in a railway accident in Minnesota in 1873 and that she was – finally – a widow. Harry was shielded from the truth, growing up believing that his father had been 'killed in battle', a story he would often repeat to the media. It would be years before he discovered the truth.

Hardly surprisingly, all the love Lois had left to give was centred on her young son. The two of them found genuine pleasure in each other's company and became such great friends that they continued to live together until the day she died. When things got bleak, they played a game called 'Suppose', which involved imaginary plots about success through endeavour. 'Suppose' they could afford a cottage with a bay window? Even 'suppose' they were able to live in a castle with lots of servants? Though a pious woman who attended church regularly and abhorred alcohol, Lois was always happy to go to a new play or concert and was an avid reader, a pleasure she imbued in her son.

Mrs Selfridge continued her career as a teacher, becoming the headmistress of Jackson High School, where the education of the town's young was entrusted to her capable care. The most important thing she taught Harry was never to fear failure. She was fond of saying, 'Why should you worry about failing? There's always something else to try and you can excel in that instead.' She taught Harry to be gracious. She taught him impeccable manners. Finally, she taught him the importance of appearance. She would check his fingernails in the morning and again before supper – not that he needed much checking. From an early age Harry was fastidious, and he loved nothing better than wearing a clean shirt to school and polishing his boots until they gleamed.

When Harry wasn't dreaming about castles or maintaining his modest wardrobe, he had his head in a book, devouring stories by James Fenimore Cooper and Nathaniel Hawthorne, along with his favourite, *Struggles and Triumphs*, the well-thumbed autobiography of the great circus showman Phineas T. Barnum. The rags-to-riches story of Barnum inspired Harry to dream of a future far away from Jackson. In many respects the two were very similar. Barnum had a rare gift for publicity. His spectacular museum in New York drew the public in their thousands and he became rich by entertaining them. Like Barnum, Selfridge had the ability to suspend disbelief. His tricks – entertaining people in a great store that was, in a way, just like a circus tent – created such confidence among his friends, family and financial backers that for years they refused to accept that his extravagant, destructive side was gradually eroding his ability to run his business empire.

All that lay ahead. At the age of 10, Harry started to earn cash in the time-honoured way, by delivering newspapers. Next he took over a bread round, and finally he took a holiday job at Leonard Field's dry-goods store where he stocked shelves and carried parcels for $1.50 a week – cash he promptly handed over to his mother. When he was 13, he and a school friend, Peter Loomis, produced a boy's monthly magazine called *Will o' the Wisp*. Harry threw himself into the magazine, hustling for advertising from local tradesmen and promising them a 'guaranteed circulation from all the boys at school'. Years later, Loomis recalled that 'Harry sold space to a local dentist who owed us 75 cents. When he didn't pay up, Harry got him to extract a troublesome tooth for free to square the debt.' His experience of publishing *Wisp* not only gave Harry a life-long passion for the business of publicity and promotion, it also introduced him to the power of the press – something he never forgot and which he played to his advantage throughout his career.

Loomis's father ran a small bank in Jackson, and when Harry left school at 14, he got a job there as a junior book-keeper, earning $20 a month. A tough taskmaster called Mr Potter taught him to write a neat ledger, as Harry later recalled in a letter to Loomis: 'He didn't exactly inspire or encourage, but he did rub things in so hard that you could never forget them.' Jotting down figures became an engrained habit, and Harry's lists make fascinating reading. In just one of his silver-clasped, cream vellum private ledgers dated 1921, he noted in an immaculate hand that on 3 June he lost £1,198 playing poker and gave 'the Hon. Angela Manners £5.5/-' (presumably a charity donation), while in July – somewhat mysteriously for a man who owned his own department store – he spent £476 17s. 6d. at the Irish Linen Company in the Burlington Arcade.

It has been said that at around this time Harry studied for the entrance examinations to the Naval Academy in Annapolis,

Maryland, but failed his physical test because he was too short. Harry was always sensitive about his height – he was a shade under 5 foot 8 inches and wore lifts in his custom-made boots to give him an extra half inch – but that fact alone wouldn't have prevented him joining the Navy, for they required only that candidates 'be not less than 5 feet'. It is more likely that he would have failed because of his eyesight. He was notoriously short-sighted, and as a consequence wore glasses for all reading and writing, initially a metal-rimmed pince-nez and later thin gold frames. He had the most brilliant, clear blue eyes and would fix people with a beguiling stare that could be disconcerting to those who didn't realize that he could hardly see them otherwise.

Harry soon left the bank and moved to Gilbert, Ransom & Knapp, a local furniture factory, where he became a book-keeper. Unfortunately, the business was already waning and went into liquidation a few months later. Being unemployed wasn't an option, so he took work at a dollar a day in an insurance business in Big Rapids, a small town several hundred miles away.

Whatever influences inspired Harry Selfridge in his quest to create a seductive shopping experience, he certainly didn't find them in Big Rapids. He was never a fan of country pursuits, and fishing and fur-trapping were pretty much all Big Rapids offered by way of recreation in those days. Neither did he drink much. What Harry enjoyed was playing cards – especially poker – and Big Rapids was almost certainly where he honed his game. At one point, boredom is rumoured to have prompted him to study law – via a correspondence course – but he subsequently admitted that it was a 'complete disaster'. In one thing, however, he remained constant. In the office he was always impeccably dressed. Years later, when Selfridge had become famous and the American press serialized his life story, an old acquaintance from Big Rapids recalled that Harry has always looked 'as if he had just come out of a bandbox'.

Harry Selfridge returned to Jackson late in 1876 with $500 he had 'saved from his earnings', although given his predilection for poker it was more likely to have been the winnings from a few lucky hands at cards. He then drifted from one dreary job to another, culminating in eighteen months at a local grocery store. By the time he was 22, he was desperate to move on. But how – and to where? Salvation came through his ex-employer, Leonard Field, who was persuaded to write a letter of introduction to Marshall Field in Chicago. Marshall was the senior partner in Field, Leiter & Co., one of the biggest and most successful stores in the city. Young Harry would ultimately help make it one of the most famous in America.

Selfridge used to say that his interview with Mr Field lasted a matter of minutes and that the man was 'so cold it made him shiver'. Terms were discussed, with Harry claiming he agreed a weekly wage of $10 as a stock boy in the wholesale department basement – but the pay at the very bottom of the ladder he determined to climb was certainly less than that.

Variously described as 'dignified and quiet', and so taciturn he was nicknamed 'silent Marsh', Field had little time for anything other than work. How a man so devoid of personality could have been so successful in the business of sales, where the ability to communicate and motivate is crucial, is a mystery. Field cared little for what he called 'frivolous methods', running his business the way he lived his life. Dry, humourless and puritanical, albeit always courteous, he was the antithesis of Harry Selfridge. They complemented one another, but although Selfridge worked for Field for over twenty-five years, they were never friends.

To call Marshall Field merely 'successful' is an understatement. By 1900, his recorded annual income was $40 million a year (nearly $800 million today) and when he died in 1906, he left an estate worth $118 million (over $2 billion today). A large part of his fortune came from real estate and his early investment in railroad stocks. He was also an original and significant investor in the Pullman Company, backing George Pullman's imaginative concept of luxurious comfort while travelling by train. Given that the journey from Chicago to New York alone took twenty hours, it is small wonder that Pullman's deluxe dining-car, called 'The Delmonico' after New York's swell restaurant, was so successful. Only the rich could travel in his cars, while the really rich bought and customized their own private Pullman carriages – the private jets of their day – fitting marble bathtubs, over-stuffed velvet sofas, piped organ music and, the height of one-upmanship, taking along an English butler to ensure the service was smooth.

The nucleus of Field's wealth, however, came from shopping. The towering department store on State Street was a Mecca for Chicago residents, but as with all the early nineteenth-century 'great store' successes, it was the wholesale department that laid the foundations of the Field fortune, supplying people in small townships all over the Midwest with whatever they needed, from dress fabric to carpets, petticoats to parasols.

Marshall Field was a farmer's son who grew up in Conway, Massachusetts, where the whole family had to help on the land. As neither he nor his elder brother Joseph had any feel for farming, both took what was virtually the only route out of rural life – working as salesmen in a dry-goods store. Marshall's first job was in Pittsfield, Massachusetts, but in 1856 he headed west to join his brother Joseph in Chicago – though it's doubtful whether the neat and tidy, church-going young man of 21 realized what was going to hit him when he got there. Reminders that Chicago was a frontier town were everywhere in the sprawling mass of timber buildings that stretched along the shore of Lake Michigan. Mud was the main topic of conversation – it was so deep that it oozed over the boardwalks, clogged wagon wheels and ruined ladies' clothes. Not that there were too many ladies in Chicago. Local men searching for a bride would 'go East' and, having found a suitable partner, return to Chicago, placing a notice in the local newspapers with the address of the new marital home. Enterprising local dressmakers would often be among their first callers. Having examined the bride's trousseau, the dressmaker would then go from door to door presenting her compliments – along with her newly discovered knowledge of the 'latest fashions from the East'.

For those prepared to take risks, business opportunities were spectacular. William Butler Ogden – who became Chicago's first Mayor – bought a tract of land in 1844 for $8,000, selling it six years later for $3 million. Mr Ogden was nothing if not enterprising. When financing for the Illinois and Michigan Canal dried up he ensured bonds were issued to raise the necessary cash. Always a step ahead, in the same year the canal was opened, he built Chicago's first railroad.

In 1856, Marshall Field had no money with which to buy land or open a store. Instead he took a job at the wholesaler's Farwell, Cooley & Wadsworth, one of the many firms busy shipping dry goods out via Chicago's burgeoning railroads to where the tracks ended in emergent new townships – where women were desperate for everything from cottons and calico to sewing threads and buttons. Field went 'on the road', meeting local merchants, sizing up the business potential and diligently doing his duty by Mr Cooley, whose efficient book-keeper, Levi Z. Leiter, was also busy in the back office, entering their profits in the ledgers. When Potter Palmer, arguably Chicago's most successful merchant, gave up wholesaling to concentrate entirely on his retail division, the polite Mr Field picked up most of his clients – at the same time keenly observing the progress of Mr Palmer's impressive new store on Lake Street.

Chicago's ladies were determined shoppers. In the pre-war financial slump they bought at discount, so much so that *Harper's* caustically advised husbands to 'observe your wife shopping if you would know her. She may be sweet in the parlor, but she is like a ghoul at the counter.' In fact there was very little else for women to do in Chicago other than shop. There were no beauty parlours, no restaurants – or certainly none where women could eat – and only one theatre. Servants took care of the housework and the kitchen. The only thing that ladies could do outside their home – other than attend activities organized by their local church – was to shop for clothes and household materials. Feminists have long raged about the consumer culture, but the early women's champion Elizabeth Cady Stanton was quite clear on the subject. While she deplored the excesses of wealthy women 'who only lived for fashion', she also implored women to seek independence through masterminding the family budget: 'go out and buy' she would shout from the platform at conventions and meetings, urging women to seize the initiative in equipping their household and clothing themselves – whether or not they were paying the bills.

Marshall Field was a man with a searing ambition to make money. All his life he judged opportunity strictly by prospective returns – and when the elderly Mr Wadsworth retired, the chance of buying into a partnership was irresistible. When the Civil War began, Mr Farwell, the sole remaining original founder, welcomed Marshall Field as a full partner. Three years later, in another management shuffle, the business was taken over completely by Field and Levi Leiter, who became partners. Somehow – despite working an average sixteen-hour day – Marshall Field found the time to meet and marry Nannie Scott, and their son, also named Marshall, was born in 1868. By this time, the Field fortunes were firmly established.

Retail historians today praise Marshall Field as one of the trade's 'founding fathers', but arguably his quantum leap to success came from buying other people's businesses rather than founding his own – and the business that really propelled him forward was that belonging to Potter Palmer. Ten years after he had opened his store, Palmer was making $10 million a year. He was wealthy, but not healthy. In 1865, worn out and worried by gloomy advice from his doctors, Palmer sold the majority equity in his business to Field and Leiter for $750,000 and moved to Paris, leaving the two men with a platform rivals could only dream about.

Palmer was soon back in Chicago enthusing over Baron Haussmann's spectacular rebuilding programme in Paris where wide, elegant boulevards had replaced narrow streets, and the installation of a modern sewage system and transport had finally made Paris 'shopper friendly'.

He knew that if Chicago was to have a world-class shopping district, then its stores needed a better environment. Getting out his cheque book he bought up buildings on State Street, parallel to the lake shore, until his holdings were a mile long. Lobbying the city council to widen the lane into a boulevard, at a stroke he single-handedly reoriented the centre of Chicago from Lake Street – which ran by a foul-smelling river – to State Street, which he virtually owned. He demolished the run of 'shack' shops and saloons along it to build commercial properties, and subsequently leased his prime six-storey corner site to Field & Leiter for $50,000 a year.

Potter Palmer married in 1870. As a wedding gift to his young bride Bertha Honoré, he built a hotel and named it the Palmer House. Eight storeys high, with 225 rooms fitted out with Italian marble and French chandeliers, it was Chicago's most sumptuous building. The hotel never took a paying guest. In 1871, fire swept through the city. An area of three and a half square miles was ravaged, 300 people died and 90,000 were made homeless – nearly a third of the city's population. Among the buildings destroyed were Palmer's hotel and Field & Leiter's new store. Luckily, Marshall Field and Levi Leiter were well-insured. Having recouped most of their losses, they moved to a temporary site, from which they did a roaring trade in Chicago's post-fire renaissance.

It took well over a year to clear the debris left by the great fire. Businesses had to 'make do and mend', and many men set up offices in their own homes as Chicago picked itself up and started a massive rebuilding programme. Field and Leiter bought a property on Market Street where they established their wholesaling headquarters while considering their future. At the same time, Potter Palmer was planning his new 'dream' hotel. To raise the money, he sold a parcel of land on State Street for $350,000 to the calculating men who ran the Singer Sewing Company and who were busy using the phenomenal profits from selling their patented sewing machine to diversify into property.

As a result of Isaac Singer's machine and Ellen Demorest's invention of the first paper patterns, many American housewives were becoming competent dressmakers. Observing this trend with unease, the legion of professional dressmakers upped the stakes by affecting fancy French names and even learning a word or two of the language, which never failed to impress their customers. For the newly affluent woman, however, all this home-centred activity was dull. Fashion, etiquette and beauty manuals and magazines were now pouring from the printing presses, establishing new trends at almost breakneck speed. Women wanted to go out and buy for themselves, a fact that had not escaped the property division of the Singer Company who spent over $750,000 on an elegant white marble-fronted building on the corner of State Street and Washington. In fact it was so elegant, the great Alexander Stewart himself was rumoured to want it for a Chicago outpost of his New York store. He didn't get it: instead it was leased to Field & Leiter who moved in during the autumn of 1873 just as the New York stock market crashed and a deep recession struck America. It was not an auspicious start.

~

GIVING THE LADIES
WHAT THEY WANT

'Judge not a man by his clothes, but by his wife's clothes.'
Sir Thomas Dewar

Fashion designers and marketers live in hope that a trend will develop credibility and become a bestseller. Then of course they crave a new one, because in reality, fashion succeeds as a business precisely because its obsolescence is inevitable. For true devotees, the cycle lasts a mere six months and the launch of a new look necessitates all sorts of changes. But even today, it is rare for one's entire wardrobe to become dated overnight. Not so when the cumbersome crinoline and matronly bonnet were consigned to history.

By the early 1870s no truly style-conscious woman in society would have been seen dead in hoops – she had to change her wardrobe from top to toe as a totally new look swept into fashion. To the delight of the drapery retailers, its replacement, a revival of the eighteenth-century *polonaise* – best described as a masterful combination of cinch and pouf – also required substantial amounts of material. Women poured themselves into a tight-fitting, short-waisted bodice with even tighter sleeves, worn above drawn-back, bunched skirts puffed at the rear into an elaborate bustle. The whole outfit, often overwhelmed with a profusion of ruches, ribbons and fringes, flew in the face of the emergent dress reform movement, which despaired at the complexity of women's wardrobes.

In the second half of the nineteenth century, the supreme master dictating trends was Charles Frederick Worth. Born in Lincolnshire, Worth spent some time on the shop floor at Swan & Edgar's in Piccadilly and several years working for leading silk merchants in both London and Paris. He opened his own salon on the rue de la Paix in 1858 and found fame by dressing Princess Pauline von Metternich and the Empress Eugénie. Monsieur Worth was sufficiently egotistical to think of himself as all-powerful – fashion titans usually do – but he wasn't the first celebrated royal designer. That honour goes to Rose Bertin, dressmaker and milliner to the ill-fated Marie Antoinette. Rose Bertin's celebrated skills were surpassed only by the astonishing bills she presented to the Queen. But even though she sent model dolls wearing miniature versions of her gowns to princesses at other royal courts in Europe, her reputation was restricted to just a few hundred people. Thanks to the growing influence of magazines in America, Worth was the first designer to become internationally famous.

He was the designer of choice for the wives of the super-rich – his were the original 'red carpet' gowns, created for women who made an entrance and whose husbands' bank balances could stand the cost. His favourite clients were American since they tended to order several gowns at once and never queried the design or the price. Worth used to say 'My transatlantic friends are always welcome – they have the figures, the francs and the faith.' The thrifty French grandees on the other hand – such as the Comtesse Greffuhle, one of Proust's models for the Duchesse de Guermantes in *A la recherche du temps perdu* – ordered individually and, worse, would have their dressmaker make 'alterations' so that the gown could be worn for longer.

Worth revolutionized the business of fashion by presenting his collection on live models in Paris to a slavishly devoted audience, which included most of the 'Wall Street wives'. Travelling to Europe – particularly to Paris – was an annual event for the American rich, enabling them to stock up on art and antiques and visit Worth's salon. Unfortunately for Worth, the Franco-Prussian War put paid to their travels. Worse still, his most famous client, the Empress Eugénie, went into exile in England, his sumptuous salon was requisitioned as a hospital, and the bitter siege of Paris left people more worried about food than fashion. News filtered out that Parisians were eating their horses, cats and dogs, and *Le Figaro* reported that the chefs at the Paris Jockey Club showed culinary initiative in making 'quite a good salami from rats'.

In the uneasy aftermath of the war, Worth reopened. Ably assisted by his son, Jean-Philippe, before long his business reached such dizzy heights that he had over 1,200 staff on his payroll. His master-stroke was to follow the money by taking his collection to New York and Rhode Island. There, as 'the king of fashion', his appearances resembled a state visit as society scrambled to have him as guest of honour at their cocktail receptions and dinners. Orders were then placed to be made up in Paris and shipped back to America.

There wasn't a name from the Gilded Age that Worth didn't dress, and a wardrobe by Worth became the sine qua non for rich American girls who were keen to acquire a titled British husband. Worth's lifestyle mirrored that of his clients, and his beautifully dressed wife and two elegant sons became part of the Worth publicity machine which whirred so effectively that J. P. Morgan himself considered Worth a friend and is said to have cried when he died.

Having virtually invented the crinoline, Worth was equally pleased to get rid of it, as once more he changed the way women dressed. Drapers owed Monsieur Worth a debt beyond price. As each fashion plate of his latest gown was published, women would rush to buy material and commission a similar model. At Field & Leiter alone in the mid-1870s, there were 300 girls sewing in the top-floor workrooms, all busy making gowns for the wives of Chicago's rich, while copies of Worth's newly styled and lavishly trimmed jaunty hats flew out of the millinery department.

Despite the back bustles, which involved purchasing a collaps-ible framed contraption called a 'dress improver', women were finally discovering the delights of lighter lingerie, as ultra-heavy boned and back-laced corsets were replaced by less cumbersome underpinnings.

Corsets were still boned, but the most popular, unaccountably named 'The Widow Machree', was a curve-inducing, front-fastening model with kid-covered hooks and eyes. For the main part, women's dresses were still buttoned up – at least during the day – but the décolleté evening gowns that were now emerging required new uplifting underwear. For those embarrassed about their meagre embonpoint, help was at hand from the Elastic Bosom Company which, having patented their padding, proudly announced that 'in case of shipwreck it would be impossible for the wearer to drown'. In an astute move at a time when virtually all sales staff were male, Marshall Field employed women to work in the store's burgeoning lingerie department, which meant that ladies could be accurately measured and fitted without embarrassment: particularly important as over-tight corsets could cause anything from fainting fits to uterine and spinal disorders.

Field's brother Joseph had by this time been dispatched to England where he set up a company outpost in Manchester, the idea being that he would source new products, imports having cachet among the store's wealthier clientele. Joseph was a dull, miserly man, given to wearing his overcoat in the unheated office and entirely lacking in the glamour associated with fashion, so it isn't surprising that his purchases had a mixed reception. He did, however, send back all sorts of specialist textiles including Nottingham lace and Paisley shawls. Field & Leiter sold lace tablecloths that cost $1,000 a time, when the average weekly wage was $10, but they had plenty of customers who could afford them and who were not at all perturbed by the prohibitive import duties that added so much to the price.

Recession hadn't halted the relentless progress of the rich in Chicago any more than it had held back the 'Robber Barons' of New York. Chicago manufactured, packed and shipped the thing that mattered most – foodstuffs – across America and over the ocean to Europe. By the end of the 1870s, the city was deafened by the sound of building as offices, warehouses and transport terminals sprang up alongside the shanty towns that housed the rising flood of immigrants from Europe. The building boom was financed by the new élite, who were also busy building themselves palatial new homes, their principal requirements being that the result should be impressively large, have the requisite ballroom, and not be anywhere near the city's riff-raff – Chicago was infamous for its brothels and booze. The city's rich colonized their own safe havens, settling in Calumet Avenue, Prairie Avenue or a little further south in 'Millionaire's Row' on Michigan Avenue.

Field himself moved his family (young Marshall II now had a baby sister called Ethel) to Prairie Avenue, commissioning the celebrated architect Richard Morris Hunt to build him a merchant's mansion. Unusually for a Chicago commission, Field asked Hunt to 'keep it simple'. Hunt, more used to clients such as the Vanderbilts (for whom he designed 'The Breakers', their faux-Italian Renaissance palace in Newport, at a cost of $11 million), was unable to exercise his imagination. Unlike the ostentatious Pullman home, or Cyrus McCormick's vast and awesomely unattractive house nearby, Hunt's three-storey dwelling for Field was a model of restraint. It was also the first house in Chicago to be wired for electricity, which shone brightly on the yellow silk-covered walls. Even so, the house was always described as being bleak and cold. It wasn't a happy home.

Mrs Marshall Field could have become one of Chicago's leading hostesses, but she seems never to have had the inclination. A gentle soul married to a man with absolutely no sense of fun, she was prone to chronic migraines and spent an increasing amount of time recuperating in the South of France, more than happy to leave Chicago's social set to compete for the exalted role of leader. That honour went to Bertha Honoré Palmer, who became the undisputed 'Queen of Chicago' just as *the* Mrs Astor was the 'Queen of New York'.

Young Bertha (who had been just 21 when she married 44-year-old Potter) had youth, good looks, quantities of money courtesy of her indulgent husband, and a sister married to President Ulysses S. Grant's son Frederick, which gave her a cachet that money couldn't buy.

Bertha adored jewels – her favourites being diamonds and pearls – and she soon had a prodigious quantity of them, seemingly often wearing them all at once. Potter enjoyed this visible display of excess as much as Bertha did, being prone to remarking fondly, 'There she stands, with half a million on her back.' Actually, it was more like half a million round her neck and another half million on her head: one of Bertha's famous 'dog collars' was set with 2,268 pearls, while her favourite tiara contained 30 diamonds each as big as a quail's egg.

Given that she was pin-thin and petite, Mrs Palmer stood up very well to the rigours of running Chicago society, which she controlled with a rod of iron. At grand functions such as the entrance march to her annual Charity Ball, Mrs Palmer was flanked by the ladies who acted as her deputies and who ran the various 'sub-divisions' of the city. The Palmers themselves ruled the North-side from their awesome turreted castle where, in a show of extreme control, there were no exterior doorknobs – guests had to wait until a servant opened the door – and where the privileged few could ride to the upper floors in the first elevators installed in a private home in Chicago.

Mrs Palmer had a great fondness for Worth gowns and for Paris, where she maintained a home, just as she did in London where the Palmers held court in Carlton House Terrace. Perhaps it was just as well they had three large houses, for they owned an awful lot of art. Always at the cutting edge of fashion, Mrs Palmer was an early patron of the Impressionists. In one single year she famously bought twenty-five Monets, and she loved her Renoir *Acrobats at the Cirque Fernando* so much that it travelled with her wherever she went.

By 1877, Bertha had only to step over to Field & Leiter to buy a new gown by Worth, the store's Paris agent having bought twelve models for Chicago's first private orders from the great man. But before they could be delivered, the store went up in smoke. People mourned its loss as they would have done the death of a relative, and the *Chicago Tribune* produced a fine obituary: 'The destruction of St Peter's in Rome could hardly have aroused a deeper interest than the destruction of this splendid dry goods establishment ... this was the place of worship for thousands of our female fellow-citizens. It was the only shrine at which they paid their devotions.'

Yet another temporary site was hastily found and while Field and Leiter anxiously debated their future, the Singer Company started to clear the rubble and rebuild. Confident that it was the best site in town, Field himself suggested not only moving back in but also buying the building. Levi Leiter was reluctant. He didn't understand the new retail business; he was a traditional wholesaling man. Wholesale, he argued, was less complex to run and made much more money – in 1872 retail sales stood at $3.1 million against wholesaling at $14 million. Field disagreed. The cachet of running a prime retail site was what kept the wholesale customers loyal – one was inseparable from the other. Eventually the partners offered $500,000 to Singer, who immediately rejected it. It was $700,000 'take it or leave it'. Field was in New York on a business trip when Singer contacted Leiter for his final offer. Brusque and stubborn to the end, Leiter wouldn't budge, losing the prime site to the ambitious Scottish duo, Sam Carson and John Pirie, who leased it at $70,000 a year. Field was furious and rushed back from New York to salvage the mess. He won – as he always did – but it cost him Singer's original purchase price of $700,000 plus an extra $100,000 to buy Carson Pirie Scott out of their lease. He didn't forgive Levi Leiter and he didn't forget.

Field & Leiter moved into their new, spacious six-storey building in November 1879 where 500 assistants on the floor served Chicago's best customers. Field used to say it was 'everyone's store', and everyone came, from the celebrated actress Lillie Langtry – famous for her sexual exploits in England – to Carrie Watson, who knew a thing or two about sex herself, given that she ran Chicago's most exclusive brothel. In keeping with the style of her 'house' – a three-storey mansion with more than twenty bedrooms plus a bowling alley and billiard room in the basement for those waiting to be served – Carrie's girls were beautifully dressed. They 'received' in ball gowns, fluttered their fans in the most charming way and peeled off layers of exquisite underwear, all of which made Carrie Watson one of Field & Leiter's most valued customers.

There was no such excitement in the basement of Field's Market

Street wholesale building where young Harry Selfridge had just started his new job. Such thrills as he got were from reading the newspapers – which he devoured daily – or from visits to the theatre where he watched stars such as Lillie Langtry while nurturing dreams of his future. He didn't have long to wait. Within the year, his boss, the immaculately dressed and fastidious John Shedd, sent Selfridge 'on the road' selling lace. Shedd, who would stay with Marshall Field throughout his career, ultimately becoming President on Field's death in 1906, had joined the business as an enthusiastic wholesaling junior in 1871. He was organized, methodical and a gifted salesman who loved beautiful things. When Selfridge joined, Mr Shedd was running the lace department, one of the most profitable in the division. Shedd and Selfridge would become the two men who between them revolutionized the firm.

The Field & Leiter 'linemen', as they were known, were legendary. They were given a budget to 'entertain' alongside their suitcase of samples and swatches, and if they surpassed their target of $100,000 each year they received a bonus. No one knows if Selfridge hit the target, but we do know he hated the job. After three years he had had enough. Harry Selfridge – always urbane – knew he was an urban man and wanted to live in Chicago. Requesting a transfer to work in retail, he moved over to the State Street store in 1883.

It has always been said that Harry Selfridge worked on the shop floor, but his son Gordon claimed he never did: 'My father did not start in retail as a clerk. He was in unofficial charge of the advertising department.' Perhaps that is why Field – while acknowledging that Selfridge was articulate and in tune with the media – never thought of him as a true merchant. That accolade was reserved for Mr Shedd, already on the path to becoming 'heir apparent'. Selfridge was the store's 'ideas man' and if those ideas made money, that was all well and good. Selfridge took his role as copy-writer seriously. His copy seems dated now but for the time it was enormously refreshing. Field ads didn't lie; they were always honest, perhaps a touch self-important – but above all, they were reassuring about quality, value, respect and commitment to service. As Chicago boomed, the message went out to the public that Field & Leiter was a comforting place to be.

For all Field's lack of charisma, he was polite, calm and dignified, exuding a quiet confidence. He prided himself on caring for the customer and drilled his staff never to hustle or harass. Walking through the store one day he found an assistant quibbling with a customer over a return. 'Give the lady what she wants,' Field remarked. He was equally calm when ousting Leiter, his partner of fourteen years, who exited the business with a cheque for nearly $3 million, leaving Harry Selfridge to write ads that announced the store would henceforth be called 'Marshall Field & Co.'.

Levi Leiter took to his forced retirement rather well, moving his wife and family to Washington and setting up home in a Dupont Circle mansion, where he nurtured his property portfolio while his wife nurtured marital ambitions for her three young daughters. Despite their handsome dowries, not even Mrs Leiter could have predicted the glittering future of her eldest daughter Mary, who married George Curzon in 1895. When her husband subsequently took up his appointment as Viceroy of India, Lady Curzon, as Vicereine, occupied the most important position ever held by an American in the British Empire.

Back in Chicago, Harry Selfridge would prove Levi Leiter wrong. The future lay not in wholesaling but in retailing. The real consumer revolution had begun.

THE CUSTOMER IS ALWAYS RIGHT

'Remember always that the recollection of quality remains
long after the price is forgotten.'
Harry Gordon Selfridge

Harry Selfridge had a deep-rooted belief in the power of advertising. To him, it was the engine that drove the retail machine, and his faith in it never wavered. Through good times and bad, the Selfridge policy was to spread the word through the media.

His first aim was to get people through the doors. 'Getting them in' became his mantra. Once they were inside he believed in giving them comfort, courteous service and, above all, entertainment as an enticement to buy. If, having reeled them in like fish on a line, he lost some, he reckoned he could always catch them another time.

Harry was brash, bold, impulsive and imaginative, qualities which did not go down well with Marshall Field's incumbent retail general manager, J. M. Fleming, to whom Harry was appointed as personal assistant in 1885. Harry's brief from Marshall Field was to propose – and subsequently implement – new ideas. Mr Fleming was of the old school, formal in manner, traditional in outlook, bowing to every ritual and rule that had 'built the business'. Harry thought him stubborn and old-fashioned.

A year or so earlier, Harry Selfridge had been to New York – a trip apparently taken at his own expense by way of a working holiday and one which had a profound effect on him. He noted the uniformed greeters at Lord & Taylor, saw the crowds hunting for bargains at

Macy's and admired the fashionable clothes at the Bloomingdale Brothers' East Side Bazaar. All had benefited in one way or another from the influence of Alexander Stewart (though his own business had, after his death in 1876, subsequently collapsed). Convinced he could make his own mark on Marshall Field, Harry looked at what was already there and set about improving it.

He had a good base on which to build. Field himself had embraced the era's new technology, removing the old-fashioned gas lamps and wiring the six-storey store for electricity in 1882. He had even installed telephone lines, albeit only five for the whole building. The store also had a fine reputation in the community. Field's promoted their 'fair price' policy, always claiming they offered good value.

Realistically, very few consumers had the faintest idea how much goods were worth. For most, the acquisition of non-essential goods was such a new adventure that if they had the money, they willingly paid the price. In many instances – particularly for luxury items – the store buyers were encouraged to set prices at what they thought the market could afford to pay. Prices were intended to cover all costs and they included an additional 6 per cent paid to the wholesale division – from whom the retail store sourced most of its goods – and a charge levied by Mr Field against the rental value of the space each department occupied. When all these costs were covered, departmental heads then had sales targets to meet, above which they made a bonus.

The store was also becoming much more service-orientated. Free local deliveries had already been introduced, as had a 'storing' point where parcels were kept while customers browsed in other departments. There were still only two elevators, but each was as comfortable as a private Pullman car, with plush bench seats, carved panelling and ornate mirrors. Otherwise customers used the impressive sweeping staircase which was twenty-three feet wide and easily accommodated the 'back-bustle and train' dresses then in fashion. Staff called customers 'Madam' or 'Sir'. They weren't allowed to hustle for sales, eat, spit, swear or chew tobacco on the shop floor. In reality, they enjoyed the status their jobs conferred as much as customers enjoyed the status of shopping there. But the refined atmosphere was too rarefied to suit Selfridge who, at 29, was young enough to crave change, and astute enough to know it was waiting to happen.

His first target was lighting. Despite the large central skylight and new electric lighting, the store, replete with vast amounts of mahogany panelling, was gloomy, so he quadrupled the number of hanging globes. Then, uniquely for Chicago and very possibly any other retail store in the world, he lit the windows at night, so creating the new art of evening 'window shopping'. Considering communication crucial, he increased the number of telephone lines, installing a central switchboard operated by female telephonists, with extensions into each major department.

Next he turned his attention to the fixtures. Shopping, he reasoned, should be both a visual and a tactile experience, one best enjoyed in a moment of private self-indulgence and enjoyment and not requiring a sales clerk to unlock a cabinet. So he put central displays in the aisles, folding stock on tables so women could touch and feel a cashmere shawl or a pair of fine kid gloves that they were thinking of buying. He lowered the old-fashioned wall units and ripped out the steep shelves, installing instead back fixtures that staff could reach without ladders. He also reduced the height of the counters, bringing them down to customer-friendly levels, with deep drawers for storage underneath to save staff wasting time making trips to the stock room.

Field may not have appreciated the significance of these moves, but Chicago's acclaimed architect Daniel Burnham certainly did. Burnham – best known today for his iconic Flat Iron building in New York – was the man who helped shape late nineteenth-century Chicago. He also became Selfridge's hero. Harry – whose greatest hobby was collecting architectural drawings – called him 'Uncle Dan', and it was he who later helped visualize the Oxford Street store. Just after Burnham's firm had completed a massive new development for Marshall Field & Co. in 1908 (a dream job that created the twelve-storey building that exists today), he wrote to Selfridge in London with news of their solution to the shop-fitting: 'the fixture question, which I am sure has been solved in this, as in no other store in the world, owes much to your early efforts'.

There was no stopping the man staff called 'mile-a-minute Harry'. He printed souvenir booklets for the 1884 Presidential Conventions held in the city and invited all the delegates to visit the store, reminding them that their shopping would be delivered to their hotels. When the city began to pay school teachers by cheque, he set up a special in-store bank to cash them – ignoring criticism from the media that he was enticing teachers to 'spend more freely in the store as they had cash in their purses'.

Ever the publicist, he also more than quadrupled the store's newspaper advertising budget and booked Chicago's first ever full-page advertisements. The advertisements always had a story – aggressive advertising never interested Harry Selfridge. He preferred to use persuasion, and the text of the advertisements was peppered with his quaint, quirky and deeply felt moral opinions. Nor would he use lurid headlines or false offers on prices. A typical trick of the day was to advertise delivery of 'a special line at exceptional prices'. When customers arrived, they invariably found that what they wanted had mysteriously sold out but that there was something similar at a higher price. Harry Selfridge never endorsed such trickery. He never promised more than the store could provide and he focused on 'service with a smile'.

Shoppers responded to what they felt was sincerity, feeling they were part of the equation in making a choice about their purchases. In truth, women are instinctively shrewd shoppers, but in choosing Field's they were acknowledging that they found subtlety more seductive than bullying. Selfridge told the staff to treat customers 'as guests when they come and when they go, whether or not they buy. Get the confidence of the public and you will have no difficulty in getting their patronage.' He was right.

His message to both the public and the staff was that there was contentment, even fun, to be found in shopping (and working) at

Marshall Field. His critics sneered at him, laughing about his 'little notices' pinned on the wall in the canteen which set 'daily targets':

'To do the right thing at the right time in the right way'
'To do some things better than they were ever done before'
'To know both sides of the question'
'To be courteous; to be a good example; to anticipate requirements'
'To be satisfied with nothing short of perfection'

In reality, his methods where hugely motivational, and this at a time when – particularly in England – store staff were more likely to read a notice outlining cash fines levied for being late on the floor or for being seen by the floor-walker to miss a sale.

Selfridge himself was never a bully, but he was a disciplinarian. He liked to think of himself as a great general marshalling his troops: he once famously said at a staff meeting that he endorsed the idea of uniforms and 'wouldn't mind wearing one himself'. He drilled the staff constantly about the need to be polite and clean (nails, shirt collars and shoes were randomly checked), and if he found a dusty surface when touring the store, he would simply scrawl HGS on it – a sure signal for staff to get out the dusters. He never raised his voice and he never reprimanded anyone in public. He didn't crack jokes and he never, ever gossiped. But he had an aura. Just being around him was heady stuff. Homer Buckley, who worked in the shipping department at Field's, still remembered the impact Selfridge made on him over sixty years later: 'he would drop in at your desk, sometimes all of a sudden, sit there and talk ten minutes, ask about this and that, never talk down to you – the result was you'd be thrilled for a week. I would literally walk on air after he'd done this at my desk. I never met a man capable of putting such inspiration into his employees.'

In 1885, having already instigated the first twice-yearly mark-down sales, Harry implemented a real coup in convincing Marshall Field to open the lower ground floor as the store's 'bargain basement'. Shoppers today are so used to discounts that it is hard to imagine what an impact it had. Chicago's wealthy were regular customers, but by now the city's population had grown to 700,000 and Selfridge longed to give ordinary people what the rich enjoyed. He didn't just target those on low incomes making a special purchase – perhaps lace for a Confirmation dress, or ribbons to trim a hat to wear at a wedding – he also believed that customers from the young, professional classes, making their way on $15 or $20 a week, would soon be able to 'move upstairs'. The bargain basement was much more than a vehicle to shift slow-moving retail stock, although of course it helped to clear the shelves, creating an aura of exclusivity around the store's core merchandise. Promoted as offering 'even better value' – Selfridge abhorred the word 'cheap' – the bargain basement rapidly became a destination for thrifty shoppers who could buy special lines that were subsequently introduced to complement the full-priced merchandise on the upper floors. The new floor was so successful that by 1900, it had a sales turnover of $3 million and had inspired a raft of competitors to copy the idea.

Originally, when presenting his case for the bargain basement, Selfridge had argued the cause of aspirational immigrants, who had an acute sense of 'Sunday Best'. This was a step too far for Field, who had a deep mistrust of immigrants and shuddered at the idea of them shopping in his store. To Field and his cronies, mass immigration, especially from Germany, meant the spreading of socialism, with its inevitable demands for workers' rights, reduced hours and higher pay. Though Field treated his own staff well, he abhorred the idea of unions. Staff who showed signs of militancy were dismissed immediately.

By the mid-1880s, there were well over a thousand staff at Field's. They worked a minimum nine-hour day, six days a week, ate well in the staff canteen and received a 6 per cent discount on their own purchases – not that many of them could afford to shop there. Field's paid less than average: a starting salesman received a weekly wage of $8, the elevator boys $4 and the cash boys $2. But a job at Marshall Field's had cachet, and the store staff considered themselves infinitely superior to the city's factory, sweatshop and railroad workers. When Chicago's railwaymen had rioted during the great railroad strike in 1877, Field staff were mobilized and issued with rifles to use against the threatening 'rabble' if they had to.

A decade later, when McCormick's workers walked out and mob violence swept the city, Chicago's burgeoning – and sometimes brutal – police force didn't need assistance from amateurs. Field himself watched the growing influence of the unions with unease. He reluctantly allowed his delivery men to join an emergent new transport union – the embryonic group that would evolve into the mighty Teamsters – but he nurtured a deep-rooted dislike of what he called 'lawless strikers', so much so that union leaders who came to shop in the store were asked to 'take their business elsewhere'. His protégé Harry Selfridge likewise mistrusted – and avoided – unions throughout his career.

Chicago's rich generally showed a blissful disregard for the poverty of their workers and continued their pursuit of extravagance. They ensured their details were recorded in the *Bon Ton Directory* whose pages listed 'the Most Prominent and Fashionable Ladies Residing in Chicago'. Among them was Mrs Perry Smith, wife of the Chicago & North Western Railway vice-president, who delighted in showing guests visiting her new mansion the butler's pantry, which was equipped with three taps – one for hot water, one for cold, and one for iced champagne. Such material excesses rather appealed to Sarah Bernhardt. When the celebrated actress swept into town to perform at McVicker's Theater, she was accompanied by a hundred pieces of luggage, her pet tiger cub and her lover of the day, a handsome young Italian known only as Angelo. Chicago's *grand dames* refused to receive her, but despite their snubs she said she 'found the city vibrant and exciting'. Not everyone agreed. George Curzon, touring America in 1887, thought Chicago 'huge and smoky and absorbed in the worship of Mammon in a grim and melancholy way', though that did not prevent him from subsequently marrying Levi Leiter's daughter.

By 1887, having driven Mr Fleming to early retirement, Harry

Selfridge was appointed retail general manager of the store. His increased salary enabled him to move his mother from Jackson to Chicago, and they both settled into a house in the city's Near North Side. Mrs Selfridge now had a maid to do her housework. She also had a carriage, whose groom drove a pair of matched chestnut horses to take her around town. The carriage was nowhere near as glamorous as Potter Palmer's imported French *char-à-banc* with its leopard-skin covered seats, nor as distinctive as the brothel-owner Carrie Watson's famous snow-white equipage with bright yellow wheels that was pulled by a team of four glistening black horses, but for Lois Selfridge, it was more than she had ever dreamed possible.

Her son meanwhile made impressive improvements to his own habitat within the State Street store, where he furnished a spacious office. By contrast, Field's office was so small and bleak that George Pullman called it a 'cubby-hole'. Field's routine never varied. He arrived by carriage each morning – setting down two blocks away so he could be seen walking to work – and spent most of the morning going through paperwork before touring the sales floors. He lunched at the Chicago Club, sitting at the 'millionaires table' with friends such as George Pullman and Judge Lambert Tree, and would then walk to the Merchants Loan and Trust Bank – an enterprise in which he held most of the shares – before calling in at the wholesale head-quarters, housed in a magnificent seven-storey building covering a whole city block.

For all his tacit support of the retailing enterprise, it was the wholesale division that interested Field the most – mainly because it made the most money, but also because his travelling sales force reported back from far-flung towns in the Midwest on everything from the state of transport to local politics, land prices and immigra-tion. Distilling this information gave Field an invaluable insight into commercial progress in rural America, which proved crucial to the investment strategy of his own portfolio. On most days, Field would spend an hour with John Shedd, by now manager of the wholesale department and already, in Field's eyes, a masterful merchant.

In 1888, John Shedd and Harry Selfridge were sent on a two-month business trip to Europe. They went to Germany, France and England, where Marshall Field now had offices in Nottingham as well as Manchester. For Selfridge the trip was a catalyst. He was impressed beyond measure with Au Bon Marché in Paris, where he filled two notebooks with ideas, and captivated by the merchandise on sale at Liberty's, particularly the ultra-modern, floaty chiffon 'teagowns' and other aesthetically inspired embroideries much loved by Liberty's more bohemian customers. In fact he was so entranced by the Arts & Crafts movement that when he returned to Chicago, he badgered Marshall Field to allow him to open a William Morris department.

In London, the two men lunched at the Criterion, dined at the Café Royal, attended the famous Gaiety Theatre and visited several English stately homes. It seems likely they went to Compton Verney in Warwickshire, where Marshall Field's daughter Ethel lived with her husband Arthur Tree and their young family in a mansion rented from Lord Willoughby de Broke. Here Harry Selfridge could stroll in gardens laid out by Capability Brown and admire the distinctive hand of Robert Adam who had remodelled the property in 1762. It was all a far cry from Chicago, not to mention Ripon, Wisconsin, and it almost certainly marked the beginning of what would ultimately become his grand passion for living in 'the stately homes of England'.

Back in Chicago, Selfridge determined to make sweeping changes and dreamed of opening branches in New York, Paris and, most importantly, London. Field indulged him – up to a point – but he refused to entertain any ideas of expansion abroad. He did, however, extend the store in Chicago, acquiring three buildings along State Street between the original store and the Central Music Hall, enabling Selfridge to open major new departments. The first was dedicated to children's wear and was partly inspired by the 'Kate Greenaway' collections that Selfridge had seen in Liberty's and by the middle-class trend for formal children's clothes spawned by the runaway success of Frances Hodgson Burnett's bestseller *Little Lord Fauntleroy*. Next came 'Fine Shoes' (mass-produced quality shoes were a recent innovation thanks to the American invention of a 'last-cutting' machine) which stocked shoes and boots in coloured leathers as well as basic black. The store also started to sell paintings, gifts and picture frames, and Selfridge opened service departments to clean customers' gloves, mend their glasses and restring their pearls.

The only thing missing was somewhere to sit, which Selfridge resolved by persuading Marshall Field to agree to an in-store restaurant. Given that there were so few places in Chicago where women could eat out by themselves, it isn't surprising that the store 'tea room', as it was first called, was a runaway success. Originally set up with just fifteen tables served by eight waitresses, within the year it was enlarged to cope with the 1,200 customers who ate there daily. It did not make a profit in the strict sense of 'numbers', but the add-on value in terms of service and keeping the customer in the store was incalculable. The lunch menu, devised by Selfridge with the assistance of a young Chicago cook called Harriet Tilden, was simple but delicious: chicken-pot pie, chicken salad, corned beef hash, cod fishcakes and Boston baked beans, and orange fruit salad served in the orange shell. When the original kitchens could no longer cope with demand, Miss Tilden co-ordinated a group of home cooks who pre-prepared the dishes and delivered them each morning. As the in-store restaurant expanded, so did the kitchen space, but Harriet Tilden's cooks were later put to good use when she opened her own business called 'The Home Delicacies Association', which catered for parties, receptions and society dinners throughout Chicago.

The restaurant was busy from the minute it opened for coffee in the morning, and the ritual of 'Afternoon Tea' at Field's became ever more fashionable. Tiny sandwiches were served in a basket trimmed with a ribbon bow, and the menu included gingerbread slices and the house speciality, Field's Rose Punch (ice-cream with a berry sauce), which came with a red rose on each plate. This was a typical Selfridge touch. The symbolism of flowers was an important part of nineteenth-century sentimentality. Magazines and the endlessly popular etiquette manuals were full of features on 'the meaning of flowers', and the most admired flower of the day was the full-blown, gloriously rich and sexy red American Beauty rose, named after the equally curvaceous, gloriously proportioned stage star Lillian Russell.

The increased activity in the store soon paid dividends. During the six years of Harry Selfridge's management, retail turnover increased from $4 million to $6.7 million. This, Selfridge reasoned, was fine for Mr Field, but he now wanted more for himself. Emboldened by his success, he audaciously asked Field to make him a partner in the business. The atmosphere in Field's office must have been electric as the elderly, reserved owner faced his cavalier, conceited young manager. Realizing 'mile-a-minute Harry' might otherwise leave, Marshall Field bowed to the inevitable. He made Selfridge a junior partner and personally lent him the $200,000 needed to 'buy himself in', while allocating him a share of just under 3 per cent of the total annual profits and increasing his annual salary to $20,000. The combined package meant that at the age of 33 Harry Selfridge was now making today's equivalent of $435,000 a year.

Harry revelled in his new position. He had always been beautifully dressed, but now his frock coats with their silk-faced lapels became even more immaculately tailored. He loathed dirty shirts, changing his at least once and sometimes twice a day. He had special high-cut wing collars made to disguise his unusually thick neck and he always wore the widest possible silk tussore ties with a very large, soft knot. A gold fob watch on a chain, a gold-rimmed pince-nez and a rose boutonnière, carefully chosen from the vase of fresh blooms placed on his desk each morning, completed his outfit. Some of his colleagues found him unbearably conceited – indeed, the only modest thing about him was his height – but he was still head and shoulders above most people working in the retail business.

Selfridge's private life at this time remains a mystery. His mother was his main companion and they were often noted in the press as 'attending the theatre'. Who else kept him company we do not know, but it seems likely that he paid for his sexual pleasures. Vice in Chicago being organized with the same efficiency that characterized more legitimate activities, there were any number of extremely elegant 'houses' which men like Harry Selfridge could frequent without the slightest scandal ever being attached to their name. Any of the celebrated Carrie Watson's twenty girls would have been delighted to welcome him, as would those working at Lizzie Allen's famous 'House of Mirrors' or 'The Arena', blatantly operating on Michigan Avenue where the local millionaires – and their sons – could make convenient visits.

Then, quite suddenly and unexpectedly, Harry became engaged to Rosalie Amelia Buckingham. His bride-to-be has been described as a 'Chicago debutante'. She was indeed a debutante when a teenager, but by the time she met Harry she was nearly 30 and had spent several years working as a successful property developer. Rosalie had learned her craft from her father, the property investor Frank Buckingham, who was also a member of the exclusive Chicago Club. Mr Buckingham had died in the early 1880s, leaving his 23-year-old daughter enough money to venture into development herself.

In partnership with her brother-in-law, Frank Chandler, Rosalie bought land on Harper Avenue in Hyde Park, then a rural outpost of the city. This was no small venture. Rosalie planned and oversaw the building of forty-two villas and 'artists' cottages', the villas each with a 45- or 50-foot frontage and a driveway to reach the stabling at the rear. It was an enlightened development, including a business block with a drugstore, a family grocery store, a café, a reading-room and even a public hall for lectures and concerts. The houses looked out on the park lagoons and lake, with the east side of the development being built sixty feet away from the railroad tracks, which the railroad company was expected to landscape in harmony with the general plan. The architect for the development was Solon S. Beman, the designer of the famous 'Pullman model town', where George Pullman corralled his employees. But Rosalie's villas were not intended for factory workers. They were elegant, spacious middle-class homes in what was the area's first planned community. Miss Buckingham was no giddy debutante.

Harry and Rosalie married on 11 November 1890. He was 34 and she was 30. Harry Selfridge was not a religious man in the conventional sense. Brought up a Presbyterian, as an adult he leaned towards Unitarianism. He believed deeply in 'salvation through good character and hard work' and championed 'improvement through education': his favourite motto was 'Life is what you make it.' In Rosalie, he found a like-minded spirit. The wedding ceremony gave her a foretaste of what life with a showman would be like. It was held at the non-denominational Central Church, housed in the Central Music Hall, just down the road from Marshall Field and one of the few venues in Chicago capable of seating the thousand guests on the happy couple's list. A choir of fifty – whose musical programme was conducted by the Director of the Chicago Musical College, Dr Florenz Ziegfeld – sang to the sound of the music hall's impressive organ, backed up by an orchestra of strings and harps. A display team had laboured to create the central aisle and roof as an exact replica of Ely Cathedral – a romantic curiosity which the newspaper reports failed to investigate but which they would have discovered was in honour of the bride's ancestors who had arrived in America from Cambridgeshire – and the hall was filled with the scent of 5,000 roses. More roses and a mass of lilies and foliage were wired around the pillars and the tiered boxes. The whole event was as spectacular as those later staged by Ziegfeld's son – also called Florenz – when he became the impresario behind Ziegfeld's Follies in New York. Indeed, many at the wedding thought the whole thing was a folly, but Harry Selfridge loved every glorious minute of it. His bride wore an ecru *duchesse* satin gown with exquisite antique lace cuffs falling from elbow-length sleeves. It wasn't made by Worth, but it was a beautiful dress, set off by an impressive necklace of blue diamonds – her gift from the bridegroom.

The couple left on their honeymoon accompanied by Lois Selfridge – a fact which didn't seem to perturb the new Mrs Selfridge in the slightest. It was just as well the two women got along because they would live together in various homes for the rest of their lives. An impressive array of wedding presents reflected the couple's status – not to mention the size of the guest list – and included a valuable parcel of land on the shores of Lake Geneva, a wealthy enclave ninety miles north of Chicago, presented to them by Rosalie's sister and brother-in-law, who owned a summer house next door. There Harry and Rose – as he always called his wife – would build a mock-Tudor country house with large greenhouses where Harry tended his favourite roses and prize orchids. Harry Selfridge now had two women to idolize, and they in turn both loved him unconditionally.

~

FULL SPEED AHEAD

'We live in an age where unnecessary things are our only necessities now.'
Oscar Wilde

On some days it seemed to Harry Selfridge that he was riding the crest of a wave, on others that he had crashed to the beach. At home, there was sadness for Rose and Harry when their first child – a daughter they named Violet – died a few months after her birth. Selfridge masked his grief by throwing himself even more energetically into his work, while Rose recuperated quietly. Having excelled herself with the development of Rosalie Villas, it might have been expected that she would continue working. But she didn't. In an era when women craved their independence, Rose seems to have been content at home. She had married a tornado of energy and at times seemed to find it all rather exhausting.

City officials were buzzing with plans following Chicago's coup in winning the bid to host what was officially known as 'The World's Columbian Exposition', America's celebration of the 400th anniversary of Christopher Columbus arriving on its shores. Chicago had flourished its cheque book to beat off stiff competition from New York, Washington and St Louis. In April 1890, President Harrison approved an Act of Congress to provide for 'an international exhibit of arts, industries, manufactures, and the products of the soil, mine and sea, in the city of Chicago', and invited the 'nations of the world to take part'. In much the same way that London's Great Exhibition of 1851 had launched the emergent trend of consumerism, Chicago's World Fair would establish it as an irrevocable part of daily life.

This was the event Chicago had been waiting for – not least the property speculators who rushed to buy land. Harlow Higginbotham (the senior partner in charge of finance at Marshall Field) was appointed as President of the Fair, and Daniel Burnham was designated as overall Director of Works. They knew when the Fair was going to be – 1892 – and they soon decided where, selecting a vast 630-acre site on the South Side, covering Jackson Park and the Midway Plaisance. How it would all happen was less easily decided. A group of the country's leading architects convened to plan the buildings. Headed by Burnham, the group included Richard Morris Hunt (of Astor, Vanderbilt and Field house fame), Charles McKim of the hallowed New York partnership McKim, Mead & White, Frederick Law Olstead (who had laid out New York's Central Park), and Chicago's own celebrated Louis Sullivan. They apparently started to argue at their very first meeting, with the eastern group advocating classicism and Chicago's Louis Sullivan, modernism. Furthermore, it soon became clear that the plans laid down couldn't possibly be completed in time, and the public opening of the Fair was postponed to 1893.

There being a lot to do, Chicago's great and good set to work. First, Mayor Carter H. Harrison had to get re-elected. He had already served a straight four terms, so the city's residents knew what they were getting – Harrison was a hard-drinking, keen gambling man. Sure enough, when he won, albeit by a narrow margin, he announced he had 'laid down two hundred barrels of good Chicago whiskey that could kill at the distance of a mile' for official hospitality. In New York, Mrs Astor's arbiter of etiquette Ward McAllister was horrified, writing in *The World* 'that it is not quantity but quality that visiting New York society will care about'. Uneasy about the menus, not to mention the wines, McAllister advised the city to 'import a number of fine French chefs as a gentleman who has been accustomed to terrapin and pâté de foie gras would not care to dine on mutton and turnips'. His pronouncements on Chicago's seeming inability to organize a banquet caused a furore, with the local press calling him a 'head butler' and a 'New York flunky'. McAllister, not to be outdone, unleashed a further barrage of criticism: 'It takes nearly a lifetime to educate a man how to live. These Chicagoans should not pretend to rival the East in matters of refinement – their growth has been too rapid for them to acquire both wealth and culture.'

McAllister, who had originated the concept of Mrs Astor's famous 'Four Hundred' (in reality the number of people who could comfortably fit in her ballroom), was obsessed with decorum, dancing and décor. Convinced that the rich of Chicago couldn't dance a quadrille, he was particularly caustic about the design of the millionaires' mansions, where the ballroom was often relegated to the third floor and, worse, accessed by an elevator: 'In New York, the opinion is that the approach to the ballroom should be as artistically effective as the room itself. We don't go to dance by going up in an elevator.'

Chicago, proud of its meaty menus and its elevators, ignored most of his pontificating, but jibes about dancing touched a nerve. Help was on hand courtesy of Eugene A. Bournique's Dance Academy where Mr Bournique, more used to teaching children their first ballet steps, was kept busy teaching the intricacies of ballroom etiquette to their parents. The city echoed to the sound of construction. New hotels were built, existing ones redecorated; new restaurants opened and, as the city's gaming dens hastily planned an expansion of their floor space, demand for roulette wheels rocketed and a new factory had to be opened to cope with the orders.

Mrs Potter Palmer, as the city's leading lady, was appointed chairman of the Board of Lady Managers in charge of their own Women's Building. Even in the face of the growing influence of the women's movement, such a project was a radical step for America, and Mrs Palmer determined it would be noteworthy. The Lady Managers hired a female architect, Sophia Hayden, to create their pavilion, planning a series of rooms to show everything from cookery demonstrations to the latest in home technology, interior design, arts, crafts and even a model kindergarten. It was agreed that concerts in the auditorium would only feature the work of women composers and that exhibitions would display the achievements of women in the arts and sciences and in the professions. Last but not least, the pavilion would exhibit the very latest in fashion trends, together with exhibits of rare jewels and antiquities borrowed by Mrs Palmer from her wealthy, titled friends in Europe. Everything in fact that a woman could want or need – except cosmetics.

Not that entrepreneurs involved in the embryonic business of beauty didn't want to exhibit. Madame Yale, famous for her lectures on 'The Religion of Beauty, the Sin of Ugliness', was keen to promote her products. But Mrs Palmer and her committee were utterly determined that she should not. Rouge and lipstick were, said Mrs Palmer, 'not things we wish to dwell on or emphasize'. In banning Mrs Yale, Bertha Palmer was following the mores of the day, which determined that cosmetics were 'not respectable'. Ladies like Mrs Palmer took care of their skin with soap, water and a face-mask made with old-fashioned oatmeal. They may have tried Harriet Hubbard Ayer's exclusive 'Recamier' cream – Mrs Ayer herself being from a good Chicago family – but more often than not they were content with a greasy lanolin-based cream made up by the local pharmacist. Given Chicago's brutal winter weather, they would almost certainly have used lip salve (one excellent local recipe included hog-fat, a useful by-product of Chicago's stock yards), and eyebrows were plucked and waxed. Finally, a light dusting of fine powder would have been applied to avoid shine. Further than that, they would not go.

As a consequence, in smart stores like Marshall Field's, the toiletries department was of minor significance. It sold hand mirrors, brushes and combs, hair accessories, eau de cologne and a wide range of beautifully packaged scented soaps. Neither did Field's attempt to enter the business of hairdressing or offer beauty treatments such as manicures and massage, which were the fiefdom of small, individual beauty parlours. Field's held out against the onslaught of cosmetics for a long time, though others soon succumbed. As early as 1897, the

Sears catalogue offered its own line of cosmetics, including rouge, eyebrow pencils and face powder, while Harry Selfridge himself would famously go on to open England's first major cosmetics department in 1910.

With 25 million visitors expected to attend the Fair, Marshall Field astutely set a retail expansion plan in motion. Early in 1892 he began to buy buildings to the east of the store, commissioning Daniel Burnham to design a new nine-storey annexe, which had to be ready in eighteen months. Despite his awesome workload overseeing the erection of more than two hundred buildings for the Fair, Burnham managed to bring the new Field project in only two months over deadline, and by August 1893 it was open for business.

Harry Selfridge became minutely involved in planning the layout and fitting of this new space of more than 100,000 feet, which ultimately gave the store an overall total of nine acres. Under Burnham's expert tutelage, he received a master class in building, lighting and shop-fitting. Technical innovations included the installation of thirteen high-pressure hydraulic elevators and twelve separate entrances with revolving glass doors. Interior fixtures included lavish hand-carved mahogany counters trimmed in bronze and, in a welcome first for shoppers, a majestic suite of ladies' lavatories. There were now a hundred different departments at Marshall Field's, all of them dressed to the nines to welcome the international visitors who were touring the Fair and who, inevitably, were also drawn into the store.

For Selfridge, 1893 was a momentous year. In addition to the World Fair and the expansion of Field's, he and Rose had a baby daughter, Rosalie, born on 10 September – which explains why Rose was absent from most of the festivities connected with the Fair: when pregnant, ladies of the day never socialized in public.

Harry was among the welcoming committee that greeted the Duke of Veragua – a direct descendant of Christopher Columbus – and his Duchess when they arrived in Chicago in May for the opening celebrations. Despite his lofty titles, among them 'Admiral of the Ocean Sea', the Duke was a man of modest means who bred Arab horses at a stud farm outside Madrid. Flattered at being met by an escort of the United States Cavalry, and delighted by the lavish hospitality and media attention accorded him and his Duchess, the Duke began to overstay his welcome. Two weeks grew to three and then a month. The organizing committee, panicking at the cost of hosting the ducal couple, suggested it was time to leave. The Veraguas finally agreed to go, but not before the Duke had intimated that the same military escort that had met them on arrival should also see them off at the station. The organizing committee, with no remit to provide a second escort, were saved by an enterprising member who kitted out a team of amateur actors as hussars, mounting them on black horses and equipping them with swords. It did the trick nicely.

Running the Fair involved considerable diplomacy as tempers flared and egos exploded. The mighty Steinway Piano Company had refused to exhibit, so the committee banned its pianos from being used by any of the dozens of orchestras playing throughout the Fair. This didn't worry the young musician Scott Joplin, who was practising his new 'rag-time' tunes on a rickety upright in a local saloon, but it did alarm the great pianist Ignacy Paderewski who refused to play on anything but a Steinway. The impasse was broken when the Fair's musical director had the foresight to smuggle in a Steinway, resulting in such a row that the poor man was forced to resign.

The next Spanish grandee to sample Chicago hospitality was HRH the Infanta Eulalia – daughter of Queen Isabella II and a haughty young woman who was fond of remarking that 'in Spain there is Nobility – or nothing. We do not recognize the middle classes.' With the World Fair being targeted at exactly that group, her visit was destined to be tricky. Eulalia and her husband Prince Antoine arrived at the station in George Pullman's own private railway car – somewhat late having made an unscheduled stop in Pennsylvania, where Eulalia had sent out for a fresh supply of Spanish cigarettes. To the delight of Chicago's booming tobacco industry – and the distress of Bertha Palmer who loathed smoking – the Infanta puffed prodigiously, even enjoying a cigar after dinner. Her much-publicized habit prompted an enterprising local firm to box up Cuban cigars with her picture on the lid, unfortunately promoting her to 'Eulalia, Queen of Spain' in the process.

The Royal party was allocated a glorious suite at the Palmer House Hotel, stuffed full of antiques and tapestries to make them feel at home. Legend has it that the Infanta at first refused to meet Mrs Palmer on the grounds that she was merely 'the wife of my innkeeper'. What is certain is that wherever the Infanta went, she was always late. Keeping Spanish-style hours, she didn't arrive at the gala reception held at the Palmers' home in her honour until 10.15 p.m. Once there, however, she was invited to take up position on a velvet throne set on rugs impregnated with rare perfumes where she held court until the small hours, while John Sousa's band kept the party entertained.

Chicago's South Side had blossomed into a glorious mass of pearly-white grandeur, shimmering by the lake like Camelot, with the gilded domes of its 'Court of Honour' (as the classically styled principal building was called) twinkling in the sunlight. The team of artists and architects who had created this model 'White City' as an awesome show of corporate power and consumerism allowed themselves to be described as 'the greatest meeting of minds since the Renaissance'. In reality, apart from the central, anchor buildings in stone, the whole was mainly done by smoke and mirrors. Most of the buildings were temporary edifices made from a mixture of plaster, cement and jute fibre, all painted white. Critics called them 'decorated sheds' but even the sternest opponent couldn't fail to be secretly impressed. Thousands of daily visitors travelled on the newly built South Side 'L', an elevated railroad that dropped them off at the Jackson Park Terminal where they could walk through Louis Sullivan's monochrome, futuristic Transportation Building before touring the Fair on its own elevated electric railway.

An off-site 'amusement area' in the Midway Plaisance, segregated from the exhibition halls but an integral part of the concept, offered round-the-clock excitement. The most thrilling was a ride on the 'Giant Wheel' built by the brilliant young design engineer George

Ferris. The Fair's organizing committee had long wanted something to 'top' the Eiffel Tower, which had dominated the 1889 Paris International Exposition. After months of indecisive bickering, they eventually settled on the Ferris concept with the proviso that George Ferris should fund not only the plans and specifications (which alone cost him $25,000) but also the construction costs. Ferris and his team worked round the clock through the severe Chicago winter. When they had finished, his triumphant wheel towered majestically to a height of 266 feet, giving the passengers who paid 50 cents to ride in one of its 36 carriages – each big enough to hold 40 people – a view of three different States from the windows. During the nineteen weeks the Ferris wheel operated, it carried nearly one and a half million people and was the greatest single attraction at the Fair. Tragically, the strain of raising the cash and the stress of building the wheel exhausted Ferris. He died destitute and alone in a Pittsburgh hospital just three years after his prototype wheel had astounded the world.

Other than the Ferris wheel, the biggest draws at the Midway Plaisance were Buffalo Bill Cody and his 'Wild West Show', and Fahreda Mahzar, an exotic dancer who called herself 'Little Egypt' and who performed her signature belly dance – the 'hootchy-kootchy' – wearing layers of transparent chiffon which, as one eager reporter noted, 'showed every muscle in her body rippling at the same time'. 'Little Egypt' wasn't the only one flexing her muscles. Assigned to tour Europe to procure military bands to play at the fair, Florenz Ziegfeld Jr, showing his potential for showmanship, had brought back the acclaimed German strongman Eugen Sandow, who subsequently became the father of modern-day body building. Flo put him under a management contract and masterminded his performance at the Fair. Sandow started his act lying in a black velvet-lined box, his body dusted in white powder, and then slowly rose from it like a muscled classical God, dressed in little more than a leopard-skin loincloth. Some women were so overcome at the sight that they fainted – even Bertha Palmer was persuaded to 'touch' Sandow's rock-hard muscles, pronouncing them 'very impressive'.

During the six months of the Fair, there wasn't a visiting VIP who didn't make their way downtown to Marshall Field, where Harry Selfridge personally conducted them around the store. Field himself was usually nowhere to be seen when these celebrity visits were made, finding them as distasteful as he did talking to the press. Field neither liked nor trusted journalists, whereas Harry instinctively understood the power of publicity, giving them all the help he could. Harry was now being described in the newspapers as the 'genial personality in charge of the retail division of Marshall Field', and his job there fitted him like a second skin.

As the Fair drew to a close, visitors could reflect on what they had seen. First and foremost, they had been exposed to the wonders of electricity, in itself an icon of technological advance. They had drunk the world's first carbonated drinks, eaten the world's first hamburgers, admired the world's largest cheese – which weighed in at thirteen tons – and bought the world's first pre-packaged tea, courtesy of the Scottish grocery magnate Thomas Lipton. Visitors had sent picture postcards to friends using the world's first commemorative stamps, enjoyed cookery demonstrations involving new products such as Quaker Oats and Aunt Jemima's Pancake Mix, and fallen in love with the bicycle. Some had heard Dvorak's 'New World Symphony' which he composed for the Fair, while others had seen Anschutz's 'electrotachyscope' project the world's first moving images. Mayor Harrison, receiving the plaudits of his colleagues on Mayor's Day, 28 October, must have felt justifiably proud, but the ebullient Mayor didn't live long enough to enjoy the plaudits. He was assassinated that night by Eugene Prendergast, who in his defence subsequently pleaded insanity. Prendergast lost his case and was executed.

The World Fair had a profound impact on Harry Selfridge who, having witnessed at first hand how to entertain a crowd, later became devoted to showing all manner of technical innovations to a captivated audience in London. The Fair itself, quite apart from being the precursor of global theme parks from Coney Island to Disney World, also so enchanted the young writer L. Frank Baum that he turned its 'White City' into his 'Emerald City' of Oz.

The World Fair was symptomatic of changes taking place everywhere in the western world, particularly in women's lives. The World's Congress of Representative Women had met in Chicago during the Fair, where over 150,000 women flocked to listen to Elizabeth Cady Stanton and Lucy Stone speak. Fresh ideas poured forth from a huge number of newly successful women's magazines. Women in Chicago now travelled alone on the cable street cars and elevated trains. There were changes too in fashion. Women would have to wait another decade to abandon their corsets, but there was an important shift in the shape and weight of clothes as more and more women took to wearing two-pieces and blouses.

The 'jacket-and-skirt' combination had first been seen in America during the Civil War. Women in the intellectual and professional classes had continued to wear it, calling it their 'emancipation suit'. Dress reformers also adopted front-buttoning soft underwear as pioneered in fine knit by Dr Jaeger and in cotton by Dr Kellogg. The leisured classes and newly rich, however, had relentlessly clung to the formality of the back bustle both by day and by night, until the 'two-piece' with its faintly military cut and gored skirt was given a huge boost when it was adopted by the Prince of Wales's beautiful wife, Princess Alexandra, whose every move in fashion was eagerly watched in America. For once the trend hadn't originated from Worth. It was the British tailoring genius Charles Poynter of Redfern who made the suits for the Princess – in tweed for shooting parties and in navy blue and white grosgrain for yachting. The waist was still cinched, but the bustle had disappeared, and the sleeves were puffed from shoulder to elbow and then narrowed from elbow to wrist.

The trend for what the stores referred to as 'tailor-mades', along with the ornate, high-necked blouses that went with them, triggered the mass production of much better-quality ready-to-wear. Marshall Field's still had its own in-house workrooms for hand-made clothes, but bulk stock, for them as for other stores, was now sourced from the clothing factories and sweat shops of New York and Chicago.

America's 'new woman', as the media styled her, energetically took to sport, particularly tennis, which in itself created a fashion trend. Players wore softer skirts, with a plainer 'shirt-waist' blouse and an unbuttoned cotton-drill jacket. Nothing typified this image more than the drawings of the graphic artist Charles Dana Gibson. The 'Gibson Girl' was officially launched in 1890 and for the next twenty-five years she came to represent the ideal female form in the United States. The tall, rangy and patrician young woman styled by Gibson, with her casually up-swept hair and *sportif* clothes, had a huge impact on fashion. Women wanted to look, dress and live their lives like her.

Women also took enthusiastically to dance as an acceptable form of exercise, in particular adopting the 'stretch and body poses' movement programme originally pioneered by the Frenchman François Delsarte, which became a huge craze in America. Not that 'doing Delsarte' meant breaking a sweat, it was more about grace and control. His system was the precursor of contemporary dance as pioneered by Loie Fuller and her disciple Isadora Duncan, who naturally chose Chicago – acclaimed as the most progressive city in America – to launch her professional career in 1895. When she auditioned at Chicago's leading variety house, the Masonic Temple Roof Garden, Isadora so impressed its manager Charles Fair that he booked her on the spot. Knowing his audience, however, the cigar-chomping Mr Fair doubted that her dance programme would hold them. 'You might do the Greek thing first,' he suggested, 'then change to something with petticoats and frills so you can do kicks.' With only her 'Grecian' shift in her luggage – and no money for shopping – Fair sent Isadora to see his friend Selfridge.

Selfridge was enchanted with Isadora, overseeing her selection of red gingham, white organdie and lace ruffles for her outfit. Billed as 'the California Faun', Isadora was a sensation, and, having dressed her, Selfridge was in the audience to watch. Some people later said he undressed her too – she was after all a believer in free love, and Harry was an attractive man, with a tendre for dancers and a wife who was often to be found 90 miles away, supervising the construction of their imposing mock-Tudor house on the shores of Lake Geneva. Whatever the case, Isadora Duncan and Harry Selfridge remained friends until she died.

Field himself continued to add to his property portfolio, one particular acquisition having a certain poignancy. In 1898, Levi Leiter's only son Joe, who so far had excelled himself solely in playing high-stakes poker, decided to gamble on making his own fortune by attempting to corner the world's wheat market, buying all he could on margin. When the Chicago meat baron P. D. Armour needed 9 million bushels in a hurry he contacted young Leiter, who refused to sell. Armour wasn't going to be pushed around by 'an uppity kid'. He sent a fleet of ice-breaking tugs over the frozen lake north to Duluth, buying wheat for himself and an extra 9 million bushels, which he poured into the market. Young Joe Leiter's margins were called in and he ended up owing $10 million. With his son facing certain bankruptcy and possibly prison, Levi Leiter had to liquidate assets fast, among them a valuable parcel of land on the corner of State Street, housing the site of department store Schlesinger & Mayer, for which Field paid his ex-partner $2,135,000.

The Leiters' financial disaster had a dramatic impact in London, where Leiter's daughter Mary, now Lady Curzon, was putting together the sumptuous wardrobe required for her forthcoming position as Vicereine of India. It wasn't only her clothes and jewels that were needed. George Curzon required an impressive wardrobe of uniforms, and the couple were also expected to pay the outgoing Viceroy for his wine cellar, horses, carriages and silver plate. Curzon, who had little money of his own, had always assumed his rich father-in-law would be able to provide everything necessary. All he got from Levi Leiter was £3,000 and a new tiara for Mary, leaving him in the embarrassing position of having to request an advance on his salary.

Back in Chicago, by 1900, 14 million tons of cargo were passing through the port. Over 500 miles of street-car tracks – called 'street railroads' – threaded their way through the city, and the elevated railroad was packed every day. Automobiles were also slowly beginning to make an appearance, though to visitors it must have seemed as if everyone was riding a bicycle as the new craze for cycling swept the nation. Happily for women cyclists their skirts didn't sweep the ground. When Lillian Russell took to cycling – on a custom-made Tiffany gold-plated machine, with mother-of-pearl handlebars and her initials worked in diamonds on the wheels – she wore a cream leg-of-mutton sleeved cycling suit with the skirt shortened by three inches, which set an unstoppable fashion trend.

Fashion also had a huge impact on Marshall Field. Since the World Fair, Field's had imported over $3 million worth of goods annually from around the world. By 1900 the retail division alone turned over an astonishing $12.5 million. With the store severely short of space, that year Field acquired the rest of the buildings in the block, including the Central Music Hall where Harry and Rose had married, enabling him to demolish the building on the original site and replace it with an enormous twelve-storey structure, retaining only the comparatively new annex. Once more Daniel Burnham and his team swung into action, and once more Harry Selfridge was flying with excitement. At every stage of the development he booked advertisements to inform shoppers about progress, at the same time reassuring them that Field's was 'committed to fair prices and good value'. Selfridge was busier than ever at work, and Rose was busy at home with their two daughters – Rosalie's sister Violette was born in 1897 – and their son, Gordon, who was born three years later. Their fourth child, another daughter called Beatrice, born in 1901, would complete their family.

Advertising had become a major tool in the promotion of retail. The industry with which Selfridge had experimented in the early days was now virtually unrecognizable. Nationally, the biggest spenders were the food companies and the tobacco industry, but businesses producing toiletries and soft drinks were not far behind. By 1899, eighty companies were making, or beginning to make, automobiles, and advertising agencies were keenly anticipating the day when cars would appear on the pages of influential magazines. In the meantime, they had to make do with the bicycle, and for the first time ever women were shown outside the home in a non-domestic setting riding their bicycles.

Advertisements for Marshall Field were, like most retail pages, booked locally rather than nationally, with newspapers being the biggest beneficiary. Indeed, the growth of retail advertising paralleled the growth of the big city newspapers, which created arts, event and fashion features by way of reciprocal editorial. Following company policy, Marshall Field pages never appeared on Sunday, this being still a day devoted to family, friends and Church.

The first phase of the six-year building programme opened in 1902. Marshall Field's was a monument to new technology with over 50 elevators, 15,000 fire-sprinklers, thousands of feet of tubing for the pneumatic cash-carriers, and a cold storage vault with room for 20,000 fur coats. There was a library, a first-aid room with a trained nurse, an information bureau, a concierge service to book theatre tickets and hotel rooms, a crèche where mothers could leave their children in the care of trained nannies, and seven restaurants. Harry Selfridge had supervised every inch of the project from the miles of carpets to the hundreds of mirrors. He hadn't forgotten the staff either. Now numbering 7,000, they had a special canteen, recreation rooms, locker rooms, a gymnasium and their own library. He instigated a three-day training system whereby new salespeople were given an intensive course in manners and in how to make the customer feel at home.

John Wanamaker, the famously enlightened Philadelphia retailer who was then the owner of America's largest emporium, came to visit, and even he was impressed. In the first three days of business, more than 150,000 people came through the doors and were given special celebration souvenirs costing over £10,000. Marshall Field's old mentor Potter Palmer wasn't there to share his triumph. Palmer had died that year, leaving an estate worth over $8 million to his wife

Bertha, even setting aside a sum for her next husband 'because he'll need it'. In the event, Bertha remained a wealthy widow. Field was dumbstruck when he heard that Palmer's fortune had passed directly to his wife, bypassing their son. 'What on earth does she need with all that money?' he asked. 'One million dollars is quite enough for any woman.'

Field was increasingly isolated. His estranged wife was dead. His brother Henry was dead. Many of his friends were dead. He never entertained in his vast, empty house. His children and grandchildren lived in England. He eschewed the poker circle at his club – gambling, in his opinion, was a weakness. His only activity was work – and playing the occasional round of golf. Peter Funk, a colleague who had the courage to speak his mind, said to him: 'Marshall, you have no home, no family, no happiness, nothing but money.'

Harry Selfridge had played a huge part in masterminding the development of the retail division and in helping to create Marshall Field's fortune, but despite his lavish lifestyle, he was still merely a salaried man. When the business was incorporated as a private limited company in 1901, Field allocated 6,000 shares to Harry, but John Shedd got more, which irked him.

In the winter of 1903, with the retail division's annual turnover now at $17 million, profits a shade under $1.5 million and the next phase of development being planned, Selfridge lobbied Marshall Field for more. It wasn't just about money. He craved recognition. Gambling on the fact that Field would give him what he wanted (including the renaming of the business as 'Marshall Field & Selfridge') he made his bid – and lost.

Field turned him down, and with that, Harry Selfridge made plans to leave.

5

~

GOING IT ALONE

'Our deeds determine us, as much as we determine our deeds.'
George Eliot

In the early 1930s, Harry Gordon Selfridge had his portrait painted by Sir William Orpen RA. The artist captured his subject looking contemplative and dignified, pen in hand, studying what might perhaps have been a financial statement. Among the large collection of treasured family memorabilia packed away into trunks and boxes at the home of Simon Wheaton Smith, Harry Selfridge's great-grandson, is that same portrait turned into a jigsaw puzzle. Nothing could be more apt in trying to fathom Harry Selfridge. The man was puzzling indeed.

In 1903, he was living in considerable comfort with his wife and family in their imposing house at 117 Lake Shore Drive, and at their even larger weekend home on Lake Geneva. He was a respected member of the business community, running what was virtually his own fiefdom at Marshall Field where he was doing a job he loved and receiving ever-increasing profits by dint of his shareholding. Selfridge had great faith, indeed an almost messianic belief, in what *he* thought was the right way forward commercially. But he forgot one salient fact. It wasn't his business.

Nancy Koehn of Harvard Business School, one of the world's leading authorities on entrepreneurial history, has made an extensive study of Marshall Field & Co. 'Selfridge,' she says, 'deserves a lot of credit for bringing Field along, and helping him understand new developments in retailing.' On the topic of Harry's complex personality, Professor Koehn says: 'He was pushy, exuberant, with panache and vision.' However, she adds that what killed the partnership was Harry's overweening ambition. 'Field would have looked at his extravagances with a pursing of the lips – everything from the size of his office to the scale of his lifestyle – all this from a man with no visible investments, who lived solely off the business.'

Chief among Harry's ambitions had always been that Marshall Field should expand beyond Chicago. Disillusioned by Field's refusal to open in New York, Selfridge set his sights even higher. Having made several buying trips to England, and being increasingly enamoured with the business opportunities he saw there, he lobbied Field to open a branch in London. Marshall Field himself knew England well. Indeed, his daughter Ethel (recently divorced and now married to naval officer David Beatty) lived there, as did his son Marshall II. Visiting them was one thing, opening an overseas business quite another.

Harry also wanted to adjust the system whereby the store buyers had first and foremost to source from the wholesale division, to whom they paid a 6 per cent levy on all goods. In the early days, there had been advantages in sourcing bulk goods – especially household linen, hosiery and other basics – from the division. It was quick, easy and, even with the levy, cost-effective. But fashion and accessories were a different matter. Selfridge had long felt that the wholesale offerings were simply too conservative, too 'safe', and not in keeping with the needs of Chicago's increasingly sophisticated shoppers. He wanted the store's retail buyers to have a free hand in where – and from whom – they ordered their stock. The idea was anathema to Marshall Field and, unsurprisingly, won little support from John Shedd, the altogether calmer, more conservative favourite of Field, who ran the wholesale department.

Finally, there was the question of a change in name for the store. Field was growing old and his son played no part in the business, while Selfridge had poured every ounce of energy he had into the store. His achievements had been spectacular – in his own mind he *was* part of the store – and he wanted his name over the door.

There were few colleagues Harry Selfridge could talk to. He wasn't a man who shared his intimate fears and feelings easily. The hierarchical structure at Marshall Field was dominated by the original, elderly partners who were Field men to the core, and he was at odds with his one potential ally, John Shedd. There was, however, one person who was always ready to listen and offer shrewd advice. His best and most loyal friend was his mother. To outsiders, Madam Selfridge seemed to be merely gentle, dignified and kindly. To those who knew her better, however, she was something else entirely. The costume designer and artist Grace Lovat Fraser, who later became close to the Selfridge family in London, wrote: 'Madam Selfridge was white-haired and tiny. Always dressed in black with lots of exquisite lace, she seemed the embodiment of a classic sweet old lady. But her appearance was misleading, for though she looked frail she was strong and hardy, had a keen brain and was an excellent business woman. For all her deceptive fragility, she could be unobtrusively formidable and was a very important influence in her son's career.'

Harry's mother's support was crucial. No doubt buoyed by her belief that he should strike out on his own, when Harry heard that the nearby store being built for Schlesinger & Mayer was discreetly on the market, he made a spontaneous decision to raise the funds and buy it himself. The formal records of the transaction have vanished. Some say he raised enough money from bankers to buy the freehold for $5 million. That seems unlikely given that Marshall Field himself was the freeholder. Field rarely, if ever, sold investment property, and he certainly wouldn't have sold it to Harry Selfridge. Others infer that Selfridge simply took over the lease, which at the time was owned by David Mayer and the property developer Henry Siegel, who had bought out Leopold Schlesinger a year or so earlier.

What is certain is that Harry's new store was, and remains today, a beautiful building. Designed by the pioneering commercial architect Louis Sullivan – who numbered Frank Lloyd Wright among his staff

– in collaboration with the engineer Dankmar Adler, the twelve-storey, terracotta-clad corner site, with its elaborate ironwork ornamentation on the lower façade, had taken five years to complete. By the time it was finished, Adler had died, Sullivan's practice was in decline and Mayer was broke.

In the spring of 1904, as building work neared completion, Henry Siegel must have been only too pleased to consign the lease. For Selfridge, it was a huge step. He was risking everything on a single throw, but for a man with a gambler's soul, who lived and worked in the then capital city of gambling, it was worth it. Selfridge was now faced with the task of stocking and staffing his own store, as well as finding tenants for the upper floors. He also had to explain his decision to Marshall Field. The atmosphere in Field's office that day must have been icy. Having admitted that he was leaving, and that he had bought Schlesinger & Mayer, Selfridge offered to stay and train his replacement. Field's chilly reply to the man who had worked for him for twenty-five years was: 'No, Mr Selfridge, you can leave tomorrow if it suits you.' With that, Harry cleared his desk.

When the paperwork involved in his settlement from Marshall Field was completed, Harry Selfridge had liquid assets of well over a million dollars as well as ownership of two substantial houses. His plans made news, but neither he nor Field gave much away about what had happened. Interviewed by the media, Selfridge merely talked about 'his great desire to become head of a business of my own', saying he was 'absolutely confident of success' and that it was 'time to take the step as he had just turned 40' – shaving eight years off his age. Marshall Field remained tight-lipped when journalists questioned him about the loss of his star executive. Indeed, he rarely talked about it even to his own colleagues, other than saying to John Shedd, 'We'll have to get another office boy.' Selfridge was more gracious. Field had been a huge part of his life, the dominant albeit distant father-figure he had craved to please. He never forgot him. When he opened Selfridge's in London, a portrait of Marshall Field took pride of place in his office.

With a fanfare of brass-band music and flags flying, Harry G. Selfridge & Co., Chicago, opened its doors on 13 June 1904. It was an auspicious time to be opening a new business. Affluent consumers had taken to the road in their new automobiles and were driving them out to newly opened country clubs where they eagerly took up the fashionable game of golf: both hobbies necessitated extensive, not to mention expensive, specialist wardrobes. Automobiles had hit the city like a whirlwind. In 1900 there had only been 100 permits issued for motor vehicles, but by the time Harry Selfridge opened his store, there were nearly 1,500 registered drivers in Chicago. The City Council, perturbed by the trend for 'scorching', as driving fast was called, set a speed limit of ten miles per hour and required drivers to have 'full use of arms and legs and be free of a drug habit'. In a city where rich and poor alike enjoyed their drink, no mention was made of alcohol.

Selfridge had long specialized in store windows that presented a themed story. Now his beautifully dressed opening displays paid homage to the latest fashion in ladies' and gentlemen's 'motoring clothes'. Female mannequins were dressed like the subjects of Sir William Nicholson's exquisite painting *La Belle Chauffeuse*, in duster coats, huge gauntlet gloves and big hats tied under the chin with a chiffon stole, while the male mannequins were shown in 'go faster' goggles and belted tweed driving jackets. Picnic hampers and leather-strapped luggage completed the picture.

Selfridge must have gone through a great deal of anguish in the run-up to the opening. It would have been hard for him travelling to work each morning, walking into his own elegant building, but wishing it was the bigger one down the road. Twenty-five years at Field's were not easily forgotten. Bonds had been forged which could not easily be broken. He later explained his emotions during those troubled times to a journalist from the *Saturday Evening Post*: 'I was extremely miserable competing with my own people – the people with whom I had spent so many happy and gloriously exciting years. I tried to beat down the feeling, but my unhappiness increased.'

Selfridge tried everything he could to energize his new staff but they simply couldn't meet his impossibly high standards. 'There's no one here who knows *how* to do it,' he told his wife sadly, perhaps only now realizing how skilful the vast back-room team had been at Marshall Field.

After being forced to leave so abruptly – no presentation, no gifts, no party, no recognition *at all* for what he had done over twenty-five years – Selfridge became a man dispossessed. Always the eternal optimist, now he became depressed. Suddenly, life at Harrose Hall, his country house on Lake Geneva, where he could tend his greenhouses full of rare orchids took on a new allure. Just three months after starting his new business, he made a spontaneous decision to sell up and retire. He called his ex-colleague John Shedd for help and advice. Shedd came up with the reputable retailers Carson, Pirie & Scott, who were anxious to relocate, and arranged a meeting between Sam Pirie and Harry Selfridge. The canny Mr Pirie struck a hard bargain, offering Selfridge – who had wanted a $250,000 premium over and above the original cost of his lease – $150,000 plus his supplier liabilities. Desperate to get out, Harry accepted.

Not unsurprisingly, Harry found retirement dull. He pottered around the grounds at Harrose Hall, tending his roses and orchids, and spending time with his young family. But it wasn't enough. He bought himself a steam yacht which apparently rarely left its moorings, and attempted to take up golf, a game which he played abysmally badly. His friends urged him to take up public office, which in Chicago would have been a challenge in itself. The idea didn't appeal. 'No politics for me,' he said, 'it's too much like being put in the pillory.' He would probably have agreed with a reporter from the London *Daily Mail* who, after visiting the city, had written: 'Chicago presents more splendid attractions and more hideous repulsions than any city I know. Other places hide their dark side out of sight – Chicago treasures it to the heart of the business quarter and gives it a veneer.' He couldn't have put it better himself. Chicago's tycoons were ruthless. Harry Selfridge was never really part of their world.

Despite being a manager *par excellence*, to most of them he would always remain 'Field's ex-office boy'.

Selfridge had a cavalier attitude towards money. He lived extravagantly, spent prodigiously on those he loved and had a belief that all would always be well – regardless of what he owed. In later years, when his personal overdraft had reached monumental proportions, one of his bankers in London remarked, 'Mr Selfridge seems to enjoy the sensation of debt.' In Chicago, with his family and perhaps his age in mind, he took out a high-level life insurance policy. He also tried his hand at investments. Invited to put money into the White Rock Soda Company – carbonated drinks being all the rage – he turned the offer down as being too closely associated with diluting whiskey. However, he did decide to invest in a gold mine. In the winter of 1904, he became President of the Sullivan Creek Mining and Milling Company, providing the finance to drill for gold at the Calico mine in Tuolumne County, California.

It all started off rather well. The Chicago firm of Allis-Chalmers – then the world's largest manufacturer of mining equipment – was on board advising Selfridge as to what equipment would be needed, and the mining expert William Chalmers seemed impressed with the initial geological data from what was a rich gold area. Drilling tests and surveys went on throughout the spring of 1905, with Selfridge paying all the costs.

That summer the Selfridge family left to spend a season on the French Riviera. There, letters arrived from America requesting more money for equipment and wages. Then came the news that Selfridge had longed to hear. They had found gold at 190 feet – enough to send for assay, and enough to convince Selfridge that he was about to become very rich. Late in August, he settled his family at the Ritz in Paris, while he went to London on business. He had a meeting to attend.

At the age of 71, Marshall Field suddenly had a spring in his step and a smile on his face. He'd put a smile on the face of Europe's most important jeweller's too as he shopped for a sumptuous collection of diamonds and pearls – presents for his new bride, Delia Caton. Mr and Mrs Arthur Caton were friends of Marshall Field who, it was always said, had long held a *tendre* for his neighbour's attractive, elegant wife. When Arthur died in 1904, Field seized the moment and proposed to Delia. They sailed to England in July 1905 and were married on 5 September at St Margaret's, Westminster. Selfridge's trip to London was timed precisely so he could visit Field – and not just to congratulate him on his new marriage.

Two earlier biographies of Selfridge have claimed that he went to see his old boss with an audacious offer to take over the Chicago store. Nancy Koehn flatly rejects the idea: 'Selfridge could never have raised that amount of money, and even if he could, Field would never have sold.' However, the talk at the time was that Harry Selfridge had the support of the mighty J. P. Morgan himself in his planned acquisition, and that Field was sufficiently intrigued to agree to 'look at' his proposals. Whether Selfridge was looking at London in his own right, as he later claimed, or whether he was proposing an outpost of Marshall Field there, we'll never know. But one way or the other, any hopes of doing business with Mr Field were about to be destroyed.

The newly-wed Fields returned to Chicago early in October that year, taking with them Marshall's son, his wife Albertine and their young family. Also en route back to America were the Selfridge family. By the time they got home on 10 October, news had arrived that the gold mine was barren. What little gold there was would be too expensive to excavate. By the time the company was wound up, Selfridge had lost $60,000 or, in today's money, just under $1,200,000.

In November, tragedy of a far greater kind struck the Field household when Field's troubled son died in hospital from a gunshot wound to the stomach. Not unnaturally, the family claimed one of his guns had been discharged accidentally. Others said he had committed suicide, while the talk of the town was that he had been shot by one of the girls at the city's most notorious brothel, the Everleigh Club. Owned by two genteel Kentucky sisters, Minna and Ada Everleigh, the brothel was the ultimate in luxury. The sisters had been just 21 and 23 when they opened their 'house', dedicated to servicing the desires of Chicago's wealthy men. Ada did the hiring. 'I talk with each applicant myself,' she said proudly in the promotional brochure she circulated. 'Girls must have worked somewhere before coming here – we do not take amateurs.' Indeed they didn't. The Everleigh Club girls were not merely beauties in ball gowns. They were expertly trained in the art of flattery, good conversation and even better sex, and several of them married extremely well. The Club had Silver and Copper Rooms for the mining kings, and the Gold Room was refurbished each year with real gold leaf. An ensemble of violin, cello, piano and, occasionally, a harp provided soothing music. The kitchen was run by superb chefs, and the cellar stocked with the finest champagne – Minna didn't serve red wine, reasoning it made the customers sleepy. On Christmas Eve, the sisters would give a special party exclusively for the 'gentlemen of the press'.

The Everleigh Club of course also offered gambling, and the stakes were high. Minna was convinced men preferred gambling to girls, so she placed a thirty-minute limit on roulette and dice. The club was never raided – the sisters paid the police well for their protection – and its opulent tranquillity was rarely shattered, except on one memorable occasion, when the rabidly anti-smoking campaigner Lucy Page Gaston stormed in yelling, 'Minna, you can stop your girls from going straight to the devil – you must stop them smoking cigarettes.'

Although father and son had never been close, Field was grief-stricken. He carried on working – supervising the next phase of the momentous rebuilding programme at the store – and playing his weekly round of golf. On New Year's Day 1906, though it was bitterly cold, he and three friends played eighteen holes, traipsing knee-deep through the snow in search of their special red golf balls. By the next day he had developed a sore throat but insisted on travelling to New York with his wife and valet. By the end of the week he had contracted severe pneumonia from which he never recovered, dying in his suite at the Holland House Hotel.

Field had planned his will very carefully. Determined there would be no squandering of his hard-earned fortune, he had set up complex trusts. On the death of the immediate beneficiaries, the capital would revert to the Field estate, and his grandchildren would not receive the bulk of their money until they were 50. His daughter Ethel meanwhile became seriously rich, enabling her to spring to her naval husband's defence when he was threatened with disciplinary action following the straining of his ship's engines. 'What, court martial my David? I'll buy them a new ship!' she exclaimed. In the event, the Navy relented, but Ethel's $6 million inheritance did buy her husband a Scottish grouse moor, a hunting lodge in Leicestershire, a steam yacht and a mansion in London. Four years later, at the age of 39, David Beatty became the youngest admiral in the Royal Navy since Horatio Nelson.

Harry Selfridge mourned Marshall Field deeply. Whatever low points their strained relationship had reached, Field had been Selfridge's mentor. His death marked the end of the great era at Marshall Field. Potter Palmer was dead. Levi Leiter was dead (leaving Mary Curzon a very rich woman). As specified in Field's will, John Shedd became President of the store, continuing with the expansion plans laid down by the founder. For Harry Selfridge, at the age of 50, the time had come to consider his future.

~

BUILDING THE DREAM

'L'Angleterre est une nation de boutiquiers.'
Napoleon Bonaparte

In 1906, no one meeting Harry Selfridge for the first time would have dreamt he was 50. He looked a decade younger, talked with endless enthusiasm and exhausted people half his age with his boundless energy. Not that he exercised to keep fit. 'Thinking is enough physical exercise for me,' he used to say. When he was pondering some major – or even minor – decision, he would sit in his swivel chair, turn it towards the window, lock his hands behind his head, and stare into the distance. No one ever dared interrupt him. When he'd decided on the outcome, he'd swing round quickly and say, 'Right, here's what we'll do, let's get on with it.' And that was that. Once he'd made up his mind, he never changed it.

Craving a new challenge, and encouraged by his close friend Walter Cottingham, of the Sherwin-Williams Paint Company (an enterprising firm whose motto was 'Cover the Earth'), Selfridge made up his mind to move to London and open his dream store. The awesome Selfridge energy swung into operation. Letters were written, cablegrams sent, telephone calls made to friends and acquaintances, meetings arranged. He was back at work and loving it. As far as his family were concerned, if he was happy, they were happy. They were probably relieved to see him so energized, and didn't mind at all when he took off for London, staying first at the Savoy Hotel and thereafter renting an elegant furnished apartment in Whitehall Court, an imposing mansion block with a spectacular view over St James's Park.

One of the essential requirements for gracious living in Edwardian London being live-in servants, a Scottish couple, Mr and Mrs Fraser, moved in during March that year, Mrs Fraser as housekeeper and Mr Fraser first as valet and later butler. The Frasers were to be part of the fabric of Selfridge family life for the next two decades. Fraser fitted the stereotype of the British butler perfectly. Depending on his mood, his manner would swing between the unctuous and the supercilious: a family friend described him as 'a cross between Disraeli and Micawber'. In 1921, when the Selfridge family had just moved into the palatial splendour of Lansdowne House, Fraser answered the bell and found a distinguished elderly gentleman on the doorstep proffering a flat box. The visitor was Monsieur Pierre Cambon, the ex-French Ambassador to the Court of St James, who on his return visits to London always called first at his old friend Lord Lansdowne's house, bringing with him a gift of a very ripe Brie. Confronted by a strange servant, Monsieur Cambon asked if Lord Lansdowne was at home. 'I've never heard of him,' said Fraser, suspiciously sniffing at the parcel, 'and he certainly doesn't live here.' Monsieur Cambon – and presumably his cheese – beat a hasty and confused retreat.

From the moment he arrived in London, Selfridge was determined not to be thought of as a 'flash Yankee', a type viewed with grave suspicion by London's business community, who were still reeling from the dubious antics of the transport tycoon Charles Tyson Yerkes, known to have been a contemporary of Selfridge in Chicago.

Backed by American money, Yerkes had arrived in London in 1900, aiming to feather his nest by developing the city's underground railway system. Having manipulated his way into gaining control of the Metropolitan District Railway, Yerkes audaciously mounted a 'rescue' bid for the half-completed Bakerloo line. The Bakerloo had been left stranded when its original founder had committed suicide by swallowing cyanide following his conviction for fraud. Yerkes (the inspiration for Theodore Dreiser's trilogy on corrupt financiers) subsequently added the Charing Cross, the Euston & Hampstead and the Great Northern, Piccadilly and Brompton Railways to his portfolio, as well as financing the building of the Lots Road power station to supply the burgeoning electric lines. Discovered to have been falsifying the accounts – his speciality being to pay massive management charges into his private bank account – Yerkes fled to New York, where he died in 1905. He left behind him a network of deep tunnels yet to be completed and, in many circles, a deep-rooted mistrust of American methods of business. It was all close enough for Selfridge to be alarmed at being thought of as anything less than punctilious in his business dealings.

Anxious for the business of retailing to be taken seriously, and partially as his own armour against a potentially hostile environment, Selfridge adopted a formal style, dressing as though he was a merchant banker rather than merely a merchant. He didn't retreat into frock coats, but the pearl-grey, braided morning coats he had favoured in Chicago were now toned down to darker shades of charcoal and black, worn with either striped or plain trousers. He remained faithful to his signature high-cut stiff collars and added a classic white 'slip' to frame his waistcoat, and in the evening he was immaculately kitted out in white tie and tails. There was always a sense of formality about his clothes – no one could ever remember seeing him dressed in anything even remotely casual.

Knowing what he wanted to do was all very well. Knowing where to do it was the next challenge. His criteria were space and easy access. Bond Street as a location was fleetingly considered and then rejected as too narrow to suit his craving for scale. Regent Street was dismissed due to restrictions on size imposed by the Crown Estates. He seriously considered the Strand, finding a site that appealed, but negotiations over a lease apparently collapsed. Being a man obsessed with beautiful buildings, the allies he found to search for the ideal site were all acquaintances involved in building and architecture. Among them was the young architect Delissa Joseph, who not only designed stations for the Underground Electric Railway Company but who also had a friend called Samuel Waring – who was interested in meeting Harry Selfridge.

By 1906, Samuel Waring was not only Chairman of the leading furniture manufacturer and retail business, Waring & Gillow, but also a director of a specialist building firm called Waring & White, a business run in association with the noted American construction engineer, James G. White. For Harry Selfridge, who needed an investment partner, Waring offered an irresistible combination of technical expertise and much-needed cash. Waring & White, under the skilful direction of the architects Charles Mewes and Arthur Davis, had just completed construction of the Ritz Hotel, London's first steel-framed building. Selfridge, like Waring, was a guest at the hotel's splendid opening-night dinner, where no doubt they discussed their plans to shake up London's retail establishment. The two men, both spontaneous, super-charged, insomniac workaholics, quickly – in hindsight perhaps too quickly – agreed terms. In June that year they formed a company called Selfridge and Waring Ltd with capital of £1 million in 100,000 preference shares at £5 each, and 500,000 ordinary shares at £1 each. Selfridge had 150,006 shares and Waring 150,001.

The partners settled on a site towards what was at that time the 'dead end' of Oxford Street, where Waring owned some properties he was prepared to see demolished. Selfridge saw the potential of the site immediately. It was conveniently placed for the mansions of Portman Square, near enough to the fashionable *demi-monde* residents of St John's Wood, and ideally placed to capture the public travelling on the Central Line which, having opened six years earlier, now carried 100,000 people a day between Shepherd's Bush and Bank. With stations at Holland Park, Notting Hill Gate, Queen's Road (renamed Queensway in 1946), Lancaster Gate, Marble Arch, Bond Street, Oxford Circus and beyond to St Paul's, the Central Line was the dream line for West End retailers.

From the very beginning, Selfridge visualized his store as stretching from Duke Street to Orchard Street – as it does today – although he had to wait until 1928 until that happened. But he also hoped it would reach right back to Wigmore Street, forming a double island site. To begin with, however, he had to make do with what they could get, which meant acquiring the leases of the adjoining jumble of small shops, tenement housing and a much-loved local pub, the Hope Arms, adjacent to some run-down warehouses and a busy stable-yard on the corner of Duke Street. Above all, they needed the consent of the landowners, the Portman Estate, as well as planning permission from St Marylebone Council. There was an enormous furore when plans were announced. From the fuss the locals made – especially those who drank in the Hope Arms – one would have thought Harry Selfridge was demolishing Buckingham Palace. Instead, he planned to build his own palace.

Selfridge moved into offices on the opposite side of the road at 415 Oxford Street and started to plan his development. He was never happier than when poring over architectural drawings. When it came to turning them into reality, however, he faced obstacles on a daily basis. He was used to the speed of Chicago where building regulations and permissions were quickly settled with a handshake – albeit one often accompanied by a wad of money. Now he had to face London's ponderous bureaucrats.

Selfridge was his own project manager, beating a regular path to see both the Chairman of the St Marylebone Borough Council works committee, Edward Hughes, and his colleague, the district surveyor Mr Ashbridge. Turning on the full power of his affability and charm, Selfridge impressed them enormously, particularly as he attended each meeting in person. Hughes would later say: 'He would bring his persuasive powers to bear and he often succeeded in convincing us that his was the correct view.'

Selfridge's original concept was a neoclassical six-storey building with a dramatic central tower. The first drawings were prepared by a young American trainee architect called Francis Swales, who had studied at the Ecole des Beaux Arts in Paris and served as an intern at the offices of the revered Jean-Louis Pascal. Selfridge, enchanted with the result, carried the drawings with him everywhere. 'I fingered them so frequently that they got dog-eared. I had frontal elevations and side elevations and floor maps – I couldn't bear to be parted from them. The result was I almost wore away the pockets of every suit I possessed.' Copies of the beautiful drawings by Swales were sent to Daniel Burnham in Chicago, who was retained as the originating architect.

Busy completing an impressive new twelve-storey store for John Wanamaker in Philadelphia, Burnham was not told that planning restrictions in London at the time forbade any building higher than a modest 80 feet from pavement level. Burnham's elevations were proudly presented to the council – who promptly rejected them. The reaction back at the great man's office was predictable. Young Mr Swales was quickly replaced by the London-based architect Robert Atkinson, who was well versed in the 'Chicago School' having worked in America but who also knew enough about the complexities of London planning regulations not to make any more expensive mistakes. Out went the six floors and tower and in came an 80-foot-high building with five vast upper floors and a deep basement that would provide additional trading space beneath them. Selfridge now had the best team of architects that money could buy. The trouble was his money was running out.

It had cost a lot – in excess of $500,000 – to get to the starting-block. Buying out the leases of surrounding properties had been much harder, and taken far longer, than Selfridge had thought possible. It had also been expensive, yet at no time did Samuel Waring put his hand in his pocket. All the money was Harry's, and he was feeling the strain. Not that anyone could tell. He smiled, joked, hosted dinners, went to the theatre and commuted to America to see his family. The publisher Charles H. Doran met Selfridge several times on transatlantic voyages during that period. Selfridge was delighted to be in the company of a fellow American who listened patiently to his new friend's woes about archaic planning laws and complex fire regulations.

After what Selfridge himself described as 'an interminable time spent in lawyers' offices' and nearly a year after Selfridge & Waring was formed, the site was finally cleared and excavations began. The foundations were dug deep enough to support extra floors or even his tower should regulations change, and Harry Selfridge dug deeper into his pockets to pay for it all. Still Sam Waring hadn't parted with a penny. He was even making money from Selfridge, who had by now cashed in one of his last remaining assets, selling his Lake Shore Drive house. Harry had also donated his precious orchid collection to Chicago's Lincoln Park and had moved his family to England, where they leased Waring's magnificent country estate, Foots Cray, in Sidcup, Kent.

Waring & Gillow were commissioned to make Harry an imposing desk, but the building programme was so slow Selfridge began to doubt he would ever have an office in which to put it. One chilly November day, in a move intended to obtain publicity as much as to inspire progress, Selfridge arranged for a band to play outside the building site. For months now he had talked to the press about his plans – how exciting they were, how big the store was going to be, how daring it was. His 'music while you work', however, succeeded in making headlines of the wrong sort. The police arrived, claiming that the band was creating a public nuisance, and ordered it to stop playing.

For Sam Waring, it was the last straw. From the beginning he had baulked at the scale of his partner's plans. When he first saw the drawings he offended Selfridge by asking if it was to be a shop or a Greek temple. Some of his frustration is understandable. As Harry's grandiose schemes progressed, the various architects produced over 12,000 blueprints. For Waring, the project was becoming more trouble than it was worth. The relationship between the two egotistical personalities, which for months had existed at a level of simmering hostility, now collapsed completely, with the inevitable result that Waring abruptly withdrew from the partnership. For Harry Selfridge it was a catastrophe. He was left with a deep hole in the road into which he had already sunk over a million dollars and he simply didn't have the money to continue alone. As building came to a halt, Selfridge was left looking bleakly at what the press described as 'the largest building site London has ever seen'. Disputes between the ex-partners led to litigation that was subsequently settled out of court. Selfridge said little in public, only remarking to a journalist that 'We had crossed the Rubicon, and my money largely paid for the ferry.'

London's established retailers must have been delighted at Selfridge's embarrassment, but Selfridge himself remained composed, never doubting for a moment that he would find a way through. He carried on compiling data on London and its inhabitants – how they travelled, where they lived, what they read, where they shopped. Huge ledgers in the Selfridges archives show how methodically he undertook this research. Every newspaper and magazine is listed with its price, readership and ownership. Reports were compiled on the stock and sales techniques of rival retailers. He gathered information obsessively, so much so that by the time Selfridge's opened to the public, there wasn't much he didn't know about the demographics of his customer base. He called it 'scientific' planning. Today we would call it the cutting-edge of market research.

Looking back at the brief years of the Edwardian era, it is all too easy to think life was just a round of country house parties, endless servants and extravagant living. To a certain extent it was all of these things. But while the rich led a seemingly charmed life, a great swathe of the populace lived in poverty and the middle class had not yet fully succumbed to the temptations of shopping for anything other than what they needed. Much of this was changing fast – and Selfridge knew it. A new group of men were finding their way into the inner circles of power – men like the grocery tycoon Sir Thomas Lipton, the trade magnate Arthur Sassoon and the financier Sir Ernest Cassel. There was already talk about the newly elected Liberal Government's plans to 'tax the rich', and intense political discussion about helping the poor. Most significantly, elements of the middle class were beginning to break established boundaries. Shopping for them wasn't just about formal clothes, mourning clothes, maid's uniforms and other household necessities. They wanted luggage to take on their travels, fashionable clothes to pack, photographic equipment to record their activities, sporting equipment and all the things associated with a more mobile life. This was the target audience Selfridge had envisioned for his altogether more egalitarian store. It was also a group many of London's existing retailers had not yet identified.

No one who met Selfridge at the time would ever have known he was a whisker away from financial disaster. He always put on a show, never more so than when money was tight. The end of 1907 was a difficult time in which to raise money. Wall Street was in disarray due to the collapse of the Knickerbocker Trust Company. In Britain high unemployment and unease on the London Stock Exchange sent share prices tumbling and pushed up the bank rate to 7 per cent. There was also a widely held view that London already had enough shops. Harrods, D. H. Evans, Whiteley's, John Barker, Debenham & Freebody's, Swan & Edgar *et al.* already catered for London's shopping needs. Could there possibly be room for yet another store?

Buoyed by his almost divine belief in financial salvation, Selfridge believed there was. Relief came just three months later in the shape of the genial tea tycoon John Musker who, along with his partner Julius Drew, had made a fortune through the Home & Colonial grocery chain which had originated in Liverpool. Musker had happily acquired the trappings of wealth, indulging in the expensive hobby of owning and breeding racehorses and acquiring a beautiful house called Shadwell Park in Thetford, Norfolk, where he maintained a fine stud. Musker was happy to invest in what Selfridge eagerly described as 'London's first custom-built department store'. In March 1908, Selfridge & Co. Ltd was formed, with capital of £900,000, made up of 400,000 preference shares and 500,000 ordinary shares at £1 each. Curiously the arrangement was finalized by a deed executed in France over a sixpenny stamp, a move reported by the *Financial News* rather cynically as 'saving Mr Selfridge the sum of £2,000 in stamp duties'. Selfridge, a firm believer in the adage 'all publicity is good publicity', ignored the sarcasm.

Builders were back on site within the month. Interestingly, Selfridge continued with Waring & White, for the benefits of the talented Mr White far outweighed any lasting resentment towards Waring. He also employed the Swedish engineering firm of Kreuger & Toll, along with their innovative structural engineer Sven Bylander – although communicating with the genius 'man of steel' was tricky as he spoke barely a word of English. Ivar Kreuger happily translated for Selfridge, who delighted in keeping the press up to date about progress on what was described as 'the first fully steel-framed retail building in England'. Since working with steel was much quicker than with iron, he also anticipated 'an exceptionally fast ten-month building programme'. Architects today owe a great debt to Harry Selfridge and his team of construction experts. Largely thanks to their endeavours, the antiquated 1894 London Building Act was rewritten to sanction steel-framed construction, and from that point onwards steel became the pre-eminent structural material.

While sightseers thronged Oxford Street to watch the giant crane lifting 125 tons of steel a week, Harry Selfridge set about recruiting his senior management team. He meticulously planned an 'organizational chart' – essentially the entire structure of the business at a glance – showing who was responsible for what, from the shop floor right through to the staff rest-rooms. Nothing, absolutely nothing, was left to chance. There was to be a staff doctor, a visiting staff dentist and a 'supervisor of staff athletics'. Transport departments were set up with 'motor drivers' as well as horse-drawn vans. Glove cleaning (just one of the many services to be offered by the store) would be out-sourced. All this and more was recorded on the massive document pinned to the wall in Harry's temporary office.

Three key posts were filled by Americans: C. W. Steines became controller of merchandise, William Oppenheimer directed the store's interior layout and fixtures, and Edward Goldsman took charge of the window displays. Before Selfridge, window-dressing in London had been haphazard. More often than not, windows were left dark at night. Some of the bigger stores had a nominal display manager, but visual presentations were rarely planned to a theme and never colour co-ordinated. In most cases, it was merely a case of showing the diversity of stock, which often involved putting one of everything in the window. The result, as Andrew Carnegie had said, was 'just jumble'.

Exactly as he had done at Marshall Field, Selfridge broke the established practice of folding merchandise away behind glass cabinet doors. Goods were to be freely on show throughout the internal floor space. The store's windows would tell their own story. There were twenty-one of them, twelve of which contained the largest sheets of plate glass in the world, and as far as Selfridge was concerned, each was a blank canvas waiting to be painted to perfection. Edward Goldsman was allocated enough studio space to house props and given sufficient staff to cope with what was listed on the organizational chart as 'flags & scenic work; interior & side aisle displays; main windows; flowers & palms'. The resulting displays – some of which wouldn't look out of date today – were visual masterpieces that defined the concept of creative window-dressing ever after.

The other senior management executives taken on in those heady, pre-opening months were all British. Selfridge interviewed them at length, caring less for references than for his own judgement. He had his foibles. He wouldn't employ men who were too tall or had a skinny neck, and he loathed scruffy shoes or anything less than perfectly manicured hands. Those who passed the test included Frank Chitham, who came from the Scotch House to oversee the launch of men's 'quality ready-for-wear coats and suits' – imported from the USA and in themselves a revelation – while the chief accountant Arthur Youngman was recruited from Debenham's. The staff manager Percy Best came from Hayes & Candy, and the systems manager (not a modern title as one might think, but actually used by the store in 1909) Alfred Cowper from the 'delivery & receiving' sector of Whiteley's. For all of them, leaving jobs with established firms to join the maverick American was a gamble, though perhaps less of one in the case of Whiteley's, where the once great business was in disarray following the founder's much publicized death earlier that year, William Whiteley having been murdered by a deranged young man called Horace Rayner, who claimed to be his illegitimate son. Given Mr Whiteley's habit of exercising *droit de seigneur* over the female staff, the surprise is that there was only the one claimant for paternity.

Despite the temptations of running a store that eventually employed over 2,000 young women – some of them exceedingly attractive – there was never the slightest suggestion that Harry Selfridge ever flirted with his female staff, never mind having an affair with any of them. The idea would have horrified him. To him, the staff were an army to be marshalled onwards to victory. He revelled in their adulation, but intimacy of any sort was out of the question.

Nonetheless, in the autumn of 1908, Harry found time for the occasional pleasurable, lingering lunch or supper with several women, among them the beautiful ex-Gaiety Girl Rosie Boot – the Marchioness of Headfort – who became a lifelong friend, and Lady Sackville, the châtelaine of one of England's great Elizabethan houses, Knole. Victoria Sackville, who had captivated Harry when the Selfridges were living in Samuel Waring's house, Foots Cray, in Kent, had a penchant for rich men, especially rich American men. She was also politically adept, articulate and devastatingly attractive, having inherited her Spanish dancer mother's dark, sultry eyes and sensual mouth. Her daughter, the writer and gardener Vita Sackville-West, would later say: 'If ever the phrase "to turn one's heart to water" meant anything, it was when my mother looked at you and smiled.' Lady Sackville also owned a charming gift shop called Spealls, in South Audley Street, where she sold expensive lamp shades and pretty bric-a-brac at inflated prices to enthusiastic American visitors.

On his regular theatre outings, however, Harry was generally accompanied by his wife Rose who, along with their children and Madam Selfridge (as Lois was always called), were now living in a palatial eighteenth-century house at 17 Arlington Street, leased from the widowed Countess of Yarborough. Selfridge may not have wanted to be thought of as flash, but he was more than happy to be thought of as rich. Surrounded by the impressive Yarborough sculpture collection – including masterpieces by Bernini – and their even more impressive library, London's most talked-about American family blithely settled into British life in the grand manner.

Arlington Street was an aristocratic enclave, colonized by the scions of Britain's finest families, where their Robert Adam and William Kent houses were known by name – Rutland, Wimborne, Zetland, Yarborough – rather than by number. In general they viewed change with suspicion – Ivor Guest, Lord Wimborne, had grumbled furiously at the disruption caused by the building of the Ritz, which overlooked his gardens – but taxes were taking their toll and Lady Yarborough for one needed the rent. Not all the Selfridges' neighbours were as tolerant as the charmingly unorthodox Duchess of Rutland and her daughters, Marjorie, Letty and Diana Manners, who lived next door in an equally beautiful house, today the site of the Caprice. The Duchess, quickly realizing that Mr Selfridge intended to staff his private office with well-connected young men of impeccable background, suggested her great friend Viscountess de Vesci's nephew Yvo as being 'just right for the job'. He was hired within the week.

Of course, no one really knew how much – or how little – money Selfridge actually had. It was said that his wife's family were rich and it was known that he had worked with Ethel Beatty's father, Marshall Field, and had been in business with Lord Curzon's father-in-law, the late Levi Leiter. (Leiter's other daughters, Daisy and Nannie, had become respectively the Countess of Suffolk and the Hon. Mrs Colin Campbell.) Selfridge, master of illusion, would simply smile and say they had all been 'marvellous people'.

That autumn the press eagerly reported on progress, fed by daily bulletins. The *Daily Graphic* quoted Selfridge as saying, 'We have broken all previous building records and without any overtime of consequence ... we built 80 square feet on the corner to the top of the great columns, including the steelwork of the storey above, in two weeks and five days.' It was an awesome sight and a frightening climb for those invited by Selfridge to tour the site. Among them was the publisher Evelyn Wrench, who noted in his diary: 'I climbed the girders with him and felt dizzy doing so.' Wrench, a distinguished traveller who would go on to found the Overseas League and the English-Speaking Union, was tremendously impressed with Selfridge. 'He certainly is one of the most forceful Americans I know. I feel sure that, granted good health, he will revolutionize the drapery and large store business in this country.'

Not all the press reports were positive. The drapery trade press were particularly sceptical about the size of the project and the sales turnover needed to sustain it, while other reports were frankly scathing about Selfridge's concept. Most criticisms had a distinctly anti-American bias. The *British Weekly* wrote: 'A crusade has been started to force on London superfluous luxuries such as those over-stocked across the Atlantic.' But in the main, the press warmed to Harry Selfridge because he, unlike virtually any other British businessman, courted them assiduously.

Selfridge had arrived in London at a point when the popular press was becoming ever more powerful. Lord Northcliffe, in particular, had astutely recognized what the growing reading public wanted out of their daily newspaper. His *Daily Mail* was appealingly priced at just a ha'penny and packed with a unique mix of scandal, social gossip, competitions and opinionated features by some remarkably fine writers. Northcliffe was not the first proprietor to discover this potent combination. George Newnes had started his phenomenally successful pictorial weekly magazine *Tit-Bits*, featuring short news 'bites' peppered with pictures, in 1881, and it soon had a circulation of over half a million.

Just as Northcliffe felt that a newspaper intended for mass readership had to be exciting, so Harry Selfridge felt the same about his shopping venue. From his earliest days in business, Selfridge had understood, as few other men really did, the value of constant publicity and how to make the best use of it. While doing so, he forged relationships with reporters, gossip-writers, editors and proprietors alike. One of his closest friends – a fellow Wisconsin-born American who had settled in London – was Ralph Blumenfeld, an ex-*Daily Mail* man and now editor of the *Daily Express*. Rarely a week went by when the two men didn't lunch or dine together, and rarely a day passed without them exchanging a letter or telephone call. Selfridge respected the press and perhaps even feared them. He once told his advertising manager: 'Never fight with them, never fall out with them if you can possibly avoid it, they will always have the last word.' He was right to be cautious, and his caution paid off. Years later, when he was deeply in debt, his life in shocking decline, the media largely left him alone.

Selfridge astutely hired an ex-journalist called James Conaly as his press officer and set up a special 'press club room' for reporters to use when they were in the West End. Invited journalists had their own keys, and the room was equipped with typewriters, telephones, stationery, a fully stocked bar and the guarantee of some sort of human-interest story for them to phone through to the news desk on a daily basis. Editors were given hampers at Christmas, flowers at Easter. There was even a diary kept that listed birthdays so a special gift could be sent, and wives were always guaranteed the best table in the store's Palm Court Restaurant. But it wasn't merely efficient media handling that endeared much of Fleet Street to Harry Selfridge – his unwavering belief in advertising meant they also made money.

During the opening week of his store, Selfridge hit London with an advertising campaign the like of which it had never seen. Thirty-eight richly illustrated advertisements drawn by some of the most well-known graphic artists and cartoonists, including Sir Bernard Partridge of *Punch*, appeared on 104 pages in 18 national newspapers. The campaign caused a sensation, with even *The Times* declaring it marked an epoch in the history of British retail advertising – perhaps regretting having vetoed Harry's attempt to book its entire front page for the launch. The cost of such a campaign was enormous. The store spent an astonishing £36,000 in just seven days – in today's terms nearly £2.35 million! That excluded production costs – and Bernard Partridge didn't come cheap. To the chagrin of London's advertising agencies, all the work was handled internally. The in-house creative department produced the artwork and Harry Selfridge personally selected the space, insisting that he receive the 10 per cent discount usually given to agencies.

In those days most stores merely booked a modest series of quarter-pages. Harry Selfridge created a whole new source of income for news-papers – and they loved him for it. It wasn't just the sheer volume of his spending that made waves. Uniquely, his advertisements weren't about products: they were a mission statement about his philosophy of shopping. Not everyone liked them. One advertising trade paper called them 'high-falutin' nonsense' while another dismissed them as 'piffle'. Other reactions ranged from admiration to derision at Harry's sentimental, idealistic text:

> We have every pleasure in announcing that the formal opening of our premises – London's newest shopping centre – begins today and continues throughout the week. We wish it to be clearly understood that our invitation is to the whole British public and to visitors from overseas – that no cards of admission are required – that all are welcome – and that the pleasures of shopping as those of sight-seeing begin from the opening hour.

In promoting the 'pleasures of shopping', in calling the store a 'shopping centre' and, more significantly, in talking about 'sight-seeing', Harry Selfridge was putting into place things we take for granted today. Art exhibitions in-store? Selfridge did it in 1909. Cookery demonstrations in the kitchen equipment department? Selfridge did it in 1912. But nearly a hundred years ago, these were visionary ideas. It was almost as if H. G. Selfridge was being advised by his new friend H. G. Wells. He made mistakes of course. Given the rising tension between Britain and Germany, his advertisement headed 'Greetings to the Fatherland' was perhaps unwise. All in all, though, his advertisements, with their lack of pressure to buy and their reassuring messages about fine quality, convenience and comfort, superb service, fair prices and above all fun, broke new ground.

Against all the advice from his army of technicians scrambling to finish the store interiors in time, Selfridge fixed the opening day for Monday, 15 March 1909. No one believed the store would be ready. Indeed a journalist escorted round the premises reported that 'disorder reigned supreme'. The 1,800 staff worked throughout the weekend until midnight on Sunday, frantically unpacking and arranging stock in over a hundred different departments. In the store's magnificent windows, hidden until the opening by ruched silk theatre curtains, Edward Goldsman had created exquisite fashion displays inspired by Watteau and Fragonard. The staff gasped with admiration – and then gasped in horror when the newly installed sprinkler system erupted, flooding most of them.

Water was the biggest problem. Outside there was too much – on the opening day it poured with rain – and inside there soon wasn't any at all. As thousands of people streamed through the store, doing everything from using the impressive bathrooms to drinking water with their lunch, the 400-foot-deep artesian well pumps gave way under the strain. In desperation, the manager of the hairdressing department fled upstairs to the restaurant, commandeering all the soda siphons to rinse out shampoos.

Staff positioned by the Oxford and Duke Street doors counted in 90,000 people on the opening day. In a nice theatrical touch by Selfridge, who always got on very well with the local constabulary, over thirty policemen were on hand outside to handle the crowds. For the most part those who came were just looking. Actual sales totalled a meagre £3,000, well under target. Selfridge himself didn't mind. Or if he did, he didn't show it. As far as he was concerned, the opening day was a bit like the opening night of a play. It was the reviews he was waiting for. Did people like the store? Would they return? Would it be a long-running success?

There wasn't much not to like. The place was a marvel. There were six acres of floor space with no internal doors. Instead there were wide, open-plan vistas – perhaps not quite as open as Selfridge had wanted but, given onerous fire restrictions, still a revelation for London retailing. Nine Otis lifts, each six foot square, whisked passengers from the toy, sports and motoring departments on the lower ground floor to the restaurant on the top floor. The store was brilliantly lit and flooded with the scent of fresh flowers. Floors were carpeted in the house 'signature green' which was also used for everything from the commissionaires' uniforms to the smart delivery vans. There was a library, fully stocked with all the latest magazines and newspapers; a silence room (for respite between exhausting bouts of shopping); a branch post office (for mailing letters and cards written on complimentary store stationery); an information bureau; and, in a forerunner of today's concierge services, staff on hand to book everything from train tickets or seats at a West End show to a hotel suite or a steamship state room on a passage to New York. There was a first-aid ward with a uniformed nurse in attendance (her clothes supplied by the in-store nurses' uniform department); a bureau de change; parcel and coat drop-off points; sumptuous ladies' and gentlemen's cloakrooms; a barber's shop; a ladies' hairdressing salon that also offered a manicure service; and even a chiropodist. The huge restaurant served lunch to people entertained by an orchestra, while men – though not women – could escape to their own smoking room. Harry Selfridge had thought of everything.

His competitors were dumbfounded at the amount of space given over to services. Surely the point of a shop was for people to buy things? The Selfridge philosophy, however, was first to get them in, then to keep them there. Thereafter they would buy. As he said in one of his advertisements, the store sold 'all merchandise that Men, Women and Children wear' and 'almost everything that enters into the affairs of daily life'. At that point, he meant more or less everything other than food and wines. Those would come later. Neither did he sell furniture, or at least not beds, wardrobes or dining-tables and chairs. Some thought this was the result of his 'deal' with Waring who, after all, was also a furniture retailer. In reality, as Selfridge later said, it was because margins were better on decorative home furnishings such as lampshades, glass, china, silver, cutlery, lacquer screens and rugs. Waring meanwhile had sent over the impressive desk destined for the Chairman's impressive fourth-floor corner site office. He also sent a bill, which Selfridge avoided paying for the next three years.

Lord Northcliffe himself visited that week, shopping incognito, and was so pleased with the service he received that he wrote to Selfridge praising the skill of the salesman, saying that the chap in question – a young man by the name of Puttick – 'was destined to go far'. Selfridge quickly dictated a reply, signing it for the first time with what thereafter became his business name: H. Gordon Selfridge.

Looking at earlier letters, it is evident his signature changed too. It was almost as if he'd been practising a brand-new sweeping flourish of letters. Now he had a new name, new handwriting, a new store and a new life. But old habits remained.

Somehow, in all the frantic months of preparation, Selfridge had found time to become initiated into that select band of brothers, the Freemasons. He joined Columbia Lodge 2397, whose membership was exclusively made up from the American community in London. Among the distinguished list of Columbia Founders was Henry S. Wellcome, the American pharmaceutical millionaire, who cordially received 'Brother Gordon Selfridge' to the Lodge. Brotherly love however would soon be irrevocably strained when Wellcome's wife Syrie and Harry Gordon Selfridge started their tempestuous affair.

~

TAKE-OFF

'A store which is used every day should be as fine a thing and,
in its own way, as ennobling a thing as a church or a museum.'
H. Gordon Selfridge

Over a million people were counted into Selfridge's during the
opening week. From that moment on, both the store and the
man became famous. 'Selfridge', wrote one columnist, 'is as much one
of the sights of London as Big Ben. With his morning jacket, white
vest slip, pearl tie-pin and orchid buttonhole, he is a mobile landmark
of the metropolis.' There was always a small crowd waiting outside to
see him arrive at work each morning at 8.30 a.m. An observer recalled
that 'he was received in respectable silence by the bystanders, who
always waved at him'. Selfridge would doff his hat and proceed inside.
He took his private lift to the fourth floor and walked briskly down
the corridor lined with framed press editorials and advertising tear
sheets to his north-east corner office suite. There his personal staff –
Thomas Aubrey, his private secretary, and two typists – would already
be going through the first post.

Harry's morning unfolded in a series of rituals, each performed
with precise timing. Though he usually shaved at home, in the store
the American-equipped barber's shop sent up an assistant to give
him a scalp rub and trim and hot towel wrap, and to lightly wax
his moustache and eyebrows, while a manicurist buffed and filed his
fingernails.

The young salesman from the menswear department who acted as his in-store valet would bring up several freshly laundered cream silk shirts and hang them in the cedar-wood closets, where a second set of dress clothes was ready in case he wanted to change at work before going out for the evening. His high, Cuban-heeled black patent boots – made to order by Alan McAfee of Duke Street, with in-built 'lifts' to give him an extra half-inch – were rubbed with a chamois cloth and, finally, his black silk top hat was carefully brushed.

The restaurant supervisor delivered a pot of weak China tea and a bowl of fruit, pausing to discuss the menu for any guests due for lunch in his private dining-room. A florist arrived from the flower department with a selection of roses and orchids from which Selfridge carefully selected a rose for the crystal vase on his desk and an orchid for his boutonnière. Three times a week, huge vases of flowers were carefully arranged in his inner and outer offices and the dining-room. Selfridge adored highly scented flowers and was fastidious about their care, always checking the water to ensure it was topped up and pausing to snap off a dead bloom.

Refreshed, he would then deal with the early morning post, the first of five enormous batches that arrived daily from the Remittance Office, which handled all the store mail. He would go through important letters with Mr Aubrey and then, at 9.15 a.m., run through the day's engagement diary with his Social Secretary. At precisely 9.30 a.m. he would don his hat and walk the store's six acres, the monarch of all he surveyed.

Department managers frantically telephoned ahead to alert staff, who would instinctively straighten up and smooth their clothes, trying not to look self-conscious. Harry would stop and have a word here, ask a question there. He never asked anyone how they were, loathing any mention of even the mildest ill-health. 'Tell me ...' was always his opening question, 'how is this selling?' or 'has this gone well?' He knew *exactly* how it had been going, for the previous day's sales reports were on his desk first thing each morning, but he wanted to hear it from them. On his instruction, staff always called him 'Mr Selfridge' to his face, never 'Sir'. He actively disliked that formality.

Any letters signed 'I remain, sir, your most obedient servant', in the manner of the time, made him wince. For the most part, his staff referred to him as 'the Chief'.

As he made his rounds, he would scribble notes about things that annoyed him or queries to be followed up on his shirt cuff in pencil: not for nothing were there spares in the office. He never criticized anyone in public – and rarely praised them either – but he would nod and smile faintly when he heard good news. Then, looking at his watch – always set five minutes fast 'so I've got five minutes longer to live' – he would move on to the next department. Nothing escaped his eagle eye, from a stain on the carpet to a blunt pencil. If he found dust he simply paused and wrote HGS with his fingertip, just as he had always done at Marshall Field. It wouldn't be there for long.

His presence, however, lingered long after he'd left and the staff would talk about his 'walk' for the rest of the day. Sometimes they would get a reminder, by way of a yellow telegram envelope that arrived at their work station. Originally, Selfridge had reasoned that they would jump to open the envelope thinking they had been sent a telegram. Once the staff had figured out the system they were even quicker to open it, never knowing if it was good news or bad but aware that it was a personal message from 'the Chief' exclusively for them.

Harry's tour took more than an hour. By the time he got back to his office he had seen over a thousand people. Within a decade that number had grown to well over three thousand and ultimately it would rise to over five. He engaged with them all. For a lot of them, it was the highlight of their day. The man himself – imbued with a glamour lacking in any other retailing chief – was why they worked at Selfridge's. The store was a theatre, with the curtain going up at nine o'clock every morning. Like every impresario before or since, Harry Selfridge was checking that his cast was in order, with the stage set for the next performance.

The rest of the morning was spent studying buyers' reports and stock inventories, meeting the advertising department staff, planning window displays or on the telephone. The store had 120 lines to the Mayfair Exchange and 600 internal extensions. Selfridge regarded all embryonic telecommunications systems as an essential business tool. He had offered the National Telephone Company the opportunity to open a branch exchange in the store, but they turned him down, instead giving the store the distinctive telephone number 'Gerrard One' by way of compensation. As telephones spread through London, Selfridge's was the first store to sell the equipment and also the first to advertise on the cover of the telephone directory – no one else had thought of it.

Harry's office door was – in theory – always open for people who wanted to see him. In reality, Thomas Aubrey carefully guarded the inner sanctum. Generally affable, Selfridge could at times be tetchy. Executives called to meetings would get a signal from Mr Aubrey, who used a coded system – 'North Wind', 'North East Wind' or 'Gale Force Wind' – so that they knew what to expect. They also soon learned that he hated, absolutely hated, long meetings. In a move designed as much to unnerve people as to structure his time, he would place a large hour-glass upside down the minute someone entered his office. Turning towards them with his vivid blue eyes fixed in a pene-trating gaze, he would ask 'What can I do for you?' Fifteen minutes, he reasoned, was long enough for most issues. It wasn't so much that 'time is money', more that 'time is precious'. He was fixated by it. He was 53. He wanted to be 30 again.

Given the *froideur* with which London's established retail busi-nesses had reacted to Selfridge's grand opening, it is curious how many of them swiftly recalled anniversaries of their own to celebrate that year. Peter Robinson, D. H. Evans, John Barker, Swan & Edgar and Maples all staged events that enabled them to send out elaborate cards and entertain their customers. Even the mighty Harrods succumbed, deciding they couldn't wait a minute longer to celebrate their 75th Jubilee by hosting a series of grand concerts led by the London Symphony Orchestra. Selfridge was hugely amused at their arithmetic, for though their founder Henry Harrod had opened his original small shop in Stepney in 1835, he hadn't acquired ownership of the Knightsbridge site until 1853. Sir Alfred Newton, the Chairman of Harrods, visited Selfridge to pay his compliments. Their meeting, seemingly friendly, ended with Sir Alfred saying: 'You'll lose your money.'

Selfridge may have remembered that remark some weeks later when the store was deserted for days at a time and takings were meagre. A reporter from the *Evening News*, who found himself virtually alone on an upper floor, bumped into Selfridge himself who, full of bravura, simply said: 'We've not provided half enough lifts – it doesn't do to keep people waiting.' While the *Evening News* remarked on 'his unconquerable optimism', there were other, less appealing, press notices. The *Anglo-Continental Magazine* puritanically observed: 'Selfridge's employs every art to lure the feminine element into those extravagances which work ruin and misery at home.'

In some respects the magazine had a point. In an era when the average household rarely had access to credit, many families still only bought what they could afford. Selfridge's, more than any other store in England, spearheaded the revolution that changed people's perception of shopping, perhaps most significantly by involving his customers less in 'ruin and misery' than in the real pleasure of purchasing something, however modest, and being made to feel special while doing it. When the store opened, all visitors (as he preferred to call customers) received miniature silver keys as a gift 'so they would feel at home'. 'I want to serve the public courteously, efficiently, expeditiously and with absolute fairness,' he told the respected American journalist, Edward Price Bell. As a consequence, his customers lacked for nothing. Lord Beaverbrook, not an easy man to impress, would later remark that 'Gordon Selfridge pioneered the art of pampering.' He was right. People went to Selfridge's to buy something they wanted rather than something they needed.

What Harry Selfridge himself needed at this point was money. He had an annual payroll bill of over £120,000 to meet, interest to pay on his £350,000 loan from John Musker, an annual ground rent of

£10,000 and increasing National Insurance costs, not to mention a huge promotional budget to underwrite. It was hardly surprising that his finances were precarious. Discussions were under way with interested parties about a stock issue, but it was proving hard to finalize. Frank Woolworth, the American 'dime store' multi-millionaire, was in London at the time, exploring his own planned expansion in England. He wrote to colleagues back in America:

> Stores here are too small and shallow. Customers do most of their shopping from the windows. The moment you go in, you are expected to buy and to have made your choice from the window. They give you an icy stare if you follow the American custom of just going in to look around. Selfridge's is the only department store that looks like an American establishment. He has spent an enormous amount of money and may make a success in time. He has been trying to float some stock in his corporation but without much success. Most Englishmen think he will fail. There seems to be a prejudice against him – in fact against all foreigners invading this territory. We will have no walkover here.

Selfridge himself was saddened by what he felt was 'a certain hostility, originating with our competitors'. It was said that several senior staff had specifically applied for jobs at the behest of rivals and were reporting back on new systems and turnover figures. Certainly, some members of staff were fired abruptly within a matter of months. Selfridge hotly denied that this was due to commercial espionage, explaining that those let go hadn't 'responded to our training methods or house rules'. These were carved in stone: no gratuities or suppliers' kick-backs were to be taken, punctuality and presentation were of paramount importance, and staff were expected to adhere to a strict dress code.

There were no second chances at Selfridge's. One mistake meant instant dismissal. The staff didn't seem to mind. There were five applicants for every available job, wages were a little higher than elsewhere, staff facilities were unique for the time and – significantly – there were no fines. An early employee, who worked there for over thirty years, recalled: 'There was a feeling of kindness pervading the store right from the start – it was always a happy place.'

Selfridge may have upset a lot of people in London, but he genuinely wanted to make Oxford Street the pre-eminent shopping street in the world. It was proving harder than he had thought and he admitted his ideal would be to have 'Harrods on one side of us, Whiteley's on the other, and Swan & Edgar facing us. Then we should all do better.'

There were daily discussions about how to increase footfall. Determined to attract men into the store – either accompanying their wives and girlfriends or shopping themselves – Selfridge opened a rifle range on the roof terrace. Paintings that had failed to be selected for the Royal Academy's Summer Show were exhibited in the store. 'Artists have a hard enough time making a living,' said Selfridge, 'and anyway, there might be some undiscovered treasures amongst them.' As it happened, there weren't, but he was always keen to explore new ideas. Even his children weren't allowed to leave the breakfast table until they had each made at least three suggestions. Rosalie, Violette, Harry Gordon (always called Gordon Jr) and Beatrice were now 15, 12, 9 and 8 respectively. Their upbringing was unusual to say the least. Their contemporaries didn't breakfast with their parents, let alone discuss business ideas, nor did their fathers own stores that provided the unheard-of treat of ice-cream sodas for tea.

Grace Lovat Fraser, a friend of Rosalie's, spent a lot of time at Arlington Street. The atmosphere was 'lively and informal, with the house always full of young people, of whom gentle Mrs Selfridge was very fond'. Grace became very close to the children, often joining them on trips to matinées organized by their grandmother, whom she described as 'unobtrusively formidable' and 'unquestionably the head of the household'. Rose Selfridge didn't share her husband's passion for London or its nightlife. Neither did she care for the rigid formality of the era. Even Jennie Jerome, Winston Churchill's mother and an early 'dollar princess' who was a member of Edward VII's set, wrote in her 1908 diary: 'In England, the American woman is looked upon as a strange and abnormal creature with habits and manner something between a red Indian and a Gaiety Girl.' Admittedly, Jennie had a snake tattooed around her wrist and a penchant for lovers younger than her own son, whereas Rose Selfridge wasn't in the least flashy and loved nothing better than being at home with her family. Rose missed Chicago, travelling back there three, or sometimes four times a year to see her sister.

The children had very different personalities. According to Grace, 'Rosalie was quiet and gentle, like her mother, while Violette was outgoing, pretty and given to improvising unexpected amusements which were indulgently regarded by the rest of the family.' Violette, the 'wild child' of the family, once famously bluffed her way into her father's office, disguised in a blonde wig, and solicited a fairly generous cheque from him for a fake charity.

The girls went to Miss Douglas's school in Queen's Gate, had dancing classes at Mrs Wordsworth's, and learned to curtsey and to speak 'very pretty French'. Young Gordon meanwhile was sent away to prep school. Groomed from an early age to join the business, his holidays filled with private tuition, even as a child he often appeared at his father's side for photo opportunities. The store was the children's playground. The three girls were treated like little princesses in the toy department, the pet department, the girls' clothes department and especially the confectionery department. Gordon Jr and his friends probably preferred the vast lower basement, where men stoked the coal furnaces that heated the steam radiators throughout the store, or Irongate Wharf in Paddington, where the delivery vans, carts and horses were kept.

The children led a very international life compared to many of their classmates. Summers were spent in Chicago, while in winter they went to St Moritz to ski and skate. In London, they cycled around town, played tennis and took judo classes, activities for which they were dressed by the store where sports clothes and equipment were stocked in depth.

While sportsmen now wore lighter clothes, women were still covered from chin to ankle, or from chin to knee in the case of swimwear. In 1909, Mrs Charlotte Cooper Sterry, who had previously won the Wimbledon Ladies' Championship five times, said: 'To my idea nothing looks smarter or more in keeping with the game than a nice white skirt – about two inches off the ground – white blouse, white band and a pale coloured silk tie and white collar.' What she didn't say was that she was – as all women were – still wearing a corset, although the newly introduced 'sports corset' was a smaller affair, made in cotton, shaped like a waist-cincher and much more lightly boned. It took what had originally been introduced as a child's garment – the ribbed cotton liberty bodice – to liberate sportswomen from corsets when an enterprising manufacturer made them in adult sizes, marketing them as a lighter-weight cover-up.

Women who played golf fared little better. The struggle between the new woman's enthusiasm for golf and her clothes became so acute that special golf courses were laid out with short holes as they couldn't hit a long drive wearing a tightly cut jacket. At this point, Burberry – having made their name with special weather-proofed motoring clothes – came to the rescue with their 'Ladies' Free-stroke Coat with patent *Pivot* Sleeve and adjustable skirt'.

There's little evidence to suggest that the Selfridge girls enjoyed country pursuits – understandably, given that their father didn't even own tweeds, once famously annoying his hostess by turning up for a weekend in the country still wearing his usual formal coat and striped trousers.

Above all, the family talked together, with Madam Selfridge marking up interesting passages in the morning and evening newspapers for daily discussion round the dining-table. Selfridge was a fond father, indulgent towards his children and himself indulged by his devoted wife and mother. Edward Price Bell, who knew them in both Chicago and London, observed that his home and family 'provided [Selfridge] with emotional riches of astonishing affluence'. Despite all this, it wasn't enough. Selfridge had a compulsion for conquest – whether in work, or with women.

Financial security came three months after the opening of the store when, despite some scepticism in the City, Selfridge succeeded in raising money through the company's share offering. The originating £900,000 capital was split into £400,000 worth of 6 per cent cumulative preference shares at £1 each, and £500,000 worth of ordinary shares at £1. Selfridge himself owned well over 200,000 preference and 300,000 ordinary shares. There was a further offer of £400,000 worth of 5 per cent first mortgage debentures at £100 each. Selfridge, having alerted investors 'not to expect dividends for a year or two', immediately went out and bought sixteen adjoining buildings, increased his advertising budget and hired 200 new members of staff.

Though the store was too new to have earned a place in London's fashion hierarchy, customers were drawn by the depth of accessories beautifully displayed in individual departments: parasols, coq feather boas, trimmed millinery, handkerchiefs, gloves and lace. Selfridge's also specialized in shoes, sold the most mouth-watering tea gowns and had some of the best-stocked children's wear and corsetry departments in town. Servants' liveries, nurses' uniforms, even clothes and dog-collars for the clergy – Selfridge's sold them all.

It was a good beginning, but it wasn't enough. Existing stores already had an established customer base. Harrods served 'society' and the classier end of the artistic world – Oscar Wilde, Lillie Langtry and Ellen Terry had been among the first to sign up for monthly credit accounts when Harrods launched them as early as 1884. Swan & Edgar was the store of choice for actresses, dancers and the *demi-monde*, all of whom ordered delicious clothes made in their workshops under the supervision of the talented Ann Cheriton. Swan's real claim to fame came when W. Somerset Maugham used it as a model for his fictional 'Lynn & Sedley' in *Of Human Bondage*, paying the floorwalker Gilbert Clarke 30 guineas to give him a blow-by-blow description of the rigours of retailing, right down to the depressing and dirty staff hostels.

Older established firms were invariably steeped in dark mahogany and staffed with imperiously mannered floor-walkers. There was very little of the theatrical about Debenham & Freebody, whose chilly Carrara marble halls in Wigmore Street were an oasis of genteel respectability serving upper-middle-class women who booked in at 'Madam Pacard's Dressmaking Department' for their special gowns.

Virtually all these clothes were hand-sewn, machines only being used for linings and petticoats. Selfridge's, like all the 'better stores', had their own workrooms where seamstresses specialized in different sections – sleeves, bodices or skirts. 'Made on our own premises' was the benchmark of quality, although ever-increasing demand put additional pressure on production space and staff costs, leading to a marked increase in 'sweated labour'.

There were very few prestigious ready-made clothes available, other than cloaks and capes, which didn't need fitting. The one exception was that mainstay of the Edwardian wardrobe, the beautiful blouse, which retailed at an average price of 2 to 3 guineas. Small, specialist manufacturers made up most of the lace and pin-tucked blouses and provided most lingerie – robes, lace-trimmed petticoats and camisoles. Such establishments might employ anything from a dozen to fifty girls, usually young, almost always immigrants, who earned somewhere between 5 and 15 shillings a week. The girls often worked in appalling conditions, and the poor light and close work ruined their eyes. *Makers of Our Clothes*, published after the 1906 Anti-Sweated Labour Exhibition organized by the Cadbury family's *Daily News*, describes the gruellingly long hours and low pay of people in workshops or at home, whose skills with a needle were the only way they could keep a roof over their head. Very few customers stopped to think how the clothes they were buying had been made.

A lot of women used the department stores to buy part-made pieces, particularly unhemmed skirts and dresses with an open seam at the back, as clothes were not yet graded by size. Those with sewing skills or good local dressmakers bought 'dress lengths' or 'blouse lengths' ready cut, and of course all the trimmings from the haberdashery department, while the more affluent had made-to-measure 'Paris models' replicated by the store's workshops. Whether the gown in question was a paid-for model from Paris or simply been lifted from the pages of a magazine rather depended on the store in question, but regardless, a woman fond of fashion had to be 'fitted and pinned', devoting hours each week to the process.

Selfridge's never set out specifically to target the grander women of the Edwardian era, who still sourced their clothes in the more rarefied, opulent surroundings of court dressmaking establishments such as Redfern, Reville & Rossiter and Mascotte in Park Street, the latter owned by the socially well-connected Mrs Cyril Drummond. Arguably London's first famous designer was the equally well-connected Lady Lucy Duff Gordon – known as Lucile – who had her own fashion house. She created her own distinctive look and had a flair for publicity – helped by the fact that her sister was the famously risqué author Elinor Glyn.

Lucile eagerly adopted celebrity dressing, designing a wardrobe for the actress Lily Elsie in her role in *The Merry Widow*. She was also the first London designer to use live models, to colour co-ordinate accessories to outfits, and to deliver clients' orders packaged in bold striped boxes with ornate labels almost as sumptuous as the clothes inside. Selfridge's, with its 'house green' used on everything from the colour of their delivery vans to the store carpets, came closest in such stylish co-ordination.

The department stores were quick to copy Lucile's ideas. Harrods promoted 'a display of gowns on living models' for their 1909 Jubilee shows in their 'Costume Department', but while the store called itself the 'Shrine of Fashion', the truly fashionable worshipped at Lucile's. No record exists of the full guest-list for Lucile's ground-breaking show held earlier that year, which she called 'The Seven Ages of Women'. Her house mannequins included the statuesque beauties Hebe, Phyllis and Florence, as well as the incomparable Dolores who went on to become a famous Ziegfeld showgirl in New York. Among the audience were Queen Marie of Romania, Lillie Langtry, Queen

Ina of Spain, Bertha Potter Palmer, Ethel Field Beatty, Margot Asquith and what the media called 'every society woman in London'.

Change in fashion had been a long time coming. For over a decade Edwardian ladies had been poured into their favoured boned 'S-Bend' corsets, which created a lush embonpoint and a curvy *derrière*. The beautiful Mrs Keppel, the King's mistress *en titre*, had herself now swelled to Junoesque proportions, whereas the Queen, at 64, still had a hand-span waist and porcelain complexion, albeit one liberally covered in make-up The Queen's use of cosmetics was unusual. Lipstick, eye-shadow and mascara were still generally taboo and worn only by show-girls and good-time girls. Stores sold toiletries, which included scent, hairnets, brushes and combs, cold cream, face powders, tiny booklets of *papier poudre* sheets and even the odd pot of rouge, but such things were generally tucked away in a discreet part of the building – at Selfridge's at the back of the lower ground floor, next to 'trusses and bedpans', and at Harrods up on the first floor. All that was about to change.

Fashion was being disseminated with increasing speed, spilling out of the pages of the ever-growing number of magazines and news-papers. In Paris the new 'lean line' had just been launched by Paul Poiret, whose influence ultimately banished frilled and flounced petti-coats and whose hobble skirts heralded the reinvention of what went underneath. Out went curved corsets and in came underpinnings specifically made to contour a long, lean and straight body. Poiret was fond of saying he had 'liberated women' by introducing the brassiere and banishing boned bodices. In reality, real Poiret devotees wore long, hip-hugging foundation garments under skirts so tight they could hardly walk.

Poiret found an enthusiastic following among the British fashion élite. The Prime Minister's wife Margot Asquith invited him to present his collection at a special show for her friends at No. 10 Downing Street, where Helena Rubinstein herself was on hand to supervise the models' make-up and apply some rouge to Mrs Asquith, who had a penchant for cosmetics. Unfortunately the press took violent exception to this French invasion, creating such a furore that questions were raised in the House of Commons. The media were equally critical: 'Not only does Mr Asquith refuse his own people the right of protection, but he facilitates the intrusion of foreign merchandise by allowing exhibitions in the residence which has been paid for by the nation's trade.' The Prime Minister's wife, for once unusually subdued, was subsequently to be found at Lucile's, while Monsieur Poiret basked in the publicity and department stores furiously copied his designs.

One fashion that didn't change was big hats. If anything, they got even bigger and were trimmed with a profusion of feathers and flowers. Big hair on the other hand was being toned down. Selfridge's sold a huge selection of false hair-pieces but the latest trend, thanks to Charles Nestlo's Permanent Wave Machine, was for waving. 'Girls Prefer Curls' said the ads, which meant that at the store's hairdressing department – featuring the most modern equipment in London – the ten senior stylists were kept busy curling. They were also colouring, thanks to the Frenchman Eugène Schueller's new hair dyes.

Clothes had also changed colour, no longer confined to a palette of sweet-pea tones or Royal Mourning Mauve. Thanks to the Fauve movement in Paris, strong, bold shades had finally swept back into fashion.

In July 1910, London's grandees were treated to a Russian *divertissement* hosted by Bertha Potter Palmer at her palatial home in Carlton House Terrace. Harry and Rose Selfridge were among the guests who saw Anna Pavlova and her partner Michel Mordkin perform, with Pavlova wearing a sumptuous scarlet satin and gold tissue appliquéd robe designed by Ivan Bilibine. Dance in various forms inspired huge fashion trends, just as dancers like Anna Pavlova, Isadora Duncan and the notorious Maude Allan – famous for writing an illustrated sex manual for women – became style icons. When Maude Allan made her debut in *Vision of Salome* at the Palace Theatre, a production loosely based on Oscar Wilde's equally notorious *Salome*, she wore what Lady Diana Manners described as a 'wisp of chiffon'. Maude also wore ropes and ropes of faux pearls, triggering a craze for fake jewels. Selfridge's hastily opened a large costume jewellery department, which annoyed their Mr Dix and Mr Tanner, who presided over real stones in the store – but the fashion for fakes became an unstoppable trend.

The biggest impact on fashion through dance, however, undoubtedly came from Sergei Diaghilev's Ballet Russe, launched at the Theatre du Châtelet in Paris in the summer of 1909. The stunning sets designed by Alexandre Benois and Leon Bakst prompted a sea-change in home décor, triggering vibrancy in everything from paint colours to curtains and cushions.

Selfridge's was in the right place at *exactly* the right time. Almost every day, it seemed as if the press was reporting a new invention or a new feat of bravura, but nothing captured the imagination of the public more than aviation. In the six years since Wilbur and Orville Wright had first taken to the air at Kitty Hawk in North Carolina, the thrill of flight had taken hold. Newspapers – in particular Northcliffe's *Daily Mail* and George Holt Thomas's *Daily Graphic* – saw aviation as a means of boosting circulation, between them offering thousands of pounds in prizes to those who could make or break flight records. The fact that most entrants were opportunist self-publicists, with little hope of getting their machines off the ground, never mind into the record books, didn't matter. It all made good copy.

The French, having invented the hot-air balloon in the eighteenth century, were understandably keen to set their own aviation records. By 1907, the Voisin-Delagrande biplane had made it into the air, while in 1910, the colourful self-styled Baroness Raymonde de Laroche became the first woman in the world to receive a pilot's licence. Most exciting of all, the Frenchman Louis Blériot flew into the history books as the first man to fly over water. On a cloudy day in late July 1909, he soared into the air above Calais in a monoplane driven by a three-cylinder engine, attached to a two-bladed propeller, and headed for England.

Blériot's epic journey – which lasted just forty-three hair-raising

minutes – was sponsored by the *Daily Mail*, who had enticingly offered
£1,000 as prize money. Waiting on the Kent coast was an enthusiastic
French reporter waving the *tricolor*, a *Daily Mail* photographer and
newsman – and Harry Gordon Selfridge. A deal was struck. Louis
– grateful apparently for some hard cash – agreed that Selfridge
could exhibit his plane in his store for four days. It has been said that
Selfridge was conveniently motoring in Kent that morning and just
happened by. His son, however, said he had planned the coup like a
military exercise, driving down to Kent having already made arrangements to transport the plane back to London. Whatever the case,
young Gordon, confined to bed with a bad cold, missed the excitement. It seems unlikely that Lord Northcliffe would have allowed his
prize-winning pilot – not to mention his plane – to be whisked away
so promptly unless he had agreed in advance. Given his acquaint-
anceship with Selfridge and the publicity that a four-day exhibition
offered the *Mail*, he had nothing to lose.

Blériot's plane, so fragile-looking that one observer said it seemed
to be 'all leather straps and balsa wood', left Dover on an open railway
wagon and arrived at Cannon Street Station at four in the morning.
There was no motorized delivery van large enough to carry it, so the
aircraft made its journey somewhat ignominiously by horse and cart
to the store, where it was installed in the hastily cleared 'bag and
trunk' department on the lower ground floor, protected by a wooden
barrier and guarded by six reserve police constables around the clock.
Having spent hours on the telephone to Fleet Street, Selfridge was
assured of headline-breaking news that would coincide with the
store's opening that morning. He had also booked advertisements,
styling them like news announcements: 'Calais – Dover – Selfridges,'
screamed the copy. 'The Blériot aeroplane, which flew the Channel
yesterday, is on view, free of charge of course, on our lower ground
floor. The Public are cordially invited to see this wonderful epoch-
making machine.' Anticipating a rush of hot-blooded males, he
tactfully added 'Reserved space for lady visitors' underneath.

It was the best show in town. Blériot's plane was seen by 150,000 people, among them MPs who were given a special viewing, as were members of the House of Lords. On Thursday that week, the store stayed open until midnight to accommodate the crowds. Competitors called it a 'cheap stunt'. Stunt it was – but it certainly wasn't cheap. It was a classy, clever, extravagant, *glorious* piece of marketing genius, which at a stroke established Harry Gordon Selfridge as the showman of shopping. From that point on, his business started to take off.

~

LIGHTING UP THE NIGHT

'Dance, dance, dance, till you drop'
W. H. Auden

For a trend to develop credibility and profitability, it has to become something that everyone is doing, however briefly. In 1910, 'trend-spotters', as today's consumer consultants are called, would have had a field day. Science was sexy. Almost all the inventions or technological refinements that were emerging in the late Edwardian era acted as a trigger of change: the aeroplane, the motor car, the telephone, colour printing, the advertising poster, graphic design, product packaging, refrigeration, processed food, recorded music, electricity, the camera, the embryonic cinema, even the six-hour boat to France. And of course there was the all-powerful popular press which, by promoting each one, helped create new consumer demand.

In 1910, the public were dancing to big-band music, smooching and sighing to the lyrics of songs such as 'I wonder who's kissing her now' and then buying phonograph wax cylinders to play the music at home (the cylinders were often sold with recording attachments, which gave the added excitement of being able to make a voice message). Professional musicians grumbled about the quality of the sound which had a tinny echo – John Sousa, by now a world-famous band-leader, scathingly called the cylinders 'canned music' – but it didn't stop them flying out of the new phonograph department at Selfridge's. Obsolescence being the life-blood of retailing, however, the complex cylinders were soon superseded by pressed discs in paper sleeves, courtesy of Columbia Records: the big hit of 1910 at Selfridge's was 'Land of Hope and Glory', recorded by Clara Butt.

For young couples, music and dancing were an escape from stifling restrictions at home. Increasingly, independence came simply from having somewhere else to go, such as the Lyons tea shops where a respectable young man could take his girl. Yet the morality of the time still insisted that men and women should not be featured together. When Selfridge's advertised their restaurant with a picture of a couple looking seductively at one another over the cutlery, it broke new ground.

Independence also came through transport. In London this included the expanding Underground system and the newly introduced motor buses which were rapidly replacing their horse-drawn predecessors. On the route down Oxford Street, the conductor would shout out 'Selfridge's' as the bus pulled up at the stop outside. Selfridge's booked bus-panel advertising, but there was never any name on the façade of the store. Selfridge, believing that signs would interfere with its architectural symmetry, reasoned that by now everyone knew his building. Instead, there were just two discreet plaques at each end of the window bays. He had long hoped that the Bond Street tube station might be renamed 'Selfridge's', and constantly lobbied his close friend, Albert Stanley, the influential Managing Director of the Underground Electric Railway Company. Mr Stanley would smile indulgently whenever Selfridge raised the topic and then gently reject the idea.

The store was now lit until midnight each night, shining like a beacon in the dark smoggy street, the window displays advertised as 'being part of the city's entertainment', designed to 'introduce the new art of window shopping'. Unfortunately, the vast piles of tantalizing merchandise freely displayed inside – dozens of sponges, mountains of scented soap, layer upon layer of embroidered handkerchiefs – also encouraged shoplifting. As more and more thieves were arrested, local magistrates accused Selfridge's of 'pandering to kleptomania'.

Selfridge himself was curiously uncommunicative about shoplifting. It was almost as though he refused to believe people could steal and wanted the whole messy business to go away. He hated being associated with it. When a thief was on trial, his public relations staff were instructed to call the newspapers and ask them not to mention Selfridge's by name but merely to write 'at a West End store'.

Dance continued to enchant and enthral, as did the dancers. When Anna Pavlova made her first public appearance in London at Shaftesbury Avenue's Palace Theatre in April, it was rumoured that Selfridge was *à deux* with the queen of the *pas de deux*. He had first met her the year before and went to see her perform several times, sending her baskets of flowers that were as tall as she was, if not taller. They were seen having supper together, Selfridge immaculate in white tie and tails, and Pavlova in a 'magnificent sable wrap', the inference being he had provided it – though since she was being paid £1,200 a week, she could easily have afforded to buy her own. Selfridge's certainly stocked sables in the fur department, and the couple's lingering tour of the store was later vividly recalled by a staff member. But then 'the Chief' was often to be found escorting famous women, a visit to Selfridge's being a sine qua non for visiting celebrities who all signed their names with a diamond-tipped stick on a specially dedicated glass window panel in Harry's office. His advertising manager, A. H. Williams, who later wrote a book about his two decades at the store, was adamant that not all these liaisons were of an intimate nature, claiming that Selfridge was merely a generous host and escort, albeit one hopelessly captivated by fame. Yet the rumour that he was a roué refused to die.

Royalty's own roué, King Edward VII, died in May 1910 and was deeply mourned. Thousands of people got up before dawn to line the route of the funeral procession, hoping to catch a glimpse of his coffin. As the cortège wound its way through London, with his dog Caesar faithfully following behind, many members of the public wept. No one was really in the mood for shopping, and business slipped back at almost every shop and store, except ironically at the grand fashion houses where staff were busy making elaborate dresses for Royal Ascot in, to paraphrase Henry Ford's slogan for his Model T car, 'every colour, so long as it's black'. There were some who felt Ascot should be cancelled that year, but the race meeting went ahead in what famously became known as 'Black Ascot'.

A few weeks earlier, Selfridge's had published their figures, which revealed a mixed year. The Blériot effect had by now worn off. Selfridge dipped into his personal funds to the tune of £28,500 to pay the 6 per cent interest due to preference shareholders. The store's figures were not well received, even though it was clear that the enormous sums invested in the store would obviously take time to recoup. Many stores in Oxford Street – even crusty old Marshall & Snelgrove – admitted that their business had 'dramatically improved since the opening of Selfridge's'. Yet the man himself got a poor financial press.

Fortunately for Selfridge, his new best friend Sir Edward Holden, Chairman of the Midland Bank, chose to ignore it. Sir Edward, having become the Midland's General Manager in 1891, had spear-headed such an aggressive expansion programme that at the peak of his friendship with Selfridge in 1918, he was presiding over what was then the largest bank in the world. Sir Edward's vision for international expansion meant he frequently travelled to America, a country he admired and where at one point during the early 1900s he had considered opening branches in New York and Chicago. While that idea never materialized, in 1905, uniquely among British banks, he had the foresight to open a foreign exchange department. Sharing Harry's belief in the lucrative prospects of the widening travel market, Sir Edward was an enthusiastic supporter of his grand plans.

It wasn't just the store's cash deposits that impressed Sir Edward – although on busy days the counting-house staff shuttle 'over the street' from the store to the Midland branch opposite was very gratifying – it was the unstoppable faith, the fanatical enthusiasm with which Selfridge embraced the new era's potential.

As always, Harry's arguments were persuasive. He had a masterful command of statistics, using them in a way rarely seen in business at that time. He gathered impressive evidence from his staff, many of whom were sent out daily armed with notebooks and pencils to record everything from the number of people getting off buses outside to the numbers entering rival stores. Rarely a day would pass without Selfridge talking to Sir Edward about his plans, his hopes, his dreams. He couldn't do any of it without money, and Sir Edward Holden and the Midland Bank had plenty of that to offer. The staff, meanwhile, were becoming used to the mercurial personality of 'the Chief' who didn't hesitate to make spontaneous decisions about dramatic departmental changes.

In 1910, fresh from a visit to Paris where he saw ranges of cosmetics and perfumes openly on sale in the stores, Selfridge decided to expand the beauty department, which until then had been part of the pharmacy department. The cosmetics industry had already begun to form an identity beyond the stage and the street. Independent young women were experimenting with make-up, although since coloured cosmetics were still controversial, the problem wasn't so much about wearing it but rather not wearing too much. New, better-quality products were now being made by Richard Hudnut, Helena Rubinstein and Bourjois, all producing finer-ground, purer-tinted face powders and rouge. The *London Journal of Fashion* noted that 'rouge, discreetly put on, forms a part of every *toilet* as worn by fashionable women, although some amongst these are beginning to use their face powders somewhat too heavily. The startling effect of contrast, by making the lips vividly red and the face very pale, greatly ages a woman. Still … almost everybody uses scarlet lip-salve.'

Even though an unstoppable trend was underway, Selfridge's sold very little red lipstick, and then only discreetly. The initial purpose of the relocated department was to sell perfume. Selfridge, who adored scent, could identify most of those on the market, and one of his undoubted attractions to women was that he enjoyed talking about such things. He knew if a woman was wearing Houbigant. He loved Guerlain. Firmly believing that perfume heightened the senses,

Selfridge wanted to offer the experience to everyday shoppers. Placing perfume inside the front doors of the store was a master-stroke, having the added advantage of disguising less pleasant odours: not everyone made personal hygiene a priority, and the smell of horse manure and exhaust fumes from the street could be overwhelming.

Selfridge wasn't the first to perfume a public place. In 1870 at the famous Gaiety Theatre, where the impresario John Hollingsworth had presided over a glamorous chorus line of 'Gaiety Girls', the perfumer Eugene Rimmel, otherwise known as 'The Scenter of the Strand', perfumed the pages of the theatre's programmes. More erotically, he installed special nozzles to perfume the water in the foyer fountain. A night out at the Gaiety was heady stuff in more ways than one.

Selfridge's set about putting boxes of face powder side by side with rouge, and swansdown powder puffs next to manicure sets, but above all at that time, they sold perfume. Pure perfume was still vastly expensive. A crystal bottle of fine fragrance could cost up to £3 or even more, an impossible amount for those earning 10 shillings a week. But thanks to the chemist Georges Darzens's discovery of the 'glycidic method' of synthesizing aldehydes, delicious smells could now be replicated at affordable prices. This meant that Selfridge's could sell bottles of 'Lily of the Valley' priced at 1/6d. The customers of course knew nothing about synthetic chemicals – they were just happy it smelled nice.

All this interest in femininity meant that Selfridge himself became a figure of fascination for all sorts of women. He was an avid 'first-nighter', always sending flowers to a favoured actress. There was no difficulty in choosing what to send as a gift to his favourites – he had a store full of such things. He was also gaining the reputation of being generous when the women in his life had financial troubles. Late in 1910, it seems the flame-haired author Elinor Glyn turned to Selfridge in her own hour of need.

Harry had met Elinor not through her sister Lucile but through their mutual friend and her neighbour in Essex, Ralph Blumenfeld, the *Daily Express* editor who not only championed her work but also paid well to publish it. Unhappily married, Elinor had for some time been having an affair with Lord Curzon, himself now a widower after the untimely death of his wife Mary Leiter in 1906. It was always an affair destined to end in pain. Curzon had great political ambition, three young children and an expensive lifestyle to maintain. Glyn was married in an era when divorce was unthinkable, and worse, she earned her income writing outré novels. When Curzon ended their relationship in the late autumn of 1910, Elinor was desolate. She was also broke and owed money to Curzon – a debt he expected to be repaid.

Throughout his life, Selfridge was attracted to successful, independent and famous women. He responded to a brittle sense of humour, was susceptible to girls in gorgeous clothes and, one suspects, was sexually aroused by being 'treated mean'. Elinor Glyn pushed every button.

Elinor met up with Selfridge in Paris that autumn. In her diary she called him 'the American Napoleon', admitting that she treated him with indifference despite being flattered by the attention he paid her. He took her out, made a huge fuss of her, no doubt paid all her bills, and ensured she lacked for nothing. It must have amused Selfridge to hand over money that would repay Lord Curzon. He always enjoyed the web of connections with his past.

A quintessential 'sugar and sin' Edwardian character, Selfridge never let his true devotion to his family get in the way of collecting beautiful arm-candy. While he was seeing Elinor Glyn, he also began an affair with Syrie Wellcome, the fall-out from which would come home to haunt him.

Syrie was the daughter of Thomas Barnardo, the pious philanthropist who established the Dr Barnardo's Homes for orphaned children. In 1901, at the age of 22, Syrie exchanged a controlling father for an equally controlling husband when she married the dour 48-year-old American pharmaceutical millionaire Henry Wellcome. Theirs was a bitterly unhappy and violent marriage, which left her physically as well as mentally scarred.

As Masons, Wellcome and Selfridge subsequently became part of the same close-knit circle. In the manner of the day, men of a certain social standing often dined out without their wives. They had their clubs – Selfridge joined the Reform – and attended endless dinners and speaking events connected with their business interests. But from time to time, wives joined husbands at formal banquets. Syrie, more inclined towards fashionable and bohemian society, and bored by such gatherings, must have been grateful that Harry Selfridge was often on hand to relieve the tedium. He wasn't a man known for his sense of humour but he did have a sympathetic ear and gave women his undivided attention. He also liked spoiling people. The combination was irresistible.

When her troubled marriage finally collapsed in 1909, Syrie, armed with a generous annual allowance of £2,400, set about launching herself in society. Beautifully dressed, brittle and, although no beauty, an attractive woman with a flawless complexion, she was 30 and ready to have fun. Officially, she was chaperoned by her widowed mother, a woman who was quite prepared to see her daughter enjoy herself whatever the cost to her reputation. Syrie herself was beginning to form the disciplined good taste that would ultimately evolve into a career as an interior decorator. Initially, however, she spent money rather than made it – and her tastes were expensive. Even an allowance of £2,400 a year wasn't going to go far, so when Harry came calling, she was happy to see him, gladly accepting his gift of the lease of an expensive house in York Terrace West where she lived with her mother. Their three-year on-and-off affair wasn't just about the money he generously provided. Harry had wonderful contacts which undoubtedly helped her career.

People close to Selfridge always believed that it was the chase and possession of his beautiful companions that Selfridge enjoyed, the act of conquest being more important than that of sex. Whatever the case, Syrie and Selfridge entered the relationship with their eyes wide open, perfectly matched in what they wanted and needed from their liaison. There was talk that Syrie was frigid, but Rebecca West, who knew a thing or two about sex herself, was dismissive of such rumours. 'Their relationship,' she said, 'was certainly a love affair. But they were lovers only when it suited them.' For a while it suited Harry very well. But there was never any suggestion that Syrie was his sole companion – he was often seen in the company of other women.

None of the senior staff seemed aware of the curious double life that 'the Chief' was leading. That would come later. They did know he worked long hours, arrived early each morning, enthused about work above almost everything else, and was bursting with ideas. Though he maintained a dignified distance from his female staff, nothing about women escaped his attention. On one daily tour he noticed that a sales assistant had bad teeth. He arranged for her to see the staff dentist and his attention turned to toothbrushes. Disappointed with what was on offer in the store, he found the best bristle brush supplier in Europe and bought up the entire stock. Selfridge always bought in large quantities. Suppliers gave him good prices and the press gave him good headlines.

Keen to popularize book-buying, he opened a huge 'popular' book department, run in conjunction with W. H. Smith. Selfridge ordered 60,000 velveteen-covered copies of the Book of Common Prayer, pricing it at 1 shilling. Next came the Selfridge Bible, then the Selfridge World Atlas, the Selfridge Dictionary, the Selfridge Encyclo-paedia and the Selfridge Cookery Book, all bought in blocks of at least 50,000 at a time and keenly priced. The department was designed to have the feel of a library, with tables and reading lights for customers. In a move rare for the time, Selfridge advertised his book department, calling it 'the most comfortable bookshop in all Europe'.

In an attempt to emulate the success of budget shopping at Marshall Field, Selfridge's opened their 'Bargain Basement' in 1911. It was promoted as the 'place where the thrifty housewife can shop to her advantage', and though it didn't have the impact of its American predecessor, slowly but surely it generated a steady profit. The Basement stocked legitimate 'seconds', bought-in bargain lines, discounted sale stock from the upper floors and occasionally truly wonderful hats marked down in price – all piled on tables where customers scrambled to find a bargain. Nothing was individually wrapped and removed for delivery. Bath salts for example were simply poured into a brown paper bag with a big scoop and handed over. The main difference between the Basement and the upper floors was not one of price – there were good-value lines on sale elsewhere in the store and good-quality things on sale in the Basement. But upstairs there was premium staff service and goods were delivered. Downstairs, customers generally served themselves and took home what they had bought. That in itself was unusual. If there was one thing that stood out in the golden age of retailing as practised by the great department stores, it was that everything, absolutely everything, was delivered. Customers never had to carry anything themselves. Purchases were taken to the dispatch department, marked up with an address label and delivered to wherever they had to go.

In the sweltering heat of 1911 – the hottest year in living memory – came the Coronation of King George V and Queen Mary. Selfridge regarded the event as being as important as the World Fair in Chicago. This was his opportunity to make Londoners take the store to their hearts, to tap into the natural affection that the people held for the Royal Family and to prove to everyone that here at least was one American with a heartfelt respect for great British traditions.

Selfridge intended to decorate the exterior of his store as if it were a civic building, not just with bunting and flags, but in a grandiose scheme that would reflect both the glory of the monarchy and the glory of shopping at Selfridge's. He spent hours consulting with the Royal College of Heralds over every minute detail, planning the elaborate décor that would symbolize and honour the concept of royalty past and present. The result was an astonishing sight. A plush red velvet frieze edged with thick corded gold ran along the top of the Ionic columns. The new King's monogram was embroidered in gold thread in the middle of each section and hung with gold-embroidered medallions emblazoned with royal emblems. Twelve-foot high shields bore the arms of previous kings, and each shield was surrounded by helmets and gauntlets, halberds and flags, while gilt papier-mâché lions guarded the base of each column. Waxed red and white roses symbolized the houses of Lancaster and York, and at the junction of Duke Street and Oxford Street there was a colossal gold crown. Every shield and portcullis was illuminated, and an astonishing 4,500 light-bulbs lit up the night sky. It cost a fortune and hopefully impressed Sir Edward Holden.

The press were certainly impressed, especially since Selfridge had invited the younger members of the extended Royal Family to watch the show from the first-floor balcony. As the royal procession returned from St Paul's Cathedral, came down Oxford Street and drew level with the store, the King and Queen turned and waved to assorted members of the Teck and other German grand-ducal families, as if the store itself was receiving the Royal seal of approval. The newsreels particularly enjoyed this *coup de théâtre* and the staff were so puffed up with pride they talked of little else for weeks. Whether courtiers were as enthusiastic is doubtful. The British were pretty good at putting on their own show. They didn't need an American shopkeeper to do it for them.

Selfridge was becoming known for making too much noise. He tried too hard, and the new Royal couple were traditionalists. Though an avid shopper, Queen Mary preferred to patronize Harrods, John Barker and the very sedate Gorringe's in Buckingham Palace Road. Despite Selfridge's yearning for Royal patronage, she never once visited the store in his lifetime.

That Selfridge himself was a snob is undeniable. Nothing delighted him more than when his wife's application for member-ship of that august body, the Daughters of the American Revolu-tion, was accepted, proving her family's long American lineage. Yet his snobbery was complex. He genuinely sought recognition for his staff as members of the 'profession of retail' and he was bitterly upset when, for example, the store director Percy Best sought member-ship of his local golf club and was rejected. But his passion for self-aggrandizement was too much for the establishment. Being in trade was one thing. Being publicly proud of it was something entirely different.

Not that Selfridge himself was particularly concerned about criticism from establishment figures. By now he had his own, increasingly influential circle of friends: Albert Stanley (now Lord Ashfield), Ralph Blumenfeld, Thomas Lipton and Thomas Dewar, whom he fondly called 'Tom Tea' and 'Tom Whisky'. He discussed spiritualism with Sir Oliver Lodge and played poker with Sir Ernest Cassel, dealing his own heavily embossed cards and using his own beautifully engraved mother-of-pearl chips. His admiration for Sir Oliver Lodge extended to his being given his own reserved table in the store's Palm Court Restaurant, where on most days he would take tea and meet informally with his fervent admirers. Lodge spent his time in distinguished company. Friends and 'believers' of the noted physicist – a brilliant scientist and inventor who was also deeply involved in psychic phenomena – included Sir Arthur Conan Doyle, H. G. Wells and Jacob Epstein. The restaurant staff would hover uncertainly around his table, in part curious, in part nervous, for the great man readily admitted he believed in the spirit world and was known to take part in séances.

By nature more practical than spiritual, with his interests firmly rooted in the present – and the future – Selfridge seems unlikely to have shared Sir Oliver's zeal for the afterlife, although he did have a 'near death' experience early in 1911 after a serious car crash in the Lake District. He was unconscious for over forty hours – long enough for his family to be gravely concerned – but then woke up quite suddenly, pronounced himself 'fit as a fiddle' and two days later, to the astonishment of colleagues who later said he had 'wished himself well', went straight back to work.

After the accident, perhaps feeling more in touch with his own mortality, he seemed even more hyper-charged than usual. From that point on, he developed insomnia, rarely sleeping more than four or five hours a night, although he did take brief cat-naps during the day. Time was the thing. Like the White Rabbit, he rushed around looking at his watch. He was always very nearly late, creating havoc with travelling companions by seemingly enjoying arriving at the boat train just as the departure whistle was being blown. There just weren't enough hours in the day to get everything done. Things were planned to the last second and he was a brilliant judge of timing, in more ways than one. When the *Daily Mirror* invited eighteen well-known figures to see if they could judge precisely how long a minute took to pass, only two of them got it right. One of them was Harry Gordon Selfridge.

Selfridge was always keen to investigate anything new. As he was a regular commuter to America as well as a devotee of the White Star shipping line, it might have been expected that he would have considered joining the maiden voyage of the *Titanic* in April 1912. His daughter Rosalie was by this time at Finch in New York, in those days a small 'post-graduate' finishing school which offered the daughters of the rich a grounding in art and music, lectures on world affairs and advice on hiring and firing servants. Rose and Harry had in fact crossed the Atlantic in January and had plans to go again in June. Selfridge himself often went over every couple of months, but in April that year, assisted by their faithful butler and housekeeper Mr and Mrs Fraser, they were busy moving from Arlington Street to their new house at 30 Portman Square. As always with Selfridge's English homes, it was a house with a history, having been the family home of George and Alice Keppel throughout 'Mrs George's' affair with Edward VII, who had been a constant visitor.

The sinking of the *Titanic* stunned the world, not least because it shattered people's faith in advanced technology. Among the 1,523 people who died in the catastrophe was Isador Strauss, the owner of Macy's in New York, who had visited Selfridge in London just a few days earlier. The elderly Mr Strauss went to his death accompanied by his devoted wife who, having been offered a place on a lifeboat, refused to leave his side. Harry Selfridge also mourned his friend W. T. Stead, the editor of the *Pall Mall Gazette*, who had often dined with the family at Arlington Street. Stead was another member of Sir Oliver Lodge's coterie and himself a great believer in psychical research. He had often dreamed about drowning, and just before boarding the ship he wrote to his secretary, 'I feel as if something is going to happen and that it will be for ever.'

Among the survivors were Lucy and Cosmo Duff Gordon who were bound for Lucile's New York showrooms. Elinor Glyn was at her house in Green Street when news of the catastrophe started to filter through. Desperate for news of her sister and close to hysteria, she immediately rang Ralph Blumenfeld's office. She needn't have worried. Lucy and her husband had managed to get into a lifeboat, despite the convention of the day that priority should go to women and children. More disturbing was the subsequent news that the boat wasn't even full and did not turn back to pick up other passengers. The Duff Gordons were bitterly attacked in the press, and gossip-mongers had a field day. Some said Duff had hastily piled on some of his wife's exotic clothes and masqueraded as a woman to secure his place (unlikely, given that he had a full beard). Others claimed that Lucy had insisted he stay with her, which is more plausible. When the Duff Gordons were called to account for their actions at an inquiry, they were vindicated, but Lucile's reputation in London never really recovered and she moved the hub of her fashion business to New York. Duff and Lucy soon separated, but both were haunted by the experience. For years afterwards, the accusation that they had deserted a sinking ship followed them wherever they went. Only today, ninety-five years later, has the truth come out with the publication of a letter from her maid, proving that luck had been on their side in being ushered by a crew member on to a virtually empty boat.

Social responsibility was high on Harry's agenda, and he regularly hosted charitable events in the store. An auction or fashion show held in the name of a good cause had the added attraction of bringing the rich, the titled and the famous together. That April, a fund-raising auction in the Palm Court Restaurant was held in support of the *Titanic* 'Disaster Fund', hosted by the celebrated actress Marie Tempest. Theatrical stars were a natural choice for Selfridge who was addicted to the stage. They attracted the right sort of press attention and they were happy to sign customers' autographs.

One of Harry's favourite plays – not least because its theme was fashion – was *The Madras House*, written and produced by Harley Granville-Barker. Selfridge admired the young, ultra-fashionable playwright/producer enormously, buying blocks of tickets for all his productions and distributing them among the staff who felt compelled to attend whether they wanted to or not. For Granville-Barker, whose intriguing work often received mixed reviews, Harry's generosity was a boon. For the store's staff it was a mixed blessing.

By now store turnover was up and profits were slowly but steadily rising: in 1912 to £50,000, in 1913 to £104,000, and in 1914 to over £131,000. Selfridge, having made a bet with Sir John Musker on meeting targets, was soon proudly driving a new Rolls-Royce. The financial press attacks had eased. *The Economist* commented on the latest figures: 'Not a roaring success, but the business is increasing.'

At the morning meetings, the ideas were still coming thick and fast. 'Merchandise' or gift vouchers were introduced. Sluggish morning trade was improved by special price-point promotions that ended at noon. A pet department opened, with special emphasis on the Selfridge family's favourite pug dogs. During the 1912 eclipse of the sun, customers were invited to watch the excitement from the roof garden. Though they were given coloured glasses for protection, most preferred to watch the reflection in the well-stocked fish ponds. Roger, the boiler-room cat – perhaps divining the fish – padded eight floors up from the sub-basement but then fell off the roof. Thousands of Londoners mourned his passing.

The death of the 'company cat' had been announced by 'Callisthenes', Harry Selfridge's new pet. The pseudonym appeared at the foot of a column which was published each day in the *Morning Post*. The column also appeared at random each day in various other newspapers, particularly *The Times*, the *Daily Telegraph*, the *Evening Standard*, the *Daily Mail* and the *Daily Express*, as well as the late Mr Stead's *Pall Mall Gazette*. 'Callisthenes,' explained Selfridge, 'was the original Public Relations man' – in fact a relative of Aristotle who, having caught the eye of Alexander the Great, was invited to join him on his expeditions as official historian.

The 'Callisthenes' column, usually about 500 words long and discreetly signed off with 'Selfridges & Co. Ltd', reflected 'the policies, principles and opinions of this House of Business upon various points of public interest'. All sorts of topics were covered, from Harry Selfridge's grand passion for a Channel Tunnel to the store's concern at the volume of traffic in Oxford Street. From time to time the column was given over to a celebrity pleading a cause: one early writer was Elinor Glyn.

Most other retailers were bemused by 'Callisthenes', unable to understand why Selfridge paid for such oblique advertising. In reality, the columns were often fascinating, sometimes sweetly sentimental but always sincere, and they drew people into the Selfridge's 'family'. *New Age* magazine howled with laughter, calling them 'utter cant', but 'Callisthenes' forged a place in the daily life of Londoners until 1939.

One topic ignored by 'Callisthenes' was female suffrage. The retail industry is often cited as being among the first to offer women career opportunities. In reality, most women only worked on the shop floor, though in Selfridge's, charmingly dressed in white pantaloons and faux-Russian tasselled boots, they also operated the lifts. There were of course 'lady buyers' – a particular breed of women who struck fear in the heart of manufacturers – among the staff at Selfridge's, and several of them were in charge of large budgets. Miss Nellie Elt, for example, was in charge of the cosmetics floor. But during Selfridge's lifetime and for long afterwards, no woman ever got anywhere near executive level, sat on the Board of Directors or was involved in investment planning.

Whether the suffragettes who went on the rampage in 1912, throwing bricks through West End store windows, did so as a protest against the lack of women in key jobs or merely as a protest against their lack of the vote was never raised in 'Callisthenes'. Whatever the case, they wreaked havoc and caused thousands of pounds' worth of damage. Even Liberty's was attacked, to the distress of the store director who mournfully told the *Evening News*, 'Women have regrettably turned against the shrines at which they usually worship.' Curiously, Selfridge's was not touched. Perhaps Harry, as an American, seemed more sympathetic to their cause, or maybe they had heard about the charming bronze plaque unveiled on the roof terrace by Madame Selfridge which said: 'This plaque is a tribute to women's work in the establishing of this business and is set up as a permanent record to their splendid loyalty and the quality of the service they have rendered'. Either that, or the suffragettes knew the vast plate-glass windows were virtually impregnable.

The night before Christmas Eve 1912, a musical revue called *Hello Rag Time!* burst on to the stage at the London Hippodrome. It was a storming success, appealing to all tastes – Rupert Brooke admitted to seeing the show ten times. Its thumping music and its snappy, sexy chorus girls parading down the 'joy plank' through the cheering audience heralded the dawn of dance mania. The sell-out show was a display of uninhibited, unashamed fun. Rag-time was American through and through, as American as the two ice-cream soda departments that opened that season at Selfridge's, where on an average day they got through 4 gallons of lemon squash, 4 gallons of chocolate, the same of coffee and 240 quarts of cream. The two departments were equipped with brand-new brine ice freezers and a new piece of technology called a Lippincott carbonator that whipped up 100 gallons in less than an hour. There were soon queues of customers standing in line for seats. There were queues too at the Hippodrome the following year when *Hello Rag-Time!* was replaced by *Hello Tango!* This was an altogether different type of show. The Latin American dance became just as much of a craze, but its unashamed eroticism attracted criticism from many who felt it was sleazy.

Selfridge's hosted a charity costume ball on the roof, where the social set enthused over a tango demonstration by Maurice and Florence Walton, London's premier dance duo. Selfridge's were quick to stock tango shoes and tango dresses, slit high up each side. The Bishop of London denounced the new craze as 'shocking', but respectable ladies soon started to host 'tango teas'. Those yearning for something even more decadent went to the Cave of the Golden Calf, a breathtakingly avant-garde nightclub just off Regent Street, decorated with exotic murals painted by Wyndham Lewis, where a Negro jazz band played in a smoke- and dope-filled haze and customers danced as if the music would never stop.

9

~

WAR WORK, WAR PLAY

'One should never give a woman anything she can't wear in the evening.'
Oscar Wilde

One morning early in 1914, Lord Northcliffe swung round from the desk at which he terrorized his secretarial staff at *The Times* and snapped: 'How are we going to pay for a war?' Warming to his theme about the need for economy, he declared that women were 'spending too much on nightdresses!' Word that the increasingly eccentric Northcliffe was about to launch an anti-consumer crusade flew around the building. *The Times*'s advertising manager, James Murray Allison, having just set in motion a sales initiative to secure more revenue from retail advertising, was so alarmed he found the courage to visit the inner sanctum and plead his cause. The last thing he wanted was for his irascible boss to turn against shopping. North-cliffe's outburst had been triggered by a Board of Trade report citing an increase in consumer spending and a commensurate increase in the manufacture of women's clothing, an industry in which nearly 800,000 women themselves were now working.

Fashion was making news and the stores were making money – stores in the West End, that is: those in the suburbs were suffering. The *Financial World*, picking up on their plight, noted that 'before the advent of Mr H. Gordon Selfridge and the perfecting of the motor-bus, much money now taken in Oxford Street was spent in the suburbs'.

Financed by the Midland Bank, Selfridge had repaid Musker's

loans and bought him out. With investment capital at his disposal, he spent a quarter of a million pounds acquiring not merely the 'fancy goods' shop William Ruscoe at 424–426 Oxford Street, but also the eight adjoining shops that had belonged to the long-established draper's Thomas Lloyd & Co. in order to begin his grand expansion plans.

Not everyone was pleased. People bemoaned the passing of Lloyd's, one elderly customer fondly recalling, 'It was the sort of place where ladies bought antimacassars for their horsehair furniture.' Negative editorials appeared about large stores crushing small shops, a criticism that in one form or another still rumbles on today. Selfridge himself countered the criticism, saying that investment was essential to create jobs and, as he put it, 'to diffuse as much sunshine as we can among all people, whose combined loyalty and labour make business possible'.

The wholesalers who made a lot of business possible were less keen on his methods. Selfridge's was beginning to bypass the middle-men and go straight to the manufacturer, where the sheer volume of their orders ensured enormous discounts. Selfridge himself was fond of making grand statements about the business of retailing, and about his own store – proudly boasting that it was now 'the third biggest attraction in town after Buckingham Palace and the Tower of London'. Adamant, as always, that his business existed not merely to make money but to bring a whole new experience to women shoppers, he declared: 'I want them to enjoy the warmth and light, the colours and styles, the feel of fine fabrics.'

There were those who sneered – in particular G. K. Chesterton, who took every opportunity to mock what he called 'the sentimentality of Selfridge'. Yet those close to Harry never doubted he meant every word. Arthur Williams later recalled: 'I don't remember *ever* hearing him utter an insincere remark.' His staff, now totalling nearly 3,000 people, never doubted him. They had gladly contributed to the cost of a bronze bust cast by the noted sculptor Sir Thomas Brock as a gift for 'the Chief' to celebrate the store's fifth birthday, presented to deafening applause at a huge gathering held at Queen's Hall, Langham Place.

Harry's affair with Syrie Wellcome meanwhile was waning. Syrie had recently met the writer W. Somerset Maugham and was now juggling her affections between Maugham, Selfridge and a dashing army officer called Desmond FitzGerald (who subsequently dumped her to marry Millicent, the Duchess of Sutherland). Her complex love life imploded on the first night of Maugham's play, *The Land of Promise*, which Syrie had promised to attend as his guest, not realizing that the date clashed with the grand house-warming party she was hosting to celebrate her top-to-toe redecoration of the Regent's Park house provided by Selfridge. Having had to deal with florists and caterers, she was late for the theatre, putting Maugham in a foul mood which worsened when he found Selfridge holding court at the party afterwards. A persistent story, much used by Maugham's biographers, is that Selfridge, still besotted with her and disconcerted by the appearance of a rival, offered the astonishing sum of £5,000 a year for her upkeep, the inference being he wanted fidelity. It is more likely that Syrie was trying to save face. There had never been any suggestion that she was his sole possession. That wasn't Selfridge's style. The truth is that her benefactor had fallen for the charms of the petite French *chanteuse* Gaby Deslys.

Usually cheerful around the store, where one of his favourite sayings was 'there's no fun like work', Selfridge could be moody. He was capable of going off people very quickly for no apparent reason. This habit was generally confined to his girlfriends or the beaux of his daughters, but he did occasionally turn on members of his growing staff. A case in point was Miss Borwick, an elegant and extremely competent senior knitwear buyer whose department was always in profit. Selfridge called her into his office and – so the story goes – fired her abruptly. After years of service, the weeping Miss Borwick was given a month's pay and told to leave. It was the same with Syrie Wellcome. Uneasy about her talk of divorce, and tiring of her temperamental moods, he left her in her luxuriously appointed house, filled with the expensive furniture he had provided, and moved on to pastures new. Maugham was left to pick up the pieces.

Sir George Lewis, Oscar Wilde's solicitor and an old friend of Maugham, tried to warn the writer that there would be a scandal. 'You're to be the mug to save her,' he wrote, explaining that Selfridge had left her and, worse, that she was deeply in debt. When divorce proceedings were initiated by Henry Wellcome the following year, Selfridge, who could easily have been cited as co-respondent, escaped unscathed. Wellcome would never have put a brother mason through that indignity, and in any event, Syrie was now pregnant with Maugham's child.

The prospect of war with Germany hung in the air. The media was full of disturbing stories. Sir Maxwell Aitken, the thrusting Canadian-born British MP who was energetically buying his way into the Pearson-owned *Daily Express*, regularly lunched with Ralph Blumenfeld and Selfridge. They talked of the growing threat in Europe, the terrible, unresolved violence in the Balkans, the bitter unrest in Ireland and, to Aitken's mind, the inadequacies of the Prime Minister, H. H. Asquith. Harry's increasing prominence came in part from the store's huge advertising budget, but also from his willingness to air his opinions on life as he saw it at a growing number of civic, charitable and educational conferences and dinners. He particularly admired the Rotarians, travelling on their behalf to Glasgow, Liverpool and Dublin, where he delivered his talks in a soft American accent, regaling the audiences with anecdotal observations based on topics often covered in 'Callisthenes'.

Invariably, he was asked about America and the mood in mighty Chicago. Selfridge kept in touch with his Chicago contacts, proudly sending his annual accounts to Harry Pratt Judson, President of the University, who wrote back saying: 'Your Chicago friends are following your English career with great interest.' Rosalie had made her debut there at the end of 1913, and the city's press was full of stories of the balls, receptions and teas held in her honour during her stay, all complimenting her on her 'American patriotism' in making her debut in her home city and not in London. It might have been expected that Rosalie would, at this point, have taken a job, if not in her father's own store – that being exclusively reserved for Gordon Jr, now a pupil at Winchester – then perhaps in journalism. As a teenager, she had followed the family tradition by writing and producing her own edition of *Will o' the Wisp*, modelled on the newspaper once produced by her father. She even sent a copy to President Theodore Roosevelt, receiving a charming note on a picture of the White House in return. But none of the three Selfridge daughters ever took a paid job during their father's lifetime.

Early in 1914, Selfridge's hosted an enormously popular 'Dominions' exhibition featuring Canada, Australia, New Zealand and South Africa. So many people crowded into the Palm Court Restaurant that the press office calculated they would have made a single file stretching for twenty miles. Visitors saw at first hand the delights of life in these far-flung countries, and more than a few admitted they were thinking of emigrating to them. Rudyard Kipling used the exhibition as his theme for a lecture at the Royal Geographical Society, saying that in the not-too-distant future it would only take four days to fly to Australia. The topic of aviation was rarely far away: exhibition-flying at Doncaster aerodrome was all the rage; industrialists were busy planning the building of aircraft; and England's first acclaimed aviator, Claude Grahame-White, who ran the Hendon Flying Club, could hardly keep up with demand for lessons.

In March 1914, Selfridge's raised £300,000 with an issue of 6 per cent cumulative preference shares. The offer was so oversubscribed that it closed by midday. A delighted Selfridge told the *Evening News* that his wholly owned ordinary shares were 'not for sale at any price'. He was busy planning the opening of his first Food Hall at premises acquired on the opposite side of Oxford Street, and also devising yet more charts and graphs showing growth, stock turnover and depreciation. He even had a card index for every staff member, showing his or her personal capacity and performance.

The staff had become used to his exacting standards. As well as obligatory morning staff training sessions for the whole workforce, anyone under the age of 18 – and many were – had to attend compulsory evening classes four nights a week. They were given lectures, slide shows and demonstrations, and when they had 'qualified' in the sense of completing the course, certificates and prizes – usually a signed book – were handed out at a strawberries-and-cream garden party on the roof terrace. Proud parents were invited to witness the passing-out parade at which their young son or daughter received a ribbon-tied certificate from Mr Selfridge himself.

Interviewed about his staff training methods, Selfridge said: 'I consider it good policy, as well as good principle, to take your assistants as far as possible into mental partnership with you. Make them feel a real interest in the business. Pay a premium for good ideas and good suggestions from assistants. They should realize that they are part and parcel of a going concern, and sharers – definite sharers – in the success of that concern.' Warming to his theme he continued: 'Make their life as happy as possible. Feed and pay them well. Make them contented. To grind the life and soul out of a miserable white slave is sheer bad business policy.'

The wages paid seem ridiculously low. A 16-year-old in the cash department earned only 5 shillings a week. But if that same youngster's figures weren't out by more than a ha'penny for a month at a time, he or she would get a 10-shilling bonus. If the figures were still accurate after three months, that amount rose to 30 shillings – a huge sum at the time and one which certainly concentrated the mind. Junior sales staff averaged £1 a week before the First World War, with 3d in the pound on top in sales commission. Paid overtime was rare, there was no pension scheme, and sick pay was at the discretion of the management. But all staff had the opportunity to rise up the hierarchy. Selfridge left notes on the staff-room bulletin boards: 'Merit will win'; 'We want intelligent, loyal, happy, progressive employees'; 'Do unto others as you would have them do unto you'; and his favourite 'Do it now!' They usually did.

Meanwhile, the affair between the retail prince Selfridge and the showgirl Gaby Deslys was intensifying. He had always had a curiously juvenile attitude towards stage stars. A showman by instinct, he responded sensitively and sensually to the atmosphere of the theatre, where the women who performed sang him a siren's song.

Gaby Deslys was 31 when she met Selfridge, and already famous for a string of love affairs with rich admirers including the young (but by now deposed) King Manuel of Portugal, Prince Wilhelm of Germany and the original Wall Street Robber Baron Jay Gould's son, Frank J. Gould. She was a sensation both on and off the stage. Born in Marseilles in 1881, she had moved to Paris where she worked her way up the musical revue ladder until, at the time she met Selfridge, she was probably the most famous personality in show-business – in today's terms hovering somewhere between Marilyn Monroe and Madonna. Gaby was adored by shop girls, chambermaids, secretaries, Lords, Ladies – and Harry Gordon Selfridge. Her dancing wasn't bad. Her singing was pretty mediocre. Her comedy acting was adequate. But somehow the whole added up to utter magic.

Deslys had first come into Harry's orbit when she launched the winter season of 1912 at Alfred Butt's Palace Theatre in Shaftesbury Avenue. Her review, entitled *Mademoiselle Chic*, involved her playing a *demi-mondaine* trying to choose between love and money, in one scene stripping down to her underwear. London's theatregoers hadn't had as much excitement since Maude Allan last took to the stage. Gaby was a material girl. Money mattered to her. She once famously said she would only dine with a man 'if they paid £50 for the pleasure of her company at supper' – sex not included. Rich men showered her with jewellery. Yet while she took a lot from them, she also earned a lot herself and was a tough negotiator. On one American tour she was paid $3,000 a week, and when she signed with Adolph Zukor's Famous Players Company to make a film in Paris, she was paid a fee of $15,000 plus 5 per cent of the gross. Not a bad deal for a fortnight's work.

Gaby Deslys was at the forefront of fashion, and her clothes made headlines. She wore Poiret's hobble dresses and Doucet's soft lace robes. Her extravagant show costumes were designed by Etienne Drian and lovingly made in Paquin's workshops. Drawn by Erte, photographed by Jacques-Henri Lartigue, endlessly written up by *Tatler*, Gaby was a celebrity before the word was invented. A youthful Cecil Beaton recalled being enchanted by her: 'She was a successor to the grand Parisian cocottes of the nineties on the one hand and, since she was such a famous theatrical figure, the precursor of a whole school of glamour that was to be exemplified twenty years later by Marlene Dietrich.'

Gaby's signature was her hats. She did big hats to such extremes – huge feathered and ribboned cartwheel confections – that she needed a second cabin on Atlantic crossings just for her millinery. The more outlandish the hats, the more the public loved them. Gaby's hats – indeed Gaby herself – so influenced Beaton that years later, when he was working on *My Fair Lady*, Audrey Hepburn's memorable millinery and the entire black-and-white Ascot scene were inspired by Gaby's hats.

Gaby's stage partner was the slick-haired and handsome Harry Pilcer. A superb dancer, Pilcer worked tirelessly on developing Gaby's skills. Their specialist routine, known as 'the Gaby Glide', was so athletic that on one memorable occasion her legs were wrapped round Harry's waist.

In those heady months before the war, young people were dancing as though their lives depended on it. Whether at smart supper-clubs in New York, in steamy nightclubs in Paris, or at tea dances at Lyons' Corner House, couples were perfecting their fox trot. The American vaudeville actor Harry Fox had invented what was originally called 'Fox's Trot', although it never made him any money. Poor Harry Fox drifted in and out of stage revues demonstrating his dashing steps, was briefly married to the dancer Jenny Dolly and then stood by while the celebrated international dancers Vernon and Irene Castle made his dance their own.

The Castles were the forerunners of all modern ballroom dancing. The idols of Fred and Adele Astaire, they had an immense influence on fashion. Irene was the first famous woman to bob her hair, wearing Lucile's floating dresses *sans corsette* as she whirled around the floor. The famous artists' agent Bessie Marbury had discovered the pair in Paris in 1914 and moved them to New York that year, establishing the elegant Castle House dancing school where society ladies learned to shed their inhibitions. The couple danced divinely to the new syncopated music that was sweeping New York, where everyone seemed to be humming the young composer Irving Berlin's 'Alexander's Rag-time Band'.

Back in London, the band in Selfridge's Palm Court Restaurant had to work hard to keep up with the pace, and the phonograph department could hardly meet demand. The store's latest gadget, their external 'electric moving news strip', flashed out details about the latest hits available in the store to the awed public watching from the pavement outside. The news strip also relayed everything from the weather forecast to the latest sports results, while ticker-tape machines inside punched out information on stock-market moves. Meanwhile, boys of all ages hovered around the newly installed seismograph in the hope that an earthquake would strike in some remote part of the world.

Tatler eagerly reported that Selfridge's had recruited some aristocratic new staff – albeit just for the day. Lady Sheffield, Lady Albemarle, Viscountess Maidstone and the Duchess of Rutland – helped by her daughter Diana – took up duty behind the sales counters, with all profits from their efforts going to benefit an educational charity for young mothers in Stepney. The 'divine Diana' Manners, having sold ribbons all morning, moved to silk stockings in the afternoon, demonstrating how fine they were by pulling them up over her arms, a sight of such fatal charm that one male customer bought a dozen pairs on the spot.

Education of a different sort was on offer when the store presented the latest state-of-the-art technology in what was called 'A Scientific and Electrical Exhibition – admission free'. Among the wonders on show were an automatic telephone exchange, a vacuum ice-machine, an X-ray machine and newly invented electric cookers. A complete installation of wireless telegraphy allowed messages to be sent to and received from Paris. Most thrilling of all, the young and eccentric inventor Archibald Low set up his latest gadgetry. Low had already demonstrated his 'Televista' at the Institute of Automobile Engineers in May that year, where an enthralled Harry Selfridge had been in the audience. Low's machinery was crude and underdeveloped, but it was the first demonstration of what would eventually become television. *The Times* reported that 'if all goes well with this invention, we shall soon be able, it seems, to see people at a distance'. Low never continued his experiments with television. John Logie Baird would have that distinction, and in 1925 the results of his pioneering work were also demonstrated at Selfridge's.

On 1 August 1914, Germany declared war on Russia and, two days later, on France. On 4 August, Great Britain declared war on Germany and so the long-anticipated war finally began. The British Army, with a reported strength of just over 700,000 trained men, was overwhelmed with new recruits. By the end of September 750,000 men had joined up. At Selfridge's, where 1,000 of the 3,500 staff were men, over half enlisted at once. Selfridge guaranteed that any male employee 'serving his country' would have his job back when he returned.

Those remaining formed a House Corps, drilling with rifles on the roof. Rifle practice was offered to all female staff and they were encouraged to enrol in self-defence classes. The whole store hummed with patriotic activity. The Palm Court Orchestra played 'Rule Britannia' twice a day, and war-work charities were given space and offered discounts on knitting wools for blankets, with free afternoon tea provided for the 'sewing circles'.

Just as elsewhere in the country, the shortfall in staff at Selfridge's was made up by recruiting women. Over half a million in England fled the servants' quarters and sweatshops to work in munitions factories, man buses and drive ambulances. Their newfound freedom put money in their pockets. A young female munitions worker earning

£3 a week (£120 today) and often still living at home had serious spending power.

By the autumn, people flocking to the cinema each week were being informed of what was happening on the Front by newsreels. The newsreels were no more accurate than the 'War Windows' at Selfridge's, in which maps of various campaigns were given pride of place. War reporting quickly fell victim to propaganda, and proud mothers had little or no idea what was actually happening to their young sons. They just kept sending food parcels.

Selfridge's futuristic white marble Food Hall had opened in its own dedicated building opposite the store some months earlier. It looked more like a science laboratory than a grocery supplier and focused heavily on hygiene. Only very limited – albeit artistic – displays of fresh food were on show, the rest being kept in refrigerated cold rooms. Customers ordered from individual booths, marking up printed sheets listing all stocked provisions. Displays of tinned food, as well as the newly popular processed items such as Marmite, Heinz Tomato Ketchup and Fry's Cocoa, were for show purposes only. Customers carried nothing away – all orders were delivered the same day from warehouse space off-site.

The Food Hall had a consulting service to help hostesses plan menus. There were daily demonstrations on the art of laying a table and arranging flowers. While wives were engrossed in etiquette, their husbands could browse in the wine room or the temperature-controlled cigar room. W. W. Astor's *Observer* declared it to be 'yet another achievement of the ceaseless energy and genius which is part of the enterprise of Selfridge's'. But the concept was so ahead of its time as to be frankly terrifying and the place was practically deserted. Reluctantly accepting defeat, Selfridge installed a more familiar, food-friendly layout which thereafter worked commercially.

Like the 'Callisthenes' columns, most of the Chief's speeches were written for him. He would then amend the copy, often to the despair of his writers, who grumbled that he was too ponderous. But when one of his staff, Herbert Morgan, came up with the phrase 'Business as

Usual', nothing was changed. It summed up exactly how Selfridge felt about his business during the war. He used the slogan so often that it became a catchphrase, famously adopted by Winston Churchill who in November 1914 declared: 'The maxim of the British people is business as usual.' Selfridge, a great fan of his fellow Freemason, was delighted.

It might have been expected that Selfridge would have been given a job during the war. Though an American and therefore, until America entered the war in 1917, a neutral, he longed to do something useful. But the British Government never asked him. The French Government were more astute. They invited him to act as their purchasing agent in equipping the army with underwear – a contract said to have been worth over a million pounds – which he did gladly, waiving all commission. In an interview with the *Westminster Gazette* he said: 'War requires two forces; one of men who fight, another to carry on the work of making and providing. The order of the day must also be advertising as usual.' Fleet Street applauded him, none more so than Horace Imber, in charge of advertising at Lord Northcliffe's *Evening News,* when Selfridge signed the biggest order ever placed with a British newspaper to run 150 daily half-page advertisements. Imber, a larger-than-life character who sported white spats and a monocle, was called 'Lord Imber' by Northcliffe because, he said, 'he's better at business than most of us real members of the House of Lords'. Mr Imber already drove a Rolls-Royce, otherwise Northcliffe might have given him one in gratitude for the Selfridge coup. There was a rumour he had won the pages throwing dice with Harry: the deal was certainly a huge gamble and not one in which his store managers had much faith.

They needn't have worried. Business at the store was, in real terms, rather good. A particular effort was made to dress the windows, which dazzled during the day. At night, thanks to the Defence of the Realm Act, they went dark. DORA had been passed in 1914, creating emergency powers for all sorts of measures that the Government felt necessary in a time of war. The Act allowed for the requisition of property, applied censorship, controlled labour, commandeered economic resources 'for the war effort', shut off street lighting, darkened shop windows at night – and closed public houses for all but five and a half hours a day. The working man, reasoned the Prime Minister, if he wasn't already fighting for King and Country, should be working on the factory floor, and preferably be sober at the time.

Selfridge thought all his staff should be on the shop floor, but it wasn't beer that was the problem, it was tea. Walking the floor one afternoon with the store director Percy Best, he noted that a department seemed understaffed. 'Where are they?' he asked. 'At tea,' came the reply. 'No more tea breaks,' said Selfridge firmly, whereupon Mr Best said, 'No more staff.' Reluctantly, Selfridge gave in.

Selfridge himself was often to be found taking tea with Lady Sackville at her bijou house in Green Street. Their friendship had endured, much to the delight of her friends who benefited from Harry's largesse in sending lavish food parcels to her London town house when she was entertaining. 'Mr Selfridge sent me some wonderful ice-cream sodas for dessert,' she wrote in her diary, while another entry recorded, 'At *last* I have got Selfridge's to import peach-fed Virginia hams, there is nothing like them.' The hams in question had made a perilous journey across the Atlantic, part of the huge amount of supplies being sent to war-torn Europe by neutral America.

America's continuing neutrality was intensely debated in Britain. Selfridge wrote to Harry Pratt Judson in Chicago, grumbling furiously that the 'American Government was trying to please the pro-German party and to assist the astute Jews who are largely in charge of the copper business in America, to dispose of their supplies to Germany'. He went on: 'The feeling exists here – unfairly perhaps – that America's first thought is to chase the dollar.' The press was reporting that American merchants were shipping cotton, foodstuffs and copper to Germany, a policy he found distasteful, perhaps forgetting that America, being neutral, was free to ship anything anywhere it wanted – including Virginia hams to his store.

Pratt Judson was quick to retaliate, pointing out that the great majority of Americans sympathized with the Allies 'because they believe that Germany and Austria really aim at the mastery of Europe and ultimately of the world'. However, he also pointed out that 'American citizens have a perfect right to sell contraband of war to either belligerent and will do so unimpeded by the American Government. Of course, they do that subject to the risk of capture and condemnation.' Whether Selfridge liked it or not, there would always be merchants involved in war profiteering. He just hated the thought that anyone might associate him with it.

There were of course many legitimate merchants who just needed to ship their goods, among them the American Frank Woolworth. By the time war broke out, Woolworth was operating over forty branches in Britain. When the Germans invaded France, Woolworth was trapped in Paris and had to scramble to find a ship to get him home safely. For Woolworth, the war presented serious problems of supply. Much of his merchandise was sourced in Europe – particularly Christmas decorations, toys, confectionery, musical instruments, clocks, watches and perfumes, variously made in Germany, Switzerland, Austria, Russia, Belgium and France. Woolworth's had both German and French offices and warehouses, from which goods were sent for consolidation in Liverpool before being shipped to America. Tons of goods were now stranded in the English port, and Woolworth appealed to the First Lord of the Admiralty, Winston Churchill, for permission to take empty hold space in Atlantic convoys. His request was refused: if America wasn't prepared to support the British Empire in the Great War, then Americans would have to forgo such luxuries. They didn't have to go without for long. The enterprising Mr Woolworth simply transferred production of all such things to America, where factory staff were trained to copy the previously imported ranges.

The Selfridge family, holding American passports, were free to travel wherever and whenever they wanted. Harry's wife, mother and children went to Chicago. Harry himself went regularly to Paris and even, on one occasion, to Germany, a trip that caused endless speculation in the media. The visit was made to assess the situation at his

German offices, but also in the interests of design. In March 1915, an exhibition of German goods was staged at the Goldsmiths' Hall, under the banner of 'A Proposal for the Foundation of the Design & Industries Association'. The exhibition focused on the aesthetics of goods, hitherto available from Germany, whose manufacturers had long championed industrial design. Earlier attempts by the Government to encourage British manufacturers to replicate blockaded goods had failed. Examples presented at Board of Trade exhibitions were frankly shoddy. This project was different. It sought to promote excellence in design and to encourage British manufacturers to be more creative. Among the original patrons and instigators of the scheme were St John Hornby of W. H. Smith; Fred Burridge, Principal of the Central School of Art; Frank Warner, the silk manufacturer; H. G. Wells; Frank Pick of the London Underground; and H. Gordon Selfridge, all of them committed to 'a more intelligent demand amongst the public for what is best and soundest in design'. Even *The Times* approved. 'Entirely practical,' they reported, 'not vaguely artistic.'

Early in 1915, Gaby Deslys moved permanently to London, preparing for the opening of her new show, a revue called *Rosy Rapture*. The besotted Selfridge bought the lease of a house for her in Kensington Gore, filling it from top to bottom with rugs, linen, silver, china, crystal and other expensive ephemera from the store. Vast baskets of flowers and hampers packed with delicacies were delivered daily by a Selfridge's motor-van. He also topped up her already bulging jewel boxes with diamonds and a sensational necklace of black pearls. When *Tatler* photographed the star 'at home', it remarked on her chinchilla fur bed rugs and the scenting of her rooms with Rigaud.

London suited Gaby like no other city, and Londoners adored her. As *Rosy Rapture* went into rehearsal, it became the talk of the town. It wasn't just Gaby who attracted attention. The revue had been written for her by J. M. Barrie. The distinguished author of *Peter Pan* and *The Admirable Crichton* was fêted wherever he went, but he was shy and lonely. A year earlier he had become entranced by the petite, fluffy, feminine Deslys. To him, she was like a living doll – a blonde, beautiful child-woman. Fascinated by the music hall, Barrie offered to write something special just for her. London's chattering classes were agog.

That Barrie wanted to experiment with the music hall was not surprising. In the aristocratic venues of the West End such as the Alhambra, the Empire, the Palace Theatre and the Hippodrome; in the huge bourgeois music halls of the less fashionable boroughs such as the Hackney Empire; even in a rickety venue down a murky alleyway in the East End, the public in their thousands gathered to sing, clap and laugh at the curious mix of comedy sketches, dancers and chorus girls who supported the legendary leading ladies – whether Lottie Collins belting out 'Ta-ra-ra-boom-de-ay' or Marie Lloyd's brilliant *double entendre* that 'she'd never had her ticket punched before'. The music halls were not licensed by the Lord Chamberlain's Office and could therefore get away with risqué performances not possible in the regular theatre. At the time Barrie was writing *Rosy Rapture*, they were also acting as recruitment centres for the Army. Young lads hearing Marie Lloyd singing 'I didn't like you much before you joined the army, John, but I do like you, cockie, now you've got yer khaki on!' enlisted the next morning.

Barrie's hopes for his show were dashed. It wasn't cheerful enough for an audience that craved humour. Despite a couple of songs from Jerome Kern and some innovative use of cinematography by Barrie, the show was a flop. Barrie didn't attend the opening night, having just heard of his close friend Guy du Maurier's death in action and the loss of his adopted son, George Llewelyn Davies. But Arnold Bennett was there. He wrote to Hugh Walpole: 'Went to the 1st night of Barrie's eccentricity. It was a frost & most of it extremely poor. Selfridge, the official *amant* of Gaby Deslys, was in a box with his family.'

Selfridge's family may or may not have known about the affair, but his staff most certainly did. Gaby toured the store like the diva she was, helping herself to anything she wanted, the bills, as always, being charged to 'the Chief's private account'. On one memorable day she lost her tiny pet dog and sat sobbing hysterically in Harry's office until he sent her home and set about masterminding what his secretary called 'Operation Dog'. Missing notices were posted up, the police were informed and a substantial reward was offered. The pampered pooch was eventually found.

Barrie meanwhile, rattled by the poor reviews, had cabled his friend and mentor Charles Frohman in New York, asking him for help in putting *Rosy Rapture* to rights. Frohman obligingly booked a passage on the *Lusitania*. The ship sailed from New York on 1 May, loaded with munitions for the war effort. Just off the coast of Ireland, it was torpedoed and sunk with the loss of 1,200 lives – including that of Charles Frohman. *Rosy Rapture* closed at the end of the month.

Somerset Maugham meanwhile had high hopes that his new play, completed while he was living in Rome in 1915, would be a success. He had crafted his story about an amoral, lascivious and depraved group of rich Americans and decadent British aristocrats very carefully, dipping his pen in acid to excellent effect. In *Our Betters*, Pearl Grayston, a rich American woman married to a British peer, has manipulated herself into becoming London's leading hostess. Her lover Arthur Fenwick – who conveniently provides the money for the lavish entertaining – is a snobbish, elderly American war profiteer. Pearl's girlfriends are drawn from a motley bunch of rich Americans who have acquired themselves British titles and gigolo boyfriends. Maugham's character Pearl was based on a combination of the society hostess Emerald Cunard and Victoria Sackville, while Arthur Fenwick was very obviously Harry Gordon Selfridge – right down to his soft voice and distinctive mannerisms.

The Lord Chamberlain was so concerned at the anti-American thrust of the play that he sent it over to the Foreign Office for Sir Edward Grey to read. The response was to ban it, the material being considered so offensive it would be detrimental to the efforts being made to persuade America to join the war. If Selfridge was unaware of the plot then, he certainly heard of it in 1917, when *Our Betters* opened to rave reviews in New York. When the play finally opened in London in 1923, it was a sell-out. Selfridge's humiliation lasted for months. Maugham had exacted his revenge.

The business of shopping continued apace, as did the business of publicity. A writer from a distinguished arts and literary magazine, *The Academy*, was given the store's 'VIP tour' by the Chief himself, who proudly pasted the resulting editorial into one of the huge press-cuttings books that he always maintained personally, right down to writing the captions and dating the pages. The *Academy*'s report was full of admiration: 'Outside all is war sensationalism, stress and danger. Inside the store all is beauty and order … [there is] a pervading sense of well-being and efficiency. It made an impression that lingers … of piles of dainty fabrics, of colour … of capable young women who have replaced our soldiers at the door and in the lift.'

In fact, the lifts at the store had always been operated by uniformed girls who were as good-looking as those in the best chorus line. The 'Selfridge's Red Cross Corps' were also particularly well kitted out, their uniforms being specially tailored to fit. Women were now driving the motorized delivery vans – many of which had been transformed into ambulances – and, in an effort to save petrol, holding the reins of the store's horse-drawn carts. Women were on guard as commission-aires, in green woollen great-coats, braided caps and huge gauntlet gloves. Wherever there was a job in the store that had been done by a man who had enlisted, a woman took it over – some even stoking the boilers. The shortage of men was affecting most households. Servants – especially footmen – were in short supply, much to the annoyance of Winston Churchill's mother, who so disliked parlour-maids that she transformed her two into 'foot-maids'. The girls wore black skirts with smart swallow-tail coats and evening waistcoats, white shirt-fronts, winged collars and black ties.

Selfridge's was always putting on a show of one sort or another. Phil Mead, Hampshire's star county cricketer, was hired to lead 'Cricket Fortnight', while less cheeringly, a few days after the Germans had used chlorine gas at Ypres, the store's pharmacist demonstrated its stinking toxicity by mixing spirits of salts with chlorate of potassium in front of a fascinated crowd on the roof terrace. Anxious mothers flocked to the pharmacy to buy supplies of bleached cotton gauze, elastic and extra-absorbent cotton wool to send out to their sons, along with packets of morphine that were readily sold and always used. The Duchess of Rutland – seemingly a constant presence in the store – opened an Art Exhibition in aid of the War Seal Foundation, one of the endless charities that kept upper-class women busy. The Duchess had hoped to open a hospital in France – her daughter Diana had solicited a donation of £2,000 from 'dear Mr Selfridge' – but the plan fell through. Diana instead became a nurse, while the Duchess confined herself to two rooms of their Arlington Street house, turning the rest into a hospital.

By 1916, Asquith's Government was in disarray. Having resigned over the disaster at Gallipoli, Churchill had gone to the Western Front. The war was escalating. Zeppelin raids had begun and the U-boat campaign was edging Britain towards the brink of starvation. The country yearned for dynamic leadership. They got it in December when David Lloyd George became Prime Minister, in part thanks to the machinations of Sir Max Aitken whose reward was a peerage. Ennobled as Lord Beaverbrook – and by now the owner of the *Daily Express* – he would soon become Minister of Information, but even his own newspaper couldn't print the truth about what was really happening. There was still no job for Selfridge, despite his friend Sir Albert Stanley being appointed as head of the Board of Trade. Late that year, Selfridge moved his family to the country, taking a lease on Highcliffe Castle in Christchurch on the Hampshire coast. Officially, their move was due to the threat of the Zeppelin raids. Unofficially, it was due to Harry's heightening affair with Gaby Deslys.

10

~

CASTLES IN THE AIR

'Business carried on as usual during alterations on the map of Europe.'
Winston Churchill

The store published record year-end figures for 1917, with profits of £258,000 (over £10 million today) mainly achieved, said Selfridge on announcing the results, 'by an increase in household goods and cheaper clothing while luxury goods and expensive women's wear has fallen off'. A year earlier, Condé Nast, the owner of American *Vogue*, had taken the view that even if women weren't buying luxuries, they would still enjoy looking at them. He launched a British edition at the price of 1 shilling a copy, perhaps not understanding that the women with the most disposable income were working in munitions and reading *Tit-Bits*. With the upper classes showing their customary thrift and the middle classes strapped for cash, launching the glossy magazine hadn't been easy. *Vogue*'s fashion editors responded with features explaining 'how it is possible to have a smart wardrobe even with the handicap of a limited income'. Shortages meant higher prices everywhere – the cost of food had risen by 65 per cent and clothing by 55 per cent. The Government Food Controller had imposed fixed prices on basics such as bread and jam which Selfridge delighted in undercutting, using his 'Callisthenes' column to hammer the point home. There were, however, no discernible cuts in his own household budget – he was living in customary style at 30 Portman Square and spending prodigiously on renovating Highcliffe Castle.

The Highcliffe estate had originally been acquired by King George III's young Prime Minister, the Earl of Bute, who, having the advantage of a very rich wife and a taste for beautiful buildings, commissioned Robert Adam to design several for him. These included Luton Hoo, Lansdowne House and Kenwood in London, and a seaside mansion, then called High Cliff, where in 1773 he laid out exotic botanical gardens. High Cliff was left to Lord Bute's youngest and favourite son, General Sir Charles Stuart, but sadly for Sir Charles, without the money to maintain it. He demolished the property, sold the contents and also parted with most of the land.

His son in turn, also called Charles and a distinguished diplomat, vigorously set about restoring his inheritance, gradually reacquiring the land his father had sold. While *en poste* in St Petersburg he ordered timber; in Spain he commissioned bricks; as British Minister in Lisbon during the Peninsular War he sent instructions about the purchase of the remnants of the original mansion, by now a notorious smuggler's den. When he was dispatched to Paris to choose a house for Lord Wellington's anticipated sojourn as Ambassador, his unerring eye settled on Princess Pauline Borghese's *hôtel* in the rue du Faubourg St Honoré – still the British Embassy today. On his own subsequent appointment as Ambassador, he delighted in attending the auctions taking place in the capital after the fall of Napoleon's regime. Among other treasures, he bought furniture and carpets from the estate of the gallant Marshal Ney, stonework from the Norman Benedictine abbey of St Peter at Jumièges, and a complete window of sixteenth-century stained glass from the church of St Vigor in Rouen. His pièce de résistance was a gloriously carved oriel window from the Grande Maison des Andelys, where Henri IV had sat with his dying father. Twelve huge barges were needed to ship his acquisitions back to England, and it took him another five years to build the impossibly romantic Highcliffe Castle, completed in 1830. Now ennobled as Lord Stuart de Rothesay, he divided his life between Highcliffe and his London town house in Carlton House Terrace, where he installed the bed on which allegedly the Empress Josephine had died.

At the time Harry Selfridge took the lease, Highcliffe had passed to a Rothesay cousin, Major-General Edward Stuart Wortley, who had fought with distinction in Sudan, Egypt and Afghanistan. Major-General Wortley had been sent back to England after the first day of the Somme for the simple reason that his regiment hadn't lost enough men, the inference being that he had shown 'a lack of offensive spirit' in somehow keeping his men back. Eddy Wortley subsequently spent the rest of the war training troops in an Irish backwater.

Harry Selfridge found Highcliffe's history irresistible, but for the Stuart Wortleys the castle was an expensive headache. Never rich, they were delighted with the offer of £5,000 a year in rent, and even more pleased when Selfridge set about fitting modern bathrooms, installing steam central heating, and building and equipping a decent kitchen. Rosa Lewis, the eccentric owner of the Cavendish Hotel and one of London's most sought-after private caterers, wouldn't have recognized the place. When she was in charge of catering for the Kaiser's three-week stay with the Stuart Wortleys in 1907, she had had to bring in portable cookers.

All in all, it is thought that Harry spent £25,000 (£1 million today) on improvements at Highcliffe in the six years he rented the property, during which time the Stuart Wortleys decamped to a modern Edwardian villa they owned nearby called Cliff House. The Selfridges adored living at Highcliffe where, poignantly for Harry, Mary Leiter Curzon had recuperated from a bout of pneumonia before making her last trip to India. Rose and her elder daughters Rosalie and Violette joined the Red Cross, working initially at Christchurch Hospital. When America joined the war in the spring of 1917, Rose opened a tented retreat, the 'Mrs Gordon Selfridge Convalescent Camp for American Soldiers', in the castle grounds. Beatrice meanwhile was sent to St Mary's Wantage, and Gordon Jr, now in his final year at Winchester, applied to read Economics at Cambridge. When the family travelled to Highcliffe, they did so by train from Waterloo, alighting at Hinton Admiral, a tiny station nearby built on the wealthy landowner Sir George Meyrick's estate, from which he had the right to flag down any passing train to board or disembark his guests. Selfridge usually motored down on Friday evenings, his chauffeur Arthur Gardener drawing increasingly scarce petrol from the store supplies before loading the car with provisions.

The bracing sea air was a tonic for Rose, who herself was subject to bouts of pneumonia. But while she grew her favourite Liberty roses at Highcliffe, her husband was seen squiring Gaby Deslys around town, where it was rumoured that he intended to fund the lease of her own theatre. Gaby was helping to raise money for the French Relief Fund and inviting wounded soldiers to tea at her Kensington Gore house, with Fleet Street in attendance. True to form, Gaby wasn't Harry's sole companion. Teddie Gerrard was wowing audiences at the Vaudeville Theatre in a show called *Cheep*, in which she sang a little ditty that went, 'Naughty, naughty Gerrard One'. The use of the store's famous telephone number was not lost on some of the audience, who were aware she was being seen arm-in-arm with Selfridge. Not that Miss Gerrard herself came cheap – she had a great fondness for furs and, regrettably, an even greater one for opium, which ultimately played havoc with her career. One scene in the show was called 'Goodbye Madame Fashion', with the chorus kitted out in wartime work-wear. Ironically, the shortage of textiles helped launch the career of the woman who would come to dominate fashion for decades to come, when Coco Chanel introduced her simple dresses made up in jersey material sourced from Rodier at her shop in Biarritz in 1915.

Events in Russia, where the Tsar had abdicated, were much in the news and watched by the Selfridge family more keenly than most. Rosalie had become close to a Russian called Serge de Bolotoff, whose family had moved to Paris before the war. Calling himself an 'aviation engineer', Bolotoff had been something of a pioneer when in 1908 he designed a large triplane, built at the Les Frères Voisin factory. Serge knew all the players in aviation's tight-knit world, being advised by Blériot and backed by a consortium of rich individuals, including Admiral Lord Charles Beresford. Before the war, the de Bolotoffs had moved to England, where Serge's mother (there being no mention of a Mr de Bolotoff) now called herself Princess Marie Wiasemsky and set up home in a series of grand, rented houses, first Kingswood House in Dulwich and later Kippington Court in Sevenoaks. Serge continued with efforts to get his plane off the ground. Trials were held at Brooklands, but the monumental triplane collapsed when the undercarriage disintegrated on take-off. Bolotoff's machine was moved to a nearby shed where it languished until the start of the war, subsequently vanishing when the army commandeered Brooklands.

Serge went on to advise the German Albatross Biplane Company and in 1912 became their British sales agent, struggling to make sales against the home-grown De Havillands. The Albatross meanwhile became the aeroplane beloved by Baron von Richthofen and his famous travelling circus. The Red Baron's planes, manned by his star pilots, were sent to fly across various parts of the line to boost the morale of German troops, who watched in awe from the trenches as their heroes looped the loop in fragile 'birds' made of canvas and wood that could barely fly at 100 miles per hour. It was a breathtakingly exciting time to be working in aviation. Developments seemed to happen daily. Initially, planes were only used for observation, but when the French pilot Roland Garros bolted steel deflectors to his propellers, enabling guns to be fired, and the German-employed Dutchman Tony Fokker improved the interrupter gear which made firing even more reliable, the aeroplane became an offensive weapon, with dashing pilots delighting in notching up aerial 'kills'.

On the outbreak of war, Serge, having hastily resigned from the Albatross Biplane Company, offered his services to Russia instead. By the time he met Rosalie, the Imperial Russian Government that he had signed up to serve no longer existed. Whether he actually still drew a salary from his desk job at the Russian Government's Naval Aviation Department in London is impossible to say, but it seems unlikely. Rosalie, a rich man's daughter, did not worry about the future prospects of the man she loved, but her father was more pragmatic. Clearly keen to put some distance between the young couple and thinking his family would benefit from some travel, in 1917 Selfridge planned an extraordinary journey for them in the middle of a world war. Their intended escort was to be the equally extraordinary man, Joseph Emile Dillon.

Dillon, by now a regular weekend visitor to Highcliffe, was a highly regarded foreign correspondent of the *Daily Telegraph*. He spoke over a dozen languages fluently, had witnessed epic events from the 1900 Boxer Rebellion in China to the 1905 Russo-Japanese War, and was consulted by Allied governments around the world. His particular speciality was Russia, where at one point he had been confidential adviser to the Tsar's Prime Minister, Count Witte.

By 1917, Selfridge was pushing Dillon to accept payment to take his family travelling: 'I am extremely anxious if possible to complete plans – a trip to America, say anywhere from the 15th of August. A fortnight or more spent in that country, then sailing from San Francisco for the Hawaiian Islands, a day or two at Honolulu and further sailing to Japan, then to China, then perhaps Singapore and arrival at Calcutta about the 1st January would be roughly what I would like to see done.' Dillon politely declined the offer, explaining that the situation in Russia made it impossible for him to be out of touch for long. Selfridge tried again. 'I very much hope that in a week or so you will see your way clear to changing your mind. We are most anxious that you and Mrs Dillon should be the leaders of the party.' In the event, the trip never materialized. Rose busied herself with her hospital, Rosalie continued her courtship, and Selfridge himself went shopping.

A lover of sculpture, he was an eager bidder against the American newspaper magnate William Randolph Hearst at Christie's 'sale of the century' when artefacts, jewels and books belonging to the impoverished aristocrat Lord Francis Pelham Clinton Hope were sold. Lord Hope, the Duke of Newcastle's brother, had become a bankrupt in 1894 and had steadily been selling off his possessions ever since. First to go was a clutch of Dutch old masters, then in 1902 the famous – and famously cursed – blue Hope diamond, which netted him £120,000. Finally, in July 1917, the contents of his property, Deepdene in Surrey, were put up for sale. They included items from the family's extensive collection of porcelain and books, and quantities of ancient Greek and Egyptian sculpture and pottery.

All the notable collectors attended the sale. Lord Cowdray acquired a prized statue of Athena for 7,140 guineas. The international dealer Joseph Duveen bought anything he could get his hands on. Sir Alfred Mond, Chairman of Imperial Chemicals, bought four pieces, while Lord Leverhulme bought in bulk, picking up no less than fourteen pieces. Selfridge bid energetically against Henry Wellcome for a Roman statue of Asclepius that was said (probably erroneously) to have come from Hadrian's Villa at Tivoli. Wellcome's agent withdrew at 1,400 guineas and Selfridge got his prize for 1,700 guineas. In a pleasing tussle against the obsessive collector Mr Hearst (via his London agent), he also bought a statue of Zeus for 650 guineas, while a statue of Apollo Hyacinthus, long thought a favourite of the sculptor Canova, rounded off his shopping list at a cost of £1,000.

At the store, there was an ambitious event to mount a sale of War Bonds, with cash prizes offered to winners whose tickets were entered into a special draw. Selfridge's 'Bonds' were printed, permission from the Postmaster-General obtained, posters designed, advertisements booked and Mrs Lloyd George herself invited to pick the winning tickets. By the day of the draw, 20 December 1917, the response had been so overwhelming that the store had to hire an extra forty cashiers to cope. The promotion, which cost Selfridge around £11,000 to mount, raised the astonishing sum of £3.5 million pounds for the war effort.

Next came a book launch. Craving gravitas for 'trade and traders', Selfridge had long planned a book of his own on the topic. Ghost-written by his old friend Edward Price Bell and published by John Lane, it was entitled *The Romance of Commerce* and covered the history of trading giants from the Fuggers of Augsburg to the Mitsuis of Japan. The book was launched in December at a dinner hosted by John Lane, but it presented Fleet Street with a dilemma. Newspapers were anxious not to offend the country's most valuable

1. Harry Gordon Selfridge married Rosalie Amelia Buckingham on 11 November 1890 in an extravagantly orchestrated ceremony held in Chicago. They spent their honeymoon in Newport, Rhode Island.

2. Lois Selfridge, Harry's mother, in 1906 at the age of 71. Friends remarked that 'she seemed the embodiment of a classic sweet old lady, but she was unobtrusively formidable'.

3. Harry Gordon Selfridge, seen here *c.* 1910, was always immaculately groomed and tailored. His taste was for formal clothes and he was rarely seen in anything remotely casual.

4. Oxford Street at the corner of Duke Street, *c.* 1907,
before the construction of Selfridges.

5. Selfridge dreamed of building a double-island site, extending from Oxford Street,
flanked by Orchard and Duke Streets and stretching back to Wigmore Street.
The architects, Sir John Burnet and Frank Atkinson, executed a series of ideas
incorporating a dome, intended to be 'as important as that of St Paul's'.

WE HAVE EVERY PLEASURE IN ANNOUNCING THAT THE FORMAL OPENING OF OUR PREMISES—LONDON'S NEWEST SHOPPING CENTRE—BEGINS TO-DAY AND CONTINUES THROUGHOUT THE WEEK.

WE WISH IT TO BE CLEARLY UNDERSTOOD THAT OUR INVITATION IS TO THE WHOLE BRITISH PUBLIC AND TO VISITORS FROM OVERSEAS —THAT NO CARDS OF ADMISSION ARE REQUIRED—THAT ALL ARE WELCOME—AND THAT THE PLEASURES OF SHOPPING AS WELL AS THOSE OF SIGHT-SEEING BEGIN FROM THE OPENING HOUR

SELFRIDGE & CO.
OXFORD STREET, LONDON. W.

6. One of the series of spectacular advertisements to launch Selfridge's, drawn by leading illustrators and artists of the day such as Byam Shaw (this drawing by Sir Bernard Partridge), which formed the biggest retail advertising campaign ever seen in England at that time.

7. Horse-drawn buses were a familiar site on London's streets until the end of 1911, when the London General Omnibus Company replaced the service with motor buses. Selfridge's name could be seen everywhere – except on the front of the store.

8. The light and bright store interiors, with high ceilings, spacious aisles and wide vistas, were unlike anything ever seen before in London. If Selfridge found dust on one of the glass counters, he scrawled his initials – HGS – on the surface. They wouldn't be there for long.

9. Harry Selfridge on the roof terrace of the store in 1911, with (*left*) the fashionable playwright Harley Granville-Barker and (*right*) the fashionably dressed author Arnold Bennett.

10. Selfridge's created the concept of visual display as we know it today. Their window-dressing, under the direction of the American display manager Edward Goldsman, was raised to a pinnacle of perfection.

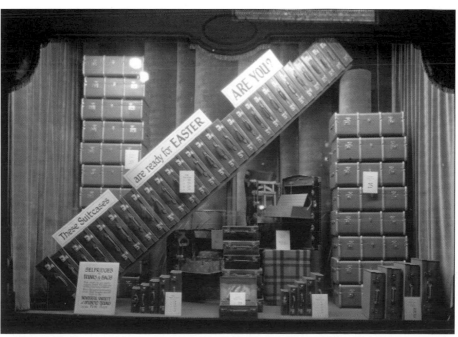

11. Advertising copy often focused on family values – as well as good value – and promoted the concept of 'having a family day out at Selfridge's'. This image was part of a colour series created for popular women's magazines.

12. Film director Frank Capra – in London for the opening of his film *You Can't Take It With You* in 1938 – signs the famous autograph window in the Chairman's office, observed by Harry Selfridge and his son Gordon Jr. Celebrity guests had been writing their names with a diamond-tipped pen since the window was inaugurated in 1919.

13. The Otis Elevator Company launched the first step-type escalator at the Paris Exposition in 1900. By 1921 their engineers had refined the system to create the design we know today. Escalators revolutionized customer-flow through department stores. This escalator was installed at Selfridge's in 1926, the most up-to-date model in a London store at that time.

14. Harry and his daughter Rosalie, photographed at Chicago's Grand Passenger Station in 1911. The family travelled back once, and often twice, a year to Chicago, where their arrival was always a local news item.

15. In 1928, Harry's daughter Violette and her aviator husband Jacques de Sibour flew in their tiny Gipsy Moth on a daring trip to go big-game hunting in Indo-China. En route they mapped a new trail over the Burmese jungle down to Bangkok. Obliged to travel light, Violette (seen off here by her father at Stag Lane Airport) still packed a black lace evening dress and a dozen pairs of silk stockings.

16. The French *chanteuse* Gaby Deslys, described by Arnold Bennett as 'the official *amant*' of Harry Selfridge in 1915, and as famous for her hats as for her singing and dancing.

17. Highcliffe Castle, Christchurch, leased by the Selfridge family as their country home from 1916 to 1922. Selfridge spent today's equivalent of £1,125,000 on modernizing it to suit his tastes. Rose Selfridge and her daughters ran a hospital for wounded American soldiers at the castle during the First World War.

18. Harry Selfridge playing his favourite game of poker on board his yacht, *Conqueror*, c. 1930. He always used heavy, mother of pearl chips – thought to bring good luck – and his own, specially made cards embossed with his initials.

19. Jenny (*right*) and Rosie Dolly, otherwise known as the Dolly Sisters, who danced their way into Harry Selfridge's life in 1925.

20. In 1935, Harry Selfridge's last love interest was the Swedish-French actress Marcelle Rogez. When their affair ended in 1938, she moved to Hollywood, where she met and married the film director Wesley Ruggles.

21. From exhibiting aeroplanes such as Louis Blériot's to the Sopwith *Atlantic*, Selfridge's promoted aviation at every possible opportunity. In 1919, the year Harry Selfridge made the world's first commercial air flight travelling from London to Dublin, he also staged a fashion show of leather flying suits on the Observation Tower on the store's roof.

22. In 1910, anticipating the emergent trend for cosmetics, Harry Selfridge opened the first dedicated perfume and cosmetics hall on the ground floor of *any* department store. Buyer Nellie Elt presided over what became the store's most profitable department and is seen here, *c.*1925, standing by the Elizabeth Arden counter. The temperamental cosmetics tycoon and Mr Selfridge became life-long friends.

23. During the founder's lifetime, Selfridge's adorned the exterior of the store for the Coronation of King George V, the Jubilee of King George V and, most sumptuously of all, the Coronation of King George VI in May 1937, shown here.

24. Harry's steam yacht, designed by Camper & Nicholson and first registered in 1911, weighed over 850 tons, was 211 feet long and slept twenty in considerable comfort. Used as an Armed Patrol Yacht in the First World War, Selfridge acquired the yacht in 1927, renaming her the *Conqueror*.

25. Harry Selfridge had a meteoric rise to fame and fortune, but died virtually penniless in 1947. With no money to pay for a dignified headstone, the man who created one of the most distinguished buildings in London was buried by his family in a humble grave.

26. A moment that Harry Selfridge would have adored: Madonna at Selfridges on 11 November 2004 for the launch of her first children's story book, *The Adventures of Abdi*.

retail advertiser, but it was clear that the book was both wordy and worthy, and getting reviews was going to be tricky. Ralph Blumenfeld, Selfridge's old friend and ally at the *Daily Express*, having opted out of the dinner on the grounds of ill-health, solved the problem by cleverly inviting Sir Woodman Burbidge, the Chairman of Harrods, to review Harry's beloved book.

Burbidge had recently inherited both his title and his job on the death of his father, the equally highly regarded Sir Richard, about whom Selfridge had written a glowing obituary. He reviewed the book cautiously, tactfully saying that in it he found 'something of the vision splendid'. Meanwhile Selfridge's press office worked overtime organizing interviews with 'the Chief', which he gave in his office surrounded by no less than seventy-seven leather-bound ledgers and accounts books from the Medici family archives in Florence, some of which dated back to Cosimo de' Medici himself and which he had bought at Christie's. Those on the store 'gift list' were usually sent food hampers, perfume or cigars at Christmas, but in 1917, whether they liked it or not, they received a copy of *The Romance of Commerce* painstakingly inscribed by Selfridge.

Early in 1918, at the behest of Lord Northcliffe, head of the British War Mission to the United States, Selfridge crossed the Atlantic. Northcliffe announced that 'Mr Selfridge has gone, at the urgent request of American business leaders, to explain our problems of supply.' Northcliffe's reward for his role was a viscountcy. Selfridge, who had to pay his own expenses, received no reward other than the realization that, as he rather sadly observed on his return, 'in America, the captains of business constitute a greater factor in the life of the nation than is the case here'. Still, he continued to do his best for his newly adopted country, offering to pay 'for all war shrines erected within a mile of us' and putting up £500 in prize money for a competition run by the store for 'ploughmen showing the best results using the new farming technology'. The top prizes were won by Titan tractors, made by his old friend Deering's International Harvester Company, who happily lent models to display in the store.

The war was going badly and desperation was in the air. By now there was hardly a family in Britain who had not lost someone they knew or loved, and in May, tragedy struck at Highcliffe. Rose Selfridge contracted pneumonia and died just one week later. Grief-stricken, Harry sought comfort in organizing her funeral at the simple parish church of St Mark's with military precision. The store's seamstresses travelled to Highcliffe to sew a blanket of fresh red roses to cover the simple oak coffin, while American soldiers from the convalescent camp formed a guard of honour, their leader carrying a Stars and Stripes flag woven from red carnations, white narcissi and bluebells from the Highcliffe woods.

Less than three months later, Rosalie quietly married Serge de Bolotoff in the chapel of the Russian Embassy in Welbeck Street. Since the family were still in mourning, the wedding was a small affair. The bridegroom however, showing his own flair for publicity, ensured that he and his mother were given ample coverage by handing a note out to the press explaining that they were 'direct descendants of Prince Rurik, who had founded Russia in the ninth century'. Not that anyone had even *heard* of Rurik, but a Prince – any Prince – had tangible glamour in the wake of the Russian Revolution.

Serge's mother attracted more attention than the bride. Madame Marie de Bolotoff – to call her correctly by her married name – was a petite, blonde bombshell with extravagant tastes. Already a beneficiary of the legendary Selfridge generosity, she was delighted by the marriage. She had separated from her husband some years earlier and, with four children to support, had decided that life would be much easier if she had a title. She hadn't entirely made it up. Instead, in about 1908, she persuaded the Tsar to allow her to use the title Princess Wiasemsky, claiming descent through maternal relatives.

Serge and Rosalie's grandson, the guardian of a mass of family documents, tactfully admits that 'there was a substantial argument about her claim to the title' but points out that Marie had some powerful friends ready to back her claim, among them Lady Tyrrell, the wife of the Foreign Office Under-Secretary, who took an oath that she had seen the

Tsar's decree. Another supporter was Marie's friend Sofia, the estranged wife of Admiral Kolchak, whose evidence also played a part. Harry, satisfied that his beloved eldest daughter would ultimately inherit a title, gave his blessing along with a lavish thirty-six setting Crown Derby dinner service for their use while living with him at Portman Square. A flat of their own might have been more useful. But he liked his family around him and, given he paid, that's where they stayed.

In October 1918, Joseph Dillon finally went to America, without the Selfridge family but armed with letters of introduction to several of Harry's powerful Chicago friends. 'Over here,' wrote Selfridge, 'we feel he is the best informed man in the world of European politics.' Selfridge himself went to France, making a tour of the battlefields at the invitation of General 'Black Jack' Pershing As the year drew to its end, the huge job of clearing the battlefields began and soldiers started to return home. At Selfridge's, the store kept its promise to take back its own serving men. By the time the Armistice was signed, nearly a thousand had returned.

In the wake of Rose's death, Selfridge kept himself busy. As early as 1915, he had announced that a new extension would be designed by the architect Sir John Burnet, whose brief was to incorporate a majestic tower. The concept of a tower had always formed part of Harry's grand plan for Oxford Street. After five years or so of lobbying, the Portman Estates and St Marylebone Council finally consented, at the same time agreeing to a plan drawn up by the engineer Sir Harley Dalrymple-Hay for a tunnel running under Oxford Street.

Sir John Burnet, who had designed the King Edward VII Galleries at the British Museum (completed just before the war), found that he and his team were part of an extended group. Selfridge's policy was always to hire several people to do the same job in the hope that one of them would get it right. Among the architects was Albert Miller, who at this point moved to London from Chicago to work full-time at the store.

Selfridge relished the new project, giving a mischievous speech to the London Society in which he declared that 'All around us in Oxford

Street are numerous little shops that should be burned because they are so ugly.' Warming to his theme, he went on to tell the *Evening Standard*, 'I shall try to build something that is good. A store used every day should be as ennobling a thing as a church or a museum. I love to look at a beautiful building.'

He bought on board yet another architect, the fashionable Philip Tilden, who was putting the finishing touches to Port Lympne, Philip Sassoon's house overlooking Romney Marsh. Tilden executed various drawings for the Oxford Street tower, none of which came to fruition. No more did Sir John Burnet's elegant efforts. 'Forget it. Forget it,' snapped Selfridge when a journalist asked him about the future of the much-publicized 450-foot tower. The difficulty of bringing his scheme to fruition was clearly irking him.

At the same time, however, Tilden was set to work on a project dear to Harry's heart. Having acquired Hengistbury Head, a tract of land of outstanding beauty with a glorious view of the Isle of Wight, from his Highcliffe neighbour Sir George Meyrick, Harry planned to build his own castle. The project created unease in the local community. Hengistbury Head was recognized as one of the most important Bronze Age archaeological sites in Europe, and any plan to build on it was bound to be controversial, especially since Selfridge grandly announced that it was going to be 'the largest castle in the world'.

Over the next five years, Tilden lovingly – and expensively – set about drawing Harry's dream. The two men formed a close friendship, and Tilden later recorded how impressed he had been by 'the magnitude of [Selfridge's] imaginative thoughts'.

The plan involved a huge castle, with a smaller, private house below. Drawings were made for cloistered gardens, a winter garden, a Galerie des Glaces as at Versailles, dining-halls capable of seating hundreds, 250 bedroom suites and a domed central hall that would be seen from far out at sea. It was intended that artists from all fields would be able rent space at Hengistbury Head and work there surrounded by beauty. It was a strangely noble idea, but the locals hated it. Some said Selfridge was building a factory on the site, others that he intended to create a theme park with a Wild West show. Selfridge assured Christchurch Town Council that 'he would work with archaeologists during construction and he would take steps to prevent erosion of the Head and always allow the public access'. Tilden meanwhile executed hundreds of drawings, admitting that the only way he could cope with the design was to develop it section by section. Whenever Selfridge was asked how, or when, the plan would be executed or what it would cost, he refused to be drawn. Tilden later recalled that he would simply look at his interrogator 'with a cold, clear, blue and calculating eye, thrusting out his chin with never a glimmer of a smile'.

In March 1919 Selfridge's celebrated its tenth birthday and Harry went on a spending spree. A swathe of impressive advertisements marked the anniversary. Lord Northcliffe in particular took note, writing to his managers: 'I feel we all owe a great deal to Selfridge for the way in which he woke up the drapers. He should be helped in every possible way.'

Flush with funds from a new issue of 500,000 preference shares, and with post-war building restrictions curtailing the Oxford Street development programme, Selfridge expanded into the provinces. He was convinced that the drapery stores presented a unique development opportunity and he bought businesses in Liverpool, Leeds, Sheffield, Gloucester, Peterborough, Reading and Northampton.

Selfridge was a man in a hurry. When he went to Dublin on 25 June to negotiate a deal to buy the city's old-established draper's Brown Thomas, he reasoned that the journey by train and ferry would take too long. So he flew. The chartered plane, a De Havilland Airco 9 piloted by Captain Gathergood, winner of the Aerial Derby, took off from Hendon just after lunch, touched down in Chester for refuelling and tea, and arrived in Dublin in time for dinner. It was the world's first commercial flight. Back at Hendon the next afternoon Selfridge told the press: 'This only shows what possibilities there are now in high speed aerial transport to the businessman in a hurry.' Reading about it in a rival paper, Lord Northcliffe was furious, shooting a note off to his staff: 'Why no reference to Selfridge's air journey to Dublin? It was the first business flight.' He might also have asked why Selfridge was proposing to buy a business in Dublin at a time when the city was under curfew and Michael Collins and his IRA men were battling it out on the streets with the brutal Black and Tans. Selfridge, however, felt that the city presented a 'wonderful opportunity'.

From that point on, Selfridge became addicted to aviation, and the pioneering commercial airline Aircraft Transport & Travel flew him not just to Highcliffe but also around the country to visit his growing empire. As always, he milked the press potential for all it was worth, putting a Handley Page seventeen-seater passenger plane fuselage on show in the store as the back-drop for a fashion show of the latest leather 'flying clothes'. At a time when flying was still a dangerous business and uninsurable, his bankers and his board members might have queried the wisdom of 'the Chief' – at the age of 63 – gallivanting around the skies. But such exploits were part of the Selfridge magic. He was on a roll, and no one could stop him.

At home, the loss of Rose had been a crushing blow. At work, the loss of his genial mentor Sir Edward Holden, who died in the summer of 1919, was another. Sir Edward's portrait joined that of Marshall Field in Harry's imposing office, where he had a new lady in his life. It had taken two years to find a suitable replacement for the inimitable Cissie Chapman who had been his personal secretary since 1914, leaving to take over the store's Information Bureau. Indeed, Selfridge – who had got through an entire battalion of temporary staff since her promotion – was beginning to think she was irreplaceable. Then he found Miss Mepham. Calm, organized, efficient, tactful, loyal and discreet, Hilda Mepham was exactly the right woman to look after Harry Selfridge – and she did so until the day he left the store. She shared the outer office with an urbane young man called Eric Dunstan, who had joined the staff as his Social Secretary. The well-connected Dunstan had spent two years in Fiji working for a Colonial Governor and a period in the Conservative Party's headquarters. He was also discreet, which, given some of the requirements of his job, was probably just as well.

With commercial construction curtailed, Selfridge turned his hand to residential development. Encouraged by his friend Sir Harry Brittain, the newly appointed Conservative MP for Acton, Harry made his own public-spirited contribution by forming the non-profit-making Victory Construction Company. His plan was to build 300 inexpensive brick and concrete dwellings. Admitting that 'they were not very lovely', they would, he said, 'be easy to run and would serve as a temporary resting place for those whose lives have been disrupted until they see better days'. Each of the five-roomed, semi-detached houses on Lowfield and Westfield Roads was priced at £310 and offered initially to Acton residents. In the end, only seventy were built before the scheme went awry due to escalating costs, but it was a fine gesture.

Allied victory, meanwhile, was being discussed at the Paris Peace Conference, held at Versailles. As the protracted negotiations neared completion, Selfridge planned a special celebration. His creative director, Edward Goldsman, was dispatched to Paris where he was given special access to sketch and photograph the famous Hall of Mirrors, using Louis XIV's marvel as the theme for the store's 'budget no option' décor planned to coincide with the signing of the Treaty of Versailles. It wasn't just about window displays. The store took the decoration right out into the street, laying out a 'Court of Honour' in front of the main building, with imposing plaster columns and bas-relief figures holding shields and flags. Even the lamp-posts were decorated. Selfridge's was no longer just a part of Oxford Street. To the thousands of people who flocked to see the decorations, it had *become* Oxford Street.

~

VICES AND VIRTUES

'A store should be like a song of which one never tires.'
H. G. Selfridge

As the new decade arrived, the band in the store's Palm Court played all the latest hits at the daily *thés dansants* and the place was packed. To some observers, it was astonishing how many people had so much time in the day to dance. Why weren't they at work? But at a time when jobs were proving increasingly difficult to find, very often dancing *was* a job. A lot of unemployed ex-officers danced for a living. There was many a 'gentleman escort' available to take a turn on the floor with a war widow, while the impresario Albert de Courville used to boast that several of the more talented chorus boys in his revues at the London Hippodrome held either the MC or the DSO. Honours, however, didn't pay the rent.

At Selfridge's there was no cover charge in the Palm Court – Harry reasoned that those who came to dance might do a little shopping in between numbers. At the Piccadilly Hotel or the Café de Paris, the charge was 4 shillings for 'afternoon tea and dancing', while at the swankier Savoy, it was 5 shillings. For the lonely, a mere 2 shillings bought tea and sympathy at the Regent Palace or the Astoria Dance Hall, where girls were rumoured to offer more to those who wanted it. The lost and the louche went to Kate 'Ma' Meyrick's Dalton's Club in Leicester Square, which really was a pick-up place and where for the price of £2, 'Ma's' girls would offer a lot more than sympathy. When Mrs Meyrick subsequently appeared in court on vice charges, part of her defence was that 'the West End was a regular hotbed of lawlessness' and that 'her girls' were just 'bringing cheer to some of the terribly disfigured boys home from the war'.

The big musical hit of the moment was 'Ain't We Got Fun?' but as Mrs Meyrick had so aptly put it, for a lot of people, life wasn't much fun. Most young men, regardless of their social background, were struggling to rebuild their shattered lives after the horrors of the war. Demobbed with brutal haste and little if any government support, many of them faced a bleak future. Some were so shell-shocked that nothing but prescribed morphine, cocaine or the illicit but widely used opium could numb the pain. Others, haunted by the blood and gore of the trenches, simply drank their memories away. Large numbers of young men, without much education other than being trained to kill, joined gangs in London, where there were rich pickings to be had from protection rackets. Petty crime – pick-pocketing and bag-snatching in Oxford Street, shoplifting in the stores – was on the increase. At Selfridge's, where the open-plan floors were particularly vulnerable, dozens of extra store superintendents were hired to keep a watchful eye.

The media took to blaming all the woes facing society on 'drink, dancing and drugs', especially the latter which made for better copy. When the young and rather pretty dancer Billie Carleton died in late 1918 of a cocaine overdose, her companion, the fashion designer Reggie de Veulle, was charged with her manslaughter and viciously attacked in the press. In the end, the rather pathetic Mr de Veulle was found innocent of anything except 'having an effeminate face and a mincing little smile', whereupon he disappeared into obscurity. Meanwhile, the real culprit was found to be a Chinese immigrant, Lau Ping You, a drug dealer who worked for Britain's biggest supplier, Brilliant Chang. The tabloid press whipped itself into a frenzy over the 'yellow peril in Limehouse', while mothers were warned not to let their daughters 'go anywhere near a Chinese laundry or other places where the yellow men congregate'. In 1920, only six years after the Army had first handed out tablets containing cocaine to its troops, the Dangerous Drugs Act banned the drug altogether.

The clergy ranted from the pulpit about the licentiousness of the dancing youth (though Victor Sylvester, the undisputed king of the Black Bottom, was a vicar's son); organizations such as the London Council for the Promotion of Public Morality warned of the growing influence of the uncensored cinema; and the influential Temperance Movement urged even stricter licensing laws. Most of the young people in question took absolutely no notice. All they wanted to do was dance. But as far as officialdom was concerned, dancing went hand in hand with drinking. While Lloyd George and Nancy Astor, the country's first woman MP, who both loathed 'the demon drink', would have been delighted to see alcohol banned in Great Britain – as it had been in America to disastrous effect – they had to rely on DORA instead. The wartime law was dusted off and made more stringent still. It became illegal to get a drink anywhere after 10 p.m. without food, and anywhere at all after midnight. Such absurdities only succeeded in driving dozens of flourishing nightclubs underground – quite literally, as most of them were in dank cellars.

Such attempts to enforce a new morality had little effect. Everyone converged on club-land. Rich war profiteers, the *jeunesse dorée* up from Oxford and Cambridge, the young British royal princes, a clutch of their dispossessed European royal cousins – all sat side by side with newly rich provincials up from the suburbs, dancing and drinking till dawn, their night out all the more thrilling because it might end in a police raid.

Before the war, apart from the odd glass of sherry or a celebratory glass of champagne, pre-dinner drinking had hardly existed. Wine was drunk with food, never on its own, women would rarely drink spirits and men passed round the port. Then cocktails arrived. 'Cocktail time' seemed to begin anywhere from 12 noon to 5 p.m., with people giving cocktail parties, eagerly exchanging recipes for the perfect Martini, and praising barmen who made a great White Lady.

Not everyone approved. The distinguished restaurateur Monsieur Boulestin said: 'Cocktails are the most romantic expression of modern life, but the cocktail habit as practised in England is now a vice.' It was a vice to which even the otherwise fairly abstemious Harry Selfridge took. Pre-war he would nurse a glass of champagne for an entire evening. During the war, he joined the King who declared Buckingham Palace a 'dry zone' and gave up drinking altogether. But post-war, Harry took to having 'a cocktail or two' before dinner. He also took to eating a prodigious amount of food while dining which resulted – as was noticed by one of his inner-sanctum office staff – in him taking to wearing a corset. Selfridge's meanwhile joined in the craze for cocktails by selling shakers, fancy ice trays, cocktail napkins, recipe books, martini glasses, gold swizzle sticks, olives and all the paraphernalia of the drinker – right down to the white mess jackets that the barmen wore.

It wasn't just the fashion in drink that changed. Clothes were changing too. The influence of the once great Paul Poiret was waning. He was still making sumptuous clothes and was still surrounded by an eccentric coterie – the poet Max Jacob, a gifted amateur astrologer, liked to advise his friend on the colours he should wear so as to be in conjunction with the planets – but his style was about to be eclipsed. When fashion revived in Paris after the war, the look was distinctly less dramatic. Coco Chanel, poised to become the defining leader of style, declared: 'I make fashions women can live in, breathe in and look younger in.' The latter effect made her clothes irresistible. Everyone wanted to look younger, including Harry Selfridge. Now 64, he seemed utterly determined to push back time, travelling to Vienna for treatments with Serge Voronoff, whose anti-ageing experiments with monkey glands were exciting other youth-conscious luminaries such as George Bernard Shaw, Helena Rubinstein, Augustus John and Winston Churchill.

Thousands of women had found war work and the utility clothing that went with it a liberating experience. The watchwords in fashion were 'simplicity', 'modernity' and 'freedom'. Many women now widowed or without much prospect of marriage were having to become self-supporting through need as much as choice. They wanted clothes for work rather than for leisure, but above all they needed clothes that worked for them – less ornate, less contrived and certainly less expensive. Mechanical methods originally devised to cut material for military uniforms were quickly adapted to produce ready-to-wear clothing – chiefly coats and suits – which transformed not just the clothing industry but also the jobs of many women working in it, as unskilled and semi-skilled machinists took over what had previously been made by hand.

The lean, short shift dress of the quintessential Twenties flapper was actually a mid-decade innovation. Its precursor was a low-waisted combination of droop and drape in soft fabrics such as lamé, panne velvet and crêpe de Chine, often tied with a deep sash at the hip. All those lush, Edwardian curves were now out, and as corset sales slumped by two-thirds, the underpinnings industry had hastily to reinvent itself. Although Dorothy Parker famously quipped 'that brevity is the soul of lingerie', there was still quite a lot going on underneath. To flatten the bosom, women bought Symington's side-lacer camisole-style bra, wore a straight-cut camisole or, in an emergency, simply taped their bosom down with a crêpe bandage. The more mature, used to some support and still priding themselves in standing up straight, wore the longer-line corset pioneered for the pre-war straighter skirts, while the young and more athletic favoured a lighter-weight 'corselette' and even took to wearing garter belts. The cotton industry was in disarray as layers of servant-starched petticoats were discarded in favour of a simple petticoat shift – usually in satin or silk. Then, in 1924, there arrived the working girl's greatest saviour, rayon.

At the beginning of the Twenties hemlines moved up by about eight inches, revealing gleaming silk stockings, coloured kid-leather shoes, the hitherto unseen shape of a lady's leg and, in the case of Lady Londonderry, the grand political hostess of the day, the surprising fact that she had a snake tattoo from her ankle to her knee.

Stockings were no longer just black or white. With the introduction of synthetics, artificial silk stockings also came in skin-tones of flesh and beige. They weren't as nice to wear as silk, but they were less than half the price and very practical. Selfridge's was actually prosecuted for falsely selling synthetic stockings as 'real silk'. The store vigorously protested that it was the fault of the supplier but agreed to refund disgruntled customers nevertheless. This incident was one of the rare occasions when anyone in the office saw 'the Chief' lose his temper. He loathed confrontation and hated arguments, thinking them a waste of energy, but any misrepresentation of goods ran against his entire business philosophy. He prided himself on accuracy and his copywriters were never allowed to put a false spin on store promotions or use misleading price promotion tricks.

Selfridge himself may have been an early adopter of ethical advertising in respect of price and value, but his creative team was part of the swelling army of copywriters and image engineers who helped to build an ideology of consumerism. The seductive hum of shopping was in the air. Women were wearing make-up (no more lipsticks under the counter), flashing their powder compacts in public, using moisturizer and worrying about wrinkles, smoking cigarettes and gargling with Listerine, listening to all the latest records at home instead of playing the piano, and going out unchaperoned. They still wore hats – *everyone* still wore hats – but the hats were getting much, much smaller, and the hair underneath them was changing.

Long hair was out. Short waved hair, as pioneered by the film star Gloria Swanson, was in. At Selfridge's, the hairdressing department (now seating fifty clients at a time) was busy all day using the latest waving machines – price 3 guineas for shingled hair, 4 guineas for long. Hairdressing had by now become big business. Most of the original stylists from Selfridge's early, innovative department had left to open their own salons, 'colour, cut and curl' then as now being a profitable business. But even in a smaller salon, marcel waving cost at least 2 guineas, so anyone who couldn't afford a week's wages to wave their hair did it at home with tongs heated on a tiny spirit stove.

Women's magazines were settling into their stride. *Harper's Bazaar*,

Good Housekeeping, Vogue, Queen, The Lady, Tatler and *Woman Magazine* – the latter edited at one stage by Arnold Bennett – were essential reading and always available at the best hairdressers. Who ever was making or selling something fashionable was starting to advertise it seriously, although full stand-alone pages were still rare. Most stores ran quarter-pages, crammed with copy and cluttered with a multitude of different typefaces, usually accompanied by a deadly dull sketch produced by an art-agency draughtsman struggling to show the projected bestseller at Arding & Hobbs or Pontings.

High-style fashion illustration on the other hand had become recognized as an art in its own right – at its peak exemplified by the Russian émigré Erte's glorious work for *Harper's Bazaar*. Erte, Tamara de Lempicka and George Barbier, whose inspired work for the pre-war *Journal des Dames et des Modes* had helped establish the trend, were at the height of their powers. It didn't last. The illustrators would soon be eclipsed by photographers, with Baron de Meyer, Edward Steichen and George Hoyningen-Huene dominating the field.

Selfridge's advertising was aimed at the high-circulation daily newspapers, but when the store did place advertisements in magazines, Harry Selfridge made sure the pages were uncluttered and the message was clear. One early page in *Vogue* typifies the style:

> *Vogue* is a beautifully-printed Journal and this typographical beauty lies in the excellence of its type and composition … its paper, *its every detail.* Selfridge's endeavours to be an admirable Store by striving for excellence in its many departments, by insisting on variety and newness and novelty in its merchandise … on charming courtesy and delightful service … by studying every one of the thousands of details which go to produce the great 20th Century Store.

The establishment, on the other hand, was rather wary about all this newness. Old habits and grand manners died hard, and the old guard were disconcerted to find their racy daughters borrowing their motor-cars, footmen whistling in the corridors and their maids 'dressed to the nines' rushing off to Selfridge's or Swan & Edgar's on their afternoon off. That the latter did so was hardly surprising. Maids could now afford to go shopping, for their wages had more than doubled since the war and a good maid could earn £2 10s. a week plus her keep. Chauffeurs, much in demand as the rich changed their carriages for cars, earned £4 10s. a week, their accommodation provided in the stable mews above what were now garages.

The great landed families were feeling the pinch as death duties and taxation on unearned income took their toll. The profligate Duke of Manchester was declared bankrupt; the Duke of Portland threatened to close up his huge Nottinghamshire mansion, Welbeck Abbey; and even the fabulously rich Duke of Westminster was realizing assets, selling Gainsborough's exquisite *Blue Boy* and several other important pieces to Joseph Duveen. The sale, which caused an outcry among art experts and the public alike, netted 'Bendor' a useful £200,000 to go towards maintaining his yachts, horses, houses, wives and Coco Chanel, one of his more famous mistresses. Duveen stated firmly that the painting was not going to America: 'I have bought it for myself. It is my wish the picture should remain in this country.' He had in fact pre-sold it to the American railway magnate Henry E. Huntington and his wife Arabella for $620,000, reassuring her that the picture would clean up well when she expressed concern that the subject of the painting 'wasn't *quite* as blue as she had thought'. The Duke of Devonshire moved from his vast London palace, Devonshire House on Piccadilly – where developers were planning a 'super-cinema-restaurant' complex – to a mere mansion in Carlton Gardens, while his father-in-law the fifth Marquis of Lansdowne rented out his magnificent London house which came with twenty servants, including a nightwatchman who guarded the private passage that ran through to Berkeley Square. News that Lord Lansdowne's tenant was none other than Harry Selfridge raised eyebrows among London's élite. 'Think of it,' said Sir Gilbert Parker, 'Selfridge in Lansdowne House. It's *appalling*.'

It was certainly intriguing. The cost of renting and maintaining one of London's largest houses was phenomenal. At a time when an average family could live reasonably well on £500 a year, Selfridge was paying £5,000 to rent his new London home, plus £5,000 a year for his lease on Highcliffe. On top of that there were servants' wages and his high living expenses, covering everything from food to flowers, travel and, last but not least, generous entertaining. All this supposedly came out of the £40,000 that Harry earned each year, but in reality, the store provided a lot more. What wasn't charged to 'the Chief's' personal account was set against 'public relations and entertainment', which neatly covered food, wines and the dozens of boxes of Corona cigars, specially imported from Havana for Selfridge and distributed to grateful friends such as Ralph Blumenfeld. Selfridge enjoyed living like a lord. Now he lived in a lord's mansion.

Like the estate at Highcliffe, Lansdowne House had originally been owned by the Marquis of Bute, though he never actually lived there. In 1765 he sold the partly finished Robert Adam property to the Foreign Secretary, Lord Shelburne. Shelburne – later the first Marquis of Lansdowne – had battled valiantly to conciliate the American colonists during the War of Independence. Having failed in the task, he resigned from government and consoled himself in the time-honoured way by travelling through Italy and, advised by the antiquities dealer Gavin Hamilton, acquiring beautiful things. By 1782, he was back in power as Prime Minister, and the second Treaty of Paris, which conceded America's independence, was drawn up for signature by Benjamin Franklin in Robert Adam's exquisite Round Room at Lansdowne House.

Thus the Selfridge family, formerly of Ripon, Wisconsin, and Chicago, Illinois, settled into one of the most famous and historically important houses in Great Britain, living surrounded by ceilings and panels painted by John Francis Rigaud and Giovanni Cipriani, entertaining in rooms where Dr Johnson had dined and where the country of their birth had ceded from Great Britain. Max Beerbohm drew a cartoon of the Marquis obsequiously showing Selfridge around Lansdowne House: 'Statuary, sir? Majolica, all the latest eighteenth-century books – this way.'

A highly valued client of the Midland Bank, Selfridge now had the undivided attention of no less than three of their senior general managers. Sometimes collectively, sometimes individually, Mr Frederick Hyde, Mr S. B. Murray and Sir Clarence Sadd would lunch with Selfridge in the store or motor down for meetings at Highcliffe, where in 1920 the quiet little town of Christchurch had acquired an imposing new pillared and porticoed branch building. That same year, the Midland managed a new issue of 1 million 10 per cent preferred ordinary shares of £1, which was subscribed seven times over and which brought the company's share capital to £3.55 million. When Eric Dunstan prepared the Chief's entry for *Who's Who*, he listed him as Managing Director. Furious, Selfridge scratched it out, shouting: 'Damn it, man, I own the place!' The trouble was, he didn't.

What impressed the bankers was the breadth of his ideas and the speed with which he put them into action. They liked his expansion into the provinces. They admired his diversification, such as the move into food via the launch of the John Quality grocery chain, with branches in, among other boroughs, Westminster, Kensington, Ealing and Acton. Above all, they liked his catch phrase, 'Best Value in London: Always', and the fact that he was unafraid to make markdowns. As if foreseeing the financial slump of May 1920, Selfridge had pre-empted disaster by reducing the store's stock by 10 per cent, advertising price cuts aggressively and adding 'spot offers' and 'an additional 10 per cent off prices on selected items'. This sort of mid-season sale was unheard of, and it rattled his competitors. For the first time, Selfridge used the 'fear factor' in his copywriting, talking of global trading difficulties and increases in the price of raw materials. Such comments, said his critics, were decidedly 'un-public-spirited' and 'deliberately designed to encourage stockpiling'. Ignoring them all and determined to clear dead stock, Selfridge relentlessly ran the promotion for five months.

He also instructed his buyers to cancel anything and everything that was late, and to cut purchasing budgets for the autumn season. 'Never talk to suppliers about discounts,' Selfridge told his buyers, 'till you have secured rock bottom price – then go for best discounts and dates. Keep a poker face and always preserve freedom to trade hard.' Manufacturers who had enjoyed the store's bulk-buying policies were distraught as orders were slashed to the bone. Defending his actions in the trade press, Selfridge said: 'Retailers cannot be expected to assume the risks of production – all business is more or less speculative.' Arguments raged about 'Selfridge's war on prices' as the local Chamber of Commerce – even the Board of Trade – waded in to complain. Selfridge, who was always impervious to criticism, didn't care. He has judged the economic situation accurately. The Mutual Communications Society – the retailers' own forum for monitoring credit and debt – was now meeting weekly, not monthly. The post-war economic boom had been short-lived. By 1921 unemployment had risen to over 2 million. The only shop a lot of families were visiting was their local pawn shop.

Meanwhile, Selfridge's staff continued to receive bonus payments if they met targets and to enjoy 'benefits in kind' that were the envy of their friends. The store director Percy Best escorted fifty personnel on an eight-day junket to Paris; 5,000 employees danced the night away at what the press called 'A Selfridge Revel' at the Albert Hall; and over 45,000 shares were set aside for an employee purchase scheme. If some noticed an increase in the Chief's yellow envelopes hitting their desks, they didn't mind, though some of the messages in them were becoming a little odd – one blouse buyer was asked: 'What great thought have you had today?' Selfridge was a great believer in the value of surprise and was quick to defend his shock tactics: 'It's important to give people new angles, it jerks them out of a rut.' They didn't always work. When he sent a tin of spinach to senior buyers before the spring sale, with a note saying 'Let us see if the result is as beneficial as it always is to Popeye', very few appreciated the gesture.

To those who knew him well, Selfridge seemed to be becoming markedly more frenetic. Like the 'mile-a-minute' Harry of earlier years, he was bursting with ideas but would set staff on to a project only to drop it at the last minute. His insomnia was becoming worse and he took up 'yoga breathing', extolling the virtues of deep inhaling and exhaling as being 'completely invigorating especially when tired'. Not that Harry ever seemed tired. His mid-afternoon cat-nap seemed to set him up for the rest of the day, and he partied late into the night as though he dreaded the thought of sleep or of being alone. How he missed Rose. Plans for Hengistbury Head were a diversion and visitors to his office would be shown drawings of the proposed castle, which jostled for space with schemes for the new store extension.

Friends were bemused by his grand plans for the castle. Lord Beaverbrook, on being given the 'virtual tour', said: 'No one has yet discovered this castle, for it exists only on paper. When Selfridge requires mental relaxation, he may be found poring over the plans which are to be the basis of this fairy edifice – moat and parapet, tower, dungeon and drawbridge, are all there, only awaiting the Mason of the future to translate them into actuality.' Ralph Blumenfeld was worried. 'He plans to build a wonderful castellated palace which shall be the most beautiful architectural effort of modern history,' he wrote in his diary, 'yet I feel it will remain in the region of dreams.'

When at Highcliffe for the weekend, Harry would write letters at the study table that had once belonged to Napoleon, paste up his scrapbooks and put flowers on Rose's grave. Dinners were hosted by his mother, who at the age of 86 still enjoyed a party. Philip Tilden later wrote: 'Old Madam Selfridge was an ideal for us all. A hostess of the rare old school of American propriety, all lavender, lace and an exquisite link with bygone standards. It was a privilege to know her. She was the soul in all the world that her son loved best.' Although mother and son were very close, shared literary pastimes and talked about business and investments, she wasn't privy to his innermost thoughts. He was an intensely private and inhibited man and would never have had the courage to open up to her about the extent of his gambling or his escalating expenses. She would have known of his strange sex life – mothers and wives almost always know when the men they love are behaving badly. But he was a grown man – indeed almost an old man. She couldn't change him. So she continued to do what she did best. She dined with him at Lansdowne House, putting a shawl round Canova's *Venus* not because the bare breasts offended her but because 'it made her feel chilly'. She was at his side at the High-cliffe fête at which a revelling crowd of 5,000 people enjoyed brass bands, a jazz dance competition, fortunes told by an Indian mystic and even a beauty contest – won by Miss Phyllis Palmer of Bournemouth who proudly collected her prize of £10 from Mr Selfridge. He himself impressed guests with his unerring eye in judging the weight of a giant cheese to the nearest ounce. Mother and son went to Wimbledon each season, never missing the matches of the French tennis star Suzanne Lenglen who had won the ladies' singles championship every year since 1919. She astounded the audience with her athleticism and, with her short hair, short *plissé* jersey tennis dresses, short white ermine warm-up coat and, most exciting of all, her glorious suntan, she had an equally electric effect on fashion.

In June 1921 the family celebrated the marriage of Violette to the French Vicomte Jacques de Sibour in a ceremony at the Brompton Oratory attended by 1,200 guests. In truth, Harry wasn't keen on his daughter's choice of husband. De Sibour had caught Violette's eye a year earlier in the store, where he was working rather than doing his shopping. De Sibour's father and step-mother lived on the Isle of Wight, where they had met Sir Thomas Lipton and had thereby moved into the Selfridge family orbit. Jacques was dashing, attractive and brave – during the war he had flown with the French Air Force. He was also unemployed. His father, perhaps hoping retail management was a career with prospects, asked Selfridge to give him a job. Less than three months later, when Jacques got engaged to the boss's daughter, he promptly resigned, saying he preferred to pursue 'prospects in aviation'. Violette and Jacques rented a flat in London and another in Paris. They also invested heavily in a coffee farm in the White Highlands of Kenya, later notorious as 'Happy Valley'. Selfridge, of course, paid for it all.

When Harry was interviewed, he was always happy to talk about his work, the store, his son, his eldest daughter, even his mother, but he rarely discussed his two younger daughters. In the extensive archives there are dozens of photographs of him with Rosalie, her husband Serge and their daughter Tatiana. There are a handful of him with Violette, mainly taken when she and her husband set off to fly round the world in their Gipsy Moth plane called 'Safari'. There are few photographs of Gordon Jr and even fewer of his youngest daughter Beatrice who later married Jacques de Sibour's elder brother Louis, a man even more attractive than his brother, also beautifully dressed – and also with little visible means of support.

In truth, Harry was not close to his children. He gave them money of course – he was always more than generous – and he gave their husbands money too. He also gave Rosalie and Serge a home, albeit not one of their own. Serge, always experimenting in the hope of patenting some potentially profitable piece of motoring gadgetry but never quite succeeding, gladly accepted the hospitality. In reality, he and his mother Marie happily sponged off Selfridge. Serge and Rosalie's grandson Simon Wheaton-Smith is also convinced that 'the entire family, certainly my Uncle Gordon, and almost anyone else, would have been afraid of him. He always got things his way – and he paid all their bills.'

The entire family lived a curious life partying together, and often travelling together – but seemingly not talking much. Certainly Gordon Jr's affair with a very pretty girl from the toy department was never discussed. Not even when she had their first child in 1925, and then a second, third *and* fourth. Gordon Jr continued to live the high life as a bachelor in a Mayfair apartment with cowhide-covered banquettes and soft lighting, while Charlotte Dennis, the mother of his children, looked after them in a house in Hampstead. Selfridge refused to acknowledge the relationship. As far as he was concerned, it simply didn't exist. Whatever hopes and dreams he had cherished for his only son, they hadn't included marriage to a girl who worked in the toy department.

Having left Trinity College, Cambridge, with a third-class degree in Economics, Gordon Jr had joined the store in 1921. Working there was always his destiny. Arnold Bennett vividly recalled an early visit to the inner sanctum during the war:

> There is a small closed roll-top desk in his room. It is his son's aged 16. Boy now home for holidays from Winchester. He was upstairs learning accountancy. He takes a boxing lesson every day at 12.30. His father showed us photos of him at his desk in various attitudes, including the attitude of dictating to a girl-clerk. I continue to like Selfridge.

Gordon was moved through the business at break-neck speed. He spent a few months learning the ropes in packing and delivery, then a year working for the highly regarded Merchandise Manager, Thomas Anthony. By 1923, he was managing the menswear department and by 1924, at the age of just 23, he had a seat on the main board. By the time he was 25 he was Managing Director. Mr Anthony meanwhile had moved to Harrods.

Whatever his son's responsibilities, Harry still controlled promotion, advertising and publicity. No one ever came between Selfridge and the media. His zeal for booking space continued unabated – although to some observers it seemed he was more concerned with the number of pages appearing rather than what he put in them. In 1922, he went a step further, seriously considering becoming a newspaper owner himself, when he apparently attempted to buy *The Times*. Lord Northcliffe had died in extraordinary circumstances in August that year, with even his foes showing discretion about his sad final weeks. Northcliffe had lost his mind. Convinced he was in danger of being poisoned by a German gang, he had taken refuge in a hut on the roof of the Duke of Devonshire's house in Carlton Gardens, where he kept a gun under his pillow.

Selfridge's friend Edward Price Bell, at the time the London correspondent of the Chicago *Daily News*, described Harry's attempt to acquire a newspaper in letters to his editor in America. 'All his peculiar vanity and ambition are enlisted in trying to get it,' wrote Bell, explaining that the funds would come from 'what one might call international-amity or world-friendship money from those who want to bring about a closer union of Great Britain and the United States. He [Selfridge] seems to be able to get as much money as he wants for any purpose.'

Harry's dream wasn't quite as wide of the mark as might be imagined. He had influential friends, among them Sir Harry Brittain, the MP for Acton, founder of the Empire Press Union and President of the British International Association of Journalists. He also knew Brittain's colleague, Evelyn Wrench, founder of the Over-Seas League and the English-Speaking Union, who would go on to edit *The Spectator.* Another connection linked both Brittain and Wrench. The former had, in 1902, founded the Pilgrims' Society, a dining club whose 'strictly invitation only' membership was exclusively formed from an élite group of wealthy British and American businessmen, bankers and politicians. Their aim was then (and remains today) 'to foster good-will, good-fellowship and everlasting peace between the US and Great Britain'. The super-rich, power-broking Pilgrims would have had unimaginable resources readily available to back the right sort of people. The trouble was that while Harry had strengths, he also had one weakness. It wasn't women that worried these men, rather the fact he was a profoundly addicted gambler. Such a vice made him vulnerable. *The Times* passed into the capable hands of one of the leading Americans in Britain, Colonel J. J. Astor (later Lord Astor of Hever), and Harry's Hearstian visions of a newspaper empire remained a dream.

Unlike William Randolph Hearst, who was devoted to only one mistress, Marion Davies, Harry scattered his largesse, evidence of which came up for auction in Paris when, following her death, Gaby Deslys's jewels – including her sensational black pearls – were sold. She was only 39 when she died from the after-effects of traumatic surgery for a throat tumour, and her estate was wound up in a blaze of publicity. The contents of the house that Harry had acquired for her raised an astonishing £50,000 as dealers and collectors scrambled to bid for Gaby's belongings. Harry's generosity proved a good investment for his girlfriends. In 1922, Syrie Maugham put his gifts on the block, selling the expensive furniture bought for the Regent's Park house to finance her new interior design business and decorative antiques shop in Baker Street.

As a rich, eligible widower, Harry Selfridge could have wined and dined any number of equally eligible and elegant women. But for the man who was at heart a showman, seemingly only showgirls would do. In 1922, his affection was focused on another French *danseuse*, Alice Delysia, the highly paid star of Charles B. Cochran's London review *Mayfair and Montmartre*. Unfortunately for Mr Cochran, Alice caught a throat infection and had to withdraw from the show, a debacle which cost C. B. over £20,000. What she cost Harry Selfridge, we will never know.

C. B. Cochran and his stage director Frank Collins were part of the innermost Selfridge circle. The store promoted theatrical productions through its window displays, invited stage stars to make presentations at events in the Palm Court, and was happy to loan furs and jewels for photographic sessions. When Selfridge wanted new uniforms for his beautiful bevy of lift girls, Cochran's office was asked about 'new design talent' in town. Recalling a polite, albeit nervous young designer who had visited recently, Mr Collins thought his work might suit Selfridge. The appointment arranged, the young man anxiously presented twenty carefully prepared sketches, looking hopefully in Harry's direction. 'Go away, my boy, and learn to draw,' Selfridge told Norman Hartnell. Sir Norman, who would become Britain's most famous fashion designer, recalled the incident in his memoirs, adding: 'Later I grew to admire and like him. He would send lovely ladies to be dressed by me, and his guineas well recompensed me for that early humiliation.'

The lift girls got their new clothes – designer unknown – while the lifts themselves got new doors, designed by the sculptor Edgar Brandt whose work Selfridge saw at the Paris Salon des Artistes Décorateurs in 1922. Adapted from Brandt's piece in bronze, *Cicognes d'Alsace*, the magnificent doors were not actually cast in bronze but were made from raised and formed sheet steel and wrought iron, mounted on plywood and painted with a mixture of varnish and bronze powder. It was beauty on a budget, but only an expert could tell.

Selfridge loved Paris. Commuting regularly on the boat train, he would visit his great friends Théophile Bader and Alphonse Khan, the owners of Galeries Lafayette. He lunched with his French banker, Benjamin Rosier of Banque Suisse et Française, saw his young grandson Blaise de Sibour and spent his nights playing baccarat for high stakes at François André's exclusive club Le Cercle Haussmann. It has often been said that Harry's gambling only began in earnest when he took up with the Dolly Sisters in the mid-1920s, But he had *always gambled* and he knew where to go.

At first it was Monte Carlo, where the casinos operated by the Société des Bains de Mer ruled supreme, but Monaco was too far to go for a weekend. Having banned gambling in 1837, the French Government, bowing to pressure, reinstated it in 1907, with the result that Grand Casinos were built in Nice, Deauville, Cannes and Biarritz. For the most part under the aegis of the man known as 'the Casino King' of France, Eugène Cornuché, they offered baccarat and chemin-de-fer – roulette then being the exclusive fiefdom of Monte Carlo. Cornuché, keen to boost his casino in Cannes, hired sixteen glorious girls from Paris, dressed and bejewelled them, and installed them at his tables with enough chips to convince other gamblers that they were genuinely playing the game. Nicknamed the Cornuchettes, his team players became both rich and famous – one married a French duke. In Paris, however, such things weren't allowed. For years, the city banned women from gambling. Playing the tables in Paris was never about fun and flirting, it was about serious money.

In England, where gaming was banned, there were illegal gaming clubs, just as there were speakeasies in America. But outside private weekend house parties, British gambling was controlled by men just as tough as those running liquor in America, and there was little pleasure playing in an uneasy atmosphere of sinister violence. Still, Harry indulged in London. For a compulsive gambler – especially one who liked to hold the bank at baccarat – there wasn't much choice. His private ledger shows the extent of his losses. In 1921, he listed fifteen payments in less than five months, totalling an astonishing £5,000, each made to his private secretary Eric Dunstan. It must have been 'money owing'. Dunstan's job was to deliver it.

Years later, when a journalist was writing a feature about Selfridge, he asked an employee who knew him well what he was *really* like. 'Oh a genius, totally brilliant all week at work – but at the weekend he was someone completely different,' came the reply. At work through the 1920s Harry hardly put a foot wrong. In October 1922 the store hosted the first of its celebrated 'Election Night' parties. Store events are commonplace now, but then it was unheard of to entertain after hours. The black-tie dancing party with supper before the results – a Conservative victory which meant Andrew Bonar Law became Prime Minister – followed by bacon and eggs for breakfast was a wild success. Champagne flowed all night, the barber's shop was kept open to refresh the men with hot towels, while Lady Curzon, the Duchess of Rutland, the Russian Grand Duke Michael and the actresses Gladys Cooper, Alice Delysia and Anna May Wong danced, it was noted in the press, 'with vigour'.

Selfridge adored statistics and busied himself with data collected by his Information Bureau. He knew, for example, that 15.3 million people had shopped in the store in 1922. He also knew that his newly uniformed waitresses – now wearing trousers – could take 'nine steps more per minute to get to the kitchen than they could in a skirt'. Speed didn't cut any ice with critics of women wearing trousers. One cleric raged against Selfridge from his pulpit, quoting Deuteronomy: 'The woman shall not wear that which pertaineth unto a man.' The vicar was wasting his breath: before long women wouldn't be wearing very much at all.

Having put up with three years of delay over his planned store extension, in March 1923, when political change heralded the lifting of commercial building restrictions, an intriguing group of men gathered on the roof of the old Thomas Lloyd building adjacent to the store. Led by Selfridge in his customary morning coat and silk top hat, the team wielding pick-axes for the photographers included Sir Woodman Burbidge (Harrods), Mr John Lawrie (Whiteley's), Colonel Cleaver (Robinson & Cleaver) and Mr Barnard (Thomas Wallis's). That such a group gathered to celebrate the expansion of a supposed rival indicates how popular Selfridge had become. The business of retail had changed radically since Selfridge's arrival in London. Indisputably, he was the accelerator of that change.

On 26 April, the Duke of York and Elizabeth Bowes-Lyon were married at Westminster Abbey in front of 3,000 guests, the women glittering with jewels, the men with decorations. That night, the Marchioness Curzon hosted a Charity Ball ('by kind permission of Mr Gordon Selfridge at Lansdowne House') for Queen Victoria's Jubilee Institute for Nurses. The guest-list resembled the pages of *Debrett's*, with an occasional leaf taken from the *Almanach de Gotha* – it was a wonderful opportunity to entertain a host of visiting royals in town for the wedding who might otherwise have had nowhere to go. For the price of 3 guineas a head they could dance to Paul Whiteman's orchestra, drink champagne all night courtesy of Perrier Jouet and admire each other's court decorations. Patrons of the event included the Duchesses of Sutherland, Somerset, Norfolk, Grafton, Beaufort, Northumberland, Abercorn, Westminster and Portland, as well as the Marchionesses Salisbury, Anglesey, Londonderry, Linlithgow, Carisbrooke and Blandford. Then there were the Countesses (from Bathurst and Beatty to Lonsdale and Shaftesbury), the Ladies (Ribblesdale, Islington, Desborough and Guinness, among others), and finally the mere knights' wives: Lady Lavery, Lady Tree, Lady Cunard. The Prince of Wales was expected, though sadly he failed to arrive, but the Royal Princes Henry and George were there, along with King Alfonso of Spain.

As the royal procession was moving through to dinner, a very drunk, near-naked Isadora Duncan bounced through the crowd and threw her arms round Selfridge, slurring: 'Harry darling, how *are* you?' Selfridge stayed calm, hissing an aside to the omnipresent Eric Dunstan that he should 'get *rid* of her' before moving through to dinner. Isadora however slipped away, disappearing up a back staircase to the ballroom where the band was playing rather romantic waltzes during the supper interval. When Dunstan eventually found her, she was wafting around in the middle of the floor, dress and arms flying, and with them a valuable terracotta knocked off its pedestal. Dunstan dutifully picked her up, carried her to a car and drove to the Cavendish Hotel where, as he later said, 'I believe the resourceful Mrs Rosa Lewis locked her in a room.'

Back at Lansdowne House, the band played on.

12

~

MAKING WAVES

'I discovered that men will pay anything to be amused. Pleasure and amusements
are the only things in the world where the buyer rarely counts the cost.'
Kate Meyrick, nightclub owner

Whether it was a teenager spending 7/6d of his savings on a crystal radio kit, or any one of the legions of enthusiasts reading *Amateur Wireless* while they fiddled with knobs in the hope of hearing the Savoy Havana Band live from the hotel ballroom, Britain had become besotted with radio. It had been hesitantly launched in 1920, when the *Daily Mail* sponsored a recital by Dame Nellie Melba broadcast live from Marconi's Chelmsford works. While commercial radio was poised to take America by storm, most of Britain's frustrated radio fans had to spend the next two years with little service to speak of, thanks to the Postmaster General's misconception that Marconi's station 2MT, run out of a hut in Writtle, 'would interfere with air to ground controls in matters of aviation'. The cheery voice of ex-Royal Flying Corps Captain P. P. Eckersley, the country's first radio presenter, was thus strictly rationed to just fifteen minutes a week.

Marconi were soon granted a second licence, setting up a call sign, 2LO, at the company head office in the Strand where the transmitter was housed in an attic room and the aerials were strung between towers on the roof. Then, in the summer of 1922, a hybrid between commerce and government called the British Broadcasting Company Ltd was formed. Marconi's 2LO was transferred to the BBC in November and sales of 'licences to listen' soared from 10,000 to

500,000. By 1924, 2LO's newly updated transmitter was installed on the roof of Selfridge's, where Mr Wragg, the buyer for the new radio department, was kept busy trying to keep pace with customer demand for wireless sets. By 1927, over two and a half million homes would own one. Selfridge's was a launch pad not merely for unstoppable consumer trends but also for employees involved with them. Just three years later, Mr Wragg left to help set up a business called Rent-A-Radio, which ultimately evolved into Radio Rentals, with a shop on virtually every high street in Britain.

Newspaper publishers, many of whom felt threatened by this new way of disseminating news, refused at first to publish programme listings. Seizing an opportunity to highlight the store's 'public service programme', Selfridge rode to the rescue, using the 'Callisthenes' column to inform readers when they could hear their favourite music or listen to the news. It struck a chord. Within the week, national newspapers followed suit and thus their 'radio pages' were born. Although enamoured with the potential of radio, Harry refused to accept a manufacturer's offer of £3,000 in cash to display their latest model. He abhorred the concept of concessions, telling Mr Wragg, 'If we did this sort of thing, we should eventually discover that someone else was running our business. Next, they would demand the right to dress our windows to suit themselves, then where would we be?'

The store meanwhile positively hummed to music. The phonograph department wired up a player to serenade the workmen busy on the Oxford Street extension, who were cheered along while they worked to the big hit of the moment, 'Fascinating Rhythm' by Jelly Roll Morton. When Selfridge himself visited the Palm Court for tea, the band struck up with 'I'm just wild about Harry', which was always guaranteed to raise a smile.

He needed cheering up. Somerset Maugham's play *Our Betters* had opened at the Globe Theatre to rave reviews. For the next twelve months Selfridge was parodied six nights a week and during matinées. He claimed he never saw it – just as William Randolph Hearst said he never saw *Citizen Kane* – but it's hard to believe he didn't slip in one evening. Every mannerism of 'Arthur Fenwick', the character based on Selfridge, was chillingly accurate. Eric Dunstan, a close acquaintance of Maugham's confidant Gerald Haxton, was told that Maugham and Syrie had invited Selfridge out to lunch years earlier 'so Willie could get the detail right'. Selfridge never talked about Syrie, who was herself now bitterly unhappy in her sham of a marriage. Indeed he never talked about any of his mistresses. Those members of staff closest to him – Dunstan, Miss Mepham and Mr Williams, by now the store Sales Manager – were never privy to his innermost thoughts. Williams would later say: 'He wasn't a man who either invited or gave confidences. He had a monumental detachment from all matters of personal concern.'

The Government meanwhile was in disarray. Bonar Law, his health failing, resigned in May 1923 and in December there was another General Election and another party in the store. The 1,200 guests, who included the Asquiths, the Churchills, Jack Buchanan, Gladys Cooper, Lady Headfort, the beautiful Lady Lavery, the Ranee of Sarawak and the Hollywood hero Charlie Chaplin, danced to music from the famous band-leader Ambrose and his Embassy Club Band. Fifty telephone operators manned special lines bringing information in from around the country. As news of one close count was supposedly coming through, the famous music-hall comedian and emergent film actor Leslie Henson took the microphone. 'No change,' he said to cheers from the audience, as he pulled out his empty trouser pockets and shook them. The real results were posted up on a cricket scoreboard by six pretty girls. Those watching outside on the street crowded round the 'electric newspaper' which lit up the results in blazing lights. In fact they caused such a bottleneck in the street that the police insisted the store close it down.

To the consternation of many wining and dining at Selfridge's, the collapsing Conservative vote resulted in a hung parliament, and Britain's first Labour Prime Minister, Ramsay MacDonald, moved into Downing Street. The Selfridge family were also on the move. Their lease on Highcliffe had expired and the castle was discreetly put up for sale by the Stuart Wortleys. Country weekends were now spent in the open environs of Wimbledon Park, where Rosalie, Serge and their daughter Tatiana had moved into the once grand but now rather shabby Wimbledon Park House. The heavily mortgaged mansion – originally built for the 4th Earl Spencer, who owned the Manor of Wimbledon – belonged to Serge's mother, Marie Wiasemsky. Desperately short of money, she had recently been taken to court by an irate servant owed three months' wages of just £12. Rosalie and Serge, clearly hoping Selfridge would fund them, struck out on their own, taking over financial responsibility for the vast property. Serge, already popular in Wimbledon where the family hosted an annual fête and a historical fancy dress gala, had become something of a local hero when locals read press reports about him diving to rescue a mother and child from the sea near Boulogne.

The deeds of the house were in the name of Prince Wiasemsky, Serge having adopted the title. The principal branch of the Wiasemsky family, headed by Prince Vladimir, was not amused. Vladimir, his married sister Princess Lydia Wassiltchikoff and his mother had escaped the turmoil of the Russian Revolution, and settled in the South of France, but his two brothers had not been so lucky: Prince Boris was murdered by his estate workers after having his eyes gouged out, and Prince Dimitri was shot. Memories of these atrocities were still fresh, so it is hardly surprising that Prince Vladimir was less than impressed when the 'self-styled Prince Serge Wiasemsky', as he caustically called him, took it upon himself to form a movement called the Russian National Progressive Party. When Alexis Aladin, leader of the Russian Peasant Union, was in London that year for talks with Ramsay MacDonald, he shared a platform with Serge who told the *Sunday Times*, 'the land of Russia belongs to the people. My party has no connection with, and totally disagrees with and disapproves of the monarchical group.' By this he meant the Romanovs rather than his own supposed ancestors the Rurikids. The exiled Romanov Grand Duke Michael, who had previously enjoyed the Selfridges' hospitality, declined an invitation to their next party.

Whatever Serge thought of the ill-fated Russian monarchy, he relentlessly clung to his own title, hobnobbing with other Russians who had married well, among them Prince Serge Obolensky and his bride, the 20-year-old Alice Astor, who had inherited a trust fund of $5 million when her father went down with the *Titanic*. Young Tatiana Wiasemsky made an angelic bridesmaid when Prince George Imeretinsky married the society beauty Stella Wright.

Meanwhile, Harry Selfridge had also parted with Harrose Hall on Lake Geneva, reportedly selling it for a tidy sum. The sale prompted his elderly mother to make a trip to Chicago to see the house once more, visiting old friends both there and in Washington. Chicago, cheerfully described in the hit song of 1922 as 'That Toddlin' Town', was a city under siege. By the time Lois Selfridge arrived in November 1923, it was reported that over 60 per cent of the city's police were involved in one way or another in the liquor business. Al Capone had established himself as a leading light in organized crime, his own employees running over 160 bars and gambling houses. Capone, having 'seen off' three rival families with an assortment of weapons ranging from bombs to Thompson sub-machine guns, was driven around town in a $30,000 bullet-proof Cadillac flanked by posses of armed hoodlums. Madam Selfridge, a life-long supporter of Prohibition, could now see for herself what it had created – a speakeasy life of violence and crime, swinging along at a fast and furious rate.

Her trip lasted three months. Although she was away for Christmas, Harry sent out a card to store staff, showing mother and son together in the library at Lansdowne House. The card also bore a message: 'What a wonderful privilege it is to live – to see – to hear – to think – to learn!' His mother, however, did not have long to live. In Washington the following February, she contracted pneumonia. Harry rushed over to America and brought her home on the SS *Berengaria*. They landed at Southampton on Saturday, 23 February, but by the Monday she was dead. Her funeral took place at St Mark's in Highcliffe, where she was buried next to her daughter-in-law Rose. The store, draped mournfully, albeit exquisitely, in black, closed for the day, while the tiny Hampshire parish church was filled with flowers sent by, among others, Mr and Mrs Adolph S. Ochs (owners of the *New York Times*), John Lawrie (the Chairman of Whiteley's), the Blumenfelds and Mr and Mrs John Shedd from Chicago. There was also a spectacularly beautiful bouquet bearing an engraved card from 'La Princesse de Monaco'. The 26-year-old Princess Charlotte had sent equally stupendous flowers to Rose's funeral five years earlier and was evidently a close friend of the Selfridge family. Though no trace exists of the origins of this intriguing relationship, Princess Charlotte was certainly in need of friends.

Charlotte had always been sneered at by Monaco society. Her mother, Marie Louvet, had been a cabaret singer in an Algerian nightclub when she first met Prince Louis II of Monaco, then an officer in the French Foreign Legion. Their illegitimate daughter Charlotte Louise was born in Algeria in 1898, and her lonely upbringing was financed by her father. Since Prince Louis never married, young Charlotte became, dynastically speaking, the last chance for the Monaco ruling family. In the absence of an heir, the throne would pass to a German cousin, and with it would go the Grimaldi share of the lucrative profits from the casino. So, by special decree, Charlotte was formally adopted by her father, created a princess, and hastily married off to the 'dandy' Count Pierre de Polignac who, during their uneasy marriage, fathered Prince Rainier and Princess Antoinette. The dynasty now being secure, profits made in what Somerset Maugham wittily described as 'a sunny place for shady people' continued apace. Selfridge himself, although he gambled at Monte Carlo, preferred the vast municipal casino in Nice, where he kept his own apartment and where, for a while, the exotic Princess Charlotte lived until she set up home with René Gigier, France's most infamous jewel thief. She and Harry would remain friends until his death.

An inveterate traveller, Selfridge liked nothing better than rushing to board the boat train at Victoria for the journey to Paris. He was an early passenger on the Calais–Nice–Rome Express, whose clattering wooden sleeping cars took travellers south to the newly fashionable summer playgrounds of the sun-seeking rich; and he was ecstatic when in December 1922 the new First Class-only Calais–Méditerranée Express service – known simply as *le train bleu* – was launched.

Years later, a senior guard on the boat train from Victoria recalled Mr Selfridge fondly: 'He crossed nearly every week, either to Le Touquet or on to Paris … he once went all the way to Cannes just for six hours' sunshine. He was the most remarkable person – brisk, methodical and so original. He had the gift of getting to sleep immediately but would jump up in the morning, brush his hair and be fully alert – the only passenger to think of bringing his disembarkation card on board pre-prepared and to put his American passport in a coloured silk folder so it could be easily identified.'

In April 1924, the vast extension to the store was officially opened. Much to Harry's annoyance, there was still a gap between the original, eastern building and the new section that was being argued about by builders, bankers and borough councillors, but below ground, the Bargain Basement stretched unbroken from Duke Street to Orchard Street, covering an area of three and a half acres. Most of the upper-floor departments were replicated 'below stairs', where customers enjoyed keen prices, cool white walls, white marble floors and, for the first time in England, cool air, courtesy of the very latest in American mechanical wizardry, a 'comfort cooling' system. Air-conditioning was the quantum leap that created a comfortable environment out of artificial, windowless spaces. To London's shoppers in 1924, it was a revelation.

When King George V opened the vast British Empire Exhibition at Wembley later that month, Selfridge's had nineteen speakers wired around the store so customers could hear the King. One chap taking tea in the Palm Court Restaurant was so awed he stood to attention. 'It's *the King* speaking,' he said. In the days of silent films, people were enchanted by the wonders of radio. Wembley Stadium itself was built as the centrepiece of the BEE, as the vast exhibition was fondly called. Ironically for Selfridge's, part of the enormous plot of land that had been compulsorily purchased had been the original location of the store's staff sports club. With the money from the enforced sale, Selfridge bought a fifteen-acre plot in Preston Road, between Wembley and Harrow, where the staff held teas, supper dances and quiz nights in a handsome pavilion after a hectic Saturday and Sunday afternoon of football, netball, cricket and tennis matches. Over 27 million people poured into Wembley to see the exhibits, travel on experimental railways, inspect a coal mine, visit an amusement park and buy such things as the first ever commemorative stamps issued by the Post Office – which were also on sale in the Selfridge's branch post office on the store's fourth floor.

Selfridge, who had used the concept of a post-war World Fair as the central theme of his many after-dinner talks to various business groups, might justifiably have felt hurt at not being invited to join the Exhibition Organizing Committee. He made up for it with his own displays in the store, where Empire 'flags, emblems and decorations' were on show in a vast department selling ephemera such as printed cotton Union Jacks priced at 1 shilling a dozen and portraits of the King at 1/11d each. Selfridge had long celebrated Empire Day with a staff party on the roof, and to inaugurate the BEE he invited Lord Beaverbrook to entertain the staff with what turned out to be a rousing speech.

Harry Selfridge believed in engaging emotionally with his workforce and he had an innate understanding of the importance of ritual for customers and employees alike. He made a point of observing Armistice Day. Each year since the war, on 11 November, a bugler had stepped out on to the central balcony to sound the Last Post at 11.00 a.m. After a two-minute silence came the Reveille. It was a moving experience for all who heard it, and it continued each year until Selfridge was evicted from the store. Creating 'experience' was central to his beliefs. His critics said it had less to do with shopping and more to do with theatricals. But he knew – as few other retailers did – that emotion and experience formed a huge part of what customers craved. 'The whole art of merchandising,' he said, 'consists of appealing to the imagination. Once the imagination is moved, the hand goes automatically to the purse.' Years later, one of his directors, Frank Chitham, who left to work for D. H. Evans, said, 'He had the closest insight into customer psychology. When he was expressing ideas they came alive in your mind.'

After the morning tour, there was usually an ideas session in the Chief's office where his desk was flanked by the Stars and Stripes and the Union Jack. Reports on new trends in England and France or new gadgetry from America that he might usefully use in Oxford Street were discussed. Sometimes he would just sit for a while, hands clasped behind his head, looking out of the window at the clouds high above Oxford Street. No one ever dared interrupt him. And then the ideas would flow. Some were prosaic. If he saw that it was going to rain he would have someone call to check on the number of raincoats and umbrellas and ask that extra stock be put on to the floor.

In the new men's department, opened in 1924, the ex-world champion Melbourne Inman challenged Tom Carpenter at the billiards table. An ice rink was opened on the roof terrace where the American champion ice skater Howard Nicholson and his partner Freda Whittaker – the Torville and Dean of their day – enthralled the public, helping to establish the trend for skating. Poppy Wingate, England's first female professional golfer, gave demonstrations in the ladies' sportswear department. All these events were supported by linked merchandise displays often marked at 'special prices', which invariably ran for the rest of the week. The events made news because Selfridge's press room was open to all, whether news reporters or sports or women's page writers. Once they had met and photographed whichever sports star or stage star was in the store that week, only one task remained: the celebrity in question had to sign the Chief's autograph window with the diamond-tipped stick before a chauffeured car whisked them back to their hotel. Finally, their visit was reported in the store's own house magazine, *The Key*.

In what the press called the 'Ball of the Season', in the early summer of 1924, Selfridge threw open the doors of Lansdowne House for another Royal Charity Gala, this time to raise funds to endow hospital beds. The guest list included the British royal princes Henry and George, their cousins the Marquis and Marchioness of Milford Haven, Princess Marie Louise and Princess Helena Victoria. The seat of honour, however, was given to Princess Serge Wiasemsky (née Rosalie Selfridge), and her cameo, charmingly drawn by Rex Whistler complete with coronet, adorned the front cover of the programme. Selfridge pulled out all stops to put on a show: Garrard's and Carrington's loaned gold plate; no less than five champagne houses kept supplies flowing freely through the night; a jazz and classical band played; and Ivor Novello's mother – herself a noted musician – put her celebrated Clara Novello Davies Male Choir through their paces for the society audience.

More of a café society crowd poured into the store at the end of October, to celebrate at the third General Election night party when 2,000 guests whooped it up on both the roof-top ice rink and the ballroom roller-skating rink. Fearful of gate-crashers, the store's smarter staff – drawn from the growing band who had attended public school – were on duty at the entrance to vet, and sometimes veto, the arriving guests. Those admitted included Joseph Pulitzer Jr, Freda Dudley Ward, Sir Gerald du Maurier, Ivor Novello, Barbara Cartland, the Asquiths, the Aga Khan, the McAlpines, the very rich Lady Louis Mountbatten, and Marshall Field's equally rich granddaughter Gwendoline and her husband, the Scottish baronet Charlie Edmonstone. The hottest actress in town, Tallulah Bankhead, was there with the best-selling author Michael Arlen, whose book *The Green Hat* was top of the lists in every lending library. 'The whole *world* was at Selfridge's,' enthused *Tatler* breathlessly.

That night the Conservative Party won the General Election and the Bright Young People who would personify the Roaring Twenties came of age. They couldn't have cared less who won the election; they just wanted to have fun. The next five years would be spent battling with the new Home Secretary, Sir William Joynson-Hicks, who tried his best to stop them. Called 'Jix' by the cartoonists, who mercilessly lampooned him, Sir William was a High Victorian disciplinarian who represented everything about the establishment that the young loathed.

Jix loathed a lot of things, particularly 'non-registered aliens'. When he discovered there were 272,000 of them in Britain, he instigated a visa system so strict that merely travelling without the precious document meant a spell in prison before being shipped straight back home. He didn't care much for sex either – especially any forms of affection in public, which to his eye were 'gross indecencies'. He viewed most modern authors, artists and sculptors with grave suspicion, unilaterally censoring their work. A life-long teetotaller who had yearned to see alcohol prohibited, he also had an absolute fixation about nightclubs, calling them 'drug-filled sewers of society', while contemporary dancing was a 'disease against civilization'.

When an overseas visitor, awed by the scale of the Home Secretary's impressive office and vast staff, asked Sir William what he did there, Sir William replied: 'It is I who am the ruler of England.' To a certain extent he was, at least as far as law, order and licensing were concerned. In all these things, he was ably assisted by his treasured friend DORA. Many who yearned for the Defence of the Realm Act to be modified to suit the times, waited in vain. Jix took it out, dusted it down and applied its regulatory powers with relish. The police were instructed to take a stern view of public morality and an even sterner view of nightclubs. Naturally, they made mistakes. A girl arrested in Liverpool and charged with being a prostitute turned out to be *virgo intacta*. When the former Liberal MP Sir Leo Money was arrested and charged for merely sitting next to a young woman on a bench in Hyde Park, his case was dismissed. Sir Basil Home Thomson, ex-Chief of London's CID and one-time head of British Intelligence, was less fortunate. Found in a compromising situation with an actress called Thelma de Lava, he declared in his defence that he was researching material for a book on vice in the West End. The magistrates were unimpressed and fined him £5 with costs.

Harry never needed to risk a romp in the park – his children were now grown-up and had an insouciant attitude towards his affairs – but the matter of a visa was pressing. To obtain one he enlisted the help of friends in high places – Sir Reginald McKenna, Chairman of the Midland Bank, various members of the Masonic Lodge frequented by the Home Secretary, and Ralph Blumenfeld, editor of the *Daily Express*. The latter was popular with Sir William, not just because his newspaper adopted a strict view of morality, but also because he had founded the Anti-Socialist Union, a group heartily approved of by Jix. Thus Selfridge acquired a letter on Home Office stationery allowing him residential status. Things weren't as easy for his son-in-law Serge, whose Russian National Progressive Party was thought rather dubious. Conveniently, however, Alexander Onou, head of the Russian Refugees Permit Office in London, came to the rescue, issuing 'Serge de Bolotoff, Prince Wiasemsky' with the necessary photographic identity card confirming his refugee status.

In many ways, the jazz decade suited Selfridge. He had the ability to enter into the mood of the moment and was always enchanted by youth, which kept him if not literally, then certainly figuratively, on his toes. 'Let me see, Mr Selfridge,' said a reporter from the Manchester *Daily Dispatch* in 1924, 'you're sixty I believe?' The answer was merely an agreeable smile. He was 68. Had he coupled the dignity of age and experience with youthful zest, his life might have taken a different turn. As it was, surrounded by a circle of sycophants and an eager press, he believed he was invincible. With no one to restrain him, his hedonistic cravings raged unchecked. By 1925, he had crossed the line.

Fuelled by the unrelenting fashion for everything new, business was booming. Since it had first been seen in the Broadway show *Runnin' Wild*, the charleston had quite literally swept everyone off their feet. In London there were charleston competitions and charleston clothes. Flimsy underwear, especially Directoire knickers and silk chemises, beaded headbands, feathered fans and the essential 'flappers'' footwear – shoes with a powder compact in the jewelled buckle, whether for cheeks or cocaine – flew out of Selfridge's. Skirts were short and nights were long. Dance halls and nightclubs were crowded, and parents of all classes despaired of their offspring's passion for dancing. Even the King was alarmed, writing to his wife, 'I see David [the Prince of Wales] continues to dance every night and most of the night. People who don't know will begin to think that either he is mad or the biggest rake in Europe. Such a pity.' Young people didn't think anything of the sort. They loved the informality, the energy and the gaiety of the Prince; they loved him *because* he danced. Such things, however, are not founded on substance. As the Prince of Wales became famous for his clothes, his lifestyle, his girl-friends and his aura of celebrity, he too was heading for disaster.

London was awash with nightclubs, much to the anguish of the Home Secretary who did his best to close them down, but the clubs – particularly those patronized by the Prince of Wales – reigned supreme. The list was endless. On Thursday nights, the Prince himself could usually be found at the Embassy, essentially a dining club with a tiny cheek-to-cheek dance floor, where he smooched with Freda Dudley Ward to music played by Bert Ambrose and his orchestra. A more bohemian, theatrical crowd hung out at Wardour Street's Fifty Fifty, the Hambone or the rakish Uncle's in Albemarle Street. Arnold Bennett, a keen nightclub aficionado, was a fan of the Gargoyle and Kate Meyrick's Silver Slipper, with its glass dance floor and twinkling mirror globes, while those who really wanted kicks headed to another of Mrs Meyrick's clubs, the infamous 43 in Gerrard Street. The 43 also had a distinguished clientele: even the Prince of Wales went from time to time, but it was really the haunt of European royalty – all those lost souls who had also lost their crowns – along with racing drivers, pilots and sportsmen like Steve Donoghue the jockey and 'Gorgeous George' Carpentier, the achingly handsome boxer. The 43 was frequented by people who lived on the edge – the serious gambler Major Jack Coats, the international financier Ivar Kreuger (who had been involved with Selfridge's construction all those years ago), the theatrical and property entrepreneur Jimmy White and London's richest asset stripper, Clarence Hatry. Michael Arlen, Avery

Hopwood, Jessie Mathews and Tallulah Bankhead were regulars – and a young Evelyn Waugh would sit quietly at a side table observing the sights, later immortalized in his novels.

Everyone in town went to the 43. When Rudolph Valentino paid a visit, wearing, in the very latest fashion, a short, fitted tuxedo jacket, he was mistaken for a waiter. He took it well apparently, picking up a bottle with a flourish to pour drinks for several delighted guests. The house champagne sold at £2 a bottle and the dance hostesses cost considerably more. Ma Meyrick presided over the door, taking 10 shillings a time from patrons eager to hear Sophie Tucker belt out a song or Paul Whiteman's star musicians jam late into the night.

All this fun came at a cost, however, especially to Mrs Meyrick. Since she had launched her first club after the war, she had been arrested several times, fined thousands of pounds and served two six-month sentences in Holloway. She was the bane of the Home Secretary's life and the target of the leading light in London's Police Vice Squad, Station Sergeant George Goddard. Fortunately for Ma, Sergeant Goddard proved to be a man of extravagant tastes, which he found hard to meet on his police pay of £6 a week. His weekly wage was supplemented with a brown envelope containing £50 in crisp £1 pound notes courtesy of Ma, with the same amount paid by her friend Mr Ribuffi, the owner of Uncle's. Every Friday afternoon, Sergeant Goddard would head to Selfridge's where he carefully placed the envelope in his personal safety deposit box. It couldn't last of course. Shopped by an envious colleague, Goddard was eventually caught in 1929. He tried to explain away a large house in Streatham, an extremely comfortable car and £12,000 in cash in his Selfridge's deposit box by saying he had made the money 'selling confectionery on the side at the British Empire Exhibition', but he was laughed out of court. Goddard, Mr Ribuffi and Ma Meyrick were all sent to jail – Ma herself getting fifteen months' hard labour.

Selfridge himself was more of a Kit Kat Club man. The expensive premises had opened on the Haymarket early in 1925, complete with the requisite big band but also with a line-up of gorgeous girls in a showy cabaret. The Kit Kat too was raided and then closed down. In an attempt to circumvent the law, it subsequently reopened as a 'cabaret restaurant'. To celebrate the event, the club's Chairman, Sir Charles Rothen JP, engaged a dazzling dancing duo called the Dolly Sisters to perform on the opening night – and among the guests was Harry Gordon Selfridge. It wasn't the first time he had seen the girls in action. They had been on the London stage in a C. B. Cochran show called *The League of Notions* in 1921, when Harry had carefully noted in his ledger that he had spent 17/6d on a ticket. After seeing them again four years later at the Kit Kat, he began an affair with Jenny – some say with both sisters – which, by the time it fizzled out in 1933, had cost him quite literally millions of pounds.

Jenny and her sister Rosie were identical twins. Hungarian by birth – their real names were Jansei and Rosika Deutsch – they were born in 1892. They moved with their family to America where the girls trained as dancers, going 'on the road' as entertainers when they were just 14. The Dollies got their first big break when Flo Ziegfeld signed them up in 1911. By the time they hit London they were 29 – rather old to be playing ingénues, but they did it well.

The twins specialized in synchronized 'tandem' dancing, their movements 'mirroring' each other so they blended into one – as indeed did the girls. The only way to identify one from the other was to listen to them – Jenny giggled more. She had been briefly married to the creator of the foxtrot, Harry Fox, and in post-war Paris she performed various outré dance numbers with a professional partner, Clifton Webb, while Rosie specialized in a particularly erotic form of flamenco. On the whole, though, the girls danced – as they did most other things – *à deux*. With their penchant for jewels, a passion for gambling and a fondness for rich men, they were quickly nicknamed 'the Million Dollar Dollies'.

Their act was especially popular with the gay crowd (both happy and homosexual) and with the sex tourists who frequented the club world of Paris, where nightlife was more lavish and louche than in London. In the French capital Elsa Maxwell, the supreme party-organizer of the period, ran a club called the Acacia in partnership with the fashion designer Captain Edward Molyneux. There Jenny would dance, making her entrance each night in a cloak of fresh gardenias. The sisters apparently regarded London as stuffy, preferring to perform in Paris and throughout France. In reality, their déclassé behaviour meant they weren't accepted socially in a city that still regarded public performers which a shiver of unease. To call them uninhibited would be an understatement. As a cub reporter on the *Sunday Times* Charles Graves recalled interviewing them after a performance of *The League of Notions*: 'I knocked on the door and they said in chorus, "Wait a minute." I did so. "Now you can come in," they called. I entered. Both were stark naked.'

During their first foray on to the London stage, the Dollies had been squired around town by Sir Thomas Lipton. In reality, the genial Sir Thomas, although keen on promoting a reputation as a ladies' man, was uninterested in women and happily returned home each night to his live-in companion, his loyal secretary John Westwood. During their Kit Kat season, when the Dollies found escorts who were more interested in their charms, it was share and share alike. Lord Beaverbrook's daughter, Janet Aitken Kidd, recalled in her memoirs that 'my father and his friend Harry Selfridge were batting Jenny and Rosie back and forth between them like a couple of ping-pong balls'. The Dollies were a *succèss fou*. They were painted by the artist Kees Van Dongen; Edouard Baudoin hired them to promote the opening of his divinely chic Casino Sea Bathing Club created out of a tattered wooden shack in Juan-les-Pins; and Cecil Beaton drew them for *Vogue* while playing chemin-de-fer at Le Touquet. The Dollies, in short, were the first celebrities to be famous merely for being famous.

While fame meant a lot to Selfridge, fashion hardly touched him. He wasn't part of the 'designer world' nor was he on Condé Nast's lunch list. He spent a fortune on entertaining, but he was frugal when it came to buying his own clothes. Arnold Bennett, killing time between appointments one day in the store's basement, met Selfridge 'wearing a rather old morning suit and silk hat. He at once seized hold of me and showed me over a lot of the new part – cold-storage for furs – finest in the world. Then up in his private lift to the offices and his room, where I had to scratch my name with a diamond on the window.'

The signature window, the Chief's pride and joy, was by now a *Who's Who* of fame and included Charlie Chaplin, Fred Astaire, Douglas Fairbanks Jr, Suzanne Lenglen and Michael Arlen. During his working day, Selfridge was still orderly and in control, working longer hours than men half his age. But he was playing hard too, delighting in showing off his conquests. He would walk the store with Suzanne, or Jenny, or Fanny Ward – just as he had done with Gaby – helping them to chose various things and telling the staff to 'send the bill upstairs'. One wonders what the sales girls, earning a few pounds a week, thought about their ageing, albeit much-revered boss blithely signing off shopping worth hundreds – sometimes thousands – of pounds for his famous lady friends. Were they impressed by contact with celebrity? Absolutely. Did they talk about it when they got home? Definitely. Did it sadden them to see a doting old man fussing over rather greedy women? Almost certainly.

The life of the store continued apace. During the week of Selfridge's sixteenth birthday celebrations in 1925, it is estimated that over a million people came through the doors. To mark the occasion, Selfridge sponsored an innovative fifteen-minute radio broadcast by the actress Yvonne Georges from the Eiffel Tower on the couture collections in Paris. This early attempt at commercial radio was the brainchild of an ex-Flying Corps radio wizard, Captain Leonard Plugge. Sadly for Selfridge, when the research survey notes were completed, only three people admitted to having heard the broadcast. Captain Plugge, cheerful in adversity, went on to launch the pirate radio station Radio Normandy as well as making a fortune perfecting the first motor-car radio.

Meanwhile, some shoppers in the store stumbled across history in the making as they watched the young Scottish inventor John Logie

Baird demonstrate his 'televisor'. Baird had struggled long and hard to get recognition for his work. Calling in at the *Daily Express* in the hope of explaining the principles of television to the science editor, he was met with the response: 'For God's sake go down to Reception and get rid of a lunatic who's down there. He says he's got a machine for seeing by wireless. Watch him – he may have a knife!' At Selfridge's, where they were more enlightened, Baird was paid £25 to demonstrate his apparatus, for one week, three times daily. Since he was penniless, the money was a godsend.

It was a time of change not just outside the business but inside it too. Staff were leaving. Well-trained and experienced, they were able to command high salaries elsewhere. Percy Best went to the traditional drapers Schoolbred's, while the three Americans went home, the display chief Edward Goldsman rejoining Marshall Field, although he returned at vast expense once a year to mastermind Selfridge's Christmas windows. Crossing the Atlantic in the other direction, young Ralph Isidor Straus of the then family-owned Macy's in New York, who was studying for an MBA at Harvard, joined the store as a hard-working summer intern. Eric Dunstan left to work for Syrie Maugham, who had by now moved to Grosvenor Street. It wasn't a happy experience. Dunstan soon moved out, saying: 'I cared little for her décor and less for her.' His replacement in the Selfridge inner sanctum was Captain Leslie Winterbottom, late of the Hussars, who stayed with the Chief until 1939.

In 1925 the Chancellor of the Exchequer Winston Churchill presided over a return to the gold standard. The aristocracy were being hit hard by death duties – on the Duke of Rutland's death, the Duchess had to put their Arlington Street mansion up for sale – while the newly rich were awash with money. For those with an eye for acquisitions, mergers and debt reconstruction, there were fortunes to be made. Selfridge himself would soon become part of that trend, making him rich beyond even his dreams. But what would he do with the money?

Meanwhile, Mr Asquith had finally accepted a peerage, becoming the Earl of Oxford. From the stage of a hugely successful revue called *The Punch Bowl,* Norah Blaney sang to an applauding audience:

Mr Asquith now is an Earl
Oxford is his seat:
But Mr Selfridge still remains
The Earl of Oxford Street.

13

~

TOUT VA

'The chains of habit are generally too small to be felt
until they are too strong to be broken.'
Samuel Johnson

In the mid-1920s, a leading business magazine, *Expressions*, wrote:
'To the best of our knowledge, no one has ever dared to refer to
Mr H. Gordon Selfridge as a shopkeeper. He must be given credit
for teaching London and the rest of the country that serving the
public is business of the highest order.' As the growth in consumerism continued, the Drapers' Chamber of Commerce inaugurated
a summer school in Cambridge, offering courses in 'new methods
of merchandising, display and window dressing'. Their star speaker
was Selfridge himself, whose talk centred on his favourite themes of
in-store entertainment, customer service and value for money. 'The
first,' he said 'will get them in, while the second and third will keep
them there.' He concluded by giving the students the same mantra
he always gave his own staff: 'There are six useful things for notable
success in business – judgement, energy, ambition, imagination, determination and nerve. But the greatest of these is judgement.'

In the context of business decisions and planning, his own
judgement appeared to be as sound as ever, his critical faculties
seemingly unimpaired by the frivolity of his after-hours escapades.
At 69, he still arrived at work early. He still walked the store. He
still controlled board meetings with a brisk 'Any business? No? Well
then, let's move on, shall we?' leaving his directors more often than

not merely nodding their agreement. The much more lively monthly meetings with buyers and senior sales staff continued as they had always done, with the Chief singling out individuals whose departments had exceeded their targets and making them blush with pleasure at his praise.

The potential of television had excited him. 'This is not a toy,' he said, 'it is going to be a link between all peoples of the world.' He was also convinced of the long-term future of the motor-car, commissioning the civil engineer Sir Harley Dalrymple-Hay to prepare a feasibility study on the logistics of building an underground car park in Portman Square and enlarging the store's fleet of motorized delivery vans. Cars were beginning to clutter the streets. By the mid-1920s as many as 51,000 motor vehicles and 3,300 horse-drawn carriages were passing round Hyde Park Corner each day and one-way traffic systems were introduced to help traffic flow. Nothing was too much trouble for Selfridge. When an American friend complained about the quality of the coffee in the Palm Court Restaurant, Selfridge had the brand changed. Walking in St Marylebone, he observed the local fire brigade practising on a piece of waste land. He wrote to offer them practice facilities in the store, and in return got the smog-soiled façade cleaned for free. Of course, there were those who knew things were getting out of hand, not least A. J. Hensey, head of the Bought Ledger Department, whose job it was to draw up cheques to cover the Chief's costs. The ever-discreet Mr Hensey who, in his own words, witnessed Selfridge 'going gaga' over various women, wasn't merely in charge of payments: he drew up cheques for generous pay-offs when the affairs ended.

Selfridge excelled in blurring the lines between professional and personal entertainment, ensuring his guest lists included influential businessmen and, unusually for the era, businesswomen such as his friend Elizabeth Arden, whose range was by now the top selling line in the store. Since moving into Lansdowne House, he had already hosted some glamorous soirées, but during 1925 he upped the pace, dispensing largesse on a spectacular scale. The media were always invited to cover such events, though they were allocated special tables rather than seated with the VIPs. Selfridge also shrewdly included the American media correspondents based in London, thereby guaranteeing coverage not just in New York and Chicago but coast to coast, courtesy of *Time* magazine who found his lifestyle irresistible. The store display department took charge of flowers and décor, the food halls delivered provisions, and restaurant staff were on hand to supplement his own domestic staff. The Stars and Stripes flew at an American-themed Rodeo Night where, after a supper of char-grilled hamburgers, fries and ketchup, washed down with a dozen different beers had been served in the Sculpture Court, enthusiastic guests were taught square dancing and watched Red Indians doing lasso demonstrations.

At another party, to honour the newly arrived Japanese Ambassador, the display team created a Japanese water-garden which ran down the centre of the vast dining-table. Checking the area in the afternoon, Selfridge noticed there were no goldfish. A series of frantic forays by taxi to the store's pet department soon ensured that fifty fish were happily swimming among the water-lilies. Satisfied with the result, Selfridge went upstairs to change into his customary white tie. Then disaster struck. The paint on the sides of the artificial pond had poisoned the water and the fish started to die. Selfridge immediately sent to the store for a dozen bicycle pumps and ordered his staff to pump oxygen into the water to revive the survivors. It was a good idea, but it didn't work. Happily, the Ambassador remained blissfully unaware of the drama and spent a delightful evening in the company of, among other dignitaries, the Home Secretary Sir William Joynson-Hicks, enjoying arias performed by an Italian soprano and watching Hawaiian 'hula-hula' dancers shimmy to a native band.

Whatever happened at home was usually a spin-off from an event that had taken place in the store. A dinner hosted to honour the tennis player Suzanne Lenglen followed the launch of her book, *Lawn Tennis: The Game of Nations*. Suzanne was still playing at her usual fast and furious pace, fortified by her customary brandy rather than barley water between sets, and Selfridge and his daughter Rosalie had been in their Centre Court seats to watch her win the Wimbledon Women's Singles for the fifth time. Suzanne's teaching manual had been eagerly awaited by her fans who swamped both the store's book department and the sports department, where the very latest in short tennis skirts and her signature salmon-coloured jersey *sportif* turbans flew off the rails.

Personal appearances by sports stars were promoted in the London newspapers, and Selfridge continued to advertise heavily in the national press, though not in *Vogue* – the store's regular pages having been cancelled after a tiff with the management. Harry Yoxall, *Vogue*'s business manager, recalled the incident in his memoirs. Towards the end of 1924, when the magazine's page rate was increased from £36 to £40, he was summoned to Oxford Street. Yoxall, finding Selfridge 'wearing his hat in the afternoon, always a bad sign', braced himself for battle. 'I am an old man now,' said Selfridge, 'and have few pleasures left in my life, other than that of buying space at a lower price than anyone else enjoys. Now, if you will let me have my advertisements at £37 10 shillings, I'll give you an order for twenty-six pages.' Rather courageously, given that the magazine was losing around £25,000 a year, Yoxall refused to compromise, with the result that *Vogue* lost a client. They pretty soon lost an editor too when Dorothy Todd, the sapphic 'thinking woman's heroine', was fired for her overly artistic and intellectual approach. Her replacement was the much more fashion-orientated Mrs Alison Settle of *Eve* magazine, who, along with her senior fashion editor, Dorothy Todd's most intimate friend Madge Garland, between them secured British *Vogue*'s role as the arbiter of fashion.

Selfridge was uninterested in the comings and goings of the growing band of influential women who wrote about fashion, leaving such things to his public relations department. What Mrs Wish of the *Daily Express* thought of the store's latest season's dresses was of little concern to him – he felt more at ease in conversation with the paper's editor Ralph Blumenfeld or its owner Lord Beaverbrook. In any event, fashion editors in those days did as they were told, and one way or the other, the store was constantly making news. The press were never short of a story. Sophie Tucker sang at a Dance Week which featured the young and beautiful Jacob Epstein model, Oriel Ross, who melted hearts playing the piano. Ivor Novello, the actress Evelyn Laye and the diva Marie Tempest launched the spring sale. An electronic scoreboard delivered the results of that year's Test Match at the front of the store, once again bringing Oxford Street to a standstill, while the American golf professional Walter Hagen gave advice to fans on their swing, and the pilot Alan Cobham's plane – in which he had flown to Africa and back – was put on display.

Returning from an adventurous trip to Russia with Rosalie and Serge, Selfridge demanded that Mr Yoxall pay him another visit. Selfridge had scoured the station bookstalls in Constantinople before boarding the Orient Express and discovered only one English title. 'Which one do you think it was?' he asked Yoxall. Magazine circulation *circa* 1925 being a haphazard affair, Yoxall hadn't the faintest idea but replied hopefully, '*Vogue*?' 'You're right,' said Selfridge, 'and I don't think my great store should be out of such a magazine.' He promptly reinstated his order for twenty-six pages, failing to notice that in the meantime *Vogue* had upped the price per page to £48. Mrs Settle and Miss Garland were soon commissioning the young and struggling photographer Cecil Beaton to take celebrity pictures. Beaton took his film to the patient Mr Barnes in the store's photographic department, noting in his diary: 'I've been giving Selfridge's nearly all the developing. This morning I traipsed for the fifty millionth time to get the results of Edith Sitwell.'

Vogue also commissioned illustrations and text from Beaton, who quickly turned his attention to the most glamorous pastime of the period – gambling. Before long, Beaton's witty little drawings of the chic set who frequented Deauville, Le Touquet, Biarritz and Cannes were a regular feature in *Vogue*, with titles such as 'The Season at Le Touquet – An Exotic World of Sophisticated Elegance'. Anyone who was anyone relentlessly played the tables. Being seen playing the right game at the right casino was as important as being seen in the right nightclubs. In the French casinos throughout the 1920s, no one yearned to show off and be seen more than Jenny and Rosie Dolly, and their passion for gaming infected Selfridge. He had spent decades hiding the extent of his habit, but when his mother died, the final restraint was lifted. In Jenny and Rosie he found his soul mates. With them he crossed the line between habit and addiction. It wasn't just about sex. It was about dealing a six and a three – or any other numbers that made the magic nine of the winning hand at baccarat.

In the post-war era, the heady combination of sun, sea and gambling in France was all the rage. And even if you didn't play, you could pay to watch those who did. All you needed were some evening clothes and the sum of £3, for which, on presentation of your passport, you could enter a casino. A further few pounds would buy dinner and a bottle of wine, and the opportunity to dance to the band which played until the small hours of the morning. For another payment of £4 10 shillings, those who cared to watch fortunes being won and lost were allowed to step beyond the ropes and stanchions and enter the *salles privées* where those for whom gambling was a way of life spent their evenings. There, the powerful players showed they could afford to lose as well as win.

Among those who could well afford to lose were the Aga Khan, Major Jack Coats, the Duke of Westminster, a clutch of Rothschilds, the Belgian financier Jacques Wittouck, Marshall Field III, the Kimberley diamond mining millionaire Solly Joel, King Alfonso of Spain, the Kings of Sweden and Denmark, Indian maharajas and their various wives, the automobile magnate André Citroën, the cognac producer James Hennessy, the Canadian tobacco tycoon Sir Mortimer Davis and various super-rich war profiteers. Millionaires from Chile, Argentina and America flocked to the tables, although after the revolution the impoverished Russian grand dukes weren't able to play unless they had hooked a rich lover to foot the bills. When Coco Chanel finished her affair with Grand Duke Dmitri Pavlovich, who had been earning a precarious living as a champagne salesman,

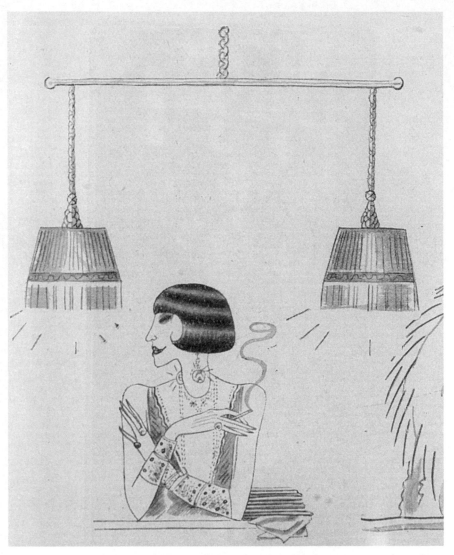

Above and on the facing page: The Dolly Sisters at the tables in Le Touquet, 1928, by Cecil Beaton (Cecil Beaton/Vogue © The Condé Nast Publications Ltd)

she passed him on to a wealthy girlfriend, saying: 'You can have him. These Grand Dukes are too expensive to keep.' In fact Dmitri had introduced Coco to Ernest Beaux, who created Chanel No. 5 for her, so the poor man had more than earned his keep.

Each season, the gambling group migrated *en masse* to their chosen habitat. In the summer it was always Deauville, Le Touquet or Biarritz, in the winter, Monte Carlo, Cannes or occasionally Nice. The casinos of France were run by Eugène Cornuché – who had made his fortune through Maxim's restaurant in Paris – and his protégé and ultimate successor, François André. Between them, these men instigated the concept of the luxury resort hotel, with its sumptuous seaside casino, its elaborate floor show and its six-course foie gras and caviar dinner. They also shrewdly invited women into the casinos and bars, and for over three decades they watched people lose their money. For the truth is that gamblers always lose. Monsieur Cornuché and Monsieur André, however, couldn't lose. Although during their era Monte Carlo held the monopoly on roulette, the French casinos offered both baccarat and *chemin de fer* – and the baccarat bank was run not by the casinos themselves but by a syndicate of Greeks headed by the fearless Nicolas Zographos, who paid the casinos for the privilege of controlling the cards. When Zographos died in 1953 he left a fortune of £5 million, every penny of it made from baccarat. When Harry Gordon Selfridge died in 1947, he left just £10,000, having ploughed his way through a fortune estimated by some to be as much as £3 million.

Nicolas Zographos changed the face of twentieth-century gambling when he sat down at the baccarat table in Deauville in 1922 and quietly said: '*Tout va.*' For those playing against him, the sky was, quite literally, the limit. He and his colleagues had put together a pool of 50 million old francs (£16 million today), which was more than enough to get them started. Although they had some alarming moments over the next few years as the richest of the rich played furiously against them, they kept their cool and ultimately their money. Someone once asked Zographos why he did it. His answer was 'It's like morphine.'

For the Dolly Sisters, gambling was indeed a drug, one on which they had become hooked as teenagers in America. There they had been squired by the legendary sugar-daddy 'Diamond Jim' Brady, who took them to the private members' Canfield Casino at Saratoga in upstate New York and out to Coney Island. By the mid-1920s, having each discarded a husband, they were commuting effortlessly between Paris, New York and the French casino resorts where they regularly took bookings to appear in cabaret. When they had finished on stage, the twins, known variously as 'the Pep Sisters' or 'the Gold Diggers', continued the show at the tables.

The girls had expensive tastes. When they were flush, they bought jewels, but what they liked most was gifts, and they perfected the art of acquiring them. Apparently, one of their favourite tricks was to strip off all their jewels, passing them to a friend, and sit looking discon-solate at the tables. When a wealthy duke, maharaja or banker asked why they were so downcast, they would say they had 'lost everything, right down to their last bracelet'. Not for nothing did every important jeweller have a boutique in the casino resorts. Following their display of crocodile tears, the Dollies could expect deliveries from various admirers by morning. They didn't invest sensibly like their actress friend Pearl White, who on her retirement bought property and opened a bar in Paris and a hotel and casino in Biarritz, where she wisely ignored the tables. Nor were the Dollies as indulgent with money as their gambling contemporary, the French actress Maude Loti, who used to light her cigarettes with 1,000-franc notes and relax each day by shooting off blank cartridges in her bathroom. However, the girls variously earned, won, spent and lost a fortune. As a result, they were always in need of a rich companion.

When Jenny and Rosie met Selfridge, he wasn't actually that rich. He lived like a lord and spent prodigiously, but it was really all show. So when the opportunity came for him to make some serious money – apparently at no risk to himself or his beloved store – he grabbed it with both hands. In early 1926, the idea of forming the Gordon Selfridge Trust was put to him by James 'Jimmy' White, a man who had made a fortune from property (among other deals he had bought and rapidly sold Wembley Stadium after the British Empire Exhibi-tion), boxing promotion and share speculation. White was a bluff and tough Lancashire man, an ex-bricklayer with a thick accent, profane language and a bad temper. Yet somehow the softly spoken, mild-mannered Harry Selfridge – whose strongest expletive was 'My stars' and whose pet phrase was 'As sure as God made little green apples' – became very taken with him. White and he had been nodding acquaintances for years, having first met at National Sporting Club boxing events at the Café Royal. Their paths continued to cross at various nightclubs such as the Kit Kat and the Silver Slipper, and at Daly's Theatre, the much-loved musical comedy venue recently acquired by White as part of his burgeoning 'leisure' portfolio. Jimmy

White's great hobby, apart from making money, was racehorses, which were kept at his flourishing Foxhill stables in Surrey.

White had a friend whose family owned two London stores – John Barnes of Finchley and Jones Brothers of Holloway. Strapped for cash and scrapping amongst themselves, the family wanted out. White's Charterhouse Investment Trust brokered a deal whereby both stores were bought by Selfridge's as part of the existing 'Provincial Stores' group. From this evolved White's grand scheme to make his friend a rich man and earn himself a sizeable cut. The retail sector was in favour with the City. Many of London's leading stores had posted good profits – Harrods, Barkers, D. H. Evans, Dickens & Jones and Liberty's all claimed a record year. Only Whiteley's seemed to be suffering. Pre-tax profits at Selfridge's for 1925 stood at £500,000. Selfridge, with his unerring grasp of statistics, was able to tell the media that the store had been dealing with up to 200,000 transactions a day; that it had handled its largest amount of cash sales ever, and that stock had turned over a record number of times.

The department making the most money was perfumery and cosmetics. Pulling out a powder compact to strike a pose had by now become the epitome of sophisticated chic, just as shingled hair, cloche hats, ever-shortening skirts and shiny stockings were now the height of fashion. An astonishing 800 films a year were now coming out of Hollywood, and there was hardly a young woman in the country who didn't follow the fashions set by film star heroines such as Clara Bow, Louise Brooks and Greta Garbo. Elinor Glyn, herself now working in Hollywood, had famously coined the phrase 'The It Girls', which perfectly summed up the brittle mood of the moment. Manufacturers were quick to use the latest synthetic fabrics, now available in a whole range of colours thanks to better-quality industrial dyes, to produce affordable ready-to-wear clothes. Fashion, with all its essential accessories, was no longer merely a perquisite of the rich. It was finally on the move among the masses.

Investors were learning to like the business of fashion and beauty, representing as it did so much spending of disposable income. In

December 1925, an impressive prospectus outlining the formation of the Drapery and General Investment Trust had resulted in over £2 million being raised by its creator, the smooth-talking, high-living businessman Clarence Hatry. Regarded in the City as a 'boy wonder', Hatry had started his career as an insurance broker. He made a fortune in war profiteering and by the 1920s was living in a Mayfair mansion with a swimming-pool in the basement and spending weekends on board the *Westward*, then one of the largest yachts in the country. Clarence Hatry ran a complex clutch of companies under his umbrella vehicle, the Austin Friar Trust, with a peer of the realm – the Marquis of Winchester – on the board to add the requisite cachet.

Hatry's Drapery Trust scheme was centred on family-owned department stores, which were mostly now run by the second or third generation and mainly operated in provincial towns. Though rich in property assets, they often lacked capital for modernization. Such stores represented ripe pickings for Hatry. He took dozens of them into his Trust, promising not just investment but also central buying services, product information and trend reports, management expertise and promotional packages. Within a matter of weeks, Hatry had taken out £1.8 million in charges in a bewildering series of sub-deals and costly service contracts, leaving dozens of stores in limbo and wondering whether it had all been worth it. It would take another four years before Clarence Hatry's world crashed around him but his money-making scheme was the model for Jimmy White in his deal with Selfridge, which they launched in the autumn of 1926.

Selfridge saw in the New Year escorting Fred and Adele Astaire's mother to the ball at the Royal Albert Hall. Busy with plans for his daughter Beatrice's wedding, he eschewed his normal week skating in St Moritz for a quick dash to Cannes where, side by side with Jenny and Rosie Dolly, he watched the epic tennis tournament between Suzanne Lenglen and the American champion Helen Wills. Later that night, despite being ill, Jenny and Rosie took their customary seats at the Winter Casino baccarat table, flanked by a pair of nurses in mufti to pass medicine and brandy. Back in London a day later,

Selfridge walked his daughter up the aisle at the Catholic church in Spanish Place where she married Count Louis Blaise de Sibour.

In May, when the TUC voted to back the depressed and disgruntled miners, the first general strike in British history began. For the miners, already struggling to survive on a few pounds a week, being asked to work longer hours for reduced wages was the last straw. For the public, led by the tabloid press to believe there would be anarchy, the whole event seemed to pass in a haze of anticipation of violence that never materialized. King George V took exception to suggestions that the strikers were 'revolutionaries', saying, 'Try living on their wages before you judge them.' As it turned out, he was right. The strike somehow seemed rather civilized. Enthusiastic volunteers drove the trains. Society ladies like Lady Diana Cooper folded copies of *The Times*, while Lady Louis Mountbatten manned the telephones at the *Daily Express*. At one point, a group of miners were seen playing football with the police. Through it all, the group the *Daily Mail* had dubbed 'The Bright Young People' danced the night away, filling their days and nights with endless fun. When treasure hunts became all the rage, they stormed through Selfridge's, leaping over counters and rushing up and down in the lifts. Selfridge didn't mind. It was good publicity and anyway, the treasure hunters all came from 'good' families.

Selfridge loved hiring people from 'good' or famous families, at one point trying to persuade Arnold Bennett's young nephew to join the firm. 'I don't know about your going to Selfridge's,' Bennett wrote to his nephew, 'it doesn't seem to me a very good idea.' Count Anthony di Bosdari, an old Wykehamist friend of Gordon Jr, was hired to work in the advertising department. Bosdari's claim to fame – other than being a distant cousin of the King of Italy – was that he was the best dancer in London. At a time when dancing really mattered, this was a useful qualification. Count Bosdari's snappy suits and fleet footwork caught the eye of Tallulah Bankhead. Within weeks, the two were engaged, and Bosdari bought his famous bride-to-be an expensive diamond necklace. Not being the kind of girl to keep a man with no money, when the invoice arrived marked for her own attention, she wisely called the wedding off. Despite the publicity – or maybe because of it – her ex-fiancé kept his job. Harrods had recently booked a series of bus posters saying 'Look in at Harrods'. Bosdari suggested booking a series to be pasted alongside them, saying: 'I'd rather look in at Selfridge's' but the Chief reluctantly turned the idea down as being too bold. The Count soon solved his own financial problems when he left to get married, having hooked a rich young Chicago heiress called Josephine Fish.

Anthony di Bosdari was a regular at the Café de Paris, the Embassy, the 43 and the Silver Slipper. By now there were literally dozens of such clubs, all doing a roaring trade. The faster the Home Secretary tried to shut them down, the quicker they reopened. Selfridge's commissioned the BBC 'disc jockey', Christopher Stone, to supervise the selection of top dance hits of the day recorded under the store's own 'Key' record label and pressed by Decca, while within the store, music played as though it would never stop. The young élite adored the ditty written in their honour:

> We mean to spread the Primrose Path
> In spite of Mr Joynson Hicks
> We're People of the Aftermath,
> We're girls of 1926
> In greedy haste, on pleasure bent
> We have no time to think or feel,
> What need is there for sentiment,
> Now we've invented Sex-Appeal?
> We're young and hungry, wild and free,
> Our skirts are well above the knee,
> Come drink your gin, or sniff your snow,
> Since Youth is brief and Love has wings,
> And time will tarnish, 'ere we know
> The brightness of the Bright Young Things.

Before the General Strike, Selfridge's had mobilized a hand-picked team to protect the roof-top radio masts and made plans to transport staff to work in their delivery vans. Even so, Selfridge himself saw no reason to cancel a planned trip for fifty of his buyers to visit top American stores and examine merchandising techniques, generously including W. R. Adams, the store's wines and beverages buyer, in the junket. Quite what Mr Adams hoped to learn in Prohibition America is hard to fathom, but he was graciously received by, among other senior store owners, Bernard Gimbel of Gimbel Brothers, who hosted a jocular 'dry' lunch for the touring group.

By the summer, the Selfridge family were in Deauville, where their father was *à trois* with the Dollies. The two girls were seen in violet wigs and matching violet chiffon and net frocks, and photographed taking a much-publicized dip in swimsuits trimmed with waterproof ostrich feathers. The besotted Selfridge bought each twin a pair of four-carat fine blue diamonds, instructing Cartier to set them on the back of a pair of matched tortoises. The ballet dancer Anton Dolin, dining with the Dollies at Deauville, recalled that after a particularly heavy session at the tables, at which both sisters had 'lost a lot', a beribboned box of pearls for Rosie and a diamond bracelet for Jenny arrived from Selfridge with a note saying: 'I hope these will make up for your losses, darling girls.' Dolin was speechless. '*Your* losses indeed!' he exclaimed to Elsa Maxwell. 'It was *all* Selfridge money!'

By now, the Dollies' stage career had peaked. The previous autumn they had suffered a run-in with the celebrated Parisian 'Queen of the Night' Mistinguett, arguing over their scene in her big revue at the Moulin Rouge. Realizing during rehearsals that they were being parodied in a particular sketch, they pulled out of the show and promptly filed a law suit for 500,000 francs, claiming damages for loss of work and saying that the script wasn't 'worthy of their status' and was demeaning to their reputation. The court case dragged on for a year, with the Dollies ultimately winning a settlement, but it left a bad taste in the theatre world. Just as Selfridge had always said 'never cross a newspaper', so the Dollies should have realized that it was unwise to cross Mistinguett. She got her own back two years later when she discovered a pair of divinely handsome Norwegian drag artists called the Rocky Twins and trained them to perform as the 'Dolly Sisters' to utter perfection. No one, it's said, could tell the difference.

Throughout the spring and summer, Jimmy White had been breezing in and out of the fourth floor inner sanctum at Selfridge's as he, Harry and his son plotted their deal. 'Hello Pop,' White would bawl out on arriving for another cigar-filled, whisky-drinking session. Harry's staff had never, ever heard anyone be that familiar with the Chief and worried at the influence the rash, brash White appeared to have over their boss.

By September 1926, the Gordon Selfridge Trust, in the name of Selfridge and his son, was established. Formed to acquire the ordinary share capital of £750,000 in Selfridge & Co. Ltd, the Trust was capitalized at £2 million, with one million 6 per cent preference shares of £1 each and one million ordinary shares of £1 each. Father and son retained 900,000 of the ordinary shares. The issue was launched in a blaze of the publicity, with the store hosting a fashion show for city investors who watched appreciatively as gorgeous models burst out of giant hat boxes on a flower-decked stage. Selfridge himself chaired the press conference, saying: 'A modern business should aim at building an edifice that will last for ever.' When one reporter had the temerity to ask him how old he was, Selfridge sidestepped the question: 'I retired once at 40. I don't intend to do it again. I've been told by my very conservative business adviser this Trust is the right thing to do.' To believe Jimmy White was a conservative adviser was extraordinarily naïve, but when Selfridge was on a roll, nothing could stop him.

Later that year, the Selfridge dynasty's domain grew still larger when Selfridge Provincial Stores Ltd was launched with capital of £3.3 million. Once again the deal had been put together by Jimmy White and once again, it was over-subscribed. The new company swiftly went on a spending spree, buying the charming and long-established, albeit now run-down store Bon Marché in Brixton, together with

Brixton's second store, Quin & Axten, Holdrons of Peckham, Barrats of Clapham and Pratts of Streatham. The financial press were bemused at the high prices paid to acquire these suburban stores and equally concerned at the guarantee of a 7 per cent dividend on the ordinary shares for ten years. Father and son ignored it all, delighting in the fact they were now rich. At the age of 26, H. Gordon Jr became Managing Director of the Provincial Stores Group, while his father celebrated by installing Otis escalators in the Oxford Street store. He also gave Jenny Dolly a thousand shares in his newly formed business and bought a horse called Misconduct, the first of several steeple-chasers he would acquire from White's Foxhill stables, which raced under the store's distinctive dark green colours. Not to be outdone, Gordon Jr ordered a custom-made teak-decked speed boat he called *The Miss Conduct* and took to piloting his own Gipsy Moth plane when visiting his regional empire.

Early in 1927, the Dollies' much-publicized Paris show *A vol d'oiseau* closed after a run of only eight weeks. In future, their fame would derive from their appearances at the gaming tables where Selfridge was spending more and more time with the dazzling duo, and spending more and more money on them. Jenny's jewels became legendary. Thelma, Lady Furness, a future mistress of the Prince of Wales and no stranger to good jewellery herself, observed Jenny playing the tables at Cannes: 'I have never seen so many jewels on any one person in my life. Her bracelets reached almost to her elbows. The necklace she wore must have cost a king's ransom, and the ring on her right hand was the size of an ice cube.' Cecil Beaton also saw Jenny at work, this time at Le Touquet:

> The greatest thrill in this sensational playground is the vision of Jenny Dolly playing baccarat at the high table. Here is a sight which will go down in history, for in years to come old doddering bores will weary their grandchildren saying I am old enough to remember Jenny Dolly looking rather like a guttersnipe as well as a regal queen, my dears, literally *harnessed* with colossal jewels of incalculable worth, sitting

sphinx-like as she won or lost the most vast of fortunes. Her coolness. Her grimaces, the movements of her arms and her diamond-smothered hands. Her hundreds of cigarettes, cups of tea, coughing and shoulder-shrugging are all part of her 'tableside' manner which has been brought to a pitch of technical perfection. Every other woman pales before her and is silenced in awe of envy!

After the Dollies had effectively retired from show business, Rosie was briefly married to Sir Mortimer Davis's son Morty Jr (who regrettably turned out to be less rich than she had thought), while Jenny divided her time between Jacques Wittouck, the Belgian financier with a bulging wallet, and Harry Selfridge. Between them, they indulged her every whim. She acquired a tumble-down house in Paris which was expensively rebuilt and decorated, and a château at Fontainebleau, where the long hall was lined with softly lit glass jewel cases exhibiting her trophies. Most weekends, Selfridge would take the boat train to France, carrying a two-quart thermos jug filled with Jenny's favourite chocolate ice-cream. He also bought a luxuriously fitted steam yacht called the *Conqueror* which was moored in Southampton Water, permanently crewed and ready for sailing instructions. The trappings of success rested easily on his shoulders. He basked in the adulation of his staff and was lionized by the press as chairman of England's largest retailing business.

When Jimmy White came calling again in 1927, Selfridge welcomed him with open arms. It was a fatal mistake. White's big plan was that Selfridge should buy Whiteley's of Bayswater, which had been ailing for some time. Selfridge knew the property well. It was the store he had most admired on his first trip to London decades earlier. Indeed, he was close to John Lawrie, who had been chairman since old Mr Whiteley had been murdered by his supposed illegitimate son in 1907. Whiteley's two legitimate sons, however, found the prospect of a wealthy retirement alluring. Having invested in a brand-new building, they had spent the last fifteen years presiding over a declining store in a declining area. Bayswater had become dismally run-down, its once elegant properties subdivided into crowded boarding-houses, or lived in by the elderly shabby-genteel. The best-known addresses were those used as drug dens. This was no place to run a smart store.

John Lawrie was close to Jimmy White. Both men knew that Selfridge, for all his apparent self-confidence and his heartfelt passion for retailing, was no hard-nosed businessman. Telling Selfridge that if he bought Whiteley's he would own 'a whole mile of windows' and would, as 'the youngest store-owner in London', have acquired the city's oldest store, White moved in for the kill. Whiteley's was not the oldest store in London (Swan & Edgar had opened in 1812), and Selfridge was no longer young, having just passed his seventieth birthday. But the prospect was irresistible and the deal – reported to have cost £10 million – was done. An official announcement of the takeover was made on April Fool's Day. At the shareholders' meeting a little old lady stood up and asked querulously if Whiteley's annual dividends would remain at 25 per cent. Selfridge assured her that they would and that he would guarantee them for fifteen years. 'She reminded me,' he said rather mournfully some years later, when the real cost of his rash promise had made itself felt, 'of my dear mother.'

By June, Jimmy White was dead. His cut from the Whiteley's deal, however big, hadn't been enough to save his crumbling empire. Having made a desperate gamble on oil shares bought on margin, he lost the last of his money. He ended his life by swallowing prussic acid and left behind a curious suicide note: 'The world is nothing but a human cauldron of greed. My soul is sickened by the homage paid to wealth.' Selfridge, who took his death hard, was one of the few mourners at White's funeral. Another suicide reported in the press just a few weeks later may also have caught his attention. William Jones, whose family business, Jones Brothers of Holloway, was sold to Selfridge in the first deal brokered by Jimmy White, had shot himself, his death attributed to depression.

Leaving his management team with the task of turning round Whiteley's, Selfridge took off for several weeks on a triumphant public relations tour of America. Meanwhile, the company laid on free shuttle buses between Selfridge's and Whiteley's, with singing conductors to cheer up the passengers. But they remained worryingly empty. At Selfridge's Mr Miller, the store's resident architect, was busy with plans to fill in the centre of the main façade, paving the way for the formation of a further eleven acres of floor space. Footfall was up – people had clamoured to see Sir Alan Seagrave's record-breaking Mystery Sunbeam car – but profits were down.

In the autumn of that year, Selfridge was back in America, this time to give a speech at Harvard Business School in celebration of his gift to the Baker Library of his priceless Medici manuscripts. The loss of the beautiful documents didn't seem to worry Selfridge. Much as he had loved them, he enjoyed recognition as an élite donor to Harvard's library more.

That autumn, Isadora Duncan died at the age of 50. She had spent her last pathetically drunken years in Paris and Nice, always hoping she would at last break into films by writing scripts. Certainly, her death was as dramatic as anything on screen – she was strangled by her own chiffon scarf in a car driven at speed by the young, handsome Italian mechanic Benoît Falchetto. She had danced beautifully, and Selfridge loved beauty. At a talk he gave to students at Liverpool University's School of Architecture, he said: 'I will tell you the five most beautiful things in creation. First a beautiful woman. Then a beautiful child. A beautiful flower, a beautiful sunset and … a beautiful building.'

His own beautiful building in Oxford Street was completed in 1928, when the huge cantilevered canopy of bronze and glass, supported by two free-standing Ionic columns set in a vast canopy of Portland stone, was unveiled to an admiring public. An enormous three-ton bell, cast by Gillett & Johnston, was installed high above the parapet, while Sir William Reid's impressive bronze frieze of sculptured panels bordering the rear wall of the loggia won him a silver medal from the Royal Society of British Sculptors. *Architectural Design & Construction* called it 'the most imperial building in London'. For Selfridge, it represented a lifetime's achievement.

Adding to his racing stable, Harry bought the much-fancied Ruddyman (Misconduct, having fallen badly in the Grand National, had had to be destroyed), placing him with Captain Powell's stables at Aldbourne in Wiltshire. Powell also trained Rex Cohen's horses. Cohen, the owner of Lewis's of Liverpool, would meet up with Selfridge at the races and exchange friendly nods and tips. There was always a camaraderie amongst the drapers, although Selfridge was virtually alone in attending John Lewis's funeral in June. The reclusive, miserly old retailer was 93 when he died and left strict instructions that he was to be buried in his wife's unmarked grave, that his staff should not mourn him and that the store should stay open as usual.

John Lewis's death marked the passing of the last of the original London store owners. The men now in charge were younger, more ambitious, more in tune with the rise of consumer society. Most of them took business seriously, and many of them had learned their craft working for Harry Gordon Selfridge. The trouble was, Harry himself was now spending his time playing.

14

~

FLIGHTS OF FANCY

'There is nothing so enthralling as the conduct of a great business. It is the most
fascinating game in the world – and it brings no sorrow with it.'
Harry Gordon Selfridge

Harry Selfridge's favourite time of day was the quiet hour or
so spent with Mr Miller, the store's resident architect, poring
over plans and elevations. Since the early 1920s, bit by bit he had
begun to acquire parcels of land fronting on to both Orchard Street
and Duke Street. The latter area was used as warehousing and
workshop space and was connected to the main store by a tunnel
running under Somerset Street. By 1928, with enough property in
place to create an enormous rear extension, Mr Miller was preparing
detailed applications for planning permission. Wherever possible,
Selfridge bought plots stretching back to Wigmore Street, always
believing that one day he would realize his dream of an entire
'double island' site. By 1930, as his jigsaw puzzle of prime property
pieces increased – finally taking in St Thomas's Church and the old
Somerset Hotel for £100,000 – the Marylebone Works Committee
recommended that the Council accept Selfridge's application for an
initial £3 million scheme to extend fully on the Duke Street side.
As ever with Harry's hopes and dreams, however, there were strange
anomalies. Sometimes he let valuable options lapse. Quite often,
he invested thousands in buying a plot, despite knowing that it was
useless unless he could get space to the left or right and that such
an acquisition might be problematic – one grumpy hairdresser held

out for over twenty years. At other times, he seemed content simply to gaze at the drawings.

It might have been expected that, having become rich, Harry would finally build the castle on Hengistbury Head. Philip Tilden, who by now had completed hundreds of drawings, waited for the call. It never came. Distracted by the Dollies, his yacht, his horses – and his dreams of a triumphant palace in Oxford Street – he let the plans gather dust, leaving seabirds to circle undisturbed over the peaceful cliff top. Each week, flowers were placed on Rose and Lois's graves in the equally peaceful churchyard at St Mark's, and each quarter, the costs of the sexton who tended the plots were paid from the Selfridge family account.

In bustling Oxford Street, where the magnificent front entrance was now installed, Selfridge turned his attention to developing the roof-top space, already used as an exhibition ground and containing the ice-rink. Now it was announced that Selfridge's was creating 'the biggest roof garden in the world', its construction to be masterminded by the urban garden expert Richard Suddell. When it opened over Whitsun in 1929, the beautiful displays stretched the entire length of the roof on Oxford Street, and the heady scent of roses, lavender, thyme and hyacinths filled the air. For the next decade, 30,000 bulbs would be planted each autumn, ensuring a spring flowering of snowdrops, crocuses, tulips and daffodils. The roof housed ornamental ponds, a water garden, a winter garden, a paved vine walk, a cherry tree walk and clematis-covered gazebos. The technical achievement in constructing such beauty was impressive: the earth, rock, stone, turf, fountains and plants required together weighed over 1,800 tons. Plants and bulbs came from the company nursery, installed at the Preston Road staff sports ground, where greenhouses and flower beds were lovingly cultivated by eight gardeners. The roof-top oasis was crowded all day, with restaurant service available for morning coffee, lunch and afternoon tea.

Flowers were an important part of the Chief's persona. He loved giving them and he loved receiving them. Each year, on his birthday in January, the staff would contribute towards vast floral baskets and bouquets, presented with full ceremony to their beaming boss. Not everyone enthused about the whip-round for the ritual, one irate member scrawling 'Balls to Gordon Selfridge' across the message on the staff notice board. Lord Woolton, the Chairman of Lewis's of Liverpool, was not impressed by such excess: 'His room was filled with flowers, as though they had been placed on an altar. He asked me whether my staff in Lewis's paid such testimony to me, and when I said "never a daisy", he said "you ought to give them a hint".' Lord Woolton, whose firm would subsequently acquire Selfridge's in the 1950s, wrote presciently about Selfridge: 'He had commercial vision and courage of a high order, combined alas with personal vanity and pride in being a public figure, which has ruined so many men who have lost a sense of proportion in the exaltation that comes from surrounding themselves with yes-men.'

He was right of course. Tucked away in an archive file is a record of a conversation between Selfridge and a close business friend, John Robertson, the advertising manager of the *Daily Express*. The two men were long-time poker partners, and Robertson had become used to watching Selfridge settle a business deal by flipping a coin. Soon after the group's acquisition of Whiteley's, the normally ebullient Selfridge seemed particularly low, admitting to Robertson that they had uncovered some serious problems ranging from missing inventory to merchandise too old or damaged to sell. Asked if he had made the deal 'subject to contract following a valuer's survey', Selfridge admitted he hadn't done any due diligence: the deal had gone through at speed and on trust. When Robertson suggested Selfridge sue Whiteley's bankers for misrepresentation, the response was: 'No. I cannot do that. It would not make me look very smart to have bought a business without safeguards.' He tackled the problem by asking his old colleague Alfred Cowper – the store's first systems manager – to run Whiteley's and he set up a new joint supply company. But the cracks in the empire were beginning to show.

Early in 1929, Selfridge staged an exhibition of 'English Decorative

Art' at Lansdowne House, opening the event with a charity viewing attended by Queen Mary. A month later the property was sold. One by one, the stately homes of London were being turned into apartment blocks or hotels – the Duke of Westminster's Grosvenor House, the Duke of Devonshire's Devonshire House, the Duchess of Rutland's Arlington House and, most recently, the Earl of Morley's beautiful Dorchester House on Park Lane, which was sold to the McAlpine family for £500,000. It was, as the press remarked, the end of an era. Lord Lansdowne had already sold a vast tract of the garden to the developers of the Mayfair Hotel. Now, tempted by escalating property prices, he sold the house to American developers for £750,000. Selfridge had to move. Addicted to grandeur, he leased the Earl of Caledon's residence, 9 Carlton House Terrace, taking it fully furnished, along with the Earl's staff of fourteen. The society hostess Emerald Cunard had recently moved on to Grosvenor Square, but illustrious neighbours still included the young Prince Aly Khan, the Earl of Lonsdale, the Duke of Marlborough, Lady Curzon and Loel Guinness MP. Selfridge was also treading the hallowed turf of the late Mrs Potter Palmer, who had once lived in the street.

In Carlton House Terrace, Selfridge hosted large post-theatre suppers, served in the newly fashionable buffet style. Each week, a horse-drawn van would arrive from the store with prodigious quantities of food and drink. Store porter Fred Birss was 14 when he was on the Carlton House run, and he later recalled a typical delivery: 'six cases of champagne, a dozen cases of whisky, six turkeys, four hams, 24 lbs of butter, a dozen loaves of bread, two boxes of cigars and several soda siphons'. This was the Monday order. The larder was replenished on Thursday, with smaller deliveries often made daily. Motorized vans also drove down to the Hampshire coast to provision the *Conqueror*. The cost of maintaining the yacht was enormous. In 1928 Selfridge spent nearly £17,000 on her (wages and victualling alone cost £8,264 3s 6d). The yacht was used to ferry the family to Deauville and Le Touquet in the spring and summer, calling in at the Isle of Wight en route, where Selfridge once famously annoyed the

Royal Yacht Squadron by tying up at the Royal buoy. But when he was going to Cannes or Nice, he continued to use *le train bleu*, only occasionally taking a Mediterranean cruise.

Harry's addiction to the Dollies continued. It has been said that he wanted to marry Jenny, although his daughter Rosalie always denied it. But whatever his intentions, he lost his head, possibly his heart and certainly his wallet. They played at Le Touquet, a resort long favoured by the British smart set where by 1929 the casino was reported to be the most profitable in the world. They played at Deauville, a more international, café society sort of place, where Selfridge rented a 'cottage', as the large houses were always called, furnishing it beautifully and indulging the twins' whims by throwing raucous parties which even he sometimes found overwhelming. One guest, present at what he described as 'a pretty riotous affair', later recalled that 'The only restful thing in the place was the furniture and that white-haired old man, sitting all alone on the sofa.'

Above all, the trio gambled at Cannes, where stories of their gaming became the stuff of legend. *Time* reported Rosie winning £32,000 in a single afternoon. On the same day, however, Jenny lost. Down by £4,000, she stayed at the table until she hit a winning streak and finished £45,000 up. But two hours later she apparently lost the lot. The Dollies attracted attention wherever they went. From Cannes, *Vogue* reported: 'When one is tired of dancing, there is the gambling: in the baccarat rooms the Dolly sisters cause the greatest stir, with crowds six deep standing to watch them play. They wear the most *wonderful* diamonds, both with their little jumper suits by day and their sequin capes and feathered helmet hats by night. The sisters shout over the table, inhale a hundred cigarettes and win or lose hundreds of thousands of pounds ... spectators stand dumb with admiration.'

Jenny adored being known for her gambling almost as much as she had enjoyed being known for her dancing. 'If I don't know anything else,' she said gaily to a reporter, having pocketed £5,000 at Biarritz, 'I know *huit* and *neuf*.' The arrangement she had with Selfridge was simple. If she won, she kept the money. If she lost, he covered her debts. The film producer Victor Saville recalled boarding *le train bleu* at Cannes when the Dollies were on the platform waiting to greet Harry, who had boarded at San Remo. Selfridge alighted, hugged the girls, handed them a diamond necklace each, and got back on board. In the dining-car later that evening, he overheard a fellow passenger exclaiming: 'You should have *seen* the Dolly sisters last night. They lost £25,000 in two sessions. I wonder who the silly old fool is who's protecting them? There must be someone, mustn't there?' Saville and Selfridge, heads down, quietly immersed themselves in their dinner.

Very little of this activity ever hit the British press. Given that Selfridge was chairman of a public company, the famous and fashionable chronicler Lord Castlerosse could – maybe even should – have covered the story in his *Sunday Express* gossip column 'Londoner's Log'. But Castlerosse was astute enough never to expose Lord Beaverbrook's friends, who included the Prince of Wales. Not that the Prince wasn't in the press. He was probably the most photographed person in the world at the time, and his every move made news. The British media, however, were loyally discreet about his penchant for married women. By now the Prince's affair with Freda Dudley Ward had ended and he was deeply involved with Thelma Furness.

Frighteningly sophisticated at just 24, the American Thelma and her sisters Gloria (married to Reggie Vanderbilt) and Consuelo (married to Benjamin Thaw, First Secretary at the American Embassy in London) were just the sort of women the Prince of Wales liked – funny, fearless, just a touch fast and charmingly devoid of deference. The Prince liked to dance, to sing along to the latest records, to talk about fashion – a topic that absorbed him almost as much as collecting stamps absorbed his father – but by now he had become disenchanted with touring the world and being on show. While the brusque shipping magnate Viscount 'Duke' Furness spent his days hunting and shooting in Melton Mowbray, his wife Thelma and the Prince of Wales spent their nights out on the town. They dined at the Ritz and danced at the newly fashionable hot-spot, the Café de Paris, where to avoid any hint of scandal they were rarely alone, their innermost circle of friends including the Duff Coopers, the Mountbattens, Prince George, and Major 'Fruity' Metcalfe and his wife, Mary Leiter Curzon's daughter Alexandra.

Weekends were spent at the Prince's newly acquired bolt-hole, Fort Belvedere in Great Windsor Park, where for the first time in his life, he felt truly at home. The Fort was *his* house, not a royal house, and he later admitted to 'loving it like no other material thing'. Thelma Furness loved it too, helping him decorate and working with her lover in the gardens, hacking down overgrown laurels. She claimed to have 'introduced him to the proper delights of Christmas', finding a twelve-foot Christmas tree and shopping at Selfridge's for the baubles: 'Being American they had absolutely the best decorations.' Christmas at Selfridge's was an opulent and emotional affair. The store was decorated throughout and smelt of cinnamon and spices, choirs sang carols, and the staff usually received a bonus along with an ornate card from the Chief.

Thelma also took charge of the Prince's Christmas shopping, buying dozens of presents for his servants and senior staff. Many of them were bought at Selfridge's where the store superintendent, the ever-patient Mr Peters, would escort her around the departments. The ritual went on for several years, the only change being that in due course Lady Furness was replaced by Mrs Simpson. Mr Peters liked Wallis Simpson – 'I found her a very charming lady' – and admitted that they became quite friendly. As the efficient and apparently thrifty Wallis spent three days tackling the task, pen in hand, ticking off items from her lists, he certainly had time to get to know her. Since she lived for a time in Bryanston Square, and later in Cumberland Terrace, Selfridge's was her local shop and Selfridge himself issued instructions that she was to be well looked after.

There was very little the store didn't sell. If something wasn't in stock, someone went out that day to source it. Selfridge's blended tobacco, allocating a special number for repeat orders. In the cloakrooms, attendants polished shoes, changed laces and sewed on buttons – all free of charge. There was a philatelic department so fine it would have impressed even the King. The travel bureau booked journeys by train, boat and plane, organized hotels and even arranged for luggage to be sent on ahead to await its owner's arrival. The information centre answered the most obscure of queries. The store stored, shipped, dry-cleaned and mended customer's clothes, shoes and soft furnishings. Virtually anything could still be made to measure. The switchboard dealt with 40,000 calls a day, and delivery vans covered a million miles a year.

In 1929, invitations went out for the 30 May General Election night party. For the first time, women under 30 were able to vote. Ironically, it was the hated Home Secretary William Joynson-Hicks who had made that possible when, a year or so earlier, in a sparsely attended evening session, he had agreed to a Private Member's Bill that committed the Conservative Party to enfranchising 'men and women on the same terms'. His deed came back to haunt him when, through what came to be known as 'the flapper vote', the Conservatives lost the election. In fairness to the Home Secretary, bigger political issues than his fixation with nightclubs influenced the public. With high unemployment, recriminations about the General Strike, rising prices and, for the first time, a genuine three-party fight between Lloyd George's Liberals, Ramsay MacDonald's Socialists and Stanley Baldwin's Conservatives, it was a tough election.

The election-night party at the store was a wonderful affair. Arnold Bennett arrived early, stayed late and described it all in a letter to his nephew:

> There must have been 2,000 people at that show. There was plenty of room for them, plenty of loudspeakers, two bands and as much Cordon Rouge as the entire 2,000 could drink, besides solid sit-down suppers for all who wanted it. I wanted it. The whole affair was magnificently organised.

Bennett, a socialist, had real cause to celebrate that night. The cartoonist David Low, however, caught glum faces with his pen, and one observer, watching the huge crowds dancing and drinking, reflected as much on the decline in manners as on the loss of Tory seats when he said: 'It is the end of an age. Our World is going out.' Propped up by the Liberals, Ramsay MacDonald returned to No. 10, little realizing what he would soon have to face.

Times were changing fast. What had been modern was suddenly becoming obsolete. As always, film and fashion led the way. Hollywood studios fitted sound stages and dozens of panicking movie stars were sent for voice tests. Many failed. You could take a beauty out of Brooklyn, but even MGM's magic couldn't take Brooklyn out of her voice. Household names vanished overnight and a whole new generation of mellow-toned movie stars filled the screen. In Paris, women wearing short skirts fidgeted in their seats at Patou's show when the designer – who among other celebrities dressed the Dollies and Suzanne Lenglen – launched his longer lengths. Madelaine Vionnet had already introduced her stunning, bias-cut evening gowns – deceptively simple slivers of charmeuse – which, eagerly adopted by Hollywood costume designers, became the quintessential look of the decade to come. For the first time ever, couture collections featured *sportif* daywear. Hermès launched its signature headscarf, and along every smart coastal promenade – to the confusion of many a maître d'hôtel struggling to uphold a dress code – women took to wearing beach pyjamas. As the androgynous, cropped-haired girl of the 1920s evolved into the soignée, sophisticated woman of the 1930s, many mourned her passing. The flapper had, after all, been great fun.

As if signalling the financial catastrophe to come, in September 1929 the police arrested Clarence Hatry, whose business empire – reported to have been worth over £10 million – turned out to have been built on shifting sands. News of the financier's disgrace echoed across the Atlantic, where the Dow Jones – having hit an all-time high – shuddered and fell back. Hatry had been massaging the company books for some time, but now he was caught issuing forged stock certificates. Remanded in Brixton and refused bail, he was sentenced to fourteen years' imprisonment. Some financial analysts predicted the end of the great bull market. Others ignored the warnings at their peril. In October 1929, Wall Street was swimming in debt. By the 29th, it had collapsed and $9 billion dollars was wiped off the stock market in a matter of hours. The impact in America and Europe was not felt by consumers for some months, but major retailers and manufacturers, already jittery about reduced spending patterns, were worried, and with reason. Recession would soon turn into the Great Depression.

In London, the hedonistic lifestyle of the young and carelessly rich came to an end. As if a portent of the misery to come, the winter of 1929 was one of the coldest in history. Hundreds of people died and Kate 'Ma' Meyrick, incarcerated in a freezing Holloway prison cell, developed chronic pneumonia. Selfridge himself refused to panic. He'd lived through enough recessions in America to know what people wanted in time of crisis – on the one hand a bargain and, on the other, a little luxury. The display manager Leslie le Voi was briefed to make the window themes ever more exotic and exciting, featuring everything from newly installed city traffic lights to the world's first television set, Baird's 'televisor'. In February 1930, the store announced record figures, with pre-tax profits of £480,000. Eternally optimistic, Selfridge told *Business* magazine, 'Business is still largely what you make it. By reiterating that business is bad, people hypnotize themselves into a state of apathy. We broke all our past records in fifty-nine departments during October, and almost as many in November. New methods of selling, new channels of distribution, new ways of advertising are transforming our performance.'

By now, mark-downs weren't just on offer in the Bargain Basement but were promoted throughout the store on separate eye-catching 'Bargain Tables'. The tables – tidied by the hour – were never allowed to get tatty. Goods purchased from them were wrapped and tied with the exclusive 'Selfridge knot' just as though they had been bought at full price: those who bought for less were never made to feel cheap. One manager exclusively controlled the reduced stock offerings, coping with what Selfridge himself called 'the peculiar problems of merchandising bargains in every department outside of the traditional sale-time'. The store came of age in March with twenty-first birthday celebrations. Decca records pressed a souvenir disc of massed bands playing 'The March of the Gladiators', while the Chief's gift from his loyal troops was an impressive bronze plaque in his honour, set into the pavement in the main entrance loggia. Worn thin by the footfall, rarely noticed by people pushing to enter the great doors, the plaque is still there, its quasi-religious inscription echoing that of Zola's 'great cathedrals':

> Laid by members of this store in admiration of him
> who conceived and gave it being
> 1909–1930

The store might be 21, but no one, not even his children, really knew how old Harry Selfridge was. 'I don't want to rest,' he said when asked about retirement, 'I want to go on – and on – and on!'

Showing a younger man's enthusiasm for technology – especially aviation – he applauded Amy Johnson at the dinner hosted in her honour by the Hon. Esmond Harmsworth of the *Daily Mail* to celebrate her epic flight to Australia. Selfridge's was by now inexorably linked with aviation, swiftly negotiating rights to display Amy's green De Havilland Moth first in Oxford Street and then at their key provincial outpost, Cole Brothers in Sheffield. The store also launched its very own aviation department, where keen customers could order a bespoke Moth and buy the very latest in everything from flying suits to safety equipment. Studying the feasibility of an autogyro landing-space on the roof, Selfridge commented: 'This is the way the rich will want to come shopping.' For sheer glamour, flying was hard to beat. Lady Heath flew from the Cape to Croydon, as did Lady Bailey, while the redoubtable 64-year-old Duchess of Bedford set off for the Cape in her tiny Spider, saying it 'helped her tinnitus'.

Flight, whether solo or piloted, wasn't without very real danger.

In July 1930, an air taxi carrying the Marquis of Dufferin and Ava, the society hostess Lady Ednam and three others returning from a weekend at Le Touquet, crashed. Broken bits of fuselage – not to mention broken bodies – scattered over a Kent cherry orchard. Reporting the accident, the media showed especial interest in jewels worth £65,000 that were lost in the crash. In October, the giant R101 airship came down, killing Lord Thomson, the Government's Minister for Air, along with forty-five other passengers. Four years later, the by then seasoned pilot, the 'Flying Duchess' of Bedford, took off from Norfolk and was lost at sea.

Harry's daughter Violette and her air-ace husband had flown from Stag Lane aerodrome in 1928 on an adventure to hunt big game, circumnavigating the world in their Moth, *Safari II*. Ignoring the challenges of such an epic journey, the *Daily Mail* excitedly reported that 'Violette Selfridge will fly wearing trousers'. She also packed a lace evening gown and twelve pairs of silk stockings in her luggage – hunting guns and fishing tackle being conveniently shipped ahead by the store.

Violette and her husband returned safely, but her brother Gordon Jr was less fortunate, crashing his Moth into a tree. Apart from a few bruises, only his pride was hurt, but his father insisted he get rid of the plane, putting it up for sale in the store aviation department where it was snapped up for £450 by a young man called Oscar Gardener. After just twenty hours of tuition, Mr Gardener headed for home – in New Zealand. Selfridge devoted a 'Callisthenes' column to the very modest Mr Gardener's amazing achievement, telling awed readers that after a hair-raising journey via Syria and India, he landed safely in Western Australia before crossing to Sydney, thereafter shipping his rather bruised and battered Moth home to Christchurch. By the middle of the decade, however, the adventures of the lone aviator were coming to a close and with them the store's short-lived aviation department. The rickety, reckless charm of the 'string and sticks' light aeroplane had had its day. Stronger machines were on their way, destined to play their part in a war.

Retailing of a different kind was preoccupying Harry Selfridge. Jenny Dolly had opened a lingerie shop on the Champs-Elysées in Paris. This was no ordinary boutique but rather an astonishing blend of boudoir brash, glitz and glamour. Pink-gilt bedroom furniture created by the designer and artist Jean-Gabriel Domergue included a mirrored bed considered glamorous enough even for Jenny who, according to *Variety*, 'knew a thing or two about beds'. Exquisitely embroidered bed-linen was said to have 'kept a couple of convents working for months', while the display of intimate apparel – wispy pieces of black chiffon, silk stockings and a fine selection of jewelled garter belts – was 'enough to make you think sinful thoughts'. Harry was seen beaming broadly at the opening night party, while the guests sipped gin slings and dunked salt crackers in caviar, and Selfridge's star mannequin, Gloria, wafted through in silks, satin and lace, a chinchilla coat casually flung over her shoulders, and Jenny's fabled black pearls, once owned by Gaby Deslys, round her neck.

'Glorious Gloria', as the press called her, had been under contract to Selfridge's for four years. The most successful commercial model of her era and the original catwalk star, she was the first 'Ovaltine Girl', and her image was printed on posters and postcards throughout the country. When Gloria appeared in the Palm Court fashion shows, she caused a sensation, not least because when she posed, smothered in jewels and furs, the press office would hire bodyguards for her photo-calls – as much to protect her as what she was wearing. Among the staff it was rumoured that she had an affair with the Chief. They were certainly close, and as 'the face of the store' she accompanied him at dozens of events, everything from air-shows to premieres. Whatever their earlier relationship, however, in the early 1930s they were simply good friends. Besotted by Jenny Dolly, however cruel, casual or calculating she might be, Harry always came back begging for more.

During the opening week of Jenny's boutique, Gloria stayed at her Paris town house and in a 'girls together' moment shared Jenny's bedroom. Each morning, Selfridge would knock, and come in in his silk dressing-gown, carrying a breakfast tray. He'd then sit on the edge of Jenny's bed, butter her toast, pour coffee and chat about the shop and plans for lunch as though none of them had a care in the world. Sometimes Jenny would smile. At other times she'd violently push away the tray, yelling at him to get out. Mario Gallati, the famous restaurateur who ran the Caprice and the Ivy, was fond of Selfridge, who had dined there for years, 'dominating the table, erect and stern, looking every inch the formidable tycoon'. It was a different story when he was with Jenny, whose tantrums were well known at the Ivy. 'Mr Selfridge would ring me up before bringing her to dine, ordering the most elaborate meals and the finest vintage wines. All Jenny's favourites were prepared for her – then she'd decide to have a hamburger.' According to Mario, 'Selfridge was like a gauche schoolboy with her. When she made a scene, going off in a huff, he would sit there, eyes downcast ...'

As the Depression took hold, Jenny's de luxe lingerie shop haemorrhaged money. At Selfridge's, things were little better. Selfridge, faced with a weekly wages bill of £155,000, refused to cut costs. The staff repaid him by offering to work until 7 p.m. without overtime – a gesture which thrilled Selfridge as much as it annoyed the hierarchy at the National Union of Shop Assistants. Defying the Depression, with his usual sangfroid he urged local and regional investment. 'Let's make Marble Arch the focal point of an avenue as magnificent as the Bois de Boulogne,' he told the *Daily Chronicle*, while suggesting that councillors in Brighton should 'dream a future' for the town by opening cafés and restaurants and making it 'more tourist friendly'. In the meantime, money was tight. Harry sold over 300 acres of Hengistbury Head to Bournemouth Council, with the proviso that they would never build on it, but retained 33 acres – complete with planning permission – for future use himself. Store profits were down. Trade suppliers, already used to slow payments from Selfridge's, now had to wait longer and longer.

In 1931, the store celebrated the installation of 'The Queen of Time', a magnificent eleven-foot-high bronze statue flanked by winged figures symbolizing Progress and surmounted by a stupendous clock. Designed by the sculptor Gilbert Bayes and the store's architect Albert Miller, 'The Queen' was hailed as a 'horological masterpiece'. *Lilliput* magazine thought otherwise, printing a little ditty:

Hickory-dickory-dock, a mouse ran up Selfridges' clock
It didn't expect such a bizarre effect and it never got over the shock.

While the Chief's watch was five minutes fast, it was always said that the store clocks were kept five minutes slow, though the management later denied it. On the wall near the Information Bureau was a row of accurate clocks, each showing the time in a capital city overseas and part of what was described as the store's 'time-honoured tradition of keeping customers informed on all things of interest'. Time had run out for many of Harry's friends, however. Sir Thomas Lipton, the America's Cup challenger who was only granted membership of the Royal Yacht Squadron in his old age, died without ever setting foot in the place. Harry's old flame Anna Pavlova died of pleurisy in January 1931 at the untimely age of 45. Arnold Bennett was also dead. Harry missed him greatly. Ever since Bennett had written his early novel, *Hugo: A Fantasia on Modern Themes*, loosely based on a combination of Harrods and Whiteley's, Selfridge had hoped he would write about the store. He wasn't alone. Trevor Fenwick, of Fenwick's of Newcastle, also lobbied Bennett in 1930. The author replied: 'The idea of writing a novel about a department store has suggested itself to me many times during the past ten years. Mr Selfridge has offered to place the whole of his establishment at my disposal, and has urged me to do such a novel. But I do not think I shall ever write it ... I have had enough of these vast subjects.' There may not have been a book, but there would be a film, when the producer Victor Saville used the store as the live background for his film *Love on Wheels*, made in 1932.

Time had also run out for Ramsay MacDonald. Faced with a tidal wave of unemployment – two and a half million by the end of 1930 – and having reached a deadlock over the financial crisis engulfing Britain, MacDonald was persuaded to form a National Government. With the Conservatives pressing for a public mandate and MacDonald himself being expelled from the Labour Party, the only solution was a General Election. In October 1931, the country headed for the polls again, and Selfridge's, true to form, put on a party. Jenny Dolly flew in to be at Harry's side when he received over 3,000 guests in the store. The store's Sales Director Mr Williams recalled that 'Jenny wore bracelets on both arms from wrist to elbow. As she moved, they flashed prismatic lights from emeralds, rubies, sapphires and diamonds.' Winston Churchill, C. B. Cochran, Emerald Cunard, Prince and Princess Galitzine, the Rajah of Sarawak, Noël Coward, Prince and Princess von Bismarck and a rather sozzled Rosa Lewis escorted by Charlie Cavendish were among the crowd who danced to Jack Hylton's orchestra and were entertained by Cossack dancers, Jimmy Nervo and Teddy Knox of the Crazy Gang, and the Australian jugglers and gymnasts, the Rigoletto Brothers.

When the votes were counted, the Conservatives had 470 seats, Labour 52 and the Liberals 33. As the National Government's Prime Minister, MacDonald spent the next four years isolated from his colleagues and at the beck and call of the Conservatives. Among a rash of new, independent political parties that had put up candidates at the election, Sir Oswald Mosley's New Party failed to win a single seat. Undeterred, the Mosleys were among the guests at the election-night party, where Lady Cynthia – as with all Levi Leiter's granddaughters – was always assured of a warm welcome. Sir Oswald seemed to have an unerring attraction for the Curzon women, marrying one, sleeping with both her sisters and rumoured to have had an affair with their step-mother. In troubled times, Sir Oswald attracted support from some who responded to his rabble-rousing speeches. Selfridge himself, grumbling at an American Chamber of Commerce luncheon about trade tariffs, government intervention and red tape, declared: 'What the country needs is a strong leader, an inspirer.'

Puzzling contradictions were a Selfridge trait. In support of a massive 'Buy British' campaign launched by the Prince of Wales, he invited the Mayor and Master Cutler of Sheffield to exhibit in London, giving them 6,000 square feet to display the city's steel products. At the same time, however, he filled the store's front windows with a million pounds' worth of diamonds, presented in burglar-proof showcases. Quite what prompted Selfridge to promote himself as the 'King of Bling' when unemployment was rife is hard to fathom. People were looking – 27,000 crowded into the store to watch the American Bridge champion Ely Culbertson's team play the British champion 'Pops' Beasley in a sound-proofed room and nearly as many watched the 'Miss England' contest staged at Selfridge's – but they weren't buying much. Figures were down. There were murmurings in the City as well as rumours of Selfridge's excessive losses at the gaming tables in France.

By now Jenny Dolly's foray into fashion had failed. The closure of her shop also marked the end of her relationship with Harry Selfridge. On a misty morning in March 1933, she crashed her car near Bordeaux, fracturing her skull and badly disfiguring her face. Her career as a femme fatale was finished and her famous jewels went up for auction that autumn to raise money for, among things, major plastic surgery. They only fetched $300,000, with Jenny tearfully acknowledging that 'people got beautiful things for next to nothing'. Among the treasures that went were the black pearls once worn by Gaby Deslys and the 'ice cube' 51.75 carat diamond bought for Jenny by Harry Selfridge in 1928.

In London, Harry's own financial affairs made waves when, at a troubled annual general meeting, an irate shareholder asked about the 'Chairman's Account' which owed £154,791 to the company. Selfridge stood up and said: 'I will reduce the matter as soon as possible. I admit I have been wrong.' The trouble was he couldn't reduce it. He also owed money to the Greek Syndicate, where even Nicolas Zographos wasn't immune to the Depression. A lot of Zographos's high rollers had faded away. Major Jack Coats had committed suicide in his Park Lane apartment and others no longer travelled to gamble. With casino earnings throughout France down 75 per cent, the Syndicate sold on their debts. For Selfridge, this was a situation fraught with danger. Whatever he owed – and it's rumoured to have been over £100,000 – was now being chased by extremely hard men. Liquidating assets, he sold his remaining parcel of land on Hengistbury Head and, in a move that alarmed his Board of Directors, he claimed thousands of pounds in arrears of salary for his titular role as Chairman of Whiteley's, a store he rarely even visited. His daughter Rosalie, who had hoped he would cover their heavy mortgage on Wimbledon Park House, was destined to be disappointed. The bank foreclosed on the Wiasemskys, forcing their return to Carlton House Terrace. Gordon Jr meanwhile continued to live the high life, his photograph appearing in *Tatler* either alongside his plane or alongside a beautiful woman, such as the actress Anne Codrington. Staff would shake their heads, murmuring 'like father, like son'.

Financial catastrophe was claiming more and more victims. Ivar Kreuger, the store's original construction engineer who had subsequently become an industrialist known 'as the richest man in the world', killed himself rather than face accusations of fraud to manipulate the markets. Yet few outsiders observing the apparently seamless operations at Selfridge's would have guessed there was trouble. For the architects and builders who had been working on the new Duke Street extension it was another matter. The extension had originally been planned to have four storeys above ground and two below. Now, because of financial constraints, it stopped at the first floor, albeit reinforced to allow for higher storeys that came later. Work on site being too slow to satisfy Selfridge, he came up with the original idea of using explosives. Half a pound stick of gelignite did the trick nicely, blasting ten tons of clay effortlessly out of the way.

The extension, which used 5,000 tons of Middlesbrough steel to create three and a half acres of extra floor space, finally opened in March 1933. It was nicknamed the SWOD by staff because it encompassed Somerset, Wigmore, Orchard and Duke Streets. The low flat roof was put to good use: Lord Clydesdale's Westland PV-3, which he had triumphantly flown over Mount Everest, went on show, and Suzanne Lenglen arrived in town to demonstrate her skills on the newly fitted *En-Tout-Cas* court. Suzanne and Selfridge's relationship was as tempestuous as her tennis. The Chief's personal store messenger, the teenage Ernest Winn, recalled having to deliver a letter from Selfridge to Miss Lenglen's rented flat nearby. 'She finished reading and started to scream and scream … I didn't know what to do … so I just stood there, watching and waiting. I was pleased I was so small the way she was swinging her arms about, I might otherwise have been decapitated.'

Selfridge continued to 'put on a show'. He spent excessively on advertising. He became a financial patron of the new Business School at Harvard University. He chartered an Imperial Airways four-engined plane for an aerial VIP New Year's Eve party with a live in-flight fashion show. He stabled horses that didn't win races and, very charmingly – given he couldn't afford it – he paid Messrs Gillett & Johnston to replace the fabled Great Bell of Bow, which, having rusted beyond repair, had been silent since 1928.

The store celebrated its Silver Jubilee in 1934. *Draper's Record* wrote: 'He has not merely transformed Oxford Street into one of the world's finest shopping centres, he gave a lead to the entire store trade.' At a banquet hosted in his honour by fellow-traders in the borough of St Marylebone, held at the Grosvenor House Hotel, Harry was presented with a beautifully illuminated 'Book of Signatures' containing a heartfelt message: 'From the first you have been a pioneer, and, even in difficult and disheartening times, have had the courage to go forward. Your energy and enterprise have brought fame to your firm, and have added to the prosperity of the community.' Behind his glasses, Harry Selfridge's eyes filled with emotion.

The year 1935 marked another Silver Jubilee, that of King George V and Queen Mary. Selfridge busied himself planning another set of majestic external decorations, much as he had done so for their Coronation. They were utterly magnificent and they cost a fortune. Created by the noted architect and graphic designer William Walcot and the store's own resident design expert, Albert Miller, their theme was 'Empire'. A huge statue of Britannia towered 80 feet above the roof top, attended by two golden lions, flags flew and trumpeters blew.

In one of his many interviews with the *Daily Express* Selfridge had said: 'It isn't the making of money that's the chief motive with me. It's the great game that's the thing. There is nothing so enthralling as the conduct of a great business – it's the most fascinating game in the world – and it brings no sorrow with it.'

Unfortunately, the making of money *was* the chief motive of one of the company's major shareholders – the Prudential Assurance Company. To them, retailing wasn't a game, it was a business. Disturbed not merely by falling profits but by the profligate extravagance of Mr Selfridge, the 'men from the Pru' decided they had to put a man on the Board. They found him in Mr H. A. Holmes, who for many years had laboured diligently at the Midland Bank before becoming the finance director of the India Tyre and Rubber Company. Little did Selfridge know just how much sorrow he would bring.

15

~

OVER AND OUT

'Tis better to have loved and lost than never to have loved at all.'
Alfred, Lord Tennyson

In early October 1935, Harry headed for America. His support for Harvard had not gone unnoticed by Dr Silas Evans, the enterprising President of Ripon College, Wisconsin, who had awarded Harry an honorary doctorate. Accompanied by his daughter Violette, Harry was royally fêted in the town of his birth, and at a civic luncheon held in his honour, Mayor Harold Bumby announced the renaming of a special town recreation space as 'Selfridge Park'. Ripon's newspapers made much of the visit and described Harry's successful career in great detail. Being less certain about the status of the pneumatic young blonde accompanying him, they merely described her as 'a family friend'.

A few days later, when Selfridge arrived in Los Angeles, *Time* magazine revealed his companion to be the 'French-Swedish actress Marcelle Rogez, who Harry Gordon Selfridge was intending to bring to the notice of Hollywood'. Miss Rogez, Harry's latest – and last – serious love interest, had great ambitions for a Hollywood career. Observing them lunching together at 20th Century Fox, the film gossip-columnist Louella Parsons wrote: 'The elderly, yet venerable-looking Mr Selfridge had such beautiful manners. He stood when Marcelle got up, pulling back her chair, bowing slightly to her at the end of the meal, walking out behind her – showing old world courtesy rarely seen in this town anymore these days.'

It was reported that Harry was hoping to raise finance on his trip. If that was so, he was destined for disappointment. To American bankers in the midst of the Great Depression, Selfridge represented a bygone era of 'success through excess' in retailing investment. With promotional budgets stripped to the bone, spending money to make money had become unfashionable.

Back in London, and accompanied by the pulchritudinous Miss Rogez, he hosted another election-night party. The eclectic guest list was, as always, a masterful combination of politics, Fleet Street, society and show business. Friends like Lord Beaverbrook, Winston Churchill and Lord Ashfield were joined by Douglas Fairbanks Jr, Noël Coward, Ivor Novello, the actress Madeleine Carroll (fresh from her role in the film of John Buchan's *The Thirty-Nine Steps*), and the Duke and Duchess of Roxburghe. The President of the Royal Aero Club, Sir Philip Sassoon, escorted the rabidly right-wing and very rich Lady Houston, whose enthusiasm for aviation was eclipsed only by her enthusiasm for Benito Mussolini. The fashion designer Elsa Schiaparelli put in an appearance, as did the interior designer Elsie de Wolfe and, surprisingly, Syrie Maugham. The party went on into the small hours. To Lady Londonderry's dismay, her almost inseparable companion Ramsay MacDonald lost his seat, and Stanley Baldwin returned to power as Prime Minister. It was the last election-night party that the store would host.

Missing from his life was Harry's old friend Lord Riddell, Chairman of the *News of the World*, who had died a year earlier. Selfridge had been full of admiration for his boisterous newspaper. In 1933, he had helped broker a deal between the store model Gloria and the *News of the World*, who serialized her racy 'top model memoirs' for an 'undisclosed sum'. It wasn't the first project they had worked on. On one occasion, Selfridge's had sponsored a fashion design competition run by the *World*, offering a cash prize and promising to showcase the winner's outfit in the store. A panel of designers and stage celebrities met in the Palm Court for the judging session and a lunch, at which the actress Sybil Thorndike had agreed to present the prize.

Unfortunately, she hadn't learned her lines. Standing up to make her speech, she gushingly enthused: 'This is the most wonderful event. But then, I have always thought that the *Sunday People* is the most wonderful newspaper ever published.' As the unstoppable Miss Thorndike continued to eulogize the *News of the World*'s bitter rival, Lord Riddell sat frozen faced, quietly decimating his bread roll.

Newspaper editors were allocating an increasing amount of space to reporting on fashion, which in itself was receiving an enormous boost from the cinema as women sought to emulate the glamour they saw on the silver screen. Ready-to-wear clothing was now widely available, and copies of work from designers such as Balenciaga swept into the shops, Madge Garland of *Vogue* observing, 'Coats admired in the February Paris collections can be found this autumn at Jaeger.' Those who couldn't afford to buy what they wanted bought the best-selling paper patterns of all the new silhouettes from Paris. Fortunately for retailers, there was still a clear divide between day and night: women dressed for dinner, wore the ubiquitous 'little black dress' for cocktails, pinned diamanté dress clips to their necklines and wouldn't dream of leaving the house without wearing a hat and gloves. The bias cut, the pyjama suit and cruise-wear were all the rage, while the daring adopted Elsa Schiaparelli's surreal style. Admittedly, not every shopper in Selfridge's took to her cheeky chapeaux with a lobster perched on top, but her influence, in everything from hand-knit swimsuits to ornate embroidery and even fantasy buttons, was unde-niable. Intent on outstripping her bitter rival Coco Chanel, 'Scap' was planning her own perfume. Called 'Shocking' and seductively packaged in a bottle based on Mae West's curves, it was launched in 1936 and showcased at Selfridge's.

The 1930s also marked a new era in that profitable department store staple, underwear. Dunlop's chemists had managed to transform latex rubber into a reliable elastic thread, which was in turn trans-formed into the girdle. With entire new ranges of underpinnings on the market – including Warner's first 'cup-sized' brassiere – manufac-turers hastened to claim that corsetry fitting had become a 'scientific' art and trained saleswomen to fit and measure accurately. So seriously did women take to this system that the process of acquiring new underwear could now take an hour or more. Gossard launched their 'Gossard Complete', a boneless foundation garment that could be worn under a backless evening gown, which, since it fastened with side hooks and bars, was promoted with the appealing copy-line 'No maid required.' Only the rich or those lucky enough to have a devoted family retainer still had a personal lady's maid. Meanwhile, thanks to labour-saving devices such as electric cookers, lighter-weight vacuum cleaners and improved washing-machines, domestic tasks could be handled without an army of servants. This was probably just as well, because not only could most people no longer afford to hire them, but young girls no longer wanted to be parlour maids: instead they took jobs as cinema usherettes or waitresses or worked behind the ever-expanding cosmetics counters in department stores.

Selfridge and his store were hardly ever out of the press. In the autumn of 1935 he was profiled in depth by *Reader's Digest* and his 'official' biography, sympathetically written by William Blackwood, was serialized in Chicago's *Saturday Morning Post* and thereafter in England in *The Passing Show*, a once successful but now somewhat ailing society features magazine. Neither the magazine's title nor its diminishing status was lost on the new member of the Board, Mr Holmes, who watched all this self-aggrandizement with unease, later saying: 'Selfridge wanted to go on being king of his own castle, even though it was beginning to tumble.'

There was, in the beginning at least, very little Andrew Holmes could do, other than watch – and wait. He made his own tours of the store, fretted over the payroll of the group's 15,000 employees, queried expenses and sat in on board meetings at which Selfridge would blithely state, 'Minutes agreed unless objected to – business closed,' before ushering everyone out of his office. If Selfridge felt uneasy about Mr Holmes, he didn't show it. Confident that he carried a majority vote, he simply ignored him. By and large Harry's life – within the store at least – continued as before. Staff were summoned to his presence by a twinkling trio of bright blue lights, part of a clever internal security system set up throughout the store. He toured each morning, and again in the afternoon. Miss Rogez continued to shop until she dropped. Most importantly, plans went ahead for the relo-cation of the food hall from the site on the far side of Oxford Street to custom-designed space in Orchard Street. Just before Christmas 1935, Selfridge went to inspect progress on the new site. Gazing up at workmen painting the ceiling, he took a step forward and toppled twelve feet from the edge of the floor on to scaffolding below. At first, witnesses thought he was dead, but he escaped with little more than concussion and a bruised hip, though he was confined to bed for a week. That Christmas, as the health of the King rapidly deterio-rated and he too took to his bed, for the second year running Wallis Simpson arrived at Selfridge's to do the seasonal gift shopping for the Prince of Wales.

King George never recovered, dying at Sandringham on 20 January 1936. His son David, now King Edward VIII, continued to go dancing with Wallis, herself by now a glittering example of Cartier's skill, wearing priceless stones remounted in ultra-modern settings. Their venue of choice was still the Embassy Club, where not much had changed either except the music. Syncopated jazz had been eclipsed by the 'swing time' sound as perfected by Benny Goodman's orchestra and by the show songs of Rogers & Hart, Noël Coward and Cole Porter. The new King-Emperor could still be seen at the Ritz and the Savoy, and he still went to stay with his close-knit circle of friends, but increasingly he spent most of his time at his beloved Fort Belvedere, deluding himself that he could marry Wallis Simpson and keep his throne. The British press continued to be discreet, despite the Court Circular revealing that in June 'Mrs Simpson' was present at a dinner party held at St James's Palace – Mr Simpson being tactfully elsewhere.

That summer, Wallis and the King went on a Mediterranean cruise aboard the luxury steam yacht *Nahlin*, but there was no cruising for the Selfridge family. Harry had had to sell the *Conqueror*. He had also moved house, departing reluctantly from Carlton House Terrace and moving into an apartment in Brook House on Park Lane, where, ironically, Syrie Maugham was busy decorating another sumptuous flat belonging to Mr and Mrs Israel Sieff of Marks & Spencer. Brook House had been built on the site of the mansion owned by Harry's old friend Ernest Cassel, which had subsequently been sold to developers by his granddaughter, Edwina Mountbatten. The Mountbattens themselves had moved into their much-photographed thirty-room penthouse, accessed by a high-speed lift, in June. Making plans to install Marcelle Rogez in an apartment nearby, Harry oversaw the decoration himself, becoming the bane of the builders and exhausting his private secretary Leslie Winterbottom, who struggled to cope with the Chief's demands. Top of his wish-list was a black bath, which proved hard to find. Making daily visits to the flat to check on progress, Selfridge badgered the foreman in charge of the search. 'Now, look here, Sir,' he replied, 'it isn't that easy. But if you want to put a black lady in here, we'll soon find a white bath for her.' The joke was lost on Harry, who returned to the store demanding that Winterbottom change the builders.

Earlier that year, Selfridge's had put on an ornate display to celebrate its twenty-seventh birthday, lighting up the exteriors with an enormous 2-ton rotating globe. Gifts such as silver keys or oak seedlings had always been given out to celebrate special anniversaries (Selfridge himself called them tokens of esteem), but this time customers were merely handed morsels of an enormous birthday cake. In June, shoppers surged into the newly opened food hall. By the time the doors closed, a central display of tinned salmon had been so depleted by shoplifters that only a dozen or so cans remained. The staff dithered about telling the Chief, who loathed the very mention of theft. When in the end they did, Miss Mepham recalled that 'the news rather crushed him. He simply couldn't believe the worst of his fellow man.' Whether due to the endless promotions, the new food hall or the increase in summer holiday shopping as travellers headed to sunnier shores, business that year picked up considerably, resulting in a year-end net profit of £485,000.

Neither Selfridge nor his son was accustomed to restraint. Gordon Jr bought himself a new plane, which *Time* magazine reported as having cost $45,000. He flew his expensive toy to Spain – at that time in the midst of a bitter civil war – taking the de Sibours along for the ride. Lacking his father's finesse in handling the press, his interview with *Time* on his return rather backfired, his escapade being described as 'Sportsman Selfridge having swank fun'. It was also noted that he had stayed safely the other side of the border when Jacques de Sibour courageously returned to rescue thirty stranded American tourists the following day. Whether the trip was wise or foolish, Mr Holmes clearly didn't like it, any more than he liked Gordon Jr flying around the country on business trips. Mr Holmes believed in taking the train.

With the date of Edward VIII's Coronation set for May 1937, and curiously ignoring the gossip about the King and Wallis, Harry started to make plans to deck the façade with the most sumptuous decorations London had ever seen. Exactly as with King George V's Coronation and subsequent Jubilee, he spent hours at the College of Heralds, poring over every detail.

Harry was now 80. He had always believed his mental agility would push back the years, and to an extent it did; but physically he was in decline. At a film premiere at the Regal Cinema in Marble Arch he fainted. When press photographers caught the moment, his embarrassment was made public in the *Daily Sketch*. Just a few weeks later he fell heavily while trying to vault a roped stanchion in the store's restaurant. His own trusted senior staff were also becoming old. Some, like the endlessly discreet Mr Hensey in Accounts and the urbane jewellery buyer Mr Dix, who had recently presided over the opening of England's first store counter selling Mikimoto cultured pearls, retired. Others, like Freddie Day who had spent his career buying trunks and luggage, died. The Chief's trusted confidant, A. H. Williams, left to open his own advertising agency which failed to perform as he had hoped: Williams later ruefully admitted that 'It was Selfridge who made us what we are.' The architect Sir John

Burnet died. Ralph Blumenfeld suffered a bad stroke and spent less and less time in Fleet Street. Lord Ashfield too was ill with a severe eye complaint. Selfridge wrote to Blumenfeld:

> I wish dear fellow you were well enough to come to America with me this autumn. Albert [Lord Ashfield], as you know, seems much improved after treatment in France. So, of the Three Musketeers, when Albert gets in good shape, two of us will pull you around and we will again be ready for the fray. Your friend, Harry.

Selfridge always attended funerals, wrote kindly letters to widows and sent flowers and fruit to the sick. He even visited an incurably ill retiree every week to play a game of cards. The store and its staff meant everything to him. Walking the vast acreage with Williams a few months earlier, the Chief said poignantly: 'This is our life, without it we are nothing.'

Children pouring on to the store roof for the arrival of Father Christmas that year were enchanted when he flew into town in his own aeroplane, triumphantly making a low loop-the-loop above them. Just a few minutes later, as if by magic, he appeared in a vast motor sleigh, riding up Oxford Street waving a star-spangled banner, and bringing the traffic to a standstill. By the time he emerged with his sack from a faux chimney built on the roof, the mesmerized youngsters were beside themselves with excitement. The performance, honed to perfection over the years, ran like a well-oiled machine. It was all very charming – not to mention profitable – and was repeated, albeit less elaborately, in all the Selfridge group stores. Usually, the Chief himself attended many of these performances, but this year he was confined to bed after an accident in which a fire-engine crushed his Rolls-Royce. He therefore missed a visit to Jones Brothers in Holloway. It was probably just as well. That year, Father Christmas ran amok, swinging his fists instead of his sack, and started to beat the children over the head.

The panic in the toy department at Jones Brothers was nothing to that in the display department at Selfridge's where ornate banners, hand-embroidered in gold thread with the insignia of the new King, had been arriving from specialist workshops charged with the task of producing perfection. The trouble was no one knew what to do with them.

On 3 December Wallis Simpson had awoken to find her photograph emblazoned across the front pages of every newspaper in England. People were aghast. Was *this* the woman their King wanted to marry? The press had worked hard to create an image of a blue-eyed Prince Charming. Now, led by the implacable *Times* Editor Geoffrey Dawson, they set about destroying him. They also set about destroying Wallis Simpson. On 10 December, after weeks of speculation and frenzied press reports, the King abdicated. Angry protestors stoned Wallis's house in Cumberland Terrace while she frantically packed her suitcases and trunks. That evening, under the cover of darkness, the trunks were transported to Selfridge's where Ernest Winn supervised their stacking in a corner of the dispatch department. Recalling that curious moment of history in the making, he later said: 'We were told to keep things quiet and not tell anyone what we had in Despatch … some special people were coming to collect it in a few hours. As we were roping it all up, some of the messenger boys were unhappy. It wasn't so hard to understand … we didn't want to lose our King. When we'd finished with Mrs Simpson's luggage we just stared at each other sadly.'

Harry Selfridge spent a miserable Christmas, comforted only by his faithful pug dogs and attended by his dutiful daughter Rosalie who, along with Serge and Tatiana, was also living in Brook House. Mr Priestley, his favoured barber from the store, came over each morning at 9.00 a.m. to shave him, Rosalie slipping him 5 shillings on his way out. He didn't even have Marcelle Rogez for company. She had been cast in the British-made musical *Big Fella* and was now busy filming with Paul Robeson.

At the store, the Coronation decorations had to be changed. Out went the insignia of King Edward VIII and in came those of King

George VI and Queen Elizabeth. Carved panels celebrated England's history since the Roman invasion and the exploits of national heroes such as Drake, Clive and Wolfe. Selfridge believed passionately that the Coronation would be 'the event of all times' to lift London out of its gloom, and the decorations took on an almost mystical meaning for him. Supremely confident that hundreds of thousands of people would flock into town, all of them keen to buy new clothes and souvenirs, he restocked the store and hired extra display staff. The resident architect Albert Miller, the sculptor Sir William Reid Dick and Professor Ernest Stern – a Romanian film production designer with a *tendre* for gilded opulence – created the most extraordinary scheme that Oxford Street had ever seen. Selfridge's became the most decorated building in Britain.

Harry had spent a colossal £50,000 on the pageantry, but not everyone appreciated the result. E. M. Forster wrote scathingly in the *New Statesman*, 'The decorations reminded me of nothing so much as a vulgar old woman, who has trotted out every scrap of her finery for an unaccustomed airing,' while *Punch*, playing on the 'more royal than the royals' décor, ran a cartoon showing a policeman telling an elderly lady: 'No Madam, I understand Mr Selfridge will not be appearing on his balcony tonight.'

Hundreds of thousands did visit London and many of them blocked Oxford Street to gaze in awe at the store. But they didn't spend their money. Takings were nowhere near expectations. Perhaps hurt by the insults hurled at Wallis, the Americans simply didn't come, and the British weren't in the mood to buy – it was almost as if they were grieving at having been rejected by the man they had idolized. For a while at least, his brother was simply second-best. It took six weeks to dismantle the finery, which was packed away and stored in the sub-basement. Selfridge himself remained tight-lipped, while Mr Holmes was infuriated by the cost of it all. The two men were now barely speaking to each other.

That same month, Harry Gordon Selfridge became a naturalized British citizen. Some said it was because he hoped for an honour in the King's Coronation list; others murmured about new, onerous American taxes imposed on Americans living abroad. Those closest to him knew it was simply because he wanted to become British. He wrote proudly to his friend Blumenfeld: 'It is 31 years next Sunday since I came to London. Now I will be a true Briton and now I shall have to try to begin to act like a gentleman. As ever, Gordon.'

He had, of course, always behaved as a gentleman – never more so than in 1927 when he had promised a little old lady that Whiteley's would pay a guaranteed 25 per cent dividend for the next fifteen years. His promise had cost him dear. A decade later, the annual figure had reached £500,000. Profits were down. People were beginning to worry about the prospect of war. As the share price of the Gordon Selfridge Trust and Selfridge Provincial Stores Ltd declined, *The Economist* wrote: 'Selfridge Group prospects have occasioned special concern.' Harry went to America, ostensibly to launch the publication of his now famous 'Callisthenes' column in the *New York Herald Tribune* but also to see bankers. His old friend Jules Bache was uncharacteristically gloomy about trading prospects, and Elizabeth Arden, with whom he lunched, was visibly moved by his dilemma, writing immediately to her London manager, 'It's a shame to see him so worried, we must give him every help possible.'

Back in London, he placed advertisements that declared: 'There will be no slump. Let us kill the whole depressing idea by laughing it off.' Yet he knew, better than anyone, that price was a powerful persuader. Throughout the country, customers were flocking to Marks & Spencer who, since they had registered their St Michael trademark in 1928, had moved rapidly to capture the hearts and minds of middle-market shoppers with their 'quality and value' offerings. The chain now sold food, and some stores even had cafés. In a move that caused some annoyance at Selfridge's, Simon Marks attracted a lot of publicity by launching a swathe of 'staff benefits' which included subsidized canteens, health and dental services, hairdressing, rest rooms and even camping holidays – all of which Selfridge's had been offering since the day the store opened, except perhaps the camping:

Selfridge's staff preferred the company's skiing holidays. One thing the mighty Marks & Spencer did offer, however, was a staff pension scheme. Selfridge had never believed in compulsory pensions, feeling people should save for themselves. Regrettably, he hadn't practised what he'd preached.

In the meantime he raised the bar by opening an even bigger bargain business, located in the store's empty property across the street, calling it 'John Thrifty'. It offered service with a smile, though customers had to carry their own shopping home. Staff still observed the store's rules: no customer was called 'Miss' or 'Dear', and staff themselves were called 'assistants'. They were told to 'walk tall' through the floors, encouraged to attend the long-established courses in 'Voice Culture and Personal Magnetism' and, as always, urged to give 'the utmost attention to the care of hair and hands'. The staff still loved the Chief. While newcomers didn't quite share the evangelical zeal of their older colleagues, their affection for their mentor was tangible.

Harry still gambled, but his days as casino king were over. In the spring of 1938, he went back to Deauville with Marcelle, only to find he wasn't welcome. In refusing him credit, Nicolas Zographos was in fact doing his one-time high-roller a huge favour. Harry could no longer afford to lose. He never went back, confining his gaming to poker, playing with his monogrammed cards and mother-of-pearl chips. He was visibly moved by the news of Suzanne Lenglen's death in July from pernicious anaemia at the age of only 39. That summer, he rented the Duke of Devonshire's seaside villa, Compton Place at Eastbourne, and summoned his children and grandchildren for what would, in effect, be their last luxury holiday spent together. Gordon Jr's four children were not among the house party, and neither was his wife. Selfridge still refused to acknowledge them and Gordon Jr was still happy to hide them away. Tatiana Wiasemsky was now 18, Violette's son Blaise was 15 and her daughter Jacqueline 5. It was the last family holiday Violette and Jacques de Sibour would spend together. Their already fractured marriage broke apart soon after, leading to divorce. Beatrice fared no better in her marriage to Jacques's brother Louis. Two years later, they too divorced. At the end of the year, Harry's Christmas card showed a picture of his cherished 'celebrity window', the latest diamond-tipped signature being that of the Oscar-winning film director Frank Capra, who had visited the store while in London to promote his latest movie *You Can't Take It with You.*

In 1939, with his unerring eye for a brilliant idea, Selfridge launched a ground-breaking television department with a major in-store exhibition. Convinced of the power of television, for years he had enthused about the latest technology: 'Television is here – You can't shut your eyes to it!' ran his advertisements in the London and national press. The store offered the most comprehensive range ever put together in the new business of broadcasting, showing many models two months before they were exhibited at the New York World Fair, including those by Pye, Cossor, G. E. C. Ferranti, Marconiphone, Baird, His Master's Voice and Ekco. The seductive sets were priced from 23 guineas and, for those on a budget but who couldn't resist temptation, Selfridge's offered their own hire purchase terms.

As always with Selfridge's, it wasn't just about selling television sets but also about education and in-store entertainment. The store invested £20,000 in setting up a fully operational studio in the Palm Court which, in conjunction with the BBC, ran a live studio facility where visitors could see celebrities being filmed and, most appealing of all, where they could enter competitions to appear on screen themselves. Dancers, singers and comedians were encouraged to apply for a screen test, while eager mothers queued up to enter their daughters for children's dance contests. Fashion shows introduced by Gordon Jr were screened on fifty television receivers strategically placed throughout the store that broadcast at 11.00 a.m. each day. There were even make-up demonstrations to show how to eliminate shine before facing the camera. The Chief had thought of everything.

Selfridge's had earned a unique place in retail history in championing television ever since Baird's pioneering demonstration in 1925, but nothing could have prepared the public for the excitement of seeing themselves on screen. Thousands of visitors poured into the Palm Court, scrambling to be part of the excitement. Yet curiously the media coverage was lacklustre. Only *The Times* got the point of it all, but even then merely reported that 'the Exhibition was an interesting and, indeed, exciting occasion'. Sadly for Harry Selfridge, the excitement was short-lived. On the outbreak of war in September, the BBC ceased transmission. Manufacturers' skills were redirected towards weapons of war, and broadcasting wouldn't resume until June 1946.

Selfridge was among the many who knew war was inevitable. On his frequent trips to Germany where the store had long maintained a buying office, he witnessed at first hand Germany's ruthless persecution of the Jews. Sensitive towards their plight, and with many Jewish friends of his own as well as customers who used the Kosher food department and the Hebrew section of the book department, he wanted to do something to help. Throughout the spring of 1939, he devoted dozens of 'Callisthenes' columns to the topic of 'What Refugees Can Do for England', being particularly supportive of German Jews seeking a safe haven.

At Brighton Technical College, in a hall so crowded that loudspeakers had to be rigged up outside for the overflow, he gave a talk to students, explaining that 'much intelligent work is being done under the dictators Hitler and Mussolini and unless we of the democracies are going to do the same amount of work and use the same effort and intelligence, we are going to be beaten'. The young students were enthralled, the local *Argus* reporting that 'they cheered and applauded until it echoed around the hall'.

Selfridge received another remarkable ovation at the shareholders' meeting, despite the fact that he owed the store over £100,000 and the board's announcement that no dividend would be paid on ordinary shares. One colleague said he 'positively glowed with faith in the future', while a reporter remarked that 'he didn't look a day over sixty '– cheering news for a man who was now 83. Having finally been invited to Hollywood, Marcelle Rogez left London that year. Now Harry was, and would remain, alone.

On a business trip to America, Andrew Holmes was entertained by the new men in power at Marshall Field, by now also a business losing money. Asking about 'mile-a-minute Harry', Holmes was told: 'He was the greatest sales promoter and publicity man the store ever had. Quite the perfect showman.' To Mr Holmes, who didn't believe in showmanship, this merely confirmed his belief that 'Selfridge's greatest illusion is that he was a merchant, which possibly explains many of his mistakes.' On holiday early that fateful summer, Mr Holmes met the owner of an important carpet company, whose main topic of conversation was their long overdue account. Faced with what he described as 'a withering blast', Holmes went back to London and examined the books, discovering that many suppliers, used to waiting patiently for six months to be paid, were now expected to extend credit for over a year. A lot of them couldn't afford it. Worse, some were threatening legal action.

At some point that summer, Harry had a serious argument with his son, their uneasy relationship collapsing into acrimony. Playing politics, Gordon Jr said: 'Something has got to be done about my father.' In August, the Group Finance Director and latterly Company Secretary, Arthur Youngman, always devotedly loyal to the Chief, retired after thirty-one years in the job. His departure signalled a Board reshuffle and the appointment of a Holmes protégé, Arthur Deakin.

The store had spent the summer preparing for war. The Civil Defence Unit ordered 5,000 sandbags, tons of sand and timber, hundreds of rubber boots, respirators and steel helmets, waterproof overalls, gas masks and two and a half tons of bleach powder, to be used to extinguish fires. Staff underwent training under the direction of the indefatigable director Mr H. J. Clarke, who energetically put his 'emergency squad' through their paces on the roof and at the Preston Road sports ground. On 2 September the Wehrmacht marched into Poland. At 11:15 a.m. on 3 September the Prime Minister Neville

Chamberlain announced that the country was at war. Sandbags were piled around the Chief's private entrance at the rear of the store, and he was photographed going to work with a gas mask slung over his shoulder, smiling broadly for waiting photographers and saying it was 'business as usual'. Rapid adjustments were made to stock inventory. Vast quantities of blankets were ordered and Nellie Elt astutely bought in quantities of lipsticks and boxed soaps. Handbags 'designed to carry gas masks' were hastily put on sale and, for the lucky few, there was an exciting addition to the hosiery department – imported nylon stockings.

In a portent of things to come, the 'Callisthenes' column ceased publication on 2 September. For the past fifteen years, the column had been written by the journalist Eisdale MacGregor, but the last article, called 'A Final Word', was written by Selfridge himself:

> Their spirit of happy enthusiasm and of good cheer is hardly consistent with the sterner atmosphere of war. The articles have endeavoured to dignify that fine thing called business and surround it with strong and unbreakable bands of integrity. With this, then final word – final for the moment – we conclude this long, interesting and, we hope, character-building series.

In reality, the column's closure was due to a massive cost-cutting exercise being orchestrated by Mr Holmes, who was now poised to get rid of the most extravagant expense of all – Mr Selfridge. Gordon Jr vanished on an extended trip to America, staying away for over a month. Senior staff, curious about his absence, gossiped among themselves. When the blow came, most of Selfridge's inner circle had been expecting it for weeks – everyone, that is, except the Chief. Miss Mepham greeted Mr Holmes with professional politeness when he appeared at the door to the inner office on 18 October. She wasn't invited to take notes. At the meeting that followed, Holmes pointed out some salient facts. Selfridge owed the store in excess of £118,000. He owed the Inland Revenue in excess of £250,000 in back taxes. In addition, he had personal, undisclosed debts to the Midland Bank. All this was secured against his shareholdings in the company. He owned no freehold property, the store paid his costs at Brook House, and he had no company pension. Selfridge was given an ultimatum. Either he retire, relinquishing all form of executive control, or the company would demand immediate repayment of his debt. He was offered a pension of £6,000 a year free of tax on condition he gave his shares back to the business. He had no choice but to accept.

Selfridge sat silently as Andrew Holmes on behalf of the Prudential Insurance Company stripped him of his life's work, ending everything he had held dear by handing him the draft of a resignation letter which he was asked to approve on the spot. Always dignified, with that same remote quality that for decades his colleagues had yearned to penetrate, Harry Gordon Selfridge initialled his life away. Miss Mepham sat outside, knowing – as all good secretaries always do – exactly what was going on.

The Board issued an abrupt and clumsily worded announcement to staff and the press:

> The time has come when Mr Selfridge feels that he should relieve himself from the duties of detail [*sic*] management and he has therefore asked his colleagues to accept his resignation. Advancing years and their accompanying penalties have been bringing the wisdom of this step to Mr Selfridge for quite a long time … his resignation has been received with the greatest possible regret and at the same time, in view of his unique association with the company since its foundation [the Board] have invited him to accept the title of President of the Company.

Harry spent a day or so composing his own leaving letter, which was circulated to the staff on 21 October:

> The time has come when I must relinquish the management of this great and beautiful business … which I created and founded over

thirty years ago. My proverbial three score years and ten have long since been passed, and I have concluded, with much thought and great regret, to resign my several posts of Chairman and Managing Director and retire from the Boards of this Company and its subsidiary and associated companies ... I have assumed the somewhat nominal title of President. This will not carry with it a controlling voice, but will put me in the position of an adviser when desirable ... And now, my friends, I am taking a bit of a holiday. It is not that, but let us call it so. Another of my regrets is that if one of these raids occurs while I am away, I shall not be here to share it with you. During the last war I was in London continually and declined to allow the German bombs to interfere with my usual routine ... wish me then, a good trip and a safe return to you all, and, as the man in the movies says – 'I'll be seeing you'. We can then again shake hands and talk about the yesterdays and the tomorrows.

And, as long as I live, my great love for this business and my deep feelings of friendship for the members of the staff will remain undimmed by time.

By the time the letter was circulated, he was gone. He couldn't bear to say goodbye. Two weeks later he boarded the SS *Washington* for his last trip to America.

The great building in Oxford Street was no longer the store of H. G. Selfridge. The name plates were swiftly put back up outside the building, and advertisements no longer showed the apostrophe in the title. Having pensioned off the father, Mr Holmes turned his attention to the son. If Gordon Jr had been under the impression there would be an enhanced role for him, he was wrong. There was no place in the business for the man whom *Time* relentlessly referred to as 'a playboy'. Mr Holmes restructured his job brief, obliging him to step down from his directorships of Whiteley's and the Gordon Selfridge Trust, leaving him as titular head of the provincial stores. Three months later, the provincial stores were sold to John Lewis of Oxford Street. Gordon Jr left the business, reportedly furious at the rapid dismantling of the empire. Within a matter of months he moved with his wife and children to America where he took a job at Sears Roebuck in Chicago.

Back in London, Selfridge found that not everyone had written him off, particularly the media. Newspaper proprietors gathered together to host a New Year's luncheon in his honour, where he sat with Ralph Blumenfeld, by now known as 'the father of Fleet Street', and Lord Ashfield, who spoke glowingly of his friend's 'transformation of Oxford Street', adding that perhaps he should after all have agreed to name Bond Street tube station 'Selfridges'. A powerful group of retailers applauded the post-lunch talk: Sir Montague Burton, Trevor Fenwick, Frederick Fenwick, Sir Woodman Burbidge of Harrods and L. H. Bentall. Everyone said Selfridge looked well. He wasn't. But he knew how to put on a show.

Surprising as it may seem, he still went into the store on most days, taking the lift once exclusively reserved for him but now designated for all directors and stubbornly sitting in his office, where he and Miss Mepham went through the ritual of 'let's pretend'. They pretended there were letters, memos, invitations or meetings. In reality there were none. He would still don his top hat and walk the store where staff, though pleased to see him, were also embarrassed. They didn't know what to say. What *could* they say? He was said to be 'making plans'. Why, no one could really fathom, but word went out that he had dreams of starting a new enterprise, and Mr Holmes struck again with a letter:

> It was clearly the intention of the Directors and especially in the minds of their advisers that for practical and psychological reasons, you would vacate the Managing Director's accommodation so as to give complete freedom to the new Management ... I am instructed by the Board to ask you to be good enough to arrange for such personal possessions as you would wish to be removed before the 26th April ... one other matter which the Directors view with some concern is that you are contemplating commencing independent business

activities … they do object and deprecate very seriously that such negotiations should be conducted from the store address.

In case Selfridge didn't get the point, he was given the use of a small office in Keysign House, a company property across the road, his pension was cut by a third and the services of Miss Mepham were withdrawn.

In May 1940, Selfridge was honoured by the dedication of a bronze plaque and illuminated scroll, to which the owners of forty-one stores subscribed and which was unveiled at a luncheon given in the store's Palm Court Restaurant. In thanking those present, Harry said: 'I realize my generation has pretty nearly lived out its life.' Conspicuous by his absence was Mr Holmes.

When the Blitz began, London braced itself. During one raid the store roof was hit by bombs that started a fierce fire. Most of the upper windows were shattered, including the Chief's much-loved signature window. When he went to inspect the damage, the old man broke down. It was the first time anyone had seen him cry. He continued to spend several hours a day sitting alone in his empty room on the opposite side of the street, writing letters to various acquaintances in authority, offering his services 'for the war effort' and hoping – in vain – that he might be given some useful work. Eventually he stopped coming.

In January 1941, just a few days before his eighty-fifth birthday, the Board stripped Harry Selfridge of his title of President and, with year-end net profits at an all-time low of only £21,093, slashed his pension yet again. Now living on a meagre £2,000 a year, Harry, Serge and Rosalie vacated Brook House and moved to a two-bedroom flat in Ross Court, Putney. In June that year, isolated and alone in Hollywood, Jenny Dolly committed suicide, hanging herself with the sash of her dressing-gown.

In August, Harry's cherished collection of rare French and English books was auctioned at Sotheby's. The family were struggling to make ends meet. While Serge spent his mornings drinking in the Green

Man, Rosalie could be found from time to time visiting a rather dubious antiques shop in the Lower Richmond Road, where she was forced to sell their valuables for hard cash. Her father spent his days reading correspondence, sifting through archives and playing the odd game of poker with the ever-cheerful Mr Robertson of the *Evening News*.

As Oxford Street was pounded by bombs, the store continued to be hit. The ground-floor windows were bricked up, the roof garden was left in ruins and the Palm Court Restaurant, the scene of so much excitement over the years, was decimated by fire and closed for ever. In 1942, the store's ex-star model Gloria once again made headlines when she was found dead in her Maida Vale flat, apparently having suffered a heart attack from an overdose of slimming pills.

Putting on a cheerful front, most of the family reunited at the King's Chapel in the Savoy in June 1943 to celebrate Tatiana Wiasemsky's marriage to Lieutenant Craig Wheaton-Smith. The wedding was followed by a small reception at Claridge's, the hotel where once Harry Selfridge had always had the best table. Later that summer, his 21-year-old grandson Blaise de Sibour, a pilot with the French Normandy Squadron flying sorties against the Germans, was shot down and killed in Russia. Violette de Sibour subsequently settled in America where she went to work for Elizabeth Arden. Conscious of his own mortality, Harry became reconciled with his son and grandchildren in America. He was increasingly frail and would sit by the fire in Ross Court, shuffling papers and burning his private letters while Rosalie looked on in despair.

On some days he would stand at his local bus stop on Putney High Street, his rheumy blue eyes searching the road for the arrival of a No. 22. Virtually deaf, his mind rambling, he hardly spoke. Harry Gordon Selfridge had retreated into his own private world, full of memories no one could share. Still wearing curiously old-fashioned formal, shabby-genteel clothes, his patent leather boots cracked and down-at-heel, his untidy white hair falling over a frayed shirt collar, his by now battered trilby pulled low, he moved stiffly, aided by a

Malacca cane. On the bus, he would carefully count out the pennies for his fare, buying a ticket to Hyde Park Corner, where he got off to wait for a No. 137 bus, quietly telling the conductor 'Selfridge's please.' Seemingly lost in memories of past glories, unrecognized by anybody, the old man shuffled the length of the majestic building before crossing the road to the corner of Duke Street. Stopping there, leaning heavily on his cane, he would look up to the roof of the store and along to the far right upper corner window, as though searching for something. Miss Mepham met him one day when he was suffering from a virulent attack of shingles and was in great pain. She fled back to her office, so distressed that she wept. Sometimes, when he was standing on the street, a hurrying pedestrian would bump into him. Once he fell heavily. On one pitiful occasion the police arrested him, suspecting he was a vagrant.

As he looked up at his great store in those desperate days of the war, Selfridge had no idea that deep below the ground, in the sub-basement he had had blasted out of the London clay, men from the US Army Signal Corps were on round-the-clock shifts protecting a top-secret telecommunications installation. Bell Telephone's X-system, codenamed Sigsaly and at the cutting edge of cryptography, was housed in what High Command felt was one of the most secure sites in London. Scrambled conversations between the men of war plotting and planning D-Day, indeed almost all communications on behalf of the British Government and the Allied forces, took place in that guarded room deep below Selfridges. How proud he would have been.

He would also have been proud to know that a perspiring subaltern returned to Company HQ after marching his platoon for many hot and weary miles on 'training' somewhere in England, to find his company commander and the CO sitting looking very pleased with themselves, holding a piece of paper. It turned out to be *The Times* crossword. 'Just finished it,' said the CO. 'We thought it had beaten us though, eh Major?' 'One blessed word,' replied the Major, 'but we rang up Selfridges Information Bureau and they knew.' Of course they did. Shortly thereafter, Mr Holmes closed the Information Bureau down.

Harry Gordon Selfridge died peacefully in his sleep at Ross Court on 8 May 1947. He was 91. Following his funeral, held at St Mark's Church, the local newspaper reported on the many floral tributes. Among them was a large wreath of red and white roses from Miss Rosie Dolly, the message simply saying 'from Rosie and Jenny', and a huge bouquet with a card saying, 'In memeory of a great citizen of the world who loved humanity' from the President, directors, vice-presidents and executives of Marshall Field and Co., Chicago, USA.

In his will, Harry left jewellery and what remained of his sculpture collection to his three daughters. He had once said: 'When I die, I want it said of me, "He dignified and ennobled commerce" ' His family had no money for a headstone to honour the man who did just that – and it never occurred to Selfridges to pay for one. Instead, he lies in a humble grave near his beloved wife and mother in the quiet churchyard of St Mark's in Highcliffe, where leaves from the over-hanging trees gently fall around their tombs.

~

FAST FORWARD

'He who will not economize will have to agonize.'
Confucius (551–479 BC)

A s there is evidence to show that chains of retail stores were operating in China several centuries before the birth of Christ, it's safe to assume Confucius was talking from first-hand experience. It's strangely comforting to know that agonizing over buying some delightful, extravagant frippery is nothing new.

Shopping today defines our lives as never before. 'Not only is shopping melting into everything, but everything is melting into shopping,' wrote Sze Tsung Leong, one of Rem Koolhaas's students at Harvard's Design School, where the urban retail planners and designers of tomorrow learn how to tackle customer flow. It's a daunting task. Shopping takes more of our time, occupies more of our space, employs more of our workforce and – so it's said – fills our thoughts more than anything else. Not unsurprisingly, it also takes a large slice of our money. For every £10 earned in the West, £4 or more is estimated to go on shopping.

As an activity, shopping dominates the developed world to such an extent that merely examining where and how we shop has become an industry in its own right. The embryonic systems of market research practised by Harry Gordon Selfridge nearly a hundred years ago have evolved into a sophisticated business which traces our every purchase through credit and loyalty cards as well as electronic point-of-sale systems, the ubiquitous in-store cameras and, less appealingly, a system called 'smart-shelf surveillance' where almost invisible hidden cameras watch our every move, judging reactions as we pick up – and maybe put down – a particular product. It doesn't stop there. In the insatiable quest for tracking and profiling consumers, electronic chips smaller than a grain of rice can be embedded into a product, and the 'shopping spy' business is very excited about a new conductive ink, which means boxes can be 'read' wherever they are. All this information floods into centralized databases, where what we buy, what time of day or night we buy it, and how much we spend are ruthlessly analysed.

Surveillance aside, an entire sector has also grown up offering advice and trend predictions, with experts readily available to make pronouncements on our desires and dreams. Even ultra-fashionable companies, those the ordinary mortal may assume might know 'what's hot and what's not', actually pay trend-trackers and sometimes (take a deep breath here) even psychic advisers to predict their future. A whole breed of consultants called 'cool hunters' really does exist – although given the speed with which the jargon changes, by the time this book is published they may well be called something else. What won't change is that their services don't come cheap. Such businesses earn millions of pounds a year in fees, and specialists in the prediction business are flown around the globe to present concepts to business forums and marketing conferences discussing 'the role of retail and consumption in contemporary society', where once they might have talked about the threat to world peace. One common thread links all these gurus. They are trying to find ways of keeping us spending.

Where and how we spend our money is rapidly changing, so rapidly in fact that it's hard to keep up with it, and sometimes equally hard to keep pace with the discarded, dying and derelict formulas left floundering in the wake of modernity. That consumers, after having so much of everything, crave something different isn't entirely surprising. It is quite normal to want new experiences, and thus 'the experience of shopping' in its own right has become the focus of sophisticated attention. One thing most of these pundits have been predicting for years is the demise of the department store. Yet despite customers flocking to individual designer shops, tapping out their wish list on the Internet, scouring the high street or preferring to raid the growing phenomenon of designer factory outlet villages, it seems we still have a soft spot for stores – at least if they are speciality ones. The 'one-stop shop' still has a role to play, although ensuring it does so to a packed house increasingly requires skilful management, a genuine respect for visual creativity and very big budgets.

For most people of a certain age, talking about department stores – those 'great cathedrals of shopping' – brings misty-eyed memories of youthful trips to town escorted by grandma to buy a new winter coat. The nostalgia factor – increasingly important in our Internet-linked, digital-television-watching, brand-conscious world – plays hard with stores, and many a mother today takes her children to see twinkling Christmas lights and Santa Claus because that is precisely what happened to her when she was little. Memories of haircuts at Harrods, ice-cream teas and the ubiquitous school uniform list flood back to me as I write this – and memories are a powerful trigger for affection.

Affection alone, however, doesn't fill a vast retail space at the wrong end of town, and as cities have shifted their axis, vast stores have often been stranded, waiting hopefully for regeneration programmes which often arrive too late to save them. Sometimes the buildings have been lost for ever, more often than not redeveloped into a mix of office and retail space, and occasionally put to more imaginative use – such as in Los Angeles where the glorious art-deco building that was formerly the high-fashion destination-store for Hollywood stars, Bullock's Wilshire, is now home to the Southwestern Law School's Leigh H. Taylor Library. Neither will today's youthful, fashion-savvy consumers shop if the merchandise mix is wrong. Customers used to the comfort factor of smaller niche boutiques (or even the bland convenience of a mall) are reluctant to shop in a tatty, tired environment. Investing in infrastructure is crucial to success today and that is precisely why so many stores have failed. Tip-top lighting, clean, bright spaces, wide aisles and the requisite glamorous ancillary services such as cafés, bars, restrooms, personal shopping services and motivated floor staff all have to be in place. It costs serious money to keep prime sites afloat, and over the past two decades the over-hyped term 'flagship' store has become a euphemism for a once great business that has lost its way simply because refitting and modernization were low on its agenda. Small wonder so many of them have closed.

Rodney Fitch, founder of the design agency Fitch, who has spent his career in global retail design, is in no doubt about the downward trend in mainstream department store retailing. Stating unequivocally that the share of total consumption attributable to stores has been falling, he says that 'most of them fail on value, convenience, innovation and customer experience'. Fitch is quite clear as to what makes a winning department store. In his view it is 'one that goes beyond just product to deliver a different shopping experience' and for him, Selfridges does this today. 'It is part store, part destination, part cultural centre,' says Fitch. That description fits to a T not only the dream of the founder, whose opening-day advertisements proudly stated that 'the pleasures of shopping as well as those of sightseeing begin from the opening hour', but also that of the present-day owners, the Weston family.

There's a satisfying buzz about Selfridges today – the hum of money and confidence and, for those who can take the pace in the giant 650,000 square-foot space, sheer, unadulterated fun. This in itself is the essence of the whole 'store-shopping' issue. When so many stores have been bought and sold, stripped of their assets and had equity taken out in one way or another, it's gratifying to see a business that isn't necessarily about what can be taken out but that focuses on what can be put in. In the case of Selfridges, the present owners aren't short of investment capital. In 2003, the Canadian food and specialist retail billionaire Galen Weston and his family won control of Selfridges (at that time still a public company) at a cost of £600 million. The store is now a private company, and the Westons take a long-term view. The store's CEO Paul Kelly (who has worked for the Westons for twenty-two years and who ran the Weston-owned store Brown Thomas in Dublin for ten years before moving to take over the helm at Selfridges), says: 'It's about growth in a planned way. The Westons have bought this business for ever and I am answerable to the family, not some guys who want a return in 12 or 18 months.' Not that the company need worry too much – in 2006, when sales reached £538 million, Kelly told *Drapers' Record* that 'our profit margin should be the envy of retailers around the world'.

The Westons acquired something rare: a truly magnificent building that was fully extended by the mid-1920s and that has survived virtually intact since it opened in 1909. Selfridges is a store built by a man who loved beautiful buildings. In 1990, when the Prince of Wales gave a speech at the American Institute of Architects' gala dinner in Washington, he said: 'There are one or two buildings in London which stand out by their quality and which, upon further examination, turn out to have been designed or inspired by Americans. The first store to rival your department stores – Selfridges on Oxford Street – has never been bettered as a civilized piece of retail development.' Dan Cruickshank writing in the *Independent* about the store's design and construction, also praises its power and longevity: 'Historicist façades masking non-traditional construction need to be more than a skin-deep panel clipped over a steel frame if they are to last. Much of the power and dignity of the Selfridge's elevation is derived from the fact that its stone columns and cornice, bonded into blue-brick piers, are authentic pieces of solid construction, fully integrated with the load-bearing steel frame behind. This is what gives the great store its sense of authenticity ... it is why Selfridge's remains Oxford Street's one architectural masterpiece.'

Selfridge himself was acclaimed for creating Oxford Street as one of the world's most important shopping thoroughfares. That Oxford Street today is an overcrowded, touristy nightmare is a great sadness. Plans to improve the flow of traffic – even perhaps to eliminate traffic altogether – have often been mooted, while trams, elevated walkways and other expensive schemes are currently being discussed. Although Selfridges offers its VIP customers a dedicated entrance into the Personal Shopping suite from the store car park, the less fortunate have to brave the throngs outside. One thing is for sure, something has to be done, and Selfridges, along with Marks & Spencer and John Lewis, is part of the steering committee debating what to a lot of Londoners is a very real crisis. Scott Malkin, Chairman of Value Retail plc, the enterprising American who brought top-end designer factory outlet shopping to Great Britain when he opened the acclaimed Bicester Village in Oxfordshire, is a third-generation member of a distinguished property-developing family. His view is that 'Selfridges must of necessity turn Oxford Street into an advantage; and it can only do so by seizing control of the street, at least in proximity to its own store. All the great retail streets, from Rodeo Drive to Bond Street, are only as good as the definition imposed upon them by their dominant retailers.' Years ago, Harry Gordon Selfridge actually owned and operated shops opposite the store. He also had plans for an underground tunnel, an underground car park in Portman Square and a helipad on the roof. Tackling the problems of traffic is nothing new.

In the meantime, the architect Eric Parry has been briefed to work on a restoration programme to restore the façade of Selfridges to the level of grandeur established by its founder. To this extent, permission has been granted by Westminster City Council to reinstate the full-height windows along the Oxford Street frontage as well as the Duke Street side, restoring them to their original magnificence and recalling the days when they were famous for being 'the largest store windows in the world'. Selfridges will also refit retractable awnings – another of the founder's innovations – which will reduce the high level of glare, often so bright you can't properly see the displays.

Naturally enough, the thought of enhanced window space excites the creative director Alannah Weston who admits that the windows are her passion. 'They are the thing I love the most, they reflect the rhythm of the floor,' she says. To this extent she shrewdly hired the highly regarded production designer Michael Howells as visual consultant to create some show-stopping windows: his golden fantasy for Christmas 2006 was particularly enticing. Alannah's enthusiasm is contagious and her respect for Harry Gordon Selfridge heartfelt. 'Retail is all about change and we'd like to think that Selfridges is always ahead of the curve,' she says. 'Retail theatre is very much Gordon Selfridge's legacy and we are constantly looking for creative ways to entertain our customers. More people today visit cultural institutions than attend sports events, so we find that collaborations with individuals working in the visual and performing arts are extremely fruitful. Today, if you don't try to capture your customer's imagination and offer a unique experience, what is the point? You might as well be in an airport shopping mall.'

Andy Warhol once said: 'Close a department store today, reopen it in a hundred years and you have a ready-made museum.' In the case of Selfridges, if that happened, visitors might think they had stumbled into Tate Modern. Alannah Weston is no mere art enthusiast. She is deeply knowledgeable and surrounds herself with like-minded friends and helpers. There aren't many stores who have their own 'art adviser' on the team, as Weston does with the highly respected curator and consultant Bettina von Hase. Since Weston took up her in-store post in 2003 (she also commutes to Canada, where she is creative director of another family-owned division, Holt Renfrew, and to Ireland to oversee Brown Thomas), she has pushed the envelope in terms of creating an edgy, cool art concept as a crucial part of the design mix. Her friend Sam Taylor Wood designed early windows; in 2006 the Chinese installation artist Song Dong built a biscuit city and invited customers to devour it; and in the spring of 2007, in support of the Victoria and Albert Museum's exhibition 'Surreal Things: Surrealism & Design', Selfridges not only took up the theme for its windows but also, among other events, had the artists Dadadandy design and launch a scentless perfume in the store complete with gorgeous girls who spritzed the customers.

Critics of Selfridge himself say he was more about style than substance, that he was a showman and not a merchandiser. He was indeed a supreme promoter, a natural publicist who believed in high-spirited events and exhibitions to 'get the customer in'. He also believed passionately in pleasing them once they got there. It's hard to compare then and now – product differentials are so huge – but as Rodney Fitch says, 'he bought a sense of theatre and scale to retailing and was a giant of the market place'. Peter Wallis, the social commentator who co-authored the *Sloane Ranger Handbook*, readily admits that Selfridges is his favourite place to shop and 'that Selfridge himself had fantastic energy and ambition and was a brilliant publicist – but perhaps more an impresario than a shopkeeper'. Even though Selfridge was better known for publicity, having minutely examined his ground-breaking innovations in customer care, staff training, stock control systems and faultless cleanliness, I find it hard to call him anything less than an inspired shopkeeper. And with the world's customers now so spoilt for choice, the theatrical element of competitive retailing seems to be the only logical way forward. There's nothing more boring than being bored.

It has also been said by some observers that despite all the 'show' at Selfridges today, sometimes the merchandise doesn't match up to the magic box of tricks used to lure people into the store. But look carefully and most of the covetable brands are there, alongside a contemporary medley of younger collections, some unexpected, directional fashion names and a lavishly redesigned menswear department. In a move Harry Gordon would have appreciated, they even have a cigar room. The point about Selfridges today, however, is that it doesn't set out to be purely a fashion-led store. Alannah Weston likes to describe it as 'a large speciality store': 'Where else can you buy a Lanvin dress, eat sushi, have your eyebrows done, your teeth whitened and buy parmesan?' It is, in line with the founder's concept, a much more egalitarian place than say Harrods, which still caters so magnificently for the rich, or Harvey Nichols which is all about high fashion and which specializes in stocking highly individual collections from designers whose provenance is less well known. Suzy Menkes, the industry's high-priestess of fashion reporting, who writes for the *International Herald Tribune*, also cites the fact that 'Selfridges is a true multi-cultural store ... which reflects the international flavor of London as much in its multi-ethnic staff as its multi-ethnic customer base'.

This too is an important part of the mix. Due to the sheer scale of the building, as well as its international reputation, Selfridges has to appeal not just to Londoners or out-of-town shoppers (although in England at least there are branch stores in Manchester and Birmingham) but also to the millions of tourists who flock through the doors, who represent 22 per cent of sales and who, in Weston's words, divide into 'both shopping travellers and fashion tourists'.

Up until the very end of the 1970s – in some stores even until the 1980s – if you mentioned the words 'shopping traveller' to a department store buyer, they would have thought you meant a tourist on the lookout for a good-quality Scottish cashmere twinset. In the strange time-warp of shopping in post-war Britain, stores stagnated for decades. While one or two tried to respond to the 'swinging 60s' fashion revolution, in reality (with the exception of Woollands in Knightsbridge), fashion was boutique-led, championed for decades by today's longest-surviving designer destination, Browns in South Molton Street. Britain had no shortage of home-grown designers – among them, Gerald McCann, Gina Fratini, Marion Foale and Sally Tuffin, Ossie Clark, David Sassoon, Zandra Rhodes, Bill Gibb, Mary Quant, Jean Muir and John Bates – but it wasn't the department stores that were snapping up their work.

The stores had purchasing power, but it was used on blankets, bed linen, canteens of silver cutlery, wedding dresses, serviceable suits and the 'dressy department' (almost always called 'After Six') rather than on designer clothes. Good solid British brands like Jaeger, Burberry and Aquascutum had a visible presence, but not many people in the fashion industry today can recall a time when British clothing manufacturers such as Reldan and Rembrandt held sway.

Even then, in those pre-international designer days, fashion had an aura about it. My mother's best friend was a magazine fashion editor who wore gloves, a hat and prodigious amounts of mascara and who lunched at the Ritz with the then Harrods Press Officer, Laurie Newton Sharpe. Just listening to them talking about it all seemed irresistibly glamorous. But it wasn't all like that. Eric Newby's brilliantly funny book *Something Wholesale: My Life and Times in the Rag Trade* portrays a more realistic picture of stout lady buyers squabbling among themselves over who would book an order for that stalwart combination of matching 'dresses and jackets'. Would it be the suit buyer or the dress buyer? Department stores weren't so much *Ab Fab* as *Are You Being Served?* Socially, the provincial department store general manager was on a par with the city's lord mayor, playing golf with the leading bank managers, dining with fellow Rotarians and handing out prizes at the grammar school sports day.

By the time shopping went turbo-charged in the early 1980s, the stores were slowly waking up. Inspired by what was happening in New York, where Bloomingdales, Saks and particularly Bergdorf Goodman and Barney's were leading the way in showcasing designer ready-to-wear, shoes and accessories, Harvey Nichols and Harrods swiftly followed suit. It was the beginning of a retail revolution but, as always with revolutions, there were victims. Among them were many well-known store names in London, Paris and New York that simply couldn't compete when designer labels – initially more than pleased to be showcased in multi-brand stores – began to want their own personal identity and started to open their own stand-alone sites. Whether on Rodeo Drive, Madison Avenue, Bond Street or Sloane Street, the arrival of branded shops with bodyguards standing outside muttering into walkie-talkie headsets shook the stores to the core. Many of them simply never recovered.

While all this was going on, Selfridges was still slumbering. There is, however, as experts agree, always a moment when a 'singular person' comes along and effects change. In the case of Selfridges, it was Vittorio Radice, the man hired by Sears in 1996, who fired the first shots. When he arrived there was still a department called

'Better Misses'. He threw it out. 'Better Misses,' said Radice at the time, 'makes it sound as if there is a "Worse Misses", and anyway, to a woman today these departmental definitions are outdated.' His predecessor had introduced the distinctive yellow plastic bags (today made of more environmentally friendly paper), but the building itself looked neglected. 'The façade was filthy, there was lino on the floor, and the store was riddled with fluorescent lighting tubes and exposed, old air-conditioning pipes running everywhere.' He cleaned it up, fitting huge central escalators (Radice adores escalators, saying they add a real 'wow' factor), installing big brand concessions alongside a mix of labels such as Prada Sport, Earl and Calvin Klein Jeans, and adding cafés and restaurants where people actually wanted to meet and eat. It was no easy task, but he did it well and today he looks back on his time there with great affection. 'If you move things with integrity,' he says, 'you will involve and inspire people.' Suzy Menkes has written that the 'transformation of Selfridges into an epicenter of cool started when the retail wizard Vittorio Radice created a *souk* of brands with his exceptional Director of Fashion, Susanne Tide Frater'. Scott Malkin agrees: 'Innovation occurred at Selfridges with Vittorio Radice because an unusual talent was allowed to slip into a position of power and revitalize an existing venue.'

Change happens and nowhere does it happen faster than in the fashion business. After an ill-fated stint at Marks & Spencer, Vittorio Radice is now weaving his magic at Italy's most traditional department store group, Rinascenti. The Westons, who had apparently been eyeing up Selfridges for some time, bought themselves a business on the cusp of success. That they have moved it so far, so fast, does them great credit, especially when one considers there is competition coming from all sides – not least the Internet.

So many trends in shopping today are led through innovation in technology – not for nothing is the Apple Store a destination of choice – that it isn't surprising that Internet sales are booming. What is surprising is that what started out as a niche business founded by Nathalie Massanet, an ex-fashion editor from *Harper's & Queen*, turned into not just a success but in some respects, potentially a real alternative to designer shop supremacy. Net-a-Porter.com was launched in June 2000. As its CEO Mark Sebba has observed, 'At first the luxury brands were sceptical because the net had developed as a place for discounting.' No longer. At the end of 2006, Net-a-Porter reported £37.2 million in sales. It is a tight operation which focuses heavily on perfect packaging (compensating in part for the fact that shopping on line cannot be a tactile affair) and swift delivery. Both are crucial to success. 'Our customers are spending a lot of money and they want to be pampered,' explains Sebba. 'They want to feel they are receiving a present, even if they ordered it for themselves. Orders are all hand-delivered – the business runs its own fleet of drivers in London and New York – and returns are collected.' This type of service is, of course, a busy woman's dream. At Net-a-Porter, if they know their customer's credit and the customer orders before 1.00 p.m., a cocktail outfit for the evening's unexpected after-office soirée is delivered that same afternoon. Nothing could be easier, especially for those who loathe going out shopping – and there are many of us – but who still crave beautiful things. Conversely, in Tokyo, where shopping is a serious pastime, at the towering new Gucci stand-alone store (part of the luxury group Pinault-Printemps-Redouté), everything is geared to the tactile, time-consuming in-store shopping experience. Leather pads are rolled out when presenting handbags, there are monogrammed Gucci robes in the dressing-rooms – and even Gucci chocolates in the café. In a symbolic gesture to Japanese rituals, the act of purchase itself is called 'the selling ceremony'. Gucci decline to give figures as to what their 'shrine to shopping' has cost, but as it is on the world's most expensive patch of real estate (valued at £6,686 per square foot) and as the Prada store on Aoyama built in 2003 is estimated to have cost $80 million, one can be certain that the store represents one of the biggest investments Gucci has ever made in retail space. Gucci, like Louis Vuitton and Prada, includes culture in the mix. Vuitton have opened a museum above its Champs-Elysées store, while Gucci have an art gallery and exhibition space in the Ginza. When Rem Koolhaas was designing the Prada Epicenter (the new term in Prada-speak for flagship) in New York, in space that was originally occupied by the Broadway Guggenheim, museum signs were left intact during building, thus emphasizing the premises as a cultural institution. In many respects it is just that. Among the shoes and handbags is a giant staircase which, at the push of a button, rotates to become an auditorium for performances, film projections and lectures.

Meanwhile, back in Oxford Street, where arguably a lot of this 'shopping experience' actually started, if it's a Tuesday morning, Paul Kelly is getting ready to walk the store and talk to the staff, a task that can take up to three hours and something he readily admits he loves. 'The floor is where you get the feel of the business,' he says. Kelly believes the heart of a retail business is the day-to-day trade. 'Customers have to see good product and good service – you have to treat every day as though it is a Saturday. To us, the most important thing is the customer.' Kelly dismisses a lot of the mystique that has built up over the business of retailing during the past decade. 'It's a simple science,' he says, 'but people are trying to make it complicated.' At Selfridges, Kelly and Alannah Weston work as a team: she focuses on creative development while Kelly, a lifelong retailer, takes care of the basics, the business and the detail – and no detail is too small. If he finds dust, he scrawls 'Paul Kelly was here' in it, just like Harry Gordon Selfridge did before him. He's proud of the store's diversification and the huge amount of entertaining activity that goes on in it. 'You can even have your fortune told,' he says, clearly wryly amused at the thought. 'The Psychic Sisters do great business in the basement – it's astonishing who goes to see them.'

One senses that Paul Kelly doesn't need tarot cards to point him in the right direction. At Selfridges, Kelly, Alannah Weston, the Deputy Chairman Allan Leighton and the owners Galen and Hilary Weston form a close-knit team. Alannah's parents are very much involved. 'They see every plan, every visual, every material sample for every capital project we embark on,' she says. The family share a passion for good lighting. 'My father believes, as I do, that human beings crave natural light. Apart from giving one more energy (which we all require when doing a serious shop), it allows the customer to orientate herself in the store which reduces stress.' One of the distinguishing features of the original great department stores was lighting, and the Westons' insistence on its importance follows a great tradition.

The Westons are, by all accounts, a modest family and their glamorous lifestyle is essentially a private one. In England they live at Fort Belvedere, the Duke of Windsor's favoured retreat, and they have extensive property in Florida and elsewhere, but you won't see them endlessly featured in the media. The family foundation donates generously to charity, and they count the great and the good as well as the rich and the famous among their friends. Although their retail empire includes everything from supermarkets to Brown Thomas, Holt Renfrew, Heals and Fortnum & Mason (it even includes Primark), they clearly love Selfridges. When I interviewed her, Alannah remarked: 'Harry Gordon Selfridge once said, "When I die, I want a round coffin so I can turn in my grave if I want to." If he saw Selfridges today, I don't think he'd be turning in his grave, do you?'

I don't, but if he saw the once throbbing building that used to be called Marshall Field in Chicago, he most certainly would. In a move that has distressed a lot of people in Chicago – and indeed elsewhere – when the business passed into the hands of the Federated Stores Group, the owners of Macy's, they changed its name. Nancy Koehn of Harvard is bemused by the move. 'It is inconceivable that they could have renamed Marshall Field as Macy's. It's like having a perfect body and chopping the arms off. It isn't just a heritage site, it's a heritage name, part of the fabric and history of the city. Interestingly, there is a quiet withdrawal by the local community from shopping in stores that have been "stolen" from them. Unless they reconsider this, they might never recover.'

Comfortingly for London, Selfridges hasn't been stolen from anyone. In fact, it has been given back.

NOTES

I have been fortunate to have been able to draw much information from the magnificent Selfridges Archive held at the History of Advertising Trust www.hatads.org. uk (hereafter referred to as HAT). I am also grateful to Simon Wheaton Smith, Harry Gordon Selfridge's great grandson, who not only provided many family anecdotes but also made available his exceptional collection of treasured family memorabilia. The letters between Elizabeth Arden and her London manager, Teddy Haslam (1922–47), have been an invaluable source in respect of her relationship with Harry Gordon Selfridge and the store. I would also like to thank Gordon Honeycombe for permission to draw from his book *Selfridges: Seventy-Five Years: The Story of a Store.*

On a personal note, I have found Elizabeth Ewing's books *Dress and Undress* and *The History of 20th Century Fashion* of inestimable help in researching the fashions of the period and must also recommend Fashion-era.com (text by Pauline Weston Thomas) which has been a fascinating and informed source. For those interested in the history of British retailing, I would recommend *Shops and Shopping* by Alison Adburgham.

During the time he lived in London, in relation to his business dealings, Harry Gordon Selfridge was generally known as Gordon Selfridge. His family and close friends, however, always referred to him as Harry. For the main part, he signed his letters to friends both in England and America as Harry. I have chosen to refer to him by that name.

The notes that follow show the principal sources on which I have drawn in order of appearance in the text. Books are listed by author and title only, but further details may be found in the Bibliography. It is my hope that by early 2008 a website will be in place on which additional detailed information on sources will be available. Owing to constraints of space, only brief details of sources are given below.

Accurate valuations on the correct value of the pound and dollar in the early part of the twentieth century to today are hard to pinpoint. I have followed official guidelines which indicate that pre-First World War, £1 was worth £65 today. It subsequently dropped to £40 and settled at £25 post-war, until the Great Depression. Throughout this period, the exchange rate for the dollar was approximately $5 to £1. For further information see Measuring Worth www.measuringworth.com and the Inflation Calculator www.westegg.com/inflation.

Selfridges have kindly granted permission for use of many of the photographs reproduced in this book. Every effort has been made to trace copyright holders and to clear copyright permission. If notified, the publishers will be pleased to rectify any omissions in future editions. Any omissions of fact or errors are the author's own.

Introduction
Emile Zola, *Au Bonheur des Dames*; Alison Adburgham, *Shops and Shopping*; Reginald Pound, *Selfridge*; Lois Banner, *American Beauty*; Erika Rappaport, *Shopping for Pleasure*; Lloyd Wendt & Herman Kogan, *Give the Lady What She Wants*; Axel Madsen, *The Marshall Fields*; Lloyd Morris, *Incredible New York*; Michael B. Miller, *The Bon Marché*; Selfridges Archives, HAT.

Chapter 1: The Fortunes of War
Stephen N. Elias, *Alexander T. Stewart*; Lloyd Morris, *Incredible New York*; Lloyd Wendt & Herman Kogan, *Give the Lady What She Wants*; Robert W. Twyman, *Potter Palmer*; Emmett Dedmon, *Fabulous Chicago*; Family Archives of Simon Wheaton Smith; The George Washington Masonic National Memorial; Robert W. Twyman, *The History of Marshall Field & Co.*; Selfridges Archive, HAT; John Tebbel, *The Marshall Fields*; Nancy F. Koehn, *Brand New*; Ishbel Ross, *Silhouette in Diamonds*.

Chapter 2: Giving the Ladies What They Want
Diana de Marley, *Worth*; Gail MacColl & Carol Wallace, *To Marry an English Lord*; Elizabeth Ewing, *The History of 20th Century Fashion*; Elizabeth Ewing, *Dress and Undress*; Madge Garland, *A History of Fashion*; Elizabeth Ewing, *The History of 20th Century Fashion*; Alistair Horne, *The Paris Commune, 1871*; Emmett Dedmon, *Fabulous Chicago*; Notes from Gordon Selfridge Jr, HAT; Lloyd Wendt & Herman Kogan, *Give the Lady What She Wants*; Robert W. Twyman, *The History of Marshall Field & Co.*; Nigel Nicolson, *Mary Curzon*.

Chapter 3: The Customer is Always Right

Gordon Honeycomb, *Selfridges*; Reginald Pound, *Selfridge*; Robert Hendrickson, *The Grand Emporiums*; Axel Madsen, *The Marshall Fields*; About Inventors.com: Lightbulbs, Lighting and Lamps; Letter from D. H. Burnham & Co., Selfridges Archives, HAT; Emmett Dedmon, *Fabulous Chicago*; Brenda Warner Rotzoll, 'The Other Bertha Palmer', *Chicago Sun-Times*, 16 March 2003; Perry R. Duis, '*Challenging Chicago*'; Lois W. Banner, *American Beauty*; Nancy F. Koehn, *Brand New*; (on Rosalie Villas) Jean F. Block, *Hyde Park Houses* (text extracts courtesy of the Hyde Park Historical Society, Chicago; further information provided by Trish Morse, University of Chicago); Family Archives of Simon Wheaton Smith; Daughters of the American Revolution, Washington, DC; Author visit to Ely Cathedral; *Chicago Tribune*, 12 November 1890, p. 3.

Chapter 4: Full Speed Ahead

Emmett Dedmon, *Fabulous Chicago*; David F. Burg, *Chicago's White City of 1893*; James William Buel, *The Magic City*; Dennis Bell, 'The Man Who Invented the Wheel and Paid the Price', retrieved from the Internet; Rita Kramer, 'Cathedrals of Commerce', *City Journal*, New York, Spring 1966; Lois W. Banner, *American Beauty*; Lindy Woodhead, *War Paint*; Robert D. Tamilia, 'The Wonderful World of the Department Store', Ph.D., University of Quebec; Reforming Fashion, 1850–1914, costume.osu.edu/Reforming-Fashion; John Burke, *Duet in Diamonds*; Morell Parker, *Lillian Russell*; Peter Kurth, *Isadora*; Nigel Nicolson, *Mary Curzon*; Family Archives of Simon Wheaton Smith; Axel Madsen, *The Marshall Fields*; Vincent Vinikas, *Soft Soap, Hard Sell*; Duke University Advertising Research Project.

Chapter 5: Going It Alone

Family Archives of Simon Wheaton Smith; Chicago Public Library; Author interview with Nancy F. Koehn, Harvard Business School; Grace Lovat Fraser, *In the Days of My Youth*; Thomas Yanul, 'The Untold Story of Schlesinger & Mayer', retrieved from the Internet; *Encyclopedia of Chicago*, entry on Carson Pirie Scott & Co.; Nancy F. Koehn, *Brand New*; Reginald Pound, *Selfridge*; Selfridges Archives, HAT; Lloyd Wendt & Herman Kogan, *Give the Lady What She Wants*; Perry R. Duis, '*Challenging Chicago*'; *Saturday Evening Post*, Chicago, March 1935; Emmett Dedmon, *Fabulous Chicago*; (on gold mine) Family Archives of Simon Wheaton Smith; Selfridges Archive, HAT.

Chapter 6: Building the Dream

Selfridge Archive, HAT; Notes from Eric Dunstan, HAT; (on Charles Yerkes) 'A

Brush with History', National Portrait Gallery; John T. Slania, 'Loop Dreams', retrieved from the Internet; 'Receiver Named for Yerkes Estate', *New York Times*, 7 April 1909; Peter Watts, 'London's Underground History', *Time Out*, 17 April 2007; 'Mrs Harry G. Selfridge', *Chicago Daily News*, 8 June 1907; Emmett Dedmon, *Fabulous Chicago*; Reginald Pound, *Selfridge*; Gordon Honeycombe, *Selfridges*; J. B. Priestley, *The Edwardians*; Article on James Gilbert White, *Cornell Alumni News*, retrieved from the Internet; Selfridges Archive, HAT; J. B. Priestley, *The Edwardians*; (on Kreuger & Toll) Notes in Selfridges Archive, HAT; Letters from Waring & White to H. G. Selfridge, HAT; Susan Mary Alsop, *Lady Sackville*; Kate Jackson, *George Newnes and the New Journalism in Britain*; Simon Jenkins, *Newspapers: The Power and the Money*; (on the store's opening) Selfridges Archive, HAT; The Library and Museum of Freemasonry, London (correspondence with Emily Greenstreet).

Chapter 7: Take-off

Selfridges Archive, HAT; Reginald Pound, *Selfridge*; Author conversation with Oliver Musker; John K. Winkler, *Five & Ten*; Grace Lovat Fraser, *In the Days of My Youth*; (on Violette) Notes from Eric Dunstan, HAT; J. B. Priestley, *The Edwardians*; Elizabeth Ewing, *The History of 20th Century Fashion*; W. Somerset Maugham, *Of Human Bondage*; Alison Adburgham, *Shops and Shopping*; (on Bertha Palmer and Anna Pavlova) Museum of London; (on Blériot) Reginald Pound, *Selfridge*; Notes from Gordon Selfridge Jr, HAT; Gordon Honeycombe, *Selfridges*; *The Globe*, 26 July 1909.

Chapter 8: Lighting up the Night

Project on 'The City', Harvard Design School Guide to Shopping; J. B. Priestley, *The Edwardians*; (on Pavlova), Staff notes, HAT; Letters between Sir Edward Holden and H. G. Selfridge, HAT; Reginald Pound, *Selfridge*; Lindy Woodhead, *War Paint*; W. J. MacQueen-Pope, *Gaiety*; International Perfume Museum, Grasse; Eugene Rimmel, Evanion Catalogue, British Library; The Letters of Ralph Blumenfeld, House of Lords Library; Letters between Ralph Blumenfeld and H. G. Selfridge, HAT; Meredith Etherington-Smith & Jeremy Pilcher, *The 'It' Girls*; Richard Fisher, *Syrie Maugham*; Gerald McKnight, *The Scandal of Syrie Maugham*; Notes from Eric Dunstan, HAT; Selfridges Archive, HAT; (on Sir Oliver Lodge) Staff notes, HAT; Daughters of the American Revolution, Washington DC; A. H. Williams, *No Name at the Door*; Selfridges Archive, HAT; J. B. Priestley, *The Edwardians*.

Chapter 9: War Work, War Play

Reginald Pound, *Selfridge*; Elizabeth Ewing, *The History of 20th Century Fashion*;

Selfridges Archive, HAT; A. H. Williams, *No Name at the Door*; Jeffrey Meyers, *Somerset Maugham*; The Letters of Ralph Blumenfeld, House of Lords Library; University of Chicago Library and Selfridges Archive, HAT; Family Archives of Simon Wheaton Smith; Gordon Honeycombe, *Selfridges*; James Gardiner, *Gaby Deslys*; Cecil Beaton, *The Glass of Fashion*; Irene Castle, *Castles in the Air*; Elisabeth Marbury, *My Crystal Ball*; Selfridges Archive, HAT; Reginald Pound, *Selfridge*; Susan Mary Alsop, *Lady Sackville*; The Woolworths Virtual Museum; John K. Winkler, *Five & Ten*; Denis Mackail, *The Story of J. M. B.*; *Letters of Arnold Bennett*, Vol. II, 1889–1915; W. Somerset Maugham, *Plays: One*, introduction by Anthony Curtis; Barbara Cartland, *We Danced All Night*; Selfridges Archive, HAT.

Chapter 10: Castles in the Air

Selfridges Archive, HAT; Condé Nast Library; (on Highcliffe) Background information provided by Ian Stevenson; 'Highcliffe Castle, Hampshire', *Country Life*, 1 May 1942; Correspondence between Dr E. Dillon and H. G. Selfridge, HAT; Papers of Dr Joseph Emile Dillon, Stamford University Library; (on Serge de Bolotoff) Family Archives of Simon Wheaton Smith; Selfridges Archive, HAT; *New York Herald* (Paris), 20 May 1906; *Legendary Aviators and Aircraft of World War One*; Author correspondence with Mr T. F. Boettger; E. Charles Vivian, *A History of Aeronautics*, retrieved from the Internet (further information provided by Brian Riddle, Royal Aeronautical Society); (on the Hope Sale) Department of Manuscripts and Special Collections, Nottingham University, and information provided by Ian Jenkins, Curator of Greek and Roman Antiquities, British Museum; also Geoffrey B. Waywell, *The Lover and Hope Sculptures*, and Jonathan Scott, *The Pleasures of Antiquity*; Harry Gordon Selfridge, *The Romance of Commerce*; The Letters of Ralph Blumenfeld, House of Lords Library; Selfridges Archive, HAT; John Lane Papers, Harry Ransom Humanities Research Center, University of Texas, Austin; Family Archives of Simon Wheaton Smith; Reginald Pound, *Selfridge*; Documents (including *Barton Breezes*) provided by Ian Stevenson; *Bournemouth Daily Echo*, 16 May 1918.

Chapter 11: Vices and Virtues

Alan Jenkins, *The Twenties*; Kate 'Ma' Meyrick, *Secrets of the '43'*; Ronald Blythe, *The Age of Illusion*; Condé Nast Library; Stella Margetson, *The Long Party*; Notes from Gordon Selfridge Jr, HAT; A. H. Williams, *No Name at the Door*; Elizabeth Ewing, *The History of 20th Century Fashion*; Selfridges Archives, HAT; Reginald Pound, *Selfridge*; Condé Nast Library; Stella Margetson, *The Long Party*; Barbara Cartland, *We Danced All Night*; Andrew Barrow, *Gossip*; Information provided by Ian Jenkins, Curator of Greek and Roman Antiquities, British Museum; Selfridges Archive, HAT; *Daily*

Express, 31 May 1920; Reginald Pound, *Selfridge*; Ralph Blumenfeld, *Diaries*; Philip Tilden, *True Remembrances*; *Bournemouth Daily Echo*, 25 May 1920; Information provided by Ian Stevenson; Violette de Sibour, *Flying Gypsies*; Staff notes, Selfridges Archive, HAT; Correspondence of H. G. Selfridge, HAT; Arnold Bennett, *Journals*, Vol. II, p. 159; Trinity College Library, Cambridge University; Reginald Pound, *Selfridge*; Charles Savoie, 'The Mysterious, Super-élite Pilgrim Society', May 2005, retrieved from the Internet; Anne Pimlott Baker, *The Pilgrims of Great Britain*; Notes from Eric Dunstan, HAT; James Gardiner, *Gaby Deslys*; Norman Hartnell, *Silver and Gold*; Joan Kahr, *Edgar Brandt*; Mary Blume, *Côte d'Azur*; Charles Graves, *None But the Rich*; Kate 'Ma' Meyrick, *Secrets of the '43'* ; Selfridges Archive, HAT; Family Archives of Simon Wheaton Smith; Notes from Eric Dunstan, HAT.

Chapter 12: Making Waves

Alan Jenkins, *The Twenties*; Ronald Blythe, *The Age of Illusion*; Staff notes, Selfridges Archive, HAT; Information provided by Ian Stevenson; Information provided by Merton Council; *Kelly's Directory, 1925*, *Bournemouth Daily Echo*, 26 February 1924; *Time Magazine*, 23 September 1929; Selfridges Archive, HAT; Reginald Pound, *Selfridge*; Family Archives of Simon Wheaton Smith; A. H. Williams, *No Name at the Door*; Ronald Blythe, *The Age of Illusion*; Reginald Pound, *Selfridge*; Kate 'Ma' Meyrick, *Secrets of the '43'*; Gary Chapman, *The Delectable Dollies*; *The Picture-goer*, April 1921, courtesy of Exeter University; Elsa Maxwell, *I Married the World*; Janet Aitken Kidd, *The Beaverbrook Girl*; Mary Blume, *Côte d'Azur*; 'Inventing the French Riviera: The Early Days of Radio Normandy', www.ibcstudio.co.uk; The Diaries of Ralph Blumenfeld; Gordon Honeycombe, *Selfridges*.

Chapter 13: *Tout Va*

Selfridges Archive, HAT; Staff notes, Selfridges Archive, HAT; Letter from Elizabeth Arden to Teddy Haslam, April 1926; Reginald Pound, *Selfridge*; Family Archives of Simon Wheaton Smith; (on Suzanne Lenglen) www.tennisfame.org; Mary Blume, *Côte d'Azur*; Harry Yoxall, *A Fashion of Life*; Caroline Seebohm, *The Man Who Was Vogue*; Condé Nast Library; Gordon Honeycombe, *Selfridges*; Richard Buckle (ed.), *Self Portrait with Friends: The Selected Diaries of Cecil Beaton, 1926–1974*; 'The Riviera Season', *Vogue*, 22 February 1928, illustrations by Cecil Beaton; Charles Graves, *None but the Rich*; Axel Madsen, *Coco Chanel*; Gary Chapman, *The Delectable Dollies*; Alan Jenkins, *The Rich Rich*; *Time Magazine*, 11 and 25 April 1927; Maurice Corina, *Fine Silks and Oak Counters*; Selfridges Archives, HAT; Ronald Blythe, *The Age of Illusion*; Stella Margetson, *The Long Party*; Andrew Barrow, *Gossip*; Selfridges Archive, HAT; Elsa Maxwell, *I Married the*

World; Gloria Vanderbilt & Lady Thelma Furness, *Double Exposure*; (on gaming) Author interview with Professor Gerda Reith; (on Maude Loti) *International Herald Tribune*, 1925; Charles Graves, *None but the Rich*; Gary Chapman, *The Delectable Dollies*; Mistinguett, *Mistinguett by Mistinguett*; A. H. Williams, *No Name at the Door*; Reginald Pound, *Selfridge*; Kate 'Ma' Meyrick, *Secrets of the '43'*; 'The Season at Le Touquet', *Vogue*, illustrations by Cecil Beaton; Staff notes, Selfridges Archive, HAT; *Time Magazine*, 1 August 1927; Gordon Honeycombe, *Selfridges*.

Chapter 14: Flights of Fancy

Philip Tilden, *True Remembrances*; Letter to Mr Skinner, Selfridges Archive, HAT; Reginald Pound, *Selfridge*; A. H. Williams, *No Name at the Door*; *Memoirs of the Rt. Hon. The Earl of Woolton*; Staff notes, Selfridges Archive, HAT; Charles Graves, *None but the Rich*; Gary Chapman, *The Delectable Dollies*; Roy Moseley & Victor Saville, *Evergreen*; Ronald Blythe, *The Age of Illusion*; Stella Margetson, *The Long Party*; Alan Jenkins, *The Twenties*; Selfridges Archive, HAT; *Time Magazine*, 12 March 1928; Arnold Bennett, *Letters to His Nephew*, p. 268; *Business Magazine*, January 1930; *Time Magazine*, 24 March 1930; Gordon Honeycombe, *Selfridges*; *Time Magazine*, 24 September 1928; Violette de Sibour, *Flying Gypsies*; Author correspondence with Mary Gardener; *The Scotsman*, 5 November 1930; 'Callisthenes', 'An Aeroplane Which We Sold', *The Times*, 29 November 1930; Gary Chapman, *The Delectable Dollies*; 'Gloria's Memoirs', *News of the World*, 31 May 1932; *Time Magazine*, 21 July 1930; (on Ivar Kreuger) Dale L. Flesher, *National Forum*, Autumn 1997, retrieved from the Internet; Letter from H. G. Selfridge to Ralph Blumenfeld, Archives; *Time Magazine*, 25 August 1930; Reginald Pound, *Arnold Bennett*; Daphne Thynne, *The Duchess of Jermyn Street*; Selfridges Archive, HAT; *Milwaukee Journal*, 7 September 1932; *Time Magazine*, 14 March 1932 and 17 July 1933; Selfridges Archive, HAT.

Chapter 15: Over and Out

Milwaukee Journal, October 1935; *Daily Tribune Chicago*, 22 October 1935 (cuttings provided by the Wisconsin History Society); *Time Magazine*, 4 November 1935; A. H. Williams, *No Name at the Door*; Election Party Guest Lists, Selfridges Archive, HAT; (on Sibyl Thorndike) A. H. Williams, *No Name at the Door*; Condé Nast Library; Underwear advertising, Selfridges Archives, HAT; *The Passing Show*, 28 September 1935; Gordon Honeycombe, *Selfridges*; Reginald Pound, *Selfridge*; (on Wallis Simpson) Ronald Blythe, *The Age of Illusion*; (on the sale of the SS *Conqueror*) National Maritime Museum & correspondence, HAT; Staff notes, Selfridges Archive, HAT; (on Gordon Jr's flight to Spain) *Time Magazine*, 17 August 1936; H. G. Selfridge letters to Ralph Blumenfeld, Archive; (on Father Christmas)

Business & Finance Magazine, 20 December 1936; (on 'Callisthenes' in USA) *Time Magazine*, 18 October 1937; Coronation Décor Catalogue, Selfridges Archive, HAT; H. G. Selfridge letters to Ralph Blumenfeld, Archive; Reginald Pound, *Selfridge*; (on gambling) A. H. Williams, *No Name at the Door*; 'Television Is Here: You Can't Shut Your Eyes to It', Selfridges Archive, HAT; (on Holmes) Gordon Honeycombe, *Selfridges*; Staff notes, Selfridges Archive, HAT; (on Gordon Jr.) Reginald Pound, *Selfridge*; Staff notes, Selfridges Archive, HAT; (on war stocks) Notes from Nellie Elt, HAT; Letters from board of directors, Selfridges Archive, HAT; (on sailing to America) *Time Magazine*, 13 November 1939; (on post-retirement luncheon) *Store*, February 1940; (on restructuring the business) *Time Magazine*, 3 February 1941; (on life in retirement) Family Archives of Simon Wheaton Smith; Notes from Mr Robertson, Selfridges Archive, HAT; Sotheby & Co. catalogue, 11 August 1941 ('sale of valuable French and English Books, Property of a Gentleman', under which he had written H. Gordon Selfridge) provided by Maggs Bros.; Information on 'Sigsaly', Selfridges Archive, HAT; Obituary, *The Times*, 9 May 1947; (on funeral) *Bournemouth Echo*, 13 May 1947; Last Will & Testament of H. G. Selfridge.

Chapter 16: Fast Forward

Project on 'The City', Harvard Design School Guide to Shopping; Alok Jha, 'Consumers against Supermarket Privacy Invasion and Numbering', *Guardian*, 19 July 2003; Author interview with Rodney Fitch; 'What's In Store for Selfridges?', *Scotland on Sunday*, 18 May 2003; Author interview with Paul Kelly; Interview with Paul Kelly, 'Building on Success', *Sunday Telegraph*, 26 November 2006; *Retail Week*, 27 April 2007; Interview with Paul Kelly, *Drapers' Record*, 5 May 2007; The Prince of Wales, 'Accent on Architecture', speech delivered at the American Institute of Architects Gala Dinner, Washington, DC, 22 February 1990; feature by Dan Cruickshank, *Independent*, 12 February 1992; Author interview with Scott Malkin; Author interview with Alannah Weston (additional information provided by Selfridges); Interview with Alannah Weston, *Sunday Times Business*, 23 July 2006; Feature by Lucia van der Post, *Financial Times: 'How To Spend It' Magazine*, Issue 170, November 2006; Suzy Menkes, 'Surreal Selfridges', *International Herald Tribune*, 5 June 2007; Author interview with Peter Wallis; Author interview with Alannah Weston; Author interview with Suzy Menkes; Ernestine Carter, *20th Century Fashion*; Eric Newby, *Something Wholesale*; Author interview with Vittorio Radice; Suzy Menkes, 'Surreal Selfridges', *International Herald Tribune*, 5 June 2007; Author interview with Mark Sebba of Net-a-Porter; Vanessa Friedman, 'Gucci's Temple to the "Selling Ceremony"', *Financial Times*, 11 November 2006; Author interview with Paul Kelly; Author interview with Alannah Weston; Author interview with Nancy F. Koehn, Harvard Business School.

BIBLIOGRAPHY

All books were published in London unless otherwise stated.

Adburgham, Alison, *Liberty's: A Biography of a Shop* (Allen & Unwin, 1975)
—— *Shops and Shopping, 1880–1914* (Allen & Unwin, 1964)
—— *Victorian Shopping* (David & Charles, Newton Abbot, 1972)
Allan, Tony, *Americans in Paris* (Bison Books, Chicago, 1977)
Alsop, Susan Mary, *Lady Sackville: A Biography* (Weidenfeld & Nicolson, 1978)
Appel, Joseph, *The Business Biography of John Wanamaker* (Macmillan, New York, 1930)
Arlen, Michael, *The Green Hat* (Collins, 1924)
Artley, Alexandra (ed.), *The Golden Age of Shop Design, 1850–1939* (Whitney Library of Design, New York, 1976)
Baker, Anne Pimlott, *The Pilgrims of Great Britain: A Centennial History* (Profile Books, 2002)
Banner, Lois W., *American Beauty* (University of Chicago Press, Chicago, 1983)
Barrow, Andrew, *Gossip* (Pan, 1978)
Beaton, Cecil, *The Glass of Fashion* (Weidenfeld & Nicolson, 1954)
—— *Self-Portrait with Friends: The Selected Diaries of Cecil Beaton, 1926–74*, ed. Richard Buckle (Weidenfeld & Nicolson, 1979)
Benjamin, Thelma, *London Shops and Shopping* (H. Joseph, 1934)
Bennett, Arnold, *Journals* (Stratford Press, 1933), Vols. II and III, 1922–8
——*Letters of Arnold Bennett*, Vol. II, 1889–1915, ed. James Hepburn (Oxford University Press, Oxford, 1968)
——*Letters to his Nephew*, ed. Richard Bennett (William Heinemann, 1935)

Bennett, Richard, *A Picture of the Twenties* (Vista Books, 1971)

Black, Jean F., *Hyde Park Houses: An Informal History, 1856–1910* (University of Chicago Press, Chicago, 1978)

Blume, Mary, *Côte d'Azur: Inventing the French Riviera* (Thames & Hudson, 1992)

Blumenfeld, R. D., *Diaries, 1887–1914* (Heinemann, 1930)

Blythe, Ronald, *The Age of Illusion: England in the Twenties and Thirties* (Hamish Hamilton, 1963)

Bowlby, Rachel, *Just Looking: Consumer Culture in Dreiser, Gissing and Zola* (Methuen, 1985)

Bret, David, *The Mistinguett Legend* (St Martin's Press, New York, 1990)

—— *Tallulah Bankhead: A Scandalous Life* (Robson Books, New York, 1997)

Browne, J. Crawford, *The Early Days of the Department Store* (Scribner's, New York, 1921)

Buel, James William, *The Magic City* (Arno Press, New York, reprinted 1974)

Burg, David F., *Chicago's White City of 1893* (University Press of Kentucky, Lexington, 1976)

Burke, John, *Duet in Diamonds: The Flamboyant Saga of Lillian Russell and Diamond Jim Brady in America's Gilded Age* (Putnam, New York, 1972)

Calder, Robert, *Willie: The Life of Maugham* (Heinemann, 1989)

Callery, Sean, *Harrods: The Story of Society's Favourite Store* (Ebury Press, 1991)

Cantor, Eddie, and Freedman, David, *Ziegfeld: The Great Glorifier* (Alfred H. King, New York, 1934)

Carter, Ernestine, *20th Century Fashion: A Scrapbook, 1910 to Today* (Eyre Methuen, 1975)

Cartland, Barbara, *We Danced All Night* (Hutchinson, 1970)

Castle, Irene, *Castles in the Air* (Da Capo Press, 1958)

Chalmers, W. S., *The Life of Beatty* (Hodder & Stoughton, 1951)

Chapman, Gary, *The Delectable Dollies* (Sutton, 2006)

Chase, Edna Woolman, *Always in Vogue* (Victor Gollancz, 1954)

Collas, Phillippe and Villedary, Eric, *Edith Wharton's French Riviera* (Flammarion, Paris, 2002)

Cooper, Lady Diana, *The Rainbow Comes and Goes* (Riverside Press, Cambridge, 1958)

Corina, Maurice, *Fine Silks and Oak Counters: Debenhams* (Hutchinson, 1978)

Cowles, Virginia, *The Astors* (Alfred A. Knopf, New York, 1979)

Cruikshank, R.J., *Roaring Century* (Hamish Hamilton, 1946)

Curtis, Anthony, *Somerset Maugham* (Weidenfeld & Nicolson, 1977)

Dale, Tim, *Harrods: The Store and the Legend* (Pan, 1981)

Dedmon, Emmett, *Fabulous Chicago* (Random House, New York, 1953)

Ditchett, S. H., *Marshall Field & Company: The Life Story of a Great Concern* (Scribner's, New York, 1922)

Duis, Perry R., *'Challenging Chicago': Coping with Everyday Life, 1837–1920* (University of Illinois Press, Chicago, 1998)

Elias, Stephen, *Alexander T. Stewart: The Forgotten Merchant Prince* (Praeger, Westport, Conn., 1992)

Etherington Smith, Meredith, and Pilcher, Jeremy, *The 'It' Girls* (Harcourt, Brace, Jovanovich, San Diego, 1986)

Ewing, Elizabeth, *The History of 20th Century Fashion* (Batsford, 1974)

——*Dress and Undress: A History of Women's Underwear* (Batsford, 1978)

Ferry, John, *A History of the Department Store* (Macmillan, 1960)

Fisher, Richard, *Syrie Maugham* (Duckworth, 1978)

Fraser, Grace Lovat, *In the Days of My Youth* (Cassell, 1970)

Gallati, Mario, *Mario of the Caprice* (Hutchinson, 1960)

Gardiner, James, *Gaby Deslys* (Sidgwick & Jackson, 1986)

Garland, Madge, *A History of Fashion* (Orbis, 1970)

Goldring, D., *The Nineteen Twenties* (Weidenfeld & Nicolson, 1945)

Graham, J. A. Maxtone, *Eccentric Gamblers* (Mowbrays, 1975)

Graves, Charles, *None but the Rich: The Story of the Greek Syndicate* (Cassell, 1963)

Gray, Stuart, *Edwardian Shops and Stores in London: A Biographical Dictionary* (Duckworth, 1985)

Green, Martin, *Children of the Sun: A Narrative of Decadence in England after 1908* (Basic Books, New York, 1976)

Gregory, Alexis, *The Golden Age of Travel* (Cassell, 1991)

Halliday, Stephen, *Underground to Everywhere* (Sutton, 2001)

Hartnell, Norman, *Silver and Gold* (Evans Bros., 1955)

Hendrickson, Robert, *The Grand Emporiums: The Illustrated History of America's Great Department Stores* (Stein & Day, New York, 1933)

Herndon, Booten, *Bergdorf's on the Plaza* (Knopf, New York, 1956)

Hess, Max, Jr, *Every Dollar Counts: The Story of the American Department Store* (Fairchild, New York, 1952)

Honeycombe, Gordon, *Selfridges: Seventy-Five Years: The Story of the Store* (Park Lane Press, 1984)

Horne, Alistair, *The Terrible Year: the Paris Commune, 1871* (Macmillan, 1971)

Ishbel, Ross, *Silhouette in Diamonds: The Life of Mrs Potter Palmer* (Harper & Brothers, New York, 1960)

Jackson, Kate, *George Newnes and the New Journalism in Britain, 1880–1910: Culture and Profit* (Ashgate, Aldershot, 2001)

Jefferys, James, *Retail Trading in Britain, 1850–1950* (Cambridge University Press, Cambridge, 1954)

Jenkins, Alan, *The Rich Rich: The Story of the Big Spenders* (Weidenfeld & Nicolson, 1977)

——*The Twenties* (Heinemann, 1974)

Jenkins, Simon, *Newspapers: The Power and the Money* (Faber, 1979)

Kahr, Joan, *Edgar Brandt: Master of Art Deco Ironwork* (Harry N. Abrams, New York, 1999), foreword by François Brandt

Kidd, Janet Aitken, *The Beaverbrook Girl* (Collins, 1987)

Kinross, Lord, *The Windsor Years* (Viking, 1967)

Koehn, Nancy F., *Brand New: How Entrepreneurs Earned Consumers' Trust from Wedgwood to Dell* (Harvard Business School Press, Harvard, 2001)

Kurth, Peter, *Isadora: A Sensational Life* (Little, Brown & Co., Boston, 2001)

Leslie, Anita, *Edwardians in Love* (Hutchinson, 1972)

Lieven, Prince Peter, *The Birth of the Ballets Russes* (Allen & Unwin, 1935)

MacColl, Gail, and Wallace, Carol, *To Marry an English Lord* (Workman, New York, 1989)

Mackail, Denis, *The Story of J. M. B., Sir James Barrie* (Peter Davies, 1941)

McKnight, Gerald, *The Scandal of Syrie Maugham* (W. H. Allen, 1980)

MacQueen-Pope, Walter James, *Gaiety: Theatre of Enchantment* (W. H. Allen, 1949)

Madsen, Axel, *Coco Chanel* (Bloomsbury, 1990)

—— *The Marshall Fields* (Wiley, New York, 2002)

Manley, P. S., *Clarence Hatry* (Abacus, 1976)

Marbury, Elisabeth, *My Crystal Ball* (Hurst & Blackett, 1924)

Marcus, Stanley, *Minding the Store* (Little Brown, New York, 1974)

Margetson, Stella, *The Long Party: High Society in the 1920s* (Gordon Cremonsi, 1974)

Marly, Diana de, *Worth: Father of Haute Couture* (Elm Tree Books, 1980)

Masters, Anthony, *Rosa Lewis* (Weidenfeld & Nicolson, 1977)

Maugham, W. Somerset, *Of Human Bondage* (Heinemann, 1934)

——*Plays: One* (Methuen Drama, 1997)

Maxwell, Elsa, *R.S.V.P.* (Heinemann, 1952)

——*I Married the World* (William Heinemann, 1955)

Meyers, Jeffrey, *Somerset Maugham: A Life* (Vintage, 2005)

Meyrick, Kate, *Secrets of the '43'* (Parkgate Press, 1933)

Miller, Michael B., *The Bon Marché: Bourgeois Culture and the Department Store, 1869–1920* (Allen & Unwin, 1981)

Mistinguett, *Mistinguett by Mistinguett* (Elek Books, 1954)

Morris, Lloyd, *Incredible New York: High Life and Low Life* (Bonanza Books, New York, 1950)

Mosely, Roy, *Evergreen: Victor Saville in His Own Words* (Scholarly Book Services Inc, New York, 2002)

Newby, Eric, *Something Wholesale* (Picador, 1985)

Nichols, Beverley, *The Sweet and Twenties* (Weidenfeld & Nicolson, 1958)

Nicolson, Nigel, *Mary Curzon* (Weidenfeld & Nicolson, 1977)

——*Portrait of a Marriage* (Weidenfeld & Nicolson, 1973)

Obolensky, Serge, *One Man and His Time: The Memoirs of Serge Obolensky* (Hutchinson, 1960)

Parker, Morell, *Lillian Russell: The Era of Plush* (Random House, New York, 1940)

Peiss, Kathy, *Hope in a Jar: The Making of America's Beauty Culture* (Henry Holt, New York, 1998)

Porter, Roy, *London: A Social History* (Hamish Hamilton, 1994)

Pound, Reginald, *Arnold Bennett* (Heinemann, 1952)

—— *Selfridge* (Heinemann, 1960)

Priestley, J. B., *The Edwardians* (Heinemann, 1970)

Raphael, Frederic, *Somerset Maugham and His World* (Thames & Hudson, 1978)

Rappaport, Erika Diane, *Shopping for Pleasure: Women in the Making of London's West End* (University of Princeton Press, Princeton, 2000)

Roberts, Cecil, *The Bright Twenties, 1920–1929* (Hodder, 1970)

Ross, Ishbel, *Silhouette in Diamonds: The Life of Mrs Potter Palmer* (Harper & Brothers, New York, 1960)

Roux-Charles, Edmonde, *Chanel* (Collins, 1989)

Schiaparelli, Elsa, *Shocking Life* (Dent, 1954)

Scott, Jonathan, *The Pleasures of Antiquity: British Collectors of Greece and Rome* (Paul Mellon Centre, USA, 2003)

Seebohm, Caroline, *The Man who was Vogue: The Life and Times of Condé Nast* (Weidenfeld & Nicolson, 1982)

Selfridge, H. G., *The Romance of Commerce* (John Lane, 1917)

Sibour, Violette de, *Flying Gypsies* (G. P. Putnam, New York, 1930)

Siry, Joseph, *Carson, Pirie Scott: Louis Sullivan and the Chicago Department Store* (University of Chicago Press, Chicago, 1988)

Souhami, Diana, *Mrs Keppel and Her Daughter* (Flamingo, 1977)

Stansky, Peter, *Sassoon: The Worlds of Philip and Sybil* (Yale University Press, New Haven, 2003)

Tebbel, John, *The Marshall Fields* (Dutton, New York, 1947)

Thomson, George, *Lord Castlerosse* (Weidenfeld & Nicolson, 1973)

Thynne, Daphne, *The Duchess of Jermyn Street* (Eyre & Spottiswoode, 1964)

Tilden, Philip, *True Remembrances: The Memoir of an Architect* (Country Life, 1954)

Twombly, Robert, *Louis Sullivan: His Life and Work* (Viking Penguin, 1986)

Twyman, Robert W., *The History of Marshall Field & Co.* (University of Pennsylvania Press, Philadelphia, 1954)

—— *Potter Palmer: Merchandising Innovator of the West* (University of Pennsylvania Press, Philadelphia, 1951)

Vanderbilt, Gloria, and Furness, Thelma, *Double Exposure* (Hamilton, 1961)

Veblen, Thorstein, *The Theory of the Leisure Class* (Macmillan, 1899)

Vickers, Hugo, *Cecil Beaton* (Phoenix Press, 1985)

Vinikas, Vincent, *Soft Soap, Hard Sell: American Hygiene in an Age of Advertisement* (Iowa State University Press, Ames, 1992)

Waywell, Geoffrey B., *The Lever and Hope Sculptures* (Gebr. Mann Verlag, Berlin, 1986)

Wendt, Lloyd, and Kogan, Herman, *Give the Lady What She Wants: The Story of Marshall Field* (Rand McNally, Chicago, 1952)

Westminster, Loelia, *Grace and Favour* (Reynal, New York, 1961)

White, Palmer, *Poiret* (Studio Vista, 1973)

Williams, Alfred H., *No Name at the Door: A Memoir of Gordon Selfridge* (W. H. Allen, 1956)

Wilson, A. N., *The Victorians* (Hutchinson, 2001)

Wilson, Edmund, *The Twenties* (Macmillan, 1975)

Wilson, Sandy, *The Roaring Twenties* (Eyre Methuen, 1976)

Winkler, John K., *Five & Ten: The Fabulous Life of F. W. Woolworth* (Robert McBridge, New York, 1941)

Woodhead, Lindy, *War Paint: Helena Rubinstein and Elizabeth Arden, Their Lives, Their Times, Their Rivalry* (Virago, 2003)

Woolton, Frederick James, *The Memoirs of the Rt Hon the Earl of Woolton* (Cassell, 1959)

Yoxall, Harry, *A Fashion of Life* (Taplinger, New York, 1967)

Zola, Emile, *The Ladies' Paradise (Au Bonheur des Dames)* (1883)

ACKNOWLEDGEMENTS

Harry Gordon Selfridge left the store in 1939, and died aged 91 in 1947, so the chance of my meeting anyone who knew him in his prime, or worked with him from the early days, was never feasible. Biographers, however, depend on luck as well as their own judgement, and I was lucky with the treasures I found in the magnificent Selfridges archives which are not merely extant but are catalogued and maintained in immaculate order at the History of Advertising Trust in Norfolk.

The archive collection contains not just the old press cuttings books – with virtually every clipping personally noted by HGS himself – but also lists and notebooks, his private ledger, letters, photographs, personal ephemera and store catalogues, price lists, promotional material and advertisements. Over the years, friends, family and retirees have donated all manner of additions, and Sue Filmer, HAT's guardian of the collection, adds to it as her modest budget allows, with the result that it is one of the finest examples of British retailing history in existence today.

In the early 1900s HGS invested in a gold mine, at one point being told by the engineers that they had struck a seam. Sadly, it was worthless, but I struck my own seam of pure gold when Sue Filmer passed me a folder full of notes gathered by the store management in 1951 when they had the idea of publishing an official biography of Harry Gordon Selfridge. At that time, Selfridges was owned by Lewis's of Liverpool, who agreed to finance the project. The book went through a series of three prospective authors and at least two publishers and agents before the finished work, *Selfridge* by Reginald Pound, was finally published in 1960. The project was co-ordinated by the redoubtable Miss Mepham, who had been the gatekeeper to HGS's inner sanctum. She was the one woman still alive who had intimate knowledge of what his son later described as 'the several sides of my father'. She stayed at the store until 1957 and thanks to her diligence virtually all the senior retirees still alive between 1951 and 1957 were interviewed in depth to gather stories about HGS. Very few of them lived to see the finished book, but their contribution lives on.

Charles Clore's company, Sears Holdings Ltd, acquired Selfridges in 1965. It is precisely because of take-overs and mergers that archives are often lost, deliberately destroyed or simply thrown away. Not so under Charles Clore and his deputy chairman Leonard Sainer, who put in place a budget, an archive room and a devoted archivist, Victor Yates, who presided over the memorabilia with efficient enthusiasm. The result of that initiative is now at HAT and without it, this book could not have been written. So, to the management and staff of the History of Advertising Trust, and in particular Barry Cox, Margaret Rose, Chloe Veale, Sue Filmer and David Thomas, go my grateful thanks.

In 1956, A. H. Williams, who had worked for Harry Gordon Selfridge for twenty-eight years, wrote an affectionate book called *No Name at the Door*. Sears also commissioned the broadcaster and author Gordon Honeycombe to write *Selfridges*, celebrating seventy-five years of the store in 1984. Both books have been invaluable and informative sources.

No documents, however detailed, can substitute for seeing things for oneself. For that reason I would like to thank Sindee Hastings at Highcliffe Castle in Hampshire, which following shocking decline is now owned by Christchurch Borough Council and is currently undergoing extensive, sympathetic restoration. Sindee and I donned hard hats to tour the cellars and old kitchens in 2005, enabling me to understand castle life at the time the Selfridge family lived there. For those interested in Highcliffe's fascinating history, I urge you to visit www.highcliffecastle. co.uk which gives excellent notes and a list of books published about the castle. I owe thanks to Sindee for introducing me to the local historian Ian Stevenson. He has worked tirelessly to provide me with facts about the castle and Christchurch during the early 1920s. He has also sent copies of press cuttings, verified details and arranged for Mr D. M. Booth to take the photograph of Harry Selfridge's grave which appears in the plate section. Thanks also to the Reverend Garry Taylor of the charming St Mark's Church at Highcliffe, Beverley Morris of the Hampshire Records Office and S. C. Munsey at the Hampshire Local Studies Collection.

Although Selfridge's tenure is recognized by a blue plaque, Lansdowne House today bears little resemblance to how it was when he lived there. Butchered beyond belief by various developers, it is a shadow of its former glorious self, existing today as a members' club. The Yarborough Mansion in Arlington Street has also long since vanished. But one begins to understand something of the lifestyle of Selfridge and his neighbours the Duke and Duchess of Rutland if one walks past the Ritz Hotel and the hotel's recently acquired (and magnificently restored) adjacent property Wimborne House, and on down the street towards the Caprice restaurant, where I enjoyed several lively lunches with contributors to this book. Selfridge was a devotee of both the Caprice and the Ivy, and Mario Gallati's memoirs proved an invaluable source.

Chicago as a city during the late nineteenth and early twentieth century came alive to me both through Emmett Dedmon's superlative book *Fabulous Chicago* and Perry R. Duis's equally evocative essays collated in *'Challenging Chicago': Coping with Everyday Life, 1837–1920*. Enthusiastic experts hastened to search out answers to complex questions and to trace rare photographs and facilitate permissions. In particular I would like to thank Trish Morse whose wonderfully descriptive 'Midway Plaisance Walking Tour' enabled me to trace Rose Buckingham's property development project; the Hyde Park Historical Society; the staff at the Chicago Public Library, in particular Lorna Donley and Teresa Yoder at the Harold Washington Library Center; and most especially Rob Medina of the Chicago History Museum.

Elsewhere in America I was assisted by: Laura Linard of the Baker Library at Harvard; Mandy Shear, Faculty and Research at Harvard Business School; Geraldine Strey of the Wisconsin Historical Society; John Dorner of the Illinois Lodge of Research Library; Mark Tabbert of the George Washington Masonic National Memorial; Rachel Hertz at the Harry Ransom Humanities Research Center, University of Texas, Austin; Stephen Showers and Marybeth Roy of Otis; Darcie M. Posz of the Daughters of the American Revolution; Mattie Taormina and Polly Armstrong at Stanford University Library; and Lauren Robinson-Brown at Princeton University. The author Pauline Metcalfe, who was writing her own biography of Syrie Maugham at the time that I was writing about Syrie's one-time lover H. G. Selfridge, sent cheering emails offering information, as did her editor Mitch Owens. Patricia Erigero, a specialist on the history of race-horses, advised on the Selfridge stable of steeplechasers, and Arnie Reisman and Ann Carol Grossman gave support, advice on books to read and suggestions on people to talk to. I am particularly grateful to Professor Nancy F. Koehn of Harvard Business School who not only made time to be interviewed but also couriered copies of her HBS paper on Marshall Field to help me meet a deadline.

Gary Chapman, author of *The Delectable Dollies*, has been both enthusiastic and helpful in giving freely of information, as have the authors Anne Sebba in respect of her book on Jennie Jerome and James Gardiner who wrote devotedly about Gaby Deslys.

In my quest for links between Harry Gordon Selfridge and his friend Arnold Bennett, I would like to thank Helen Burton at Keele University and most particularly

John Shapcott of the Arnold Bennett Society who was kindness itself in supplying all manner of detail. Janice Francoise at Southwark Library provided information about Kingswood House; and Sarah Gould at Merton Libraries and Heritage Services went to endless trouble to check details about the Wiasemskys' tenure at Wimbledon Park House. The noted genealogist Timothy Boettger provided his expertise on Russian titles, and Ian Jenkins, Curator of Greek and Roman Antiquities at the British Museum, educated me on both the Hope Sculpture Collections and the splendid collections once kept at Lansdowne House. Denise Summerton at the University of Nottingham provided information on the Hope Sale. Dr Gerda Reith of Glasgow University took time to explain the intricacies of the gambler's mentality. From Australia, Mary Garden provided information about Mr Garden's epic flight to Australia in the plane he bought at Selfridge's. At Condé Nast in London I would like to thank Nicolas Coleridge, Harriet Wilson and her team, and Brett Croft, who runs the Condé Nast Library, for undertaking so much copying and putting up with my erratic schedule. I must also thank Annie Pindor of the House of Lords Record Office, Jane Rosen of the Imperial War Museum, the Bill Douglas Centre for the History of the Cinema and Popular Culture at the University of Exeter and the staff at the London Library.

A special thank you to Suzy Menkes, Rodney Fitch, Peter Wallis, Vittorio Radice, Scott Malkin and Mark Sebba, all of whom took time to answer questions about retailing today in the context of the department store and H. G. Selfridge.

I am most grateful to HRH The Prince of Wales for permission to quote from his 1990 speech 'Accent on Architecture', given at the American Institute of Architects gala dinner, and to Amanda Foster, Press Officer to the Prince of Wales and the Duchess of Cornwall.

Harry Gordon Selfridge's great-grandson Simon Wheaton Smith was generous with his time, memories of his mother and grandparents, and his precious family archives. I would also like to thank Gordon Selfridge Jr's daughter, Jennifer MacLeod.

Friends and contacts who have sent information, given advice and encouragement, and even on occasion done my shopping during the many months I was glued to my computer include: Alison Cathie, Oliver Musker, Simon Rendall, Giles Chapman, David Burgess-Wise, Karen Wheeler, Alisdair Sutherland, Samantha Conti, Robert Harding of Maggs Bros., Sarah Standing, Melissa Wyndham, Stephen Lawler, Ju Ju Watenphul, Tim Leon-Dufour, Margaret Muldoon, John Rendall and Susan Farmer. In France, Charlotte and Chris Milln, Tener and Patsy Eckleberry, Carole and Alan Henderson, Ewart Bremer, Sophie Allington, Jorge Guillermo, Michael Dobson, Felix Anaut, Carey Good and Jean-Claude and Kattaline Pavlosky proved what friends and neighbours are for.

To my husband, who has put up with a lot over the past three years, special thanks for his discerning eye in selecting photographs. He read chapters from the very beginning, as did my son Max. Both laughed in the right places and gave wise advice. Ollie (who himself once worked at Selfridges) preferred to wait for the finished book but has cheered me at every turn. My sister Nikki, her daughter Julie and her grandson Jake, who was born while I was writing this book, have all played their part in keeping the home fires burning.

This book wouldn't have happened without the support and enthusiasm of my agent, Lucinda Prain at William Morris Associates, who always believed in the story. Caroline Michel, Eugenie Furniss and Lucinda at WMA are a formidable team to have batting on your side. At my publishers, Profile Books, Andrew Franklin deserves a special mention for resolving the book's title and suggesting the format for the end chapter. Profile are lucky to have Gail Pirkis on board, and I am lucky to have had her as my editor. Her wisdom, tact and graceful editing, not to mention her patience over some fraught moments while writing this book, have kept me going. Thanks also to Penny Daniel and Nicola Taplin who managed the book through its final stages and to the most knowledgeable, eagle-eyed indexer any biographer could ask for: Douglas Matthews. My thanks, too, to Rebecca Gray and Anna-Marie Fitzgerald for spearheading the publicity with such enthusiasm.

Finally I must turn to Selfridges where the creative director Alannah Weston must have been astonished to get a letter from out of the blue, telling her that I was writing a book about the founder and that I hoped they would 'help me out'. She took it well. Nothing has been too much trouble for the staff at the store who have been kindness itself and have allowed me to explore every nook and cranny of the place. They have answered innumerable questions, their lawyers have given copyright approval and the press office has checked details for me around the clock. I saw the wonderful Madonna picture when walking down the executive corridor to visit the chief executive Paul Kelly: in a flash it was mine to use in the plate section. To Alannah Weston, Mr and Mrs Galen Weston, Paul Kelly, Christine Watts, Sally Scott, Sue Minns, Caroline Parker, William Rae, Elisa Young and Lucy Willis, not forgetting the inimitable Michael Howells, go my heartfelt thanks. I hope you enjoy reading this book as much as I have enjoyed writing it.

INDEX

1925

CONFIDENCE
--- --- ---
THE ABSOLUTE
CONFIDENCE OF
THE PUBLIC IS
THE GREATEST
AND MOST
PRIZED ASSET
OF THIS HOUSE
OF BUSINESS.

1924

EFFICIENCY
--- --- ---
MEANS DOING
THINGS WELL
AND QUICKLY.
WE APPLAUD
AND ENCOURAGE
IN OUR YOUNG
PEOPLE THIS
FINE QUALITY.

BEYOND INDIGO

By the same author

One Hundred Shades of White
Gypsy Masala

PREETHI NAIR

Beyond Indigo

HarperCollins*Publishers*

This novel is entirely a work of fiction.
The names, characters and incidents portrayed
in it are the work of the author's imagination.
Any resemblance to actual persons, living or dead,
events or localities is entirely coincidental.

HarperCollins*Publishers*
77–85 Fulham Palace Road,
Hammersmith, London W6 8JB

www.harpercollins.co.uk

Published by HarperCollins*Publishers* 2004
1   3   5   7   9   8   6   4   2

A catalogue record for this book
is available from the British Library

ISBN 0 00 714348 6

Set in Sabon by Palimpsest Book Production Limited,
Polmont, Stirlingshire

Printed and bound in Great Britain by
Clays Ltd, St Ives plc

Thank you to whoever is responsible for making flowers pop up when I most needed them. To my family and friends, especially to Avni, Esperenza and Tricia whose constant support, encouragement and enthusiasm cannot help but inspire me. To my friend and agent Diana Holmes for believing in me and finally a big 'thank you' to all the team at HarperCollins.

To my Dad and Amma.

'There are always flowers for those who want to see them.'
HENRI MATISSE

2nd December 1999

I know now that hurtling a saffron-stained coconut over London Bridge at six-thirty in the morning should have set some alarm bells off. The tramp peered up at me from his cardboard box as if to say that I would be joining him very soon. But the Guru had said that it would remove the stagnation from my life, me being represented by a hairy coconut and the water representing flow. The Thames did not glisten at me. Well, it couldn't really as it was pitch black and probably frozen, but I believed it was glistening, shimmering even, and leading me to better things.

Looking back, the only bit the Guru got right was the symbolism. Brown woman thrown further into murky waters.

I had met this Guru the previous day. I'd like to say that I met him at the foothills of the Himalayas or somewhere exotic but I bumped into him outside Pound Savers on Croydon High Street. It was one of those really cold December days when everything comes at you from all directions; the wind, the rain, puddle-slush, the odd hailstone, and anything else nature can find to throw at you.

It had been a really hard day at work and almost unbearable to get through: my best friend, Kirelli, had died exactly

1

a year earlier. Sorting out the contract of some egotistical artist and checking the provenance of a painting for a client seemed irrelevant, so I told my boss that I had a headache and was leaving early.

'Two aspirins will clear it,' he said.

'Right, I'll get some on my way home,' I replied, with absolutely no intention of stopping off at the chemist's. I was good at pretending; it had become second nature to me because of the distinct worlds I lived in.

Having said that, there were certain parallels between the art world and the Indian subcontinent ensconced within our semi: both worlds were seemingly very secure with an undercurrent of unspoken rules and codes of conduct that were made and manipulated by a dominant few. One set fixed the price of art and the other fixed up marriages. The main difference was that the ones in the art world didn't have centre-parted hair and weren't dressed in saris, grey woolly socks and sandals.

The only way I was able to make the cultural crossover from the Hindi songs wailing from the semi to the classical music played subtly at the reception area in the law firm where I worked as an artist's representative was by pretending. Pretending to be someone I wasn't.

'Nina, Boo Williams is coming in tomorrow,' my boss reiterated before I left. This was his coded way of saying, 'Make sure you pull yourself together by the morning.'

Boo Williams was one of the artists we represented at the firm. Her sculpture of Venus de Milo made from dried fruit and vegetables had failed to win the Turner Prize so she would be needing much consolation and bullshit from me in the morning. Forget the sickie, forget grief; Boo and her heap of fruit and vegetables needed me more.

'Right, see you tomorrow then,' I muttered, grabbing my coat.

On the way back home there were no commuters hurling

2

themselves onto the tube. The carriages were almost empty and I was relieved, because if I had had a group of wet strangers pushing against me, vying for space, that would have just about done it. I sat opposite an old lady with wispy white hair. She had the kind of eyes that made me want to tell her that my best friend had died in my arms at exactly this time – two-thirty, a year ago – and that since then I had been lost, truly lost. The old lady smiled at me and a lump began to form in my throat. I got up, moved seats and sat down beside a soggy copy of the *Guardian*. The page it was turned to showed the Turner Prize winner, Maximus Karlhein, trying desperately to pose seriously. He was standing next to one of his pieces exhibited at the Tate – an old wardrobe stuffed with his worldly possessions.

I pushed the paper away feeling exhausted. It was all nonsense; people posing in front of wardrobes, passing it off as art and making headlines. Where was the feeling? The passion? And that crap – that the relationship with his wardrobe was imbued on his soul and that he had no option but to express it – which PR person had thought of that line? Art was supposed to be passionate and full of emotion, not contrived, not like an Emperor's-new-clothes scenario where a group of influential people said that the work was good and therefore people believed it was. What had happened to art? Paintings done by artists who didn't even care if they weren't known, not some hyped artist giving a convoluted explanation behind a pile of dried fruit or a heap of junk. A year on, and despite promising that I would be true to myself after Ki's death, I still participated in the circus.

Tomorrow, no doubt I would have to console Boo. What kind of name was that anyway? Knock, knock, who's there? Boo. Boo who? Don't worry, love, your apricots didn't win the Turner Prize this year but you can sell

3

them for at least five grand. That's what I would want to say, but what I would probably say was, 'Ms Williams, Boo, it's an injustice, I just can't see how you didn't win. Your concept, the use of colour is simply . . . simply inspirational.'

Was that what happened to you in life? You started off with such high hopes and ideals and then got sucked into all the bullshit and you pretended that that was reality. No, I didn't think that was the case with me – I knew deep down that life was too short to be doing anything other than what I really wanted to do; Ki had shown me that. But that wasn't the problem – there were the occupants living in the semi to consider. I had a duty to make sure that they were happy, and keeping my job as a lawyer was fundamental to their all-important list system.

Mum and Dad's short list was devoid of any kind of love or passion. Thinking about it, the Turner Prize short list and my parents' own were not that dissimilar: although the criteria was seemingly clear and transparent, the subject produced was, at times, truly baffling. In their case, the subject was a man and the objective of the list was to find me a husband. Like the art world, much went on behind the scenes that nobody really knew about. Favours were exchanged, backs were scratched and tactics employed so that the prospective candidate was over-hyped to an influential few in order to persuade them that he was the right man for the job.

The long list was drawn up by a group of well-connected elderly women in the community, whose demure presence betrayed what they were really capable of. The criteria that had been set to filter the candidates were that they had to come from a good family background, be well educated and have lots of money. One of my mum's roles was to whittle down the long list, but her primary task was to set the PR machinery in motion; to cover up any negatives, then to promote and hype the candidates and make sure they were shown to me in a favourable light. This week she had managed to get the list down to three potentials whose vital statistics were presented in the form of handwritten CVs. There was a doctor, another lawyer and an accountant left on the dining-room table for me to look at. The hot favourite (who had been put to the top of the pile) was the accountant, because he had his own property: 'Beta, this candidate was imbued on my soul.' She wouldn't use those words exactly, she would just draw my attention to his flat. So, although it was seemingly my decision to choose one, go on a few dates with him and agree to marriage, the system was clearly rigged.

However, the panel had overlooked one very important thing: an outsider was trying to infiltrate the system. A man of whom they had no knowledge had just asked me to marry him. The judges were going to have a problem. At best there would be an uproar: my dad would pretend to go into heart failure and my mum would do her wailing and beating on the chest routine. At worst I would suffer the same fate as my sister, who had run off with her boyfriend and who they had not spoken to since.

I didn't know what to say to Jean Michel when he asked me to marry him. It wasn't a question of not loving him enough; it was a question of making a decision and then facing all of the consequences, and I was too tired for all of that. So for a while I hadn't been making any decisions; not even daring to venture slightly outside my routine. There was a certain sense of safety in catching the tube to work, dealing with clients, going back home to Mum and Dad and seeing the CVs on the table.

I hadn't been thinking about anything too deeply except on days like that when I had been forced to. I mean, I knew Ki was dead, I had watched her disintegrate before me and then be scattered into the wind, but for me she was still there in some kind of shape or form. She had to be. Pretending that she was still there, looking out for me, was the only thing that had helped me hold it together, because otherwise . . . otherwise, everything was pointless.

Her death was senseless. Good people weren't supposed to die young. I had bargained hard with God and promised to do all sorts of things if He let her live, and although He didn't listen I held steadfast in my belief. It was the only thing that I could really cling to. I don't know how best to describe what this *belief* was, but it's the feeling that someone out there is listening and responding; that there's a universal conversation going on where forces of nature conspire to look after you and give you strength. Occasionally you'd get a glimpse of the workings behind the scenes and these were termed by others as coincidences or luck. And then there were signs. Signs were things like accidentally finding a twenty-pound note when you most needed it; a song on the radio that comes from nowhere and that speaks to you directly; words or people that find their way to you at just the right time. Ki promised she would send me a sign. A year had passed and she hadn't. Or maybe she had and I'd missed it. I had become far too busy to see any signs.

I got off the underground and waited for the train that would take me home.

The High Street looked tired and depressed, like it too had had enough of being battered by the rain. Among all the greyness, the windswept umbrellas and the shoppers scurrying home, I suddenly spotted colour, a vibrant bright orange. I walked in its direction to take a closer look. It was a Guru, standing calmly in the rain amid a flurry of

6

activity. I stopped momentarily, thinking that the scene would have made a good painting, and stared at the strangeness of his presence. He was wearing a long, orange robe over some blue flarey trousers and over his robe he had a blue body-warmer. As they walked past, school children were pointing and laughing at the enormous red stain across his forehead. The red stain did not strike me as much as the open-toed sandals on his feet. It was freezing, and as I was thinking that he must be in desperate need of some socks, someone called out to me.

'Nina, Nina,' shouted the man as he came out of Pound Savers, clutching his bag. He knew my dad, I had met him a couple of times but I couldn't remember his name.

'Hello Uncle,' I said, thankful that calling obscure friends of your parents 'Uncle' is an Indian thing. Any random person that you've only met once in your life has to be bestowed with this title. 'How are you?' I asked politely.

'Just buying the socks for his Holiness,' he said, looking at the Guru, 'he's finding the weather here a little colder than Mumbai. Guru Anuraj, this is Nina Savani. Nina, this is his Holiness, Guru Anuraj.'

The Guru put his hands together in a prayer pose. If I was a well-mannered Indian girl, such an introduction and the use of the word 'Holiness' would be my cue to bow down in the middle of Croydon High Street and touch his 'Holiness's' icy feet, but instead I just smiled and nodded.

The Guru held out his hand. I thought he was angling for a handshake so I gave him mine. He took it, turned it palm up and muttered, 'Been through much heartache. Don't worry, it's nearly over.'

'He's very good, you know. For years Auntie was becoming unable to have baby and now we are expecting our child,' acquaintance man interrupted eagerly. 'Guru

7

Anuraj was responsible for sending child,' he beamed.

The Guru's warm smile spun out like a safety net as he told me my life would improve greatly in two weeks. Although his smile was warm I chose to ignore the fact that it was full of chipped and blackened teeth. If I had paid attention to his dental hygiene it could have given me some indication towards his character and all that was to follow without having to take his palm – 'cleanliness being next to godliness' and all that – but as he made promises of being able to remove the stagnant energy which was the cause of much maligned obstacles, I chose not to see the warning signs. I wanted him to tell me more but the Guru had his socks to put on. He'd also spotted the grocer roasting chestnuts, and indicated to acquaintance man that he might like some.

Before he left, he delved inside his robe and handed me a leaflet. 'Call me,' he said, staring intently into my eyes.

'You must call him, his Holiness only gives out his number to the very special people,' added acquaintance man. I took the leaflet and said goodbye to them both.

When I got home, Hindi music was blasting from the television set and both my parents were doing their normal activities. My mum was in the kitchen making rotis and my dad was in the sitting room, with a glass of whisky in one hand, newspaper in the other, looking like an Indian version of Father Christmas with his red shirt, white beard and big belly. He was the only person who was not engulfed by the enormous Land of Leather sofa.

'Good day, Nina?' he asked, turning back to his newspaper.

'It was really crap. Crap day, crap client, just awful.'

'Good, good,' he replied. My dad had very selective

hearing and only chose to hear the words he liked or words that were of some threat to him. 'Home early, no?'

'We were all made redundant.'

He put his glass down, threw his newspaper to the floor and looked at me. Redundancy was his worst nightmare. I had to be a lawyer; years of both time and money were invested in this and it was pivotal to the list system (the spin on candidates worked both ways so I too was lying on someone's dining-room table). That was what he sold me on, the fact that I was a lawyer working for a reputable firm, and also that I was tall and quite fair-skinned, but he omitted the fact that I had one humungous scar down my left arm and that I couldn't really cook.

By my parents' standards, twenty-seven was far too late to be getting married, and my mum was truly baffled by it, saying to my father that I was one of the prettiest girls on the circuit and there was a queue of men waiting to marry me. But I had managed to fend them off so far by telling them that things were changing and men were looking for women who were settled in their careers; it wasn't like the olden days when they just wanted to know your height, complexion, and if you had long hair down to your back. It was, however, getting to a stage where this argument was wearing thin. As my dad said, at this rate I would be heading towards retirement: hence more and more weekly CVs.

'What?' he shouted.

'I said I had a headache.'

'I thought you said redundant.'

'No, just a headache.'

'Thank Bhagavan,' he sighed, glancing up to one of the many incarnated god statues.

My mum came out of the kitchen, rolling pin in one hand. 'What headache, beta? It's because you are not eating properly.'

'I think I'll just go to bed, I'll be fine, Ma.'

'Not eating with us?' she asked, looking over at the dining-room table and fixing her gaze on it. 'Rajan Mehta. He's thirty-one, an accountant. He's got his own flat in Victoria . . .'

My heart sank. I turned my back and began walking up the stairs as she shouted, '. . . three bedrooms and two bathrooms.'

I couldn't put off the inevitable. I had to tell them about Jean Michel, and tell them soon. He was away on a business trip in New York and as soon as he got back we had to sort something out. I picked up the phone to call him and put it down again; he was having back-to-back meetings so it probably wasn't the best time to call. I flicked through my address book to see who else I could phone. I had friends, of course, but nobody I could open up to. Since Ki's death I had kept all my other friendships on a superficial basis: nobody knew what was really going on inside my head as I refused to go through that kind of closeness again only for it to be snatched away. I flicked through the pages once more. No, there was no one, no one who had an inkling that anything was wrong. Anyway, where would I start? The fact that I did not allow myself to cry, that I was desperately missing Ki, that I hated going into work, or that I didn't know whether to marry Jean Michel?

Suddenly, a thought occurred to me.

'Did you send that Guru for me, Ki? Is that what you meant when you said you'd speak to me? Was he a sign?'

I pulled out the leaflet and read: 'Guru Anuraj, Psychic Healer, Spiritual Counsellor and Friend.'

I dialled the number. He gave me an appointment to come and see him the very next morning. I had a shower and went to bed.

*　　*　　*

It was five-thirty in the morning when I drove to the address he had given me. I didn't want to tell my parents that I was going to see the Guru as it would have sent my mother's thoughts propelling into all kinds of directions and that was dangerous. So when she spotted me up and about very early in the morning I told her I was driving up to Leeds for a client meeting; the lie, believe me, was for her own protection.

I know it was an odd time but my mum always said that, supposedly, between four and seven in the morning are when prayers are most likely to be receptive – that's when she annoyed all the neighbours with her howling and chanting.

'Kavitha, why you can't you learn to sing like the Cilla Black?' my dad would ask her.

'I *am* singing.'

'This is not the singing, see, neighbours have written letters doing complaining,' my dad said, producing letters that contained handwriting which appeared remarkably similar to that of his own.

'This is all for Nina, so she will find a good man, coming from a good family,' my mother replied.

'No, only man who comes will be police.'

But she continued unabated by threats of the council charging her with noise pollution. Because, for her, if it produced the desired result it would all have been worth it.

When I arrived I knocked on the door as instructed. A short man opened it and took me to the dining room where he asked me to take a seat. He said that the Guru was with someone and would see me shortly. I was nervous and excited; seeing the Guru was the first positive step I had taken in a long while. Admittedly, I was also feeling slightly apprehensive, not about being in a stranger's house but about what the Guru might say, so I focused on the decoration in the dining room and, like Lloyd Grossman, studied the clues and imagined what sort of family lived there. Half an hour later the man came back and led me to another room. I knocked on the door and went in.

Warm jasmine incense and soft music and candles filled the room, and on pieces of colourful silk stood statues of gods in all different sizes. The Guru acknowledged me by nodding his head and asked me to remove my shoes and take a seat opposite him on the floor. I did so nervously.

'Date of birth?' the Guru asked swiftly.

'Fourth of September, 1972.'

He proceeded to draw boxes, do calculations, and then, like a bingo caller, he reeled off some numbers which, he said, were the key events that had marked my life: aged six, an accident with the element of fire which had left deep scarring. I looked at my right arm; it was well covered, how could he have known that? He continued: aged eighteen, a romantic liaison which did not end in marriage. At this point he raised his eyebrow. Aged twenty-five, another. I saw how this could look bad to a holy Guru who believed in traditional values and the sanctity of just one arranged marriage so I avoided eye contact.

'A Western man?' he questioned.

I nodded.

He shook his head. 'It is being serious?' he asked.

I nodded again.

'Parents knowing?'

I shook my head.

'Parents not arranging anything?'

Parents were very busy arranging things. Last week the hot favourite was a twenty-nine-year-old investment banker, this week it was thirty-one-year-old, five degrees accountant Raj, the letters behind his name rolling off the page.

The Guru stopped at age twenty-six, with the death of my best friend.

'It will all change,' he promised. I fought back the tears and then he touched the palms of my hands and they began to tingle, a warm glow that made his words feel safe.

'Stagnant life now, unable to move forward, unable to take decision. See this,' he said, nodding at my palms, 'this is now flow but too much negativity in body for flow. Let it go. Let it all go.' And that's how the whole coconut-over-bridge routine came about.

It sounds bizarre now but he performed a ceremony that morning, asking permission from the gods to be able to treat me. The coconut he used in the ceremony was meant to represent me and he stained it with saffron. He did the same with my forehead so that the coconut and I were united. The river was supposed to represent new life. After mumbling a prayer, the Guru asked me to return after I'd thrown my coconut self off the bridge. I could have chosen anywhere where there was water, even the canal near where we lived, but I didn't want the coconut to sink to the bottom and find a rusty bicycle, a portent of doom if ever there was one, so I chose London Bridge.

'There will be a big change in you, Nina,' he said as I left, coconut in hand. 'Come and see me later this evening.'

After I hurled the coconut off the bridge I felt immensely relieved. I wiped the stain off my forehead and went to work, ready to caress Boo Williams' ego. I got to work only to be told that Boo was too upset to get out of bed and would be in the following day instead. Still, I was unperturbed.

Richard, one of my colleagues, commented on how well I was looking.

'I'm getting engaged,' I replied.

When the coconut had left my hands all my decisions seemed so clear. I wanted to phone Jean Michel right away to tell him that I was going to marry him. I started to dial his mobile number but decided to wait for him to come back from his trip the next day and tell him in person. Everything that day at work was effortless. I knew I wouldn't have to be there for long: once Jean and I were married I could think about other options. And my mum and dad? What would I do with them? If I looked at things optimistically, Jean could charm my mother – he could charm anyone, he was incredibly charismatic – and my mum, in turn, could work on my dad. Together we could make him come around.

Jean called me later that afternoon and I had to stop myself from blurting it all out.

'I can't wait to see you, ma cherie.'

'Me too. When you're back it's all going to change. I love you, Jean.'

All I had to do was wait one more day and all the pretence could stop.

The Guru had given me the energy to make all obstacles appear surmountable and later that evening I returned to thank him for what he had done. He prescribed one more session for the following day, just to make sure I would keep on track. How I wish I had stopped there.

The next morning the Guru's door was slightly ajar so I knocked on it and walked in. He had his back to me and was lighting his candles, humming away and swaying to Sting's 'Englishman in New York', which was playing loudly. It got to the alien bit when the Guru turned around.

14

He looked startled when he saw me and immediately stopped the tape recorder, saying that he was sampling the music that was corrupting the youth of today, and promptly changed the cassette to a whinging sitar.

'Sting is not a corrupting force,' I said. 'In fact, he's against deforestation.'

The Guru glared at me when I said deforestation like he didn't know what the word meant, but now I think about that look – eyes narrowing, brows furrowed – it was probably more that he remembered he had a job to do.

He signalled for me to sit on the floor and held my hands. They tingled with warmth again as he whispered kind words and then he began humming and chanting. Then the Guru asked me to lie down and he proceeded to touch me, moving slowly from my hands to other parts of my body, my neck, my feet; incantations and gods' names being chanted all the while as he healed the negativity that shrouded me, asking me to let it go. As he unbuttoned my clothes and took off my top, his breath became rhythmic, his chanting louder, his beads pressed against my chest. I closed my eyes, wanting to believe that I was lost between the gods' names and that none of this was really happening. It couldn't happen; a holy man wouldn't do this, he couldn't do this, this wasn't supposed to happen. His beard brushed against my skin, his fingers circled my mouth, I pretended that my trousers had not come down.

I have often asked myself why I didn't get out of there sooner and how I had got myself into such a position. I didn't want to believe what was really going on, because if I did, nothing whatsoever would make any sense – and the only thing at that point in time that I had left to hang on to was my belief. I didn't want to believe what his dry, filthy hands were doing because I would have had to concede that whoever was responsible for sending me signs had sent this Guru, who was into an altogether different kind of spiritual feeling. Nobody could be that cruel.

As he placed his salivating mouth on my lips and pulled up his robe, I smelled him, and it was this that made something inside of me snap. He smelled of coffee. I kicked him, pushed him off me and managed to get out from under him before he used his magic wand.

'No,' I shouted.

'You're cursed,' he screamed as I ran out of the door. 'Cursed, and I will make sure of it.'

How I had sunk to such depths still remains a mystery but, essentially, that is where my journey began. I was confused and desperate, feeling wholly inadequate, riddled with self-doubt and dirty. I wanted to call Jean Michel and tell him but he would kill the Guru. So I tried to block it from my mind and pretend that nothing had happened.

The train I was on stopped. Some old man with the same rotten teeth as the Guru got on. It's funny how that happens; reminders of the things you are trying most to forget. He smiled at me and I felt physically sick. My hands began to shake. 'It didn't happen,' I kept saying to myself. 'It's all in the mind, it didn't happen,' and I reached into my handbag to get a mint. While I was fishing for it I found an envelope that was marked urgent.

It was a contract that I had looked over for a client, and which had been sitting in my handbag for the last two days. I had promised to send it back the next day and had completely forgotten. But today it was all going to change. I had to hold it together.

'All change here,' announced the driver. Although

running late I was determined to buy a stamp, find a postbox, and personally post this letter. Posting it myself would be symbolic of my commitment to getting my life back on track. But, wouldn't you know, there wasn't a postbox in sight.

'You're cursed,' I kept hearing, and the more I heard it, the more adamant I became that I would find a postbox and put everything behind me.

My boss, Simon, was slightly concerned when I arrived late. I was *never* late.

'Is everything all right, Nina?'

'Fine, just fine,' I said, making my way to my desk.

I turned on the computer and looked out of the window. The buildings were grey and dreary and set against a grey winter sky. So many times I had sat looking out of this window, imagining the sky to be orange, wishing that I could soak up the rays of an orange sky, fly out of the window and have the courage to do something else, something that gave me meaning.

I had been working at Whitter and Lawson for the last three and a half years, representing all kinds of artists but mostly those who had issues over copyright or needed contractual agreements with galleries drawn up. I read somewhere that people work on the periphery of what they really want to do so that they don't have to cope with rejection. So, someone who harboured desires to be a racing-car driver would be a mechanic on a racetrack but not actually drive the car. It was like this for me in a sense: I'd always wanted to be a painter and so I worked with artists. But my job wasn't really about art, it was about making money, dealing with boosting egos. Feeling increasingly cynical and secretly thinking that I could do much better. But I couldn't – it wasn't really rejection I feared, it was disappointing my father and sabotaging his investment in the *Encyclopaedia Britannica*.

I'd known I wanted to be a painter since the age of six. My brain had always had difficulty engaging with my mouth and I was unable to fully articulate any emotion except on paper. So anything I felt, I produced in a swirl of finger-painted colours that nobody could quite manage to understand. When I found out that my sister wasn't coming back I did more of the same. My parents didn't hang the pictures on the fridge door with a magnet – they didn't know that that is what you were supposed to do with the nonsensical pictures that your children produced. They didn't even lie and tell me how good they were. Instead, the pictures were folded up and binned while my father would sit with me and read me bits from the *Encyclopaedia Britannica*, extracts that even he didn't understand. He was preparing me for a career in law, or 'love' as he mispronounced it.

His career choice for me was not based on any long-standing family tradition. He was a bus driver and I think he just wanted to give me the best possible start, and make sure I would not have to face the instability that he had suffered. That's why when the encyclopaedia man came round when I was young and sensed the aspirations my father had for me, he blatantly incorporated me into his sales pitch by saying that the books would set me on course for a high-flying career. My dad bought the whole set, which he could clearly not afford, taking on extra jobs like mending television sets so he could buy the entire set and receive the latest volume, year after year.

At sixteen, when I expressed a desire to go to art college he went ballistic and didn't speak to me for weeks. When he did it was to say, 'Nina, I have not sacrificed the life so you can do the hobby, the lawyer is a good profession. Not that I am pressurising you, not that I came to

18

the England to give you the good education and work every hour and make sacrifices.'

Put that way I could clearly see his point. So I did an art A level without him knowing about it – just in case, by some miracle, he changed his mind. He didn't and so I went to university to study law.

Whitter and Lawson was where I did my training, and I worked incredibly hard so that they would give me a job after I had finished; at least that way I could be around artists and connect with their world. Everyone around me said it was impossible, there were hardly any Indian lawyers representing artists and it was a place where contacts mattered. People said that I would need a miracle to be taken on by the firm but I busted my gut and worked every single hour I could, going out of my way to prove everyone wrong.

I remember making promises that I would do a whole series of things if I got the job, like give away ten per cent of my future earnings to charity and buy a *Big Issue* weekly. To whom these promises were made I couldn't really tell you; maybe just to myself. So I should have known that the first visible signs of wanting out was crossing the road, making out like I hadn't seen the *Big Issue* man when he was blatantly waving at me. But I pretended, pretended that I was lucky to have a job and make lots of money and be in that world. My dad always said this was what life was about – working hard, being disciplined, making money, surviving in a 'dog eating the cat' world. But then my best friend Ki died and none of that made sense anymore. An uneasiness began to set in.

Felicity, the PA, called me to say that Boo Williams was waiting for me in reception.

*　　*　　*

19

Ki disintegrated rapidly at twenty-five. She had felt a lump in her leg while she was away travelling but decided it was nothing. By the time she came back it had spread throughout her whole body. There was nothing anyone could do. I pretended it would be fine; didn't even see the head scarf and the dribbling mouth and the weight loss. She whispered lots of things to me and I made a whole heap of promises to her. I'm not sure exactly what I said, I wasn't really there so couldn't remember any of it. Not until that moment, the moment I sat at my computer thinking about how I'd not taken responsibility for anything.

What I had promised her was that I would live my life passionately and do all the things I really wanted to, not just for me but for her.

The day she told me about her condition she dropped it in like it was something she forgot to mention on a shopping list. Ki had got back from Thailand a couple of weeks earlier, and we had spent virtually every day together since. That day we were off to Brighton, and her dad was in the driveway cleaning his car.

'It's hot weather, na?' he asked.

'Good, isn't it?' I replied.

'Makes me want to go and visit some bitches.'

I looked at him as Ki came out. He continued, 'Na, beta, saying to Nina we must visit some bitches.'

'It's beaches, Dad, beaches. Yeah, we'll visit loads and we'll make sure we do it soon.'

I remember thinking that comment was strange as she normally took the piss out of his mispronunciations.

'Yours is into bitches, mine thinks I'm into porn,' I said walking back in with her.

'What?'

'I didn't realise that the Sky box downstairs was linked to the one upstairs, and I was flicking through it and lingered on a few porn channels and this lesbian talk show.

She looked at me.

'It was just out of interest, didn't know I was interrupting Mum and Dad watching their Zee TV. Then in the morning I heard my dad tell my mum to talk to me, to have a word, maybe marriage would straighten that out. So she just left a couple more CVs on the table.'

'When will you tell them about Jean?'

'Soon,' I said.

'Tell them soon, Nina, it's not worth the wait. Do what makes you happy. You'll make sure you're happy, won't you?'

I looked at her. Where did that come from?

'I've got cancer, Nina, and it's bad. Phase three, that's what they called it. Don't think they can do much with chemo but they'll give it a go.'

She said it just like that, like she had bought some new trousers from French Connection and had forgotten to tell me.

She hadn't told her parents. Outside, her dad was blissfully ignorant; bucket in one hand, sponge in another, cleaning his shiny silver car and talking about bitches, unaware that shortly his life would change forever.

I deluded myself that chemo would sort it. I knew if I bargained hard and made a whole series of promises, it would be all right. Right until the last minute I believed that. Even when she died, I held on to her, not letting go. Her dad had to pull me off her.

The phone went again. 'Ms Williams is waiting for you in reception, Nina.'

'I heard you the first time,' I snapped.

My colleagues turned and looked at me. I never lost

it. No matter what, I was always calm. Calm and reliable Nina, who worked twelve hours a day if necessary. Calm and dependable Nina, who did what was asked of her; who went to the gallery openings that nobody else in the firm wanted to go to.

I got up and went to reception to meet Boo. She was dressed in black and wore bright red boots, the colour of the dried tomatoes she had put into Venus de Milo's sockets.

'Sorry to have kept you waiting.'

'Quite,' she replied.

And that was it, the word that tipped me over the edge.

'Quite,' I mumbled.

'Yes, I've got better things to do with my time,' she replied.

'Like make apricot statues?'

Felicity looked up from behind the reception desk, shocked.

'I don't like your tone, Nina,' Boo said.

'I don't like your work, but there's nothing I can do about that, is there?'

'Nessun dorma', which was playing in reception, seemed to be playing unusually loud in my head as Boo started ranting. I wasn't really listening to what she was saying but just gazed blankly at her, watching her lips move and hearing the Guru's words telling me again and again that I was cursed. The only thought I had was to get out of there.

'Boo, Nina has been under the weather recently, haven't you, Nina?' Simon said, hearing her shouting and coming out of his office to try to placate her.

'Yes, under the weather, under a cloud, a dirty grey sky. I have to go, I have to leave.'

There was silence: the kind of silence that is desperate to be filled.

And Simon didn't stop me. Over three years at the firm, sweating blood, pampering over-inflated egos and making him money and he didn't even say, 'Come into my office, let's talk about it.'

Maybe if he had I would have stayed, because all that I needed was some reassurance that I was worth something.

'Right,' I said, getting my coat. 'I'll come back for the rest of my things later.'

'I'll make sure Felicity sends them on to you,' Simon replied.

I splashed through puddles, wandering aimlessly, feeling numb. I should have been elated, relieved at least that I had left work; but the way it had happened was out of my control, he was essentially showing me the door. After everything I had done, that's how much I meant. What would I say to my parents? Not only would I crush them by saying that I was marrying Jean but now my dad's biggest fear of me losing my job had come true. Perhaps it was better to break it to them all at once: if I didn't have a job I couldn't go through with their list system anyway so that didn't matter, and at least I had Jean. Jean would be there no matter what. He would return home later that evening and between us we could find a way to break it to them so that it wouldn't completely crush them. Things weren't that bad, I tried to convince myself. I'd just attempted to put the whole Guru thing behind me – there were good things to look forward to. Jean and I could finally settle down. I felt excited at the thought of seeing him again, having him wrap his arms around me and reassure me that everything would work out. As I had time on my hands I decided to go to his flat, make us dinner and wait for him: he was due back around six.

23

A short time later, my shopping basket was bulging with colourful vegetables. I had no idea what I was going to do with them but anything that had any colour went into the basket. Jean liked chicken so I decided to throw one in and figure out how to cook it later. I picked up a recipe book, some wine, flowers and candles and made my way to his apartment.

I smiled at the concierge as I entered the building, but instead of smiling back he glanced down at his feet.

'Busy morning, John?'

'Yes, miss,' he replied, calling for the lift. I could sense that he wasn't in the mood for chatting so I waited in silence for the lift to come down.

The tiles and mirrors reflected the huge ceilings of the apartment block and the lift was rickety and had an old-style caged door. I had always thought I'd get stuck in it. Before Jean Michel went away on his trip he had stopped the lift as we were halfway down. I had panicked. 'I'll take care of you, cherie,' he said. 'Always, you know I will. Nina, I want you to marry me.'

And although I was overwhelmed the first word that came out of my mouth wasn't 'Yes' but 'Dad'. All I could see was my dad's face, so absolutely crushed.

Jean tried not to appear disappointed. I asked for time to think about it. He said he understood, but now my head was clear I would have a chance to make it up to him.

We had met two years earlier at a party. The moment he walked in half the women in the room turned to look: he was six foot two, with blue eyes, jet-black hair and a big smile. I watched his every move from the corner of my eye and my heart jumped with disbelief as he made his way towards me.

'Are you OK?' he said in a deep, confident voice, as if he had always known me.

I turned to check that it was me he was talking to and that I wasn't mistaken: out of all the women in the room, he had chosen to speak to me.

We talked for hours and as I left he said he'd call. The days seemed interminable as I waited and my stomach did all sorts of things each time the phone rang. He called two days later, said he had wanted to phone straightaway to see if I got home safely but had held out as long as he could. There was something very solid about him: he was confident yet also excitingly passionate and spontaneous. There was no routine in our lives, no planning; things just happened.

He whisked me away from the world of the semi, Croydon and list systems, away from practicality and duty, and made me feel beautiful. He had all the qualities I lacked and when I was around him I never felt inadequate. Ki said he was what I needed; that he made me see things differently, beyond the values and concepts that had been drummed into me.

She, like Jean, was also a risk-taker, but ended up with someone who seemed safe, reliable and predictable . . . although he didn't turn out to be in the end. Ki was laid out in her coffin in her red bridal sari. Her boyfriend, who was supposedly madly in love with her, hadn't wanted to marry her, but her mother insisted that that was the way that she wanted to be dressed. Had she known towards the end that her boyfriend's visits had become more and more infrequent? He didn't even manage to make it to the funeral and three months later he was seeing someone else.

Jean Michel saw me through that period. Although my way of coping was just to get on with life and try not to think about things too deeply, I knew if I needed to talk he would listen. He always listened; he always tried to understand.

*   *   *

25

I turned the key to Jean's flat and it wasn't double locked.

'Careless as usual,' I thought. 'Goes away for four days and forgets to double-lock the door.'

I carried the shopping into the kitchen and thought I heard a noise. Maybe the cleaner was in, although it wasn't her usual day.

'Hello,' I shouted. Nobody responded so I began unpacking the shopping. The fridge had half a bottle of champagne in it along with some pâté. There was another noise.

'Hello, is anyone in?' I said, going towards Jean's room.

Jean suddenly came out, making me jump.

'Jean, I didn't know you were home. When did you get in? Didn't you hear me? I've got so much to tell you.'

He looked very pale.

'Are you ill? What's wrong?'

His bedroom door clicked closed.

'What's going on? Who's in there? Who is it, Jean?'

'No one, Nina,' his voice sounded odd. 'Don't go in there.'

I went in and saw this woman emerging like some weasel out of a hole. She had a mass of red curls and was half-dressed.

All I could think about was the concierge, party to as many secrets as he was keys. He could have said something like, 'Miss, don't go up there, the gas men are seeing to a leak, come back in a few hours.' I would have listened.

I stood there, completely frozen, trying to comprehend an obvious situation. There were no clichés like, 'It's not what you think' or 'She's not important.' In a way I wish there had been because in those moments of silence I understood that he could not possibly love me and that he loved himself much more. He expected me to say something, to do something, but I just stood there in silence, staring at him. And then I walked away.

26

I ran down the stairs and out of the building, cars beeping as I flew recklessly across the road, not caring if they knocked me down. I ran like I never wanted to stop but when my sides began to ache I couldn't go on any more. Stumbling on a bench in Green Park, catching my breath, the tears began to trickle down my face.

The only other person apart from Ki who knew me inside out was Jean. I had showed him who I truly was and he had rejected me. Was I not good enough? Was that it? Was I fooling myself that he loved me? Did he mean it when he asked me to marry him? Did I make that up too? Was it because since Ki's death I had been distant, or was it because I made him wait? He said that he would wait for as long as it took.

My arm and my chest, the ugly blotchy creases – he had pretended that they didn't matter? Did she have ugly blotchy creases that he ran his fingers down while whispering that he loved her, every single part of her? Was that it? Was he touching her, saying that he was there for her, while the Guru was touching me? Did he pretend to love me because he pitied me?

Tears streamed down my face.

'Help me, Ki, please, I need you. Show me a sign if you're around. You said you would. Please. Are you seeing all this? Are you?' Nothing came. 'You lied to me. You said you would always be with me but how can you be? If you were with me you wouldn't let any of this happen. None of this. But you're dead and dead people can't do anything, can they? I trusted you and you lied. I let you give up because you promised you would always be with me, but you deceived me just like everyone else.'

The rain began falling. I sat on the park bench thinking that there was really no such thing as fate: imagining providence having a hand was just a way of not feeling alone, a way of making sense of a pointless journey. 'I'll

27

give you one last chance. Speak to me like you said you would. Go on, I'm listening now. Do you want me to beg? I'll beg if you want.'

I crawled down onto my hands and knees. 'See, I'm begging you. Please.'

Still nothing came.

Clutching at the blades of grass I fell forward on my knees onto a patch of muddy wet grass and began sobbing my heart out, oblivious to who was watching me. I looked up at the grey, miserable sky and the bursting rain clouds. 'Fall harder, go on, is that the best you can manage? I don't care what else you throw at me, send someone else to feel me up, go on, I don't care any more. You've taken everything, everything. Do you hear me? You probably don't even exist, do you? All made up, all of it, lies.'

I sat back on the bench and was aware that I was making an awful gut-wrenching sound. The wailing came from feeling cheated by the death of my closest friend, cheated by love and the injustice of being touched up and having my faith simultaneously taken away. Unable to fight any more, I let the rain pour down on me. It soaked through my coat as I sat there continuing to think. I thought about the nature of love and how that too was a lie. Ki's boyfriend had left her to die. Jean Michel had fooled me into believing that it was possible to love. All along my parents had been right. Life wasn't about emotion, emotion was for people who had nothing better to do with their time. It was about coping and easing the struggle, being practical and realistic, that was what my dad was trying to prepare me for. Their ideas about love were practical, they left no room for emotion and no room to be hurt, let down or disappointed. They were right: romantic airy-fairy notions of love did not exist, and if they did they were impractical and could only lead to disappointment. Life was all about survival. Trust no one as everyone was out for themselves, have no expectations: that way you could not be let down.

Eventually, when I could take the cold no longer, I made my way to the train station.

I was soaking wet so that each time I moved slightly the seat made a sloshing sound. Water ran down from my hair into my face and then dripped onto my coat, which was covered in mud. A scummy dark mess of brown on a brown coat; dirty on the outside, dirty on the inside. The commuters desperately avoided eye contact with me and tried not to look when I emitted that erratic sound; that noise when you can't quite control your breathing. By the time I got to the High Street I had assimilated the day's events. I managed to go into McDonalds and clean myself up a bit and by the time I reached our road I had tried to pull myself together. When I got to the blue front door of our semi, I even managed a fake smile.

My mother was in the kitchen making rotis and my father was in the sitting room, snoozing under his newspaper despite the Hindi music blasting out of the television. Their world rotated the same way it had done since 1972 when they came to London. In the evenings, Mum rolled out the rotis and made sure they were perfectly circular. During the day she worked at a tailor's and sometimes took home extra work making Indian garments. My father had been on the same route for twenty years and wasn't taking retirement until he saw me married; something else he succeeded in making me feel guilty about.

Although I could see the connection between retirement and marriage, he managed to find a connection between marriage and most things, and if it didn't provoke a response in me he would bring out the death card. 'Tell me, who will look after you, Nina, when I die?' And if he wanted to provoke an extreme response he would say, 'Are you going to do the same as your sister?' This, however, was rare, as he did his very best not to mention her.

My sister Jana had left when she was eighteen. Her departure deeply wounded my parents as she had gone off to live with a 'white boy'. They decided the best way to handle it was to pretend nothing had happened and not to talk about her, exiling her into the recesses of their minds. The jewellery my mother had saved for her wedding was safely packed away in the hope that at some stage it could be used for me. So I knew it was madness going out with Jean Michel because it couldn't lead anywhere, but he convinced me that everything would work out and that he could win them round. Foolishly, I believed him.

Outwardly my parents hardly ever showed signs that Jana's departure had affected them, and in those intervening years many things happened but their routine remained the same. At exactly seven o'clock they would eat and by eight they would both be in bed, flicking between Zee TV and ITV.

'Didn't you take your umbrella, beta? What has happened to your coat?' my mother asked, putting down her rolling pin and handing me a multi-stained tea towel to wipe myself down with.

'I fell over.'

'Go and get changed,' she said, picking up the rolling pin and pointing it at me.

'Ma . . .'

'Hmmm . . .'

'About Raj, Ma, you know, the accountant man.'

She put down her rolling pin again and turned to look at me. Her eyes lit up like all her prayers had finally been answered.

'I'll see him. You can call his mother to arrange it.'

Why exactly these words came out of my mouth remains a mystery; perhaps it was easier than, 'Ma, I've been touched up by a Guru, I've lost my job, found my boyfriend with someone else and have accepted that Ki is dead.' Or maybe it was just that I was finally ready for the kind of stability they had: a gale-force wind could descend upon them, or an earthquake that measured eight on the Richter scale, and they would still be unaffected. In the words of my father, 'This is what the routine and the discipline are both bringing.'

I went to have a shower, vigorously scrubbing every part the Guru had touched until it hurt while I began figuring out ways to break the news to my dad that I no longer had a job.

He was sitting there in the front row when I graduated. That's when he really got into power dressing – wearing red and looking like Santa. It also gave him a certain amount of status in the community to say that his daughter was a lawyer and he would often get out the graduation photo and tears would form in his eyes.

That's why I couldn't tell them when I went back downstairs. He munched through his rotis asking if I had had a good day, not really stopping to listen for an answer but telling us about some rude passenger who had refused to pay full fare and how he 'bullocked' him and how he was tired of the 'riff-raffies' on his bus. Mum had put Raj's CV safely to one side and kept looking over at it and touching her heart as if to tell me that it would break it if I went back on my word. I couldn't eat anything so told them that I had had something after work, had had a long day and needed to go to bed.

Unable to sleep, I had lots of questions with no answers and an aching feeling of emptiness and solitude, compounded by the fact that I wanted to scream and scream out loud and not stop. But I couldn't. The day

31

had begun with the Guru's hands touching me, his fingers circling my lips, and ended with me covering my mouth, making some pathetic, muffled sounds under the duvet so that nobody could hear.

That weekend I didn't get out of bed. I was running a temperature and was in a state of complete delusion. I could hear my mum faintly in the background, pottering about, bringing food to me, mumbling something about not taking an umbrella, but I slept through it in a blissful state of illusion, imagining that I was married to Jean Michel, that everything had been a nightmare. It was only my dad's voice that managed to penetrate through my dreamlike state.

'You'll be late, Nina. Don't want to get the sack, get up, you're better now, no?'

Waking up that morning, when every part of me wanted to remain in a heap, was hell.

'You'll be late, Nina,' my dad shouted again, and then I heard him say to my mum, 'When I was her age I had to get up at five o'clock every day, even when I was sick. And I was married.' He said it like marriage had been a double punishment but my mum wasn't listening. Her mind was still on her future son-in-law.

Dad married Mum under a fog of controversy. It was controversial in the sense that he felt he had been duped. The story goes that he had a chesty cough and went to a chemist, well not really a chemist as you would expect but a shop somewhere in Uganda and that this beautiful woman served him. He was, at the time, searching for a wife and was utterly taken with her. He made a few enquiries as to her eligibility but it turned out that she was already married to the man who owned the chemist's. In true Indian style, not letting an opportunity go, the woman said she had a sister who lived with her parents in India who would be perfect for my father.

My dad, impetuous as ever, agreed to marry the sister without checking out the goods – if she was anything like her sister she would be snapped up pretty soon. When he saw my mother on the wedding day he tried to hide his disappointment but then I think he really grew to love her. That's what arranged marriages were like; you learned to fall in love. 'I was the fooled,' he joked in front of her. 'See, Nina, you're lucky, you can meet these boys and see if you likes them: me, I had no choice.' And despite the fact that he said he had no choice, they were really compatible and I could never imagine one without the other. It was hardly fireworks between them – more like a Catherine wheel which failed to ignite in the rain but then unexpectedly fizzed about a bit – but it worked for them.

I could barely open my eyes as they felt so sore. I dragged myself up, managed to have a shower, put on my suit and made out as if I was going to work, creeping down the stairs so they wouldn't have to see me. Just before getting to the front door, I shouted, 'Bye, Ma. Bye, Dad.'

'You'll be home early this evening, nah, beta? I've told Raj's mother to get him to call you at seven-thirty,' my mum said, pouncing on me from nowhere. 'Oh, what's happened to the eyes?'

'Allergy,' I replied. 'Anyway, I'll try not to be too late,' I continued, thinking of all the places I could go to kill eight hours.

She handed me an umbrella and saw me out.

My head was throbbing and my body ached. I went to a café and sat there drinking endless cups of coffee, trying to make some kind of a decision as to what to do. What was going to happen to me without Jean – he was there to cushion all the blows. What was I going to do about work? Thank God my dad had drilled it into my head about being careful with money in an attempt to prepare me for 'the days of the flooding'. Most of what I had earned was put aside. He was right: life was all about trying to make yourself as secure as possible so nobody could come along with any surprises. After hours of sitting there and thinking, I decided to drag myself to the Tate.

For a Monday morning it was busy, with people flocking to see the wardrobe stuffed with worldly possessions. Thankfully there was a Matisse exhibition on. I always liked Matisse. He also studied law and his father was furious when he said he wanted to give it up to paint. He was a great painter and didn't begin to paint until after recovering from an illness. They say it was providence that sent him that illness to set him on a different path, that only looking back do we know exactly why things have happened.

It had been almost ten years since I'd picked up a paintbrush. I could have continued to paint as a 'hobby' after I began my law degree but it was always all or nothing with me. Even when I was angry or sad and had a desperate urge to splatter the emotion across a blank canvas, I resisted and picked up my books and studied instead. Studied and did what everyone else wanted me to do, and became who others wanted me to be.

The rooms where Matisse's pictures were displayed were not as busy as downstairs. But as soon as I walked in I could feel the warmth. His pictures gave me energy, their raw emotions expressed with an explosion of pure, intense colours. There was no option but to stare at the paintings, to feel them: violets to stir feelings placed next to sunny, optimistic yellows, vibrant oranges against laconic blues and sober greens floating among a sea of passionate cerulean red. When I stared into Matisse's colours I could see other colours that weren't really there; realities that were invented; somewhere I could escape.

Matisse's paintings carried me into his world without me even realising, making me forget who or where I was. He painted windows that let you fly in and out; bold strips of colour like the green that ran along his wife's nose and made you feel you could balance on it, look at her every feature and see what he saw; hues of reality next to splashes of imagination. I wandered around for hours, drawn into his world, lost in the depths of his colour, soaking up every ray, searching for the shadows that he had skilfully eliminated. In every painting, I found peace.

I went to have lunch in the cafeteria and found that my thoughts had become calmer, and because I didn't want to think any more deeply I concentrated on the noise that the cutlery and crockery were making, watching the tourists, many of whom had pulled out their guidebooks to see which exhibitions they would visit next.

Before leaving the Tate I visited the shop and picked up a book on Matisse. I randomly flicked through the pages and stopped at one of his quotes:

'In art, truth and reality begin when one no longer understands what one is doing or what one knows, and when there remains an energy that is all the stronger for being constrained, controlled and compressed.'

I put the book back. It wasn't a sign – dead people were unable to speak.

With a few more hours to kill before going back home, I decided to take a walk in Green Park. Jean Michel didn't live too far from there and sometimes we had gone walking together. It was an effort to drag him out as he really didn't like walking. He didn't really enjoy staying in and watching videos, either, as I did. He liked finding new restaurants and eating out; he would drive halfway across the country to find a good restaurant. He loved going to the casino and betting all his money on one number. I was intrigued by his boldness, but looking back I should have known then that I would never have been enough – life with me was probably boring, with my constant refusal to go away with him and rushing off home to my parents instead. But he said we were good together, that I brought calmness to his life; but then he said many things, most of which probably weren't even true.

I switched my phone back on and the message box was full. All of them were from him, frantic messages, every one saying how much he loved me. I so desperately wanted to believe him, to speak to him and have him put his arms around me and tell me that there had been some terrible mistake, that he could explain it all, but instead I made myself delete the messages one by one. Time, that was what I needed, time to sort out my head. I bought a coffee, sat on the park bench and thought more about the quote before setting off for home.

No sooner had I turned the key, my mum was waiting anxiously, rolling pin in one hand, telling me that Raj would be calling at seven-thirty.

'You already told me that before I left,' I said.

'Good day?' my dad asked, turning back to watch the television before I had replied.

What was I supposed to say? That Henri Matisse had given me some much-needed peace.

'Yes, good day.'

I went upstairs, quickly had a shower, and bang on time the phone rang. No unpredictability there, then.

'Hi Nina, it's Raj.'

'Hello.'

There was a moment's hesitation and then he took control.

'I hear you're a lawyer and working in the city?'

'Yes, and you?' I asked in a half-hearted attempt to deflect the conversation away from myself.

'No, I'm not a lawyer,' he laughed. Well, it was more of a grunting sound. And why did he laugh? I mean, if the man thought that was humour we might as well put the phone down now.

'No,' he said, gathering himself together, 'I work for a consultancy firm as an accountant.'

There wasn't much to say to that.

'So what do you like doing?' he began again.

There was no stopping this man; he careered straight past the silences and kept on going.

Be kind to him, Nina, talk. It's not his fault, none of it is his fault. What did I like doing? Suddenly I felt a sense of panic. It was the realisation that my life up until that moment had revolved solely around Jean and work. I had to say something, and so, like an eight-year-old, reeled off a list of hobbies. 'Reading, cinema, watching TV, painting.'

'Oh, painting? What do you paint with?'

'A paintbrush,' I replied.

He laughed again. 'Very good, that's very good, I see you too have got a sense of humour. I've dabbled in water-colours but I'm not very good,' he added.

Then there was another silence.

'Seen any good films?' he asked.

I said the first thing that came into my head. '*The Matrix*.'

'I saw that on the plane to Japan.'

For the first time he had my attention. Japan? What was he doing in Japan?

'Japan?' I enquired.

'Yes, I have to travel for work and so I extend my stay wherever possible. I love to find out about other cultures. It's important to expand the mind.'

'Where else have you been?'

He listed practically half the countries in the atlas but not in a pretentious way. I stopped him at Chile and asked what it was like, and for the first time I sensed he was being himself.

'I've always wanted to go there,' I said, and to my surprise he did not come out with a cheesy line like, 'I'll take you' or 'Maybe you'll go there soon.' Instead, he said it was beautiful.

There was a pause but now it wasn't awkward.

'Perhaps you'd like to meet up?' he asked.

I had images of my mother, a protagonist in an Indian film, wailing and beating her chest in despair at the thought of me saying no, so I said 'Yes'. It would be just one meeting and then I could say it didn't work out.

'For dinner or a movie?' he asked.

Movie? Before I made a comment on his use of the word 'movie' I thought twice. It was only the Croydon multiplex and I wouldn't have to talk to him that much if we were seeing a film. 'Yes, a movie sounds good.'

'Great, I'll pick you up on Saturday, about three?'

'All right.'

'See you then, Nina.'

My mother was downstairs, eagerly waiting for me. I could hear her pacing. As soon as I came down she pretended to look disinterested, resuming the rolling-pin position. She turned around for a second and her right eyebrow signalled as if to say, 'Dish the dirt.' The other eyebrow said, 'He's a good boy, got a good job, coming from a very good family, now tell me you have arranged to meet him.'

'Three o'clock on Saturday,' I said.

'OK, OK,' she muttered as if she wasn't bothered, but when she turned back to her perfectly circular rotis I could feel her beaming.

Knowing that my parents were distracted with the whole Raj scenario, I felt less guilty the next morning about putting on a suit and pretending to go to work. Jean Michel had left three more messages. I wanted to listen to them but again deleted them one by one. Then I went back to see Matisse, the only person who I could turn to at that moment in time.

I bought the book I had seen the day before. It told me about his life and each of the paintings. It also included a commentary by critics on what he was trying to achieve, saying something about his search for chromatic equilibrium. How did they know that anyway? Maybe he wasn't trying to achieve anything except to express his feelings? Did it matter what they thought he was trying to do? What mattered was how the paintings left you feeling, not a skewed interpretation on what he did or didn't want to do. I searched the book for his own words and came across another quote: 'There are always flowers for those who want to see them.'

'Are there, Matisse?' I wondered aloud.

The cafeteria was full again at lunchtime and I found myself having to ask if I could sit next to a girl with long, mousy-blonde hair.

'Sure,' she replied in an Australian accent, smiling away. When she spotted that I had bought the same book on

Matisse as her and commented on it, I nodded and kept my head down. I wasn't in the mood for chitchat.

But she continued. 'He's just great, isn't he? And I love the quote on flowers.'

Ordinarily I might have taken this to be a sign, having just read the exact same quote, but in my jaded state I took it to be some lonely traveller who probably had no money and was trying to strike up a friendship so she could ask if she could sleep on my sofa. I imagined my dad finding her on his Land of Leather sofa in the morning.

'"There are always flowers for those who want to see them,"' she continued out loud, just in case I wasn't familiar with it.

'And weeds,' I wanted to say, but remained looking down, eating in silence.

'Nice meeting you,' she got up to leave.

'Yes,' I replied as she went off.

I sat there for a while reading. Some Japanese tourists signalled to the seats next to me to ask if they could sit there. They seemed really grateful that I said yes. I nodded, relieved that they couldn't speak any English and turned the page.

The last bit I read before heading off to Green Park was about the nature of creativity. Matisse said that creativity took courage. My dad would say creativity took a lot of lazy people who had nothing better to do all day except to waste time. The Turner Prize did nothing except confirm his perception: 'See, they fooling people and making the money. Maybe I should get Kavitha to make some patterns with her samosas and send them in.' I closed the book and caught the tube to Green Park.

Creativity takes courage.

Does it? I don't think I can take a leap of faith, not on my own, anyway. I don't trust myself. Does that make

40

sense? I've never really done anything on my own. I'm used to doing things for other people, that's what makes me feel secure. I'm used to being someone's daughter, someone's girlfriend, someone's lawyer. I'm not used to being me. I don't believe that I am big enough to make this all better. If I'm myself, I don't think I'll survive. Don't worry, I'm talking to myself, not you, Ki. Wouldn't want you to think that I'm asking you or anything. Wouldn't want you to rise from the dead or do something complicated like that.

I sat on the bench for a little while longer, then wandered around the back of Mayfair looking in gallery windows before going home.

'Good day, Nina?' my dad asked.

'We got an important client today.'

'Very good,' he said as he delved back into his newspaper. He didn't really need to know the ins and outs of 'love', just to be occasionally reassured that I wouldn't unexpectedly be made redundant; hence the addition of new clients every now and then.

It's not my natural inclination to bend the truth. I wasn't one of those types who went to school with a long skirt and rolled it up on the way there. Truth-bending is something I have learned to do out of necessity, and not necessarily to protect myself but my parents. When I was with Jean Michel I always said I was seeing Jean or staying there, but they jumped to the conclusion that he was a she and I let them believe it.

'Bring this Jeannie round,' my dad would say.

'Yes, we would like to meet her. I'll make roti and paneer,' my mum would add. It went on like this till I couldn't make any more excuses, so I got Susan, one of my friends, to stand in as her.

41

My dad liked 'the Jeannie' as he referred to her. After ascertaining what Susan's parents did and estimating their combined annual income, he thought she was a good person to mix with.

Now I looked at my dad, took a deep breath and said, 'Dad, the office is experiencing some difficulties with the phone, so if there is an emergency ring me on my mobile.' They never rang the office, but just in case.

'Hmmm.'

'Did you hear me, Dad? Fire, flood, office, call me on my mobile.'

'What fire in the office, it's not burned down, no?'

Now I had his attention. 'No, I'm just saying, in case of an emergency or if you need to speak to me, call me on my mobile.'

'Nothing is wrong, no, Nina?'

That was the moment to confess and, believe me, I wanted to, but he looked at me like he wanted reassurance that everything was OK and I just didn't have the strength to tell him.

'Everything is fine.'

'They need someone to come and fix it?'

'Fix what?'

'The phones. I can come and sort out problem.'

'No, Dad, but thank you.'

My mother was in rolling-pin position and asked me the standard questions: what I'd eaten for lunch, was I ready to have dinner, if I was going to go up and have a shower. As she returned to her rotis, I stared at her. Where was that other person she had unleashed when she raged at my sister? Did she ever think of Jana? Did she worry about what she ate and what time she was going to take her shower? She must have, I know she must have. Once I caught her unpacking the jewellery box she had packed safely away, emptying its contents and crying, but she never said anything to us, me or my dad. Instead she kept it all inside and carried on with her routine. And many times when I tried to speak to her about my sister she would turn her back to me and walk away.

After I came out of the shower, the phone rang. It was Raj.

'Hi Nina, I know we're meeting on Saturday but I just thought I'd give you a call and see how you are.'

'I'm fine,' I heard myself reply politely. It was quite a relief to talk to someone who didn't really know me, who wanted to talk about superficial things like what films I watched; someone who was unable to affect me in any way and didn't require any depth of conversation.

'How are you?' I asked.

'Good. Had a busy day. I am just going to read now.'

'What are you reading?'

'*Seven Habits of Highly Effective People.*'

'Right. And is it working? Are you being effective?'

'Hope so. What are you going to do?'

'Going down to eat and then hopefully get to sleep early. I haven't been sleeping well.'

'Don't eat too late,' he said. 'I've heard that causes insomnia because the food isn't digested properly.'

'It's not the food,' I heard myself saying. 'It's just there are lots of things going on at the moment . . . lots of . . . lots of . . .' I searched desperately for the word I was looking for but the best I could come up with was '. . . contracts.'

'Are you busy at work, then?' he enquired.

'Yes. Very busy.'

'I'll leave you to it, Nina. I just wanted to say hello, that was all.'

'Thank you,' I said as I put the phone down.

And that was the first time that I really warmed to

43

him, because practicality brought a certain amount of stability that did not require much of me.

It was time to get a new mobile phone as I was finding it increasingly hard not to listen to the daily messages from Jean. After buying the phone I went back to the Tate and back to Matisse.

The blonde girl from the cafeteria was there again, studying the paintings. She smiled when she saw me. I smiled back and wandered off into the next room before she could ask me for the sofa. She followed swiftly behind me.

'Excuse me,' she whispered.

I pretended not to hear her.

'Excuse me,' she repeated.

I turned around.

'You dropped this.' She handed me my Matisse book.

'Thank you,' I said, taking it. 'I didn't even hear it drop.'

'It's what Matisse does to you. Sometimes you can just be lost in his colours.'

That's exactly what I had thought. 'I know what you mean,' I replied. 'Is he one of your favourite artists?' I found myself asking.

She nodded.

'Mine too,' I said, wanting her to ask me another question.

But she didn't ask me anything else, just smiled politely and left.

My feet took me effortlessly around the room as I tried to see the flowers in his paintings. Even in his down-times he painted light, he painted with bold colours. Maybe that's what he meant when he said 'Creativity takes courage', that every day he showed up and painted no matter what else was happening in his life.

The cafeteria wasn't that busy as it was late afternoon. I could see the blonde girl sitting and eating a sandwich and although there were other empty seats I could have sat at, I went up to her and asked if the seat beside her was taken.

'No,' she smiled. 'My name's Gina by the way.'

'I'm Nina.'

'Nina, Gina,' she laughed. 'Pleased to meet you, Nina,' she said, shaking my hand.

'I liked that quote too,' I found myself saying out of nowhere, trying to make up for my previous unfriendliness.

'The one about seeing flowers?' she asked. 'It's beautiful, isn't it? It reminds me of my mum.'

'Is she in Australia?'

'No, she's dead.'

I put my own sandwich down. 'I'm so sorry, I really am, I didn't mean to –'

'No, it's OK, really. That's why that quote means so much.'

I wanted to ask her if she spoke to her, if her mother responded, if she looked for signs.

Instead, I asked, 'Are you on holiday?'

'No, I live here now. I'm an artist. How about you?'

'I am – was – a lawyer but I'm thinking about painting again.'

'Well, if you need a studio, I know of one going. Or if you know of anyone who needs one, let me know. I'm desperate to find someone who'll take mine for three months so I can go back to Australia.'

She said she wanted to surprise her family and escape

the winter months but hadn't managed to find anyone who was interested in subletting her studio despite placing several ads. We talked some more, mainly about Matisse, and I took her number just in case I came across anyone who needed a studio.

Later, I sat in Green Park trying to convince myself that it was not meant for me.

'Ki, Matisse talks about seeing flowers when there are none. I want to see them. Even if you're not there and you're not listening it doesn't matter. I want to believe you are. Sorry about what I said to you the other day. There's a studio that has become free. Do you think it's meant for me?'

Silence.

'That's what I thought too. What if I just tried it out for three months tops? Haven't really got anything else to lose.'

I began to feel almost excited when I thought about the possibility of having my own studio and being able to paint. The only problem with having a studio was that the level of deceit would escalate even further. I had never intended to lie so blatantly to my parents. I didn't want to, the days I was going to the Tate were just to get my head straight. Perhaps I would try broaching the subject of renting a studio with my dad. I would say that the firm had given me a three-month sabbatical so I could understand the work of my artists better. It wasn't that far from the truth, really.

My dad was upstairs in the spare room, fiddling with one of the many television sets he had, when I arrived home.

'Can sell this one for fifty pounds. Newsagent wants it for tomorrow.'

'Right. That's great.' I thought the best way of bringing

up the studio subject was by telling him what Matisse said and then at least I could start talking about painting and lead on from there. 'Dad, what do you think of this quote?'

'What?' he shouted.

I had to rephrase the sentence. 'An artist who is worth a lot of money said that there are always flowers for those who want to see them. What do you think about that?'

'He's your client?'

'Sort of.'

'Very good quote.'

'Really, do you think so?'

'Yes, that is why he is the rich. Wastes no money buying the expensive flowers from the petrol shops and saves the money that the flowers are taking. Not giving the peoples the flowers every time he is seeing them.'

I wanted to bury my head in my hands in despair. He would never understand. Even if I sat down with him and explained in great detail why it was so important to me, he just wouldn't get it.

'Thought about what you are going to wear to see Raj?' my mother asked later at dinner.

'No, I have had other things on my mind.'

She made some suggestions that I pretended to listen to. The only way I could possibly escape it all was to paint. My decision was made.

The next morning I phoned Gina to tell her that I was interested in looking at her studio. She told me to come by whenever I could that day.

It was located at the back of London Bridge, in an alley with cobbled stones that led nowhere in particular. The sign read 'Forget the dog, just beware if you disturb the artist at work'. I knocked on the door and Gina pulled it open.

'Good to see you again, Nina. Well, this is it.'

The studio was a converted garage, bright and airy as it had a skylight. There was an enormous table in the centre of the room and a smaller one on the side which had a kettle, a toaster and a blow heater that were all attached to one adapter.

'It's safe,' Gina said as she saw my eyes rest on that spot.

The walls were covered with pictures of Sydney Harbour in different sizes and forms.

'Homesick?' I asked.

'I don't think there's anywhere more beautiful than that view.'

The floor was concrete grey, splattered with colours that had managed to jump off Sydney Harbour.

'What do you paint?'

Where was I supposed to start? I couldn't say I didn't know so I said, 'Birds.'

'Any particular kind?'

'Just the flying ones.'

She laughed and moved towards her easel, remarking that that was where the light fell best. 'I'm leaving that here but if you've got your own and you want me to put it away then that's fine.'

'You mean I can really rent this studio from you?' I asked.

'If you want it, it's yours. The only thing is can you give me cash instead of a cheque. Other than that, you can have it from Monday. That gives me time to pack up my stuff but if you want to drop your things by before then, just give me a call.'

When I got home there was complete chaos. The

garments my mum had made were stuffed into black bin-liners and there were about twenty television sets on the landing. My dad was up a ladder, screaming at my mum, telling her to pass the sets to him quicker so he could put them in the attic. She was huffing and puffing and looking as though she was going to pass out.

'What's going on?' I asked.

'Inland Revenue man is outside. He's been watching the house for the last two hours. Fukkus, Kavitha, fukkus.'

'It's focus, Dad, focus.'

'Yes, I know this, this is what I am saying to her. Why you telling me, tell Kavitha, she is almost dropping the television. She doesn't know what a big problem this is.'

I looked outside the window and to my horror saw Jean's car. Jean was making his way towards our house.

'Oh God,' I muttered.

'I know, I know, that's what I thought. Help us, Bhagavan. Hurry up, hurry up, Kavitha,' he shouted.

'I'll get rid of him, Dad,' I said, running down the stairs.

As I opened the door, Jean was standing on the doorstep. I closed the door behind me and pulled him away from the house.

'What the hell are you doing here?'

'Nina, I had to see you, your phone is dead and you haven't answered any of my letters.'

'There's nothing to say except it's over.'

'Can't we at least talk about it?'

'No, not here, not now.'

'When, then?'

'I don't know.'

'Tomorrow,' he said. 'Come round to the flat.'

'No,' I said. 'Just go, Jean.'

'I won't let you go,' he said, 'not like this. I love you.'

'OK, OK, I'll call, please just leave.'

I went back into the house.

'I've got rid of him, Dad.'

'Thank Bhagavan.'

'I told him he wasn't within his rights to wait in his car and watch out for illegal activity as there was nothing illegal going on, and if he continued to wait in his car I would make an official complaint. I don't think he'll be coming back.' The lies were getting bigger, and the frightening thing was they were getting easier to tell.

'See, Kavitha, all those years to make Nina study "the love", all worth it,' he said coming down from his ladder. Then he hugged me.

Dad never hugged me. I could count the times he had on one hand. When I went to hold him he would do this ninety-degree rotation so I got the back of him and then he would walk out of my embrace. My mum never knew how to respond when I held her and would stand there like a statue, waiting for the hug to pass like it was some massive tidal-wave that would knock her over.

The next morning, I went to the bank. My dad took £300 a month from me as part of my wedding contribution. I always thought that if I married Jean this fund would cushion the blow slightly as he could keep the amount he had built up and console himself and my mother with a holiday or a new car. Mind you, they never went on holiday, but they would have had to go somewhere for a couple of weeks until the scandal died down. When my Uncle Amit's daughter began living with Roy who was black, 'the honchos' had endless rounds of secret talks to confer so they could sort out the situation. Pressure was put on my Uncle Amit and his wife; they were bombarded with CVs of every single male specimen on the planet who could be a possible replacement. When this didn't work, one of the honchos leaked the news to the wider community. I thought Uncle Amit and Auntie Asha would have to emigrate but they stood firm, attending family functions, ignoring the whispering and gossip and being shunned by certain members of the community; but they never managed to live it down. But Uncle Amit was different from my father, he didn't need the approval of the community or that sense of belonging.

'Parents taking modern approach, what can you expect?' had been my dad's first reaction to the news. Though in my dad's case this wasn't strictly true: he hadn't had a modern approach but my sister had still left. I didn't correct him. 'This is not looking after the children. What will happen to this girl? He will leave her, she will have baby, nobody will want her. Parents will die, she will live alone, nobody wants her or baby.'

So a happy life, then. 'He might not ever leave, Dad, they probably really love each other,' I replied.

'Two years I gives them. The love is not enough, Nina, you must understand this. Everyday living with someone is hard. See your mother and me, she knows me, I knows her. She is not thinking that she will one day wake up and find the Bra Pitt.'

'Brad?'

'Yah, yah, him. I knows I will not wake up and find the Cilla Black. This is life. Kavitha understands me, I understands her. We have the family, the culture, the traditions, the security. This is what is making the marriage. This is why I am working for you, I want you to have what I have with Kavitha.'

Thinking about him doing two jobs for me made me feel incredibly guilty for taking money from the bank to pay for the studio. It would only be for a month or two, just to sort my head out, just to get it out of my system.

*   *   *

51

The man at the art shop was of no help to me as I stood looking at the rows and rows of brushes and paints, and the different types of paper and canvases. When I used to paint I painted in oils best, so I went over to the oils section only to be confronted by more tubes in different colours and sizes. I hesitated for a moment. Painting with oils was not going to be practical. My mum had a nose like a bloodhound and she would smell the linseed and turpentine on me. I walked over to the acrylic section and chose the paints that I needed, and bought a dozen primed, stretched canvases and brushes. I called Gina to see if the material could be delivered to the studio later that day. She told me to come by whenever I wanted.

When I arrived she was taking down her paintings and wrapping them in brown paper.

'So have you been painting long, Nina?'

'No. I'm just experimenting. I'm not an artist or anything. I used to paint when I was younger and then I had to stop.'

'Why?'

'Family stuff,' I replied. 'But I'm taking time off just to find out what it is I'm supposed to be doing.' I didn't know why I was divulging such information but she had something about her that made you want to tell her things.

I desperately wanted to ask her about her mother. 'How long have you been here?' I asked instead.

'Eight months. I went to art school in Sydney, did a few exhibitions over there and have been going to college here, but it's hard to break into the circuit, unless you know someone or you get spotted. I do love London but sometimes it can be a really cold and lonely place.'

'I know what you mean.'

'You got family here?' Gina asked.

I nodded.

'See, that makes all the difference,' she said. 'You've

52

always got them to fall back on if things don't work out.'

'Not if you have a family like mine,' I said. 'What about you?'

'My dad is back home with my little sister. I want to surprise them for Christmas.'

'Do you believe in signs?' I suddenly blurted.

Instead of giving me the strange look of incomprehension I expected, she answered, 'Why do you think I said the quote aloud?'

There was an instant understanding that passed between us at that moment, and we didn't even have to say what it was.

'How did she die?' I asked.

'Skin cancer,' Gina replied.

'I'm sorry. My best friend died of cancer too.'

'It's the pits, isn't it? I promised my mum that I'd come to England. What did you promise?'

'That I'd paint again and everything I did I would do passionately.'

'This would be the work of my mum, you know.'

'What?' I asked.

'Getting you and me together. It's got her name all over it. Maybe your friend and my mum have got together up there and said, "These two, they need to meet." What's your friend's name?'

'Ki.'

She looked up at her skylight. 'Ki . . . Mum . . . Thank you.'

And when she did that it was the first time that I thought I wasn't losing my mind. There was someone else in the world as crazy as I was.

Gina told me she had been teaching English in Japan before her mother had fallen ill. She wasn't told how bad it was so didn't hurry home until the final stages, and then when she got home she couldn't bring herself to leave Australia again. It had taken a huge leap of faith to come to England, and she said with leaps of faith came the call to adventure. I wouldn't know about that – the biggest leap of faith before my foray into painting was going out with Jean Michel and look where that had landed me.

She said she wasn't giving up on England, just needed a rest from the rain and from trying so hard to make things work. I understood this: if I had had an Australia to go to, I would have gone there too.

The delivery men came with my paints and canvases later that day and as Gina helped me unpack we talked about death, not in a morbid way but in a way that both of us understood. I didn't want to leave the warmth of her studio. I wanted to tell her more, tell her about the Guru and what had happened, but it was getting late and she still had lots to do.

'Nearly done,' she said, unwrapping the last canvas.

'Thank you, thank you so much.'

'I've hardly done anything. If you need to use any of my stuff, like brushes or whatever else you need, just go through those boxes.'

And though I hardly knew Gina it felt as if she had always been my friend. I wanted to hug her and tell her that it would all be all right, and that she would come back to London and find that it wasn't such a lonely place. As I was thinking this she wrapped her arms around me and told me that she was sure I would find what I wanted through my paintings. She was as generous as Ki was and I desperately wanted to believe that our meeting had been orchestrated by the two people we loved.

*   *   *

On the way back home, I thought of the money spent on renting the studio and buying canvases and paint, of how one thing had led to another. Then I thought about managing the deceit. Perhaps it was better to say nothing, to stop adding new clients and blatantly lying.

As I walked in the door, my dad put down his paper and pointed to a box.

'Nina, why your work send you this big box?'

Oh God, it was my things, work had sent me all my things. Don't panic, breathe deeply, remain silent, say nothing, do not lie.

He looked at me, waiting for a response. 'Why they doing this?'

'Didn't I tell you, Dad, we're moving offices.'

'No problem in the company?' he asked, putting down his glass.

'No, no problem. Actually, we've got more clients, we're expanding so we need to move to bigger premises.' That would account for the change in telephone numbers and the technical difficulties we were experiencing.

'Doesn't make sense to me.'

'What, Dad?'

'Why they're not sending box to the new office? Why they're sending it here?'

'Feng shui.' I said the first thing that came into my head.

He looked at me, puzzled.

'Because they want us to have a clear-out of our files and our personal belongings so we don't bring old things into the new office. It's feng shui.'

'He's the office manager?'

'No, feng shui is an idea about clearing space and bringing new energies in. When you get rid of something old, something new comes in its place.'

'I always know this,' my mother shouted out from the kitchen. 'I'm telling you, since we tidy television sets and

55

put them all in attic there is change, maybe energy will bring Nina's marriage. To bring them down, it's unlucky. Bhagavan will tell you.' See, even she was prone to a bit of truth bending; nowhere in the Gita did it say 'Thou shalt keep broken television sets in the attic' or 'Broken television sets left in attic will lead to daughter's marriage.'

Dad mumbled that they wouldn't stay in the attic long, just for enough time to stop the taxman snooping around, and then he muttered, 'I have to fix the television sets and drive the bus for a living, but Fongi Shu, he tells the peoples any rubbish and he makes the money. He's not Indian, no?'

'No, it's Chinese, I think.'

'The Chinese peoples, they are the clever, very clever.'

My resolve not to tell lies was obviously not working, and seeing as I'd just told one, another one wasn't going to be so bad.

'It's been a really busy day at work. That new client is very demanding and I might have to be a bit more hands-on.'

As I heard myself saying the words I knew he wouldn't understand, but these were the only words he latched on to. He put his newspaper down again and looked at me, probably imagining me hugging my clients and them doing ninety-degree rotations away from me too.

'What I mean by hands-on, Dad, is helping the client a bit more: so, say if he is organising an exhibition in Mayfair, I might go and help him in his studio.'

I knew it made no sense but my dad only chose to hear words that he liked, hence Mayfair.

'Good, good,' he mumbled.

My mother was listening from the kitchen. 'Ma, I was just saying to Dad that one of my clients is going to want me to help with an important exhibition he has so I might have to help him a bit in his studio.'

56

I knew it was volunteering far too much information but I had to get her bloodhound nose off the trail.

'Has Raj called?' she replied.

'What!' Here I was trying to set her off the track and she was going on about the accountant. As I went back into the hall to take off my coat she followed me.

'Why don't you call him? You are seeing him tomorrow, no?' she said before giving me a chance to reply.

'I'm not calling him, why should I?'

'We don't want him to forget you, Nina. A boy like that probably has a hundred girls to choose from.'

I wanted to ask her if she was ever disappointed; disappointed at the way her life had turned out, if she ever felt passionate about anything other then her circular rotis. But instead I said that I was seeing Raj in twenty-four hours and I was sure that if he wanted to speak to me before then, he would call.

No sooner had I said that, the phone rang.

'Hello Nina, it's Raj.'

'Just a moment.' I turned to my mum. 'Ma, is that burning I can smell in the kitchen?'

'No, beta, I switched off the gas.'

'I think Dad's calling you.'

'I'm not,' he shouted.

'Ma, can I speak to Raj on my own?'

'Sorry about that Raj,' I sighed as my mother reluctantly shuffled back to the kitchen.

'That's OK. Nina, I just wanted to know if you were still all right to meet tomorrow?'

'Do you feel like going to a gallery instead?' I asked. There was a pause. 'I mean it's all right if you don't want to, we can go to the cinema, it's just that I was thinking that . . .'

'No, no, a gallery is fine. Shall we meet at the Tate?' he suggested.

I liked the fact that he suggested the Tate. Maybe he wasn't so bad after all. 'There's a Matisse exhibition on at the moment.'

'I know,' he replied.

I was impressed. 'Around three o'clock?'

'Three o'clock is fine, Nina. Shall we meet in the café?'

And he knew about the café.

I told him I'd meet him there.

I went upstairs to call Jean.

'Thank God, Nina, I have to see you to explain.'

'Do you know that there's a Matisse exhibition on at the Tate?' I asked.

'What?'

'There's a Matisse exhibition on at the Tate.'

'Is that where you want to meet me?'

'No. I just wanted to know if you knew that?'

'No. Will you meet me, Nina, just to talk and listen to what I have to say?'

'Will you promise to leave me alone if I do?'

He said he would and so we agreed to meet the next day at seven.

I woke up very late the next morning. It must have seemed like an eternity to my mum who was hanging about outside my bedroom door.

'Yes, before you ask, I'm going to see some paintings with him.'

'Paintings?' she repeated.

'Paintings?' my father interrupted as he was passing. 'If you want to see paintings you can see the paintings here . . .' He indicated the numerous pictures of incarnated gods on the landing, hung on Seventies retro wallpaper.

These were the moments when I wanted so desperately not to be related to him.

58

As I got ready to leave for the Tate, my mother stopped me.

'You can't go like that,' she said, thinking about the hundreds of girls dancing before Raj – the competition. I was wearing a pale blue polo-neck, jeans, a long black coat and had no make-up on.

'What will he think when he sees you?'

'He will think he hasn't been the fooled. Fooled, I tell you,' my dad shouted from the sitting room.

'Put at least a bit of colour on your lips. I know you don't need the make-up. I know that Bhagavan has given you a very pretty face, but it is to show you have made some effort.'

'It's not about looks, Ma, it's about what's on the inside.' This was half the problem with the list system; for me it was all too superficial. Everything was to do with the outward appearance – what you looked like, how much money you had, what job you did. Also, it wasn't as if you could go on hundreds of dates with a guy to get to know him and then say no, you didn't like him. This would be another red mark against your family name.

'But please, beta, do this for me.'

'It's the weekend, Ma,' I said and then, feeling a little guilty, I went back up and put some lipstick on.

Raj was already sitting at a table waiting for me when I got to the cafeteria. I knew it was him by the way he was fidgeting with his cup. As he looked up I didn't think 'wow' but it wasn't a heart-sinking disappointment either like it could have been, and I could see how the other ninety-nine women would find him attractive. As I walked closer to him his aftershave smelled stronger and stronger. He got up to greet me and it was slightly awkward as we didn't know whether to shake hands or kiss each other.

'Hello, Nina, how are you?' he asked, missing my cheek and kissing my ear.

'I'm fine, thank you.'

His height at over six foot had been greatly exaggerated. He was slightly smaller than me and had a gap in between his front teeth, which I was sure that my mother would say was symbolic of good fortune. He'd also overdone it with the gel in his hair and it made it look greasy.

'You're very tall,' he commented.

I didn't know what to say to that so I smiled.

'I'm always nervous about doing this,' he said.

And then he went on at great lengths about how he felt. I caught the first part of it which was that he had now got a system in place when meeting the prospective date but then after that I wasn't really listening to what he was saying, and I knew it wasn't right but I was comparing him to Jean. Jean's eyes sparkled, Raj's didn't. Raj's lips were much thinner; Ki said she never trusted a man with thin lips. It was the occasional grunting laugh that brought me back to the conversation.

'So how about you?' he asked.

How about me what? I had missed that first part of the conversation. 'Well, as you know, I'm a lawyer, as you know . . .'

'You're funny, Nina. I meant how many times have you done this?'

'Done what?'

'Meeting, on the arranged system?'

'Ohh, this?' I wanted to tell him about all the weirdos I had to see before meeting Jean, and about Jean, but I didn't as I knew if word got back to the honchos who were responsible for matching up the CVs, mine would be marked with a red pen and my mother's reputation tarnished forever. 'A few,' I replied.

'You're very beautiful, Nina, I would have thought you would have been snapped up just like that,' he clicked his fingers.

There it was; cheesy line number one. Only one person in the world had ever made me feel truly beautiful on the inside and out; what did he know? Raj sensed my irritation. 'I'm sorry, I didn't mean it like that. It came out wrong . . . nerves . . . .'

Feeling guilty at taking my frustration out on Raj, I replied, 'No, it's OK. Thank you.'

It transpired that he really had no need to be nervous as he had been on about twenty dates, had got as far as two engagements, but for one reason or another, neither of them worked out. His perseverance was commendable.

'Third time lucky,' I said like a fool.

'Indeed,' he replied, smiling.

We talked about each other's jobs, families and interests, and on paper the honchos seemed to have done their job well – he was a suitable match in the eyes of my parents at least. Raj then asked if I wanted to see the Matisse exhibition. I didn't want to say that I had visited it all week.

'I would love to. Do you like Matisse?' I asked, surprised.

He nodded.

As he got up I was distracted by the T-shirt underneath his blue jumper. It was on inside out so that the label was showing. It was probably nerves, haste or just clumsiness, but I found it almost endearing. I was definitely warming towards him, almost despite myself.

'"Creativity takes courage,"' Raj said as we entered the room.

'How did you know he said that?' I replied, astounded. Was this a sign? No signs all year and then a bloody shower of them.

He laughed and this time I didn't hear the grunting sound. 'There's a lot about me you don't know, Nina,' he said confidently.

'Can I ask you a question?'

'Ask as many as you like,' he replied.

'If you went to a casino, would you put all your money on one number?'

'I wouldn't go to a casino.'

'But if you had to, what would you do?'

'I would cover all eventualities – put as many chips on as many numbers – that way you can't lose.'

We looked at the paintings together and his favourite was *The Red Studio*, the same as mine. To my surprise I found I could have spent much more time with him, but I was aware that Jean Michel would be waiting for me and that I was already running late.

'Is there somewhere you have to be, Nina?' he asked, spotting me checking my watch.

'Yes, I'm really sorry. But I'm sure we'll meet again.'

'Look, Nina, I've met lots of people and I know that I like you and I'd really like to see you again. Tomorrow?' he asked, pinning me down with a date.

I took a moment to think about it: I did want someone who was calm, who knew what they wanted, someone who was practical yet could understand me on some level. Above all, someone who was the total opposite of Jean. And how did he know that about Matisse?

'Is it OK if I call you and let you know this evening?'

'You can call me whenever you like,' he replied.

I had said I'd meet Jean at seven but it was seven-thirty when I got to his apartment building. The concierge opened the door for me and smiled. I took the lift up and rang the buzzer.

Jean answered the door. He looked tired and just for one fleeting moment I wanted to forgive him and tell him that I had really, really missed him.

'I thought you weren't coming. I'm so happy to see you, Nina.'

Be strong, I kept telling myself.

'Come in, cherie, come in,' he said, coming to kiss me. 'Cherie' sounded stupid. I turned away so he caught part of my ear.

The lights were dimmed, candles were lit and he had made dinner.

'Why didn't you use your key?' he asked.

'Well, I don't know, let me think . . . because I might find someone else here?'

'Nina, I'm sorry, I was drunk. We got a deal with . . .'

I couldn't believe what he was telling me. 'Drunk . . .? Drunk . . .?' If he had said he was angry with me and wanted to hurt me, maybe then I could listen, but drunk?

His eyes searched mine for something he could tell me that would make it better but they couldn't find anything. He reached out his hand to touch me.

I wanted to tell him about my week, giving up work, finding a studio, but didn't know where to begin and, besides, I felt I couldn't pour my heart out to him any more.

'Do you know that it takes courage to be creative?'

'What?' he replied, perplexed.

'Creativity takes courage.'

'Does it?'

'I don't know.'

He grabbed my hand, told me that he loved me, that he was sorry and would do whatever it took to make it up to me, that it would never, ever happen again. That we could start over. He said he would do absolutely anything to make me happy. And I wanted to believe every word of it, I wanted to believe it was all going to be all right, but I couldn't because it wasn't all right. And what if my dad was correct? What if love was fleeting and understanding was what was really important. If Jean understood me, I mean really understood me, he wouldn't have done that. What if in a few years he found someone else again? I took a deep breath, moved my hand away from his.

'You'll need these back,' I said, handing him his keys and then heading towards the door.

'Nina, I love you,' he shouted.

I closed the door behind me, fighting back the tears. The sad thing was I loved him too, but it wasn't enough any more.

When I got home my mum was sitting downstairs with the contents of the jewellery box sprawled across the floor.

'All for you, when you get married,' she said glancing up at me. 'Raj's mother called to tell me it had gone very well.'

'Yes, it went well, Ma.'

I didn't need love, I decided then, I needed understanding; so I called Raj and asked him if he wanted to go for a walk in the park with me.

I wished I had had the luxury of a whole string of dates with Raj before having to make a decision but arranged introductions didn't always work like that; well, especially in our family they didn't. So if you see someone twice, especially in the space of two days, it's a given that you'll be walking around a fire with them and feeding each other sickly sweets on your wedding day, unless, that is, you want to deal with a distraught mother who says you have brought shame and disrepute on the family.

But how exactly events precipitated themselves that Sunday is beyond me. The walk in the park had gone well and by the end of the afternoon Raj wanted to know if there was possibly a future for us. At that time I couldn't answer the question but by the evening I was somehow engaged to him.

It started in my absence when my dad was going through my things looking for my car insurance papers. He had taken my car out and bumped it, and true to his impatient nature couldn't wait a couple of hours for me to get back and sort it out. While rummaging through my things, he came across letters from Jean. Letters that had been sent earlier that week, telling me how sorry he was and how much he loved me.

Putting together the fact that I wasn't married at twenty-seven, the Zee TV lesbian talk-show incident, and believing Jean to be a woman, he almost had a heart attack as he finished reading how much Jean loved me.

He screamed at my mother, calling her to witness the evidence, and told her it was all her fault, that she had spoiled me and let me get away with 'the murder'. They were both pacing the house, waiting for me to get home.

Raj had given me a lift back and, thank God, I hadn't asked him in. My dad opened the door before I had even had a chance to put the key in the lock.

'We've found out about you and the Jeannie,' he shouted. 'It is shameful. How will I hold my head in the community if anyone finds out?' he ranted as I walked in.

My mother was weeping in the corner, refusing to look at me.

'You don't understand, Dad . . .'

'No, Nina, you can not deny it,' he said, pulling out

the letters from his pocket and throwing them at me.

'It's not what you think, it's . . .'

'How can you do this to us, after everything we have done for you, it's . . . it's . . .'

'It's a man, Dad. Jean is a man. You met Susan, my friend Susan, who was pretending to be Jean who's a man.'

My mother wailed even louder, the wedding sari ripped to shreds in her mind.

'Don't worry, it's finished, and anyway, if it wasn't why would I be seeing Raj?'

As they took a moment to think about this the doorbell went.

My dad answered it.

'Hello Mr Savani.'

'Oh Bhagavan, what more today? My daughter told you I have paid all my tax bills.'

Oh God, Jean, I thought.

'Nina,' Jean said seeing me by the door. 'Who was that man who dropped you off?'

Dad looked confused as my world caved in around me.

'Nina, I love you,' Jean shouted.

My dad looked over at my mum who had gathered herself together. 'Kavitha, the taxman is saying he is in love with Nina.'

'He's not the taxman, Dad, he's Jean, "the Jeannie".' I turned to Jean. 'What will it take for you to leave me alone, Jean?'

'I won't, not until you tell me that –'

'I'm marrying someone else,' I blurted.

My mother looked at me, wiping her tears with the end of her sari.

'His name is Raj and he's an accountant,' I continued.

Jean looked at me, incredulous. 'The man in the car?'

I nodded. And then he walked away. And soon after

I'd said it, I wanted to shout out, 'Don't go, Jean, it's not true.' But my mother had somehow managed to wrap herself around me and was weeping with delight.

Dad thankfully thought that Jean had fallen in love with me the day he had met me at the door. It was understandable, he said, as I got my looks from his side of the family. Mum said that we'd have to keep it all quiet so as not to disrupt the wedding plans. But then she would say that as she kept a lot of things quiet. And me, I called up Raj later that evening to ask him if he felt he might be lucky the third time around.

My dad was right: in life you can't have everything you want – it was better to make it as pain-free as possible.

The next morning I woke up feeling very dazed, and for one moment I breathed a sigh of relief thinking that agreeing to marry an accountant and being an unemployed owner of a studio had been a nightmare. The moment I realised it was true, I wanted to smother myself with the pillow.

'What a bloody mess, Ki, suppose you're unable to help me out here?'

She would be laughing at the mess, telling me to get out of it and give Jean another chance, but it was too late – wedding plans were already being put into action.

My mum was like a contestant on *The Price is Right* who had just found out that her name had been called and was running down the steps in a state of delirious excitement. 'Get up, beta, and go to work and then you can come home early,' she said bouncing into my room. 'We have so many plans to discuss, so many things to do. Come on, beta, we've done it, we've done it.'

She pulled back the duvet and I dragged myself into the shower. Part of my job was getting artists out of contracts that appeared watertight, but this was something else: verbal agreements in the semi were binding.

I got changed into my suit, pulled out my sports bag and packed a change of clothes, a few jumpers, a dirty pair of trainers, towels and an old bed-sheet. Should I be caught I was prepared with the answer of the forthcoming charity jumble sale that the firm were holding.

'So you'll try to come home early? We have the engagement party to think about.'

'I don't know, I might go to the gym after work,' I replied as she was eyeing my sports bag.

'But the party . . .?'

'You just decide, Ma, call whoever you want. I'm running late.'

'Thank you, beta, thank you. You have made me the happiest woman on this earth and you know –'

I left before she could finish.

It was freezing cold but it wasn't raining. All the units adjacent to the studio were closed. Just outside the studio door was a grubby pair of boots. I put them to one side, unlocked the padlock and went in. The studio looked bare with no Sydney Harbours looking down over it and the emptiness heightened the absurdity of what I was planning to do. Blank canvases were stacked against the wall and one hung on the easel with a note. 'Good luck with the birds – play the tape if you get stuck.'

I stood in the centre of the room looking up at the skylight. 'You crazy, crazy woman, Nina, what have you gone and done? What are you thinking of?' I said to myself. I changed out of my suit and into my jeans and jumper, tied my hair back and put the suit on the suit hanger. The heater was already turned on full blast. What was I supposed to paint?

Tubes of paint had been laid on the table in an orderly fashion. It wasn't my natural inclination to be orderly but I had to be that way at the firm. I had to be a lot of things at the firm. I stared at the blank canvas for what seemed like hours, thinking about my family, Jean Michel, about Ki and the deep insecurities the Guru had touched. It was as if I were looking at myself in the mirror and seeing all the parts that hurt. I picked up the paintbrush with my right hand. I wasn't even really right handed but from being a child my dad had insisted on me using it, as in our culture it was considered bad manners to do anything with the left hand.

'Chi, Chi, Chi, dirty girl. Not with that hand, Nina, what will the peoples say if they see you?'

But now I rolled up my sleeve and put the paintbrush in my left hand. All down my left arm was scarring, blotchy skin that revealed my deepest inadequacies. I could have had the prettiest face in the world but it wouldn't have mattered; inside I felt ugly and worthless; inside was a gaping hole that had been left by the people I had loved the most. The Guru had found his way into that place and confirmed what I already believed. I heard his words again: 'You're cursed.'

This was the arm that I hid from everyone, that I tended not to look at. This was the arm I covered, pretending that everything was fine, but here in the confines of this space there was no deceiving myself – this was the arm I wanted to paint with. Nobody here was telling me what to do or how to do it; I could reveal everything about myself and nobody would judge me. I stared some more at the canvas and started to see black. The optical illusion of colour was like the optical illusion of life: stare at something hard enough and eventually you see what you want to see.

69

Blacks, that's all I saw: black hole, black deceit, burning black, black at the funeral, empty black nights waiting for my sister to tuck me into bed, the Guru's black teeth, his dirty black fingernails. Thick ivory black squirted from the tube directly onto the canvas. But there wasn't a hint of ivory in this black, not one shade of another colour, and with the thickest, hairiest brush I frantically covered the entire canvas with this black.

I swept my hand across the meticulously placed paints and went to get the pair of grubby boots that I had seen outside. They looked so miserable – maybe they belonged to a tramp who had rejected them. They had no laces just holes as if they had been deeply wounded. I hurled them onto the table and watched them land defeated. One fell on its sole, the other on its side.

While the paint was still wet I took another black and smeared the paint on with my fingers. I could not stop. Molten anger bubbled to the surface as I pounded the canvas with my hand and fingers, smearing black onto black, trying to find the shape of the boots on the canvas. My hand and my arm ached but I kept on pounding frantically, finding the ugly creases and the lacklustre holes where laces didn't even want to go through, until eventually I had to stop and sit on the floor.

When Ki left she took a huge part of myself with her, the part that made me believe I could be anyone or do anything, Jean Michel took away a bit more and what was on the canvas was the part that had stayed with me.

As I hoisted myself up to go and knock the boots off the table, a shaft of light reflected back from them, wanting to tell me something else.

I stared at the boots in this light. They had walked for miles and miles and had been bought at a time when people saved up to buy things for special occasions. Maybe a man had saved up for weeks to buy them for his wedding and had proudly walked down the aisle. He'd also kicked a football in them with his son. When they had been chucked out years later, he searched all over the house and every subsequent pair he bought was in a vain attempt to replicate those cherished boots.

Perhaps a woman in a charity shop had picked them out just before they were put on display for the customers. She felt that they would fit her husband and had bought new laces that matched. Polishing and wrapping them up in newspaper, she had handed the boots to her husband, swearing it was a stroke of luck that she had found them as it wasn't her turn to empty the bags that day. Shortly after that he was promoted. He would have wanted to be buried in his boots when he died but his son hadn't known that and they were discarded along with the rest of his belongings.

Finally, a tramp had come across the boots quite recently after rummaging through some bin liners. He had also come across a decent suit. In a drunken state, he had taken them off and forgotten where they were. It became his mission to find them and every day he would search a different street.

Putting the canvas I had been working on to the side, along with the dirty black brush, I cleaned my hands, took a new brush and another canvas. Without mixing the colours I thinned paint with water and washed the canvas in a sea of cerulean blue. While I waited for the paint to dry, I put on the tape Gina had left me. It was Puccini's *Madame Butterfly*. Opera wasn't really my thing but I listened to it anyway. Carried away by the waves of emotion, I sat staring at the blue and then I suddenly saw something.

Dampening a rag with water, I looked at the spot two-thirds of the way down and wiped the space. I picked up an ochre yellow from the floor and oozed a buttery mass onto the empty space. The bristles on the paintbrush swirled the pigment into two rotund shapes that resembled the shape of the boots. I didn't feel as if I were the one who was painting as the strokes were rhythmic and disconnected me from all my thoughts.

Pockets of green came through where the blue paint hadn't come off, and these were effortlessly worked into the painting. Confident red-iron laces were added and where the yellow met the red a hopeful orange shone, the same orange as the soles; the same orange as the sky I had envisaged while sitting at my office window.

The bright colours made the painting look vibrant and full of life. For the first time in a very long time, it made me feel optimistic. Is this what Matisse meant by seeing flowers when there were clearly none? If painting could create an illusion, if it could make you feel things or see things that weren't there, then this was what I wanted. At that moment I was certain of only one thing; that this was what I wanted to do with my paintings. I wanted to see magic and paint it even if it couldn't tangibly be seen. I wanted to put bold colours together, see colours that hadn't been painted and bring inanimate objects back to life.

I took white paint, squirted some onto the palette, thinned it with water and in the left-hand corner I painted the words 'For Ki'. Looking at the space in between the words and sensing that there was a great distance between them, a distance that shouldn't have been there, I inserted the letter 'u' so it read, 'Foruki'.

I cleaned the boots with a damp rag so that most of the grime disappeared. There was string in the cupboard along with brown paper, both of which I placed on the table. I cut two long pieces of string and put each of the strings through the lace holes, and when I had finished I packed them both in brown paper.

I washed my hands with soap and water but couldn't get my nails clean and kept scrubbing my fingers until they felt raw. After my brushes were cleaned and the paints neatly organised on the table again, I got changed into my suit, sprayed myself with perfume, glanced at the canvas one last time and smiled. I picked up the boots, switched off the lights and locked up the studio.

The boots were left where I had found them and then I switched my phone back on. There were two messages from my mum and one from Raj asking how I was and to give him a call back whenever I could.

On the journey back home I prepared to condense my world back into Croydon, to squeeze it back into the semi. No sooner had I walked through the door than my mum cornered me.

I panicked, thinking that she could smell the paint or would spot the state of my fingernails, and so I tried to get away from her.

'Where have you been, beta, you're very late? Have lots of things to tell you,' she beamed.

'Let me have a shower first, Ma, I've had a really busy day,' I said quickly.

She followed me upstairs and talked nonstop through the bathroom door but I didn't want to hear a word of it.

'So it's OK, then? Two weeks' time, so December twenty-sixth and second of April?' she asked, shouting through the door.

'What's OK?'

'The engagement and the wedding.'

I opened the bathroom door in disbelief. The second of April was less than four months away – what was she thinking. I hardly knew this man. 'What?'

'I spoke to the priest today and he said that was a good date and then I called up Raj's mother and she too agreed. We're all so happy.'

'It's too soon,' I shouted.

'Soon, soon,' I heard my dad shout from downstairs. 'We have waited twenty-seven years.'

'But I've phoned people and made arrangements now, beta.'

'Unmake them.'

She took out her sari-end from her midriff and before she even began sobbing, I left her there.

How could she just do that? Engagement, priest, wedding, all within four months.

There was nobody I could talk to about it except Raj so I returned his call.

'Am I glad you called, Nina. I've just heard about the engagement and the wedding date, and I didn't want you to think that it was me pushing you. Far from it, we don't even really know each other.'

'That's exactly what I was thinking.' This man was growing on me more and more.

'Anyway, when you get to find out some of my really bad habits you might want to delay it indefinitely.'

'And they are?'

'Well you'll just have to find out, won't you?' he flirted.

I giggled pathetically. This was what happened when you spent hours in a room full of paint and had no one to converse with.

We talked about his day at work, his colleagues, his friends, he asked me lots of questions but I diverted the conversation so we spoke mainly about him. I didn't want to lie so I tried to find a way of broaching the painting-by-day subject.

'Do you believe in magic?'

'Black magic?' he replied.

'No, things like coincidences. Coincidences, and also

when you take a leap of faith that other things happen almost as if you have no control over them, as if someone is helping out.' I was thinking about my transition into the art world but he took it to mean us.

'I never thought about it but I suppose in a way I do. I took a leap of faith with you and it feels right and it's all moving along almost like we have no control over it.'

Did I feel that way about him? Well, no. But there had been a sign.

'What about signs?' I asked.

'What do you mean?'

'A sign is an indication that you are doing the right thing.'

He didn't say anything.

'The sign between us,' I continued, 'was that for days, even before I met you, I was thinking about the Matisse quote – you know, the one about creativity – and then you said it to me. Out of all the things you could have said, you gave me that quote.'

'I can see how that could be a sign,' he answered diplomatically. 'It's nice to think about things that way but I work on gut feeling, Nina, and I know I'm sure about you.'

Yes, that's what I liked about him. His certainty and practicality: there was no spontaneous, impetuous behaviour, no way on earth that I would ever find him with a red-headed woman.

'So what do you think?' he asked.

'About what?'

'About getting engaged in two weeks?'

Carried along by his sense of certainty and convincing myself that all the doubts I had were not about Raj but about the superficiality of the list system, I said yes.

* * *

My mother couldn't stop kissing my forehead when I told her I'd agreed to the dates, and my dad hugged me. It was getting to the stage where I could use both my hands to count the number of times he had done that. But I knew I had made them proud; the kind of proud that studying law couldn't even come close to, and before I knew it they were on the phone, calling all their friends and relatives telling them that their daughter was getting married.

'See,' my mother said to my father after she had made the last call. 'Cleaning the house of old televisions has brought Nina a husband.'

And although he didn't want to, he begrudgingly conceded that the 'Chinaman Fongi' might well be on to something.

Early next morning, I was woken by the sound of my mum singing her heart out with prayers. Singing, though, is probably not the right word, more of a howling noise. My dad began protesting but she sang like nobody could stop her.

The journey into the studio that morning took less than an hour and somewhere during that time the sun had risen. By the time I got there it was eight o'clock. The musty smell of paint lingered in the air from the day before. After getting changed I sat in front of the easel looking at the painting of the boots. I took it down and leaned it against the table leg and put a new canvas on the easel. I sat staring at the blank canvas for hours before looking again at the black, ugly canvas from the day before. It wasn't black I saw now but grey; grey like sad skies that have the promise of another colour above them; grey like the two stone-carved elephants we had in our sitting room, brought back from Uganda. They had changed hands from the craftsman who sat on the beach making them for tourists to my tight-fisted uncle who had resold them to my father. These carved elephants were what he asked relatives to bring back every time someone returned, and despite the fact that he could now afford to go there himself, he never did.

I left the easel, put the tape on, reached for Paynes Grey and squeezed it out into an empty paint-pot. My parents had lived in East Africa after they were married and my dad took care of one of his uncle's tea plantations. Years later, when his uncle died, everything was left to my dad. The story from here on changes depending on who is telling it: my dad says that he built up the plantations across East Africa and had amassed a fortune, whereas his cousin, my Uncle Amit, says that he ran the business into the ground and the extent of the debts he had run up were not discovered because Idi Amin came to power and made all the Indians leave.

My father, having amassed a fortune or not, was told to leave it all and go. My parents' lives were turned upside down when they, along with thousands of others, were told to leave. We were bundled into a van, my dad holding my mother who was clutching onto me – her baby – and my big sister. It must have been hard: one day they were surrounded by fields, the next they were looking out onto lonely pavements.

Our world shrunk to a two-bedroom flat above an Indian restaurant in Croydon which we had to share with my dad's brother, my Uncle Nandan, and his wife, Auntie Leena. Mum and Dad had to get jobs straightaway and they took the first thing that came, out of desperation. My mother worked in a factory and my father got a job with London Transport. It must have been hard for him because he had to exchange everything he had for a bus. I don't think he ever dared to dream bigger, just in case someone took those things away too; or maybe the fight for survival in England precluded the luxury of dreaming. Whatever it was, he remained trapped in his double-decker and pinned all his hopes and aspirations onto his two girls.

At that moment in time, one of his daughters was thinking about painting elephants and the other . . . nobody knew where she was. I left the grey paint and took out the tube of Cadmium Red. It was the colour of my dad's double-decker, the colour of his favourite shirt, the colour of his pride, his sadness and his anger. Most of the canvas was covered with it except the space where I wanted the elephants to go.

My dad was close to Jana. His face lit up when she walked into the room and this must have hurt my mother because she had never had that effect on him. Jana was beautiful and had a mass of black curls. When she used to collect me from school everyone said that I had a very pretty mother.

'She's my big sister,' I would say proudly, correcting them.

Taking the pot of grey and thinning it slightly with water, I outlined an elephant shape and then painted it.

When I was little I had an obsession about cutting sheets of paper and gluing them back together. Jana was the only one who knew this, in fact she was the only one who knew most things about me as she was always with me. I loved to either cut and glue or play in the middle of the kitchen floor with my collection of Matchbox cars. Jana would watch me play while cooking for the others and waiting for them to all arrive back from their jobs.

One day, as she was making dinner, the phone rang. She told me to stay where I was, saying she would be back in a minute. I'm sure she was gone for more than a minute and I only wanted to help her. I took a chair, put it next to the cooker and stood on it so I could stir the dhal. The spoon dropped to the side just next to the blue flame and as I went to get it my sleeve caught fire. Blue quickly turned to orange which turned to black. At first I just watched the flames; they rapidly spread up my arm across my chest, and as I watched it was almost as if I wasn't there. It was the smell that brought me back – a charred, burning smell – and then I felt excruciating pain and began to scream and scream. My sister got to me in seconds but just at that moment my mother came back from work.

She took a towel, soaked it and threw it over me, and shouted at my sister to call an ambulance.

Jana was crying.

'Do it,' my mother shouted.

The rest I remember vividly not just because of the pain but because I have never seen my mother so angry. Even today I have never met again the woman she turned into that day.

'Look what you've done to her,' she screamed when my sister came back. 'You can't even look after her for five minutes, always thinking of yourself, you're so selfish. You've always been selfish. It would be better if you –'

'Ma, it wasn't my fault, I only –'

'It's never your fault, nothing is ever your fault. Go and speak to your boyfriend, don't think I don't know, go speak to him again and let her burn.'

Then my mother fell silent as she looked down at me and continued rocking me in her arms. 'It's OK, beta, mummy's here. Mummy will look after you.'

The ambulance men came and Jana was told to stay behind and wait for my father.

Later that night when I was asleep in the hospital bed, I had this strange feeling that Jana came to visit me. She told me that it was time to leave and kissed me, whispering that she would always love me.

When I got back home from the hospital she wasn't there. My dad said she had gone on holiday, and each time I asked she was still on holiday. It made no sense to me – there were no letters or phone calls – and when she'd been gone for three months, my parents said she had decided to stay where she was. One day I heard my mum and dad talking, and my dad was sobbing when my mum told him what had happened and about the 'white boy'. They both agreed never to mention her name in the house again and for the purpose of the list system – to avoid any controversy and avert scandal – she was erased.

I know it broke Dad's heart when she left and so all his attention went on me. Now when I walked into a room his eyes lit up. Everything he did, he did for me, and I tried my very best not to disappoint him. It made me feel even more guilty for the lies I was now telling him on an ever-increasing basis.

A few inches to the left, just beneath the grey elephant, I painted a smaller elephant in white. Both softened the red background in which they were set.

The tape had stopped a while ago but I hadn't noticed until I put the brush down. I played it again and sat for a while eating chocolate, packets of crisps and drinking Coke that I'd bought from the newsagent's on my way to the studio. I never ate junk but in my studio there were no rules; everything was made up as I went along.

When the tape had stopped again I decided it was time to go home. Why I took the tape of *Madame Butterfly* with me I have no idea. Maybe because the studio felt like another world, somewhere where there was peace and nothing else existed, and I wanted to bring something of this world into the semi.

*   *   *

The moment I walked through the door my mum put her rolling pin down and came at me with a list of plans and things that needed to be done.

'I'll go over it after I've had a shower.'

'Yah, but don't forget most important thing is to invite Raj home day after tomorrow. Call him now to ask him.'

'Good day, Nina?' my dad interrupted.

'Yes, you know, same old thing.'

'Good, good,' he said, returning to his newspaper.

'You'll call him, no?' my mum insisted.

After coming out of the bathroom my mum was still shouting up the stairs, making all sorts of suggestions for the engagement. I put the tape of *Madame Butterfly* on to drown her out, turning it up louder and louder with every question asked.

Dad came up to my room, banging on the door.

'What are you trying to do to me, Nina? Kill me? I have to listen to Kavitha in the morning and now you make me listen to this. Why is that lady screaming like that? She got no job or husband?'

'She's found out she's been deceived,' I replied calmly. 'Fooled,' I rephrased, using his terminology.

'No, Nina, you have been the fooled, buying such music. People they buys anything these days. Maybe I should put Kavitha on a tape and make the money. Turn the lady off or make her more quiet.'

I switched the tape off, called Raj, and went to discuss the preparations with my mum.

When I left home in the mornings it was dark and when I came home it was dark. Everything was artificially lit by streetlamps, deceitful night pretending to be day and daylight cut short prematurely and swallowed up by night. In these hours of darkness I found myself on the train, preparing myself to go from one world to another, and it was only at these times when I actually thought about the insanity of what I was doing. As I climbed up the underground steps and walked to the studio, it didn't seem so insane. And when shafts of light entered my studio it was the only thing that was real; painting was the only time I could be myself and totally free. In the studio there was no pretending to be anyone else other than who I was, no wedding, no expectations, nothing. Yet, ironically, whole realities that did not exist were created with colour. Around evening, when I looked up at my skylight and saw the grey clouds encroaching, it was time to prepare myself to be someone else.

As my train arrived at London Bridge, I put all wedding plans and what would happen out of my mind. By the time I got out of the station my thoughts were consumed with what to paint next. No one had reclaimed the boots, which were still outside, but someone had unwrapped them. The table in the studio was a mess with empty Coke cans, chocolate wrappers and crisp packets. I left it all on the table, got changed, put the elephant painting against the wall, switched the tape on and sat in front of my easel. I turned around to stare at the canvas and the little elephant.

White; white like the writing on the Coke can, the sling that protected my arm, the gobstopper Ki had once given me all those years ago, the sheet that she was wrapped in to be laid to rest. White, like innocence, anticipation; the start of something new.

On the way home from school, Jana always made sure we stopped off at the newsagent's and bought me sweets. I wasn't allowed to tell Mum and Dad this because the money she was given for housekeeping wasn't supposed to be spent on confectionery, but every day we got something and she sat me up on the wall outside while I ate. Sometimes her friend David came and sat with us. He worked in a garage across the road but I wasn't allowed to tell anyone this either.

That's how I met Ki. Ki was the newsagent's daughter and one day I saw her in his shop behind the counter. I recognised her from school and smiled. She didn't smile back; she probably didn't need any more new friends as she already had loads of them, all of them huddled around her at break-time when she got out her assortment of sweets. That's the kind of power a packet of cola cubes had back then. She had big round brown eyes and I remember thinking that my eyes would be as round as hers if my dad had a sweetshop.

The sweetshop girl ran from the counter and went to balance on a broom. I held my sister's hand like I too had something to be proud of. We saw her most days after school and that was all she did, run and balance on her broom head as if it were her most prized possession, but she never said anything to me there or at school, not even hello. But my sister spoke to her and she spoke to the owners of the newsagent's; Jana could talk to anyone.

Not until months later when I had been off school for a while and had my arm in a sling did broom girl come and talk to me. She came up to me one playtime shortly after I had returned to school and offered me some gobstoppers.

'You don't come to the shop any more,' she said.

Like she really cared. After my sister went on holiday, my mum stayed at home to take care of me and didn't know about the sweetshop. I glanced at the packet of gobstoppers being tempted at me. I said nothing. No one could buy me like that.

'What happened?' she said pointing at the sling, her cheek bulging in the shape of a round ball.

I shrugged one shoulder and she thrust the packet in my face again, took out a gobstopper and placed it in my hand. The information was worth one gobstopper.

I tried to explain the sequence of events but it must have sounded confusing, and as I got to the part about my sister I began to cry.

'Here, take them,' she said trying to console me, handing the whole packet over. And then I found her looking out for me every playtime.

The canvas was painted white.

'Do you want to be the witch?' she said when my arm got better and all that was left was the scarring. At the time, being the witch was a privilege, but I didn't know this. I assumed it was because she thought I was ugly and the scars could add to the character portrayal. But when we played with the other girls there would always be a fight as to who would be the witch and if any of the girls said anything about my arm, she'd beat them up. Those were the roles we fell into; she took care of me and I let her. I still missed my sister desperately but I grew to love my new friend.

A year later, my sister began sending letters to me at Ki's sweetshop. I don't know how she knew I'd get them, maybe she didn't as she began each letter with, 'I don't know if you'll get this, my little one.' Ki's mother secretly read them to us. Jana was living in Manchester with her friend David but didn't leave an address at the top so I could write back to her. Every birthday and Christmas she sent me a card but that all stopped abruptly when I was twelve. Every day after school, without fail, I would go into the sweetshop hoping for a letter that never came. Ki's mother would shake her head and cuddle me. Her family became mine.

Around this time, Mum and Dad bought their own house, and it was round the corner from Ki's. If I wasn't in her house, she was in mine, but I preferred to be there as her parents let us do pretty much what we wanted. If my dad was at home we couldn't really run about as he would track us down and make us sit at the dining-room table while he read bits from the encyclopaedia or *The Reader's Digest* which he'd begun to subscribe to. On Saturdays, Ki's dad would let us help him out while he went to the cash and carry. We could unwrap all the packets of sweets, drinks and crisps and then her mother would give me a carrier-bag full of stuff to take home. I'd draw her lots of pictures as a way of saying thanks. Ki's mother put them on her fridge door although I bet she wished she hadn't done that because week after week she got more and more garish pictures.

Ki and I didn't end up going to the same secondary school but it didn't matter, because after school we were inseparable. She was very popular at her school but I didn't have a gang as I was shy, very self-conscious of my scar, and was forced to wear this awful grey oversized anorak that my dad had got down the market. On top of that, I had the misfortune of having to sit next to Rita Harris, who was the class babe. One day Rita drew up a list where she paired up the girls and the boys. She decided to leave my name out as she said none of the boys would want to be paired up with me. When I told Ki about this, she came to our school at lunchtime and beat Rita Harris up and made her say sorry to me in front of everyone.

Shortly after that, things turned. I got rid of the anorak,

made new friends and began to believe in myself a little more. Even my Uncle Amit who hadn't seen me in years remarked on the change and said I had turned into a swan, though at the time I had some difficulty understanding this as he pronounced it as 'wone' – it was only after further clarification when he mentioned the ugly duckling that I knew what he was going on about.

The only time Ki and I didn't speak for weeks was when I said that she was being dumb leaving school to do a secretarial course.

'God, Nina, you've been spending too much time with your dad.'

'But you can go to university.'

'Have you ever thought that I might not want to? I don't do things to please other people.'

'You don't have to.'

'At least I don't spend my time creeping around pretending to be someone I'm not. Why don't you tell your dad you're doing an art A-level. It's spineless.'

'Spineless?' I repeated. 'You're just spoiled. You've always been a brat. Anything you want, just go ask daddy.' And as soon as I said it, her eyes looked as if I'd dropped the heaviest rocks in them.

Normally after an argument it was me that went quiet, but I couldn't handle her silences; they were of a different kind – they could completely freeze you out. Even so, every day I went to her house as normal, watched videos and listened to her tapes despite the fact she wasn't speaking to me, and chatted away with no response. Then one day, as I was telling her how I had caught my dad blowing the television a kiss when Cilla Black was on, I could tell she wanted to laugh, so I threw my arms around her.

'You're such an idiot, Nina,' she laughed.

'Dad and Cilla can always break you down.'

It was a given that we'd always be there for each other and forgive each other anything.

Ki worked for the same travel company for years. When I started at Whitter and Lawson she got into a pattern of temping and travelling until she met her boyfriend Sanjay. Her trip to Southeast Asia was to be her last before she got married.

She bought me a buddha from a market stall in Bangkok. She was in Thailand and was meant to go on to Australia, then Sanjay was going to meet her and together they'd go to South America. But Ki came home early with the pain in her leg that kept getting worse. The buddha was bought for me in haste as a souvenir.

Every time she went somewhere she got me something, as if to entice me out of my life in London. Some of the things she brought back wouldn't have got me out of Croydon.

Towards the end was the only time when I looked after her, but I had to, I had to make her fight, not let her go. She pretended she was getting better, that she was getting stronger and I believed this because I wanted to. If you stare at something long enough you can see whatever you want to.

The canvas was still blank. Where was she now? What would she be doing? Where did an energy like that go? It couldn't just dissolve into nothingness. I dented the Coke can with my fist, first in one direction and then in another; things were really so fragile. Taking thick, bright red I painted a buddha in the colours and shapes of the Coca Cola tin, adding white so there were different hues of red. It took hours and hours to replicate the detail and the dents of the can and when I looked at my watch it was seven o'clock; time to go.

Exhausted, I sat back and looked at the canvas. The painting was bright, vibrant and full of life without a trace of its fragility. Thinning the red paint, on the left-hand corner in bold capitals, I wrote 'FORUKI'. If I had to get rid of all my pictures but could keep one, it would be this one. It gave me a great sense of peace, an energy – her energy, her boldness.

I packed my things up, changed into my suit, put some make-up on and went to meet Raj.

It was on Raj's insistence that we met at Holborn tube station so he could meet me directly from work. I got there ten minutes late. He looked good in his suit, taller, and there wasn't as much gel in his hair. Raj didn't quite know what to do when he saw me so I kissed him on the cheek.

'Sorry I'm late.'

'I've just got here myself,' he replied. 'Where shall we go?'

'There's a nice Belgian restaurant here . . .' and then I stopped, thinking maybe it wasn't such a good idea in case I bumped into my old boss or some work colleagues '. . . but you normally have to book,' I continued. 'Let's go somewhere you know.'

'We'll walk over to Covent Garden, there's a nice little Italian restaurant. You don't mind walking, do you, and you do like Italian?' he asked.

'Italian's good and I love walking,' I replied. 'If I could, I would spend all day walking.'

'Me too,' he said. 'It helps me think.'

I always thought that too.

'You know there's a theory that walking balances both sides of the brain's hemispheres,' he continued. 'When you have a problem, it's because you are predominantly using one part of your brain, so when you walk the physical act of walking makes both sides of the brain communicate with each other; that's why the problem seems less of a problem when you go for a walk.'

'Really?' I asked.

'Yes,' he replied, attempting to take my hand – he caught two of my fingers instead.

I laughed nervously.

His hand was moist and I could feel it throbbing. It wasn't like Jean Michel's grip that felt firm and safe.

'How did you know that? About walking a problem out?' I asked, feeling stupid for my childish laugh.

'I have a fascination with personal development and ways we are able to improve ourselves. You know we only truly use a fraction of our potential.'

I understood all about not using potential.

Covent Garden had a real Christmassy feel; the streets were decked with lights and the shops were beautifully decorated. It was the first time in ages I felt there was something to look forward to.

'So did you have a busy day,' he asked.

'Yes,' I said. 'I got quite a bit done. Did you?'

'Not much. I was just thinking about us and this crazy scenario.'

'You can back out,' I said hastily.

'That's the thing. I don't want to. It's never felt this right.' He squeezed my hand tightly. 'And I know my friends are going to love you, Nina.'

I wanted to tell him about Ki, what had happened to her, but it didn't seem appropriate so I asked him about them.

He talked about each of them and then just as I felt he was going to ask me about my friends I changed the subject totally and asked him about the type of music he liked.

'That's what I love about you, Nina. I never know which way the conversation is going.'

By the time we got to the restaurant we had covered music, film and travel, and then we got on to the family.

My mother had asked me not to mention Jana to avert any scandal. Under this list system any family scandal would be red-penned and circled by the honchos and used against us at a later stage. But I told Raj about her and sent Jana to Australia instead, where I said she was living, happily married, and that we hardly got to see her.

'It must be hard. You must miss her,' he said.

I nodded. Later it would all come out, I thought. When I knew him well enough.

He told me that his parents were looking forward to meeting me. I checked if he was still coming around the next day to meet mine.

'I don't think I've ever seen them this happy,' I said.

'I have,' he replied. 'I mean, *my* parents. Twice before,' he laughed, with not one trace of a grunt. Raj reached for my hand across the table and it felt warmer and safer. Maybe everything would be all right.

'What's good?' I asked looking at the menu.

He ordered the food and wine for both of us. We ate, talked some more, and then it was time to go home.

He hailed me a cab and before I got in it, he kissed me. It wasn't a passionate kiss, more of a 'this is going to be just fine' type of a kiss.

The next morning as I walked into the studio I felt incredibly optimistic. The red was striking and the buddha filled my studio with a different kind of warmth. After studying him for a while I sat cleaning my brushes, organising the

90

paint and then reorganising it. I painted one more canvas white, changed back into my suit and went to Green Park.

It was cold but I sat eating a sandwich and drinking a coffee and imagined what Jean Michel was doing, and then as I found myself thinking too much about him, comparing Raj's incessant need to fill silences with Jean Michel's ability to listen or say nothing, I got up and went around the galleries in Cork Street. It wasn't fair to Raj to compare them like that – his need to talk was because we didn't know each other. As I looked through the gallery windows I envied the artists who were able to display their work. Mine wouldn't even make it to a church fete. It was only three o'clock but I went home anyway.

'Why are you home so early, beta?' my mother said coming out of the kitchen.

'You told me to be.'

'Yah, yah,' she nodded fiercely.

'I'll have a shower and I'll come down and help you.'

'No need,' she said. 'All done. You go and rest and then you can do your hair and make-up.'

I wanted to say something but instead had a shower and watched *Countdown*. My dad came in from work but before he had a chance to say anything I said, 'My boss told me to leave early today as I mentioned we had an important family function.'

'Everything at work good, Nina?'

'Yes, Dad, it's fine.' It had to be, this is what he'd sold me on, the fact that I was a lawyer with huge prospects. People like Raj's family wouldn't be interested in families like ours if it weren't for this one fact.

'Very good,' he replied. 'New clients?'

'No, as I said before, I'm just busy with one of our most important clients. He's got an exhibition coming up soon . . . in Mayfair,' I added, so it would make him think about the first part of that sentence.

'Good.'

'See, Dad, artists can earn a lot of money.'

'What?'

I knew he heard the word money. 'Money – I was just saying that artists can earn lots.'

'They are the fools the people who buy paintings. Anybody can put paint on the paper. That's why the artists need you; people are taking them to court because they realise they have been the fooled.'

Raj rang the bell promptly at seven-thirty. My mum had changed into her favourite green sari and my dad had his red shirt on. Kitchen activity had commenced the day before and an array of dishes had been cooked with the best cutlery and plates being taken out. Dad had wiped them all with a tissue and my mum had gone over it once again so fluff or marks that the tissue had left were totally eradicated. The television was off, there was no background noise and so the bell rang loud and clear. My mother and father looked at each other, then my mother got up to open the door but my father glanced over at her. 'Wait, Kavitha. I'll go, don't want him to think we are desperate to see him.' She nodded and sat back down, then my father waited a few seconds before he went to greet him.

'Pleased to meet you, Uncle,' I heard Raj say.

There was a pause and then my father said, 'Yes, good to meet the man who will make my Nina happy.'

He showed him into the sitting room.

'This is my wife, Kavitha.'

'Hello Auntie. How are you?'

She did her prayer-pose thing to which he couldn't quite respond as he had his hands full with an enormous chocolate box.

'These are for you,' he said handing them to her.

'Thank you but I really shouldn't eat them.' She patted

92

her stomach, wanting him to tell her not to be so ridiculous; that she was fine without having to lose three stone.

'Don't be silly. You're fine, Auntie,' Raj replied.

She beamed.

He then came over to kiss me on the cheek. My parents smiled at each other and my mother raised that eyebrow that could converse on its own.

'Drink?' she asked.

'Something soft, Auntie. I don't really drink.'

Didn't he guzzle a bottle of wine yesterday? 'We've got some wine if you want,' I said mischievously.

'No, Nina, orange juice is fine.'

'Whisky, Dad?' I asked. He nodded.

There was silence and then Raj said, 'So do you still work, Uncle?'

'Soon I'll retire, when Nina is settled. I have my own repair business,' I heard him say, conveniently missing out his day job.

'What kind of business, Uncle?'

'Repairing electronic goods. You are an accountant, no, Rajan? Very good. What accountant?'

'Tax,' Raj replied.

'I was having the problems with the taxman. He came to the house and then . . .' I took the drinks and burst into the sitting room before he could say anything more.

'No, Nina, the taxman . . .'

My mum skilfully interrupted by asking after Raj's mother and family. He seemed confused at the different lines of conversation.

'See where you get it from, Nina,' he laughed before turning to my mum and saying, 'they're fine, Auntie, all waiting to meet you again. My mother says it's been far too long.'

I remembered it had been too long because my dad had called her a 'snub' and didn't want my mum to socialise with her, but now they were on their way to being best friends, family even.

'And your daughter, do you think she'll make it home in time for the engagement?' Raj added.

'Of course, Nina has to be there,' my dad laughed.

'No, no, your other one.'

There was silence. Mum looked shocked.

'Australia,' I said, 'Jana's in Australia.'

'Australia. Couldn't take cold weather,' my dad added quickly, 'and then . . .'

'She got married,' I continued, knowing that if my dad were left to his own devices he would lead everyone to a murky crocodile swamp where there would be no way of back-pedalling.

'Got married to a pharmacist. I've told Raj already, Dad, so you don't have to bore him.'

'This girl,' he said, pinching my cheek, 'we will miss her.'

Mum regained her composure and asked if we were ready to eat and led the way to the dining room. She pulled out her circular rotis, which she had kept warm in the oven along with all the paneer, dhals and shak she had made, and we sat round the table.

'You're a brilliant cook, Auntie,' Raj said.

To which she promptly got up off the chair and served him another helping and a roti.

'Nina is not good,' my father stated. 'But she will learn now she's getting married – too much hi and bye to stop at home and learn good cooking.'

'That doesn't matter, Uncle, I can help.'

My dad was horrified. 'Man is not supposed to cook,' he instructed as if it were one of God's commandments. 'Man is supposed to bring home bacon or . . . brinjals,' he said, laughing at his own joke.

Raj laughed politely.

'Victoria is not far from here so you can come to eat whenever you like,' my mother added.

After we got married we would be moving into Raj's three-bedroom flat in Victoria. Although he had bought it years ago it was vacant as he still lived with his parents. He had asked how I would feel about moving to Victoria the day before and I said it didn't bother me. Only when she made this comment did the reality sink in. I had to live with a virtual stranger; I hadn't even lived with Jean.

Sensing my panic, Raj said, 'You too, Auntie, come around whenever you want to see us. I don't want you to feel like you are losing a daughter. You're gaining a son.'

That one sentence gave her enough voltage to illuminate the whole of Croydon.

'Thank you, thank you, my son.'

Seeing how happy Raj made everyone I tried to convince myself that by the time the wedding came around he wouldn't be a stranger – he would be someone I loved . . . hopefully.

The rest of the evening went pretty smoothly. Raj smiled politely at my dad's comments and mum kept getting up off her chair and serving him some more. When it was time to leave Mum wouldn't let Raj go. She became the tidal wave she so feared would engulf her, wrapping her arms around him and hugging him in to her bosom so that there was no way out. 'Thank you, thank you,' she kept repeating.

'No, thank you, Auntie,' he managed after somehow releasing himself.

'Thank you too, Uncle.'

My father shook his hand and patted him on the back, except it wasn't a pat, more of a wallop. 'We'll talk tax next time, son.'

'I'll see you out to the front door, Raj,' I said.

We got outside to the gate. 'I'll completely understand if you want to back out.'

'It makes me fall in love with you even more, Nina.'

I was taken aback by the use of the word love. Love wasn't supposed to enter into the equation – not yet, anyway.

'Oh, right,' was all I could manage and then he kissed me goodnight.

Over the next few days I painted six more buddhas on one canvas in different colours and backgrounds like an Andy Warhol picture, except it wasn't as good as the original. It was more an exercise in experimenting; placing contrasting colours next to each other and then seeing what that did to the painting. During that week I came to the conclusion that the relationship with Raj couldn't progress any further unless I was completely honest with him.

So on Friday, when I was due to meet him, I decided I was going to tell him about the other part of my life he knew nothing about. He would understand – he came across as an empathetic type of a person. Perhaps I wouldn't start from the very beginning but tell him about my three-month unpaid sabbatical which was helping me sort out my thoughts.

We had decided already that we would go to the cinema, but because Raj was running late he arrived slightly agitated and rushed and so it didn't feel appropriate to bring up the conversation on our way there.

'I am so sorry, Nina, this never normally happens.'

'It's OK if we miss it, Raj,' I said as he drove faster.

'We can't be late,' he insisted.

'It's only the cinema.'

'Yes but it's booked and paid for.'

If it had been Jean Michel we would have gone and done something completely different – plans were there to be made and broken.

Somehow we got there on time, missing only the trailers. As we sat watching *The Matrix* he grabbed my hand and I leaned against his shoulder. Nobody would have guessed that two weeks earlier we had been complete strangers.

Throughout that evening it never felt like a good time to bring up the painting subject. Would he understand? Stability, and his need for having to know exactly what was happening when, was completely opposite to what I was doing.

'Just be yourself and they'll love you,' he said as he dropped me home.

'Sorry?'

'When you meet my parents tomorrow all you have to do is be yourself, Nina.'

The way he said my name felt as if he were talking to someone else. 'I don't think they would,' I replied.

'What do you mean?'

It was the perfect opening. 'Do you ever feel that you can't really be yourself?'

'All the time.'

'Do you really?'

Just as I thought we were getting somewhere, he said, 'Except when I'm with you.'

No, not a cheesy line. I wanted a story about deception, about secrets and untruths, but he didn't have one.

'I have something to show you,' I said pulling up my sleeve so he could see the scarring. He had to ask me where I had got it and then at least we could start from the very beginning; the inability to express pain except on paper, the feelings of inadequacy, how painting made me feel that none of that really mattered because what I did with the colours made me feel good about myself as a person.

He was taken aback but then quickly said, 'Is this what you're worried about, Nina? It doesn't make a bit of difference to me.' And then I thought he was going to pull up his trouser-leg and show me a wound and ask where I got mine, but instead he gave me another cheesy line and said I was beautiful and he still couldn't believe how lucky he was to have found me.

Raj came the next morning to take me to his parents and as he parked outside in his black BMW my dad was jumping up and down asking my mum to look out of the window to see his car.

'I knew we made Nina the good match, he's a nice boy. Close the curtain now, Kavitha, he's coming to the door.'

'Hello Uncle, hello Auntie, it's nice to meet you again. You know my mother and father have asked you to come around tomorrow?'

'Yes, yes, your mother called me to tell us,' my mum beamed.

I didn't want Raj to sit down and never find his way out of the sofa so I said, 'I think we're running late. Shall we go, Raj?'

'Not even stopping for a drink?' Mum asked.

'It's not good to be late, is it, Ma, especially when you're meeting for the first time.'

'No, but remember, beta, you met Mrs Mehta at Auntie Leena's house.'

I had been about nine and at that age one auntie looked pretty much like another: centre-parted hair in bun, red dot on forehead, lots of gold jewellery and all neatly wrapped up in a sari – the wearing of socks and sandals depended on how old they were.

'Yes, but still, best not to be late.'

'Yes, Auntie, we really have to go.'

She nodded, smiled at Raj, embraced him in her bosom thanking him once again, and then we left.

One hand was on the steering wheel, the other hand was holding mine and after much conversation from him, we got to Raj's house in Sutton. I say house but it was more of a mansion. His mother was waiting for us saying that his father would be back shortly as he had gone to play golf.

'I've heard so much about you, Nina. It's so lovely to meet you finally,' she said, kissing me on both cheeks.

She was completely different from the bun and dot look I had envisaged for her. Instead she had a side-parted bob, lots of diamond rings on her manicured fingers and was wearing black chiffon trousers and a long red top.

'Nice to meet you too, Auntie.'

'Come through, come through. You're even prettier than on the photo I was sent. Normally it's the opposite. They do themselves all up, the mothers send the photos, and then they come here and you think dinner and dog.'

'Dog's dinner' was the phrase she was looking for but instead I sensed that she wasn't a woman who took kindly to being corrected. 'Thank you,' I replied instead.

She led us into the sitting room, which was incredibly spacious with minimalist furniture on oak-wood flooring. I had tried to persuade my dad to get rid of the Seventies-patterned carpets we had, and to convince him to put down some laminate flooring, but he said that it looked cheap. I wondered what Raj thought about our sitting room stuffed with brown leather sofas and the elaborate chandelier that my dad had got off a man he knew down the market. It didn't work; not that much in our house actually did work.

99

'Tea? Coffee?' she asked.

'Nothing for me, thank you.'

'Raju, will you get me some juice. Get some for Nina as well. Nina, you'll have some, no?'

I didn't get a chance to answer before Raj was sent off.

'So Nina, you're a lawyer I hear . . . for artists, no? You must come across some famous people.'

'Some,' I said.

'How interesting. Uncle and I know Ravi Shankar.'

I said I didn't represent him.

She laughed. You can tell a lot about a person by the way they laugh and hers was an elongated 'Ha', which sounded fake.

'We're all so excited about the wedding. I was speaking to your mother and we've both got it in hand. No expense spared. I don't mean to be rude but I want to give you both the best possible wedding and that doesn't always stretch to the modest wage of a bus driver.'

'He's also an electrician,' I added.

'Sorry?'

'My father, he's also an electrician.'

'Yes. We were thinking the Café Royal, and if that was booked maybe the Hilton on Park Lane and definitely no plastic plates. I find that so crude.'

Raj came in with the juice.

'No, Raju, I'm just telling Nina maybe the Café Royal for the wedding and reception.'

'Whatever Nina thinks best, Ma.'

'She has far too much to worry about with her career and this networking that they are all doing. It's agreed, then, your mother and I will take care of it.'

I thought about the other two candidates before me who had fallen by the wayside and I was positive that she had had something to do with it.

Then his dad rushed in. A nice, quiet, sedate man, the

only offensive thing about him being his chequered trousers.

'Pleased to meet you, Nina,' he said shaking my hand. 'Sorry I'm late.'

'Wash your hands and get changed,' Raj's mother ordered.

He went upstairs and came back down after a while and then we all had lunch. She'd thrown together a buffet with quiches and salads. I thought that if she served this to my father he'd be violently sick on her rosewood table as he couldn't cope with 'English food' and couldn't swallow anything that wasn't wrapped in a roti.

Raj sat next to me, occasionally squeezing my hand under the table while she fired out questions that she alternated by talking about herself. By the end of the afternoon it was decided that she would take charge of the preparations. With the speed she had us out of the door I was sure that she would be on the case that very moment.

'Nina, are you having second thoughts after meeting mine now?' Raj asked when we got outside.

And instead of saying yes I saw where the vulnerability that made him wear his T-shirts inside out had come from. Maybe I could look after him, maybe he could look after me, maybe we could take care of each other, so I said, 'No backing out now,' and squeezed his hand.

Though the days were getting a little longer the space between my two worlds was increasingly widening. I let others organise my life while I threw myself into my paintings. All the anxiety and doubts were splattered onto canvas and the more I needed to believe that it would all work out and that marrying Raj was absolutely the right thing to do, the more inanimate the objects I chose to paint became and the more I tried to bring them to life.

101

One day it was a concrete brick painted on rough strokes of green grass; the next it was a red iron-oxide bicycle wheel on fresh white snow.

The following week I went through a phase of painting houses. Derelict houses whose colours and symmetry hid their state of disrepair, and then I painted houses in the style of rich sari fabrics set against grey backgrounds, and then grey houses set against rich sari-coloured backgrounds. When I got home, a selection of engagement saris were sprawled across my bed and my mother sat waiting for me asking me to choose. Every day it was the same routine. I would fold them away, not choosing any. She just thought I was playing a guessing game with her and this heightened her excitement.

The Christmas holidays came and I couldn't paint in the studio as it would appear strange that work had not given me the customary days off, so despite the fact that I yearned to be in the studio I busied myself shopping and buying Christmas gifts for everyone – not that we ever celebrated Christmas.

Every Christmas morning as a child I'd go around to Ki's house. My mum would drop me in the morning and collect me in the evening, and though Ki's mum invited her in she was always in a hurry to get back to the garments she had to stitch. Ki's parents were also Hindu but they would still put a tree up in the run-up to Christmas and a mountain of presents for Ki would be underneath. There would always be something there for me too. Ki would open her presents before I came, bar one of them, and we would sit and open these together.

When we were seven my dad told us that Santa Claus was an invention so that people could make lots of money, but when we asked Ki's dad if that was true he said that

Santa was as real as people believed him to be. Weeks before Santa came, Ki's dad would sit and help us write letters to him and Rudolf. We had to think very carefully about what we put in these letters as they always brought us the number one item on our list. This year I couldn't face Ki's parents and put off going to see them yet another day. Instead, I handed my mum and dad their Christmas gifts.

'You should not do these things, beta,' my mum said, ripping her present open. 'We don't even celebrate Christmas.'

'They're only . . .'

'Gloves,' she said with a hint of disappointment, and then almost immediately she perked up knowing that they might only be gloves but this was no consolation prize; she could put them on and hug her real prize (her future son-in-law) in all weathers.

'Open yours, Dad.'

'I know what it is, it's a CD. You can put as much wrapping around it but I cannot be the fooled.'

He tore the wrapping open and his eyes lit up in a way that made my mother suspicious.

'Show,' she demanded.

'*You're My World*,' she read. '*Thirty-fifth Anniversary Collection*. Cilla Black.'

'Only the Cilla,' he said, trying not to appear embarrassed. And then he completely changed the subject. 'Why the English peoples are eating the ugly bird on this day? Somebody is probably telling them that this was the Jesus's favourite food and is making the money from this. They may not even be having this bird where Jesus lived.'

'Dad, not everything is about making money, sometimes people do things because they love to and there's nothing else in the world that they would rather do. Take Cilla, for example, she sings because she loves it.'

103

'No, Nina, she is singing because she is making the money.'

'But before, when she didn't have any, she was singing.'

He stopped to think about this and then said, 'Don't talk about the Cilla now, Nina, you knows your mother doesn't like her.'

Christmas passed as it did every year with my dad lying on the sofa waiting for the Queen's speech and then dozing off, looking like an exhausted, tanned Santa who had just come back from his holidays in the Bahamas. My mum was busy pottering about preparing for the engagement party that was to be held on Boxing Day.

I finally chose an orange silk sari with small gold-embroidered elephants. With anticipation, Mum picked out the jewellery, ironed the sari and brought it into my room.

'I never thought I could be this happy, beta.'

'Me neither,' I replied, thinking that the only other way I could make them any happier was by producing a child a year after the wedding. When I went to bed she came to kiss me on the forehead. The last time she did that I was six.

Early next morning the bell rang. It was the make-up lady. I couldn't believe Mum had arranged for a lady to come.

'What's the point of wasting the money trying to fool him? He already knows what Nina looks like.'

For the first time ever I agreed with my dad but Mum seemed to derive some kind of pleasure watching my hair being put up in ringlets and my skin being plastered with foundation. After I put my sari blouse on, the lady attempted to patch up the scarring on my arm with powder, and that's when I lost my temper.

104

'If they can't cope with seeing that they can stuff the wedding. Is that why you asked her to come, so she can cover that up? There are some things you just can't cover up, Ma,' I shouted.

Sensing that the entire wedding marquee she had constructed in her head was about to come crashing down, she made out as if it were all the make-up lady's fault and asked her to leave.

'I'm sorry, beta, I didn't tell her to do that.'

'Didn't you?'

'No, I just asked her to put some colour on you. No need to be upset, it will all be OK.'

My dad salvaged the situation with a diplomacy that I didn't even know he was capable of.

'This is for you, Nina, your mother and I bought this.' He opened the box and pulled out a necklace – a simple silver chain, not at all like the heavy gold pieces I would have expected.

'Thank you, it's beautiful,' I said as he put it on for me. 'It's just nerves.'

My Auntie Leena and Uncle Nandan were the only people from our side of the family who were invited to witness the actual engagement ceremony, but a whole collection of various family members and distant relatives were called to congregate at Raj's house later that afternoon for lunch. It was on Raj's mother's insistence to have it at her house as she said it was probably bigger. My uncle and aunt were both tearful when they saw me, probably because I had given them hope by agreeing to an arranged marriage – if I could do it, maybe their two younger daughters who showed absolutely no inclination would go the same way.

Raj's family came in their convoy at exactly eleven o'clock. 'Don't look out of the window,' my father yelled as he pulled down the net curtain. Two of the leading honchos responsible for the matchmaking also got out of one of the cars; they had come to preside over the proceedings. Their granny-like appearance and hobbled walk were deceptive: these women were capable of handling an AK47 and taking out any unnecessary obstacles in an instant. Raj's mother was in her full regalia and she instructed her husband to straighten out her sari as she approached our door. Behind them all was Raj, swamped in his new grey suit.

The bell rang and my father ran to open the door.

'Welcome,' he said to them all. They began taking off their shoes and Raj's mother, bewildered at the state of the carpet, kept glancing at my father hoping that he'd tell her not to bother. She looked as if she'd never stepped foot in a semi and was staring at the Seventies retro wallpaper while leaning against the door which had some dodgy Christmas lights precariously suspended around it; my father had bought them from the market especially for the engagement. I was worried that she might electrocute herself if she moved her hand any further but my mum saved her from this when she asked me to go and touch their feet. Once they had all assembled in the hall, I had to bow down to the honchos and my future in-laws. Insisting I did not need to go all the way down was also part of the whole routine but no one except my father-in-law-to-be did this.

Raj and I smiled nervously and were quickly ushered into the sitting room and asked to sit on the floor next to one another. Those who could find space made their way into the Land of Leather showroom. Raj's mother sank into her seat and had difficulty getting up when it was her turn to place before me the gifts they had brought. The honchos were getting impatient and began coughing and spluttering; it was taking too much time, they needed to be fed.

From a bag, Raj's mother took out a red sari, gold

106

necklace, silver anklets, a nose ring, some bindi and lastly a hairy saffron-stained coconut and gave it all to me. There it was, the fated coconut finding its way back; once thrown hastily over a bridge, now participating in an engagement. How events had precipitated since that day – back then I was certain that I was getting engaged, but not to a complete stranger. Jean: what would he be doing right now as I sat with this family accepting a ring from my future husband.

'It's a family heirloom,' his mother said as Raj slipped it on my finger.

It was enormous and I wondered if the candidate before me had sausage-shaped fingers. It was also very ornate, with clusters of diamonds set around a huge emerald, not at all like the single solitaire Jean had produced.

'Such thin fingers you have, Nina,' she commented. 'And I meant to ask you earlier, what happened to your arm?'

My mum, bewildered that the proceedings had taken a diversion, hastily added, 'Nina had an accident with fire when she was little. The ring is beautiful.'

'Show,' my dad indicated. As I lifted my hand to show him, the ring fell off. There was a gasp from one of the honchos – perhaps she felt it was a sign of foreboding. No one paid her any attention. Dad picked up the ring and studied it closely. 'Very good. You can see good quality diamond don't go black.'

The ring he had bought my mother under duress for their twenty-fifth wedding anniversary had turned a funny black colour and had left ugly stains on her hand. 'I paid a lot of money for that but I was the fooled,' Dad had said to Mum.

I wanted Jean to come and rescue me – to get me out of there. Raj's mother instructed Raj to get it altered as soon as he could.

Raj and I were then fed sickly sweets and that was it – we were officially engaged.

'I am the proud,' my father proclaimed, closing the ceremony. They were all given tea and savouries and then it was time to make our way over to Raj's house.

His family left first and we followed half an hour later. Everyone was talking excitedly in the car but I didn't feel like I was there with them; it felt as if it was all happening to someone else as I sat in silence looking out of the window. We parked in the drive along with a fleet of other cars and then I participated in a foot-stepping ceremony before entering his home.

Red bindi mixed with water in a bowl waited for me on the porch. My sari was lifted up as I placed my feet in the bowl. My right foot had to enter his house first and just by the door was a white sheet so that the stained footprint could tell everyone that I now belonged to Raj's family. They all clapped and cheered as my red footprint left its mark. I was now one of them. It was too late to back out.

Crowds of people came up to us to wish us well; endless streams of uncles and aunts who fed us even more sweets. Then, after lunch, a group of uncles got out their thablas and started singing and a chorus of aunts joined in. Some, like my mother, wailed; others clapped. As their clapping grew more and more frenzied, people felt that they had no option but to get up and dance. Raj sat by my side throughout it all, watching. He needed taking care of as much as I did and although we didn't know each other that well there was some level of understanding. After being fed more tea and sweets it was finally time to go home.

My parents and I got back about seven o'clock. I ran inside, grabbed my car keys and immediately went out again.

'Where are you going?' my mother shouted.

'There's something I've forgotten.'

Without getting changed, I got into my car and drove to Ki's house. I sat in my car outside her front door for ten minutes before getting out, overwhelmed with sadness. Sadness because it was Christmas and she wasn't around, sad because she wasn't there to stop me getting engaged, sad because there was only one light on at her parents' house. It had been at least six months since I'd seen her mother. Despite the fact that the house wasn't well lit, I knew she was in. 'Auntie, it's me, Nina. Open the door,' I shouted through the letterbox. She came to the door, opened it, and tears welled in her eyes when she saw me. I could barely bring myself to say hello. She held me and the two of us stood in the hallway for a while, understanding the other's pain in a way that nobody else could. It was dark inside, no Christmas tree, no lights.

She didn't ask me why it had taken me so long to come round but just wiped her tears with the end of her sari, wiped mine and then cupped my face in both her hands and whispered, 'You look beautiful.'

'I'm sorry I didn't come yesterday, Auntie, I wanted to.'

'It's OK, beta, you must be busy.'

'I'm getting married, Auntie, and I wanted to ask you and Uncle to the wedding.'

I looked over at Ki's dad. A man once so full of life, now reduced to flicking television channels like a zombie, hoping that someone, somewhere might give him some answers. He couldn't even bring himself to turn and look at me.

It was a stupid question but I asked her if she was all right. I wanted to ask her lots of other things, like if she ever had doubts, doubts about getting married, doubts if Ki was out there somewhere. Most of all, I wanted to ask

109

her if she had lost her faith along with her daughter. But I didn't ask her anything; nothing important, anyway.

Auntie said she was glad that I was getting on with my life and then she asked me if Raj was a good man.

'I think so,' I replied.

She nodded.

'Is it OK to go up?'

I had lost count of the amount of times I had asked that question. Every day, without fail, I had visited Ki, no matter how late it was or how tired I felt.

'What's changed in the world today, Nina?' Ki would ask, waiting for me. And throughout the day I would collect in great detail things that I could tell her. The way the light had fallen, if someone had made me laugh, the people I'd come across, the food I'd eaten. If nothing had happened, I'd just made it up.

'And tell me how it's going to be?'

'I'll find a way to tell Mum and Dad about Jean Michel and marry him. We'll move out of London and then at some point I'm going to paint pictures.'

'What kind of pictures?'

'Bright, colourful ones on huge canvases.'

'Where will you live?'

'Maybe in the country or by the sea. We'll have one of those old farmhouses and I'll learn to cook.'

'And?'

'You'll come to visit.'

'Yeah, I'll come and see you there. I'll always be with you, Nina, I know I will, and I'll talk to you.'

Whenever I needed to change the subject so we could avoid the topic of death, I'd ask, 'Where are we going next?' That's what we did on the weekends. We'd pretend we were in one of the countries she hadn't yet travelled to. I'd get the appropriate food just so it smelled vaguely like the place, put some music on even if it didn't

110

correspond exactly with where we were meant to be, and then I'd lie next to her and read to her about it from travelogues.

She died on the day we were in Chile. She died in my arms while I was reading to her about Patagonia; salsa was playing in the background.

I went up to Ki's room. The walls were light green and everything was in the same place as it was the day she left. Her scent still lingered. It was as if she would walk back in and resume her life at any moment. Her patchwork quilt was thrown over the bed and on top of it was a tatty dolphin. The television was still on the dresser with the remote control on the side table next to her mirror, along with her make-up box and photos.

'I'm getting married. I don't know what you think about it, you haven't said anything and if you don't think it should be him I suppose you would have let me know by now. It's still lonely without you. I didn't think it would be like this but it is. What else? I'm painting. Did a buddha for you the other day, don't know if you've managed to see it yet but I thought it would make you laugh. I'm sorry I haven't seen your mum for so long. It's been . . . well, there isn't really an excuse. Miss you, but then I know you know that.'

I blew her a kiss and went back downstairs.

'I'll make sure it's not as long next time, Auntie,' I said as I held Ki's mother and kissed her goodbye.

New Year passed without much excitement. Raj and I had dinner together to see it in. He made a toast to the first of many. Jean had sent me a card wishing me every happiness and part of me felt furious with him; if it hadn't been for him I wouldn't have been in this situation . . . and how dare he wish me luck, did he think it wasn't going to work? I was eager for the holidays to end so I could get back into the studio and forget. Forget Jean, forget the wedding, forget everything.

There was a postcard from Australia waiting for me at the studio when I arrived on my first day back. 'Sending you Sydney sunshine. Hope you are finding what you want. Gina x'

Was it what I wanted or was it all happening way too fast, as if I had no control over it? But through painting I was finding something; it was giving me a sense of peace, especially the buddha. My studio was full of dead objects brought back to life and overseeing it all was my happy buddha, breathing life into the studio. He needed to be framed. Every day I thought this but every day there was some excuse not to leave the safety of my haven. But after seeing Ki's mum I wanted her to have him: the buddha would bring light to the dark corners of her house and I knew even if she didn't like the picture she would hang it somewhere and he'd watch over her.

I started painting a left footprint on icy grey pebbles but framing the buddha was on my mind; I left the painting and wrapped up the buddha so I could take it into the frame shop around the corner. A shiny black Bentley with tinted windows was parked just outside the shop. There was an argument going on inside between a very well-dressed man and the framer: 'Mangetti won't be happy with this, you said it would be ready. He waits for no one, he'll be furious.'

I knew the name.

The framer was trying to pacify the angry man who was huffing and pacing up and down. A young apprentice swiftly came up to me and asked how he could help. I told him I needed my canvas framed. Instead of just unpacking the canvas, I balanced it on the counter and ripped it open. The ripping sound brought all eyes to the counter. The angry man glanced at me and at the buddha.

As the young apprentice went to get some sample frames out I could feel the man staring intensely at the buddha.

'Anyway, tell me how much longer you will keep us waiting?' he shouted at the framer.

'It should only be a few more minutes,' the framer replied.

The apprentice brought the frames out and I chose a silver-plated one. I was shocked when he told me the price but then it was for Ki's mum so the cost didn't matter.

Sensing my initial apprehension, the apprentice said, 'We are specialists, used by some of the best gallery owners,' and then he lowered his voice. 'I would say to ask Mr Mangetti's assistant but now is probably not the best time.' He smiled, signalling the angry man with his eyes. I left my name and a deposit.

Tastudi Mangetti was Director of the Fiorelli Gallery in Milan and also had several high-profile business interests in London. I had come across his name when representing one of my artists who was having an exhibition at the Fiorelli and his paintings had been damaged in transit. Mangetti refused to accept liability; he was just awful to deal with. What would he be doing having paintings framed in London Bridge when he could have them framed anywhere in the world? I passed the Bentley again on my way out, and seeing as I was out already I decided to go and buy myself an engagement card and a present from the people at work. It would keep Dad happy and also distract me.

The shop assistant at Selfridges was really helpful and I spent a long time debating whether we'd like a vase or a lamp. After I opted for the vase I went back to the studio and dabbled a bit with the red on the footprint, then wrapped up the vase and wrote the card out to myself, and then wrote out a card that I had bought for Gina. I was going to enclose a letter telling her how I had got myself engaged but then I thought it wouldn't make any sense to her as it didn't make any sense to me, so instead I said I hoped she was having a nice holiday and that she would have a fantastic year ahead of her. It was time to go home when I stopped to ponder what my year ahead would be like.

Both my parents immediately spotted the huge carrier from Selfridges.

'Engagement present from work,' I said holding up the bag. One lie turned into another and then another and then it didn't matter how many I told as I had become totally immersed in it. As soon as the painting was out of my system, maybe before the wedding, all the lies would stop and then I could stop feeling like such a fraud.

'Show,' my dad signalled, reaching for the carrier. He pulled out the vase and looked disappointed and I waited for him to voice it.

'This is all they could whip the round?'

'It's a really nice vase, Dad, by Marcela Lonecroft.'

He read out the card which was stuck to the wrapping paper.

'Congratulations, wishing you all the very best, Felicity, Richard, Seamon . . .'

Before he went through the whole list of names I stopped him at Simon. 'Simon is the senior partner, Dad.'

'Very good, invite them to the wedding,' he replied, returning to his newspaper.

'We don't have to invite them to the wedding. I know we are restricted on numbers,' I panicked.

'No, no, plenty of room for the peoples at work,' he replied.

Raj came around for dinner and my dad asked me to show him the vase that work had bought us. He said that his colleagues hadn't got him anything as he hadn't told anyone this time around; didn't want to tempt fate. It wouldn't have mattered if he had as I knew there was no way that fate could possibly be tempted – this was a wedding that was going to happen no matter what.

A few days later the framed picture was waiting for me and I went along to collect it.

'This painting that you brought in by Foruki,' the framer began.

'No, no, that's, "For you, Ki,"' I replied.

'That's what I said – Foruki,' he repeated. 'Japanese name, isn't it?'

He didn't wait for my answer and just as I was about to tell him that it was a dedication, he continued. The framer said that Tastudi Mangetti's assistant was so impressed with my painting that he went back to the Bentley and called Mangetti to come and have a look at it.

I stared at him in disbelief. 'What?'

He continued, 'We do a lot of work for Mr Mangetti and he came out of the car. He said it was original and was intrigued by Foruki's bold use of colour and the way he signed his painting.'

'Did he?' I asked astounded.

'He did, and he doesn't come in here for nothing. Are you Foruki's assistant?' he asked.

'No. You see it's a bit of a long story,' I began.

'You're his friend?' the framer interrupted, indicating that he didn't want to hear the long story.

'Well . . .'

'Tastudi has left his card and has asked your friend Foruki to call him.'

I thanked the framer and took the buddha back to the studio, utterly amazed at the turn of events.

'Tastudi Mangetti,' I laughed out loud, 'interested in my painting.' Looking at the signature I could see why he had thought Foruki was the artist's name. The 'F' and the 'K' were written in a sharp, elongated way that made it appear slightly oriental. I sat thinking what I would say to Mangetti if I had the courage to call him.

I couldn't say to Mangetti that it was a painting done by me; he wouldn't possibly buy any pictures if he knew it was me – a complete unknown – and anyway, I didn't have the confidence to say 'I'm Nina, the artist.' I wasn't an artist – not in the true sense. How could he possibly be interested in me? Mangetti wasn't just anyone, he set trends, but if I could just sell him one painting then I could prove to my dad that it was possible to make money from something you loved doing. What would be the best way? If I said that I was Foruki's agent maybe that would work; that would create a distance between me and the work. Besides, Mangetti might be more receptive to talking to me if I said I was the agent. Planning what I was going to say, I picked up the phone and then I panicked and put it down again.

'Breathe, Nina. Relax, distance yourself, it's not your painting, it's done by a man called Foruki. You're not selling yourself, you're selling someone else. It's not that difficult.'

I dialled the number again. My heart was thumping. His assistant picked it up and asked who I was.

'Breathe,' I kept telling myself, 'act as though Foruki is your client.'

'I'm Nina Savani. I represent Foruki.'

'Foruki,' he repeated.

116

'Yes, Mr Mangetti showed some interest in his buddha painting.'

After a few seconds he transferred me to Mangetti.

'Tastudi Mangetti.'

My heart was beating faster. 'Just be bold,' I thought, 'show no hesitation.'

'Nice to talk to you again, Mr Mangetti. It's Nina Savani, I represent Foruki.'

'When did we speak last, Ms Savani?' he asked.

'I used to represent Françoise Dubois, she had an exhibition at . . .'

'Yes, yes, I remember,' he said dismissively. 'I'm interested in buying the buddha piece.'

No, he couldn't have that one, it was for Ki's mother. Maybe I could persuade him to buy another one.

'I'm terribly sorry. That particular one is not for sale.'

'Has it been earmarked already?' he asked.

Yes, that was it, it wasn't for sale because it had been earmarked. 'Yes,' I replied, trying to sound confident.

He said he had never heard of the artist and began asking me lots of questions about him. I wasn't prepared for all these questions and in an attempt to halt them in a seemingly confident manner, I tentatively suggested we meet for lunch.

He was taken aback by the suggestion. I was beginning to lose my nerve.

'Why would I want to meet you?' he asked.

Why would he want to meet me? And at that moment I knew how Jean Michel felt when he was losing and decided to bet all his chips on one colour. I sat upright in my chair and said with certainty:

'He's about to hit the London scene. I'm sure you'll be intrigued by what I have to say about him.' People in the art world loved to know that they had made a discovery; they loved all that hype.

Mangetti said that he might be available Thursday lunchtime and asked for Foruki to be present. He said his assistant would call later to confirm the meeting.

My hands began to tremble as I put the phone down. 'You're a lunatic woman,' I said to myself. 'You lied and you did it so blatantly. What's happening to you? What kind of person are you turning into?' And instead of sitting down and finding the answers to these questions, I got up with a rush of energy feeling completely exhilarated. Getting changed, I went to meet Raj.

I was buzzing when I met Raj at Lazio's, the Italian restaurant in Covent Garden. He noticed and asked me what had happened. I was going to tell him all of it, explaining the painting scenario from the beginning, just missing out a few details like the coconut, Jean Michel and the signs. To spill everything out in one great flood would have been such a relief and then I thought about the vase that was a gift from my colleagues; where could that fit in? And all the times I sent him to Holborn tube station to meet me after work because . . .?

My mobile rang and I wanted to get it in case it was Mangetti's assistant.

'I'm sorry, Raj, I have to get this,' I said, and then spoke into the phone. 'Hello.'

'Tastudi Mangetti here.'

'Hello Mr Mangetti,' I said getting up from the table to go outside.

'Yes, I would like to meet Foruki. It's my particular interest to bring new talent to the fore. I'll meet you both at one o'clock, Thursday, at the restaurant in Brown's Hotel.'

Before I had an opportunity to say anything, he hung up.

118

I switched the phone off, taken aback. Where was I going to find a Japanese man who looked the part? My grocer was Japanese but he wasn't old – in my mind Foruki was old and, anyway, the grocer didn't look right – he had streaks in his hair the colour of his plums. That left three days to find a Japanese man. What was I supposed to do? Filled with panic, I went back to the restaurant, doing this neck-jerking thing I did whenever I was nervous or had something to hide.

'You were going to tell me what happened to you today, Nina.'

'Er . . . yes, well . . . we . . . I, I got a new client today. Except he isn't a real client. What I mean is . . .'

'He's not signed on the dotted line yet.' Raj had a habit of interrupting me. 'He will, I'm sure you'll charm him. You know, Nina, it's so refreshing to see someone who is as into their career as I am.'

'What?' I asked, seeing the opportunity to tell him pass me by.

'I'm so proud that your career is important to you too,' he said. 'It gives us more common ground.'

Forget ground, I was skating on thin ice. 'Ice,' I vocalised the last word.

Before I knew it he was calling the waiter to get me some. He was like my dad – he only acted on the words he chose to hear.

'So my career is important to you?'

'Definitely. I'm so proud of what you do,' Raj replied.

My stomach felt tight, I didn't feel hungry any more. 'Tell me about your time in Japan,' I asked, trying to find a distraction.

He happily talked about his trip to Japan while I wondered what had possessed me to ask Mangetti for lunch and about the web of deceit I was weaving – it wasn't me.

119

Pay attention to what he is saying, Nina, I kept telling myself; it might come in handy as research. But my thoughts were consumed by how important my career was to Raj and where I could find an old Japanese man within seventy-two hours who could be relied upon to say very little.

The next morning I got up late as I had supposedly taken the day off work to run some errands for the wedding.

'Good,' my mother said. 'Maybe you can help me with a few things. Wedding is less than three months away.'

'I've got some people to see.'

'What people?'

'The florist,' I replied.

'I thought Raj's mother was doing that.'

'No, we are.'

'OK, I'll come with you,' she said grabbing her coat.

'Ma, I can do this by myself seeing as you've both pretty much organised everything.'

'I'm only doing it for you, beta.'

'Are you?' I wanted to ask. This was all her disappointments cancelled out by one big wedding; her wedding, the wedding she never had, the wedding she couldn't give my sister. But I didn't say anything as she had turned around and put her coat down.

'And have you asked work for the time off to come to India with me?'

She was planning to go to India to do a whole wedding shop. And as much as I knew that if I went with her it would make every single one of her dreams come true, I couldn't go. I could not leave the studio for two whole weeks. Even if it meant that on my wedding day I'd be wearing garish colours and jewellery like BA Baracus from the A-Team.

'Ma, I don't think that work will give me the time off, not with the honeymoon and everything.'

'I will pray they give you the time – Bhagavan has listened so far.'

'Better go,' I said, feeling guilty and not wanting to involve Bhagavan in the whole proceedings.

'I see, beta, maybe want to go and have lunch with Raj after,' she said, smiling.

The grocer had some flowers; well, some dehydrated chrysanthemums. Perhaps I could buy a bunch and then ask him if he had any elderly relatives. I got in the queue and after he got an old lady her tomatoes he turned to me and asked what I wanted.

'A bunch of yellow chrysanthemums please.'

'Coming right up, miss.'

Not long before I'd be a Mrs, I thought.

'Anything else?'

I couldn't do it so I bought the flowers and walked away.

Where else could I find old Japanese people?

I stood back in the queue again.

'Forgotten something?'

'This is going to sound very strange but I'm doing some research into Japanese culture, things like cuisine, and I was wondering if I could possibly speak to your father.'

'My dad's dead,' the grocer replied.

'I'm so very sorry,' I said, turning away, wanting to run off.

'But you can speak to my mother if you like,' he added.

I imagined Foruki as an elderly woman – no, it had to be a man, but I couldn't suddenly say that his mother wasn't good enough after raking up the death of his father.

'That would be very helpful,' I answered.

'You can go and see her now if you've got time. She doesn't really go out that much so she'll be happy to see you. What did you say your name was?'

'Nina.'

'I'll give her a call and let her know you are coming around. What was it you wanted to know about again?'

'Japanese fashion, cuisine and art.'

I didn't expect him to call up and ask her there and then. I didn't expect her to say yes so eagerly either but he gave me her address and said she was waiting for me.

Three hours later I was still in Mrs Onoro's sitting room, looking at the porcelain cats she had everywhere, drinking green tea, thinking that I had a wedding to organise and an elderly Japanese man to find in forty-eight hours, but instead I was sat listening to Mrs Onoro's life story.

I had to interrupt her at some point so I asked if she knew any men.

'You want marry my son?' she enquired.

'No, no that's not what I meant. I'm getting married soon,' I replied quickly, thinking I should have phrased the question better.

Then she blushed. 'I seeing Hikito, he is a good man, but my son, he don't know.'

'Hikito?' At last, an elderly Japanese man, this was sounding promising. 'Where did you meet?'

'Hikito, he is Reiki master, met at Japanese Association talk.'

It was just getting better, a whole association to pick from!

'Would it be possible to come to this association with you, so I can get a man's perspective on Japanese culture.'

'We meet next week.'

No, next week was too late. 'What about Hikito? Maybe he can help me.'

'He don't speak much good English.'

'Perfect,' I thought. An old Japanese man who said very little – just what I was looking for.

'Can I meet him?' I asked.

'You want Reiki session?'

I didn't quite know what Reiki was but I agreed, thinking that Hikito was the one – he was potentially my Foruki.

Mrs Onoro went off to make a phone call and came back saying that Hikito could see me in an hour and that she would come along as translator.

A short while later we made our way to his house. A Japanese man came to the door. If Mrs Onoro hadn't told me that he was seventy-four I would have thought he wasn't a day over fifty. His skin was smooth and unlined and he had twinkling brown eyes that shone with wisdom. There was no mistake: here before me stood Foruki. He took Mrs Onoro's hand and he kissed it, then he looked at me and nodded.

'Take off shoes,' he instructed. They spoke in Japanese and when it went quiet I tried to ask him if he was free on Thursday afternoon but he put his lips together and his index finger to his mouth, indicating silence.

He led us to his sitting room. The curtains were drawn, there were lighted candles everywhere and the smell of incense. In the centre of the room stood a massage table that he pointed to.

What was going on? I shook my head. There was no way in the world I would let this man touch me, not after the Guru incident.

Hikito said, 'I don't hurt you.'

Tears were welling in my eyes. For some reason I had this overwhelming need to tell them about the filthy, dry hands that felt me; the Guru's heavy, rhythmic breath that made everything seem much slower and more intense; his smell. How he made me believe in him, took away whatever I had left and made me feel dirty and worthless inside. I started to cry, uncontrollably so.

They stood silently for a few minutes. Hikito gave me a tissue. 'I understand,' he said. 'Lie down,' he indicated, pointing to the table.

'I stay here,' added Mrs Onoro.

I reluctantly got on the table. 'Close eyes,' Hikito instructed.

Half-closing my eyes, I watched what he did. Hikito had his hands six inches above my head. He made a sign with his palms and then his hands went around my body from one part to another without touching it.

'Close eyes,' he repeated.

He had his hands at the soles of my feet and I could sense heat, warm heat. He slowly moved up to my solar plexus and as I experienced more and more heat I had to open my eyes to make sure he wasn't touching me.

'It's OK,' Hikito reassured.

He moved from my solar plexus to my heart and I felt someone safely holding my left hand. I wanted to open my eyes but I couldn't just in case the feeling left me.

It was the same kind of feeling that I had had as a child when I was in hospital and I thought Jana was there; warm and loving.

'Your friend here,' Hikito said. 'She say you doing good. That she always hold your hand when you think you by self and you think you by yourself a lot.'

Tears streamed from my eyes and at that moment in time there were no questions I needed to ask or anything else I needed to know. I felt completely and utterly secure, as if things were exactly as they were meant to be.

'She tell me to tell you that Chile is beautiful.'

Hikito's hands stayed over my chest and not only did I see the most beautiful colours, I held them in my heart as if they were a part of me. Indescribable hues of indigo, violet and blues, colours beyond indigo that I could not possibly describe, all of them dancing within me, making me feel safe, and then as he moved towards my head I fell asleep. A deep, undisturbed sleep that I thought had lasted for hours.

Only an hour had passed when I woke up and Hikito gave me a glass of water.

'Drink lots of water,' he said. 'You do good.'

I had no questions; I understood none of it yet somehow everything made perfect sense.

Mrs Onoro was sitting on the sofa in tears. She got up and held me, saying something in Japanese. I wanted to give her flowers but she deserved more than the miserable-looking chrysanthemums that I had.

'Thank you,' I whispered.

I couldn't bring myself to ask Hikito to be Foruki; it didn't feel right to bring him into the web of deceit, so I paid him, thanked them both again and left. As I turned to wave they had gone in.

I arrived home in the evening, still with the dreary bunch of chrysanthemums.

'Hope they are not from the flower shop where you ordered wedding flowers,' my mother said, looking disdainfully at them.

'No. Couldn't find any good ones, Ma, so I'll just leave it to you.'

'All day out to look for flowers and comes back with this,' she gestured to my father.

125

Surprisingly, he didn't comment. Just peered up from behind his newspaper, peered back down again and then said, 'There are the flowers always for peoples who wants to see them.'

'What, Dad? What did you just say then, Dad?' My heart leaped. Maybe finally he had understood. It had been a truly magical day; maybe something that I was unaware of had happened.

'Why we need flowers there in the wedding? Peoples can see them like your client who is not wasting money buying them from the petrol stations.'

'Bhagavan, help me with this man, of course we need flowers; and beta, you didn't even go and see Raj. You said you were going to have lunch with him and I told him that when he called.'

'Why?' I shouted and then I fell silent. There was no point in arguing, we were worlds apart, not even the biggest bridge would join the two worlds together. They would walk into mine and not see paintings, a Japanese healer, not notice any difference; because to them my world appeared exactly like theirs: stuffed with Land of Leather sofas, dodgy television sets, rotis and potential husbands.

'Because that's what you said. He's waiting for your call,' she replied calmly.

The sense of peace that I felt – that everything was exactly as it should be – quickly dissipated. It wasn't right, none of it – not Raj, the wedding, the lies, none of it. What I felt for Raj was a brotherly type of love, it was nothing compared to what it was like with Jean. There was never any real inclination to touch Raj; maybe to take care of him but not to touch him or to run my fingers through his hair. My dad said that attraction grows the more time you spend with someone and that he hardly noticed now the fact that my mother had 'the buckhead teeth'. Maybe it was a gradual thing. I dialled Raj's number.

'Hi Nina, Mummy said that you were coming to see me today.' He had started calling my mother that the day we got engaged. It niggled at me but my mother touched her heart every time she heard it. I couldn't quite get my lips around that for his mother so I continued to call her Auntie.

'No, she just got a bit confused.'

'What have you been doing then?'

I couldn't bring myself to tell him any of it: the search for the Japanese man, the Reiki healer. He'd be more interested about hearing how the wedding preparations were going so that's what I told him. 'I went to find a florist to do the flowers.'

'We could have done that together, baby,' he replied.

Baby? Now that did irritate me. 'No, it's best if we do other things,' I replied, meaning practical things like arranging where the guests sat and food sampling.

But instead I'm sure I heard him grunt, not laugh. 'We'll have plenty of time to do that.'

'Do you want to go and see a movie tonight?'

'No, I'm really tired but I'll see you after work tomorrow night?'

'Tomorrow, then. I can't wait to finally put the ring on your finger,' he replied.

'Yes,' I said. 'I'll speak to you tomorrow.'

'Miss you. Do you miss me?' he asked.

'Yes,' I mumbled.

Putting all thoughts of finding a Japanese stand-in out of my head, I ate some perfectly circular rotis and went to bed.

I got to the studio early the next morning and the boots had gone – I felt glad that the tramp had found them at last; perhaps it was a sign. Maybe they had disappeared days ago and it was the first time I had noticed them missing. I got changed, pulled out the dying bunch of chrysanthemums from my sports bag, put them on the table and took out the canvas that had been painted white all those many weeks ago.

I sat for hours thinking about the colours I had seen the day before, and when the light fell I began mixing paints. I mixed several colours in two palettes trying to replicate the tones in some way. Hours were spent doing this, trying to re-create warmth. Taking the chrysanthemums, I gently pulled off the petals and heaped them into a pile.

Before painting, I sat with my palm open. 'I pretended to believe, Ki, every day, even when I couldn't see. I pretended it was you but you know that, don't you? Sorry about the things I said. I'm seeing Tastudi Mangetti tomorrow and I'm scared, really scared. It's something you would do, not me. You were always far braver. Did you orchestrate that? Did you do all of this? Did you make me meet Gina? If it was you, you couldn't have chosen a nicer person. Did you send me Raj? Is there something I'm missing there? I mean, don't get me wrong, he's kind and everything but I can't quite see you putting the two of us together. Is it about not having any expectations? See, if it's that, it doesn't make sense because you always told me not to accept second best. That sounds awful, doesn't it? That makes Raj sound like a consolation prize. It's not what I meant. It's not as though I want to go back to Jean either. I don't know, maybe it's because it's all happening too fast.

'I've been up for most of the night thinking about all of this deceit; although I am lying to paint, painting makes me believe in myself again – I can't remember the last time I did. During the time that I'm here in this room, the world looks like I want it to, and when I am painting I am me, the me that you know.

'All I ever wanted was to believe that you were around so I wouldn't have to do this on my own. I didn't have the strength to do this on my own. And when it was hard, really hard, I pretended you were there and that's how I got through it. Now that I know, really know, I don't have that need to believe any more. Do you understand that? I want to let you go. It's not that I don't need you because I do, more than ever, but I want you to rest knowing that I love you very much and whenever I want to see you or hear you laugh, all I have to do is close my eyes. See, you've got me going again. I'm turning into a wuss.'

Wiping the tears, I outlined an enormous handprint on the canvas and then took the petals and individually painted them onto the handprint with hues of indigo, just as if they were lines running along a palm. Death and wastage stuck together with thick colour. I dipped my hand into the rest of the paint and covered the handprint with my palm. Then I slowly peeled the petals off one by one, leaving nothing but spaces of calm white light among a storm of indigo.

I met Raj briefly that evening for dinner and instead of yet another outright lie, I told him about an artist who painted hands.

'You can tell a lot about a person just by their hands. It's one of the first things I look at.'

'Me too,' he replied, taking mine.

'Do you?'

'Yes.'

I told him about the artist who had done a huge imprint of a hand and all the lines running across it were painted from chrysanthemum petals.

'Really?' I couldn't work out if the 'really' was out of

interest or because he didn't know what else to say.

'It was a big palm. What do they say? The bigger the palm the more generous the person. The fingers were long and delicate. This palm looked as if it should have longer lines but it didn't.'

'I love the way you get so involved with your clients' work, Nina.'

When he said that, the urge to tell him about my painting didn't seem so important. At least he appreciated that I cared about art.

'Sometimes it doesn't feel like work,' I replied.

'Every day seems like work, you're lucky.'

'Do you ever feel like you'd like to go off and do something different?' I asked.

'Not really, I don't know what else I would do except travel, but even then there is only so much travelling you can do before you start getting homesick.'

'I would love to paint,' I added, answering my own question.

'If you were to do it for a while you'd enjoy it, but then it's like most things: once you have it, it becomes boring.'

This comment struck me as odd. It didn't seem to fit in with the way Raj operated.

'Boring?'

Sensing my tone he answered quickly, 'I am just being practical.'

I didn't feel the need to broach the subject about Mangetti and so I moved on to our wedding plans. His mother had asked us to check a whole load of details like the size of the mandir, the short-listed musicians and the selection of mementos for the guests to take away; so this is what we did for the rest of the evening. After dinner he dropped me home and kissed me goodbye. It was our first proper kiss and it bothered me. It was a suction-type movement where Raj engulfed the whole of my lips and hoovered them up with his mouth. Maybe it was wrong of me to think about how Jean kissed but they couldn't have been more different so I couldn't help it.

As soon as I crawled into bed I fell asleep and dreamed about paintings, Japanese waiters and boats, along with many other things that made no sense. When the alarm went off I lay there thinking about my meeting with Mangetti.

'Get up, you'll be late,' my dad shouted.

I was immobilised by fear. What was I thinking of doing? It was ludicrous, Mangetti was a huge player in the art world. Word was that he was going to be one of the judges for the Turner Prize. He wasn't stupid. I wasn't a real artist or an artist's agent; surely he would be able to spot that.

'One day early, one day late. Twenty-five years I've been on time,' I heard him shout to my mother.

'She has a lot to think about with the wedding.'

'What's there to think?'

'Lots of things. Girl has a lot to think about before she takes a decision like that.'

She was right. It was a big decision. What if it didn't work out? What if Mangetti suspected that it was me who did the painting? He had the kind of power to make sure that I didn't step foot in the art world again, as a lawyer, an agent or even selling paintbrushes.

'It is the easy. She doesn't have to think, just do it, like me and you, Kavitha, we just do it.'

'Yes, get up and just do it, do it like you have nothing to lose,' I told myself, getting up. What about Foruki? He was still expecting Foruki. What could I say about that? It was a mess, he would see right through all of it. Think; think it through carefully.

'What is that girl doing up there? This far we make her come, we give good education and what does she do? Taking it easy now she's getting married; having the lie in. Nina, what you doing there? Enough of the lie in,' Dad bellowed.

The word 'lie' reverberated around my head. Not just a simple bending of the truth; this one was going to be one big whopper. I got into the shower and began planning. Foruki wouldn't turn up to meetings, he wasn't like that, he didn't listen to what other people said, didn't do what they wanted. He was his own person, an artist who valued himself and his work, and if he didn't feel like showing up, he wouldn't, and nobody, not even Tastudi Mangetti, could make him.

I got changed into my best suit – the suit I wore for important days at work – and while putting on my make-up tried to steady my hand. This was it – all I had to do was to act professional and it would be fine. I went downstairs.

'We didn't see you yesterday, beta. Did you eat anything?'

'Yes, had something with Raj.'

'Have the breakfast.'

I couldn't eat anything or I would be sick.

'Have to go, I'm running late.'

'What? No breakfast?' my mum asked.

'If you get up earlier then no need for this hi, bye,' my dad interrupted.

'Wish me luck, I'm dealing with an important client today.'

'Nothing to do with the luck, just hard work. When I made my money in the plantations . . .'

I left before he had a chance to go over that story again.

*　　*　　*

132

Mangetti was more conservative in his approach to art and his interest was more in paintings than installations, photography or sculptures. I sat in a café near Green Park planning meticulously what I was going to say about Foruki. All I had to do was pretend he was a very important client, and how hard was that going to be? I had pretended for the last three and a half years with clients I didn't even believe in, bullshitted about liking statues built with dried fruit, put all my emotions to one side and remained calm and professional.

Raj had once told me that in every meeting he had he visualised good outcomes, something about the body sending out chemicals that gave off positive vibes, so over and over again I imagined Mangetti agreeing to buy a painting.

It was one o'clock when I made my way nervously to the restaurant. Brown's was busy, but as soon as I walked in I knew who he was, and when I told the head waiter that I was there to meet Mangetti I knew very well where he was going to lead me. Mangetti was tall, immaculately dressed in a black polo-neck and black suit and appeared to be in his mid-forties. His nose was crooked and extremely prominent so I thought if at any time he made me nervous I would just focus on it and stare hard. My heart beat faster as I went over to meet him.

Taking a deep breath, I smiled. 'Nina Savani, pleased to meet you, Mr Mangetti,' I said, holding out my hand.

He gripped it solidly. 'Mr Foruki?' he indicated at the empty space next to me.

'I'm terribly sorry but Foruki is unable to make it. He's very introspective and doesn't like attention so he's hired me to conduct all negotiations here in London.'

I focused on his nose while I waited for him to leave. 'Really?'

I nodded.

He gestured for me to take a seat and then sat down himself.

'It's strange I haven't come across his name before.'

'It's taken me a long time to persuade him to share his art. He's only done a very limited amount of exhibitions in Japan. He doesn't do them to sell his paintings. He doesn't need to.' *You're talking too much, Nina, there's no need to go into so much detail. Let him ask the questions.*

'Come now, Ms Savani, you hardly expect me to believe that?'

Of course I didn't expect him to believe any of it. Was he going to put his napkin down and walk off?

'You're expecting me to believe that a man who signs his name so boldly on a canvas doesn't want to be known?'

'He doesn't want to be known but he wants his work to be respected. There's a difference; he has his reasons for signing so boldly,' I said, surprising even myself by how convincing I sounded.

'They are?'

Yes, what were they? 'His upbringing . . .' Oh God, what kind of disturbed upbringing was the poor man going to have to go through. *Don't go there, Nina, get back on track.* '. . . but I'm not here to talk about that,' I replied assertively.

'Is he British? Japanese? How old is he?' The more I refused to go into Foruki the more he wanted to know. That's how people in the art world worked; elusiveness equalled more hype; give it to them on a plate and they didn't want it. My boss used to term this as 'whispers', leak a little information and then act all vague and elusive so they would be left craving more.

'He's in his early thirties, was born in Britain to a Japanese mother and had to return there as a child.

134

Hence the fact that he doesn't speak English.' Having not had the heart to ask Hikito, I thought if I was desperate my grocer could step in and keep his accent under wraps.

'Every day I come across talented artists, there are thousands of them. But this one, he seems interesting. Tell me about his concepts.'

The waiter came to take our order. Mangetti ordered a bottle of wine that cost as much as my father's chandelier and his Land of Leather suite. I imagined my dad keeling over if he knew the price of that bottle. I worried about the bill – it wasn't looking good. We ordered our food. I chose the cheapest thing on the menu.

'I'm sorry, you were talking about concepts,' I said, composing myself and deflecting the answer back to him.

'Yes, when I saw that buddha painted in the form of a red Coca Cola tin, I was struck by Foruki's critique of how far the fusion of East/West culture had gone. And the juxtaposition of the subject and material – highly original.'

What was he going on about? Hardly juxtaposition, more memories of Ki's sweetshop and her souvenir. I smiled, thinking she would be laughing at all of this. Just go with it, if that's what he wants to hear, tell him that.

'Yes there is an element of social critique there but his particular interest is resuscitating inanimate objects.'

He nodded, waiting for more.

'He attempts to infuse inanimate objects with magic. All part of the upbringing, as I said, which I am not at liberty to divulge.'

'Intriguing. And the painting of the buddha, how much is it?'

'As I've said, it's been earmarked,' I replied.

The food came.

'Surely you can sell it to me. Everyone has a price, Ms

Savani?' he said, looking at me directly in the eye.

He was asking me to name a price, any price. This is what I wanted – to sell a painting – but he couldn't have that one, that was for Ki's mum. Don't buckle; don't buckle. I focused on his nose. 'I'm afraid not,' I replied.

He seemed like a man who was used to getting his way but surprisingly he didn't insist. Just as I was about to say that there were other paintings he could buy he asked, 'And where do you come into the picture?' He took a sip of wine and laughed at his pun.

'Mr Mangetti, I have come across many artists but very few have actually managed to really captivate me and lose me in their paintings. It's rare. A year ago, I was in Japan and I came across his work. I was so inspired by Foruki that I tracked him down and convinced him to come to London. There are few times in life when I have had this gut feeling so I've brought him over so his work can be shared.' *Keep going, keep going, Nina.*

He listened intently.

'I gave up a good job at Whitter and Lawson to back Foruki: I don't give up the luxury of working for a firm like that for backing people I don't completely believe in – and with Foruki I've never believed in anyone more.'

'As you know, Ms Savani, it's my particular interest to bring new talent to the fore. I'd like to see more of his work.'

I had prepared myself for this eventuality; this for me was very-best-case scenario and I honestly didn't believe it was going to happen.

'I am trying to persuade him to hold an exhibition.'

He nodded.

We finished the main course and he asked if I wanted dessert. I declined, thinking about the mounting bill; at this rate I'd have to take out an overdraft and I just wanted to get out of there while I was on a roll, but he

136

ordered something for himself along with dessert wine.

Putting my chips again on one number, I said, 'Give me six weeks. My new cards are being printed but I'll call you with a concrete date, Mr Mangetti.'

He gave me his card. 'So you won't sell any more of his paintings until I have had an opportunity to see them all first?'

'I'll see what I can do,' I replied.

He ended the conversation by telling me that he was going to Italy on business and that he would wait to hear from me soon.

'It was a pleasure meeting you, Mr Mangetti,' I said as he left.

'Call me Tastudi and the pleasure was mine.'

By that time I was so excited and relieved at how the meeting had gone that I didn't care what the bill came to, and after I had paid it I ran to Green Park.

'Yes, yes, I bloody did it,' I screamed, jumping up and down, punching the air. 'I did it.'

People stared but it didn't bother me, nothing at that moment in time bothered me, not even the fact that I had never organised an exhibition.

After getting over the initial excitement and beaming at everyone on the tube, I went back to the studio, put my painting to one side and sat in front of a blank canvas. The reality of what I had done started to dawn on me. I had told an outright lie to one of the major players in the art world and now had to organise a successful exhibition in six weeks. That was two weeks before my wedding. If it was shoddy and if Mangetti found out that I had deceived him, he had the power to make sure that I never worked in the art world again.

Don't panic, I kept telling myself, opportunities like

this never came along and I could make it work. I had to make it work. But how the hell was I going to find a venue and then make sure people turned up? I needed journalists and people from the art world. Foruki, he had to have a past, galleries in Japan that he had exhibited at – he couldn't just suddenly materialise from nowhere. What about a mailing address? Invitations? It suddenly all seemed far too much for one person. And how was I even going to begin to think about the wedding.

Do it step by step, don't panic, you can do this, you can make it work, just hold your nerve, I reassured myself. Take another leap of faith and go for it. And though I knew I was way out of my depth, and was nervous and scared, there was a certain part of me that felt totally exhilarated and alive.

I took some black paint and on the canvas I made a list.

Find venue
Office space? (Computer, phone, mailing address)
Stationery (invitations, letterheads, brochures)
Invent Foruki – will the grocer do? (Past? Profile?
  Concepts?)
Talk to all art contacts/hype to other artists
Enough paintings for exhibition? Do more?
COST???????

Money wasn't going to be too much of a problem as my dad had asked me to stop paying my monthly instalments into the wedding fund. He had also given me a three thousand pound rebate; a sort of bonus disguised as a wedding gift. Feeling that he'd better share his good fortune of finding both a groom and a mother to pay for most of the wedding he handed me a cheque: 'Wedding gift. Buy a sofa for your new house, Nina. You never lose the money on good leather sofa. I will come with you when you buy it.' His obsession with sofas had started with a flippant comment that my Uncle Amit made years ago about a man not making his mark in England until he owned a Chesterfield. This stuck in my dad's psyche and he dreamed of owning Land of Leather.

I took out a sheet of paper and elaborated in more detail on what exactly I needed to do. Treating Foruki as if he were one of my best clients I drew up a strategy. I would email Gina and ask her about galleries in Japan – she said she had lived there and so she would know. I didn't have to go into what exactly I was intending to do.

I went to the library to do some research on Japanese art and art galleries in Japan. A lot of Japanese paintings were about relating big flat areas of colour together using flat shapes. I was astounded to read that Matisse had been influenced by the Japanese style, when I – rather, Foruki – was heavily influenced by Mattisse. Was this a sign? A sign that my paintings really did have Japanese influences without meaning to? Is that why Mangetti readily believed that the painting had been done by a Japanese painter? I read on. It was plausible and it didn't seem that far-fetched when I looked at some of the pictures in the books. After I felt I had enough information to make it all hang together, I moved on to logistical planning.

The search engine threw up hundreds of names after I'd typed in 'office space, London Bridge', 'hot-desking, London' and 'printers, London Bridge'. Reading through each one carefully I wrote down contact names, numbers and addresses and then I went to Green Park, sat on my bench, took a deep breath and started calling people who rented out desk space in offices, making arrangements to see them the next day. Before I knew it, it was five o'clock and time to go.

*   *   *

139

Raj was leaving work early and meeting me at Chancery Lane so we could pick up my engagement ring, which was being altered.

He kissed me. I wanted to tell him how well the meeting had gone and so did it in a roundabout way. 'We got a really important client on board today. I said I'd help him with his exhibition.'

'Who is he?'

'A Japanese artist by the name of Foruki.'

'I think I read something about him recently.'

'Did you?' I asked, astonished. He couldn't possibly have. Was he prone to truth-bending as well or had he confused the name with someone else? 'Where did you read about him?'

'I can't remember but his name sounds familiar.'

The ring was still too big so we left it at the jeweller's and then went to Raj's mother's house.

His mother had wedding invitations sprawled across her table and was bursting to tell us that she had booked the Park Lane Hilton. 'What do you think?' she said, thrusting an invitation into my hand. 'Four hundred guests, maybe more.'

'I don't think we even know two hundred people,' I replied.

'*We do*,' she interrupted. 'So, what do you think?'

The one I was holding was embossed in gold and very simplistic. 'Which printer did you use, Auntie?' I asked, thinking maybe he could do Foruki's invites, perhaps even the other stationery.

'One of Uncle's friends. He's done some work for the Queen. Which one do you think, then? This one, no, Raju? Do you want to use our printer to do your invitations too, Nina?'

'Thank you, but we've found a really good one,' I lied,

only because I wanted to do something that she had no control over.

'He said it will take only four days to print so by the end of this week we can send them out. When is your mother going to India, Nina?'

My mum was going off to India on her own, disappointed that despite all the praying and singing Bhagavan hadn't managed to wangle it so I could go with her. Her imminent trip would make it slightly easier for me to organise the exhibition, though, and I was relieved that she would soon be gone.

'This weekend,' I replied.

'OK, OK, so we all agree on this one,' she said taking back the invitation that was in my hand. 'I have sorted out all the catering. At the Hilton they have a select list of caterers who they use so I've asked them to send me a fusion menu – you know, a mixture of East meets West – as a lot of our friends are English.'

Caterers, that was a point. Would I need food at the exhibition? What about the drink? I hadn't even thought about the drink. 'The drink,' I mumbled.

'All arranged too. We'll have an open bar. Your mother was going to take care of the flowers but if it's too much for her to do before she goes away we have an excellent florist.' Raj's mother indicated a huge vase that had some swirling twig-like arrangement going on.

'Thank you, Auntie, but I'm sure she'll be able to sort it out.' What was the point of making Raj and I wade through her endless lists if she had it all planned.

'OK then, let's have dinner,' she said.

She summoned her husband who was sitting quietly in the next room with a piercing screech, and served a concoction of curried puff-pastry followed by apple crumble and cream. My dad had suffered indigestion when he and my mother had first gone to meet the in-laws and he had made sure he ate well the next time they went to see her, muttering, 'This is why woman must know how to cook or she will kill man.'

Both my mum and dad were in bed when I arrived home.

'Beta,' my mum whispered out on hearing my footsteps. 'Beta,' she called out again in between my dad's snores.

'What is it, Ma?' I said, going into their room.

'You've eaten something?'

'I had something at Raj's house.'

'How it went?'

'His mum's got it all under control.'

'No, not wedding plans, work. Your important client?'

I was taken aback because she never asked about the specifics of work or clients but she seemed genuinely interested for a change. 'It went well, Ma, really well.'

'Good. Only today even, your father and me, we saying how proud we are of you.'

Thank God it was dark and she couldn't see my face riddled with guilt. 'There's no need to be, Ma.'

I wanted to go over to her, hold her, unburden myself and confess.

'Every need. You make us so proud.'

In a couple of months it would all be over. I would be married and then there would be no more deceit. I would have hopefully got it all out of my system and I would endeavour to be a good wife to Raj.

'Good night, Ma.'

'Sleep well, beta.'

I went to see three offices in southwest London and settled for the last one in Westminster as it had a desk with the use of a phone and computer along with a shared receptionist who would take messages in my absence. It was £200 per week and I signed the contract for six weeks. There was no going back now and I felt a sense of excitement once I had made the commitment.

The desks were separated off with huge barriers so you couldn't see what people either side or in front of you were doing. It wasn't particularly busy but those who were there had their heads down, lost in their work.

'What's your company name?' the office manager asked.

'Sorry?'

'Your company name – when you get phone calls how would you like the receptionist to answer?'

I thought for a moment. If the receptionist said Nina Savani Limited it would make the company seem small – when I called people up to hype Foruki I had to make it seem as if it was a busy, cutting-edge company.

Frantically looking for inspiration, I noticed a picture of a brown owl behind her signed Kendal. It had a solid ring to it.

'Kendal,' I replied. 'Kendal Brown.'

'There's also a divert system on the phone – I'll show you how to action that. Here's a set of keys and the pin number to use the phone. All calls are itemised and are charged separately. You choose your own computer password and let me know what it is. That's all you need to know really . . . oh, there's a kitchen area to your right so you can help yourself to tea and coffee and the toilets are just around the corner. Any questions?'

'No, not really.'

'Well, if you put your full address there and sign here, you can start using the office . . .' she looked at her watch '. . . as of now.'

I gave her the studio's address and took all the paperwork she handed me.

Sitting at my new desk and switching on the computer, the first thing I did was fiddle about on the screensaver typing the words 'GO NINA' in capitals. I laughed at my own craziness but inside I desperately wanted to succeed. I wanted the exhibition to go well. What I wanted beyond that I really didn't know, maybe just to feel as happy, as crazy and as alive as I did on seeing the words dance boldly in front of me.

Pulling out a contact sheet from my folder with names and telephone numbers that I had drawn up, I divided up the list of people on the basis of how well I knew them and how they could help. There were artists, gallery owners, curators that I had met at my time at Whitter and Lawson, some of whom I knew very well. I would begin with them and would say that I had left the firm to dedicate more time to artists I felt passionately about.

The first thing was to find a venue. None of the major galleries in London would exhibit an unknown, especially not in six weeks. Impression was absolutely everything and Foruki had to look big as well as different. Somewhere obvious wouldn't do. I thought about who on my list could help specifically with venues, then reflecting on what Raj had told me about confidence, I took a deep breath and began calling them; almost as if they were obliged to help. Raj had got this from one of the many books he had read and said that if there was a level of expectation and confidence in a person's tone then people would be more likely to be receptive.

Despite having many contacts it was harder than I thought it would be. There were few leads but eventually a promising one came from a PR company who I hyped Foruki to. The lady said she was dealing with a restaurant chain called Artusion. They had restaurants in Tokyo and New York, and were opening their first restaurant in

London soon. The concept was simple: a modern Japanese restaurant and a gallery where up-and-coming artists were exhibited. It sounded almost too good to be true. The PR lady said she could arrange a meeting; I left her my details. A restaurant/gallery was an unusual place to hold Foruki's first exhibition in London but Foruki was different. It would be an ideal venue.

I rang the artists whom I had once represented just to tell them that I had left Whitter and Lawson and casually dropped in that I was spending my time representing an up-and-coming Japanese artist. The more influential people who had heard of Foruki the better.

A few of them wanted to know if I would represent them too. I had to say that there was a clause in my old contract which stated that I was unable to take old clients with me, but I thanked them for their support and hoped that they would be able to make it to Foruki's exhibition. Later that afternoon my boss Simon called me up, curious about what I was doing.

'I'm sorry about what happened, Simon, with Boo and everything. It was inexcusable.'

'Quite out of character for you, Nina, but I suppose you had your other plans in mind.'

Is that what he thought? That I had orchestrated a departure so I wouldn't have to work my notice? I wanted to tell him that it wasn't like that – that there was no planning or scheming involved – but how else could it all be explained besides telling him the truth. 'All I can do is apologise again for being so unprofessional.'

He asked me what exactly I was doing and I talked about the artist that I had brought over from Japan and invited him along to the opening night. It was better to keep on good terms with him. Simon could make trouble for me, he could say anything about me; that I had lost it at work and was near-enough sacked.

145

Once he had established that I couldn't possibly be any kind of threat to him, he dismissed me abruptly.

'There's another call waiting. I wish you the very best in your endeavours, Nina,' he said with a touch of sarcasm.

Maybe I was a nobody in his eyes and it was a mad idea, but this made me resolve to make Foruki as big as I could.

The PR lady called back saying she had managed to fix up a meeting for the following day with the owners of Artusion. I then took a walk to see the stationer. Taking a copy of Raj's mother's wedding invite, I showed them the type of style I wanted for all my letter-heads and business cards and for Foruki's exhibition invites.

'Kendal Brown just across there like that, and the contact details here.'

'Costly,' the printer kept saying, 'especially in that style. Gold doesn't come cheap, especially if you want it embossed.' So I picked out a much cheaper version for my own wedding invites seeing as all my uncles and aunts would only need to read it once to make sure where and when exactly they were being fed. The invite would then, inevitably, be discarded or used as a coaster.

Foruki's invites couldn't be done at that time seeing as the printer didn't have all the information he needed but he said that I could pick the rest of the stationery, letter-heads and so on, on Monday. When he presented me with the bill I slipped in the fact that I would give him more business, adding that I was in charge of ordering all the company's stationery, and he gave me a discount that would have made my dad proud.

*　　*　　*

My mum was busy cooking when I got home. My dad was not all that impressed with the discount when I told him, worried more about who from work would be attending the wedding.

'Your boss will come to the wedding?'

'Hopefully, if he's not away; but Simon's said that he'll give me a few days off before the wedding,' I added, thinking that logistically the whole suit routine in the run-up to the exhibition might prove a bit difficult.

My mum rushed out of the kitchen. 'So you can come with me to India? Oh, Bhagavan, thank you.'

'No Ma, it's just in case I have to do last minute things here.'

'Your father will do them.'

He pretended not to hear her.

I imagined Dad running about organising the exhibition. 'No, it's only really me who can arrange it all.'

'Bhagavan has other plans for you, it was not meant to be. Never mind. I am doing all the cooking for your father. All you have to do, beta, is defrost the food in the morning and heat it in the microwave in the evening,' she said pointing at the many plastic containers. 'So, beta, try not to come home too late because he doesn't know how the microwave works.'

It wasn't going to be possible to get in for seven every day, not with all that I had to organise. 'I know I'll be late, Ma, it's really busy at work and they've already given me time off and, anyway, Dad's an electrician, of course he knows how it works. Don't you, Dad?'

'What?' he said, peering from behind his paper, pretending again that he hadn't heard a word.

'The microwave, you know how it works. It's just that I know I'm going to be home late and I don't want you to starve.'

He muttered something.

'Alternatively, I can ask Raj's mum to send food parcels over. I'm sure she would be happy to help, I mean she loves organising people.'

The newspaper was flung on his chair as he stormed into the uncharted territory of the kitchen, and before you knew it he had mastered the microwave, hob, and found out where the freezer was located.

The three of us sat and had dinner together and my mum commented that it had been a while since she had seen me this happy – and I did feel happy, happy and excited for Foruki and for me, I suppose. She talked about the kind of sari she would bring back and described the jewellery in great detail. My dad dropped a random comment in about *An audience with the Cilla Black* being on ITV the following week and I was thinking about what I would say on Foruki's invitations. And although the three of us were each in our separate worlds, we had never been so close; all bonded by a prevailing sense of excitement.

The next day, I prepared to meet with the owners of Artusion and the PR lady later that afternoon. To calm myself I went into the studio early and began to paint a portrait of what I thought Foruki looked like. Having him there on canvas would make him seem more real. I painted an abstract face in oranges, reds and yellow with only a slight hint of white. I didn't get time to finish it but he seemed as though he would be the kind of man I would have liked to work for; peaceful and not at all temperamental. 'I'll try and do my best for you, Foruki,' I said to the man on the unfinished canvas. Washing my hands and changing back into my suit, I made my way to the restaurant.

Situated in Mayfair and literally just around the corner from the wedding venue, Artusion was due to open in a fortnight. As soon as I stepped in I heard *Madame Butterfly* playing in the background. This was most definitely a sign. It was spacious, elegant and minimalist, designed in black, white and red. The manager, Christophe, introduced himself and led me to an office, saying that both the owners were in town and were keen to meet me.

'Emanuel Hikatari and this is my business partner Michael Hyland. I deal with the restaurant, Michael deals with the gallery.'

They both appeared to be in their early thirties. Emanuel Hikatari was tall and lean, while Michael Hyland was even taller and robust; he had a very gentle smile and a perfectly symmetrical nose. For a moment I felt like I was in one of Matisse's paintings, balancing on this man's nose and seeing every single feature: large round eyes, unusually long lashes. What were his hands like?

He held one out to shake mine; it felt warm and confident. 'Pleased to meet you.'

I couldn't quite place his accent.

'And Emily Bruce-Williams you know, of course.'

He was introducing me to the PR lady. I'd only spoken to her, never met her before, but I held out my hand as if we were life-long friends.

'Hello again, Emily.'

After the introductions Emanuel Hikatari got straight to it. 'Emily tells us you're representing a Japanese artist. His name?' he asked coldly.

'Foruki,' I replied.

'Surname?'

He didn't have a surname. 'That's what he likes to be known as.' Why was he being so hostile? Could he see through me?

'I'm half-Japanese, I've never heard of him and it is an unusual name.'

'It's a pseudonym,' I replied.

My hands felt sweaty. He turned to his colleague. 'Have you heard of this, this pseudonym?'

'No, but that's not necessarily a bad thing,' he answered. His eyes were infinitely warmer than his partner's and his voice was not arrogant. 'Where has he exhibited?' Michael asked with interest.

I couldn't lie about the Japanese galleries, they would know. So I said I discovered him in Japan and then reeled off a list of well-known artists I had represented to add credibility to what I was saying.

'Where in Japan?' Emanuel Hikatari asked.

'Tokyo, I discovered him in Tokyo,' I replied assertively. I turned and directed my answers towards Michael. 'He isn't famous, he doesn't want to be famous, I had to persuade him to come to London; and for his first exhibition here I want to find somewhere that reflects his personality – innovative yet understated.'

Emanuel interrupted, 'Can you guarantee press coverage? That's what I want to know.'

'Yes,' I said looking at him confidently, with absolutely no idea of how to get press there.

'I'll leave it entirely up to you, Michael.' He excused himself, saying he had another meeting to go to, and left.

As soon as Emanuel Hikatari left the room, the PR lady suddenly stirred to life and began twirling her long blonde hair; she too had felt the thaw. Once again, she explained the concept of Artusion and how it was important for them to find the right artist for the exhibition. She went on to say how they were maximising coverage by opening the restaurant with an installation done by the Turner Prize winner, alias wardrobe man, Maximus Karlhein.

'But after the initial PR, I want the first real exhibitor to be a painter. I don't mind if he's not famous – it's about the work. Have you brought any slides with you?' Michael asked.

'No, but I can get some to you.' I should have thought about slides but I had thought it was going to be much easier than this; it was hardly as if I was trying to get Foruki into the opening exhibition of the Tate Modern.

'Let me show you around the place,' he said getting up.

He towered above me and we walked towards a spiral staircase. He let me go first and I had a strange sensation of being able to feel his presence even though he was two or three steps away from me. It was making me nervous and I just focused on trying not to trip or fall down those stairs, and as we reached the top he glanced at my face to see my reaction.

The staircase led to an opulent yet minimalist gallery. The walls were white, it was bright and spacious with large arc-shaped windows that overlooked London. The floor was intricately done in mosaic with Japanese letters. It was perfect.

'It's not finished yet but it will be soon. I do apologise if my partner was a little short with you, it's just that there is so much left to do and so little time.'

I knew the feeling.

'So what style does Foruki adopt?'

'Abstract.' I kept the conversation to a minimum in case I said the wrong things, and although I had become something of an expert I didn't want to lie to him. He had the kind of eyes that made him incredibly difficult to lie to.

'And you, Nina, how long have you been an agent?' He didn't call me Ms Savani as he had done in the room downstairs. Was he trying to catch me off guard, did he think that I didn't sound competent? I didn't want to blow it now.

'I was a lawyer in the art industry for almost four years and gave it up recently to represent Foruki.' There, almost the truth. I wanted the conversation to end there because he was making me feel nervous and I too wanted to play with my hair like Emily Bruce-Williams.

'So you'll drop the slides off by tomorrow?'

'I'll courier them over to you,' I replied, trying in vain to sound professional. Then I looked at my watch, thinking that I'd have to find someone who would have the slides ready for the next day. 'I have another meeting to go to but it was a pleasure and I would be grateful if you could contact me as soon as possible once you have reached a decision.'

'I certainly will,' Michael Hyland replied, smiling.

I rushed off and finally managed to find someone who would take pictures of the canvases and develop them into slides for the following day.

After the man had left I attempted to finish Foruki's portrait, but saw nothing except fiery hues of red in large bold strokes so that is what I painted. His eyebrows appeared to be the only thing salvaged from this fiery storm. I couldn't stop thinking about Michael Hyland. Yes, OK, he definitely had something about him and was attractive, but that was it. Engaged people could still find other people attractive, that was no crime. Married people found other people attractive – dad and Cilla, for example. 'She's the dynamite,' he had accidentally blurted when he first saw her many years ago on *Blind Date*. Ki and I had split our sides laughing as my mother disgruntledly went to attend to her rotis.

Later that evening, Ki had probed further as to his fascination with her.

152

'I know she's good-looking, Uncle, is that why you like her?' she had sniggered.

'No, not just the looks. I respects her. She is just like me, coming from the humble beginnings, taking a risk and coming to London, also has the funny accent but this did not stop her, she still worked hard and made it.'

'But Uncle,' Ki had said trying desperately to control her laughter, 'Cilla's not an immigrant, Liverpool's not that far.'

'It doesn't matter how far, she came in a boat with only a suitcase.'

'A ferry?'

'Ferry, boat, all the same, Kirelli. I understands her.'

Understanding; understanding was what mattered and Raj and I had this. OK he didn't know about the paintings so on this basis we couldn't have a full understanding but maybe it was time to tell him.

I stared at Foruki's face; it had gone from calm and sedate to fiery. If it was an omen, it wasn't a very good one.

Raj phoned a while later to say he couldn't meet up as we'd planned because he had to take important clients who had come over from the States to dinner. I desperately needed to see him that evening, to have him put his arms around me and to know that surely attraction could grow. I wondered who else I could talk to and thought about going to see Mrs Onoro but I couldn't just turn up, and besides, I didn't want to go and see her empty-handed. Raj's mother phoned to check that the flowers were still being organised by my mum and then she wanted to speak to her to make doubly sure that all was going according to plan and on schedule. It was all on track, running smoothly, she had made sure of that; there was no room for error, none whatsoever – and especially not from me.

*   *   *

153

The next morning I went to the office and began making a list of people who could help me with PR. There were only two people on it. One of them was a free-lance journalist, the other was a PR director, both of whom I'd met at exhibitions. I called up the PR man first and I almost fell off my chair when he told me how much it would cost to run a campaign for Foruki. I didn't have that sort of money and so I called up the journalist who asked me to send him a press release. Not even sure what this was exactly, I agreed. What I needed was a step-by-step book that would tell me about PR. I added this to my list of things to buy, put everything back in my folder and then went to collect the slides.

I thought about calling a courier but it was another expense so I took the slides to Artusion myself, planning to just drop them off to Christophe. When I got there, however, Michael was in the restaurant area, talking to some workmen. I thought he hadn't seen me but just as I was leaving he called out my name.

Having made up some flimsy excuse about being in the area, he invited me to have a coffee with him and I agreed, thinking that maybe I wouldn't be so tongue-tied and could make a better job of convincing him to exhibit Foruki if I spent more time with him informally. Michael asked how long I had known him and what was so special about him that I would want to leave Whitter and Lawson to represent him exclusively. And instead of giving him the same rehearsed bullshit, I talked about Foruki as if he was someone I really, truly believed in.

'There's a vulnerability about him which he doesn't show, you can't even detect it through his paintings but I know it's there and I know this by what he paints. Mostly he paints inanimate objects and tries to see magic in them, even when it's not there; and he uses bright colours if he can, or colours that seemingly don't go together.' Lost in the analysis of my own creation, I continued, 'Sometimes he contrasts dead objects with something that is alive, hoping that . . .' Realising I was getting carried away, I ended the sentence with, '. . . Yes, hoping that it will work. This is my interpretation of what he's trying to do, he might tell you something completely different. Actually, come to think of it, he won't tell you anything at all. He's a complete recluse.'

Michael laughed. It was a gentle sort of a laugh. 'So you say you gave up working at the firm to represent Foruki?'

'Yes, because I believe in him and it is the first time I've really believed in any of my artists. And how about you? How long have you owned Artusion?'

'Five years. Emanuel and I started from scratch with nothing except my passion for art and his for food.'

'Who are your favourite artists?' I asked.

'Postmodernists like . . .'

'. . . Picasso and Matisse,' I said, finishing his sentence.

'Yes.' He held my gaze intently and I quickly changed the subject, looking away as I did so.

'So why the installation by wardrobe man? I mean Karlhein.'

'PR. Everyone's talking about him at the moment, sometimes you have to play the game to get the attention and then you can do what you want.'

He understood about the game. Maybe he would understand that sometimes you have to bend the rules in order to play, even if you really didn't mean to play in the first place. Half an hour had passed in an instant. We talked more about the art world and I could have talked to him for hours but I had work to be getting on with and so I thanked him and left. Michael said he would be in touch soon.

I went for a walk along the back of Cork Street, taking in the pictures displayed in the gallery windows. What if mine was in there one day? Mine couldn't be but what if Foruki's was? What if he was a success? What would happen then? Would I have to continue to be him? I couldn't suddenly switch and be me – Mangetti could never find out. Don't get carried away, Nina, it's a sabbatical – remember that – and then you get back to reality.

Raj and I met later that evening and I stared at him, wishing that he would just hold my gaze for once and not feel the need to fill the silences with inane chatter.

'So, baby, tell me about your day?'

I began by telling him about Artusion but he wouldn't let me finish. He interrupted me by saying that he had read about it in one of the papers but didn't think the concept would take off in London because the last thing people wanted to do after a meal was to look at paintings.

'There are people who can see paintings anytime,' I responded, surprised by his comment. 'Anyway, you love paintings too.'

'Yes,' he said, attempting to backtrack, 'but I like to know what I'm doing. If I'm going to a restaurant, I want to have dinner; if I'm going to a gallery, I want to see art.'

His argument didn't make any sense: it was such an odd thing to say for someone who liked art. 'But if you're going to a place where you know you can do both, all the better.'

'Not left your lawyer-head at work today,' he said patronisingly. 'Anyway, baby, why do we care if it's a success or not?'

And then I lost it. 'I care,' I shouted, 'and I care because it's original and it's bold to do something different and not follow the pack like sheep.' Maybe I subconsciously meant us, being herded from list to engagement to marriage, but he stopped me from going any further and tried to calm me down.

'This is our first real argument, baby.'

'No it's not, because if it was an argument you would be shouting back at me. What are you passionate about, Raj, tell me?'

'You, Nina, you. I love you.'

And hearing those words made me realise how deeply we had gotten into this. There was no turning back – love had entered into the equation, for one of us at least. How could he love me? He didn't even know me. Maybe it was me who expected too much; I expected too much and therefore was always so disappointed. There was no room to be disappointed with Raj because this was who he was; he was uncomplicated; he liked to know that a restaurant was for eating in and a gallery was for seeing art. Why was I getting so worked up? No expectation, no room for disappointment, just stability.

'I'm sorry,' I said. 'It's just been a long day.'

'I understand,' he replied.

He couldn't understand. Michael Hyland had crept into my psyche in a way that nobody, not even I, could understand.

There were hardly any people on the train when I made my way to the studio early the next morning, not even waiting for the light to begin painting. There was an

157

energy bubbling away inside of me that worked its way onto the canvas, balancing the red hues on Foruki's face. *Madame Butterfly* was playing as usual while I was working so I didn't hear the knock on the garage door until it turned into a bang. It was ten o'clock in the morning and nobody ever came to the studio, so I kept silent, hoping whoever it was would go away.

'Anyone there?' There was another bang on the door.

'Who is it?' I asked, clutching my paintbrush in case I had to stab an intruder.

'It's Michael, Michael Hyland.'

Bloody hell. What was he doing here? I put down the paintbrush, thought quickly about grabbing my proper clothes but it was too late, he had already pulled the door open.

'Hi,' he said.

I didn't even have time to roll down my sleeves; my arm was exposed. He could see the scarring. I fumbled with the sleeve, trying not to panic, trying to find some kind of explanation as to why I would be standing in a studio clearly in the midst of painting a portrait of someone who did not even exist.

'You left this at the restaurant,' he said handing over my folder. 'I thought it might be important so I looked inside for an address, hope you don't mind.'

I hadn't even noticed the folder was missing. Oh God, he must have seen my scribbled notes and the plan. 'Thank you,' I replied, not knowing what else to say and willing him to leave.

'Even more impressive than on the slides,' he commented.

'Foruki was kind enough to let me use his studio for the morning. I just dabble,' I said, flicking white paint randomly on the canvas.

He stood studying the pictures.

'Thank you for bringing back the folder. Was there anything else?' *Leave, please leave*, I willed.

'I saw the slides yesterday evening but this, this is something else. He's good, isn't he, very good. There's a tremendous warmth that comes from these pictures.' Then he turned to me, 'So do you paint here often?'

Go, just go, I thought.

'Is that him?' he continued, pointing at Foruki.

I nodded. He would know if I had done the self-portrait, I would have done the rest. He wasn't stupid. I had to get him out of the studio before he finally put two and two together. 'Like I said, Foruki has let me use the studio for the morning. I don't mean to be rude but I don't get that much time to myself so if there isn't anything else.' I signalled towards the door with my eyes.

'Why are the lines not longer on that palm?'

'What?' I replied, thrown by his question.

'That painting there, the lines are so short.'

'Because everything about the picture is so alive and the only way I . . . Ki . . . Foruki could capture the nature of death was by the length of the life, heart and fate line.'

'Did he experience the death of someone close?'

'His best friend.'

'Died young?'

I wanted desperately to tell him about Ki but nodded instead.

There was silence.

'Anyway, I mustn't keep you. I just wanted to tell you that you – Foruki – can exhibit at Artusion. There will be no charge for the food or the drink but come around when you are not so busy so we can finalise the other details.'

He knew. I knew he knew, he knew I knew he knew, but I couldn't say anything except, 'Thank you.'

'If Foruki needs help with PR, let me know and I'll tell

Emily to get on to it,' he said, glancing at the canvas behind me with the list of things to do so prominently displayed.

'I'll tell him,' I said. 'Thank you, Michael.'

A splattering of white had hit one of Foruki's eyes and it looked like a stream of tears. I know how he felt. What was I going to do? How would I explain it? What if he told someone? No, he wouldn't, he would have said something now. Out of all the people in the world, why did it have to be him? Why wasn't it Raj? I left the canvas, anxious after Michael's visit. He had seen me, me in my studio, and accepted it with no questions? Why? He understood about the lines on the palm. I had had this overwhelming need to tell him about Ki; I didn't even have this with Raj.

Raj had to come and see the studio and the pictures. Raj would restore a sense of normality but at the same time I also had to tell him everything. It wasn't right that Michael, a virtual stranger, knew; and Raj, the man I was about to marry, remained in blissful ignorance about this part of my life. I called him up and said that there was something I wanted to show him and asked him to meet me at London Bridge when he finished work. Raj wasn't good with surprises and wanted to know what it was. 'Just meet me at six-thirty,' I insisted.

It was the perfect opportunity to tell him about Foruki but I needed to see his reaction to the paintings first without telling him it was me. Deep down, I wanted him to just look at the pictures and guess. I tidied up the studio, took down the canvas with the list of things to do, packed away anything that he would know was mine, changed back into my suit, and feeling very excited I went to meet him.

'Hi baby,' he said as soon as he saw me. 'What's with the big secret?'

'It's not a secret, Raj, it's just that Foruki has left me

with the keys to his studio and I wanted you to be one of the first to see his work.'

'Do we have his permission?'

'He won't mind, just come see it with me. We won't get another chance to see it together like this.'

'If it means so much to you baby, let's go,' he said, grabbing my hand.

'Were you very busy today?'

'No, not really, what about you?'

'It was a strange day,' I said, 'I forgot some important documents at a restaurant and the owner came by to drop them off.'

'Right. Why was that strange?'

Yes, why was it strange? I was going to say that Michael could have sent Christophe or one of his staff with the folder, that he had 101 other things to do when his restaurant was about to open, and then when he came . . . 'You know, when you expect someone to behave in a certain way and they don't.'

'Is that a good thing or a bad thing?' Raj asked.

'I don't know, that's why it's strange. Anyway, Foruki wants the exhibition held there – it's Artusion.'

'We're here,' I said a few minutes later, stopping outside the studio.

'What, here?' Raj asked surprised, looking at the building. 'You'd think that he could afford somewhere better.'

'It's about what he does with the space inside, not what it looks like from the outside,' I said, unlocking the padlock and pulling the door open. 'Let me just put the lights on. So, what do you think?'

He stood as if he were taking in the atmosphere. 'It's amazing how people can work in such places.'

'What?' I asked, irritated.

'I mean what he is able to do with such space and the paintings are . . . the paintings are . . . interesting. Yes, look at that buddha. You can see there how he is trying to make a point.'

'Really?' I asked.

'Yes, baby, see there again. Andy Warhol did a picture like that about the nature of fame. This guy Fuki is trying to say that even religious concepts in today's era go through a fashion.'

I was dumbfounded. What was he going on about? 'I don't think that's what he meant . . .'

'He's obviously got some Indian influence here,' he pointed at the derelict houses painted in the colours of sari material.

At last, I thought, thinking that surely he must recognise the orange house with the delicate elephant print – the pattern of my engagement sari.

'Again, social commentary. Maybe about how cultures have fused.'

By then I was exasperated by Raj's words.

'Then this footprint,' he continued, analysing the painting of the red footprint on pebbles. 'It's possibly the mark he wants to leave, the red boldness is what he has to offer. See, all his paintings are bold and expressive.'

'It's my left foot that wasn't captured on the white sheet, the one that doesn't belong to your family,' was what I wanted to say. But instead I asked him what he thought about the palm.

'See the contrast in colours between the palm and the foot, the palm is . . .'

I wanted to save him from himself and from what I would say if he continued any further so I threw a rope to help him. 'That's the palm I was talking to you about, Raj, you know, when I said I felt the lines should have been longer but they're not.'

162

'Yes, I see what you mean. They could have been longer. He seems an interesting guy this Fuki. Is that him?' he glanced over at the portrait.

'Yes it is, and it's Foruki.' I tried to hide my disappointment. There was no moment of revelation, no spark of recognition, no comprehension of who I really was. Maybe after the exhibition I wouldn't even tell him that it had been me, and we'd just get on with our lives like normal people, living normal lives in a normal world.

'Now, baby, I've got a surprise for you too.'

'You have?' I asked.

He put his hand inside his pocket. 'I've been waiting all day to do this.' He pulled out the ring. 'There,' he said, putting it on my finger. 'It fits and it's beautiful just like you. Don't you think so?'

'Yes . . . beautiful.'

'And thank you for sharing all this with me, baby, I can see how it's important to you.'

'It is,' I said, switching off the lights and putting the padlock back on the door.

I didn't sleep all night, thinking about Raj's reaction, thinking about Michael coming to the studio. They had both seen me and my work and reacted in different ways. Raj didn't want to see me in the pictures, it was about him – how much he thought he knew about art. But then that was unfair of me to do that to Raj – if I hadn't built Foruki up so much to him, I'm sure he would have seen that it was me.

It must have been about seven o'clock on Saturday morning when my mum came into my bedroom, mumbling something about Raj's mother telling her that he had given me the engagement ring. I pulled my hand from under the duvet and waved it at her. She gasped, seeing again

163

the size of the rock, and then tried to get me up so we could all organise who was coming to the wedding. It had to be done that day as she was leaving for India that evening. I couldn't wait to have ten days where I could just concentrate on the exhibition.

My mum lifted up the duvet and practically dragged me out of bed. I went to make a cup of tea and she followed me just in case I got lost.

My dad was sitting downstairs in his red pyjamas. He was busy drawing up the guest list. Seeing several red marks across people's names I said, 'Just invite whoever you want, Dad, don't worry about my friends.'

'No, Nina. Come, sit, see what I've done. These here,' he pointed, 'they won't appreciate Hilton. We'll have a party for them here later.'

My Uncle Amit and Auntie Asha were also crossed out.

'Don't you want them to come?' I asked. 'Is it because of –?'

'No, not because of the Raw,' he interrupted.

'It's Roy, Dad, Roy.'

'For two dickheads I suffered,' he shouted.

Dad went through a phase of picking up phrases on the bus; sometimes he didn't quite get the gist of what they meant. Anyway, Auntie Asha was inoffensive and my Uncle Amit was lovely; he owned lots of factories and had helped my dad financially when we first came to London. I would never have called them that. Maybe I hadn't heard him right. 'What?'

'Two dickheads and they did nothing.'

Imagining Raj's mother keeling over upon hearing these words, I thought I'd better check to see if he knew what he was saying. 'Do you know what that means, Dad?'

'Yes, it means twenty years with no help from them.'

'Oh . . . decades.'

'Yes, dickheads, what I'm saying. Two of them,

164

struggling to make the ends meet when he could have made me the boss in one of his factories.'

'He did ask if you wanted to be supervisor.'

'They're not coming,' he said adamantly.

We went through everyone on the list and the guests were chosen on the basis of who had done what for my dad and whether they would be significantly impressed with the venue. At some point there was some crossover as some of the guests had wronged my father considerably but he wanted to show them how far he had come and so they were included. My mother just insisted on the key honchos being present.

'All done. You'll write out invitations when they come?' he said two hours later.

I went to buy my PR books and then on my way back I saw a porcelain cat that reminded me of Mrs Onoro so I bought it for her and went around to see her.

'Sorry I haven't come around sooner. I have been meaning to but it's been so busy,' I said as she led me to her sitting room.

'World too busy today,' she commented as I sat down. 'You better now? I make you some tea.'

She came back with a tray.

'This is just something I bought for you to say thank you.'

'Oh, it beautiful,' she said opening it. 'You good girl.'

No, I'm not. I used to be but now I'm turning into this serial liar, is what I wanted to tell her. 'I saw it in the shop window and I thought of you,' I said instead.

Her son, the grocer, came downstairs. 'Ma, have you seen my . . .?'

He stopped when he saw me in the sitting room.

'No, Rooney, why you no marry a girl like this? Look

165

what she bought me.' The cat was thrust into his hands.

'How's your research coming along?' he asked.

'Oh, the research, yes. I've decided to specialise in Japanese painting at the moment.'

'I don't know anything about art.'

It was then I decided that Foruki was not going to be present at his exhibition. The grocer didn't look right; he had these awful maroon streaks in his hair.

'Ma, do you know where my green shirt is?'

'I ironed and put in your cupboard. It there only.'

'Anyway, nice to see you again.' He said something in Japanese to his mother and went back up. Probably said something like 'Why are you letting crazy women into the house bearing gifts of porcelain cats?'

'He good boy really. You marry soon, no?'

'Two months.'

'He good boy?'

'Yes. I think so.'

'Only think so?'

'He is. I don't know him that well. I mean it was sort of arranged but he's nice. Talks a lot, interrupts me at times, but he's nice and he's kind. Mrs Onoro, when you married your husband, did you know he was the one for you?'

'I too young to know anything but now I can tell if person good by looking in eyes. He got good eyes?'

They were small but that was if I were comparing them to Michael's eyes, and they didn't sparkle but there was nothing bad about them.

'I glad when my husband died. He was no good man and now I free. You make wrong choice you no free.'

She left me to think about that as she went to get the tea. The irony was, despite the fact that I was marrying Raj who was solid and reliable, I had never felt freer or bolder within myself – I was bordering on reckless. It had

166

been me who was solid and reliable with Jean Michel. How was it possible to change in only a matter of months?

Mrs Onoro came back.

I enquired after Hikito. She blushed, telling me he was well and then she said, 'I wait fifty years to find a good man.'

I wanted to tell her about Michael, how he threw all my feelings into utter confusion, but I looked at my watch. Mum was going to India, I had to take her to the airport.

'I have to go.'

'You come back soon?'

'I will.'

My mother and father made it work. Although it wasn't the best marriage in the world they were still together and in their own way, they loved each other. Raj was a good man and this was the most important thing. He was practical, stable, kind, and he loved me and would never do anything to hurt me.

He came with us to the airport to see my mum off.

'See you soon, my son,' she said engulfing him. 'Look after them both, beta.'

'I will,' I replied.

There was no way out of this. I couldn't break their hearts. I just had to accept that and then maybe things would get easier and then there wouldn't be such a conflict inside myself.

The next day I spent with Raj's family and somehow found myself calling his mother 'Mummy', just as he did. Surprisingly, it was quite a pleasant day, or maybe that is the way I chose to see it. Either way, I vowed that as soon as the exhibition was over there would be no more lies and I would do my very best to be a good wife.

It was good that my mum had gone to India because when she wasn't in the house there was no more talk of weddings and it made it seem less real. I also took my engagement ring off, justifying it to myself by saying that I didn't want to get paint on it.

And Michael Hyland, I put him to the back of my mind; that electric thing he did to me whenever he was around. It had no effect on me, it couldn't – it was wrong, I was marrying Raj, that was that, it was time to focus now on hyping Foruki. All my energy had to go into making this exhibition work – it was only a month away.

I needed a strategy and a plan. I had read through the PR books. Confidence; it was all about confidence and believing in the hype. I drafted a press release and reread it and then I sat at my desk, psyching myself up to call the list of art correspondents. I dialled the first number and hung up.

'Pitching' was selling an idea. The more confident you were about a product the easier it was to sell. I believed in Foruki, I just had to make others believe in him. I dialled the number again.

'It's Nina Savani from Kendal Brown. I have . . . er . . . an artist by the name of Foruki who has his first exhibition in London coming up.'

'What makes this one unique?' the journalist asked abruptly.

'Er, his style.'

'What about it?'

I froze, not knowing quite what to say about his style and I just wanted to get off the phone, so I said I had another call to attend to and hung up.

It was a complete disaster and so unprofessional. I didn't know quite what to say and the journalist must have known that I was a fraud. It wasn't working. Maybe I should just call up Michael and ask for the help he offered. It would be good to speak to him and share the experience with someone. No. No Michael. I sat in front of my computer and the words 'GO NINA' danced in front of me. I smiled and closed my eyes and imagined Ki laughing at my half-hearted attempts. Inspired by the thought of her splitting her sides, I picked up the phone and started again.

With each call I made it got easier, and I learned more and more while making them.

'Hello, Nina Savani here from Kendal Brown. We met at the ICA last month and you asked me to let you know as soon as the Japanese painter Foruki was exhibiting.' This was the first thing I learned. Give them the impression that they already know you; they were much more receptive if they thought they knew you.

Despite the fact that they had no recollection of the meeting and maybe hadn't even gone to the ICA, most of them acknowledged me, perhaps embarrassed by their poor memories.

'Well, he has a press launch on the twenty-second of March and he's specifically asked me to send you an invitation.'

More often than not, they asked for a press release along with the invite, just to refresh their memories.

And so it went on like that until I had contacted most of the journalists on the list.

The most audacious thing I did, surprising even myself, was attending every major opening in London that week despite not having any formal invitations. While at Whitter and Lawson we received invites regularly and more often than not I had to attend these functions to network and

169

build contacts. It was the same arty crowd, mostly talking nonsense; artists making stains on serviettes which some fool would buy for a couple of thousand pounds. There would always be one or two people who looked like they didn't belong there; they were more often than not the only ones who were worth talking to.

I put on a smart black dress, caught the tube part-way to the function, then caught a cab so I felt like I hadn't just walked off the streets. My heart leaped as I prayed that the door person would not turn me away. I acted as if I had misplaced the invite or rummaged in my handbag, and, amazingly, they'd let me through. If I was lucky, someone I knew would call out my name and that didn't make me feel so bad. At the exhibitions I mingled, handed out my business card, talked about Foruki and his up-and-coming exhibition and sought out the journalists and spoke to them. It was as if I were a different person with an inner strength, poise and social confidence that even I didn't know I possessed.

There was a woman at one of the events who I really clicked with and we had a very good conversation about the artists being over-hyped and everything these days being about celebrity and not necessarily about the work. It transpired she was a producer on Radio 4 but had previously been an economist. I was desperate to share my experience of my own career change but instead listened attentively to her. We got on very well on a personal level and before she left, she asked me for my contact details.

Another thing I did were Simon's famous 'whispers', telling a few artists who I was on good terms with that Foruki was going to be the next big thing and being as elusive as I could. They, no doubt, would make enquiries with their agents, who would in turn make further enquiries. And so it went on like that for the rest of that week, talking to people, hyping to a select few, going to exhibitions until late in the evening, participating in the theatrics that went on behind the scenes. Consumed with the overwhelming desire to turn Foruki into a success, I was absorbed in the world that I was creating for him. Part of me enjoyed the challenge and I wanted to show these people that it was possible to be a nobody and play the game as they did.

Because I had been so busy I hadn't seen Raj all week. I was relieved because I didn't have to think about the wedding plans, Raj, or if my dad was surviving on his frozen-food rations. By the end of the week my wedding invitations were still lying on my desk. On Friday I sat writing out Foruki's invites and after I had done that, I quickly scribbled out my wedding invitations.

In the midst of the chaos, Michael called.

'Kendal Brown. Nina speaking.'

'How are you, Nina?'

I took a deep breath as I recognised his voice. See, he could phone me and there was no electric thing going on.

'I'm fine, just incredibly busy organising everything.'

'That's why I'm calling. Can you come in this Sunday. We can sample some food for the launch and finalise the details of Foruki's exhibition. I've put Emily onto the PR as well so we need to talk about the best way to handle that too.'

'There was no need for that, we've got it all organised,' I said, not realising that I might have sounded ungrateful – and why had I said 'we'? This multiple personality thing was being embedded in my psyche.

'I thought you might need a hand.'

'Thank you.'

'So one o'clock then?' he asked.

Raj and I had planned to go for lunch and then to the cinema that day. 'It's a bit short notice.'

'It's the only time I have available before our launch and we really need to get everything tied up.'

'Sunday it is, then.'

Before I went home I made one last call, possibly the most important call yet. I spent twenty minutes psyching myself up, convincing myself that it would all work out. I dialled the number and hung up before I actually spoke to Mangetti. After composing myself, I redialled.

'Mr Mangetti, it's Nina Savani.'

'Nina. How are you?'

Absolutely sick with nerves, I can't sleep at night because the level of deceit has just snowballed out of all proportion and now, well now I'm just running with it. That's how I really was. I sat upright in my chair and said, 'I'm very well, thank you. How are you?'

'Yes. I'm well.'

'I just wanted to let you know that Foruki's exhibition is on the twenty-second of March.'

'Let me just check my diary,' he replied.

My heart began thumping. Please be free, I thought. I'm doing all of this for you, please tell me you can come.

'Yes, that's fine. I look forward to meeting both you and Foruki.'

I thanked him and hung up.

I couldn't believe it. I wanted to cry with relief and had to leave my desk because I was so overwhelmed. 'He's coming, Ki. I've done it. He's going to come.' I posted both sets of invites on my way home.

That Saturday morning when I woke up my dad began grumbling about the starvation diet that I had subjected him to.

'Days, I tell you. I haven't eaten for days. Waiting for you, no sign, no call, nothing. Why didn't you put me in a home? At least I would have been fed.'

'I told you, Dad, I would be working late, doing overtime so I can have time off for the honeymoon.'

'This is all you are thinking about, the holidays, not if your father is well.'

'Believe me, the holiday is the last thing on my mind. Anyway, when we go to the Hilton today I know there aren't going to be any rotis, Dad, so don't start arguing about the food. Raj's mother is paying for it so we'll just let her choose.'

He grumbled something about murdering the guests with the 'poffo'. Admittedly, Raj's mother did have a thing about puff pastry but I assured him she wasn't the one cooking and I managed to convince him to agree with everything she said. The total cost of the wedding if she didn't pay for it was the key influencing factor.

Raj and his parents came to collect my father. I wanted to meet them there but Raj had insisted on driving us.

'I've missed you, baby. It's been such a busy week.'

'For me too,' I replied as he opened the car door for us.

'Raj, we're going to have to meet up later on tomorrow. It's just that I've got some bits and pieces to do.'

'I'll help you.'

'No,' I said too quickly. 'I mean it's just some things for work and then I'll meet you after.'

'That's my girl,' my father shouted. 'Always working, even in the weekends, very top in her job.'

Raj parked just across the road from Artusion. *Why?* I thought. It would be a nightmare if I bumped into Michael while holding Raj's hand with the whole family in tow.

'Isn't that the place where your Japanese artist is having his launch?' Raj asked.

'Yes, that's it. It's almost two o'clock, we'll be late,' I said, getting out of the car quickly and trying to hurry everyone up just in case we bumped into anyone.

'What artist?' Raj's mother asked.

'Oh no one in particular, just a Japanese artist who I'm representing at the moment.'

'You'll have a party there for him?'

'It's not really a party. It's an exhibition.'

'Lots of interesting people go to these functions, no, Nina? I go to music things you know, when Ravi Shankar has something on, but I've never been to an art thing,' she replied, obviously angling for an invite.

I ignored her.

'Mummy would really love to go along to something like that. You can get her an invite – it's not a problem, is it, baby? You are organising it, aren't you?'

It was a huge problem, and what was an even bigger problem was we hadn't seemed to get very far out of the car and the 'baby' thing was really starting to annoy me.

'Full of boring art-world types. You'd hate it, Mummy,' I said quickly. 'I mean, I only go because I have to for work.'

'Yah, but just for the experience, Nina, I'd love to come.'

'She'll be fine, baby, I'll bring her.'

Raj wasn't invited either.

'I'm going to be working,' I said, trying to remain unfazed, 'so I won't really get a chance to speak to you. You know how it is when you're working.'

'It will be nice to see what you do, baby, and you won't even know we are there.'

It was hard to keep coming up with objections.

'Agreed then,' his mother asserted. 'What date is it?'

'Thursday twenty-second. Won't you still have lots to do for the wedding?'

174

'All done by then. You'll come as well, no?' she said, turning to my father and asking him out of politeness. 'Dillip can't come, he normally has his golf committee meetings on Thursday evenings, no, Dillip?'

Her husband nodded.

About to have both my worlds collide and destroy each other, I quickly said, 'Dad's not really into exhibitions or art.'

'What?' he grunted.

Please God, please make him say no. You can't do this to me.

'To see Nina's Japanese painter. You'll come? It's on a Thursday night.'

'Can't see Japan man. *Astitva Ek Prem Kahani* is then.'

That's right, he never missed that, eight o'clock Thursday on Zee TV. He was in front of that box regardless of whatever else happened in the world. Thank you, God.

I took Raj to one side.

'Raj, it's a really important artist and I can't lose him so when we're there, you've got to act like you're not my fiancé. Work doesn't like it if we bring our family along to these events.'

'Completely understand. You won't even notice us, if you want we'll pretend we don't know you.'

What a nightmare. This was all I needed – his mother screeching at the exhibition. There was no way she was going to pretend she didn't know me.

'Promise me, Raj, that you'll speak to her. It's very, very important.'

'I promise, baby. We'll be invisible.'

We got to the restaurant and the waiter showed us to the table and handed us our menu. There were a selection of hors d'oeuvres to begin with followed by curried vegetables and potatoes on a bed of filo pastry drizzled in olive oil, or pan-fried fillet of salmon with mint and coriander sauce. The only thing that could really pass off as Indian were the desserts: kulfi ice-cream, gulabjam or rasmalai.

My dad sat studying the menu. 'No samosa, paneer, chana dhal, roti?'

I kicked him under the table.

'OHH . . . no samosa, paneer, chana dhal, roti. Good, good, all the greasy foods makes peoples fatties.'

We tasted it all. It was fine. However, several times Dad looked as if he would be sick but remained unusually quiet while he ate.

'Delicious,' Raj's mother exclaimed.

'It's a good menu, isn't it, Dad?' I asked when we had finished.

'Yes, it was the good. Very good,' he managed.

The heated towels came at the end and this was the part I was dreading. Dad took the towel out of the plastic wrapper and instead of just wiping his hands, he flannelled his face, rubbing it vigorously and making sure he did behind his ears.

Raj's family looked at him completely bewildered and then looked at each other.

'Ah, good, very good,' he said, handing the towel back to the waiter.

Then Dad asked him if he had any paan. The waiter didn't have a clue what he was talking about. 'Just give me the mint and water to wash the taste,' he said.

They dropped us back home. My dad headed straight for the freezer, defrosted another container in the microwave and heated it up. He sat in the sitting room waiting for *An Audience with Cilla Black* and I hovered around hoping for an opening where we could just sit and talk. There was none and so I waited for Cilla with him. When she finally came on, he clapped. Clapped really hard, knowing that my mum wasn't there to hear his adoration for her.

'Oh, the Cilla, the Cilla,' he repeated as he stood up clapping as if he were part of the audience.

She took the mike and opened by singing, 'Surprise, Surprise . . .'

He bellowed along with her as if he were on stage singing a duet: '. . . the unexpecteds hits you between the eyes . . .'

'I'm not a lawyer any more, Dad, and I'm having mega doubts about marrying Raj. There, I've said it.'

'Shhhhh, Nina, let me sing with the Cilla.'

The trees in Green Park seemed happy that spring was finally on its way; winter had seemed endless. The benches were occupied by couples enticed out by the unexpected sunshine. I know it was something that I shouldn't have done, but I put my engagement ring in my pocket before arriving at Artusion. It slid off almost too effortlessly and I justified it in my mind by thinking that I wanted to keep both worlds completely separate.

I was expecting to find it heaving with people ready to sample food but it was quiet, and then I thought it wasn't the kind of establishment like my Uncle Nandan's restaurant, where people queued for miles if you said anything was free. The restaurant was shrouded in darkness and appeared to be closed. I rang the buzzer and Michael came to open the doors.

'Come in, Nina.'

He was dressed informally in a black T-shirt and jeans. It was really nice to see him again.

'You're looking well,' he said.

I acted like I didn't hear the comment, as well was far

177

from what I was looking; it had been yet another sleep-less night worrying about Raj's mother's presence at the exhibition.

The restaurant was empty so I commented on that instead. 'And the others?' I asked.

'What others?'

'I thought that there would be a few more people.' Maybe I had misheard him when he invited me or I was getting into my dad's habit of just hearing things I wanted to. I mean, I saw what I wanted to.

'No, it's just you, if you'd like to sit here,' he said, pulling out the chair. I caught myself glancing at his hand to see if he had a ring and as soon as I found myself doing this, I diverted my thoughts. Michael went into the kitchen and brought out a platter of Japanese canapés. I couldn't believe he had gone out of his way to sort out the food just for me to try; it was a very kind gesture.

'The chef came in this morning to make them. This is maki, and this is nigiri, katsu . . .'

'I'm not really familiar with Japanese food,' I replied, adding quickly, 'I mean the first time I ate it was when we were in Tokyo.'

'You really were in Japan, then?'

It was the first true acknowledgement from Michael that he knew Foruki's real identity.

He waited for my answer and I didn't lie.

'No, I have never been to Japan.'

'It's the name of a restaurant?'

'No.'

'Help me out here, Nina – how have you been to Tokyo if you've never been to Japan?'

I wanted to help him out, but if I did, I would involve him in the deceit. And although he already knew, it wasn't spoken about, so therefore it didn't matter. And why him?

Why couldn't it be Raj who I was about to spill my heart out to?

'Nina?'

The way he called my name like that, so softly, made me feel even more desperate to tell him.

'My friend Ki and I were in Tokyo. Not Tokyo as you would know it but in her bedroom. That's what we did, she loved to travel and we pretended we were in some part of the world, not in some back bedroom that smelled of raw fish and Domestos staring at cheap red paper lanterns. It didn't matter at that stage anyway, she was ill, really ill, and she couldn't eat any of the food, couldn't swallow, and I was trying to make things better for her but I couldn't.' And though it must have sounded like the ramblings of a mad woman, he let me continue, without interrupting, without needing to add his comments.

After I'd told him all about Ki, I glanced up at him, tears in my eyes.

'I'm sorry,' I said. I didn't know what I was sorry for: sorry for unburdening myself, sorry for deceiving him, sorry that I was in tears, sorry that it wasn't Raj sitting there.

'How old was she when she . . .?'

'Twenty-six.'

'I'm sorry too,' he said simply.

The warmth in his eyes was sincere and I wanted to tell him all of it – all about the plan which had spiralled out of control.

'This all started because I promised her I would paint again. I never meant for it to get this far, you know I've never really lied, not on this scale anyway.'

'You don't have to tell me.'

He was right, I didn't have to tell him a thing, but I began at the beginning with leaving my job; Matisse's quotes; the serendipitous meeting with Gina; the suit

179

routine; going to the framer's; Mangetti's interest in the buddha painting; setting up the office. With each piece of information it felt as if a huge burden was being lifted from me. The only bits that I missed out were Raj and the wedding, because at that moment it didn't seem part of my life. That part was like it was happening to someone else and I didn't want him to know that I was getting married.

Michael looked dumbfounded. 'And you haven't told anyone else? How have you managed to keep it all in?'

'By pretending it was happening to someone else, maybe? Pretending that Foruki is real, that it was all going to somehow come together and I could pull it off if I really focused. It is the first time in my life that I have taken a risk on any scale.'

'Might as well start big then,' he smiled.

Michael knew Tastudi Mangetti, he knew most of the major players in the art world and he told me to be careful. Mangetti was renowned for being ruthless and getting his own way; if he ever found out he would make sure I would never work in the art world again. He asked me what my strategy was but there was no real strategy, just to get Mangetti to buy a few paintings and to sell the rest so I would have made a sizeable amount to tell my father about, and then I would kill off Foruki. By then, the art world would have moved on to the next artist.

'And what about you? What happens to you, Nina?'

'I haven't allowed myself to think beyond the exhibition.'

He was surprised that there wasn't more calculation to it. But that was the point, it wasn't ever meant to be calculated; I had taken one step and events had escalated and I went along with it all because it was the first time I had ventured outside my comfort zone and also because it had been a very long time since I had felt passionate

180

about something. And now it had got to a stage where it had become a personal challenge and I needed to know that I could pull it off.

Michael told me how he had gone to art school in New York but knew early on he would never make money from his work so he looked for another outlet to express himself through. He teamed up with Emanuel Hikatari whom he had met through a friend and together they had gradually built up a reputation for finding new artists. They had taken risks with many unknown artists who were later spotted and made into commercial successes. I knew he was taking a huge gamble with me because if it ever came out in public that he knew Foruki was an invention, his reputation would be ruined.

'I'll understand if you want to back out, Michael. Really I will.'

'No, I'm not even thinking about that. I want to help you. What you're doing takes guts.'

I didn't know about guts, stupidity maybe. 'Do you think creativity takes courage?' I asked.

'I would say that not being creative also takes courage. It's hard just to go through the motions and not do what you really want to do.'

I hadn't thought of it that way.

My phone began ringing. It was Raj. I looked at my watch. I'd completely lost track of time; he was probably waiting for me outside the cinema.

'I'll be there in half an hour,' I said, answering quickly.

'You have to go?' Michael enquired.

'I'm sorry to leave in such a rush, Michael.' I hadn't tried any of the food, we hadn't talked about the contract, the exhibition or any of the PR. 'We'll talk again soon.'

He said he would do whatever he could to help me.

'Thank you,' I said getting up, 'you're very kind.' What I really wanted to do was throw my arms around him

181

and thank him for really listening to me but I couldn't bring myself to, so I shook his hand and left.

Raj was waiting at the cinema and seemed irate, pacing up and down. I'd never seen him like that before.

'Where have you been?' he shouted.

'I'm sorry, I was at Artusion, trying to plan the exhibition.'

'On a Sunday? Anyway, the film has already started; we'd better go in.'

The film was *The Green Mile*, and despite really wanting to see it I couldn't concentrate as I was thinking about the conversation I had had with Michael. It had been a relief to talk to him, to feel unburdened . . . and then, feeling incredibly guilty, I held out my hand and took Raj's.

He squeezed it and whispered, 'I'm sorry if I shouted at you earlier, baby.'

I spent most of that week in the office, making more phone calls, sending out press releases. Michael called every day to see how things were coming along and if he could offer any assistance. I really did try to keep our conversations strictly professional but at times the conversation would veer off to other realms and I would find out things about him, such as he lived in New York but was in London until the restaurant was up and running. But it was the little details about him that I loved finding out about. Like how much his family meant to him – how he would try to get back to Ireland as often as he could to see his niece and nephew; that he liked to drink cinnamon coffee every morning and in this time would plan his day. Jean hadn't been too concerned about seeing

182

his family; Nantes wasn't far at all but he only saw them twice a year and he never sat and planned anything in the morning. He had always been rushing around, spontaneous and impetuous. I didn't even know what Raj was like in the mornings. And in these moments, when I caught myself thinking about three different men, I would seek refuge by burying myself in my work, and in Foruki.

Michael called to say that he was sending someone over to the studio to take pictures of the paintings for a brochure and he would come by the studio himself at some point, drop the contract around and help me pick out the paintings to exhibit. I also had wedding jobs to do like call around and find a wedding cake as this was the only thing Raj's mother had entrusted me with, but I couldn't work up the enthusiasm to do it.

On Wednesday I received an RSVP from my Auntie Shilpa accepting Foruki's invitation to see his work. At first I didn't understand but then at the bottom she had put 'Will food be available in the canapé?' Then it dawned on me that when sending out the invites there must have been some kind of mix-up – I had sent exhibition invites to the wedding guests. With visions of my relatives turning up at Foruki's launch, I began to panic; all this work only to have relatives come and cause havoc. I rushed home to retrieve the guest list and my dad's address book.

'Who's a there?'

'It's me, Dad. What are you doing at home? Aren't you supposed to be at work?'

'Feeling a bit sick,' he said, listening to Cilla's CD. 'And you?'

'I've forgotten some important documents that I brought home to read and the client needs them sent off today.'

He wasn't listening but I needed to get him out of the

sitting room so I could get the address book that was by the phone along with the guest list.

'Dad, is that the bathroom tap I can hear?'

'Go switch it off, no wasting water here,' he indicated with his hand.

I went upstairs. It would take a burglary to move him.

'Oh my God,' I screamed.

'What?'

'No!' I gasped.

'What?'

I remained silent while he made his way up, huffing and puffing.

'Have we been burgled?' I asked, looking around his bedroom.

'The burgled where?'

'Here.'

'Don't be the fool, Nina; this is the mess. You are not cleaning in the house, you doing nothing so I wait for Kavitha and then she . . .'

Before he had an opportunity to finish I ran downstairs, grabbed the address book and shouted, 'Got to go, Dad, will see you this evening.'

I got back to the office and began calling up all my relatives asking them if they had received an invitation to Foruki's exhibition. Most of them didn't know what I was talking about and congratulated me, thanking Bhagavan that I was finally getting married. Others who had received invites to the exhibition wanted to know why they couldn't come after all. It was a lengthy process to sort it all out and took the rest of that day – hours that I didn't have.

That evening, my dad and I had been invited to Raj's house for dinner but he said he was sick with a stomach bug and didn't want to make it worse. Raj's mother had her checklist and itinerary out and asked if I had managed to organise the cake.

'Yes. Raj and I will go and see them on Saturday.'

'I've organised a band to play at the reception,' she said.

'Indian music?'

'No, no, none of that. A good band, play at Daddy's golf functions. Latest pop songs.'

'If Nina wants Indian music I'm sure we can arrange it,' Raj insisted.

She ignored him. 'Pretty much all done then. When is your mother coming back from India, Nina?'

'This Saturday.'

'And she said she was speaking to her priest, no?'

'Yes, I think she's already done it but I'm not too sure.'

'Just in case he can't do it, I've organised someone. Our priest can step in at the very latest moment; Daddy and I know him very well.'

She knew everyone very well: should my mother's priest be taken ill she had a stand in; there was a stand in for everyone except the bride and groom. This wedding was going to happen no matter what.

The next morning I went into the studio to try and sort out which paintings to put in for the exhibition. There were only eight paintings which I felt were good enough to be included – I couldn't put just eight paintings into an exhibition. I had more than that but the others were experiments, some dabblings. Perhaps the best idea was to lay them all out and that way I could see how far Foruki had come.

I moved the large table to the side and laid all the pictures out on the floor in the order that I had done them, beginning with the grubby pair of black boots and ending with the hand print and then the portrait of Foruki. It went from darkness to light and in between were shades of vibrant colours; the reds from the buddha and the background of the painting with the elephants. If it were really my exhibition, I would have laid them out in this order, as each painting had a part of me and my story to tell: from the blackness and need to escape the grubby hands of the Guru to the red footprint of committing to a marriage; the inanimate bricks and stones and the constant need to believe and to keep believing and the many houses that despite being vibrant with colour still made me feel alone. But it wasn't about me any more, it was about trying to turn an unknown Foruki into a success. I began rearranging the pictures.

From Obscurity to Light, I thought. That was a good title for Foruki's exhibition, not just to describe his work conceptually but also his feelings about entering the art world from the point of being a recluse and not wanting to be known. I thought about painting a black shadow on a grey background to go alongside the picture of the boots – this could be Foruki's feelings back then and then I could end the exhibition with his vibrant self-portrait alongside the handprint.

There was a knock on the door. It was Michael. I invited him in and tried to make him feel welcome by tidying up the clutter on the battered chair so he could sit somewhere, but he said he was fine standing.

'Completely understandable. Don't want to get your suit dirty.'

'No, no, it's not that, I want to help you arrange your paintings,' he said, taking his jacket off. He was wearing a pale blue shirt with faint white pinstripes that were hardly noticeable. His shoulders were broad; they looked like they could carry the weight of the world and still remain strong.

'Before I forget, here is your contract. Get a lawyer to check it over,' he smiled, handing it over to me.

He had sturdy, dependable hands; hands that were . . . I had to stop myself thinking about them.

'Thank you,' I said, taking the envelope and putting it to one side.

We discussed what each of the paintings would mean to Foruki and he helped me rearrange them.

At times our hands brushed past each other's and I had to tell myself to get a grip as I felt like a coy protagonist in an Indian film; thinking all that was missing was the wet sari, the rain scene, and a tree for Michael to pop out from behind and for us to dance around.

'So when are you thinking of going back to New York?' I asked.

'When I'm happy that the gallery is in safe hands.'

I hoped it would take him a while to find someone to run it.

'Don't your family miss you when you spend so much time away?'

'My family are based in Ireland.' I knew this already but I wanted to know if he would say the word girlfriend. He had to have a girlfriend in New York.

'Where in Ireland?' I asked, trying to escape my thoughts.

'Galway. Have you been there?'

I told him I hadn't, missing out the fact that I hadn't really been out of London much. My dad didn't believe in holidays: 'Peoples, they pay to see anything. If I paint the house pink and put "Taj Mahal of Croydon" they'll come, you'll see that, Kavitha,' he said to my mum once after she hinted that she would love to go somewhere.

Michael began to describe Galway; rugged countryside and rough seas: 'You can't help but be captivated by it. It's one of the most beautiful places to paint. Even in winter it has something special. People say that winter is when it's at its most depressing, but when everything is seemingly dead, that's when all the elements really come together.'

Michael asked me where I was brought up. I thought about Croydon and its elements, most notably the tramp and his dog who sat on the corner of the High Street each day; and it was hard to make it sound as exciting, more so in winter, so I said London.

He told me his family had always supported him and allowed him to do whatever he wanted, even when he chose to go and study art in the States. The struggle, therefore, when he had finished was entirely with himself and trying to make a go of it alone. 'You're fortunate and they must be so proud,' I replied, thinking of my dad preparing me for my career with the *Encyclopaedia Britannica*, the path he had chosen for me and the list of men I was presented with. Perhaps it's harder when you have the luxury of choice and the struggle is internally and not externally. If Dad had said to me, 'Goes on, Nina, be an artist,' where would I have ended up? It would have come too easy. Would I have relished every moment of painting as I did now?

We could have spent hours more talking but I was aware that he had a launch to prepare for and many other things to do, besides helping me, so I thanked him for his time and said I could manage on my own. He looked surprised and I realised it sounded ungrateful and had come out all wrong but I was too proud to say that what I really meant was that I wanted him to stay for as long as he wanted to.

I understood what my dad meant when he said Cilla was like dynamite. He clearly felt attracted to her but admired her from afar, in his world of fantasy. That was what I felt about Michael. It was hard not to admire him, to be intrigued by him, but it was safe to admire him because I knew nothing could come of it; he probably

188

just felt sorry for me and thought that I needed all the help I could get. He was probably attached – there was no way a man like that would not have been attached – and anyway he would be going home to whoever was waiting for him and I was getting married.

After he left I tried not to miss his presence and began finding things to clean. I didn't have to be someone else when he was around; he saw me as I was, in my space, and accepted me. When I'd cleaned the brushes for the fifth time I decided to open the envelope and sit and read the contract. For some reason there were two contracts. One was for the artist Foruki, who was represented by me. I skimmed through it – the terms and conditions were standard and it stipulated that Foruki's work was to be exhibited for four weeks. And then I flicked through the other contract thinking that it was an addendum of some sort. My name jumped out at me where it said 'Artist's Name'. It didn't make any sense. Thinking that there had been an error I went back to the beginning and read word by word, line by line, and almost fell off my chair by the time I got to the end.

The other contract was for me; for me to have my first exhibition as myself in a year's time with Artusion. I couldn't believe it; nobody except Ki had shown that much faith in me. I read, savouring each line, each paragraph, marvelling at the possibility of having my very own exhibition, being able to share my work freely. Feelings of elation quickly returned to sobriety as a year seemed a long time away. So many things were going to happen in between now and then and having my exhibition seemed the least likely.

Stunned at his gesture, I changed out of my clothes and into my suit and went to Artusion.

Emanuel was by the entrance, giving instructions to Christophe. He stopped when he saw me. 'Michael tells me the publicity is going well.'

'Yes,' I replied.

'Good, that's what I like to hear.'

I asked to speak to Michael.

'Is there a problem, Nina?' Michael asked when I walked into his office.

'I can't accept this invitation to exhibit. I've been thinking about it and I don't want you to get into any trouble. What if someone finds out that you knew all along that Foruki doesn't exist. It's your business we're playing with and I can't do that to you.'

'If it happens, I will deal with it, Nina.'

'And why have you drawn up this contract for me?'

'Why not? You can hold your own as an artist, you don't need to hide behind anyone else, and in a year's time when this is all over and people have forgotten about Foruki's exhibition, I want you to come and exhibit with us. I mean, we are getting something here – exclusivity.'

I wanted to tell him then that it was highly unlikely because I was marrying someone else, someone who didn't even know about my need to paint or that part of my life, but instead I thanked him for his generosity and faith in me.

'Come for lunch on Sunday,' he said as I left. 'We can go over things properly then.'

'But you're not open . . . and won't you be busy with your launch?'

'We always make time for our prospective artists,' he replied.

Something had changed; someone else totally believed in me. Foruki's exhibition *had* to work. I went to the office to respond to all the telephone calls and enquiries Foruki had received. Apart from the invitation mix-up it was going well; people had begun responding, confirming that

190

they would be there. A few journalists called to ask me to reveal his real name as I had told them all that Foruki was a pseudonym. But I refused and then they wanted specific information like how old he was and where he had exhibited: the more vague I was about him, the more they wanted to know. So I just made things up that I thought they'd like to hear: tragic childhood, substance abuse, a man who had cleaned up his act and who was ready to share his talent. The gallery details Gina had given me for Japan when I'd last spoken with her were so obscure that I knew they wouldn't bother to go and check his previous exhibitions. With what remaining time I had I worked on new canvases with a different kind of light and optimism, buoyed up by Michael's faith in me.

On Saturday morning Raj came so we could go and see wedding cakes. His mother had come with him so I didn't really get a chance to sit and talk to him like I wanted to. In fact it was pointless the both of us going because she already had her heart set on a five-tier cake with a tacky couple on top who had been made from brown marzipan.

'Cute, no?'

After a few hours of shopping with them I decided I would prefer to go with my dad and collect my mum from the airport, so I rushed off.

The plane had arrived early and we spotted my mum from a distance as we entered the arrival hall. She was wearing a sari, an overcoat and some thick woollen socks and was mopping her brow with a Kleenex. Although we were waving frantically at her and my father was bellowing out her name across the concourse, she stood at the exit squinting her eyes, clutching on to her trolley and obstructing the other passengers from meeting their relatives. The trolley was stacked high with three suit-cases, two of them tied with string to fortify the contents. No doubt these contained the bridal outfits. My father and I made our way over to her.

'Ma,' I said, hugging her.

My father patted her on the back.

'Raj?' She gasped, staring at the empty space between my father and I.

'He's just sorting out some bits and pieces. I'm sure he'll come around later.'

She breathed a sigh of relief.

On the journey back home, my dad told her how he had had to sort out his own food as I was always too busy. He invited her to comment on his weight loss but as he seemed heavier she made a comment on how healthy he appeared given the fact that she had been away. Not satisfied with her response, he expressed his concerns about what would happen if she were to die first and wondered how I would look after him in his old age as I was never there. Before you knew it he was protesting, refusing to be put in a home.

'This is the way now, Kavitha. Old, take their pension, their house, and put them in the home.'

She ignored him.

'So how are you, beta? Everything going well?'

'Yes, it's more or less all organised.'

'Very good,' she smiled.

My father interjected and told her about the food tasting he had had to endure and said she was lucky she hadn't come back a widow. My mum wasn't listening; her mind was on those suitcases. Eager to unwrap the goods she had brought, she asked my father to drive a little faster.

He swore pretty much at every driver who overtook him and at times didn't bother to indicate. It was moments like these I wondered how he'd survived on the buses.

'It's the woman. They should stay in the kitchen and be banned from the road.'

We didn't comment. My mum was thinking about which saris would be best and I was thinking about what names to give the paintings.

As soon as we got home Mum went into the kitchen, got a knife and cut the string, unlocking the cases. She didn't even bother to take off her coat.

'What do you think, beta?' she said, pulling out an ornate red sari and then placing one hand to her heart.

Ki had been dressed in a beautiful, plain, embroidered wedding sari for her funeral. I wanted to cry. She would laugh if she could see this, she probably could see it and would say that it looked like something a drag queen would wear. It had sparkly bits everywhere with a kitsch gold pattern.

'It's pretty,' I said.

'And here, here are the bangles and the rest of the jewellery . . . And then I have bought this one for later,' she said, pulling out a gold thing. 'Go, go try it on.'

'I'll do it later, Ma.'

'Half the way around the world I've gone for you and you can't try it on?'

'All right, I'll do it now.'

I went up and got changed. Maybe it wouldn't look so bad if we could take some of the tassels and sparkly bits off. After I got changed, I went downstairs. My mum burst into tears when she saw me; my dad began to sob. Red, after all, was his favourite colour.

'The beautiful,' he cried.

Raj came around later and my mother sat close to him all evening.

'Nina has all her clothes,' my mum said, 'looks very beautiful.'

The BA Baracus/drag queen look was hardly what I'd call beautiful but if it pleased them then that was the main thing. 'And you, Raj, everything is done?'

'Yes, though I don't think I'll look as beautiful as Nina but everything is pretty much arranged. Mummy is happy with it all and now I just can't wait to go for it.'

'Go for it?' she repeated, more as a question about what that meant precisely.

'Yes,' he replied, 'I certainly will.'

'Meeting Raj?' my mum asked as I was sitting by the mirror putting lipstick on.

'No, just a client.'

'On Sunday?'

'It's the artist I was talking to you and Dad about.'

'It's a woman?'

'Yes,' I replied uncomfortably, sensing that this was what she wanted to hear.

Michael had invited Emily to join us, and in a way I was relieved. It was too tense and charged when were alone. I gave her a list of people who I had contacted and we talked about concentrating only on Foruki's artwork as opposed to his personal life.

'Are you sure we can't take any pictures of him? He'll be much easier to pitch if we have a photograph.'

'No, he's an enigma, he won't allow any.'

She found this fascinating and I had to give her the whole back-story that I had made up about him.

'It's fascinating,' she said. 'It's all material we can use.'

'Emily, I think at this stage all we want is an awareness,

no features, so if you bring up his name to people that you speak to that would be really helpful,' Michael said.

'Of course,' she replied and then she went through the coverage she had lined up for wardrobe man.

We had lunch together and then she had to dash off somewhere.

'I'd better be going too,' I said.

'Someone's waiting for you?' Michael asked.

I should have said yes, I should have told him about Raj, but again, I didn't.

Despite having every intention of leaving Michael there, I found myself walking in Green Park with him and then sat with him on the bench where the whole episode had really started. The grass that had been yanked out all those months ago had grown back, while winter had taken me through a bizarre series of events. Now everything had changed again. Those insecurities and doubts had gone and others had replaced them as I sat pretending that I didn't feel anything for this man. I felt strangely uncomfortable because I was myself with him and I hadn't been truly myself for a long time. It was effortless – the days I didn't know how to be me or how to express what I felt, I threw myself into my work and painted. But here I was articulating everything that had ever meant anything to me. If only things were different and I wasn't marrying Raj.

'What's wrong, Nina?' he asked, seeing the thoughtful look on my face.

I told him about the time I sat on this bench after seeing Jean Michel. He then told me about his fiancée who had left him a month before they were supposed to get married. A few months later she was married to someone else.

'Did you love her?' I asked.

'Like I've never loved anyone,' he replied.

I was going to ask him how long ago it had happened

and then I answered my own question. 'Five years ago?' The single-mindedness with which he had built up his galleries could only have been fuelled by a passion that had been redirected.

He nodded. 'Did you love him?'

'Loads.'

'Do you still think about him?'

'Yes, but it's getting better.' I didn't know if it was getting better because of all the distractions I had in my life or because of the months that had passed since Jean's betrayal, but it had been a while since he had occupied the major part of my thoughts.

'It's hard to put your heart on the line and trust again after something like that,' he replied.

'It's better not to,' I answered. 'It's all about expectation; the bigger the expectation, the harder the fall.'

'Is that why you're hiding behind an artist who doesn't exist?'

'I don't think I'm hiding. It just happened that way.'

He said that everything is planned; that we subconsciously instigate every situation we bring into our lives.

I didn't agree with that because I couldn't have planned any of this, not even subconsciously. 'If that's the case you won't believe in signs, then?'

'Signs?'

'Oh, forget it.'

'No, tell me.'

'Maybe another day.' Signs were dangerous territory. If he suddenly came out with a Matisse quote at that moment, I wouldn't know what to do.

He asked me about the scar that he had seen on my arm and I told him about my sister and how she had left.

'You never tried to find her?'

'I went to Manchester a few times, but nothing.' The more I spoke to him, the more uncomfortable I felt. It

196

was as if he was unravelling layer upon layer and eventually he would get to the real me.

'Come on, let's go, it's getting cold,' I said.

We left Green Park, walked along Cork Street looking at pictures in the gallery windows, and then I felt it was time to go home; back to reality.

There were four messages from Raj, each of them sounding more and more frantic. I switched my phone back off and eventually called him when I got back home.

'Where the hell have you been, Nina?'

'Out with a friend.'

'Your mother said you went out with your artist. Did you?'

'No, I went out with someone who's helping me put together Foruki's exhibition. You don't know them.'

'How can I if you don't introduce me to anyone?' he shouted.

'Well it's not like you've introduced me to your friends.'

As soon as I said those words, I knew what he was going to say.

'When do you want to meet them? Wednesday? Are you around then or are you going to be consumed with your Foruki.'

'Are you jealous of him? There's no need to be, really.'

And then he calmed down. 'Baby, it's just that I hardly get to see you these days and I thought the weekends were for us.'

'They are, but today I went out and I had my phone switched off . . . and that's it.'

'I'm sorry,' he said. 'So Wednesday, is that good for you – and I'll get everyone together.'

'It's fine.'

'You can bring your friends along too.'

'No, I'll let you meet them another time.'

'Really missed you today, wanted to talk to you,' he said.

'About what?'

'About nothing. That's what makes it feel so special; that I need to talk to you about nothing.'

'Well, I'm back now. Don't think I'll be going anywhere.'

And that was the sad truth, it was never going to go anywhere with Michael and not just because I was marrying Raj. Even if I wasn't I don't think I would have had the strength to love again or go through any of that, not after Jean Michel. Everything I had could be put on the line for my work, but not for my heart.

On Monday I went in early to the studio, put the music on full blast and began working on a new canvas. If I had to paint deception what colour would I give it? I slapped on some dark greens. What's worse, deceiving yourself or someone else? Red came to mind and so I picked up the red paint-pot. If you start by deceiving your-self, you inevitably end up deceiving other people. What if you didn't really mean to deceive anyone and found this big massive whopper of a lie in front of you and then everywhere else you looked there were more and more lies all created because of the need to be what other people wanted you to be. Red found itself on most of the canvas. There was no escaping it: the facts were that I was getting married to a man who I did not love and was organising an exhibition for a man who did not exist, and both of these lies had to work because there was too much at stake for them not to. If I tried and just stayed focused for a few more weeks, I could get through it. The thought of what lay ahead was more than I could handle right now.

I put my suit on and went to the office. Raj called to say that he'd fixed Wednesday evening with his friends and then Michael called to check if I could make it to the restaurant's official opening the following day; there would be an array of people from the art world. It would be another opportunity to spread the word about Foruki.

'Beta, priest is coming to talk to you tomorrow, make sure you are home early,' my mother said when I returned home.

'But I can't.'

'You must. Raj and his family are coming as well. You can tell your boss you need to leave early – you're working very hard, he will understand, just say for your wedding.'

I had to be there for the launch. There was no other option.

'Can't we make it another day?'

'No, all arranged, he's coming at seven o'clock. Make sure you are here.'

I went around to Mrs Onoro's house.

'Nice to see you again, Nina. You good girl. You promise to come see me soon and you come. I make tea.'

We sat drinking tea and talking about her family back in Japan and about Hikito.

'Mrs Onoro, when you first met Hikito, did you know he was the one for you?'

'We good friend first, we no do no pankie.'

'Pankie?'

'Hankie.'

I wanted to laugh.

'But there definitely something first time I saw him, but I no want man then I want friend.'

I knew how she felt.

'A friend of mine is opening a restaurant tomorrow

199

and I wanted to ask you if you could write something that conveys luck.'

'You want me to write good luck?' She looked bemused.

'If there's a way of saying it in Japanese or if there is a Japanese character you can use.'

'I see . . . let me think.' She went to find a pen. 'Here,' she said handing me a piece of paper. 'More or less that say "Go for it" in Japanese, no point in writing proverb. No one remember that. Which friend this for? It man friend?'

'Yes.'

'Oohhhh.'

'It's not like that.'

'What it like?'

'We're good friends.'

'I see. You happy with man you marry, no?' she asked suspiciously.

I nodded.

'I not sure you happy.'

It was time to leave before she delved any further.

'Mrs Onoro,' I said hugging her, 'I'm happier for seeing you. Thank you very much for this.'

The following day I covered a small canvas with a red background, and once it had dried I painted the Japanese characters Mrs Onoro had given me in black. Signing the painting with my own initials, I wrapped it up in brown paper, got changed back into my suit and went to the restaurant.

Christophe was rushing around and said Michael was upstairs in the gallery. I went up and he was dealing with wardrobe man and his agent. The agent was arguing with Michael because wardrobe man wasn't happy with where his installation was placed. It was supposed to be an enormous replica of a Bonsai tree made of wood, with cups, saucers, plates and cutlery hanging off it. The agent was arguing because it wasn't bang in the centre of the room.

'As I said it's a critique of how things that are seemingly small have a huge impact, and that's why it's got to go in the centre, not the side, not here, but in the centre.'

They turned to look at me when I walked in.

Michael introduced us. The agent gave me the once-over when Michael said I was representing the Japanese artist Foruki Wardrobe man was polite enough and shook my hand.

'If you'll just excuse me, gentlemen, for one moment,' Michael said, leaving them.

We went next door to his office.

'I came because I can't make it this evening.'

'Why not?'

'Family engagement that I can't get out of but I brought this for you.' I handed him the parcel.

His poise and professionalism momentarily left him as he ripped it open like a child and then he laughed. 'A Japanese character, not signed by Foruki but you.'

'You know it's my first painting signed as me.'

'It's very, very much appreciated that you've given it to me,' he said, kissing me on the cheek.

It felt as if there were a hundred butterflies in my stomach. 'You'd better get back to the bonsai tree,' I said hastily.

'Nina, please come back later and stay for one drink if you can,' he said. 'It would be a good opportunity for you to meet people and introduce Foruki's exhibition.'

And it was ridiculous but I was annoyed that he had said to come because of Foruki.

*   *   *

After tidying up my studio I went back to Artusion and on the way called my mum to say that I would be slightly late. She went hysterical and made no sense, so I asked her to put my dad on the line and I explained to him that I had to do something for an important client and my job depended on it. Nothing could come in the way of my employment, not even a priest. He told me not to worry and that he would keep the guests entertained. That was what was worrying me but maybe it wasn't such a bad idea to further expose Raj's mother to my dad. It might make her think twice about the family she was allowing her only son to marry into.

Artusion was packed with guests. The PR lady was running around Emanuel Hikatari; they were both trying to coordinate the press who wanted pictures of wardrobe man next to the Bonsai tree. There were several influential personalities from the art world present as well as celebrities who made their way into the press shot of wardrobe man on the pretext that they thought his work was fascinating and needed to tell him. I circulated among them all, listened to the chitchat and brought up Foruki's name where appropriate. Michael was extremely busy. He appeared very charismatic talking to his guests and came over to greet me when he saw me; and though I knew I could have mingled for a while longer I thought it was time to leave; they would all be waiting for me at home and Michael had guests to see to.

It was totally ridiculous. I felt jealous of all those beautiful women hovering around Michael. How silly to think that he would feel something towards me other than pity. That's probably what Jean had felt. Why was I thinking like this anyway? I wished there was a little button in my head that said stop. Stop thinking about him, you're getting married. By the time I got to the semi I had pushed all thoughts of Michael to the back of my mind.

Everybody had already congregated at home when I arrived forty minutes late. Raj's mother was furious at being kept waiting and held up her watch. My dad gestured with his hand as if to say he had done a good job in keeping them all entertained.

'I'm so sorry, the tube was stuck in a tunnel and I couldn't call.'

The priest somehow managed to get up off the sofa and my mother signalled to me to bow down and touch his feet. He wore a type of loincloth and his handy legs were exposed so while I was down there I caught a glimpse of the war wounds that he'd once told us about. Seeing as I was down anyway, I touched Raj's mother's pedicured feet, but my future father-in-law stopped me as was customary in that whole routine.

'Where's your ring?' Raj's mother asked.

Everyone turned to look at my finger. It was in my suit pocket. I had forgotten to put it back on. What could I say?

'Sometimes, when it's quite late and I'm travelling home, I take it off because . . . because I don't want to attract muggers.'

'The muggers,' my dad shouted. 'Everywhere, even tried to take television set from me.'

'We don't have that problem in Sutton,' Raj's mother commented sniffily.

I reached inside my pocket and put the ring back on.

'And what's the red things in your hair, Nina?' Raj's mother asked.

'I don't know, Mummy.' Oh God – had I gone to Artusion with paint in my hair?

My mother came over and had a good inspection. 'It looks like paint.'

'Paint?' my dad shouted.

'I was at an artist's studio today, it might have come from there.'

'But how?' my mother asked, continuing the investigation.

'Dropped or splattered?'

'Were you with Foruki?' Raj asked suspiciously.

'No.'

The priest continued slurping his tea. 'Would you like any biscuits with that or some mix?' I asked in an attempt to get away from their questioning.

'We've asked him already,' my mother said. 'He's been waiting for you for the last hour.'

'So let's not make him wait any longer.'

Raj and I sat down on the floor in front of him and he explained what the wedding ceremony would entail, what he would do and what all the symbolism meant. Then he went off track slightly and started talking to us about a young couple who he had married the year before who were having difficulties. 'It is not easy, but you must work hard. Western notion is romantic but it does not last. It is hard work, commitment and the understanding which do.'

My dad nodded vehemently and glanced over at my mother to see if she were in agreement.

The priest then branded the word 'affair' about saying that this was the Western way out of a problem and I promptly barricaded the thoughts of Michael flooding my head.

After wolfing down more savouries and declining the invitation to stay for dinner, he said it was time to go; he had to be off as he had taped *EastEnders*. My mother helped him up and then we had to do the feet routine all over again.

'Such a nice couple,' he said, pinching our cheeks. 'I know you'll be very happy together.'

This was my cue to put my hands together in prayer pose to thank him for the blessing and perhaps for Raj to slip some kind of donation into his hands for the temple funds.

'It is not necessary,' he said, taking the money.

Raj's mother wasn't very impressed by him and after he had left she said she hoped he did not ramble on as some of her guests were English and they wouldn't understand him.

'The English they likes the rambles,' my dad retorted. He then went on to tell us about a passenger he had driven that day who was carrying what looked like an Indian rice sack, which she had paid £30 for. 'You have been the fooled,' I told her. He turned to Raj's mother. 'But now it's the fashion. Give them the rambles, they likes it.'

Surely Raj's mother wanted to break down at some point and take her son back?

I had to organise a van to transport the pictures to Artusion; another addition to the list of things to do. What was becoming increasingly urgent was to find titles for the paintings. I sat for hours looking at a blank canvas, hoping that something would come, but all I felt were doubts and more doubts. How had it all got to this stage? There wasn't even the possibility of postponing the wedding; everything was pretty much organised and there wasn't a valid reason to delay things. I went to the office and sorted through the RSVPs and drew up a guest list. What if nobody came to the exhibition? I debated whether to chase the people who had not responded but then I thought it would make Foruki seem desperate: he was supposed to not care who turned up.

The phone rang. It was Radio 4; they were doing a series to coincide with the opening of the Tate Modern and wanted me to join a discussion about the relevance of the Turner Prize.

I was shocked. 'I'm sorry to be rude but where did you get my contact details?'

'You do represent Fuki, don't you?'

'Foruki, yes.'

'You were speaking to the producer about him and she said you were a good person to have on air as you were quite vociferous in your views. You said that the Turner was about hype, egos and personalities and that you represent an artist who doesn't even use his real name as he doesn't want to be known.'

'Was it an exhibition?'

'Excuse me?'

'When I spoke to your producer? Was it at an exhibition?'

'I don't know.'

I couldn't go on radio, people would recognise me, and anyway what would I say? 'I would love to participate but I'm incredibly busy at the moment. Maybe another time?'

'It shouldn't take too long. Just half an hour of your time tomorrow?'

Maybe it wouldn't be so bad; the only people I really didn't want to listen to me were Mum and Dad and this was hardly likely as any radio programme they listened to had to have Hindi songs blasting out of it. And Raj would be at work. Thinking that it might be an opportunity for Foruki to have a bit of exposure before his exhibition, I reluctantly agreed.

Michael hadn't called. We usually spoke almost every day but I didn't bother to call him either. It was best for everyone if we kept our relationship strictly professional from now on. He was kind and courteous to me as he was to everyone; I saw that yesterday at the launch. It was just in his nature. What was I thinking of?

Later that evening I went to meet Raj and his friends.

He had chosen our Italian restaurant in Covent Garden and I had got there early. I was absolutely dreading it and so had had a few drinks before they came.

Pinkie, Saf, Mel, Din and Hitin came in a group headed by Raj. I felt envious at seeing them all together and then felt guilty about feeling that way so I overcompensated with the friendliness. He introduced us all. Pinkie, one of the girls, had her arm around Raj. I wasn't jealous of this, not even annoyed; in fact I wanted her to tell me at some point in the evening that they were having a passionate affair and that she was madly in love with him but she didn't. I also wanted to dislike them but I couldn't as they made me feel very welcome in their group, going out of their way to include me in a past that I didn't share with any of them.

'Raj talks about you all the time, Nina. Are you excited about the wedding?'

'Yes.' Realising that my answer sounded flat and that it needed to be resuscitated, I started talking nonstop about the dress, the venue and how I was trying to find out where Raj had booked for the honeymoon.

'It's a surprise, baby,' he said, leaning over and kissing me.

And then we talked about how we met and what each of us felt when we first saw each other.

'I knew from the very first moment I saw her,' he said. 'You pretty much knew too, didn't you, baby? In fact it was just after the second date that we decided to get engaged.'

I thought back to his gelled hair, his inside-out T-shirt, his strong aftershave, and then Jean Michel coming to the door of the semi.

'Sometimes things just happen,' I replied.

By the end of the evening, after a few more glasses of wine, the girls were exchanging numbers with me, promising that they would call and we would meet without Raj.

On the way home, Raj suddenly asked, 'There are no secrets between us, baby, are there?'

Only about a dozen or so, I thought. 'What makes you ask me that now?'

'It's just that sometimes I get the impression that there is so much about you that I still don't know about?'

'Like what?' I asked nervously.

'Your friends.'

'If you want to meet my friends I can arrange it.'

'It's not just that; these last two weeks you've been distant.'

'Only because this new exhibition means so much and there's so much to think about with the wedding. It's a big step.'

'It will all be over soon,' he said, squeezing my hand.

'I know,' I replied. 'I know.'

On Thursday morning I made my way to Broadcasting House. How had I managed to get on to Radio 4? It just wasn't possible to instigate these things subconsciously, whatever Michael said. The other members of the panel were a Professor of Art from Goldsmiths College and one of Turner's distant relatives. I sat wondering what on earth I was doing there.

The presenter introduced the other guests first and then turned to me.

'We also have Nina Savani from the agency Kendal Brown who is currently working with an artist who doesn't want to be known; a bit of a contradiction in there somewhere?' she sniffed.

Why did she sniff like that? Didn't she believe he existed? Was there a problem? Remain calm, Nina, and answer the question like Foruki would want to, I thought.

'It's not that my artist doesn't want to be known, he just doesn't want to be bigger than his work and this is what is increasingly happening. More and more we are living in an age where it is about celebrity, hype and PR stunts, and the quality of the work is overlooked. I think Turner would be disappointed to what his name is now being associated with.'

His relative was nodding her head.

'Turner was ahead of his time and he would be rejoicing at the fact that many of these artists are ground-breaking and that they have brought art into a new dimension,' the professor interjected.

'I would hardly call a wardrobe ground-breaking,' I interjected.

The professor then replied immediately, 'Yes, but then he has added to the debate; one must ask the question "What is art?" Surely it's about having a seminal idea in history in terms of art culture?' And then he began giving some spiel about conventionalism and used long words so no one could really follow his argument. All that was going through my mind when he spoke were my father's words: 'Gives them the rambles, they likes it.'

Sensing that her boat was heading towards an iceberg, the presenter asked Turner's relative for her opinion. She quietly said she thought it was important to bring the subject matter back to paintings.

The professor was off again, saying that paintings were prehistoric and taking art backwards and I argued with him about art being about self-expression as opposed to self-absorption. It sounded good and it would have sounded better if it were true and if I was actually there as the artist.

In the closing stages of the debate, the presenter turned to me and asked me about Foruki. 'Does this mean your

209

artist would be completely averse to being on the short list for the Turner Prize?'

'Foruki, and this speaks for itself as it is not even his real name, would not want to be bigger than his paintings. I think for him he feels he would have done his job if his pictures are taken for what they are and not who he is.' The likelihood of Foruki being on the short list was as likely as my wedding being called off but it was good to make it sound as if it was a possibility; it added more kudos.

'He wants to express himself yet he doesn't want to be known?' the professor laughed.

Hold it together, Nina, believe in your argument. 'Your point being, Professor Landstein?'

He was about to go off again when the presenter hastily stepped in and closed the debate with a few last words from each of her guests. The news bulletin mercifully cut off the professor.

That afternoon the phone did not stop ringing: Foruki was in demand, people wanted to know where they could see his work. Michael called to say that people were ringing up Artusion requesting invitations to Foruki's opening night. He asked me to drop some more around if I could so Emily could deal with it.

In the evening I went to Artusion and as Christophe greeted me I spotted Jean Michel sitting at one of the tables. A sense of dread and panic filled me: why of all places was he here, and tonight of all nights? He was with a group of people and hadn't seen me so I decided to make a swift exit.

'I've forgotten something, Christophe,' I said hastily.

210

At that moment Emanuel Hikatari stopped me suddenly. 'Leaving already?' He had sprung from nowhere and had positioned himself so that he was obstructing the door.

'Yes, I was just saying to Christophe that I've forgotten something. Congratulations, by the way, on your launch,' I said, attempting to leave.

'Thank you, we couldn't have expected more.'

Then I heard his voice. 'Nina, Nina, I thought it was you. How are you?'

My heart was beating incredibly fast. 'Fine, thank you, Jean,' I said, taking a deep breath and introducing everyone.

'Pleased to meet you. Hope you are enjoying your meal, Ms Savani, I must leave you. Michael tells me it's going well and that there has been lots of press interest. Good to hear.' Emanuel left us.

Jean looked at me.

'We're having an exhibition here for one of my artists.'

'But you've left Whitter and Lawson. I tried calling you there.'

'I've set up on my own now, working for a Japanese artist,' I answered almost too quickly. Would that have sounded odd to him? Wasn't I the person who procrastinated over every decision and had to weigh up the pros and cons.

'That's fantastic, you're looking really well. It's so good to see you, Nina,' he said clasping the sides of my shoulders.

It felt very uncomfortable.

'You're looking well too,' I replied, thinking he seemed to have lost half his body weight and needed to be fed. I almost felt sorry for him and had to tell myself that he had betrayed me; he had betrayed me when I needed him the most.

'Are you still getting married, Nina?'

'Yes, in a month's time,' I said coldly.

'That's quick.'

'Better to say yes quickly before you find them with someone else.' And as soon as I'd said that I regretted it because it showed him that he still affected me and what I wanted was for him to return to his table and leave me alone.

'No more than I deserve. As long as it's not a rebound thing, you know, you can't have known him that long. All of . . .'

'. . . A week,' I replied. 'It is possible to meet someone and feel you've known them a lifetime.' And this was true – perhaps not in relation to Raj, but it was true.

'Are you in love?'

How dare he ask me if I was in love.

'Yes,' I replied defiantly. 'Anyway, I have to go. It was nice seeing you again. Take care of yourself.'

'You too, maybe we can . . .'

I walked away before he could finish his sentence, trying to hold my poise as I went up to the gallery in an attempt to show that he had not affected me.

There were a few people studying the bonsai tree. The porcelain appeared so fragile hanging off the branches, as if should a huge gust of wind come unexpectedly from nowhere it would send the whole thing crashing to the floor. Perhaps it wouldn't be the wind but a careless waiter blown into the direction of the tree. Maybe in life you have to factor in the unexpected so there is no room for disappointment. That was what my parents did; they always had a sense of mistrust about the good things that happened because they knew that the wind wasn't far behind, and that was probably why they sought stability in the things that they knew; that was why their marriage worked.

The priest was right, romantic notions of love were

fleeting. How was it possible to feel so strongly for someone and then have another person come into your life and feel the same in only a matter of months? Love was fickle, just as life was. Love led to disappointment. Raj was stable, he would always be stable and it would last because with him there was no room for disappointment; no room to get hurt.

I sat in a corner of the room watching the way the light fell and the patterns the cutlery hanging from the tree made on the floor. They were intricate patterns like the web of deceit I was weaving and I think I knew then that the biggest lie was the one I was telling myself – but then one lie led to another and everything had become so embroiled that it was just impossible to see clearly. I clung to the fact that Raj came into my life when I most needed him and there had been a sign that he was the right one.

Michael came and pulled up a chair opposite me.

I handed him the invitations.

'What's wrong?'

What could I say? That I was getting married in a month but was feeling angry that he hadn't called me earlier; that I was jealous at seeing all those women hanging around him at the launch; that I had seen Jean Michel downstairs and he had provoked feelings in me but they weren't as strong as the ones Michael did; that I was unable to do anything with these emotions except pretend that they weren't there.

'I don't think I can do this any more.'

'There have been many times when I have felt like that but you have to hold your nerve and you'll get through it. You've come this far, don't let it go, Nina. I know it will be a success.'

'You don't understand, people are going to get hurt, I can feel it, and it will be all my fault; it's just such a mess, a big mess.'

213

'Who's going to get hurt? There's only me and if it goes wrong I can handle it. I only take on what I know I can handle.' It was time to tell him about Raj. I glanced over at the tree, trying to find the right words.

'They all went for it,' he said, indicating the tree.

'I never thought I'd hear myself say this but it's not bad. All those patterns the light is reflecting on the floor.'

'It still can't beat a good painting. Have you thought any more if you are going to get a Japanese man to stand in for your artist? Because if you need anyone, I know someone completely trustworthy.'

'No, it's better if Foruki isn't present.'

'It adds to the enigma?'

'No, no more lies,' I sighed, and just as I was about to tell him about Raj he asked me if I'd eaten.

'No, but –'

'Let me go down and get one of the waiters to bring us up something.'

'I've got something I want to tell you,' I said as Michael came back.

'Me too,' he replied.

I thought it was something about the PR or to do with my paintings so I let him go first, thinking that it was better to get the superficial things out of the way.

He was struggling with his words; I'd never seen him struggle with them. 'I was thinking that if you . . .' he reached out for my hand and touched my fingers. My heart nearly jumped out and I felt as though I was going to be sick.

'. . . It's just that I'm going back to the States after your exhibition but I can stay if you –'

And before I could stop him and explain, he was interrupted.

'Just came to say goodbye, Nina.'

It was Jean Michel. I quickly took back my hand and had to introduce them both.

'Pleased to meet you,' Jean Michel said. 'I just wanted to wish you the very best for . . .' he stared at me.

'Please don't say it,' I willed, expecting to hear the word 'wedding'.

'. . . for the exhibition,' he continued. 'I'm sure it will be very successful.'

And then he left.

Jean Michel had thrown me. What I felt when Michael touched my hand made me want to get up and run. The level of intensity could lead nowhere but disaster.

'I'm sorry, I have to go,' I replied, collecting my things together.

Once I got home I called Raj. He didn't pick up the phone so I left a message. 'Raj, shall we just do something spontaneous and get married tomorrow, just go to the register office and get married? Why not? Let's do it.'

And then I went to sleep.

The phone rang early next morning.

'Nina, what is this about the register office? I know you can't wait, I can't wait either, but Mummy will go mad.'

'I was tired and it was all getting to me. You know when you just want everything to be over so you can just get on with things. Not have to think any more.'

'That's why Mummy has taken care of it, so you don't have to think; and baby, it's not long to go now.'

'I know, I know, I'll get through it.'

I went into the restaurant that morning with every intention of explaining to Michael but he was uncharacteristically aloof and wholly professional, wanting to discuss where the pictures would go and the labels that needed to be made up. Not once did he bring up what had happened the night before and when I tried he said he understood the situation perfectly and asked me to leave it. And maybe it was just better to leave it.

After going back to the studio I painted more blacks, greens and reds; a whirlwind of deceit that had to stop. And seeing the other canvases, the titles suddenly just came to me; I named them in the colour that was most predominant. The paintings would begin with black and end in indigo. The print of the hand would be called *Beyond Indigo*, colours that I knew existed but I was unable to capture. What lay beyond indigo I didn't know, but all I had to do was get through the opening night and the rest would work itself out.

On Sunday Raj's mother had invited me over for lunch so I could meet her friends before the wedding. The drive was like a BMW showroom with the personalised number-plates giving me an indication as to who would be present.

'Hi baby,' Raj said opening the door. He kissed me.

'Raj, it's not that I don't like you calling me baby but I love the way Nina sounds when you say it.' If I nicely corrected the little things that niggled me, the other things would be fine.

'But everyone calls you Nina and you are my baby.'

'But nobody says Nina the way you do.'

His mother screeched out my name. 'See,' I smiled.

Her eyes gave me the once-over and she tried not to appear too disappointed in my choice of clothes and then blew two air kisses because she didn't want her lip-gloss or her foundation to smudge. Maybe it wasn't such a bad

216

idea to have her at Foruki's exhibition; she would fit in well.

'Come in, come in, everyone is waiting for you. I've asked all the men to leave, Daddy has taken them to his golf club. Raj, you can go now too.'

He obeyed her instructions. If Raj wasn't around her too much then perhaps that would make him change too. He said goodbye to me as she hauled me into her sitting room where a group of ladies who looked like they had been cloned were sitting, waiting in anticipation.

Raj's mother went round the room introducing them but they were all pretty much identical: dripping in diamonds, sporting matching handbags and Gucci sandals with pedicured feet, a far cry from my mum's friends who sank to the bottom of the Land of Leather sofas in their ample salwars, sandals and woolly socks, and their centre-parted hair and large red dots. One set compared the price of a Gucci handbag, the others haggled over the cost of a marrow. It was mind-boggling how the honchos had managed to arrange a union between the two families and how Raj's mother had accepted my parents without deporting them from her home for entry under false pretences.

'Nina's a lawyer and works with lots of famous people. In fact we're going to an exhibition next week that she's organising for a famous Japanese Emperor.'

'What's his name?' one of them squealed.

'Foruki.'

'Yar, Foruki, I think my son deals with his investments.'

The conversation revolved around shopping, celebrities and beauty tips. They wanted superficial so I gave them superficial and even pretended to heed the advice of a pencilled-brow woman who suggested threading my eyebrows further back so that it would accentuate my eyes.

217

I almost had some depth of conversation with one of them who had her own personal Guru who was advising her on all matters spiritual. The Guru had also made her do that coconut-over-the-bridge routine.

'Is his name Guru Anuraj?'

'No, no, his Holiness is Guru Rama. You must come home one evening to meet him. He only deals with very special people.'

'Do you pay him?'

'Only donations to the temple funds.'

I told her to be careful but she took offence, saying that the problem with westernised career girls was they thought they knew it all, and then I was whisked away by Raj's mother asking me to describe my wedding outfit.

After lunch Raj's mother insisted on waiting for Raj so he could drop me home but I needed to walk and to think.

Would I be like these women in twenty years' time? Starting off with no intention of being anything like them and then finding myself looking back as one of them? There was no backing out now so it wasn't even worth thinking about. The biggest of my worries were not my parents not speaking to me but what Raj's mother would do to them if I called it off; at best they would be humiliated and never be allowed to step foot in the community. I went to my studio to paint; in painting there were always answers.

I hung up my sari in the suit holder and changed into my other clothes then began mixing colours. There was a knock on the door.

'Michael?'

The door was pulled open. First I saw a pair of boots and then long blonde hair.

'Not Michael,' an Australian voice giggled.

218

'Gina! You're back early.'

'Don't panic, you've still got the studio for another week.'

'How was it?' I asked, putting down my brush and hugging her.

'It was the best.' She looked around the room. 'Far out, you've moved on from birds. This is bloody fantastic. Has anyone seen this stuff?'

'It's a bit of a long story but I'm in the middle of organising an exhibition for Tastudi Mangetti.'

'Not *the* Mangetti?'

I nodded.

'No bloody way! Go on, tell me.'

'It's a bit complicated.'

'I want to hear; all of it.'

So I told her everything, starting with the Guru and ending with the forthcoming exhibition at Artusion.

She had her mouth half-open with disbelief.

'Why didn't you call me? Even if it was just to unburden yourself?' she said.

'I thought about it but then if I explained it all to you and said it out loud and heard myself, I wouldn't have gone through with it – it would have just seemed too insane. And then there's the rest.'

'Go on,' she said.

'My parents don't know that I'm painting. Every day I've been putting on a suit, pretending to go to work, when really I've been coming here. To throw them off the scent I arranged to see this guy who they wanted me to meet. I'm getting married next month.'

'No!' she exclaimed. 'Do you love him?'

'I think I can grow to love him if I just focus on the good stuff. I know I can. He's nice, really nice and kind.'

'Does he know about all of this?'

I shook my head.

'God, Nina, there's more to it than being nice and kind, there's honesty and . . .'

'I know, but you don't understand – the wedding is in four weeks; there are six hundred and fifty guests. It's all arranged. Mum and Dad are so proud of me. It's been the only time that I've done something that they're so proud of, and I have to go through with it, there is no way out.'

'But what about the paintings? And Mangetti's interest? I'm sure if you tell them they would be proud.'

'No, they'd be horrified. I don't know if they would be more horrified at the fact that I paint or that I have been deceiving them.'

'And who's Michael?'

'What?'

'When I knocked on the door, you said "It's open, Michael."'

'He's . . .'

'Oh no, Nina, don't tell me you've got another guy.'

'It's complicated.'

I told her all about Michael, how he had come into my life from nowhere and what he had done for me.

'But I can't do anything, I don't know what to do. How I feel about Michael is how I felt about Jean Michel and look where that got me. The right thing and the only thing is to get married to Raj. You know, the first time I met him he gave me the Matisse quote, surely that's a sign?'

'Sometimes you only see what you want to see.'

'What am I going to do, Gina?'

'Concentrate on getting this exhibition together, get through it and the rest will follow. Tell me what needs to be done – I'll help in any way I can.'

After we talked some more, she left saying that she would be back in the morning. It was a relief to have her back.

Gina was sent; Mrs Onoro was sent – these were the only things I knew for sure.

Mrs Onoro was in her dressing gown when I went to see her later that evening.

'What wrong my dear?'

'Nothing, Mrs Onoro, I just wanted to have a chat, that's all.'

She looked at her watch.

'I'm sorry it's late.'

'No it not late,' she replied, taking the watch off and banging it. 'It just that it normally tick loud, must have stopped. Come in, I make you tea.'

I sat in her lounge staring at the porcelain cats.

'There,' she said putting the tray down. 'It is about man friend who I write "go for it"? He go for it but it not right.'

I nodded. 'It's just that I don't want to hurt anyone.'

'Hurt, it part of life. Accept it part of life and it easier.'

'What about stability? Making sure that things are secure.'

'It not exist, you know that. It excuse for not doing things.'

'What about doing the right thing?'

'There no right or wrong thing; there only best decision at that time; maybe good maybe bad but you make it based on heart. You make bad decision when based on head.'

'What if you don't know what your heart is telling you?'

'You always know; sometime you don't want to listen.'

I sat a while longer talking about the plans for Foruki's exhibition. She yawned and said she would do a special prayer so it would all go smoothly.

'I'm very lucky to have you.' I told her.

'You good girl, Nina,' she said as I left. 'You welcome any time, day or night.' She looked at her watch again.

Gina came early the next morning and we began cleaning the pictures up and attaching picture fasteners. She talked about that first day she had seen me in the cafeteria at the Tate and felt compelled to speak to me, despite the fact that I seemed so totally unapproachable and moody. I told her that I thought she was a traveller who needed a sofa for the night.

'And there was that quote. Complete lunatic,' I laughed. 'You're worse than me. Who goes around cafeterias spouting quotes to complete strangers? Definitely desperate, I thought.'

Then she began mimicking the way I asked if Matisse was her favourite painter.

'And what's with that flowers quote anyway?' I asked. 'I was only trying to see flowers when there were clearly none and now this whole bloody forest has sprouted out of nowhere.'

Gina laughed.

'I mean what kind of crazy woman throws a coconut off London Bridge and expects a miracle?'

'Not crazy, just grieving,' Gina replied seriously. 'When my mum died, I went to a faith healer who blew all the negativity out of my ears.'

We looked at each other and burst into uncontrollable laughter.

'Did it work?' I managed.

'Like hell it did.'

'But you know, it isn't just about seeing what you want to see or seeing what's not there. I had the most amazing experience a few months after mum died. One night when

I couldn't sleep because the decision to go to England was really weighing on me, I felt my feet being rubbed. Mum did that when I was little and nervous or anxious about something. She's always with me, I know she is, and it's not because I want to believe it.'

I told her about the Reiki healer and Ki being there.

'So how can you still doubt, Nina?'

'I doubt to protect myself. For example, if I say that I doubt my feelings for Michael that means I don't have to make that decision, I don't have to risk anything, I don't have to fear he'll go and do the same thing as Jean. If I say that I know it's him, I just know, don't even ask me how but I do, it means an awful lot of people get hurt.

'How have I let it get this far anyway? It was one lie that has spiralled so out of control, and all because I wanted to sell a few paintings to prove something.'

'I know, Nina, but you have to make the best of it. I mean, you've got Tastudi Mangetti's interest so you've got to focus on getting through the exhibition. Try to put everything else to the back of your mind; deal with that later and just get through this now.'

Gina helped me for the rest of that week. Whenever I stopped to consider not going through with the wedding I heard my father's voice saying 'I'm the proud'; I saw my mother with the contents of the jewellery box sprawled across the floor; I heard the priest telling us about western notions of romantic love; I heard Raj saying how much he loved me; and I imagined what Raj's mother would do to my parents. All these thoughts were put to the back of my head as I focused on making Foruki a success.

The day before the exhibition we hired a van to transport the pictures to Artusion. Michael came down to the restaurant and arranged for the pictures to be unloaded and taken up. I introduced him to Gina. When he turned his back she pretended she was going to pass out and made some swooning gesture. The wardrobe man's bonsai tree had been removed from the gallery and in its place was an exotic Japanese flower arrangement.

Michael was polite and courteous but kept the conversation to a minimum. At times I could tell he wanted to laugh at some of the comments Gina and I made. We stuck to the layout Michael and I had discussed but after we had finished arranging the paintings it still didn't feel right. The colours seemed to clash with each other and even before I voiced this he said it, and so we had to rethink the whole thing. It was seven o'clock when Gina said she had to leave as she was about to begin her shift at the restaurant where she had just started working. I called my parents to tell them I would be late again.

There was an awkward silence between Michael and I that I was unable to fill. I thought about doing something drastic like pretending to fall off the stepladder so I could get his attention but on reflection thought that this was manipulative. Not that conning the entire art world wasn't, of course.

'Would you like something to eat, Nina?' he asked.

'Only if you speak to me.'

'I am talking to you.'

'Properly.'

Later, Michael went around earmarking some of the paintings. 'Just makes him more in demand.'

'But I've told Mangetti that he gets first option on all of them.'

'All the more reason to earmark them then.'

'I think I'll be at a loss as to what to do after. You can just get so lost in it all; it's like another world.'

'You'll paint more, you have an exhibition to do for us.'

I wondered if that would ever happen. Would Raj

understand my need to paint? I thought about being Raj's wife, having to produce the first grandchild soon after and painting the odd picture now and then. How would I cope? Would this be enough for me?

We ate and spoke about everything other than what we really wanted to. After dinner we got back to work.

'About the other night,' I began.

'It's all right, Nina, totally understandable, you're not over Jean.'

'No, it's not that . . .' Before I had a chance to explain Michael went to dim the lights so we could see what the gallery would look like for the exhibition. The room felt magical. Fiery oranges and reds balanced against sedate colours, bringing them to life. There were no shadows; only light.

'It's beautiful, I can't believe we've done this.'

'You've done this,' he replied.

'Thank you, thank you for everything, thank you for believing in me.' I went over to kiss his cheek.

My lips lingered on his cheek for a second longer than they should have. He turned his head slightly and his nose brushed against mine. This overwhelming impulse just to kiss him took over me – not to think about anything else but to do it. He touched the back of my neck with his hand. It felt warm and safe. I looked up at him, held his gaze and then I let him kiss me.

And for a while nothing else existed in the world but the two of us.

'I've been waiting a long time to do that,' he whispered.

I marvelled at how happy and safe I felt. He took hold of my left hand and kissed my fingers.

'I never thought that I would feel like this again,' he said. And that's when the enormity of what I had done struck me.

'Me neither,' I said, tears welling in my eyes. I knew that someone was going to get hurt and I didn't want it to be him.

'Don't cry, Nina, we'll be fine. I'll never do anything to hurt you.'

I buried my head in his arms and we held each other for a long time. It was getting very late.

'Let me take you home,' he said.

'I've got this big van that I've got to drive back home in.'

'I'll drive you.'

'No, I'll be fine. There are just a few things I need to think about, clear my head.'

He nodded. 'It's a big day tomorrow. Call me as soon as you get home.'

Michael walked me to my van and began laughing at the state of it; it was a big, dirty, beat-up van.

'It's the only one they had.'

He kissed me again.

All I thought about was Michael as I drove home. Raj didn't even enter into the equation until I got to our front door and stepped over the threshold of the semi. As soon as I got in I called Michael saying that there were things that we needed to talk about.

'After the exhibition,' he said. 'You just concentrate on getting through that.'

And that's what I decided to do, sort the whole mess out as soon as the opening night was over. It was a relief to have actually decided on something.

My dad woke me up the next morning with his shouting.

'Nina, it's seven o'clock, you will be the late.'

'Don't have to go in today until later,' I screamed back. 'What?'

I put on my dressing gown and went downstairs.

'Don't have to go in until later. We have an important exhibition on today – you know, for that Japanese man – so they've given me the morning off because I have to work in the evening.'

'We haven't seen you for days, beta, everything all right?' my mum asked.

'Fine,' I replied, thinking about the kiss, what I'd say to them, what I'd say to Raj.

'We've got new neighbours,' my dad interrupted.

'Really?' I tried sounding enthusiastic.

'Yah, look,' he pulled up the net curtains and pointed to my van.

Oh God, how was I going to explain the van? 'That's mine, Dad.'

He stared at me, completely baffled.

'As I said, we have this really important exhibition on and last night I helped transport the artists' paintings.'

'This is not making the sense to me. You still a lawyer, no? Why you taking pictures in dirty van? Artist is so poor he not got anyone to do this job. How can he afford you?'

It was the perfect opportunity to come clean with everything but it was the day of the exhibition and one more day wouldn't make a difference.

'It's a favour. I went out of my way to help.'

'It's a woman, no?' my mum asked hastily.

'Foruki, now does that sound like a woman to you?'

'Foruki,' she paused for thought. 'Yes, a woman,' she replied.

'And you still have your job? And everything is good?' my dad added.

My stomach felt as though it was tied in knots. 'What

would I be driving around in a van for if I didn't have a job, Dad?'

'Everybody want the favours today, nobody want to pay. I say no when they ask me to repair the television for nothing. This is what I say. Don't drive in dirty van, Nina. You're a lawyer, what will peoples say if they see you?'

Later I called Gina to tell her what had happened with Michael.

'I'm just amazed how you waited that long – he's gorgeous! Have you told Raj and your parents?'

'No, not yet. I'm going to leave it all until after the exhibition; then I'll deal with it.'

'Yes, you need to focus, put it to the back of your mind.'

'How?'

'Think of the consequences if you don't.'

But Raj and his mother were coming that evening. They'd see Michael – surely they'd sense that there was something between us. It wasn't right, Raj needed to be told properly. I called him up in a vain attempt to dissuade them both from coming to the exhibition.

'No, baby, I mean Nina, it's no problem.'

'It's full of boring types and I know it's not going to be Mummy's thing.'

'No, baby, she's really looking forward to it. So am I, I want to see this Foruki chap.'

'He won't be there, he rarely turns up at his exhibitions.'

'Well, we want to come to support you but you won't even notice that we are there. We'll act like we don't know you like I promised.'

'Raj, there's something else you need to know. Can we make time tomorrow evening?'

'What is it, baby?'

'It's best if we sit down and talk about it tomorrow.'

I went to the office to sort out all the last-minute enquiries. Raj weighed heavily on my conscience. None of it was intended, I never set out to hurt him or his family. Yes, his mother was controlling and domineering but she didn't deserve this. What about the wedding guests? I thought about Michael and the kiss and then about how to tell my mum and dad. They had already had their hearts broken with Jana. How could I do it to them again? How would they hold their heads up in the community? What would I say? Where would I begin? Was it worth giving everything up on the basis of one kiss. Focus, Nina, try to focus. Tonight is not about you; Michael has his reputation, Mangetti will be there, you have to pull it off otherwise it's all for nothing. One more day and then all the lying stops. Michael left several messages on my phone but I couldn't speak to him. He didn't even know about Raj. I had misled him, misled them both. It was a mess and although I tried I couldn't put it to the back of my mind.

In painting I always found a sense of peace, but that day there was none. Both worlds were no longer separate and I couldn't keep up the pretence. I went to see Mrs Onoro in desperation.

'Mrs Onoro, it's me, Nina,' I shouted through her letterbox.

She came to the door. 'Bell no working, I tell Rooney to fix it but he too busy. Maybe he find girlfriend. You think he find girlfriend?'

The association of Rooney not fixing the bell and finding a girlfriend threw me and I wondered why I was standing there when there were so many things to be getting on with.

'What time is it?' Mrs Onoro asked.

'Four o'clock.'

'I make us some tea.'

She came back with a tray. 'What can I do my dear?'

'I needed some advice.'

She smiled proudly as if I had come to the right place. 'I know keep many secret.'

'Mrs Onoro, I've told so many lies, and I've made a big mess.'

'Big mess, like when pig give birth, or big mess like . . .' She struggled to find a comparison.

'Yes, a big mess, like a really big mess.'

'To get out of big mess you stand in the centre and you accept it,' she said as if she had received wisdom from a fortune cookie.

'What if I just put it all off for a day?'

'It no matter. Big mess is big mess, today or tomorrow. Important thing to accept it.'

'Thank you, Mrs Onoro, thank you.'

'You no drink tea again?'

'I'll come back. I promise I will. It's just that there is somewhere I have to be.'

'Always running somewhere. That why big mess come. Better to stop.'

'I'll stay next time. I will.'

She was right, it didn't matter if it was today or tomorrow, the most important thing was to accept it. I went home to get ready for the exhibition.

My mum was in the sitting room waiting to talk to me when I arrived.

'Can't stop now, Ma, I'm running really late and the guests will be arriving soon,' I said, running upstairs.

After coming out of the bath I couldn't find the hairdryer. It had been by the mirror five minutes ago.

'Ma, have you seen the hairdryer?'

'What?'

'The hairdryer, have you seen it?'

'I'm not allowed to come, then?' she asked.

'Come where?'

'To see the Japan man?'

I imagined her standing in the centre of the gallery, waiting like she did at Heathrow airport, clutching onto her possessions and obstructing the guests, and a sense of panic filled me. 'But *Astitva Ek Prem Kahani* is on. You never miss that for anyone, and anyway it's a work function and full of boring people.'

'Raj's mother is going there. You are saying now she is better than me?'

'Raj's mother is only going there because she invited herself. Didn't she, Dad?'

'No big thing, Kavitha, soon she'll be part of their family anyway,' he shouted up.

'Ma, I promise you, I'll make it up to you if I can, I'll make it all up to you.'

'You have a surprise for me for the wedding?' This is what happened, this is how the whole mess started in the first place. I would say one thing and she would interpret it the way she wanted to. 'I knew it. I knew there was something going on. It's a very big surprise?'

'It's not what you think and I want you to know that whatever happens, I love you and Dad very, very much.'

She wasn't listening and went into her bedroom, opened one of the drawers and pulled out the hairdryer.

'Thank you, beta, thank you, I know you will never let me off.'

231

'Down, Ma, down.'

'Yah, I'm going.'

'No, the word's down, and anyway, about the surprise, it's not what you . . .'

She was halfway down the stairs, telling my dad about the forthcoming surprise.

Forget about letting her down, I was going to leave her in the recess of a quagmire she would never find her way out of – and my dad, what would I do to him?

'Good a the luck, Nina,' he said as I was leaving.

'What, Dad?'

'Good a the luck. We know you been working very hard for this Japan man.'

Guilt, angst and nerves all knotted in my stomach ready for one volcanic explosion, but all I had to do was to get through the evening.

I got to the gallery at six-thirty. Michael was there with Emanuel, organising the waiters.

'Ms Savani, all set?' Emanuel asked.

'Yes. Thank you.'

'Nina, there are a few things that I need to check with you. Would you mind coming into my office for a moment?'

'Sorry about not answering any of your messages,' I said once the door shut behind us.

'I figured you would be running about today. Come here, Nina.'

'No, Michael, we have to talk.'

'I know but let's leave it till later. I just wanted to give you this and to wish you the very best for tonight,' he said, handing me a box.

It was a paintbrush with my name engraved on it. 'For when you decide not to hide behind someone else.'

232

Forget about hiding behind someone else, I just wanted to go and bury myself somewhere. 'Thank you.'

'Keep your nerve and you will be fine,' he said, holding my hand.

Despite the soft music, the sound of wind chimes and running water, all I could hear was the thudding noise my heart made as we went back to the gallery. I had a sinking feeling in the pit of my stomach.

'Which papers did you say were coming?' Emanuel asked.

'They haven't all confirmed but we are expecting quite a few,' I replied, trying to sound confident, as if I had it all under control.

Bonsai tree/wardrobe man's agent was the first to arrive, followed by Gina and a group of people.

'They're mostly art students and are just gonna go around hyping. Nina, I can't stay for long as my shift begins soon but come around tomorrow when you've done the deed.'

I nodded, almost detached from everyone and everything, pretending it was happening to someone else.

Between seven-thirty and eight a steady stream of people came. They were regulars on the circuit who went from exhibition to exhibition, strutting in a panoply of colour as if they were trying to outdo the paint on the canvas. Most of them didn't come to see the paintings and made it obvious by wearing ridiculous tinted glasses that they couldn't possibly see out of. They were there to see who came into the room and who was watching them. You could tell them any old rubbish as long as you dropped a few important names in. A bit like my dad in this sense they had very selective hearing, but theirs was sometimes made worse because of the substances they had snorted.

A few 'darlings' and air kisses blew across the room; some went around appearing to study the pictures as if

233

they warranted a huge amount of intellectual thought and then added their pretentious comments. Others were fascinated by the fact that Foruki hadn't turned up to his own exhibition; I could hear all kinds of speculation as to who he was and what his concepts were.

'Emperor's descendant . . .'

'Prince . . .'

'One of the Mykoto sons . . .'

'That's his agent over there . . .'

I circulated among them all, people that I knew, people that I didn't, and told them whatever I thought they might like to hear about the artist. The professor from the radio show was in one corner of the room studying the footprint. A few journalists came, asked questions, drank more wine, and photographers took pictures. Emanuel greeted the guests he had invited. Michael circulated, talking to people and occasionally glancing at me as if to say everything was going well.

Drink flowed, the waiters took the food around and the sound of the river and chimes were drowned out as the room became more and more crowded. There were several influential people from the art world present, but no Mangetti. My boss, Simon, was there.

'Good turn out, Nina. Tell me again where you came across this chap?'

'Last year in Japan.' I told him what I had told everyone.

'I can't recollect you going to Japan.' He wouldn't as I never took holidays, just worked. 'OK,' I wanted to say, 'OK, it's all made up. There, I've never been to Japan.' But then I spotted Raj and his mother coming in.

'Excuse me, Simon, I've just seen some people that I have to say hello to.'

'I'm sorry, baby, we're a bit late. Mummy had to get something done.'

'Remember – Nina, not baby,' I added quickly.

234

'My fingers,' Raj's mum said, swishing her nails in front of me. 'It took a long time to stick on the jewels.' She pointed to some tacky sparkly bits. 'But I'll know now for the wedding time to leave at least two hours.'

'Where's your ring?' Raj asked, looking at my fingers.

'Some people here don't know I'm getting married. Remember what we talked about before?'

'You won't even know that we are here.'

And then I heard a familiar voice. I glanced up and wanted to curl up in a heap on the floor. 'What are you doing here, Jean?'

'I wanted to wish you luck.'

Raj's mother lingered as if she needed an introduction.

'Raj, if you want to take Mummy around to have a look at the pictures.'

'And this handsome man is . . . ?' she asked.

'This is Jean, a friend of mine.'

'So nice to finally meet a friend of Nina's,' Raj said, extending his hand. 'Raj Mehta.'

'Jean Michel Duval. When's the big day?' Jean asked.

Raj looked at me, surprised; nobody there was supposed to know that I'd let my fiancé come along to the launch. Why had Jean done that? Maybe now Raj would let his guard down and tell people we were getting married.

'Please don't do this to me,' I thought. 'Please just go away, all of you.'

'Next month,' Raj replied.

'Mummy, Raj, there's someone I would really like you to meet,' I said spotting Gina.

'Gina, this is Raj and his mother. Gina works for Ravi Shankar.'

'I do?' She glared at me. 'Yes, I do. Nice guy.'

She led them off to another part of the room. Raj's mother went reluctantly.

'Nina, I know you don't love him. You were with . . .'

'You don't have the right to tell me anything and if you'll excuse me, I have guests to see to.'

I wasn't enjoying any of it, trying to keep people apart so they wouldn't say the wrong thing, keeping an eye out for how much Raj and his mother were drinking so they wouldn't let anything slip, trying not to say the wrong things myself, waiting anxiously for Mangetti. It all felt like one long nightmare.

Michael was safely at one end of the room and I could hear Raj's voice booming at the other.

'See, Mummy, he probably had some Asian influence here. Maybe spent some time there . . .'

Gina came over to me saying she had to leave, her shift was about to begin.

'Definitely doing the right thing,' she said, nodding towards Raj's mother.

'I just want all this to be over.'

'It will be, soon,' she replied.

It was half past eight, Mangetti still hadn't arrived and I kept glancing over to the entrance. Michael walked over to me as if to reassure me. He put one hand on my shoulder.

Raj was looking at me and was coming over. 'God, please don't let this be happening,' I thought. My head began doing the jerking thing.

'Nina, what's wrong?' Michael asked.

'Baby, Gina doesn't work for Ravi Shankar really, does she? She said he's doing some interesting work with sculpture at the moment.'

'She does. Ravi's diversifying into other areas.'

'But baby,' he said again.

The room fell silent. All I could hear was the word 'baby', amplified and resounding around the room.

'Gay,' I turned and whispered to Michael. 'Arty type.'

But then Raj squeezed my hand. He had promised: no physical contact, no hand-squeezing, no terms of endearment – not while I was working – but no, there for all to see, he gripped it tightly.

Michael stared at Raj.

'Raj, this is Michael. Michael, this is Raj.'

'Her fiancé,' Raj said, holding out his hand.

Now two words reverberated around the room: 'baby' and 'fiancé'.

'Right,' Michael managed.

Then there was a pause that I wanted to be swallowed by. Michael looked at me with incomprehension and then his face hardened. 'I've come to check how it's all going and if you needed anything but I can see that you have everything under control so I'll leave you to it.' He turned and left.

'Very nice of him,' Raj commented and began prattling about something else.

Just as I was about to stop him, Raj's mother staggered over. 'Ravi Shankar is exhibiting next month, Gina said she'll send me an invite. Raju, you'll take me home now. Nina, wonderful evening.'

'Thank you. Raj, don't come back for me. I'll get a cab,' I said, thinking that I had to find Michael.

'No, baby, I'll drop Mummy – she's only staying at the flat in Victoria – and then I'll come back for you.'

'There's no need, really. I'll be seeing you tomorrow.'

As they were getting their coats, I ran downstairs. I caught a glimpse of Michael leaving, called out his name and then ran after him when he didn't turn around.

'Michael, I can explain. It's not how it seems.'

He turned and looked at me. 'Leave it.'

'No, you have to let me explain.'

He continued walking and ignored me.

Distraught, I went back up to the gallery. Mangetti

hadn't yet arrived. Where was he? Maybe he was stuck in traffic. He couldn't not come; not after this. The guests were leaving.

'I'm always here for you,' Jean said as he was about to leave.

The irony wanted to make me shout at him: at that moment in time, standing there in front of me, he was the only one who was there – but where had he been when I needed him?

He waited for a comment.

'Bye Jean,' I whispered as he turned his back.

Half an hour later they had all gone. The room was empty with only the mess of dirty plates, empty glasses, beer bottles and scrawled up napkins. I sat in a corner looking at the buddha and I cried. All of it for nothing: the planning, the scheming, the lies, all for nothing. It had been a crazy idea, what was I thinking of? How naïve to believe that Michael and Raj wouldn't meet each other and to think that Mangetti would actually show up. How stupid to think that the mess I had created wouldn't unravel before me.

'Oh Ki, it's a mess, a big, big mess.'

I could hear footsteps coming up the stairs. I wiped my tears.

'Michael?'

It was Raj.

'What's wrong, baby?'

'It was for nothing, all for nothing.'

'It was a success, lots of people came. OK, Foruki wasn't here but you said you didn't expect him.'

'No, it's all been for nothing. Creativity takes courage, remember, you told me that and that's all I did. I took a leap of faith, seeing flowers when there were none, that's all I did.'

He seemed confused.

'Creativity takes courage. Henri Mattise. That's who you quoted the very first time we met.'

'Did I?'

'Yes you did. You said it the first time we met, remember?'

'Oh yes, got that from a book I was reading on developing confidence. It said that . . .'

'But it was the sign, my sign, you and me,' I cried.

He looked like he had absolutely no idea as to what I was talking about.

'What about hands?'

'What hands? What are you talking about, Nina?'

'You said that hands meant a lot to you. What do mine tell you? What does that picture on the wall tell you? Or did you just pluck that out of the air as well?'

'Nina, maybe you've had a bit too much to drink. We'll talk about this later, when you're a bit more rational.'

'I'll never be rational. I'll never be who you want me to be, you don't even know who I am. This, all this, is me. ME.'

'Nina, let's just get you home.'

'I can't marry you.'

He stood still. 'What?'

'I can't,' I cried. 'I can't. I tried, I really did, but I can't.'

'It's been a long day, you're tired, Nina, you're not making any sense.'

'I can't go through with it. It's not you, it's me.'

'Nina, be practical. The wedding is next month.'

I sobbed.

'What about Mummy, the preparations? Listen, baby, it's nerves. We all have them.'

'I'm so sorry, Raj.'

'You can't do this to me,' he shouted.

'I'm sorry, really very sorry.'
He had his head in his hands.

I walked around Green Park in the dark; no Michael, no Raj, no Mangetti, nothing. All of it had been for nothing. I had left Raj feeling as worthless as I once had. We couldn't subconsciously instigate scenarios and bring them into our lives. I wouldn't have wished this on my worst enemy.

It was eleven o'clock when I arrived at Gina's house. She wasn't in. Michael wasn't picking up his phone; I had left countless messages. With nowhere else to go I made my way back home. What was I going to tell my parents? How was I going to break it to them? All their expectations detonated in one night.

They were sleeping when I got in. There was food left for me in the oven: three circular rotis with peas and potatoes. Both my parents were snoring peacefully so Raj's mother had obviously not called them. It could wait until morning; things always seemed worse at night.

I crawled into bed too tired to cry any more, too tired to reflect but unable to sleep.

In the morning, things seemed no better. My parents stirred at about five-thirty. That was the time my mother got up to do her prayers. Before she got started, my dad sent her downstairs to make some tea and when she brought it back up I thought it was probably best that I did it then.

My hands were shaking, my throat was dry.

'Beta, you're up already,' my mum called out on hearing my footsteps. 'Did you eat anything last night?'

I went into their room and sat on the bed.

'Ma, Dad, I have something I want to tell you.'

'What is it, beta?' my mother asked.

'There really is no easy way to do this and I want you to know that I tried, I tried my best to make you happy but . . .'

Mum put her hand to her heart.

Dad put his teacup down. 'You've given up work, I knew it,' he interrupted. 'Please tell me it's not this, you could have waited until you were married. What if Raj's family finds out, then what?' he shouted.

'It's not that.'

'Thank Bhagavan . . .'

'It's . . .'

'Oh Bhagavan, don't tell me she's not going to pay for the wedding. She was the one who . . .'

'I'm not getting married,' I blurted.

There was a gasp from my mother.

'April the fool in March,' my father laughed.

'No Dad, I've told Raj that I can't marry him.'

'Hare Ram,' my mother wailed, clasping both hands to her heart.

'What do you mean?' my father screamed. 'Only two weeks left, you have to. The guests, the Hilton, all organised.'

'I'm really sorry, I can't do it.'

'No choice. I felt the same when I saw your mother but there is no choice and look how happy we are now.' He grabbed her.

'I can't, I know I can't.'

My mother began blubbering.

'Kavitha, tell her she won't find a good boy coming from a good family like that anywhere. Tell her, nobody takes girls who can't cook and she's getting old now. Tell her, make her understand nobody will want to look after her.'

241

My mother was unable to speak.

'I'm not going through with it.'

'Why?' he shouted.

'Because I don't love him.'

'It's not about the love, it's about duty.'

'Then I can't do my duty.'

'Please, beta, please think, think what you are doing to us,' my mother sobbed.

'Everything I did I tried to do for you, but I've realised it will never be enough – and you know why, because what you want for me is not what I want. I'm sorry, I never meant to hurt you, never meant to hurt anyone, but I can't pretend any more.'

'Pretend? Nobody is asking you to pretend, just to marry him,' my dad yelled.

'Every day I pretend. I paint. Do you know that about me? Every day I get up, put on a suit and go to paint?'

'Paint? And the love?'

'There is no law, there hasn't been for the last three months.'

'The van,' he shouted. 'I knew this. Dickheads struggling and you telling me this? It's the Jeannie who has put the thoughts into your head.'

'Nobody has. Did you hear me, Dad? I paint, I've given up work so I can paint and when I am painting it's the only time I'm me. I don't have to be anyone else but me.'

'No, no, no,' my mother cried.

'And I might as well tell you all of it. There's someone else.'

At this stage my mum passed out.

'Jeannie,' my dad raged.

'His name is Michael.'

'Leave, leave my house,' my father screamed. 'Take your dirty van and go to wherever your sister has gone.'

I went to pack my things together and they didn't even

try to stop me. My father told my mother to let me go, that I was an even greater disappointment to him than my sister. The problem, he said, was that he had loved us too much and given us too much freedom. Maybe he didn't love us enough. If he did, he could have let us be ourselves.

Maybe loving us didn't even enter into the equation. It was all about keeping us clothed and fed and doing his best to do his duty and this was, for him, loving us. Seeing me married off was being a good father. No matter how much I argued that it was important to be happy, he wouldn't understand. Happiness was a luxury, an expectation, you weren't supposed to be happy, you were supposed to get on with it and try to make the best of every situation.

'See, Nina, you talks always about the feelings, if you talks about the feelings who will pay the bills. One day you can be happy, one day you can be sad, the feelings they comes and goes but the routine this never changes.'

That is what they clung to and by doing what they wanted me to do and what was always done I would have made them proud, but by being me . . . the only way they could handle that was by telling me to go. I understood at that moment what my sister must have felt – a complete and utter disappointment to them.

Maybe that's what happens when you are forced to move continents and come to a foreign place; you become incredibly practical and don't get attached to anything again, not even your children.

I drove to Gina's house and rang the bell. It was seven o'clock in the morning. Nobody answered so I kept on ringing.

'Go away, there's nobody in,' she shouted from her window.

'Gina, it's me. Will you let me in?'

'Bloody hell, Nina. What time is it?' She opened the door, half-asleep. 'Jesus, what's happened?'

'I've told my parents everything and they've thrown me out. Can't find Michael anywhere, Mangetti didn't show and I've crushed Raj . . .'

'Slow down, slow down. Come in.' She took my bags and led me to the kitchen.

'Your mum and dad have thrown you out and you've left that pretentious guy?'

'How am I going to manage? And Michael, he knows about Raj and he didn't give me a chance to explain. It's all gone wrong. I've hurt people, I've got no money, no job, no family, nowhere to go,' I put my head in my hands and sobbed. 'It was all just one crazy idea . . . mad . . . mad.'

'Don't worry, sweetheart, I know it's not much but you've got me. If you don't mind sleeping on the sofa you can stay here until you get yourself sorted. Let's make you something to eat and you can tell me properly.'

'I can't eat. You know he just told me to go. They both did, and when I went to speak to them they just closed the door and asked for my keys back. My mum was crying hysterically. What have I done to them? All for what? For nothing.'

'They'll come round, you'll see. The first thing you gotta do is have a good sleep, you can't think straight like this. Then have a shower, get dressed, and go find Michael.'

She made up the sofa, made me some tea, and sat down and listened to me ramble until I exhausted myself and fell asleep.

It was five o'clock in the afternoon when I resurfaced. My dad would be arriving home from work, my mum would be in the kitchen making rotis. Sleep didn't make things feel any better. I got ready and made my way to Artusion. Michael wasn't there. Emanuel Hikatari came down from his office to thank me for the successful coverage Foruki had received. I enquired after Michael but he told me that Michael had already left for New York.

No, he couldn't have gone, not without giving me an opportunity to explain, not like that.

'But I need to speak to him, about the exhibition,' I added, trying not to sound desperate.

'The gallery manager, who I believe you met yesterday, will be taking over the day-to-day running; so if he can be of help?'

'It was really Michael I needed to speak to.'

Emanuel gave me the numbers for Artusion in New York and said that he would tell Michael that I needed to speak to him.

As I stepped out of Artusion my phone rang.

'Michael?'

'No.' It was Raj's mother. 'It's true, you don't want my son?' She was incredibly calm considering she had six hundred and fifty guests and no wedding.

'I'm so sorry, Auntie, I never meant for any of this to happen.'

'Tell me, why?'

I wanted to be as honest as I could with her. 'I don't love him.'

'When does love come into it? Just marry him; these things will come later.'

'I didn't mean for this to happen.'

'Then how else has it happened? You can change it.'

'I'm sorry.'

'There is nothing I can say to make you change your mind?'

'No.'

She turned on me. 'I knew from the first time I set eyes on you that you were cheap. Look what kind of family you come from. One could hardly expect better.'

'It's got nothing to do with Mum and Dad. Don't take this out on them.'

'They raised you,' she shouted. 'What can one expect these people to raise? You cheating housie.' It was inappropriate to tell her that the word she was looking for was hussy so I let her vent.

'Who is this Michael? You're leaving my son for him? Don't think I won't make you and your family suffer for this.'

And then the words flew out: 'Maybe if you didn't spend half your life trying to control your son's life he would be happier, and maybe, just maybe, the others wouldn't have left.'

'What?' she screamed. 'I'll make sure you won't be able to set foot anywhere without people knowing how cheap you are, and I promise you, I will make you pay for this.'

I cut her off. It was probably the wrong thing to do but when was I ever good at doing anything right?

Gina wasn't home when I got back. I called home. My dad picked it up and as soon as I spoke he put the phone down. I called once more and he did the same. I waited by the phone for a few hours and tried again. My mother answered and I could hear my dad shouting in the background, 'If that is the unemployed fooler, tell her if she says there has been some mistake and that she will marry Raj she can come back.'

'You'll marry him?'

'No, Ma, but listen to me, please.'

She hung up.

I left a message for Michael. 'Michael, it's me. I never thought it was possible to fall in love with someone just like that. There, I've said it. I'm not marrying Raj. I had my reasons. Can I explain? Please, just pick up your phone and hear me out.'

He didn't call back.

It was dark; I went to the studio and stared at the blank canvas. The only thing that reflected back at me was emptiness and the bits that hurt. Taking out the blue and black paint, I mixed them together in a tin pot and then dipped my hand in it. An explosion of bluish black paint was thrown on the canvas and I swirled it around with my fingertips. Nobody cared if I returned home with dirty fingernails, nobody cared if I had paint smeared across my face or in my hair. After I'd finished I sat desperately trying to find some light in the painting but there wasn't any. No spaces between the movement that I could paint white. I stared hard.

'I know you're still there, Ki. I haven't come this far to believe you not to be but I've made such a mess of things. A really big, awful mess. I should have told him, I know I should have, but I never found the right time. I didn't even want to begin to think it was love because that kind of love hurts. It's safer not to really love someone, Ki, because they go, don't they?

'And Mum and Dad, I held on to them because I didn't want them not to love me any more, so I tried, I really did. I don't know what to do now.'

I lay curled up on the floor, crying. Paint was sprawled everywhere, across my face, hair and clothes. I must have fallen asleep there because I was woken by the studio door being pulled open.

'Hell, Nina, it's not that bad. It isn't, look, look what

they've written about you.' Gina crouched down beside me and read from the paper she was holding.

'"The enigma of Foruki. Foruki manages to capture the sense of obscurity to light on so many different levels as to be beyond simple explanation." Another one here, look. "This is a collection that must be seen to appreciate the conceptual diversity and the bold use of colour . . . "

'Nina, are you listening? What do you think?'

'I don't care any more.'

'I know, but Imogene Bailey has also given the exhibition a brilliant review. She doesn't write anything good about anyone, so it doesn't matter if Mangetti didn't turn up; all these paintings are going to sell.'

'It doesn't matter any more. Just lies; all of it.'

'You can't give up, not now. Come on, Nina.'

'What am I supposed to do? Michael's gone. He's not coming back. I have no family, no home, and a whole load of pictures done by someone who doesn't even exist.'

'Keep believing, maybe? Believe that it will all work out? That's what you say, isn't it?'

'I can't see the light between the spaces,' I cried. 'The only place I have been able to see it is on the canvas. Even when it hasn't been there.'

'We'll paint some, look,' she said, picking up the white tube. 'Let's pretend it's there and paint. Come on, Nina, get up and start again. We can do this.'

She oozed the entire tube of white into a tin and mixed it with water and dipped her hand in, and then held it out to me so she could help me up. The paint dripped from our hands onto the floor.

'You ready?' she asked.

Together, we pressed our palms onto the canvas and covered every part of it with our white prints, and after we had finished Gina washed my hands for me with soap and water.

248

'Tomorrow we'll paint flowers there. Come on, Nina, let's get you home.'

It had been incredibly hard going back to school after my accident: everything hurt, my sister had gone, she didn't drop me off or pick me up any more, there was no one or nothing to be proud of. The other children at school, perhaps sensing my self-pity, stayed away and didn't play with me. I watched from the sidelines feeling inadequate and alienated, completely unaware that someone was watching. Ki took me from the sidelines to the centre of every game, she saw something in me that was baffling even to myself. That is what Gina did too; she made me want to leave all the questions behind and start all over again, even though every part of me hurt.

The following day, like children, we went into the studio together. There wasn't really space for the both of us but Gina made it feel like ten people could fit in. We painted what we wanted to see and not what was there – huge, colourful flowers absorbing sunny optimistic colours, eliminating any signs of shadows.

Despite the fact that I had virtually no money left and was supposed to hand the studio back to Gina, she said I could share it with her for as long as I needed to. After we painted, she went to the flat and I went for a long walk in Green Park to try and sort out my thoughts. This had begun because all I ever wanted to do was paint, and that was what I decided I was going to continue to do. I would work part-time like Gina did. If even a few paintings sold from Foruki's exhibition, I would have enough money to rent my own studio and flat. I sat on the bench making plans. For the first time I could see myself being my own person, completely self-sufficient.

The phone rang while I was sitting writing notes on

the bench. There was a fuzzy background noise. It sounded long-distance.

'Michael, is that you?'

'Tastudi Mangetti here.'

'Oh, hello,' I replied disappointed. It was ironic; if he had called me a week ago I would have been jumping up and down, but now, impressing him was the thing that mattered to me least.

'Nina? Nina Savani?'

'Yes it's me. How can I help you?'

'I saw Foruki's work. I prefer to see work in the starkness of an empty room. That is when you see if it holds its own. What can I say? Interesting? Original? The use of colour is impressive.'

'Right.' When had he gone to see it? He wasn't there at the exhibition.

His tone suggested that he expected me to be more enthusiastic. 'Right?' he repeated.

'I mean, yes, I know – so how can I help you?' I asked, trying to focus.

'Foruki is good, very good. That was you I heard on the radio, wasn't it? I agreed with what you said about art now being more about the artist and moving even further away from the subject matter.'

'You did?'

'Yes. This is what I like about Foruki's work, his focus on the subject matter. I was told he didn't even turn up to the opening.'

'That's right, he didn't. He's media shy.'

'There is something that I would like to discuss with him and it is of a delicate nature. When can we set up a meeting?'

What did he want to talk to him about? Did he want to buy a painting? If he did I could rent my own studio but I couldn't produce Foruki, no more lying. 'Could you

250

give me an indication as to what it is about?' I asked calmly.

'The Turner Prize. I want him to be entered in for it but I'd like to discuss a few things with him first.'

I nearly fell off the bench. The Turner Prize? He was having a joke. Foruki and the bloody Turner Prize? Hold it together, Nina, say it's not possible – you can't pull that off, you're not lying any more. 'Mr Mangetti, I have to let you know now it may not be possible to convince him to meet with you.' I didn't want to lie, even if he was handing me the crown jewels on a plate.

'I'm sure you're skilful enough to persuade anyone, Ms Savani, and it would be to our mutual benefit. One more thing, why are all those paintings earmarked? You said you would give me first option. Are you saying that those paintings have been sold and that the buddha is still not for sale? Surely you can persuade Foruki to sell it to me?'

I felt overwhelmed. He could buy all the paintings if he wanted but not the buddha.

'That particular one is not for sale.'

'Surely you of all people could manage something? Persuade him to meet with me and I will make sure it is worth your while.'

I needed to end the conversation, I needed time to assimilate what he was saying.

'Mr Mangetti, I will call you back once I have had an opportunity to speak to Foruki.'

'I look forward to hearing back from you soon,' he replied.

What was going on? It was complete madness, Foruki being entered for the Turner Prize. No, I couldn't go that far; it was ridiculous. That wasn't supposed to happen. Mangetti hadn't even turned up to the opening night.

How could he want Foruki to be entered for the Turner? It wasn't making sense.

I thought about it on the way to Gina's house. If he was being serious I just didn't have the strength to pretend any more. He would have to take me as I was.

Gina was back at the flat, about to leave for work.

'Did you sort out the stuff in your head?' she asked.

'Sort of . . .'

'And?'

'And then Tastudi Mangetti called,' I replied.

'What did he want? Did he apologise for not turning up?'

'He wants Foruki to enter the Turner Prize.'

She spat out the cornflakes she was eating. 'Bloody hell! No! What? And what did you say?'

'I said I'd call him back.'

'Why the bloody hell did you say that?'

'Because I don't think I can lie any more. It was never meant to go this far. People get hurt. What if someone finds out Michael helped me? I can't do that to him.'

'No one is going to find out – if it ever comes out, Michael can deny it. Nina, you can't let this go. It's the bloody Turner. You've got to keep going and then when it's all over you can come clean. Think about it . . . Foruki going in for the Turner.'

'I'm not sure.'

'What's there to be sure about? Just go for it. Play them at their own game. Most of them are just full of crap anyway. When I went to the opening of Hutton's new exhibition you know what he did? He made a sculpture with cigarette butts and a few empty cartons and some idiot bought it for two thousand pounds. What kind of madness is that? Your paintings are original, Nina, it's the artist who's a fake. I've got to go to work now but please tell me that you'll think about it.'

252

'It's all I've been doing.'

'So think about it some more.'

It was like Ki making me take centre stage. At first I thought she didn't understand, I didn't want to be humiliated any further, but she just wanted to make me stronger.

After Gina left I called my mum and dad.

'Have you changed your mind?'

'No, Dad, but . . .'

'The fooler.' He hung up.

I then left one last message for Michael.

'Michael, Mangetti wants Foruki to go in for the Turner. I don't know what to do. What if someone finds out that you knew all along. Will you call me? Can we talk?'

An hour later Michael's secretary called back saying he would have no reservations with Mr Foruki entering the Turner Prize and wished him the very best with his career. That was it, nothing more.

I went to see Mrs Onoro.

'Oh Mrs Onoro,' I said hugging her, 'I don't know where to start. I've left my fiancé, my family won't speak to me and my friend Michael has gone.'

'I make you tea and you tell me properly.'

She made us some tea and I told her everything and then I asked her if she had ever pretended.

'I pretended for long time I happy when I not – at least you no have to pretend. You be yourself. Lots of people they not self because they pretend they happy when they not.'

'What about truth?'

'Hikito say you find own truth. Nobody tell you what right or what wrong. You find your own way, you do what you think is right.'

I asked if I could speak to her son, thinking that at

that moment what was right was to finish what I had started and to see it through to the end with conviction.

'Ah,' she smiled. 'You want marry him?'

'No, no. Maybe he can help me with a job I'm doing?'

'Rooney supply fruit and veg everywhere. No job too small. You wait, he come home soon.'

We talked about her childhood in Japan, how she came to England, what she wished for Rooney, and together we waited for him. Two hours later he came home. In that time I had managed to convince myself that asking him to stand in as Foruki made perfect sense.

'What's for . . . ?' He stopped when he saw me, he probably thought I was stalking his mother so I could get to him.

'Rooney, Nina wait for you.'

He looked at me suspiciously and said something in Japanese to his mother.

'No, she want big order for vegetables,' Mrs Onoro replied in English.

'It's not exactly vegetables I wanted to ask you about.'

Mrs Onoro showed no sign of leaving us alone so I could talk to him privately about being Foruki.

'Mrs Onoro, could I have some more tea please?' I asked, thinking she'd go off and make a fresh pot.

'I pour for you.' She poured the cold tea into my cup, sat comfortably back in her chair and waited for me to begin.

'Well, well the thing is I'm a painter, well, I was a lawyer before that and I sort of fell into painting. When I finished a piece, I dedicated it to my best friend Ki who died. It was because of her I started to paint again.'

Mrs Onoro nodded vehemently.

'These paintings were spotted by a very influential man and he confused the inscription with the name of a Japanese painter.'

'I no understand,' she said.

'Well, he thought that "FOR U KI" was a Japanese man and because he was so important I didn't tell him that it was me.'

'Ohhhh,' Mrs Onoro gasped. 'You lie?'

'Yes, and now he wants to enter the exhibition he thinks Foruki has done for an important prize so he wants to meet him. I don't know any Japanese men except you, Rooney.'

'Sorry, I don't want to get involved,' he said quickly. If he needed confirmation that I was a lunatic, this was it.

'I'll pay you. Ten per cent of whatever I get from the exhibition. Say if I make thirty thousand pounds that's . . .'

'Three thousand, Rooney, he do it,' Mrs Onoro said.

'You don't even have to say anything. Just talk in Japanese and a friend of mine will translate or I'll pretend to. You can think about it and tell me later if you want to do it.'

'So I don't have to paint? Just turn up, talk in Japanese and you're gonna pay me for doing that?'

'I'll pay you if he goes for it and the paintings sell. If they don't I'll pay you three hundred pounds. Either way, you don't really have to do anything.'

He took a moment to think about it and then he agreed.

'It so clever. Rooney he sell good,' Mrs Onoro added.

I called up Mangetti to tell him that we could meet him the following week. He wanted to meet at Brown's but I mentioned that Foruki would prefer it if we could meet somewhere more private. Mangetti suggested meeting at his friend's offices in Cork Street. That left five days for Rooney to be primed.

Gina arrived home late. I couldn't find a Japanese restaurant near where she lived so I bought us a Chinese takeaway and had it ready for her when she arrived home.

'Tell me you've been thinking about it?' she asked. 'It would be good to see one of us break the mould.'

'How much Japanese do you speak, Gina?'

'Enough to get me by? Why?'

'Me and you have got a lot of work to do if Rooney is going to stand any kind of chance with Mangetti.'

'That's more like it,' she replied.

'I've been thinking all evening about this and I don't know how exactly this is going to work, but maybe you could act as Foruki's translator so Rooney doesn't have to talk about art. The only way I could convince him was by telling him he didn't have to do a thing.'

'Let's get Foruki's profile right first, his background and his concepts, and then we'll deal with how we present it all to Mangetti.'

Gina and I sat up for most of the night, eating Chinese food and expanding on the profile I had given Foruki.

Foruki was a pseudonym for Ronald David Onoro. He was born in London in 1973 to a Japanese mother and a British father. His mother, Lydia Onoro, was a descendant of a Japanese Emperor who came from a very wealthy family and she was a painter. Gina suggested making her good friends with Yoko Ono but I said it was a bad idea in case Yoko was tracked down for a quote on their friendship.

'You think it will go as far as that?' she asked.

'I don't know, but when we are doing this we have to try and think of every eventuality.'

Foruki's father was Kenneth David, an archaeologist who had been sent on a project to Tokyo. Lydia and Kenneth met by chance on a bus, there was an immediate connection between them and they began talking (Lydia could speak some English). Just four weeks after their initial meeting, they married. I told Gina that it was a bit far-fetched that they married a month after meeting on a bus but she assured me that was what had happened to her parents.

The Onoro family were completely against the marriage and they asked Lydia to leave. So after Lydia married Kenneth they moved to London. A year later, Rooney was born. At this stage I wanted Kenneth to die so Lydia would be left penniless and alone with no alternative but to go back to Japan, but Gina suggested it was better if they were abandoned so there would be a whole range of emotions that Foruki could work with. I used my dad's example of what he envisaged happening to my Uncle Amit's daughter and Roy; and so their marriage disintegrated rapidly after the birth of their son, primarily due to cultural differences, and Kenneth met someone else. When Rooney was only two, Kenneth left them both. Penniless and with nowhere to turn, Lydia returned to Japan, thinking that her parents would soften on seeing their grandson. But when she arrived in her home town they refused to see her because she had brought disgrace on the family.

With no money, Lydia began selling fruit and vegetables and took her son to work on the streets with her. At night at home she would paint to escape her reality and if Rooney was awake he would enter her world of colour. There had to be this link to a fruit and veg stall just in case someone photographed him and came forward saying they'd seen Foruki down the market. We would do everything to keep him away from the press but there were no guarantees that they wouldn't track him down. If this ever happened, I could say that Foruki could do things that appeared completely eccentric like selling fruit and veg, but this was because before he started each painting he

257

needed to re-create the joy found in the formative years of his youth. It was absolute nonsense, but as my dad put it, 'Gives them the rambles, they likes it.'

We spent a long time debating whether to kill off Lydia but essentially she had to go. Gina said the colours Foruki painted with were so bold and daring, almost as if they had been let loose from a place of tremendous angst. Therefore, Foruki had to have lots of pain in his life and be unable to express his grief except on the canvas.

Lydia died when Foruki was fifteen and he was left to fend for himself. After working the whole day doing odd jobs he would transmute his feelings onto the canvas. Feelings of despair, loneliness and sadness all poured out and were given colour and life. They were hopeful pictures, he wanted to see something else other than the starkness of his reality.

His life changed dramatically after an encounter with a wealthy Japanese widow who was taken by him and his paintings. She introduced him to an influential circle, moved him into her home and paid him money just to paint for her. After years of being with her she betrayed him and left him for another artist. A period of substance abuse followed, a period where Foruki questioned his self worth, anything he could snort was up his nose. That was until he found himself in the gutter and decided that the only way was up.

Foruki had several opportunities to exhibit abroad but chose not to, that was until I came along and found his work in some back-street gallery. I asked him to come to London because all that exuded from the canvas was energy and potential.

'What were you doing in Japan?' Gina asked.

'I had been feeling disillusioned at work for a long time and always had a fascination with Japanese art and so I made a preliminary trip where I happened to stumble across him.'

'Sounds good,' Gina interjected.

It was hard to convince him because Foruki wasn't an artist who could be enticed by fame or money and there was a nonchalance to his character. He was eventually persuaded on the premise that he could explore his feelings towards one part of his heritage that he had previously denied: his Britishness. Gina suggested that maybe he came to London because he fancied me but this suggestion also had to go; it was better if his feelings towards me were ambiguous, he had to concentrate on his art.

'We've got a few problems,' Gina pointed out.

'And they are?'

'You said this Rooney bloke is Japanese; he's not half-English. Isn't that going to show?'

I thought for a moment. The Japanese thing; it only showed in his eyes as his skin was quite pale. 'We'll have him wearing sunglasses. They help him see light in a different way, he only takes them off when he's painting so the light appears even brighter and this is reflected in his work.'

'You're bloody mad, Nina.'

We had Foruki's profile and back-story down to every minuscule detail, even what kind of aftershave he would wear. The next few days I spent going to the library and taking out books on personal development. Raj had talked a lot about Neuro Linguistic Programming and the art of empathy but I hadn't really listened. He had called me twice in an attempt to persuade me to go back to him and both times I took the calls, trying my very best to explain to him my reasons for doing what I did. The last time his mother caught him in mid-conversation with me and I could hear her shouting at him to hang up 'on that cheating housie', which is what he did. There hadn't been any more calls since. In contrast, Jean Michel left several messages asking me not to go through with the wedding, that I was making a big mistake. I had already made the biggest mistake by not being honest with both Raj and Michael. There was still no news from Michael and I knew that at some stage soon I would have to give up hoping.

In two days I devoured books on NLP and learned about empathy and how you could appear to be on the same wavelength as someone. The way the books were written did not make it sound manipulative, which it patently was.

'This bit talks about the importance of body language. He's got to mimic Tastudi's gestures but so subtly that Tastudi doesn't notice a thing. This guy also talks a lot about eye contact but that's going to be difficult with the shades, but maybe if you're translating you should do the eye-contact thing with him,' I said, holding the book up. 'And also speaking in the same tone.'

'What time did you say we were going round there?' Gina asked.

'Around eight.'

I wanted to go and see Mum and Dad who didn't live too far from Mrs Onoro but it was too soon, I couldn't face the door being slammed shut in my face. And anyway, Gina was coming with me to Mrs Onoro's house to try and ascertain the extent of the work that needed to be done on Rooney.

'Come in, come in,' Mrs Onoro ushered us in.

Gina greeted her in Japanese and Mrs Onoro was mesmerised.

'Oh you pretty girl,' she said to Gina. 'And you speak Japanese.'

'Mrs Onoro, this is my friend Gina.'

'Pleased to meet you at last, Mrs Onoro. I've heard a lot about you.'

'And polite girl. You married?'

'No,' Gina replied.

'That's very good. You don't marry until you find right boy. You engaged?'

'No.'

'Rooney, Nina and her friend come to see you. Come down, put good shirt on.' She led us into the sitting room. 'I make you tea. Where you learn to speak Japanese?'

'In Japan,' Gina replied. 'I used to teach English there.'

'Rooney put best shirt on,' Mrs Onoro shouted up again as she went to make the tea.

Rooney came down in a black tracksuit. We only had four days left to transform him into a charismatic artist. 'This is my friend Gina,' I said introducing them.

When he went over to her to shake her hand I sensed that there was some raw material that we could work with; his eyes seemed to sparkle, his shoulders were pulled back so he appeared taller and confident.

'Tea here,' Mrs Onoro came in with her tray.

'Gina's going to do the translation and maybe find some clothes that are more appropriate.'

'I'm just kitting Foruki out, you know, the kinda clothes he would wear. So it would be good to know your sizes,' she added. 'And shoes, do you have any classy shoes? They are important,' Gina continued.

'Go bring down shoes,' his mother instructed.

'No,' he replied.

Mrs Onoro sat back in her chair as if he had said something deeply offensive.

'It's all right, I'll take a look later,' Gina replied.

I told him what we were planning to have him dressed in and how we were going to work on him. He objected.

261

Mrs Onoro looked at him as if he had wounded her.

'I'll think about it,' he replied.

Gina then read out Foruki's history.

'Kenneth bad man,' Mrs Onoro shouted, fully recovered. 'Good he dead. Why Foruki mother she have to die? She no good? How she die?'

'She was killed in a car crash, killed instantly so she didn't feel a thing. His mother was really nice, the best mother, but it was her time to go.'

'So sad,' Mrs Onoro replied.

'Anyway, that's his story. You have to imagine that I am Tastudi Mangetti and I'm going to ask you some questions. Say the first thing that comes into your head in Japanese and try to copy some of my gestures.'

'No bloody way,' he shouted.

'Just work with us, Rooney. See how it goes and if it's not working, leave it, but at least give it a go,' Gina said.

He seemed to respond to Gina better so I let her continue.

'Tell me what you want me to do again?' he asked.

'Answer Nina's questions by saying the first thing that comes to your head in Japanese, but when you answer try and copy her a bit. What she's doing with her hands or her head. The tone she's using. So if Nina talks softly, you answer softly. If she pauses when she's asking you a question, you pause in giving her an answer.'

'So, Foruki, how long have you been in England?'

He said something in Japanese, moved his head forward and copied me.

'That's good but maybe don't exaggerate the gesture as much. Just make it slight. Now at this point you have to wait until I translate whatever you've said into English.'

'How well do you speak Japanese?' he said.

'How well do you want me to speak it?' she flirted.

He glanced down, hoping nobody had spotted his

embarrassment, but we all had, especially Mrs Onoro who had hawk eyes. She sat back in her chair and smiled.

'We're going to be talking about art and paintings so it doesn't matter what you say, just how you say it and the body-language thing. Mangetti will just be watching you but listening to what I say and I'll talk about your – I mean Nina's – pictures so you don't have to worry about that. What you do have to do is look at me intensely and nod at me as if you agree with everything. OK, Nina, try the next question.'

Rooney seemed perplexed.

'It easy, Rooney. You copy way Nina move hand, tell her anything, then you look at Gina, wait, nod and agree,' Mrs Onoro added.

He knew what he had to do, he just found looking intensely at Gina the tricky part.

'How do you think Britain influences your work?'

He answered in Japanese.

Gina translated. 'The contrast in tones and colours are a constant source of inspiration. I can look at a grey building, set in a grey sky, and the luscious green tree standing next to it brings out the warmth of that building, a warmth that one cannot tangibly see. That is what I try to capture in my pictures.'

He nodded away and then said, 'What a load of bollocks.'

'What did he really say?' I asked.

'Rooney, you no use such bad language. Not in Japanese either,' Mrs Onoro interrupted.

He said, '*Well when it's really cold outside and it's pissing down, I hurry up and just try and shift more stock so I can go home.*'

'It's a good answer, it's how I feel when I'm in the restaurant trying to get rid of the last customers.'

'You work in a restaurant?' Rooney asked her.

Fukkus, fukkus, I heard my dad's voice. 'Focus,' I said to both of them. 'Who or what is your greatest influence?' I continued.

He copied my gestures and said something else to Gina in Japanese.

'I'm influenced by the nature of life and death, both seemingly transitory and disconnected. Life is supposed to bring joy, and death sadness, but for me life is death and death is life. They work in union with one another.'

'Do you really like Clapton?' Gina asked. 'Me too.'

'What has Clapton got to do with anything?'

'Rooney said his greatest inspiration was music and his greatest influence was Eric Clapton.'

It was working – sort of – if Gina and Rooney didn't stop every few minutes to ask questions about each other. She was taking the empathy bit slightly too far.

'And what about me influence you?' Mrs Onoro asked Rooney.

'Come here, sweetheart,' he said cuddling her. 'And of course there's you.'

'See, Gina, how my son is good boy, maybe you want go up and see his shoes?'

'Haven't heard that line before,' she laughed.

'It's all right, I'll bring them down,' he said, trying not to appear embarrassed.

Rooney went to fetch his shoes. None of them were any good. Gina was thinking of a pair of black and white ones with a crocodile-skin look. 'We're going shopping tomorrow for Foruki's clothes and shoes, come with us and then maybe you and Gina could go to Artusion to get a feel for the paintings,' I said, sensing if they got all their personal questions out of the way they could focus more on the translating part.

'OK, I'll come,' he said without hesitation.

'I spread word around in Japanese Association about

famous painter called Foruki,' Mrs Onoro said as we left. 'Gina, after this all you come back have dinner with us. You too, Nina.'

'What do you think?' I asked as we made our way home.

'You made him sound boring. He isn't boring. He's got heaps of potential.'

'You flirting with him helped.'

'I did not.'

'You did and you know you did, Gina.'

'Maybe just a little but he's cute, isn't he? Kinda shy but not, if you know what I mean.'

He was cute in the way you appreciate a My Little Pony with all the matching accessories when you're eight, cute in the way that he had managed to match his hair to the colour of his plums. 'In a purple, streaky kind of a way,' I said.

'There's more to him, Nina,' she replied. 'You'll see.'

After getting someone to mind his stall, Rooney spent the morning with Gina at Artusion while I went into a café and surfed the Internet. I read every single piece of information I could find about Tastudi Mangetti. What transpired from most of the pages was that he was incredibly well-respected and wielded an enormous amount of power in the art world both in Europe and the States. I knew this but reading it all in black and white made my stomach churn. What were we thinking of doing? If he found out, forget ever trying to exhibit in any sort of gallery, any paintings Gina and I did would be confined to craft fairs in town halls. And then my imagination began to run away. What if Mangetti was linked to the Mafia? What if he sent them to track us down after he found out that we had deceived him?

265

I imagined the Godfather knocking on the semi's door.

'Whatever you's selling me, I'm not interested, now get off.' That was my dad's standard line to strangers who came knocking. It didn't bear thinking about.

'We can't do it,' I said, meeting Gina and Rooney in Bond Street.

'Have you spoken to your dad? To Raj?'

'No, it's Mangetti.'

'What, he's pulled out?'

'No, we can't mess with him. Gina, you won't be able to sell any paintings if he finds out.'

'I'm not selling any anyway, so what does it matter?'

'It's not going to work; and what if he's got connections?'

'Connections?'

'Mafia,' I blurted.

She began laughing. 'This is what happens when I leave you for too long on your own. They're only paintings. It's not major, major; it's nothing he wouldn't do.'

'What if Mangetti finds out we deceived him and it's a question of honour?'

'I'm not even going to answer that. We had a good morning and Rooney really liked his work.'

I felt neurotic and stupid.

'It's good stuff. I'm up for it,' he said.

Up for it? It wasn't a competition to see who had the best My Little Pony.

'Rooney, do you know what you're getting yourself involved in? It's deceit – out-and-out deceit.'

'Sometimes it's best not to know, not to ask too many questions and get on with it. I want to help both of you.'

He was right. I knew what he meant by not asking too many questions. When I was at the firm there were many things that we weren't technically supposed to do, like hide the provenance of a painting due to tax implications,

266

but we didn't ask our clients too many questions and just got on with it. It was sort of a similar scenario.

Rooney made it sound so simple, they both did. 'Take another leap of faith, Nina. We can pull this off if we do a bit more work.'

The only way we could pull it off was if I held my nerve. 'OK,' I replied. 'And we all know what we're getting into.'

'Yes, and no more jitters.'

The jitters had to be kept inside – they were putting their faith in me, I had to stay strong. 'Let's do it, let's go and get some clothes for Foruki,' I said, attempting to sound resolute.

We went mainly to the charity shops in the best parts of London, finding things that might be appropriate for him. Later, Rooney came back home with us to have dinner and to try on the clothes.

'I look like an idiot,' he said coming out of the bathroom.

'Maybe we can lose the cap but you look great, just great,' Gina insisted. 'Those shades look amazing.'

The sunglasses were enormous; they covered most of his face and he was dressed mostly in black, except for his jacket and shoes. The jacket that swayed down to his ankles was purple and the shoes had a snake-skin print. And though he looked the part, there was something missing.

'Does he need some jewellery?' I asked.

'Definitely not,' Gina replied. 'He's Foruki, not Liberace.'

Being loaded up with jewellery for a special occasion was obviously an Indian thing that was embedded in my psyche.

'I know what it is,' Gina said. 'Rooney, you've got to let me dye your hair all black. It will just be for a few days and we'll dye it back. Go on, you've been great – I mean, you've let us do all this to you without moaning and it's just one last thing,' she tried to convince him.

'Well, if you really need to.'

Gina was like the Avon lady that came to our house, a person who could just convince anyone to do anything and then make them feel like it was their idea in the first place. Every time the Avon lady came to the door my dad stood with one foot behind it so there was no way she would be let in, but she always managed to get past him and convince him to buy bits and pieces for my mum.

'Kavitha, why you wasting the money, I know what you looks like,' he would say as she stared longingly at the Avon lady's coveted products.

'Yes, but wouldn't you like your wife to have a touch of Cilla about her – you know, that glamour,' the Avon lady would wink at my mum.

'You saying this is the lipstick that the Cilla buys?' he would ask, rummaging through her products.

'Sold the same one to her just last week.'

She used the same line over and over, and he would fall for it over and over again.

I missed them both so much, even their routine and the comments they made to each other. Despite the fact they had their faults there was a safety that they provided. Jana must have found it hard to stay away. Did she just get used to being without us and felt that the best way was to cut everyone off?

It had been a long day. Rooney and Gina were engrossed in conversation. I wanted to leave them to it and go to bed but I didn't have a bed, just the sofa they were both sitting on, so I fell asleep in the armchair.

*   *   *

Early the next morning I woke up startled and with no recollection of going to sleep on the sofa. This was what my angst was doing to me; making me forget things, making me hallucinate. I had dreamed Raj was really Foruki but then Mangetti had found out Foruki did not exist and was holding a gun to my head. I was frantically pointing at Raj, pleading with him to believe me, but Raj denied it and kept calling me a liar. I couldn't go back to sleep. It was 5.57 a.m., in a few more hours I was supposed to be getting married. Raj would be feeling devastated today and my parents more so. My mum probably wouldn't even get out of bed, feigning a bad headache, and my dad would be fiddling with the television sets. Was it worth putting everyone through so much just so I could paint pictures and sleep on someone else's sofa? The sofa I so feared Gina would ask me if she could sleep on those many months ago at the Tate. She was one of the kindest people I had ever met, and Rooney, I had misjudged him. Why did they believe in me so much? Maybe it was better, as he said, not to ask so many questions; maybe then I could stop oscillating between doubt and fear and just get on with finishing what I had unwittingly started. So that is what I decided to do on the morning I was supposed to be getting married. I pulled myself together and resolved to see it through to the end. If it all went horribly wrong I would accept it, as Mrs Onoro said; I would stand in the centre and accept all of it and at least, deep down, I would know that I had given it my very best.

The phone beeped and I got off the sofa. It was a text message from Raj's mother that read 'HOUSIE YOU WILL PAY'. I put thoughts about her, and about my mum sitting with the contents of her jewellery box, to the back of my mind and began making notes on all the things Mangetti could possibly ask and Gina's possible responses. I scribbled down what Rooney needed to work on and then I made Gina breakfast.

'Oh God, Nina, it's the day of the wedding. Are you OK?'

'Much better. I came to the conclusion that I have two options – to be Raj's wife or to do something extraordinary. Was it you who put me on the sofa?'

'Rooney. I took off your shoes and he picked you up and put you there before he left.'

'He's a nice guy, isn't he?'

'And witty as well,' she replied, 'in an understated, not-witty way.'

After finishing on his stall that morning, Rooney came round. Gina dyed his hair and got him to wear Foruki's clothes again. He appeared convincing.

'We've got to spend some time on refining gestures and mannerisms and you'll be perfect. When he asks you some questions that you think are difficult, make some erratic hand movements and mutter, like this. That's what I've seen some of these eccentric types do,' I said.

Rooney laughed. He had a soothing, unruffled laugh.

We sat for hours rehearsing the kind of questions Mangetti would ask and what Foruki would do.

'When you don't know what to say, if nothing comes to you or you think it's a question that requires much thought, touch your heart, pause, lower your head as if you are thinking, and then answer.'

After dinner Gina was getting out the wineglasses to show him how to hold the glass correctly, should he be offered some, when Rooney spotted her acoustic guitar behind the cabinet.

'Do you play?' he asked her.

'Yeah, just a bit.'

'Play us something,' he said going over to it.

She picked up the guitar and then sang a Tracy

270

Chapman song. Rooney asked if he could take the guitar from her and then he started strumming. First it was a chord here, a chord there, nothing spectacular. His fingers pressed firmly on the strings. They didn't seem like grocers' fingers, there were no muddy bits under his fingernails, no rough skin. He looked at Gina before tilting his head and then his fingers did their own thing. And the Rooney playing before us didn't seem like the Rooney who lived with his mum and asked her if his shirts were ironed; when he played he was a mass of potential and possibilities. He could have said he was anyone and we would have believed him. Gina's jaw dropped.

'Where the hell did you learn to play like that?' she asked in amazement.

'I was doing gigs before . . .' he stopped '. . . before my dad died, and then I decided to go back home, take over his stall and look after mum.'

Gina and I looked at each other.

'What do you feel when you play?' I asked.

'There's just me and the guitar, the rest of the world doesn't exist.'

He played us some more and we were in awe.

'It's bloody fantastic. OK Rooney, when you meet Mangetti, think about what you feel when you're playing, that it's just you and your guitar. Forget what I've told you about poise and posture; when he's asking you those questions imagine you're playing in your head and give him that look,' Gina said.

By the end of the two days Gina knew every facet of my life; she knew what each of the paintings meant to me, what they would mean to Foruki. We spent hours discussing colours, influences, thoughts and feelings, and potentially what Mangetti might ask and ways of getting around questions. In the evenings Rooney came around and I watched the chemistry between them as I pretended to be Mangetti and asked the questions. He answered all the questions in Japanese, talking about his music or fruit and veg, but Gina skilfully converted his answers and made him sound as if he were an eccentric artist talking passionately about his concepts and influences. By the end of those two days I knew that there was nothing more we could possibly do; we were as ready as we would ever be.

The following morning I could hardly get myself dressed. My hands shook as I fumbled with the buttons on my shirt, trying to fasten them.

Gina was getting dressed in one of my suits.

'Aren't you scared, Gina, not even a little bit?'

'What's the worst thing that has happened in our lives?' she asked and then she answered her own question: 'Death – so this is a drop in the ocean, it's nothing. OK we might be making someone see something that isn't there but this guy is responsible for making hundreds of people see things that aren't there. We're not hurting anyone. You can't go through life being scared or fearing what might or might not happen. You know that as well as I do, Nina, you take what comes knowing some things are inevitable. But what you can do is live every moment. The way I see it is that we've got a great opportunity here, there's nothing to be scared about – it's an adventure and we live it to the max, and whatever happens, happens.'

Ki would have probably said pretty much the same thing. They were both incredibly optimistic, full of life with boundless energy and passion. They careered past obstacles and got on with things. One was looking out for me from somewhere else and the other was here; how could I fail?

Rooney came and we all sat and had breakfast together, though I couldn't eat anything. He didn't seem fazed either, it was as if it was just another day and instead of selling fruit and veg he was selling concepts. I sat thinking of all the last minute things we needed to do.

'OK, when we arrive do your greeting, you don't have to wait for Mangetti's prompt to say something if you feel like there needs to be a sentence in there somewhere.'

'You've said that to me three times already, Nina, just chill,' he replied.

'OK, but if you get nervous about anything, anything at all, focus on his nose. Stare at it hard. It's kind of prominent, you can't miss it, and I'm sure he must have a thing about it.'

'Damn, we've forgotten something,' Gina interrupted.

'What? What is it?' I panicked.

'Aftershave, he's got to have aftershave, it's important. We should stop off at Fortnum and Mason and spray something on him.'

We caught the tube to Green Park and went to spray Rooney with aftershave.

'Remember,' Gina said, 'we have absolutely nothing to lose.'

'Right, nothing to lose,' I repeated seeing images of my dad being carted away by the Mafia.

My heart raced as we turned into Cork Street. 'He's just a client, just a client,' I kept saying to myself.

We walked into the main gallery and a middle-aged woman looked at us through her half-moon spectacles and asked how she could help.

'We're here to see Mr Mangetti. It's Nina Savani and . . .'

'Foki,' she exclaimed getting up from behind her desk. 'Delighted to meet you. Mr Mangetti is in the office, waiting for you,' she said, holding out her hand. 'Let me show you down there.'

As her high heels went click, click, click on the parquet floor, my heart began thumping even louder.

'We have nothing to lose,' I kept saying to myself. 'It will be fine.'

As he emerged from behind his desk, Mangetti looked smaller than I had remembered him.

'A pleasure to see you again, Nina,' he said, shaking my hand.

'Tastudi, this is Foruki and his interpreter, Gina Walker.'

Tastudi held out his hand. Rooney didn't take it. My heart began beating even faster and then Rooney bowed down and said something in Japanese.

Mangetti nodded and smiled and cast his eyes on Gina. I introduced them again.

'As I said, Tastudi, Foruki understands English perfectly and he does speak some English but he would just feel slightly more comfortable if his translator is present to answer for him.'

'Can understand but speaking English not very good,' Rooney said with a strange Japanese accent.

'By all means, an artist always likes to express his work in his own language. Can I get you anything to drink?'

'Water,' Rooney replied.

'Water is fine for all of us,' I replied. I needed to sit down, my legs felt as if they were going to collapse if he didn't invite us to sit down.

'Leticia, some water please,' he said to the lady. 'Please take a seat.' He invited Foruki to take a seat first.

There were enormous leather chairs that had probably

274

cost a fortune; my dad would have been very impressed. He would be on his route now, shouting at all the customers who didn't give him the right change.

'I saw your work, Foruki. I'm sure Nina has told you what I thought of it,' Mangetti began.

I left thoughts of my dad and focused.

Rooney paused, looked at me and said to Gina in Japanese, '*It's not mine but you believe what you want to. I'm actually a grocer, didn't think I'd end up being a grocer but there you go, you never know which way life is going to take you.*'

Gina turned to Mangetti and said, 'She has indeed but I'd like to say that the artist is not the owner of the painting; he does not figure in the painting; he is merely the conduit.'

That sounded good, we hadn't rehearsed that. I tried not to catch her eye and kept my gaze on Mangetti, imagining him being delighted with the answers Foruki provided. Mangetti appeared eager to follow up and was leaning forward in his chair.

'Interesting, tell me more,' Mangetti continued.

Rooney leaned forward and said in Japanese, '*Well, I had a band. We were touring Europe when my dad died. My mum couldn't manage on her own, my dad was a bit of a control freak and never let her do anything, so I decided to go back and help her out for a couple of months.*'

Gina translated. 'When I'm painting, I'm not present. I can't explain it, it's the time that I access parts of the self that I never knew existed. It is the only time when I feel the ego to be completely eradicated. At that precise moment in time it's about the painting. Nothing else exists.'

This was true; this was what Gina and I both felt. Painting was the only time when both of us felt we were truly ourselves and not pretending to be other people. Mangetti would understand this.

'That comes across. It's striking how you have managed not to allow your cultural background to permeate your work. I mean obviously the use of space and the flat surfaces would indicate a certain Japanese influence but this is not the overriding impression one is left with; I would go so far as to say that the paintings are unstilted,' Mangetti responded.

Rooney paused and then replied, *'If you had any Japanese influence in the music, we'd only really sell in Japan. I know it's not all just about being commercial but you have to have some mass appeal.'*

Gina nodded as Rooney gave his answer and turned to Mangetti. 'This is what I have discovered in Britain and that's why this particular collection is very close to me. It's not about being Japanese or British, or Indian for that matter. Art speaks a universal language; it's about conveying depth of feeling through colour and if at all possible trying to attain a neutrality or sense of peace through colour.'

Word for word, this is what we had spoken about the night before. It was sounding fluid. Maybe this would be enough to convince him. I searched Mangetti's face for traces of doubt or hesitation but there was only eagerness to continue the conversation.

'Is that attainable?' Mangetti asked.

'You've got to aim for something.'

'Aren't we always seeking?' she translated.

I thought about interrupting and adding my own thoughts to the discussion but then without being prompted Rooney went off on his own direction. *'Most blokes would think it's weird that after all this time I haven't really achieved anything and I'm still at home. I've thought about it a lot. I don't think it is the comfort-zone thing, I think if I'm not there my mum wouldn't manage.'* He touched his heart.

Gina agreed with whatever Rooney was saying and turned back to Mangetti. 'This is what my work is about; trying to find balance in an inharmonious world. Trying to find life among death, peace in turbulence and stillness in movement.'

We hadn't practised that. I began to worry until Mangetti said, 'And may I say you have done it admirably. This was exquisitely captured.'

They were doing really well but it was dangerous for Rooney to go off on tangents, it wasn't something we had practised.

Gina waited for him to do something. She glanced at me.

Nod, Rooney, nod. Please don't say anything.

Rooney went off again. *'Don't need any admiration for it. If you met her, you'd know exactly why I do it.'*

She translated. 'Thank you. And then of course there is the social commentary aspect.'

What social commentary aspect? I thought. I began to panic – stop there.

'Take the buddha painting,' she continued, giving Mangetti his own spiel about cultural juxtaposition – this is what I told her Mangetti had first said when he initially saw the painting. 'We live in a society where culture is increasingly becoming fused. I wanted to show that we are able to reach a middle ground, that both are compatible.'

'These are my sentiments and indeed this is what your work conveys. A sense of peace, a sense of understanding. Is that what you would say?'

'You have to understand what your customer wants: apples and pears, kilo there, kilo here, it's not rocket science, though, maybe it's the same in art, they want bullshit, give it to them,' Rooney waved.

'Essentially the work is a search for identity; death being part of that identity, life being part of that identity. Confronting parts of the self that are ugly and transmuting light into them,' Gina said and then added, 'Identity is not about ego, and this particular collection – *From Obscurity to Light* – is the journey I took to realise this. It's almost as if the ego was left behind and the paintings were done by someone else.'

Gina had a straight face and appeared deadly serious. I wanted to bury my head in my hands; surely he wouldn't go for it, not after she had said that, he had to know.

Mangetti leaned further across the table and seemed fully engaged. If the table hadn't been there to separate them he would have been in Foruki's lap.

'The handprint and the footprint is the only thing we have to leave; these are the only things that are alive,' Mangetti added.

Nod, Rooney, just nod.

He nodded.

'Thank you, thank you,' I thought, 'We've done it.'

Rooney turned to Gina and said something in Japanese.

Foruki would like to look at the work upstairs and give you a moment to speak to Ms Savani. This was just as we had rehearsed. As soon as they felt they had done their bit, this was what she had to say.

Mangetti turned to Rooney and said, 'I completely understand but there's something I want to ask you before you leave. Foruki, I am not easily impressed. It's not often that I come across art like this that completely enraptures me. I want to enter you into the Turner Prize. I know what your objections will be, that you don't want to be exposed publicly, but please think about it.'

Rooney nodded and said something in Japanese. If we were asked this question, Gina was going to say that he would need some time to consider it.

'I would consider it an honour,' Gina replied.

NO!, I wanted to shout.

Mangetti appeared delighted. He called Leticia on the buzzer and asked her to come down. 'Please take Mr Foruki up, he'd like to take a look at De Monte's work.'

Rooney bowed before he and Gina went up with Leticia.

The two of us were left alone in the room together. I wasn't sure if I would be able to get through the rest of it without Gina and Rooney being there. My legs were shaking and I had to put my hands on my knees to stop them jumping up and down.

'Tell me again, Nina, where else has Foruki exhibited?' Mangetti asked.

I was telling myself to breathe and to treat him as if he were any client. 'Client,' I said out loud.

'Client?' Mangetti asked.

'Yes, client.' How would I explain that outburst? 'I was just thinking that Foruki is one of the best clients I've had. So unpresumptuous, that is what I liked about him when I first met him. Sorry, getting back to your question he's only exhibited in a few galleries in Japan and, even then, he's done that anonymously. As I said, exhibitions are not really his thing and he's only been ready to share his work in the last year.'

'*From Obscurity to Light*. It was all done this year, wasn't it?'

'Yes, since he's been in Britain.'

'And that has been?'

'Nine months,' I said. After much debate, that is what Gina and I had settled on.

'Marvellous, he is such an original individual.'

'Unique.'

'I thought it would take much more to convince him to be entered into the Turner,' Mangetti added.

So did I, I wanted to say.

'What he says about ego, the nature of fame and the search for identity is so valid. Between you and I there has been so much negative press towards the Turner Prize that some of the judges and myself feel that maybe this year it's important to have a slightly more traditionalist approach. I agree with what you said, it has become all about celebrity, all about hype, so perhaps someone as noncontroversial as Foruki would bring something else to the table.'

'Although he says it's an honour, I know he would want to retain his anonymity,' I added quickly.

Mangetti nodded. 'It just makes his point even stronger. The critics will have nothing to comment on this year.'

That was one way of looking at it.

'One more thing, the buddha painting. I'll give you ten thousand pounds for it.'

Though I was desperate for the money, I refused.

'Twenty?'

Twenty thousand pounds would have allowed me to paint for the entire year without worrying. 'I'm sorry.'

'I admire your integrity,' he replied. 'And those other paintings at Artusion which have been earmarked?'

'I'll have a word with Emanuel Hikatari at Artusion,' I replied.

'Excellent. I would also like to commission Foruki to do a portrait. I'll call you to discuss the details as there's somewhere I have to be.'

Mangetti led me back upstairs. Surely this wasn't it. It couldn't be this easy.

Gina was studying one of the paintings and Rooney was hovering, flitting from one to another.

'He's into comparison,' I whispered to Mangetti.

'Foruki, it was an absolute pleasure meeting you,' Mangetti said walking over to him.

Rooney bowed his head once again.

Mangetti thanked me and accompanied us to the door.

We walked round the corner of the street and like three lunatics who had managed to escape from an asylum we began laughing. I went over to them and put my arms around each of them.

'You did it, you were both fantastic. Thank you.'

'We did it, I told you it would be a breeze,' Gina replied.

'Weren't you supposed to say he would need much convincing to be entered for the Turner, that he would have to think seriously about it.'

'Kinda got carried away there. Anyway, he's only using Foruki, he's got his own agenda. If they want non-controversial, we'll give them noncontroversial.'

'Can't believe we pulled it off,' Rooney said.

'But I thought you didn't care?'

'I only said that, Nina, because you were nervous and at that time it's what you needed to hear.'

I kissed him on the cheek. 'Thank you, Rooney, for everything.'

The paintings had all sold at Artusion. Emanuel Hikatari was delighted with the response and after the gallery had taken their cut I collected a cheque for £25,000.

'Dad, twenty-five thousand pounds,' I put this in first so he would listen to the rest of my sentence. 'Twenty-five thousand pounds, that's how much my paintings sold for.'

He slammed the phone down.

We had dinner with Rooney and Mrs Onoro later that evening and I handed Rooney a cheque for £2500.

'Just for being Foruki?' Mrs Onoro asked in disbelief.

'There's more to it than just being Foruki,' I answered. 'Rooney was fantastic.'

'Rooney available to be him any time. No, Rooney?'

'Any time.'

'Well if we get short-listed for the Turner, and that is a really big if, we'll need him again, but for now it's all over, thank God.'

'What are you going to do with the money?' Gina asked him.

'Buy a new guitar, maybe, then I'll start practising again. I've been putting it off with excuses of no money.'

'Well if you ever want to do a gig let me know because on Thursday nights the restaurant I work at has live music and I can have a word with the boss,' Gina said.

'Rooney, he do it,' Mrs Onoro volunteered.

Just as we were leaving Mrs Onoro took me to one side.

'You good girl, Nina, you good to give Rooney a chance. He got confidence back,' she said glancing at him.

'I didn't do that, he did; he was the one that gave me a chance.'

'You see he think I need him, I think he need me. Maybe I tell him about Hikito.'

'I think that's a good idea.'

She hugged me as we left and I didn't want her to let me go as it had been ages since I felt that secure; they were like my family. 'You come soon?'

'I will,' I replied.

As Gina and I made our way home she said, 'He's asked me to a concert on Sunday evening.'

'And?'

'I told him yes.'

*   *   *

282

One thing that has always been exceptionally hard for me to do is to let go, but then all the people who I loved the most were taken from me so I had no choice but to learn to let go. This time I wanted it to be different, I wanted it to be my decision and as much as I wanted to avoid the feelings of loneliness, it was time to stand on my own two feet and leave the warmth and security that Gina provided. With the money from the exhibition I decided to rent a studio and a flat of my own so I told her this once we had got home. Gina didn't want me to leave and said we could share both the flat and studio, but as much as I wanted to stay it was time to move on.

She helped me look and within a few weeks we had found both. The flat had one bedroom and it was just around the corner from Gina, and the studio was a converted warehouse in Shoreditch, split on two levels: downstairs was where I could stock all the materials and upstairs was where I saw myself painting. It was much bigger than I needed it to be and much more expensive but it felt right because I knew I would be spending most of my time there.

There was hardly anything to pack but Gina came with me to buy more paints and canvases for my new studio and helped me set up.

'This is for you,' I said as she was leaving, handing her an envelope.

'What is it?'

'Two thousand pounds.'

'I can't take this.'

I had to insist that she take it.

'Oh Nina,' she said hugging me, 'it was never about the money. It was about breaking the mould and we did that.'

'I know, but none of this would have happened without you.'

Gina had once said that when you did something out of the ordinary, extraordinary things began to happen. The other thing she taught me was – and I don't know exactly how this one works, but – once you begin to see potential in someone else, even if they don't see it, they evolve into the person you envisaged them to be.

She was right.

After Gina went I was left alone in my studio and though I should have felt excited at the thought of being completely independent, I didn't. I had this huge pang of loneliness and sadness; it was as if she had taken everyone I had ever loved with her and left me alone with a gaping blank canvas. I thought about what I'd done to Raj and his family, to my mum and dad – all of that was because I was scared to be me, to show them who I was in case they didn't love me any more. Then I thought fleetingly about Jean Michel, how I could forgive him now for his mistake but things for us had moved on.

It was with Michael that my thoughts stayed. It was so wrong not to have been completely honest with him, but I was scared by the extent of the feelings I had for him, scared to expect too much, scared in case I was hurt again. My need not to be hurt overrode everything. Picking up my paintbrush I began to paint black silhouettes and wondered what Ki would make of all of it. When I had finished I put the paintbrush down.

'Did you see? Do you think it's all crazy? I can't quite get my head around any of it, how one thing has led to another and I'm here now, the place where I've always wanted to be. I can paint and there's no one to bother me or to tell me what to do but I still feel alone and I still miss you, there is no happily ever after, is there, Ki? You get what you want and you still think "Is that it?" I think all there is, is making the best of each day. When this exhibition is over I'll take the buddha over to your mum. Maybe she'll put it in your room. I want to mess your room up, take everything that's in it away. I wish I didn't still miss you like this. A big part of me wants it to stop.'

Matisse's quote about flowers went around in my head. I thought about the new people who had entered my life in the last few months – Mrs Onoro, Gina, Rooney – and began painting colourful figures between the silhouettes, and when I had finished I didn't bother washing my hands or brushing my hair, I just went to an empty home.

Over the next few months I made several attempts to speak to Mum and Dad. I even followed my dad's bus route and waited for him at the bus stop but he closed the doors on me and drove off leaving the other passengers stranded. Being completely cut off from my family I threw myself into a world of my own, painting pictures that I had always wanted to paint, putting down feelings I was unable to express.

Mangetti had commissioned Foruki to do a portrait of him and because I couldn't go through with the whole sitting thing where Rooney would have to pretend to paint, I said Foruki didn't feel that a sitting was necessary as he worked from the vibration given off the subject matter. Despite the fact that Mangetti was paying £8000 for the commission I was unable to paint him and just kept painting flowers in all different shapes and sizes. Nothing came to me – the canvas was the only place where I couldn't fool myself.

There was still no news from Michael. Painting became everything to me; it was the only thing that I knew couldn't leave me and when I wasn't in my studio I spent time with Gina and Rooney.

Rooney began playing in Gina's restaurant and managed

to find other venues where he could perform. Gina spent more time on her own work and the world revolved like this until the day Mangetti called and left a message asking me to call him at home.

I always had my phone switched off when I was working in the studio so later that evening I heard the message. I called him back, not even thinking twice about doing it, not like the first time I called him. His assistant picked up the phone and handed it to Mangetti.

'Hello Tastudi, it's Nina.'

'Yes, Nina. How are you?'

'Very well, thank you.'

'And how is Foruki doing with my painting?'

'It's coming on well,' I lied.

'Excellent. I have some good news for Foruki,' he paused. 'We have short-listed him for the Turner.'

I couldn't believe what I was hearing. There must have been some mistake.

'Nina, are you still there?'

'Short-listed?' I repeated.

'Indeed.'

'That's very good news,' I managed. The palms of my hands began to sweat.

'The judges were impressed with his exploration of darkness and light and his attitude towards identity.'

'They were?'

'Yes, and they liked this whole idea of bringing art back to the subject matter and not the artist. Meaning no dis-respect to Foruki but he makes his point in an understated way and we felt that this year this is what the Turner needed; a little more sobriety than the circus the media turn it into.'

'Yes it does,' I replied, not knowing what to say. If he was short-listed it meant press attention on a massive scale. What would we do? 'To be honest with you, Tastudi,

I'm not sure how he will take the news – you know, with the publicity and everything.'

'We have taken this into account and have briefed the press office. The announcement will be made on June the fourteenth and they'd like you to come in to discuss how you'd like to handle this. So give them a call to arrange a time that is convenient.'

'I will.'

'Convey my regards to Foruki and I know he'll be very busy but we must do lunch soon.'

'We will,' I replied, remaining professional. 'Thank you, Tastudi.'

I hung up. I didn't know whether to scream with excitement or bury my head. This was serious. I thought it was all over. How were we going to pull this one off? I called up Gina.

'Gina, are you sitting down?'

'What's up, Nina?'

'Foruki's been short-listed for the Turner.'

'No bloody way! . . . Roon, you've been short-listed for the Turner Prize.'

'Is he there with you, Gina?'

'Yeah, he's here. Come round as soon as you can.'

There was a bottle of champagne waiting on the table when I got to Gina's house.

'I know I should be happy but I don't know if I can go through with this once more. I'm only beginning to find some kind of stability and it means more lies and deceit.'

'Nina, it's the Turner Prize. This just doesn't happen. It's a once in a lifetime opportunity and when it's all over you can come clean or kill him off, it doesn't really matter.'

'But Mangetti, I actually like him, I don't want to lie to him any more.'

287

'We've come this far, you can't back out now. What will you say to him?'

'I'll tell him the truth. He might even understand.'

'Think about this. Realistically, Foruki is not going to win. They've obviously short-listed him because he's not controversial and probably tempers all the other artists. They've done it for their own self-interest. They wanted someone with a traditional approach and you've given that to them – you're doing them a favour.

'When it's all over and if you feel the need to tell Mangetti, tell him – but just do this one more time. Do it for us.'

'What if they find out?'

'They haven't up until now, have they? Artusion was a pretty big venue, nobody found out then, did they?'

'What if he wins?'

'He won't,' Gina insisted. 'They're just doing this to shut some of the critics up but there's no way he'll win, let's be realistic. It's fixed, they like all that circus stuff, they are not going to choose a painter.'

'And if he does win?'

'Then that would be mad.'

Rooney agreed with Gina and asked me to see it through as we had got that far.

The only reason why I would go through with it again was because I had become increasingly insular in my own world and I wanted to feel the bond and the sense of excitement the three of us had created the first time we brought Foruki to life.

'Let's do it,' I said, opening the champagne.

Kendal Brown's offices were reopened the following week and the phone line activated. I met with the Tate's press office to give them more information about Foruki. His résumé was brief and had the main biographical details and a list of some obscure galleries in Japan that Gina had put together where he had supposedly exhibited. The coordinator said that they needed more to work with. 'The main point to stress about Foruki,' I reiterated, 'is his desire for anonymity and that the focus has to be on his work.'

'It is going to be fairly difficult to maintain his privacy as the press always want to interview the artist and Channel Four do a six-minute presentation about the artist and their work which is aired the evening of the prize-giving.'

'Is that obligatory?' I asked, stunned. How the hell were we going to do that?

'All the artists normally participate, even the ones who are media shy. We find the less information you give the press, the more they want, so I would advise Foruki to partake in the documentary.'

How could I have Rooney on national TV talking about his concepts? 'I'll try to talk him into it,' I replied.

'It would be for the best as his privacy is so guarded you don't want him to stand out.'

The press shots I handed over were photographs that Gina had taken of Rooney wearing a cap and enormous sunglasses. 'These are the only shots he'll allow you to use,' I said handing them over to the PR lady.

The day the short-list was officially announced, journalists began calling for specific details.

'The more I don't tell you about Foruki, the more you'll want to know; this is the point he's trying to make, that the artist is bigger than the subject matter.' I was using reverse psychology so they would feel that Foruki was so up himself that they weren't going to bother finding out anything more about him. I also slipped in some personal details that would feed their insatiable curiosity, like his father abandoning him which had marked his psyche at a very young age, beginning the journey of the search for identity and the sense of self.

I tried to field their questions without sounding too evasive but there was a journalist called Richard Morris from the *Guardian* who was much more tenacious and wouldn't let it go.

'Miss Savani, the galleries where Foruki claims to have exhibited in Japan haven't heard of him.'

My mouth went dry – of course they wouldn't have heard of him – but I was prepared for this question. 'Of course they haven't heard of him. When he's in his own country he goes under different pseudonyms. It's never about him, it's his art. In fact he doesn't even like doing exhibitions and the only way he will show his work is to go under different names.'

'So let me get this right. He has done no major exhibitions anywhere in the world and he suddenly decides to go in for the Turner, and this is a man who is media shy?'

'The only reason why he was persuaded to enter the Turner Prize was that it would be a platform for the statement he is trying to make on the nature of identity and celebrity in today's media-frenzied culture. Everyone is so obsessed as to who is behind the art that the art gets overlooked. He is trying to find authenticity in fakeness. Judge Foruki by the paintings he does and not the man he is. I have another call waiting, Mr Morris, I really must go,' I said, trying to get rid of him. 'If you have any more questions, give me a call.' I put the phone down, incredibly nervous about what he might unearth if he dug a little deeper, but I put these thoughts to the back of my mind while I tried to concentrate on what exactly Foruki would put together for the exhibition at the Tate.

Richard Morris called again later that evening.

It's the weasel, I thought as soon as I heard his turgid voice. Didn't he have anything better to investigate?

'You say, Ms Savani, that you left Whitter and Lawson so you could bring Foruki over to London.'

'That's right,' I replied, sitting upright in my chair.

'Why is it that your former boss, Simon Lawson, says that he had to let you go because you were on the verge of a breakdown?'

Simon wouldn't have said that, I knew he wouldn't have, even if he wasn't impressed by my behaviour when I left. But how else would the weasel have known? What if Simon had said that?

'There was a conflict of interest between the two of us, he's hardly going to praise me for leaving.' Yes, that was a good answer; that would cover it.

'And you say you went to Japan in May 1998 and that is where you stumbled upon your chap Foruki?'

Breathe, Nina, breathe. 'That's right.'

'Why is it that Mr Lawson has no recollection of you going to Japan at that time?'

I began to sweat. I took a deep breath and thought of the best thing I could think of. 'It was hardly something that I was going to broadcast to my boss – what I do in my personal time has nothing to do with anyone else.'

'So you're still not prepared to grant me the first interview with Foruki?'

'As I have said, Foruki doesn't court publicity and therefore I am unable to do this.'

'Right,' he replied.

The way he said 'right' made me feel incredibly uneasy.

'Is there anything else I can help you with?' I asked in a vain attempt to show him that he had not unnerved me.

'No, that's all for now,' he replied. 'No doubt we will speak again soon.'

I called Gina straightaway. She told me not to worry, that all journalists tried it on; it was their job. But I wasn't reassured; he wasn't like the other journalists who I had spoken to. I got the sense that he could see through me; he made me feel as if he knew that I hadn't told the truth and was waiting to see how long it would take before I snapped.

Thinking about Richard Morris and what he might write the next day worried me and I was unable to sleep: he had the power to ruin us – not just us, but ruin Mangetti's reputation. Every time I wanted to call Mangetti and tell him everything, I called Gina instead.

The following morning, Gina and Rooney came around to my flat with the articles that had appeared. 'See, nothing at all to worry about, Nina.'

THE NONCONTROVERSIAL SHORT-LIST
The only thing that is controversial about this year's Turner Prize is its noncontroversy. The four short-listed are a sober mix of artists: Steve Carey from Leeds sculpts nudes with garden fences; Londoner Amanda Finley models still-life using fabrics; Foruki, a British-born Japanese media-shy painter, whose work is about identity; and finally, photographer Matthew Perring from Durham whose photography captures speed and motion . . .

The only thing slightly controversial about this year's Turner Prize is the identity of one of the short-listed artists. Foruki, a British-Japanese artist, refuses to reveal his real identity as a matter of principle. Identity is one of the main statements he makes through his work and he is vehement about his art being at the fore rather than himself . . .

'It's just crazy,' Gina said as she read.

'Are you having doubts?' I asked.

'Absolutely not,' she replied. 'There's so much we can do here.'

My fears were allayed as I read on and nothing untoward had been written. Perhaps I knew it was naïve to think that he would let it go just like that but I wanted to be lulled into a false sense of security. I wanted to believe everything would work out because there was no time to dwell on what could potentially go wrong; there was only three months before the Channel 4 documentary was due to be filmed and I had a series of new pictures to paint for the exhibition at the Tate, all around the theme of identity. The biggest irony was I finally knew who I was but was doing one of the biggest exhibitions I would ever do for someone who did not exist.

For the next few months I was absorbed with my pictures. The first piece I did was a six-foot canvas with the famous image of Marilyn Monroe trying to hold down her white dress, but instead of using her head I painted a faint Japanese face. It was Mrs Onoro's face.

This piece took me weeks and after it was completed I took out another enormous canvas and painted it white.

I was going to have an elaborate gold frame around it. In the middle I painted the words 'self-portrait' in bold black letters and then signed it Foruki. On the next canvas I painted an abstract Rooney, changing his face slightly each time so by the fifth canvas his face completely dissolved and all that was left were segments of the colours used to paint the face.

The third canvas had an explosion of loud, vibrant paint. I was trying to capture the madness of what had happened in the last six months. The picture was of a rush-hour scene in the morning with a sea of commuters trying to get to work. Behind them all, on an underground poster, was a woman who was painting a picture of a man.

And the final piece in this collection was of an old man holding a newborn baby – only in these two phases of our lives do we not care who we are or what we have.

When the pictures were finally completed I let Rooney and Gina come to the studio.

'The first two are quite calculated. I thought we needed to make a strong statement about the nature of identity, and the next two . . . I don't know what they are about, it was just an emotion I had.'

'They're absolutely beautiful, Nina,' Gina said studying them. 'Really beautiful.'

The three of us spent hours discussing what each of the paintings meant and how to present it in a form palatable to Channel 4. Gina said she would prep Rooney and work on all his mannerisms so this would leave me free to take care of whatever else needed to be done.

The two of them had become very close: he was virtually living with her but he hadn't formally taken the step of moving in because he didn't want to upset Mrs Onoro, although I thought that she would have been delighted.

They were good together – they joked about together a lot and he understood her. Being around Gina had changed Rooney considerably; he had become very self-confident and incredibly decisive. Gina also believed in herself a lot more because of the support he provided. Sometimes I was envious; not because they had found each other but because it reminded me of what I possibly could have had with Michael.

A few weeks before the curators were due to arrive I went into the office and dealt with all the admin and the queries from journalists all around the world. I did stop to think about the madness but when I did that I got the jitters and wanted to call Mangetti and tell him that there had been a terrible mistake. How I could class a blatant lie as a mistake I didn't know, and so the only way my conscience would allow me to reconcile the whole scenario was by treating Foruki as if he really were my client, and this being the case I endeavoured to do my best for him.

A few days before the curators arrived, Gina came to the studio with Rooney to show me how far she had got with prepping him.

'OK Roon, just make yourself feel comfortable with the paintings and then try to talk to us about them,' Gina said. 'Make like we're the camera crew or something, don't forget what I told you and, you know . . . that pose at the end.'

'This is Marilyn Monroe,' he pointed, 'with my mum's head. She'll be dead proud, she's always wanted her face somewhere. This is my face all mixed up, suppose it's because no one knows who I am or who I'm supposed to be. Here you've got some tube scene . . . and anyone can see this old man and kid.'

I despaired. If this was the best we could do we might as well have a banner on display telling everyone that we were a bunch of fakes. 'We're not going to pull this one off. The viewers aren't stupid. Anyway, Foruki can't talk like that, what happened to the accent he was going to do?'

'Be serious, Rooney,' Gina said.

'It's not going to work,' I said, shaking my head.

'The whole question of identity is one I constantly searching for; is man a woman, is woman a man, what make him so? Is it society? Society tell us a lot of thing, make a lot of rule.'

I looked up at Rooney.

'They turn people into celebrity; they give them an identity which is false. I try to find authenticity in fakeness. Look at Marilyn Monroe; it media who dictate who is she really; inside she might be old lady.'

I smiled in disbelief as he continued. 'My work is about trying to detract from artist and what to expect, the artist merely conduit. He is not painting. That is what I try to show here. Artist dissolves before picture,' he said, pointing to the mixture of colour that had become separated from his face. It not important who paint what but feeling and statement picture leave you with. This is human emotion,' Rooney continued, indicating towards the picture of the old man and the baby. 'Pure, simple emotion. It when human kind show their true self, no need to impress anybody.'

I began to cry. 'How . . . how did you do that?'

'Gina and me, we don't waste time. She's been teaching me how to speak. We want this to work for you, Nina.'

'I haven't taught him how to paint yet,' Gina said. 'That's what we've got to focus on now, how he throws paint on a canvas and captures emotion. He doesn't have to learn the rest of it, just the initial paint-throwing bit.'

Before the curators came Rooney had mastered how

to appear to work in a style that Foruki would have been proud of.

We got Rooney ready to meet the curators. Foruki discussed at length in Japanese with the curators the work he wanted to display at the Tate while Gina translated. The curators agreed and together we decided how and when the pictures would be hung. We had a month left to practise as the paintings needed to be exhibited at the Tate by the end of October. Two weeks later the crew arrived from the production company to film Foruki at his studio.

'You're not allowed to take close-up shots of his face,' I said to the cameraman.

'But you're hardly going to see anything with that big cap and those sunglasses.'

'That is the idea, the press office told me that you have been briefed on the nature of what can be shown.'

The director came over and said some close-up shots were required. Rooney threw a tantrum and said, 'I don't know if I express myself properly but not me close up or I don't do this.'

'Artists, very temperamental,' I added.

'Quite,' he replied. 'Ian, no close-ups of the artist's face.'

The presenter introduced Foruki's work first. 'The paintings have such bold use of colour that they scream so loudly you can't ignore them; unlike the artist who wants to remain very much in the background.'

There was a shot of Rooney pretending to be working away in the background. Gina and I had taught him how to look contemplative while putting the paint onto the canvas.

We'd also taught him another move, which was to pick up various paints erratically and dip his hands into the mixture while working in a frenzy. The cameraman got a shot of this and a close-up of his hands working away.

'Could you give us a commentary?' the presenter asked.

'He's unable to speak when he works,' I added, 'he enters a world of his own.'

'We'll do a separate take with him talking later,' the director shouted.

They took various shots of his hands and his feet moving, and of the studio.

'We need some sound bites now,' the director instructed.

The presenter began asking Foruki questions.

'Foruki, why is it so important to you that the pictures appear in the foreground and the artist very much in the background, behind the work?'

We had rehearsed this question over and over.

'It's artist work that is important, not artist. People make judgements about my work when see me. I want them to look at work for itself, not for who painted it. I want them feel raw emotion.'

'Cut, we didn't quite get what emotion that was.'

Rooney had overdone the accent slightly so it sounded like 'waw'. 'Raw,' I repeated.

'Foruki, if you could just say that last sentence again, that is, "I want them to feel raw emotion."'

Gina had to leave the room as she began laughing.

Rooney did it again.

'Just talk to us about this particular collection,' the presenter asked.

'This one is search for identity. People put value and judgement on thing so Marilyn Monroe, you expect her to be certain way, but maybe she not like that at all. Media age we live in is able to create celebrity but person they create does not exist.'

He talked about each of the pictures. 'This one here is

when we show our vulnerability,' he said pointing to the painting of the old man and the baby. 'This is the only time we are truly ourselves, when we are vulnerable,' Rooney stated.

'I think we have all that we need. Thank you very much, Mr Foruki,' the director said. 'Very interesting.'

'When does this run?' I asked.

'It goes out on the night of the prize-giving between the live Channel 4 broadcast.'

That wasn't too bad, I thought. If anyone recognised Rooney it wouldn't matter as it would be all over by then.

After having spent the entire day with us, the crew left. 'Intriguing personality,' the presenter commented. 'Has something Michael Jackson-ish about him,' he said sarcastically.

'Do you think we did it?' Rooney asked when they had gone.

Gina and I burst out laughing.

'You're an absolute star.'

Two weeks later we were at the Tate gallery and the curators were assisting us and advising us as to where best to hang the collection. The other artists had already put their collections in the designated rooms.

As we were leaving I looked up at the high ceilings and the grandeur of the Tate. Rooney and Gina stopped. Each of us was struck by the enormity of what we were doing.

'What if we win?' Gina asked.

'You said it was highly unlikely,' I replied.

'That was then.'

Gina was the one who always reassured me. I pretended to hold my nerve and reassured her. 'We see how it goes, we say nothing. Maybe Foruki has enough of all the publicity and emigrates, maybe he dies – I don't know. One step at a time.'

'No, he won't win,' Rooney said. 'I just know he won't, that bloke with the garden fences is going to bag it.'

The likelihood of Foruki winning was one in four. He couldn't win; he was just used to pacify some of the severer critics; the Turner Prize wasn't intended for artists such as Foruki, it was meant to court controversy. As Rooney said, 'garden-fence man would bag it'.

I couldn't put Tastudi Mangetti off any longer. He kept calling to see when he could see Foruki again. He came to Foruki's studio the day before the exhibition at the Tate opened to members of the public. Mangetti told Rooney how impressed he was at the new collection. Rooney spoke some English, some Japanese.

'But Foruki, you speak very good English.'

Rooney nodded.

'But I know how it is when you are trying to express something that is in your heart . . . the depths of you,' he gestured. 'I feel the same way and want to speak in Italian. The work is just exquisite.'

'Thank you, Mr Mangetti,' Rooney bowed.

'And how is my commission coming along?' Among all the preparation I had forgotten that I was supposed to be painting Mangetti.

Rooney stared blankly.

'As you'll appreciate, Tastudi,' I interjected, 'Foruki has been extremely busy so it's not quite finished.'

'Seeing as I'm here, let me take a quick look.'

'No,' Rooney shouted.

'What Foruki means is he never lets anyone see work in progress, it disperses the energy around the picture,' I added quickly.

Rooney nodded. 'Not good to see half man,' he replied, 'but you take this . . .' He pointed to a canvas that I had

300

experimented on. 'It not finished but when it finished it for you.' Hadn't he just contradicted me as I'd said he never allowed people to see work in progress. I stared at Rooney, confused.

'How much is it?' Mangetti asked, staring at the red lines.

'No, it gift from me to you.'

Mangetti was assuaged.

'Most generous of you, Foruki, and I accept it with the generosity with which it is given.'

'Welcome, welcome.' Rooney shuffled about a bit as if he had somewhere else he had to be.

'I know you are busy and thank you for sharing your space with me. It must have taken a lot and I appreciate it. Foruki, it has been a pleasure as always.'

I showed Mangetti out. 'A very affable character. Nina, do you know his paintings have doubled in value?'

I just wanted to get Mangetti out of there. 'We'll talk about it later,' I said. 'When this is all over.'

Mangetti climbed into his Bentley. 'I will be in touch.'

I went back into the studio. '"Welcome"? "Welcome"? You're getting too good at this, Rooney.'

He laughed.

It was a hectic day; journalists were calling up asking if they could have an interview with Foruki and have pictures of him by his work. I said that he didn't do any interviews and the press office had pictures of him standing by his latest collection.

'But he has his back to the camera.'

'I know. Can't you think up a title: "Artist turns his back on fame", or something like that? It has been done this way intentionally,' I said.

The journalist at the *Guardian* would not let it go.

301

'So where exactly did you say Foruki had studied art?'

'I didn't and he didn't. He learned from his mother who was a painter.'

'And she is dead, is this correct?'

'Yes. It was through his paintings that he could come to terms with her death.'

'Has he found the father he came looking for?'

'Sorry?'

'You said in our last conversation that he came to find his father.'

I hadn't realised I had said that.

'Sadly, his father died a year ago.'

'And what was his name?'

'Kenneth David.'

'You've been most helpful, Ms Savani. Intriguing details you have given me, we'll be speaking again soon.'

When he hung up I felt very nervous. Something didn't feel right. I didn't speak to Gina about it as she was getting as nervous about the whole thing as I was. I did what I knew best; put it to the back of my mind and pretended that everything would be fine.

The exhibition at the Tate was going well and my fears were allayed once more when nothing sinister about Foruki appeared in the press. Journalists just focused on interviews with the fence man who sculptured nudes, and also on how sedate and noncontroversial the Turner Prize nominees were this year. Articles did appear on Foruki, but mostly about his artwork being more important than the personality. Gina kept all the cuttings and would only let me read the good things that were said about him.

'Just one more month to go and it will all be over,' I said.

'Nina, Rooney's moving in with me.'

'That's fantastic.'

'He's telling Lydia now. He's getting someone to watch over the stall part-time so he can concentrate on his music. So you don't mind?'

'Why should I mind? It's brilliant news. Mrs Onoro will be fine about it, you'll see.'

'She's only got a bloke,' Rooney said coming in.

'Did it go OK, what did she say?'

'She almost strangled me cos she was so happy and then she told me she's seeing a healer. "For your legs, Ma?" I asked, and she said, "No, for love." Anyway, she wants us to go around for dinner on Saturday night and meet him. Come as well, Nina, she's been asking about you.'

'I've got something to do,' I replied, 'but tell her I'll see her soon.'

I knew I would have been more than welcome but I wanted to go and attempt to see my parents.

Mum and Dad hung up whenever I phoned so I got Gina to call up on Friday night to say that Dad had been selected in a special draw and the prize was two tickets to go and see Cilla Black.

I could imagine him asking her what draw it was, as he didn't believe you could get anything for free.

'Our representative will come and see you tomorrow evening at six o'clock and will explain everything clearly to you.'

'What did he say?' I asked Gina as she got off the phone.

'He double-checked that she wouldn't try to sell him anything otherwise he'd tell her "to get off". When I said you wouldn't, he said he'd be waiting.'

I didn't know what made me feel more nervous, meeting Mangetti or my dad.

I rang the bell and could hear him shout out to my mother that it was for him.

My heart was racing.

He opened the door. I put one foot against it.

'Dad, let me just explain.'

'Get off, I'm waiting for lady.'

'The lady with the tickets is me. Please let me in so I can speak to you and Mum.'

'The door-to-door selling now, this is what you doing?'

'No, Dad. That was just to –'

'Dickheads suffering and now you selling door-to-door. Get off, I don't want nothing.' He was jamming the door against my foot so I had to pull it back.

'Dad, please,' I shouted through the letterbox. 'Channel Four, I want you to watch Channel Four on the twenty-eighth of November . . .' and just for that moment I wanted Foruki to win because then he might be proud of me. Then it dawned on me that he wouldn't even know that it had been me behind Foruki, and what did the Turner Prize mean to him anyway? He thought my mum could win it by assembling a pile of her samosas in the shape of the Star of India; it was for a bunch of lazy people who had too much time and money.

I walked around to Ki's house. I just wanted to put my arms around her mum and sit with her. Despite shouting through the letterbox, no one answered the door.

The 28th of November descended with the heaviness with which it was anticipated. It was raining heavily and there was the odd thunderstorm. Rooney and Gina came to collect me from the flat. Rooney had got one of his friends to drive us to Tate Britain.

'It's going to be fine, Nina, and think, after today it's all over,' Gina said. 'Are you ready for this?'

'Can't be much more prepared,' I replied nervously.

We had rehearsed what Rooney would do in the unlikely event that Foruki should win. He would say a simple thank you and depending on the level of media interest we would see what needed to be done. If we didn't win it would be fine as Foruki could just slip away into the background and nobody need know any different. I would sell some more of his paintings and he would return to Japan and probably die at some point.

I could see crowds as we approached the Tate. There were some anti Turner Prize protestors dressed up as clowns. One banner read: 'We are the bullshit detectors.' Another read: 'Turner Prize for a bunch of fakes.' My heart beat faster. They booed as we got out of the car and made our way into the gallery.

Several introductions were made in the foyer and Foruki was introduced to the fence maker who sculpted nudes and who was the bookies' favourite as well as the other artists'. They congratulated each other. Simon my old boss was there and congratulated me on Foruki's success. He said that if I ever needed a job again it was waiting for me complete with promotion. I thanked him politely. I didn't even know if Richard Morris was there but it didn't matter now anyway as this was the final hurdle and once we got through this it would all be well and truly over. Mangetti came over and introduced us to the other judges, lots of other people hovered around us and then it was time to take our seats at the table.

Gina and I sat on either side of Rooney. I looked up at the large ceilings and wondered how on earth we had got there. Drinks were served and then starters. My stomach was churning. A television camera pointed at us and we knew that we were going out live. Mrs Onoro would be at home watching nervously. I wondered whether my dad would flick the channel over from Zee and see me – maybe he would. There was a lot of hustle and bustle, people moving from their seats, nervous coughs, laughter, the sound of clinking glasses and talking which echoed loudly through the hall.

The Channel 4 presenter was trying to talk and move among the bustle and on several occasions nearly fell over. The director was introducing the fashion designer who was about to make the presentation and just as he was doing that a man with ginger hair walked over to me.

'Richard Morris, the *Guardian*.'

It was an inappropriate time for introductions so I just smiled and waited for the fashion designer to open the envelope.

'Nervous tonight then, Ms Savani?'

'Nervous for Foruki,' I said swiftly.

'One and the same,' he replied.

He had my attention.

'Kenneth David does not exist. Lydia Onoro lives at Frith Road, her son is a Ronald Onoro, a grocer. Do you have anything to say?'

I could feel the blood drain from my face. I wanted to be sick. He couldn't do this to me, not then; he could have chosen any other day, any other moment.

'No comment,' I stuttered.

I could see him go over to the judges. Please don't do this to me, not today. Tastudi Mangetti turned white, his eyes bulged, and then all I could hear was the crowd clapping and cheering and Gina saying, 'Bloody hell, Nina, we've won, we've bloody won.' Rooney got up. Mangetti stared at me. We couldn't publicly humiliate him. What was I going to do? I got up and went after Rooney.

'Think, Nina, think.' We hadn't prepared for the eventuality that this would happen on the night of the prize-giving. I followed Rooney onto the stage and I was aware that cameras were pointing at us.

'Thank you,' Rooney said, accepting the cheque. 'Thank you very much.'

The crowd clapped.

I had to say something, otherwise Richard Morris would make an announcement and Mangetti's reputation would be ruined. My legs were shaking as I leaned towards the microphone.

'There is one thing that I'd like to add.' The crowd were silent. 'There's a final piece to the collection at the Tate and he's here today – Foruki,' I announced. The crowd were unsure as to whether they had to clap. 'Take off your hat and glasses, Rooney,' I whispered while a few of them were clapping.

'What, here?'

'Yes.'

Rooney took off his hat and his glasses.

'I'd like to introduce you to Ronald Onoro. He didn't paint the pictures, I did, and I'd like to thank Tastudi Mangetti for his support in helping me with the project. We wanted to make a statement about bringing art back to its subject matter and not the artist, so I thank you Mr Mangetti for allowing me to show my work behind the Japanese character we invented.'

People were unsure of what to do and then they began clapping.

'Thank you,' I said, smiling despite the fact I felt like collapsing and have someone take me away from there.

As we climbed down from the stage, camera crews, journalists and photographers surrounded us. 'Nina, how did you come up with the idea?' 'Did you do it because you are Asian?' 'Nina, how do you feel about winning the Turner?' 'Look over here.' 'Why did you feel the need to do this?' Rooney was accosted in the same way.

'What do you do, Ronald?' 'Are you an artist?' The Communications Director from the Tate rushed over to us and told them that all questions would be answered at a press conference at nine o'clock in the morning. He then turned to me: 'Tastudi Mangetti is waiting outside for you both; it's best if you leave now.'

Gina was across the room trying to get to us but there was no way of reaching her. We left. Mangetti's Bentley was parked outside, waiting for us. The clowns were shouting at us, 'Bunch of fakes.' We were, but not in the way that they meant.

The car door was opened.

'Get in.'

Mangetti's assistant was sitting beside him.

'Were you thinking of ruining me?' Mangetti said very calmly.

'No. I'm so sorry, Tastudi. I didn't think we were going to win it.'

'Is it true about Mr Foruki's occupation?'

'Yes,' Rooney replied.

'But you came into my office and spoke passionately about your concepts; your art.'

I shook my head.

'They weren't his concepts?' His eyes were bulging, his nose seemed even more prominent.

'No, Tastudi.'

'I've been to your studio and seen your work.' He was seething but trying to contain himself; his cheeks were florid.

'It was my studio. I'm really, truly sorry – none of this was supposed to happen, you see . . .'

'What about me?' he interrupted. 'The press are going to have a field day with this. And me? What about me? Was it an attack on the establishment or just me person-ally?' he shouted.

308

'We can turn this around,' I said trying to calm him down. 'I know we can.'

'Who the hell are you to tell me what we can and cannot do. I never trusted your sort anyway, you're all swindlers, cheap swindlers, stick to what you know best.'

'Just hang on, Mr Mangetti, Nina meant none of this personally.'

'Who are you anyway? A grocer?' He looked at Rooney as if he had just found him at the bottom of his shoe and then he turned to me, utterly disgusted. 'Have my driver drop you wherever you want, I've got to get out. Be there at eight tomorrow morning or face the consequences.'

Mangetti and the assistant got out of the car. Rooney and I got out of the car as soon as they were out of sight.

'Oh God, I'm sorry, Rooney.'

'You've got nothing to be sorry about, in fact, I'm glad you did that to him.'

Gina phoned to tell us not to go to any of the houses as the press might be camping outside. 'They've been asking me all kinds of questions. I've said nothing but it's big. Nobody left, they were all waiting for answers and more press were turning up,' she said.

We arranged to meet at a Travelodge near London Bridge and decided to stay there for the night. It was a nightmare; a complete nightmare. None of it was about making anyone look stupid; if Mangetti had given me a chance to explain maybe he would have seen that. And his threat – it didn't scare me, but despite the fact that Mangetti had been obnoxious I still wanted him to look good, then everything would finally be over.

Gina met us an hour later at the Travelodge and we spent hours with Rooney discussing all the possibilities and what we could say the following day. I went to bed at three in the morning. And though I was exhausted I was awake most of the night, unable to sleep.

I thought about the fact that I had won the Turner and it baffled me. How the hell did that happen? One of the biggest prizes in art was mine. Did I win it because they felt the paintings were good or because they needed someone and Foruki's unusual profile seemed to fit the bill? It didn't matter anyway, it was all subjective. Everyone was playing a game, it was just that some people were unaware of the rules. I had found myself in the midst of it all and made the rules up as I went along. How could I explain that it was as simple as that. All I ever wanted to do was paint and be me.

It was six o'clock when I hauled myself out of bed. As I came out of the shower I switched the television on and thought I saw a shot of my parents' house. It *was* my parents' house and there was a media pack outside.

'No, they can't do this to me.' I held my hand to my mouth.

My mum opened the door, taken aback by all the flashing. She started calling out for my dad. He came to the door in his red pyjamas and had a microphone thrust in his face.

'Mr Savani, what do you think of your daughter's antics?'

Oh God, please don't let him say anything. 'No comment,' I willed. 'Say "no comment", Dad.'

'Antics?' he shouted. 'She doesn't have no furniture here, now get off.' He made some erratic gestures.

I had my head in my hands.

The ensuing scenes were cut as they returned back to the news reporter.

'We seem to have lost the sound but I'm sure it will be a story that we will return to.'

I called my parents but the phone was engaged. I kept trying in between drying my hair and after half an hour I finally got through.

'Dad, it's me, Nina, please don't hang up.'

'Oh my daughter Nina,' he said. 'I can't speak to you now because we have the television peoples filming here.'

'Is that Nina, Mr Savani? Could we possibly have a word with her?' A woman came on the line. 'Nina, your parents are giving us the first live exclusive interview. We're about to run, stay on the phone, we'd like to talk to you too.'

'I don't have anything to say. Could you give it back to my dad please?'

'Nina, it would give you an opportunity to put your side of the story across.'

'It will be put across later this morning, could you hand the phone back to my dad please? . . . Dad, don't speak to them.'

'Nina, I must go, the lady is calling me.' He hung up.

I tried ringing again but the phone was off the hook and then a few minutes later I heard his voice on the television.

'Good morning Mr and Mrs Savani.'

'Good morning,' he shouted.

Both my parents were sitting on the Land of Leather sofa. My dad had changed into his red shirt and my mum was wearing her green sari. They had obviously been briefed on what had happened. As the reporter did her introduction the camera turned to photographs of me everywhere, photos that I was sure they had got rid of.

'So here we are talking to the parents of Nina Savani, the lawyer who managed to dupe the art world by getting a grocer to stand in for her as the artist.' The reporter, realising she was getting vacuumed by the sofa, attempted to move to the edge of the seat. 'An ingenious ploy and indeed some would say cunning. We're talking live to her parents this morning. So, Mr and Mrs Savani, did you believe your daughter was an agent?'

'Of course. It's the normal. She is one because I am one.'

Oh God, I thought, he's misunderstood her: 'Not "Asian", Dad, "agent".'

'You are?' Her voice sounded perplexed.

'Can't you see that?'

Someone must have told the reporter not to continue that line of questioning as she suddenly said, 'Did you know about your daughter's scheme to fool the art world?'

I shook my head: 'Please don't say anything, Dad.'

'Definitely. I knew she was fooling them but not for one moment was I the fooled. I said fool them, do a good job and fool them.'

'Is it because you agreed on her critique of the artist being bigger than the art itself?'

He looked confused. 'What?'

She rephrased her question. 'Did you encourage her because of the statement she was making?'

'No, I said this because when you do any job you make sure you do it properly. I have always told her this.'

'Do you have any of her art here that you can show us?'

'We don't keep the pictures here, too expensive to leave in the house because of the burglars.'

'Indeed. And what do you think about what she has done?'

'I am the proud,' he bellowed.

I didn't know whether to laugh or cry and then the reporter turned to my mum.

'Mrs Savani?'

My mother nodded.

'Does she have any future plans?'

'Marriage, hopefully,' she sighed.

'Mr and Mrs Savani, thank you. Now, back to the studio.'

312

'Thank you, Sonia. I have Professor Landstein from Goldsmith University with me to talk about the nature of the duplicity.' The presenter turned to the professor.

'Professor, what is your opinion on the statement Nina Savani was making?'

'The fact that she went to such lengths is an artistic statement in itself. She has opened up the debate even further; pushing forth the boundaries as to what one deems as art and it begs the question, can one call duplicity an art form?' He began going off 'on the rambles' and she interrupted him by saying, 'For viewers who have just joined us, one of the leading stories today is the lawyer who duped the art world by . . .'

Didn't they have more important news to discuss?

I couldn't listen to it and turned the television off, got ready and switched my phone on. The message box was full. I went through them quickly; most of them were from journalists and there was one from Jean and one from my dad. 'Nina, did you see me on the TV? Did they get a picture of the sofa? They wanted us to sit in the dining room but we told them no, sitting room on sofa or no deal.' And then I could hear my mum in the background asking if I was eating properly.

I got a phone call from Mangetti giving us instructions as to where he wanted to meet us before going to the Tate. The three of us met him in a grotty café where he briefed us.

He said to say that the judges had known all along that the paintings were not done by Foruki and the point they were making with the nominee Nina Savani, aka Foruki, was the extent to which celebrity had permeated today's society, so much so that people were fascinated not just by the subject matter but by the artist. 'You are

313

clear on this?' Mangetti asked. 'You wanted to illustrate the nature of identity in today's society. You must insist that the judges were aware. Do you understand?'

I understood all of it but I wanted him to know why we did it – but he never let me explain. He wanted us to get into the Bentley with him so we could make our way to the Tate together.

'Not you,' he said, staring at Gina as she was about to climb in.

'Rooney and I will walk then,' I replied.

'You're not in a position to play with me, Nina.'

'I'm not playing, I never was, it's the three of us or we walk.' And I don't know where the courage to say that came from but I meant it literally because the side of Mangetti I was seeing was ugly and making him look good didn't seem as important as having my friend there.

'Get in,' he mumbled, not even looking at her.

A few photographers pounced on us as we got out of the car and made our way into the Tate. We were taken to a room. It was packed. Photographer's bulbs were flashing away. Rooney and I were seated next to each other, alongside Mangetti, another judge and a spokesperson from the Tate. Questions were fired at me from all directions. I stuck to the story that Mangetti had told us to say: that we had gone to such lengths to make a statement about art and the best way to illustrate the point was to demonstrate the very nature of identity. The panel were asked at what stage Mangetti knew about it and he answered: he was adamant that it was from the beginning. They were then asked if I would still receive the £20,000 prize money, as technically I was not the one who had won. They responded by saying that the work was judged on its own merit and not by the artist and therefore the prize would still go to me. There were more questions but it was the one from a lady sitting two rows from the front that stopped me for a moment. It was a lady who had wispy white hair, and she reminded me of the woman who had smiled at me on the tube a year ago. She asked me about the theme that ran through my first exhibition at Artusion and specifically about the painting of the hand, which I had named *Beyond Indigo*.

I wanted to tell her about my best friend Ki who had died in my arms two years ago – but how I wasn't lost any more. '*Beyond Indigo* is about believing and knowing that something exists even if you can't see it. It's about believing in all possibilities,' I replied.

There were questions for Rooney – who he was, what he did. It was endless. After half an hour the press conference was brought to a close.

Mangetti had his arm around me for the press shots and was smiling, and then as soon as it was over he left without saying a word to me.

Gina and Rooney invited me back to celebrate at their house but I needed time on my own to take stock of what had happened and so I told them I would catch up with them later. After successfully dodging the press, I went to Green Park. It was cold, but not as cold and wet as it had been a year earlier. The trees were looking bare. Had the leaves jumped off the branches of their own accord or were they pushed along by the wind? A year ago I was here on my knees, stripped of everything, and a year later I had finally learned to see flowers; I had kept believing even when there was clearly nothing there. And in my moments of doubting, people were sent to show me otherwise. I had defied all odds and won the bloody Turner. How mad was that? Was it because I had taken a leap of faith and done something out of the ordinary? Or was it because I was pushed and swept along? Whatever it was, on the journey I found parts of myself that I never knew existed.

315

The greatest irony in being someone else was that I learned to be me: to trust myself, to be myself. It was as simple as that. Maybe there were no concrete answers to anything, just experiences; to live each moment as it came.

There were press camped outside my doorstep so I went to the studio, packed up my paints, took down the buddha and wrapped him up. I then went to the rental company to hire the van again, loaded everything up and went to Gina's house.

Gina and Rooney were having lunch with Mrs Onoro when I walked in.

Mrs Onoro smiled. 'Ohhhhhhhh, Nina, you done so good. I saw the TV and news; you and Rooney every-where. They come looking for Rooney. I say I not know no man call Rooney. After, I go to Japanese Association and make them follow someone else, then I come here.'

'It's all so crazy,' Gina said. 'You've been on every channel, Nina.'

'I told you Rooney win prize. He always win every-thing when he was child. Lucky charm,' she said, touching her necklace.

'It's mad, I still can't believe it,' I replied. 'They are camping outside the flat and the phone hasn't stopped ringing.'

'What are you going to do, Nina?'

'I'm going to go away for a few months until it dies down.'

'You can come stay with me,' Mrs Onoro suggested.

'Thank you, Mrs Onoro, but I've decided to go to Ireland.'

'Who's in Ireland?' Rooney asked.

'Man who you write "go for it" to?' Mrs Onoro interrupted.

'No. Another experience, maybe?'

I stayed over with them all. Gina crept into my flat for me in the middle of the night to get a few things together, and in the morning I said my goodbyes.

'I'm going to make this quick as I'm not really very good with goodbyes and anyway I'm not going for long. I just don't know how to thank you all enough.'

'You don't say nothing, you good girl, Nina,' Mrs Onoro said.

'Yeah,' Rooney added. 'One of the nicest people I've met.'

Gina was silent. I looked at her and tears streamed down my face. 'Thank you for believing in me,' I whispered as I held her. 'This is for you and Rooney, open it when I go.' I wanted them to have half the Turner Prize money because without them both, none of it would have been possible.

Tastudi Mangetti called to say that for everything I had put him through the least I could do was to sell him the buddha painting. He offered me £60,000.

'I'm terribly sorry, Mr Mangetti, but "our sort" have some things that are not for sale.'

'I will make sure you are unable to exhibit anywhere – I promise you.'

'You go ahead and do that.' I hung up on him. If the Mafia ever knocked on the semi it was my dad they had to fear.

Gina, Rooney and Mrs Onoro waved me off. I went to see Ki's mum.

'Auntie, open the door, it's me, Nina.'

She came to the door.

'What happened, Nina? I saw you on the news.'

I told her the story about Ki's name being mistaken and she began to laugh and then she cried.

'She's always here with us, Auntie.'

'I know, beta.'

'There's something I want you to have.'

I went into the van and got out the picture of the buddha. She tore off the brown paper and studied it curiously, just the same way she looked at the pictures I handed her as a child.

'It's very nice,' she lied.

She came up to Ki's room with me. We hung the picture of the buddha on the wall and her mum said maybe she needed to paint the walls and wash the curtains. Then she left me alone in the room.

'I still miss you, you know, but I can still hear you laughing. Are you laughing now? Only you could have orchestrated this, it's got your name written all over it. All I asked for was a sign not to win the bloody Turner.' I blew her a kiss, 'I love you, Ki,' and then I went downstairs.

'Take care of yourself, beta.' Ki's mum kissed me as I left.

'I will, Auntie, and you take care of yourself too.'

The phone rang – it was Raj. I picked it up because that was the least I owed him.

'Congratulations, Nina, I saw it all on the news.'

'Thank you. How are you? Are you all right?'

'I'm engaged,' he said.

'That's fantastic news.'

'To Pinkie, you remember her? She was brilliant after what happened with . . . with us, and then one thing led to another.'

'I'm really happy for you, truly I am.' Pinkie would make a far better wife than I possibly could have.

'Mummy's not happy about it but Pinkie and I have decided to go away and get married.'

'Be happy, Raj. I really do wish you the very best.'

318

'Stay in touch, Nina.'

'I will.'

I drove around the corner to my parents' house, checked that no one was waiting for me there and knocked on the door, unafraid if my dad would slam it in my face or not.

My dad answered it.

'Dad.'

He smiled at me, welcomed me in and patted me on the back. 'Nina, I am the celebrity in the depot.'

'That's great, Dad, really great.'

'All day yesterday we had the crews filming us. You see six o'clock news?'

My mum came out. I went to hug her and she was inert, like the biggest tidal wave had knocked her over and washed away everything she had left.

'You're still with the Jeannie?' my dad asked.

'It's not Jean, it's Michael, and no, I'm not with him.'

'These things, they never last.'

An enormous smile spread across my mum's face. 'Raj,' she gasped. 'I prayed to Bhagavan and I knew it would work in the end.'

'I'm not with him either. There's no one, and you know what? I'm happy.'

'People will be queuing for you now that you are famous. Queuing I tells you. We might even be able to get the Kapadias' son.'

The honchos considered the Kapadias to be the crème of the community. Their son, Hiten, was a barrister.

'You can move back today,' my mum added.

'I'm not coming home.'

'What?' my dad shouted.

'I'm going away for a few months to paint.'

'We will let you do the painting in your room,' my dad said.

'No, Dad.'

My mum took her sari end out and sobbed.

'I only ever wanted you to be proud of me,' I began to cry.

'Don't cry, Nina. You made us very proud. Who can say they have been on the news at six? Who can say they are going to meet the Cilla Black?'

'Cilla?'

'Yah, part of ITV deal for first exclusive interview. I tells them, nothing comes for free, I do this if you let me meet the Cilla.'

He held out his arms to hug me. He never did that.

I held on to him and wept and then my mum did something I never thought she was capable of. She put her arms around both of us.

'Better go now, I'll call when I get there.'

'I knew that there was no artist and it was you,' my dad said on seeing the van. 'I cannot be the fooled.'

'You'll eat properly, no, beta?'

'Yes, Ma,' I said, leaving.

My phone began ringing. I parked the van and answered it.

'Nina Savani?'

'Yes.'

'Frances Evans, *Mail on Sunday*. We've spoken to a Mrs Malika Mehta with a story on how you duped her son Raj into marriage. She said that this is a pattern that seems to be recurrent with you. I just wanted to give you an opportunity to put across your side of the story.'

I threw the phone out of the van and continued driving.

* * *

6th March 2001

I travelled to the west of Ireland and settled for a few months in Galway. The landscape and beauty that surrounded me was even more spectacular than Michael had described and though the winter months made everything appear moodier that's not what I saw. I captured the energy of the roughness of the seas in vibrant reds. Beneath the grey clouds were piercing shafts of white light that made me look beyond them and see blue skies. Though the landscape was wet and damp with the rain, the raindrops glistened against luscious hues of green and when the snow came to settle I could still see the greens. Every day of these months, I painted. Solitude became part of my life and when I wasn't scared by it any more or trying to run away from it I knew it was time to go home – back to my flat and my studio.

Contrary to what Tastudi Mangetti said he would do, several gallery owners were interested in exhibiting my work. Contractually my first exhibition was supposed to be with Artusion and I wanted to exhibit there as Michael had risked so much for me.

Emanuel Hikatari had left Artusion to go back to New York and the gallery was run by a man named Stephen McCabe. We had arranged a date when he would come to my studio and go through the paintings with me. The same day I was supposed to be meeting him my mum called me to say that they had 'a very, very big surprise' for me and I had to go round as soon as possible.

'Can't we do it later this evening,' I said, thinking that I would be pushing it for my meeting with Stephen.

'No, now, beta, come now because it is a big, big surprise.'

'Ma, I thought things had changed, please don't put

321

me through this again,' I pleaded, thinking she had arranged a meeting with Hiten Kapadia, the barrister. The excitement in my mother's voice could mean only this.

'Kavitha, get off the line before you tells her,' my dad bellowed.

'Just come soon, beta. It's urgent,' she said hanging up.

There was a black Fiesta parked right outside the door of the semi. It was an understated car for the Kapadias. It had to be them because although the space was permit free, my dad never allowed anyone else to park outside his front door.

'Get off,' he would shout, holding a traffic cone he had taken from a crime scene and placing it in his space.

I knocked on the front door and instead of my mum or dad coming to answer it, a girl of about ten or eleven opened it.

'Hello Auntie,' she beamed.

I thought it was one of the Kapadias' relatives. 'Hello,' I replied.

She grabbed me and began hugging me tightly. I was slightly taken aback by this child who was showing me so much affection – did she think I was going to marry her uncle or whoever Hiten Kapadia was to her? Affectionate child was sorely mistaken.

'Bring your auntie in here, Nina,' my father shouted from the sitting room.

Nina? She had the same name as me.

My mother had the end of her sari out and was sobbing. My dad was sitting with his best red shirt on with a smile from ear to ear; the little girl went and sat beside him. There, engulfed by the sofa, was a woman with curly hair. It was no longer jet black as I recollected but had streaks of white. She was still beautiful; beautiful and elegant as I remembered her. It was my sister, Jana.

She got up. Tears streamed down her face. 'Nina,' she whispered.

I was unable to speak.

When we managed to disentangle ourselves she sat holding my hand. Jana told me she read all about me winning the Turner Prize and made contact with Ki's mum, who convinced her to call Mum and Dad.

She phoned Dad and instead of Dad claiming no relation to her, he asked to meet her again. They had met for the first time when I had been in Ireland and she had returned this morning from Germany where she was living, and was going to stay for the week.

'Why did you stop writing to me?'

'So many things happened, Nina, I will sit and explain it all.'

Jana looked over at her daughter.

'Did you give your Auntie Nina a big kiss?'

'I hugged her,' Nina said shyly.

'This girl,' my dad said, pinching her cheeks.

I did not want to leave my sister but I realised that Stephen McCabe would be on his way to the studio.

'Go and see him,' Jana said. 'We're not going anywhere.'

Reluctantly, I rushed off, saying that I would be back as soon as I could.

My thoughts were elsewhere when I got to the studio. I hadn't even arranged the pictures as I'd intended. The ones I wanted to exhibit were the ones on flowers that I'd done prior to the Turner Prize exhibition work. I was also debating whether to put in some of the paintings done in Ireland. I hadn't even taken off my coat when the door buzzer went.

'It's open,' I called out, removing my coat, trying to get my head together.

'You shouldn't leave the door open, it could be anyone.'

'Michael!' It couldn't be. I looked up and saw him standing by the door. I wanted to run towards him and throw my arms around him. He walked towards me without his hand outstretched.

'Nina,' he said very calmly, 'I know that you are doing an exhibition for us. I was in town and I've come to help select the paintings.'

'Oh, right,' I said, trying not to sound disappointed that he was there for purely professional motives. 'I didn't expect you to come.'

'Of course I would be here – I had to be, I mean look what happened the last time you had an exhibition.'

'How are you? Are you well?' I asked. He looked incredibly well; his eyes still sparkled and his face was as warm as ever.

'Yes, very well, and you?'

'My sister's back,' I blurted. 'I've just seen her now for the first time in years, it's crazy. I have a niece; they're both waiting for me at home.'

'Right . . . I mustn't keep you.'

That wasn't what I'd meant. There was an awkward silence. 'The ones I thought about exhibiting were the ones I've put out over here,' I said, attempting to sound professional.

'Have you got over the shock of winning the Turner?'

'Yes. Thank you for helping me.'

'No, we have to thank you. Since your win, business has rocketed and Emanuel is revelling in the publicity.'

'Right. Well, that's good, then.'

'Is it all working out for you? What have you been up to?' he asked, studying the various paintings.

'I've spent some time in Ireland.'

'What were you doing there?'

'About what happened . . .' I began.

'It's in the past,' he said. 'You don't owe me anything.'

Why had he come then? Was he married? Had he come to tell me that he had got married? I searched his fingers for a ring.

'So show me the work you did in Ireland, you must have done some.'

'Over there.'

He went over to the canvases. 'It's Galway. You went to Galway.'

'I've been there for the last three months sorting myself out.'

'God, Nina,' his face softened.

'I didn't marry Raj, I tried calling to explain but you never answered any of my calls, you never once let me explain. I know I made a real mess but I wanted to put it all right . . .'

'I called you a few days after you'd won the Turner and an old man picked up, saying he didn't know you.'

'Was it my dad?'

'No, some old man who said he'd found the phone.'

'What did you want to say to me?'

'That I'm really proud of what you did.'

Was that it, was that all he wanted to say?

He looked away from me and began studying one of the paintings again. It was Cashla Bay. I had gone there late in the afternoon before the sun was about to disappear; the sea was green and although it was cold, and the sky was turning black, it was still lit with possibility. I captured this with indigo – colours that were there; colours that lay beyond.

'That's where I would go to make some of my biggest decisions. When I decided to go to America I sat there for hours, thinking. When Emanuel asked me to set up Artusion with him; when I was nine and mustering the courage to ask Lisa Flynn out.' He smiled. 'It's the only place I've found where you can really hear the silence of your own voice.'

I knew what he meant. After I'd painted, I had sat there in the cold just listening.

'And so do you think that this is a sign?' Michael asked, taking his gaze off the canvas. He came towards me and held out his hand.

'Maybe, maybe not,' I said, taking it.